Cases on Chinese Unicorns and the Development of Startups

Youssef Elhaoussine
Beijing Normal University–Hong Kong Baptist University United International College, China

Henni Appelgryn
Beijing Normal Universitiy–Hong Kong Baptist University United International College, China

Lulu Wang
Business Advantage Consulting, China

A volume in the Advances in Business Strategy and Competitive Advantage (ABSCA) Book Series

IGI Global
Publishing Tomorrow's Research Today

Published in the United States of America by
    IGI Global
    Business Science Reference (an imprint of IGI Global)
    701 E. Chocolate Avenue
    Hershey PA, USA 17033
    Tel: 717-533-8845
    Fax: 717-533-8661
    E-mail: cust@igi-global.com
    Web site: http://www.igi-global.com

Library of Congress Cataloging-in-Publication Data

CIP DATA PENDING

ISBN: 9798369329214
eISBN: 9798369329221

British Cataloguing in Publication Data
A Cataloguing in Publication record for this book is available from the British Library.

All work contributed to this book is new, previously-unpublished material.
The views expressed in this book are those of the authors, but not necessarily of the publisher.

For electronic access to this publication, please contact: eresources@igi-global.com.

Table of Contents

Detailed Table of Contents

Chapter 1

Henni Appelgryn, Beijing Normal University-Hong Kong Baptist
University United International College, China

This case study examines Manner Coffee's journey in China's competitive coffee market, focusing on its strategic initiatives, market positioning, and brand identity challenges. Manner Coffee has differentiated itself by blending modern aesthetics with traditional Chinese elements, creating a unique coffee experience that resonates with local consumers. The case details how Manner Coffee has leveraged community engagement, sustainability practices, and technological innovation to build customer loyalty and drive growth. However, the company faces a significant trademark infringement issue with Josef Manner and Comp AG, affecting its brand identity and future expansion plans. Despite these challenges, Manner Coffee remains committed to delivering premium coffee experiences and navigating legal uncertainties to secure its position in China's burgeoning coffee culture. This study provides insights into brand management, market entry strategies, and the complexities of protecting intellectual property in international markets.

Chapter 2

Zizhen Wang, University College London, UK

Chapter 3

Haoyue Yu, Beijing Normal University-Hong Kong Baptist University
United International College, China

This case study examines the evolution and strategic initiatives of Hello Trans Tech, a pioneering force in China's shared mobility sector. Founded in 2016 amidst the boom of bike-sharing, Hello Trans Tech quickly emerged as a leader by leveraging innovative technologies and sustainable transportation solutions. The journey from its inception, navigating through phases of market expansion, technological adaptation, and diversification into electric vehicles and intelligent mobility systems. Key aspects include strategic partnerships with Alibaba and Contemporary Amperex Technology, its transition from bike-sharing to a comprehensive mobility platform, and its expansion into Singapore. The study also highlights the leadership of founders Yang Lei and Kaizhu Li, their vision for sustainable urban mobility, and Hello's pioneering efforts in AI-driven optimization and carbon-neutral initiatives. Through this exploration, readers gain insights into how Hello Trans Tech has reshaped urban transportation and positioned itself at the forefront of China's shared economy revolution.

Chapter 4

Zhuoyue Ji, Beijing Normal University-Hong Kong Baptist University
United International College, China

This case study provides an in-depth market analysis of Zongmu Technology, a leading player in autonomous driving and advanced driver assistance systems (ADAS) in China. It explores the evolution of the automobile market from traditional vehicles to new energy vehicles, highlighting the shift from secondary software algorithms to full-stack solutions. The case study investigates Zongmu's strategic position, the competitive environment it operates in, and the difficulties it encounters when competing against major rivals such as Velodyne Lidar and Pony.ai. It also details the company's latest developments, including the introduction of new products like FlashBot and Lightning Bao by Silkworm Bush Robotics. The study delves into Zongmu's complex shareholding structure, strategic partnerships, and future projects, such as comprehensive intelligent driving systems, wireless charging for NEVs, and smart city solutions. Through this comprehensive analysis, the case aims to explain Zongmu Technology's strategies for growth and innovation in the rapidly developing autonomous driving market.

This case explores the dynamic landscape of the autonomous driving industry, focusing on UiSee Technology as a prominent player. It examines the competitive strategies, technological advancements, market dynamics, and regulatory influences shaping the sector. UiSee Technology, founded by Ganesha Wu in 2016, emerges as a key innovator in China's autonomous driving market, navigating partnerships with major industry players and expanding its footprint in both passenger and logistics applications. The case delves into UiSee's pivotal role in advancing autonomous vehicle technologies, its strategic collaborations, and the broader implications for the automotive industry's future. It also discusses market forecasts, investment trends, and the developing regulatory framework driving the industry towards the widespread adoption of autonomous driving technologies.

This case study delves into the rapid evolution and strategic initiatives of Keenon Robotics, a pioneering force in commercial service robots. Focusing on innovative technologies such as robot as a service (RaaS), Keenon Robotics has revolutionized sectors including catering, healthcare, hospitality, and epidemic management with its diverse range of robots. The case explores Keenon Robotics' journey from its historic breakthroughs in robotic technology to its pivotal role in addressing contemporary challenges like the COVID-19 pandemic through products like the Disinfection Robot M2. It also highlights the strategic expansions into new markets and industries, such as hotels and education, underscoring the company's commitment to technological innovation and societal impact. Through insightful analysis and strategic milestones, the case explains how Keenon Robotics navigates opportunities and challenges in the burgeoning field of service robotics, positioning itself at the forefront of industry transformation.

Chapter 7

This case study examines Star Charge, a pivotal player in China's electric vehicle (EV) charging infrastructure market. Founded amid ambitious government initiatives to bolster EV adoption, Star Charge rapidly emerged under the visionary leadership of Danwei Shao. The case explores how Star Charge has developed strategically, from its unique crowdfunding approach to its current success, overcoming challenges and taking advantage of opportunities in a competitive industry where State Grid and Special Call are the dominant players. It explores Star Charge's business model, technological advancements in charging stations, and the pivotal role in supporting China's dual carbon goals. The study analyzes future projections, including international expansion strategies and technological innovations such as vehicle-to-grid (V2G) technology. Through this comprehensive analysis, the case illustrates how Star Charge continues to shape the future of sustainable mobility in China and beyond.

Chapter 8

This case study examines Medlinker, a leading figure in China's internet healthcare sector, focusing on its evolution, market strategy, and technological innovations. Founded in 2014 by Dr. Wang Shirui, Medlinker has transformed from a social networking platform for doctors to a comprehensive disease management service integrating AI-driven solutions. The study delves into Medlinker's pioneering role in leveraging MedGPT, China's first large language model for medical applications, and its strategic initiatives to enhance healthcare accessibility and efficiency. It examines Medlinker's way of doing business, competition, and market position in a rapidly growing industry with developing government regulations. Ultimately, the case explores how Medlinker continues to innovate and expand, shaping the future of digital healthcare in China.

Chapter 9
Zhenxiang Yuan, Beijing Normal University-Hong Kong Baptist
University United International College, China

This case study explores the evolution and strategic growth of WeDoctor, a pioneering force in China's internet healthcare sector. Founded amidst challenges within China's medical regulatory environment, WeDoctor leveraged technological innovation and strategic partnerships to establish itself as a leader. Beginning with an innovative appointment registration platform, WeDoctor navigated regulatory landscapes through local government collaborations, leading to the establishment of China's first Internet hospital. The study details WeDoctor's progression through germination, demonstration, theorization, and diffusion stages, highlighting pivotal strategies such as stakeholder engagement, technological integration, and policy advocacy. WeDoctor's success in gaining regulatory legitimacy and scaling innovative models underscores its role in transforming healthcare delivery through digital solutions, setting benchmarks in internet-based medical services in China.

Chapter 10
Zihui Yang, Beijing Normal University-Hong Kong Baptist University
United International College, China

This case study explores the rise of Weilong, a leading player in China's spicy snack market, examining its transformation from a regional brand to a national and international powerhouse. Led by CEO Liu Weiping and CFO Peng Hongzhi, Weilong strategically navigated challenges like intense market competition and low brand loyalty through innovative branding, extensive market expansion, and effective cultural promotion. The case details Weilong's journey from localized marketing strategies in Henan province to national prominence, leveraging digital platforms and cultural resonance to engage a youthful consumer base. It highlights key strategies such as product innovation, diversified marketing campaigns, and CSR initiatives, showcasing how Weilong capitalized on China's spicy snack craze while promoting traditional Chinese culture globally. Through meticulous market positioning and operational optimization, Weilong exemplifies effective growth strategies in the dynamic Chinese consumer goods sector.

Chapter 11

Guoquan Shihui: Reforming the Prepared Food Market Through Integrated Supply Chain and Digital Innovation... 173

Yiru Wang, Beijing Normal University-Hong Kong Baptist University United International College, China

This case study examines Guo Quan Shi Hui, a prominent player in China's new retail and prepared food market. Founded by Mingchao Yang, Guo Quan Shi Hui revolutionized the hotpot industry through innovative supply chain management and digital integration. Yang's journey from a night market entrepreneur to a billionaire showcases his strategic vision for building a robust logistics system, collaborating with over 266 ODM plants, and implementing cold chain technology for freshness. The case details Guo Quan Shi Hui's expansion from a small retail outlet to a nationwide network of 10,000 stores, leveraging multi-platform marketing strategies, including TikTok, for consumer engagement. It explores the company's franchise model success, online-offline integration, and plans for global expansion. Guo Quan Shi Hui's story underscores its leadership for blending traditional cuisine with modern business practices, setting a benchmark for industry transformation and consumer-centric innovation.

Chapter 12

Jiuxian: Revolutionizing Liquor Distribution in China Through Omnichannel Innovation 193

Ziyi Li, Beijing Normal University-Hong Kong Baptist University United International College, China

This case study examines Jiuxian's transformative journey within China's competitive liquor distribution industry, focusing on its innovative strategies and evolution into an omnichannel powerhouse. Founded in 2009 by Hao Hongfeng, Jiuxian capitalised on the burgeoning e-commerce landscape, pioneering online liquor retailing in a market traditionally dominated by offline channels. Through strategic partnerships and aggressive expansion, Jiuxian established itself as a leader, leveraging its online platform and a nationwide network of offline stores branded as "Jiuxian International Wine & Spirit Centre." The case explores Jiuxian's adaptation to market shifts, including its embrace of new retail concepts and integration of live-streaming commerce to engage a younger consumer base. Despite challenges like financial setbacks and IPO delays, Jiuxian's resilience and strategic vision have positioned it at the forefront of China's liquor retail sector, setting a benchmark for omnichannel excellence and market innovation.

Chapter 13

Ke Chen, Beijing Normal University-Hong Kong Baptist University
United International College, China

This case study explores Wenheyou, a pioneering culinary brand in Changsha, China, founded by Wen Bin. Positioned at the intersection of nostalgia-driven consumption and urban cultural preservation, Wenheyou exemplifies a strategic blend of culinary innovation and emotional engagement. Targeting young consumers, particularly post-80s and post-90s, Wenheyou revives Changsha's cultural memories through themed dining complexes like Super Wenheyou, integrating local specialties and immersive historical settings. The case delves into Wen Bin's entrepreneurial journey, from humble beginnings with a skewer stall to establishing Asia's largest lobster restaurant and expanding into multi-floor cultural hubs. Through detailed analysis of Wenheyou's market positioning, operational strategies, and community engagement initiatives, the study illustrates how Wenheyou has transformed into a symbol of Changsha's cultural identity, fostering deep consumer connections and contributing to local cultural revitalization efforts.

Chapter 14

Liu Yuan, University of Warwick, UK

This case study examines Beisen Holdings Limited's evolution as a pioneer in China's Human Capital Management (HCM) industry. Beginning with its inception in 2002, Beisen strategically embraced cloud computing and advanced AI technologies to offer integrated HCM solutions. The study traces Beisen's transition from software as a service (SaaS) to platform as a service (PaaS), culminating in the development of iTalent X—a comprehensive HCM platform. Key innovations include AI-driven recruitment, talent management, and performance analytics tools, which have reshaped HR practices for over 6,000 enterprises, including 70% of the Fortune 500 in China. Through detailed analysis of market dynamics, technological advancements, and socio-economic effects like the pandemic and demographic shifts, the case underscores Beisen's leadership and its transformative impact on the HCM landscape.

Chapter 15

Enyi Zhang, Beijing Normal University-Hong Kong Baptist University
United International College, China

This case study examines how Genki Forest has grown and changed its strategy in the competitive health drinks market in China. Founded with a vision to offer healthier beverage alternatives, Genki Forest capitalized on rising consumer demand for natural, low-sugar beverages by innovating with unique flavors and leveraging digital marketing channels. The case delves into Genki Forest's early challenges in product sourcing and its subsequent growth through effective branding, product diversification, and e-commerce expansion. Analyzing competitive pressures from established players and emerging brands, the study examines Genki Forest's strategies to maintain market leadership, including sustainability initiatives and international expansion ambitions. Through a comprehensive exploration of its development phases, market positioning, and outlook, this case provides insights into navigating the complexities of consumer-driven markets and achieving sustained growth in the beverage industry.

Chapter 16

Shuyi Feng, Beijing Normal University-Hong Kong Baptist University
United International College, China

The case study explores WeRide, a leading innovator in autonomous driving technology, tracing its journey from inception to becoming a global powerhouse in the autonomous vehicle industry. Founded by Xu Han, WeRide has strategically positioned itself through significant investments, strategic partnerships with global giants like Renault-Nissan-Mitsubishi Alliance, and continuous technological advancements. The case examines WeRide's growth strategies, including product diversification into Robotaxis, Robobuses, and Robovans, as well as its expansion into international markets with operations spanning 26 cities globally. Highlighting key figures such as Xu Han and Hua Zhong, the study delves into their pivotal roles in driving WeRide's technological evolution and market dominance. It discusses prospects, including upcoming technologies like WeRide Sensor Suite 5.2 and strategic alliances with major travel platforms. WeRide's journey highlights their dedication to revolutionizing transportation through advanced self-driving technology and valuable international collaborations.

This case study explores the development and strategic growth of Tuhu Vehicle Co., Ltd., a leading player in China's automotive aftermarket, under the leadership of MIN Chen. It provides a comprehensive analysis of Chen's extensive background in software development, data management, and the automotive service sector, highlighting his pivotal role in transforming Tuhu from a tire-changing service to a diversified O2O one-stop automobile repair and maintenance company. The case delves into Tuhu's innovative approaches, including the implementation of standardized services, the creation of industry alliances, and the launch of an open product platform. It examines Tuhu's strategic expansion, its successful IPO on the Hong Kong Stock Exchange, and its forward-looking initiatives in the new energy vehicle market. By analyzing Tuhu's business model, supply chain revolutions, and market positioning, this case provides insights into the company's unique development path, operational resilience, and its impact on China's auto aftermarket industry.

This case study delves into ByteDance, a pioneering force in global technology led by visionary founder Zhang Yiming and CEO Shou Zi Chew. It explores ByteDance's journey from its inception, driven by innovative AI technologies and a global expansion strategy, to becoming a dominant player in social media with platforms like TikTok. The case examines ByteDance's multifaceted approach, including its development of the MegaScale AI system for large-scale language model training and its strategies for navigating complex data sovereignty issues across international markets. It also analyzes ByteDance's competitive landscape, encompassing key rivals in social media, AI development, e-commerce, and cloud services. Moreover, the case scrutinizes ByteDance's leadership strategies, emphasizing its efforts in user data privacy compliance and global regulatory challenges. Through these insights, the case offers a comprehensive view of ByteDance's evolution, strategic initiatives, and the broader implications for the tech industry.

Chapter 19

Zhixuan Yu, EDHEC Business School, France

This case study explores the evolution and strategic trajectory of Xiaohongshu, a pioneering social commerce platform in China. Founded in 2013 by Miranda Qu and Charlwin Mao, Xiaohongshu has redefined consumer engagement by seamlessly integrating social media with e-commerce functionalities. Initially conceived as an online guide for Chinese shoppers abroad, the platform quickly developed into a vibrant community where users share product recommendations, reviews, and lifestyle insights. Xiaohongshu's strategic pivot on social commerce in 2014 marked a significant milestone, enabling direct product purchases within its app and fostering a dynamic ecosystem of user-generated content. The case examines Xiaohongshu's growth trajectory, challenges such as counterfeit goods, and strategic initiatives, including influencer marketing and blockchain integration. With a focus on expanding its user base, enhancing e-commerce capabilities, and exploring emerging technologies like Web3, Xiaohongshu continues to shape the future of digital commerce in China's competitive market landscape.

Chapter 20

Danyu Luo, Beijing Normal University-Hong Kong Baptist University United International College, China

This case study explores the dynamic evolution of China's audio economy industry, focusing on technological advancements, market trends, and key players, such as Ximalaya. With a historical perspective, it traces the industry's growth through distinct eras, from early audiobooks to the current era dominated by mobile internet and specialized audio services. Market data from AI Media Consulting underscores the industry's exponential growth, driven by factors like the increased demand for online learning and knowledge payment. Detailed demographic insights highlight the user composition and providing a comprehensive understanding of consumer behaviors and preferences. Central to this narrative is the pivotal role of Jianjun Yu, founder of Ximalaya, whose entrepreneurial journey and strategic vision have shaped the platform's prominence in delivering high-quality audio content. As the industry navigates developing media consumption habits and technological advancements, this case study offers valuable insights into the future trajectories of China's vibrant audio economy landscape.

Chapter 21

This case study explores the transformative journey of Mafengwo, a leading travel platform in China, from 2015 to the present. It examines Mafengwo's strategic shift from a community-based model to a comprehensive travel service platform, focusing on its commercialization efforts and expansion into transaction-based revenue streams. The narrative highlights the visionary leadership of co-founders Chen Gang and Lv Gang, who leveraged extensive data research and strategic foresight to position Mafengwo as a global travel consumer guide. The case delves into the company's innovative use of the Youyun SaaS system to enhance productivity and flexibility for travel agencies and its efforts to capitalize on the "new golden decade of freedom" in tourism. It outlines Mafengwo's launch of "new tourism methods" and its comprehensive community upgrade to meet personalized travel demands. The case concludes with an overview of Mafengwo's plans to integrate AI travel tools, underscoring the company's commitment to leveraging big data for personalized scaling in the tourism industry.

Chapter 22

This case study examines Kuaikan Manhua, a prominent player in China's digital comics industry, focusing on its strategic evolution and entrepreneurial journey under the leadership of founder Annie Chen. Beginning with a mission to foster a vibrant Gen Z content community, Kuaikan Manhua employed an "intellectual property plus community" strategy, leveraging AI and big data to enhance content creation and user engagement. The study highlights key initiatives, such as IP development, community integration through the Community World platform, and international expansion efforts, like the Columbus Plan. It also explores challenges, including regulatory constraints and shifting market dynamics, offering insights into Kuaikan Manhua's resilience and innovation in navigating these obstacles. Through this analysis, the case underscores Kuaikan Manhua's pivotal role in shaping China's digital comics landscape and provides strategic lessons for businesses operating in dynamic and competitive digital content markets.

This case study explores Keep, a pioneering company in the Chinese fitness industry known for its innovative approach to blending technology with fitness solutions. Founded by Wang Ning, Keep revolutionized home fitness during the COVID-19 pandemic by introducing interactive live classes and expanding its digital offerings. The study examines Keep's strategic adaptations amid market challenges, such as shifting from offline gyms to collaborative ventures with traditional fitness centers. It highlights Keep's successful integration of gamification and virtual events to enhance user engagement and retention. The case also delves into Wang Ning's entrepreneurial journey, emphasizing his vision to democratize access to fitness through accessible, tech-driven solutions. Through rigorous analysis of Keep's business strategies, technological innovations, and market positioning, this case study provides insights into the dynamics of digital transformation in the fitness sector and its implications for future industry trends.

This case study explores the transformative journey of Yuanfudao within China's dynamic K12 online education sector. Founded by Li Yong in 2012, it initially struggled with its business model centred around their question bank. Overcoming early challenges, they pivoted to capitalize on the burgeoning demand for online live courses, launching Fenbigongkao and subsequently integrating AI-driven solutions like Ape Search and Zebra AI. As the market evolved, they navigated regulatory changes and competitive pressures, adapting strategies to align with national educational policies and shifting consumer preference. The case examines key milestones such as strategic partnerships with Xinhua Publishing House and the launch of the Ape Learning Machine, highlighting their innovative approach to enhancing learning outcomes through technology. Analysing the growth trajectory, technological advancements, and strategic initiatives, the case offers insights into the broader implications of digital transformation in education and their role in shaping the future of K12 online learning in China.

Chapter 25

This case study examines Zuoyebang's strategic evolution from an online education platform to a leader in intelligent education hardware amidst transformative industry shifts and regulatory challenges in China. Founded by Hou Jianbin in 2015 as a spinoff from Baidu, Zuoyebang initially focused on providing K12 students with homework assistance. Overcoming industry crises and regulatory changes, the company pivoted towards developing AI-powered learning devices, leveraging its extensive data resources and market insights. The case details Zuoyebang's strategic decisions, including extensive financing rounds, workforce expansion to over 30,000 employees, and the launch of successful intelligent hardware products. It also explores future directions, such as expanding offline sales channels and continuous product innovation, highlighting Zuoyebang's adaptation to market demands and technological advancements in the education sector.

Chapter 26

This case study examines Poizon, a leading fashion e-commerce platform in China, renowned for its innovative approach to catering to young consumers' demands for authenticity, community engagement, and trend-setting products. Founded by Yang Bing in 2015, Poizon has rapidly established itself as a prominent player in the competitive market by integrating e-commerce with social elements, ensuring product authenticity through robust identification services, and fostering a vibrant community of fashion enthusiasts. The case explores Poizon's strategic initiatives, including its unique business model, technological innovations such as AR try-ons, and community-driven marketing strategies. It also assesses Poizon's competitors, the difficulties of sustaining growth in a competitive market, and the potential opportunities for changing consumer preferences and market dynamics.

This case study examines Zhuan Zhuan, a prominent second-hand e-commerce platform in China, focusing on its development, sustainability initiatives, strategic partnerships, and prospects. Founded under the leadership of Yao Jinbo from 58 Group, Zhuan Zhuan has strategically positioned itself in the circular economy by facilitating the trade of idle goods to reduce carbon emissions and promote sustainable consumption. Rigorous quality control measures, extensive user engagement via Tencent's WeChat, and partnerships enhancing logistical and financial capabilities underscored the platform's success. Zhuan Zhuan's plans include deeper integration with Tencent for user acquisition and trust-building, expanding product categories to include larger appliances, and leveraging its parent company's ecosystem to streamline operations and foster environmental stewardship. This case highlights Zhuan Zhuan's role in sustainable commerce and its trajectory towards broader societal and environmental impact in the e-commerce landscape.

Preface

In today's fast-changing world of startups, the term 'unicorn' refers to companies valued at over $1 billion. These companies show great innovation and business success. As more and more unicorns appear, China has become a major player in this area, showing its growing strength in business and innovation. *Cases on Chinese Unicorns and the Development of Startups* is a casebook that regroups a series of case studies exploring this entrepreneurial world and looks closely at the beginning, growth, and future plans of some of China's top unicorn companies.

The primary objective of the casebook is to provide a comprehensive and insightful exploration of China's most prominent unicorn companies. In a landscape dominated by swift technological innovations and dynamic startup cultures, understanding these major players' rise, strategies, leadership, and future aspirations becomes paramount. Through detailed case studies, this casebook aims to demystify the growth trajectory of these entities, offering readers a clear lens into the factors that propel a startup into the billion-dollar valuation club.

The casebook will elevate our understanding of the business ecosystem in China. By closely studying these unicorns' financial strategies, leadership dynamics, and growth blueprints, entrepreneurs, researchers, and students can gather practical insights that could be replicated or adapted in different global contexts. Additionally, as China continues to cement its position as a global economic powerhouse, understanding its business narratives will facilitate better East-West business collaborations and synergies.

The target audience spans a broad spectrum of readers with interests in business, entrepreneurship, and global market dynamics. It's particularly suited for academic scholars and researchers who are keen to understand the Chinese startup ecosystem and the factors that contribute to the rapid ascension of companies to unicorn status. Business students, both at the undergraduate and postgraduate levels, can benefit from the real-world case studies presented, giving them a practical perspective that goes beyond traditional textbook learning.

Moreover, entrepreneurs and startup enthusiasts can derive valuable insights into scaling businesses, understanding market dynamics, and navigating the complexities of rapid growth. The book can serve as a primer for international businesses and investors looking to collaborate or invest in the Chinese market, offering them a clearer understanding of the operational intricacies and cultural nuances.

In addition, business consultants and strategists can utilise the casebook as a reference for designing growth strategies, understanding leadership dynamics, and anticipating market shifts in similar ecosystems. Libraries, business schools, and research institutions would also find this casebook to be a valuable addition to their collections, facilitating both academic inquiry and practical business discussions.

Each case study in this casebook will tell the in-depth story of a different Chinese unicorn through credible and verifiable information. The cases start by giving current details about the company, like basic information, the markets they're in, the products or services they offer, and how the company is set up. Furthermore, the cases track the company's journey over time. It discusses how they grew, the main strategies they used, how they made money, and the problems they faced. This section gives a complete view of their ups and downs and how they tackled challenges. Furthermore, a big part of each company's story is its leaders. The casebook discusses their leaders, how they led the company, and any major leadership changes. Finally, funding is crucial for any startup. So, the casebook also looks at how these unicorns got the money they needed to grow. It explains who invested in them, the different funding rounds, and other strategic ways they used to raise money. Ultimately, each case study looks at what the company plans to do next.

We, the editors—Youssef Elhaoussine, Henni Appelgryn, and Lulu Wang—are excited to present this casebook. Our aim is to shed light on the unique dynamics that drive the success of Chinese unicorns and to offer valuable lessons that can inspire and inform the next generation of entrepreneurs, business leaders, and scholars around the globe.

ORGANISATION OF THE BOOK

Becoming a unicorn company is achievable for businesses in various industries through innovation, strategic adaptability, and customer-centric approaches. While technology-driven enterprises often grab the spotlight, unicorns can emerge from diverse sectors. This diversity shows that the journey to becoming a unicorn is not limited to one path; it can be achieved by any company that effectively harnesses market demands, embraces continuous innovation, and forges strategic partnerships. The successful unicorn cases described in this casebook illustrate that with the right business model, vision, and execution, companies from any industry can achieve significant growth and secure their place among the elite. Here are the cases listed below:

Chapter 1: Manner Coffee: Journey in China's Specialty Coffee Market

Chapter 1 explores Manner Coffee's strategic journey within China's burgeoning specialty coffee market. The chapter examines the company's unique positioning, blending modern aesthetics with traditional Chinese elements to resonate with local consumers. Key focal points include Manner Coffee's community engagement, sustainability practices, and technological innovations that have fostered customer loyalty and driven growth. However, the company faces a significant trademark infringement issue with Josef Manner & Comp AG, posing challenges to its brand identity and expansion plans. This chapter provides valuable insights into brand management, market entry strategies, and the complexities of protecting intellectual property in international markets, illustrating Manner Coffee's dedication to delivering premium coffee experiences despite legal uncertainties.

Chapter 2: Heytea: Revolutionizing the Beverage Industry with Innovation and Customer Engagement

Chapter 2 explores Heytea's transformative journey in China's beverage industry. The case study highlights Heytea's innovative business model, comprehensive product offerings, and strategic initiatives that have enabled it to capture a significant market share. The detailed analysis covers Heytea's customer profiles, marketing tactics, and competitive environment. The chapter profiles MIN Chen, the visionary Chairperson and CEO, whose expertise in software development and data management has shaped Heytea's growth trajectory. By understanding Heytea's operational strategies and market positioning, readers gain insights into the dynamics of the beverage industry in China and the factors contributing to the success of this leading industry player.

Chapter 3: Hello Trans Tech: Pioneering Sustainable Mobility in the Shared Economy

Chapter 3 examines Hello Trans Tech's evolution and strategic initiatives in China's shared mobility sector. Founded in 2016 amidst the bike-sharing boom, Hello Trans Tech quickly emerged as a leader through innovative technologies and sustainable transportation solutions. The chapter details the company's journey from bike-sharing to a comprehensive mobility platform, highlighting strategic partnerships with Alibaba and Contemporary Amperex Technology and expansion into Singapore. Key aspects include AI-driven optimisation and carbon-neutral initiatives, showcasing the vision of founders Yang Lei and Kaizhu Li. This chapter provides insights into how Hello Trans Tech has reshaped urban transportation and positioned itself at the forefront of China's shared economy revolution.

Chapter 4: Zongmu Technology: Autonomous Driving and Advanced Driver Assistance Systems (ADAS)

Chapter 4 explores Zongmu Technology's market analysis within China's autonomous driving and Advanced Driver Assistance Systems (ADAS) sector. The chapter covers the shift from traditional vehicles to new energy vehicles, highlighting Zongmu's transition from secondary software algorithms to full-stack solutions. The competitive environment and challenges against rivals such as Velodyne Lidar and Pony.ai are examined. The case study also details Zongmu's complex shareholding structure, strategic partnerships, and future projects, such as intelligent driving systems and smart city solutions. This comprehensive analysis sheds light on Zongmu Technology's strategies for growth and innovation in the rapidly developing autonomous driving market.

Chapter 5: UISEE: Driving Innovation Technology and the Evolution of Autonomous Vehicles

Chapter 5 investigates the dynamic landscape of the autonomous driving industry, focusing on UISEE Technology. Founded by Ganesha Wu in 2016, UISEE has become a key innovator in China's autonomous driving market. The chapter examines UISEE's competitive strategies, technological advancements, and strategic collaborations, emphasising its pivotal role in advancing autonomous vehicle technologies. Market dynamics, regulatory influences, and future implications for the automotive industry are explored. This chapter provides a thorough understanding of UISEE's evolution, strategic initiatives, and the broader impact on the future of autonomous driving technologies.

Chapter 6: Keenon Robotics: Innovating the Future of Commercial Service Robots

Chapter 6 explores Keenon Robotics' rapid evolution and strategic initiatives in commercial service robots. The chapter focuses on innovative technologies like Robot as a Service (RaaS) and Keenon Robotics' impact on sectors such as catering, healthcare, hospitality, and epidemic management. Key products and strategic expansions into new markets and industries are highlighted. The chapter underscores Keenon

Robotics' commitment to technological innovation and societal impact, showcasing its pivotal role in addressing contemporary challenges through service robotics. Through insightful analysis, this chapter explains Keenon Robotics' strategies for navigating opportunities and challenges in the burgeoning field of service robotics.

Chapter 7: Star Charge: Developing China's Electric Vehicle Charging Landscape

Chapter 7 examines Star Charge's pivotal role in China's electric vehicle (EV) charging infrastructure market. Founded amid ambitious government initiatives to bolster EV adoption, Star Charge has rapidly emerged as a leader. The chapter explores Star Charge's strategic development, unique crowdfunding approach, and technological advancements in charging stations. The company's contributions to China's dual carbon goals and future projections, including international expansion and Vehicle-to-Grid (V2G) technology, are analysed. This comprehensive analysis illustrates how Star Charge continues to shape the future of sustainable mobility in China and beyond.

Chapter 8: Medlinker: Innovations at the Forefront of China's Internet Healthcare Market

Chapter 8 examines Medlinker, a leading figure in China's internet healthcare sector. Founded in 2014 by Dr. Wang Shirui, Medlinker has transformed from a social networking platform for doctors to a comprehensive disease management service integrating AI-driven solutions. The chapter explores Medlinker's pioneering role in leveraging MedGPT, China's first large language model for medical applications, and its strategic initiatives to enhance healthcare accessibility and efficiency. Market competition, regulatory dynamics, and Medlinker's innovative approach to digital healthcare are analysed, providing insights into the company's strategies for continued innovation and expansion in the rapidly growing industry.

Chapter 9: WeDoctor: Journey to Leadership in China's Internet Healthcare Industry

Chapter 9 explores the evolution and strategic growth of WeDoctor, a pioneering force in China's Internet healthcare sector. Founded amidst challenges within China's medical regulatory environment, WeDoctor leveraged technological innovation and strategic partnerships to establish itself as a leader. The chapter details WeDoctor's progression through key stages, highlighting stakeholder engagement, technological integration, and policy advocacy. WeDoctor's success in gaining regulatory legitimacy and scaling innovative models underscores its role in transforming healthcare delivery through digital solutions. This chapter provides valuable insights into WeDoctor's journey and its impact on the future of internet-based medical services in China.

Chapter 10: Weilong: Journey from Regional Delicacy to Global Brand

Chapter 10 explores the rise of Weilong, a leading player in China's spicy snack market. The chapter examines Weilong's transformation from a regional brand to a national and international powerhouse under the leadership of CEO Liu Weiping and CFO Peng Hongzhi. Key strategies such as innovative branding, market expansion, and cultural promotion are highlighted. The chapter details Weilong's journey from localised marketing strategies in Henan province to national prominence, leveraging digital platforms and cultural resonance to engage a youthful consumer base. Through meticulous analysis, this chapter showcases Weilong's effective growth strategies in the dynamic Chinese consumer goods sector.

Chapter 11: Guoquan Shihui: Reforming the Prepared Food Market through Integrated Supply Chain and Digital Innovation

Chapter 11 examines Guoquan Shihui's revolution of the hotpot industry through innovative supply chain management and digital integration. Founded by Mingchao Yang, Guoquan Shihui's journey from a night market entrepreneur to a billionaire is explored. Key aspects include the company's robust logistics system, collaboration with ODM plants, and cold chain technology for freshness. The chapter also highlights Guoquan Shihui's expansion from a small retail outlet to a nationwide network, leveraging multi-platform marketing strategies for consumer engagement. This chapter provides insights into Guoquan Shihui's leadership in blending traditional cuisine with modern business practices, setting a benchmark for industry transformation and consumer-centric innovation.

Chapter 12: Jiuxian: Revolutionizing Liquor Distribution in China through Omnichannel Innovation

Chapter 12 examines Jiuxian's transformative journey within China's competitive liquor distribution industry. Founded in 2009 by Hao Hongfeng, Jiuxian pioneered online liquor retailing in a market traditionally dominated by offline channels. The chapter explores Jiuxian's strategic partnerships, aggressive expansion, and adaptation to market shifts. Key innovations include the integration of live-streaming commerce to engage a younger consumer base. Despite challenges such as financial setbacks and IPO delays, Jiuxian's resilience and strategic vision have positioned it at the forefront of China's liquor retail sector. This chapter provides insights into Jiuxian's omnichannel excellence and market innovation.

Chapter 13: Wenheyou: Reviving and Preserving Changsha's Culinary Heritage

Chapter 13 explores Wenheyou, a pioneering culinary brand in Changsha, China. Founded by Wen Bin, Wenheyou blends nostalgia-driven consumption with urban cultural preservation. The chapter highlights Wenheyou's strategic blend of culinary innovation and emotional engagement, targeting young consumers. Key aspects include themed dining complexes like Super Wenheyou and the integration of local specialities with immersive historical settings. Wen Bin's entrepreneurial journey and Wenheyou's role in fostering deep consumer connections and contributing to local cultural revitalisation are explored. This chapter provides insights into Wenheyou's transformation into a symbol of Changsha's cultural identity.

Chapter 14: Beisen: Transforming Human Capital Management

Chapter 14 examines Beisen Holdings Limited's evolution as a pioneer in China's Human Capital Management (HCM) industry. Founded in 2002, Beisen embraced cloud computing and advanced AI technologies to offer integrated HCM solutions. The chapter traces Beisen's transition from Software as a Service (SaaS) to Platform as a Service (PaaS), culminating in the development of iTalent X. Key innovations include AI-driven recruitment, talent management, and performance analytics tools. Market dynamics, technological advancements, and socio-economic effects like the pandemic are analysed. This chapter provides insights into Beisen's transformation into a comprehensive HCM solution provider and the implications for workforce management.

Chapter 15: Yuanqi Forest: Navigating Growth in China's Health Drinks Market

Chapter 15 explores how Yuanqi Forest has grown and changed its strategy in the competitive health drinks market in China. Founded with a vision to offer healthier beverage alternatives, Yuanqi Forest capitalised on rising consumer demand for natural, low-sugar beverages by innovating with unique flavours and leveraging digital marketing channels. The case delves into Yuanqi Forest's early challenges in product sourcing and its subsequent growth through effective branding, product diversification, and e-commerce expansion. Analysing competitive pressures from established players and emerging brands, the study examines Yuanqi Forest's strategies to maintain market leadership, including sustainability initiatives and international expansion ambitions. Through a comprehensive exploration of its development phases, market positioning, and outlook, this case provides insights into navigating the complexities of consumer-driven markets and achieving sustained growth in the beverage industry.

Chapter 16: WeRide: Pioneering Autonomous Driving Innovation and Global Expansion

Chapter 16 explores WeRide, a leading innovator in autonomous driving technology, tracing its journey from inception to becoming a global powerhouse in the autonomous vehicle industry. Founded by Xu Han, WeRide has strategically positioned itself through significant investments, strategic partnerships with global giants like Renault-Nissan-Mitsubishi Alliance, and continuous technological advancements. The case examines WeRide's growth strategies, including product diversification into Robotaxis, Robobuses, and Robovans, as well as its expansion into international markets with operations spanning 26 cities globally. Highlighting key figures such as Xu Han and Hua Zhong, the study delves into their pivotal roles in driving WeRide's technological evolution and market dominance. It discusses prospects, including upcoming technologies like WeRide Sensor Suite 5.2 and strategic alliances with major travel platforms. WeRide's journey highlights its dedication to revolutionising transportation through advanced self-driving technology and valuable international collaborations.

Chapter 17: Tuhu: Changing China's Automotive Aftermarket

Chapter 17 explores the development and strategic growth of Tuhu Vehicle Co., Ltd., a leading player in China's automotive aftermarket, under the leadership of MIN Chen. It provides a comprehensive analysis of Chen's extensive background in software development, data management, and the automotive service sector, highlighting his pivotal role in transforming Tuhu from a tire-changing service to a diversified O2O one-stop automobile repair and maintenance company. The case delves into Tuhu's innovative approaches, including the implementation of standardised services, the creation of industry alliances, and the launch of an open product platform. It examines Tuhu's strategic expansion, its successful IPO on the Hong Kong Stock Exchange, and its forward-looking initiatives in the new energy vehicle market. By analysing Tuhu's business model, supply chain revolutions, and market positioning, this case provides insights into the company's unique development path, operational resilience, and impact on China's auto aftermarket industry.

Chapter 18: ByteDance: Innovating Global Technology and Navigating Strategic Challenges

Chapter 18 explores ByteDance, a pioneering force in global technology led by visionary founder Zhang Yiming and CEO Shou Zi Chew. It explores ByteDance's journey from its inception, driven by innovative AI technologies and a global expansion strategy, to becoming a dominant player in social media with platforms like TikTok. The case examines ByteDance's multifaceted approach, including its development of the MegaScale AI system for large-scale language model training and its strategies for navigating complex data sovereignty issues across international markets. It also analyses ByteDance's competitive landscape, encompassing key rivals in social media, AI development, e-commerce, and cloud services. Moreover, the case scrutinises ByteDance's leadership strategies, emphasising its efforts in user data privacy compliance and global regulatory challenges. Through these insights, the case offers a comprehensive view of ByteDance's evolution, strategic initiatives, and broader implications for the tech industry.

Chapter 19: Xiaohongshu: Modernizing Social Commerce in China's Digital Landscape

Chapter 19 explores the evolution and strategic trajectory of Xiaohongshu, a pioneering social commerce platform in China. Founded in 2013 by Miranda Qu and Charlwin Mao, Xiaohongshu has redefined consumer engagement by seamlessly integrating social media with e-commerce functionalities. Initially conceived as an online guide for Chinese shoppers abroad, the platform quickly developed into a vibrant community where users share product recommendations, reviews, and lifestyle insights. Xiaohongshu's strategic pivot on social commerce in 2014 marked a significant milestone, enabling direct product purchases within its app and fostering a dynamic ecosystem of user-generated content. The case examines Xiaohongshu's growth trajectory, challenges such as counterfeit goods, and strategic initiatives, including influencer marketing and blockchain integration. With a focus on expanding its user base, enhancing e-commerce capabilities, and exploring emerging technologies like Web3, Xiaohongshu continues to shape the future of digital commerce in China's competitive market landscape.

Chapter 20: Ximalaya FM: Empowering the Sound Economy and the Evolution of China's Audio Industry

Chapter 20 explores the dynamic evolution of China's audio economy industry, focusing on technological advancements, market trends, and key players, such as Ximalaya. From a historical perspective, it traces the industry's growth through distinct eras, from early audiobooks to the current era dominated by mobile internet and specialised audio services. Market data from Ai Media Consulting underscores the industry's exponential growth, driven by factors like the increased demand for online learning and knowledge payment. Detailed demographic insights highlight the user composition and provide a comprehensive understanding of consumer behaviours and preferences. Central to this narrative is the pivotal role of Jianjun Yu, founder of Ximalaya, whose entrepreneurial journey and strategic vision have shaped the platform's prominence in delivering high-quality audio content. As the industry navigates developing media consumption habits and technological advancements, this case study offers valuable insights into the future trajectories of China's vibrant audio economy landscape.

Chapter 21: Mafengwo: From Travel Community to Global Tourism Powerhouse

Chapter 21 explores the transformative journey of Mafengwo, a leading travel platform in China, from 2015 to the present. It examines Mafengwo's strategic shift from a community-based model to a comprehensive travel service platform, focusing on its commercialisation efforts and expansion into transaction-based revenue streams. The narrative highlights the visionary leadership of co-founders Chen Gang and Lv Gang, who leveraged extensive data research and strategic foresight to position Mafengwo as a global travel consumer guide. The case delves into the company's innovative use of the Youyun SaaS system to enhance productivity and flexibility for travel agencies and its efforts to capitalise on the "new golden decade of freedom" in tourism. It outlines Mafengwo's launch of "new tourism methods" and its comprehensive community upgrade to meet personalised travel demands. The case concludes with an overview of Mafengwo's plans to integrate AI travel tools, underscoring the company's commitment to leveraging big data for personalised scaling in the tourism industry.

Chapter 22: Kuaikan Manhua: Empowering China's Digital Comics Landscape

Chapter 22 examines Kuaikan Manhua, a prominent player in China's digital comics industry, focusing on its strategic evolution and entrepreneurial journey under the leadership of founder Annie Chen. Beginning with a mission to foster a vibrant Gen Z content community, Kuaikan Manhua employed an "intellectual property plus community" strategy, leveraging AI and big data to enhance content creation and user engagement. The study highlights key initiatives, such as IP development, community integration through the Community World platform, and international expansion efforts, like the Columbus Plan. It also explores challenges, including regulatory constraints and shifting market dynamics, offering insights into Kuaikan Manhua's resilience and innovation in navigating these obstacles. Through this analysis, the case underscores Kuaikan Manhua's pivotal role in shaping China's digital comics landscape and provides strategic lessons for businesses operating in dynamic and competitive digital content markets.

Chapter 23: Keep: Transforming Fitness Through Innovation and Integration

Chapter 23 explores Keep, a pioneering company in the Chinese fitness industry known for its innovative approach to blending technology with fitness solutions. Founded by Wang Ning, Keep revolutionised home fitness during the COVID-19 pandemic by introducing interactive live classes and expanding its digital offerings. The study examines Keep's strategic adaptations amid market challenges, such as shifting from offline gyms to collaborative ventures with traditional fitness centres. It highlights Keep's successful integration of gamification and virtual events to enhance user engagement and retention. The case also delves into Wang Ning's entrepreneurial journey, emphasising his vision to democratise access to fitness through accessible, tech-driven solutions. Through rigorous analysis of Keep's business strategies, technological innovations, and market positioning, this case study provides insights into the dynamics of digital transformation in the fitness sector and its implications for future industry trends.

Chapter 24: Yuanfudao: Transforming China's K12 Online Education Landscape

Chapter 24 explores the transformative journey of Yuanfudao within China's dynamic K12 online education sector. Founded by Li Yong in 2012, it initially struggled with its business model centred around its question bank. Overcoming early challenges, they pivoted to capitalise on the burgeoning demand for online live courses, launching Fenbigongkao and subsequently integrating AI-driven solutions like Ape Search and Zebra AI. As the market evolved, they navigated regulatory changes and competitive pressures, adapting their strategies to align with national educational policies and shifting consumer preferences. The case examines key milestones such as strategic partnerships with Xinhua Publishing House and the launch of the Ape Learning Machine, highlighting their innovative approach to enhancing learning outcomes through technology. Analysing the growth trajectory, technological advancements, and strategic initiatives, the case offers insights into the broader implications of digital transformation in education and its role in shaping the future of K12 online learning in China.

Chapter 25: Zuoyebang: Pioneering the Future of Intelligent Education Hardware

Chapter 25 examines Zuoyebang's strategic evolution from an online education platform to a leader in intelligent education hardware amidst transformative industry shifts and regulatory challenges in China. Founded by Hou Jianbin in 2015 as a spinoff from Baidu, Zuoyebang initially focused on providing K12 students with homework assistance. Overcoming industry crises and regulatory changes, the company pivoted towards developing AI-powered learning devices, leveraging its extensive data resources and market insights. The case details Zuoyebang's strategic decisions, including extensive financing rounds, workforce expansion to over 30,000 employees, and the launch of successful, intelligent hardware products. It also explores future directions, such as expanding offline sales channels and continuous product innovation, highlighting Zuoyebang's adaptation to market demands and technological advancements in the education sector.

Chapter 26: Poizon: Redefining Fashion E-commerce through Quality, Community, and Innovation

Chapter 26 examines Poizon, a leading fashion e-commerce platform in China, renowned for its innovative approach to catering to young consumers' demands for authenticity, community engagement, and trend-setting products. Founded by Yang Bing in 2015, Poizon has rapidly established itself as a prominent player in the competitive market by integrating e-commerce with social elements, ensuring product authenticity through robust identification services, and fostering a vibrant community of fashion enthusiasts. The case explores Poizon's strategic initiatives, including its unique business model, technological innovations such as AR try-ons, and community-driven marketing strategies. It also assesses Poizon's competitors, the difficulties of sustaining growth in a competitive market, and the potential opportunities for changing consumer preferences and market dynamics.

Chapter 27: Zhuan Zhuan: Pioneering Sustainability in Second-Hand E-Commerce

Chapter 27 examines Zhuan Zhuan, a prominent second-hand e-commerce platform in China, focusing on its development, sustainability initiatives, strategic partnerships, and prospects. Founded under the leadership of Yao Jinbo from 58 Group, Zhuan Zhuan has strategically positioned itself in the circular economy by facilitating the trade of idle goods to reduce carbon emissions and promote sustainable consumption. Rigorous quality control measures, extensive user engagement via Tencent's WeChat, and partnerships enhancing logistical and financial capabilities underscored the platform's success. Zhuan Zhuan's plans include deeper integration with Tencent for user acquisition and trust-building, expanding product categories to include larger appliances, and leveraging its parent company's ecosystem to streamline operations and foster environmental stewardship. This case highlights Zhuan Zhuan's role in sustainable commerce and its trajectory towards broader societal and environmental impact in the e-commerce landscape.

IN CONCLUSION

As editors of this comprehensive case book, we are proud to present a series of case studies that offer profound insights into China's most dynamic and transformative industries. These chapters collectively underscore the remarkable growth, innovation, and resilience demonstrated by leading companies across a wide array of sectors.

The case studies of these 27 Chinese unicorn companies highlight the remarkable diversity of industries in which they operate, showcasing innovation, adaptability, and strategic foresight across a broad spectrum of sectors. These industries include Human Capital Management, Digital Content and Social Media, Retail and Food, Mobility and Urban Transportation, Digital Healthcare, Education Technology, E-commerce and Retail, Robotics and AI, Audio and Media, Electric Vehicles, and Beverages.

Human Capital Management is exemplified by Beisen, a pioneer in HR management solutions in China. Their journey from a SaaS to a PaaS model reflects the importance of strategic adaptability to meet evolving customer needs. Beisen's innovative cloud-based solutions have revolutionised the HR landscape, emphasising the crucial role of aligning technological innovation with market demands.

In the era of Digital Content and Social Media, ByteDance stands out with its AI-driven platforms like TikTok, which have transformed how content is consumed globally. Similarly, Kuaikan Manhua has carved a niche in the digital comics industry by fostering community engagement and cultural relevance, while Xiaohongshu blends social media with e-commerce, catering to the lifestyle needs of young urban consumers through user-generated content and strategic partnerships.

The Retail and Food Industry showcases significant innovation and growth. Guo Quan Shi Hui has made its mark in the hot pot industry through robust supply chain management and technological integration. Heytea has modernised traditional tea culture with creative products like cheese tea, while Manner Coffee focuses on premium, ethically sourced coffee, emphasising quality and sustainability. Weilong leverages Chinese culinary traditions, adapting them to global tastes and using technology to ensure quality and efficiency. Wenheyou taps into cultural nostalgia, blending heritage with culinary expertise to create unique dining experiences. Yuanqi Forest has rapidly emerged as a major player in the global beverage market, focusing on health-conscious products with "0 sugar, 0 calories, 0 fat" that appeal to younger consumers.

Mobility and Urban Transportation feature prominently with companies like Hello Trans Tech, which has expanded from bike-sharing to comprehensive travel-sharing platforms, and WeRide, which leads in autonomous driving technology through continuous innovation and strategic partnerships. UISEE and Zongmu Technology also operate in this space, advancing autonomous driving through technological integration and strategic collaborations.

Digital Healthcare is represented by Medlinker and WeDoctor. Medlinker integrates online and offline services with AI and technology to enhance healthcare delivery, while WeDoctor focuses on making healthcare more accessible and efficient through technology-driven solutions and strategic partnerships.

In Education Technology, companies like Keep, Yuanfudao, and Zuoyebang have transformed learning through innovative approaches. Keep combining online fitness content with social community and management tools, adapting to market trends with agility. Yuanfudao leverages AI for personalised learning, ensuring quality education despite regulatory changes. Zuoyebang has evolved from homework assistance to a comprehensive K12 education provider, emphasising user-centric development and strategic alliances.

The E-commerce and Retail sector includes Jiuxian, Poizon, Zhuan Zhuan, and Tuhu. Jiuxian has become China's largest integrated liquor e-commerce company through a hybrid business model and strategic partnerships. Poizon focuses on authenticity in the fashion market, integrating social functionalities to enhance user engagement. Zhuan Zhuan revolutionises second-hand transactions with trust and transparency, while Tuhu expands automotive services through innovation and logistical excellence.

Robotics and AI are highlighted by Keenon Robotics, which leads in unmanned delivery solutions by solving real-world problems through technological innovation. Their customer-centric business model and R&D investment have driven significant growth.

In Audio and Media, Ximalaya FM demonstrates growth by innovating its business model and leveraging data for strategic decisions. The company diversifies revenue streams and enhances user engagement through exclusive content and strategic partnerships.

Lastly, the Electric Vehicles sector is represented by Star Charge, which has evolved in the EV charging industry by adapting business strategies and leveraging innovative financing. Their focus on sustainability and technological advancement underscores the importance of aligning business operations with environmental goals.

Mafengwo has carved a niche in the tourism industry by blending user-generated content with transactional capabilities supported by big data and AI. This fusion has positioned Mafengwo as a leader in personalised travel experiences, fundamentally altering how tourism products are consumed and provided.

These case studies illustrate how these companies, across diverse industries, have leveraged innovation, strategic adaptability, and customer-centric approaches to achieve significant growth and maintain a competitive edge. The diversity of these industries showcases the dynamic nature of the Chinese market and the broad range of opportunities for innovation and development. Each company's journey offers valuable insights into the critical factors driving success in their respective fields, emphasising the importance of continuous innovation, strategic partnerships, and responsiveness to market demands.

Youssef Elhaoussine

Beijing Normal University-Hong Kong Baptist University United International College, China

Henni Appelgryn

Beijing Normal Universitiy-Hong Kong Baptist University United International College, China

Lulu Wang

Business Advantage Consulting, China

Acknowledgment

We are immensely grateful to all the authors who took part in this project and shared valuable case studies. Their dedicated efforts to gather and integrate precious information have significantly enhanced our understanding of China's market. Their contributions are not only academic achievements but also crucial for business practitioners and researchers, shaping our knowledge and insights.

We want to express our gratitude to the Faculty of Business and Management at the Beijing Normal University – Hong Kong Baptist University United International College for their support throughout this project. Specifically, Professor Adolf Ng and Dr. Darren Weng, respectively Dean and Assistant Dean of the Faculty of Business and Management. As an international higher education institution in China, the university provided an ideal environment for developing this practical research project in business. We are hopeful that the findings from this project will be beneficial and inspiring for the students.

We would like to express our gratitude to the IGI editorial team for giving us the opportunity to create this case book. They have also offered an exceptional support system to manage the publication process efficiently, especially Nina Eddinger.

Thank you all for your invaluable contributions. We are hopeful that this case book will not only enhance our understanding of China's market but also provide an opportunity for us to better understand each other, fostering a spirit of collaboration and mutual learning.

Chapter 1
Manner Coffee:
Journey in China's Specialty Coffee Market

Henni Appelgryn
http://orcid.org/0000-0001-6567-5605
Beijing Normal University-Hong Kong Baptist University United International College, China

EXECUTIVE SUMMARY

This case study examines Manner Coffee's journey in China's competitive coffee market, focusing on its strategic initiatives, market positioning, and brand identity challenges. Manner Coffee has differentiated itself by blending modern aesthetics with traditional Chinese elements, creating a unique coffee experience that resonates with local consumers. The case details how Manner Coffee has leveraged community engagement, sustainability practices, and technological innovation to build customer loyalty and drive growth. However, the company faces a significant trademark infringement issue with Josef Manner and Comp AG, affecting its brand identity and future expansion plans. Despite these challenges, Manner Coffee remains committed to delivering premium coffee experiences and navigating legal uncertainties to secure its position in China's burgeoning coffee culture. This study provides insights into brand management, market entry strategies, and the complexities of protecting intellectual property in international markets.

INTRODUCTION

Manner Coffee, a prominent specialty coffee chain in China, has rapidly emerged as a market leader through its commitment to quality, craftsmanship, and sustainability. This case examines their strategic market entry, consumer preferences, market

DOI: 10.4018/979-8-3693-2921-4.ch001

1

demand shaping, brand differentiation strategies, and the significant challenges it faces because of a trademark infringement issue.

Entering the Shanghai market with a thorough analysis of market trends and consumer preferences, the company quickly becomes a favourite among coffee enthusiasts. By prioritizing exceptional coffee quality, stylish café environments, they appeal to both connoisseurs and the broader consumer base. Chinese consumers' increasing demand for specialty coffee, characterized by unique brewing methods and artisanal roasts, has positioned favourably. To target a younger audience and stand out from Western chains, they offer popular creamy flat whites, stylish store layouts, and competitive pricing.

In line with changing consumer preferences for higher quality, their commitment to premium, ethically sourced coffee remains steadfast. Their commitment to these values has shaped market demand in China, capitalizing on the growing specialty coffee culture. By offering diverse products, customization options, and convenient ordering channels, Manner Coffee ensures accessibility and satisfaction for its customers, driving repeat business and brand loyalty.

They distinguish itself through a strategy focused on quality, sustainability, community engagement, and specialty coffee expertise. This approach attracts loyal customers who resonate with the brand's values. The company's emphasis on eco-friendliness, exemplified by discounts for customers who bring their own cups, further strengthens its appeal to environmentally conscious consumers.

Despite its success, they face a significant trademark infringement issue with Josef Manner an Austrian confectionery conglomerate. Their company's prior registration of the "Manner" trademark in China has led to repeated rejections of the trademark applications. This legal ambiguity poses severe challenges to their brand identity, consumer trust, marketing efforts, operational costs, and future expansion plans.

Consumer trust and perception are at risk, as a name change could cause confusion and scepticism. Marketing and advertising strategies cantered around the "Manner" brand would require a complete overhaul, incurring significant costs and disrupting brand consistency. The rebranding process, which involves operational costs such as logo redesign, packaging updates, and changes to the digital footprint, further strains resources.

The inability to secure a trademark puts them at a competitive disadvantage, as competitors with protected brand identities can capitalize on this instability. Legal uncertainties also pose challenges for future expansion, potentially impeding growth in new regions and affecting investor confidence. The remarkable ascent in China's dynamic coffee market underscores its commitment to quality, sustainability, and innovation. However, resolving the trademark conflict is crucial for protecting its brand identity and ensuring long-term success. By navigating this legal challenge strategically, Manner Coffee can maintain consumer trust, support marketing efforts, manage operational costs, and secure a competitive position.

From the ancient origins of coffee to its rise as a market leader in China through Manner Coffee, the journey of coffee is a fascinating tale of cultural adaptation, innovation, and strategic business acumen.

Ancient Origins to Coffee Culture

The coffee story begins in the ancient coffee forests of Ethiopia, where legend has it that a goat herder named Kaldi first discovered the potential of these beans. Upon observing that his goats became energetic after eating the berries from a certain tree, Kaldi shared his findings with a local monastery. The monks made a drink with the berries and found that it kept them alert during long hours of prayer. The knowledge spread east, and coffee reached the Arabian Peninsula, growing in popularity.

According to Husni et al., (2021, p. 221) the word "coffee" has its origins in the Arabic word "qahwah" which means "wine of the bean." The Turkish language borrowed it as "kahve." Dutch traders then adopted it as "koffie" after encountering coffee in the Ottoman Empire. As coffee spread across Europe in the 16th and 17th centuries, the word took on various spellings like "coffe" and "cophy" before eventually becoming "coffee" in English by the mid-1600s.

By the 12th century, Yemeni farmers cultivated coffee, and beverages made from roasted beans became popular across the Islamic world. The commercial production of coffee distributed beyond Yemen, starting in Sri Lanka in the 1660s, Java in the 1700s, and Latin America by 1715. This expansion deeply intertwined powerful empires with plundering lands, people, and ideas. In the 17th century, Europeans introduced coffee to Europe, and according to Weinberg & Bealer (2001), in 1883 Burton praised it as an intoxicant, a mood enhancer, a social and physical stimulant, and a digestive aid.

Coffee's Arrival in China

Coffee first arrived in China over a century ago, but remained relatively unnoticed. Farmers in southwest China cultivated Coffea arabica, but tea overshadowed coffee (Cai et al., 2007). However, for the next century, coffee remained relatively unnoticed in the country. Yet, as is often the case with developments in China, the market has undergone significant transformations in the past two decades. Though, it remained a niche product, overshadowed by the country's deep-rooted tea culture.

Modern Resurgence

In recent decades, urbanization, globalization, and changing consumer preferences have driven a resurgence in coffee consumption in China. Young urban professionals adopted coffee as a part of their daily routines, and international coffee chains entered the market, paving the way for local brands.

The data from the World Coffee Portal (WCP) underscores the remarkable growth potential of China's branded coffee shop market. According WCP (2024), their data underscores the remarkable growth potential of China's branded coffee shop market, projecting a forecasted growth rate of 11.7% Compound Annual Growth Rate (CAGR). They expect that the number of coffee outlets in China will surpass 86,300 by the end of 2028 (ECS, 2024). This highlights the increased demand for coffee and the shifting preferences of Chinese consumers. China's coffee industry has experienced a remarkable expansion in recent years, surging to a valuation of $36.7 billion in 2023 (He, 2024). The coffee industry in China, particularly in urban areas like Shanghai, has experienced significant growth in recent years. This growth is driven by factors such as urbanization, changing lifestyles, and a growing appreciation for Western-style coffee culture.

THE BIRTH OF MANNER COFFEE

In 2015, Manner Coffee (hereafter referred to as "Manner") opened in Shanghai, quickly becoming a popular haven for urban professionals. Manner made its debut as a specialty coffee chain based in Shanghai, China (Chu, 2023). Amidst the abundance of coffee shops, it sets itself apart as a rising star in China's coffee scene.

They quickly gained popularity and captivates coffee enthusiasts by its innovative approach and commitment to excellence. The vision statement is "Make Coffee Part of Your Life." Starting as a humble specialty coffee chain, Manner Coffee quickly became a symbol of quality and style in China's coffee culture.

The culture has found inspiration in the coffee escape, which embodies unwavering commitment to excellence, sustainability, and style. Delighted a generation that desires ambitious standards, affordability, and a touch of eco-awareness in their everyday coffee. Discover the captivating chronicle of a thrilling expedition into the world of flavour, and the endless prospects that lie within a single bean. It stands as a testament to the changing desires and goals of Chinese consumers.

Their ability to go beyond the ordinary and deliver something truly exceptional is the foundation of their success. Customers encompass more than just patrons. The delightful scent of freshly ground beans and the cozy atmosphere when you step into the café, beckoning you to embark on an extraordinary sensory adventure.

Despite its trendy façade and delicious espresso drinks, there is a narrative of drive, perseverance, and the unyielding mission to redefine the coffee experience in China.

It has a far-reaching impact that goes beyond its café locations. With their founder's visionary leadership, their goal is to inspire, delight, and make a positive impact in China. By implementing sustainable sourcing practices, community engagement initiatives, and prioritizing social responsibility, it is not only transforming the coffee industry.

Its legacy strengthens as it continues to grow and expand. The opening of each new café is more than just a celebration of their achievements; it is a pledge to provide customers with excellence, coffee in style. Manner shines as a symbol of hope, creativity, and connection in a world where coffee is more than a drink. The coffee devoted to daily rituals is to embrace one cup at a time.

DEVELOPMENT OF THE COMPANY

Founding Vision

In 2015, Han Yulong and Lu Jianxia, his wife, founded Manner Coffee in Shanghai, starting with a simple kiosk. Their vision was to offer high-quality coffee at an affordable price, making it accessible to a broader audience. They are from Nantong and aimed to make high-quality coffee accessible in Shanghai. In an interview with its founders, they explained the inspiration behind the name stems from a renowned movie line in Kingsman: "Manner makes man." He explained that in English, "Manner" also refers to the behaviours and habits of individuals. They strived to make coffee a delightful, recurring pleasure for customers, enhancing their sensory experience with each visit.

The CEO Yulong infused his vision into the brand. Initially a photography enthusiast, Yulong shifted his focus to coffee, refining his skills and conducting market research. However, his interest in coffee soon eclipsed his enthusiasm for photography. Despite the initial setback of his coffee venture in Nantong, disappointing interest in coffee among the locals led to its closure. Undeterred, he set his sights on Shanghai, where he embarked on a journey to refine his coffee-making skills. He has a genuine passion for coffee and a deep appreciation for its culture and craftsmanship. This passion may have driven him to explore ways to elevate the coffee experience beyond traditional coffee shops.

Inspired by his personal journey and insights gained from witnessing the growing coffee landscape, he embarked on a mission to reshape the coffee scene for Shanghai's sophisticated clientele. To capitalizing on China's thriving coffee market, which boasts a consistent annual growth rate of 15% (Mordor, 2024), per capita coffee consumption has soared in key urban hubs like Shanghai and in secondary tier cities. These trends show a shift towards consumption patterns akin to those seen in more established coffee markets.

In his background and experience prior to venturing into the coffee industry, Yulong had a diverse career trajectory that encompassed fields beyond food and beverage. His previous experiences might include roles in technology, finance, and even the arts, highlighting his multidisciplinary approach to entrepreneurship. This diverse background provided him with a unique perspective and set of skills that he could leverage in building and growing the company into the successful and innovative brand it is today. His vision stems from a desire to create a unique coffee experience that goes beyond just serving great coffee, but also encompasses atmosphere, style, and sustainability. He gained valuable experience and insights from working in the coffee industry prior to founding Manner. This experience included roles in coffee sourcing, roasting, or retail operations, giving him a comprehensive understanding of the industry and its challenges. His personal values and vision played a significant role in shaping the concept of the venture. A vision for a coffee chain committed to exceptional atmosphere, taste, and style while maintaining sustainability reflects the desire to create a business that aligns with his values and makes a positive impact on the world.

He worked as a barista and roaster to hone his expertise at a specialty coffee boutique called Café del Volcán in Shanghai. He gained knowledge to appreciate the distinctive aroma of coffee beans and mastered home brewing skills. Explore the diverse selection of premium coffee beans found all over the globe. While he immersed himself in the craftmanship, he conducted a thorough market research and diligent search for a location for the first coffee shop.

He identified a 2 square-meter space in Shanghai for his new venture. Opting for a less-travelled alley rather than a high-traffic location, he catered to the preferences of artistic-minded consumers who sought hidden gems. Satisfied with the strategic location, he priced the coffee products competitively, offering affordable options and additional perks like discounts for customers who brought their own cups. Since the launch in 2015, it has flourished, drawing hundreds of customers daily with its inviting atmosphere and value-driven approach to coffee.

Yulong's leadership and vision serve as pivotal factors behind the company's triumph, inspiring both customers and employees to adopt its values and mission. By moulding the company culture and nurturing a cooperative, innovative atmosphere, he empowers employees to contribute actively to the company's prosperity. As an entrepreneur, he has been driven by a desire to create something of his own and make a mark in the coffee industry. The chance to start a successful business from scratch, all while following his passion for coffee could have been a powerful driving force.

GROWTH

In 2021, Manner Coffee achieved unicorn status, marking a significant milestone in its growth trajectory. The influx of investment facilitated rapid expansion and innovation, allowing them to explore new markets and enhance their offerings. They are rapidly expanding in China, having announced the 1,000th store opening in October 2023 (KrASIA, 2023).

The ability to attract investment funding shows investor confidence in its business model and growth potential. Monitoring the company's funding rounds, the amount raised, and the valuation at each round can provide insights into its financial health and trajectory. Examining the identities of the investors, such as venture capital firms or strategic investors, can offer clues about the company's strategic partnerships and growth strategy. Manner Coffee secured multiple investment (CBinsights, 2024; Ma, 2021), from notable investors like Capital Today, Temasek, ByteDance, and others, driving its rapid expansion:

- October 2018, funding from Capital Today, Temasek, and ByteDance.
- December 2020, funding from H Capital and Coatue Management investment.
- February 2021, funding from Temasek, Singaporean Government investment company.
- May 2021, funding from DragonBall Capital, a Meituan subsidiary.
- June 2021, funding from ByteDance, the firm operating TikTok.
- June 2021, Capital Today, withdraws their funds and is no longer listed among its investors.

BUSINESS MODEL

Their business model emphasizes quality, craftsmanship, and sustainability. They ensure an exceptional coffee experience for their customers by handpicking premium beans from ethically responsible farms and executing a meticulous brewing process with skilled baristas.

The bedrock of quality lies in sourcing premium Arabica beans from ethically dependable farms. This guarantees that the coffee beans used in their beverages uphold the highest standards, culminating in superior flavour profiles and unwavering consistency. The brand upholds its standards of excellence by subjecting each batch of beans to rigorous quality control measures, from coffee bean harvest to the last cup served to the customer.

This unwavering commitment to quality assurance instils confidence among patrons, knowing that every sip embodies the hallmark of superior craftsmanship and uncompromising quality. Sourcing from ethically trustworthy farms represents more than just a business decision, it reflects its values, a commitment to sustainability, and a dedication to delivering an unparalleled coffee experience to its discerning clientele.

They place a strong emphasis on committed to continuous improvement and innovation in its quest for quality. This may involve experimenting with new brewing techniques, exploring different bean varieties, or refining existing processes to enhance the overall coffee-drinking experience. By staying at the forefront of coffee trends and techniques, they ensure it remains a leader in quality.

Highly trained baristas follow precise brewing parameters to extract the full flavour potential of the beans while maintaining the integrity of the final product. Whether it's an espresso shot, a pour-over, or a specialty beverage, their commitment to craftsmanship shines through in every cup. They pay careful attention to every detail, from the grind size of the beans to the temperature of the water.

They place importance on educating customers about the coffee-making process and the characteristics of different coffee varieties. By providing information about the origin of the beans, the roasting process, and the flavour profiles of various coffees, this empowers customers to make informed choices and develop a deeper appreciation for the artistry behind each cup. They earned a reputation for consistently delivering exceptional coffee that delights the senses and satisfies the soul.

The focus on innovative menu offerings characterizes it with creativity, experimentation, customer engagement, and brand differentiation. By continuously thinking expansively and introducing new and exciting flavours. The menu development process is driven by creativity and experimentation. Their team of culinary experts and coffee aficionados are constantly exploring new flavour combinations, ingredients, and brewing techniques to create innovative beverages that stand out in the crowded coffee market. This emphasis on creativity allows to differentiate itself from competitors and captures the interest of adventurous coffee enthusiasts.

They differentiate through its innovative menu offerings, which blend traditional coffee-making techniques with contemporary flavours and ingredients. By continuously experimenting with new recipes and flavour combinations, they strive to delight customers with unique and memorable coffee experiences. Whether it's a classic espresso-based beverage or a trendy specialty drink infused with unique flavours, to ensure that each item on its menu reflects a harmonious blend of tradition and innovation.

Keeping the menu fresh and exciting by introducing seasonal and limited time offerings. Seasonal ingredients, cultural celebrations, or emerging trends inspire these special creations in the culinary world. By regularly updating their menu with new and limited-time items, this encourages repeat visits from customers eager to try the latest offerings and stay ahead of the curve.

They actively solicit feedback from customers to inform its menu development process. Through surveys, social media interactions, and in-store feedback channels, gathers insights into customer preferences, tastes, and emerging trends. By prioritizing the needs of their customers, this approach ensures that the menu choices are appealing to their intended customers and adapt to changing consumer preferences. By constantly surprising and delighting customers with new and exciting flavours, creates a sense of anticipation and exclusivity that keeps patrons coming back for more. This fosters a strong sense of brand loyalty among customers who appreciate the commitment to pushing the boundaries of traditional coffee culture.

They place a significant emphasis on interior design, carefully crafting spaces that blend contemporary minimalism with traditional Chinese elements. This design philosophy creates a serene and inviting atmosphere that sets them apart from its competitors. The thoughtful layout, choice of furnishings, and use of natural materials contribute to a sense of tranquillity and sophistication, enticing customers to linger and savour their coffee experience.

Beyond the physical design, they curate an atmosphere that fosters relaxation, socialization, and productivity. Soft lighting, comfortable seating, and soothing music create a welcoming environment where patrons can unwind, connect with others, or focus on work. Whether it's a quiet corner for solitary reflection or a communal table for lively conversation, offers spaces that cater to diverse needs and preferences.

The aesthetic and ambiance of the cafes play a pivotal role in shaping the brand's identity and perception. The fusion of modern and traditional elements reflects commitment to innovation while honouring its Chinese heritage. This unique blend of aesthetics not only attracts customers but also reinforces the brand's image as a sophisticated and culturally aware coffee destination.

They focus on aesthetic and ambiance enhances the overall customer experience, elevating it from a mere transaction to a multisensory journey. They carefully curate every aspect of the environment to delight the senses and evoke a feeling of well-being. The aroma of freshly brewed coffee greets customers when they enter and can enjoy their first sip in a cozy corner. The ambiance of the shops plays a significant role in shaping the overall customer experience. With a blend of contemporary minimalism and traditional Chinese elements, this intricately woven around creating a distinct appeal within its cafes, which serves as a crucial element of its overall customer experience. The strategically located kiosks that minimized overhead costs and maximized convenience. This lean approach allowed them to offer premium coffee without the high prices associated with larger coffee shops.

With their aesthetically pleasing ambiance, the cafes serve as perfect WeChat-worthy backdrops, boosting social media engagement and word-of-mouth marketing. The surroundings of the cafes naturally attract customers to share photos of their experiences, highlighting both the delicious beverages and the aesthetic charm. The allure of the cafes' aesthetic and ambiance helps attract new customers and expand their reach through this organic promotion. Successfully integrated into the local culture by understanding and catering to Chinese tastes and preferences. They maintained a balance between offering international coffee experiences and respecting local customs.

Community engagement is not just a peripheral aspect of Manner but a core value that permeates every aspect of its operations. By prioritizing relationships, sustainability, and social responsibility, not only enriches the lives of its customers but also contributes to the well-being of the communities it calls home. The intricately intertwined with community engagement, reflecting its commitment to fostering meaningful connections and making a positive impact in the communities it serves.

Hosting a variety of community events and activities aimed at bringing people together and fostering a sense of belonging. These events may include coffee tastings, workshops, coffee exhibitions, and more. By providing a platform for creativity, learning, and social interaction strengthens its ties with the community and creates memorable experiences for its patrons. The brand cultivated a sense of community through social media engagement and customer feedback, fostering loyalty and repeat business. Their presence in relatively high-traffic areas made them a convenient and popular choice for busy professionals and students alike.

They actively seek to collaborate with local farmers, suppliers, and artisans to support the local economy and promote sustainable practices. By sourcing ingredients and products locally not only ensures freshness and quality but also contributes to the livelihoods of local producers and businesses.

They have a commitment to preserving the environment and actively implement measures to minimize their impact on nature. This may include using eco-friendly packaging, implementing waste reduction, and recycling programs, and supporting environmental conservation efforts. By prioritizing environmental responsibility, demonstrates its dedication to making a positive impact on the planet and inspires customers to adopt sustainable habits.

They engage in various social responsibility initiatives aimed at addressing social issues and improving the well-being of disadvantaged communities. This may involve partnering with local charities, organizing fundraising campaigns, or donating a portion of supports social causes. By leveraging its platform for social good, demonstrates its values of compassion and empathy while empowering customers to contribute to positive change.

They actively seek input from its customers and engage with them regularly to solicit feedback, ideas, and suggestions. This two-way dialogue not only strengthens the bond between them and its customers but also allows the company to better understand their needs and preferences. By incorporating customer feedback into its decision-making process ensures its offerings are relevant, resonant, and responsive to the community it serves for convenience.

Leveraging digital payment systems and data analytics, Manner Coffee enhanced customer experience and operational efficiency. Their minimalist branding and design resonated with the urban demographic, creating a strong and appealing identity.

They leverage technology for mobile ordering, digital loyalty programs, and data analytics to enhance customer experience and operational efficiency. This includes offering mobile ordering and delivery options, implementing loyalty programs, and engaging with customers through social media platforms to build brand awareness and loyalty. Implementing technology in its operations through various applications aimed at enhancing efficiency, quality, and customer experience. It can analyse sales data to predict demand and optimize inventory levels. This ensures that there is always the right amount of coffee beans, supplies, and ingredients on hand, reducing waste and minimizing stock-outs. Technology plays a significant role in the coffee industry, with cashless payment systems is increasingly common. Coffee chains are leveraging technology to enhance convenience and improve customer experience with cashless payment systems becoming increasingly common.

MARKET ANALYSIS

By carefully studying market trends, understanding what customers liked, and emphasizing their unique value, they successfully entered the Shanghai market and became a popular specialty coffee chain. The company thrives in a competitive market by prioritizing by offering exceptional coffee and inviting cafe environments that appeal to coffee enthusiasts.

Their dedication to quality and craftsmanship appeals to coffee connoisseurs who are in search of exceptional experiences. Their coffee commands a higher price because of the increased care and attention to detail in its production. Chinese consumers increasingly demand specialty coffee, driven by a desire for higher quality and diverse offerings. Shops with unique brewing methods, single-origin beans, and artisanal roasts are becoming more popular. Distinguished by its exceptional quality, unique flavours, and meticulous production processes.

Manner Coffee distinguishes itself by targeting a younger audience with its creamy flat whites, stylish store layouts, and competitive pricing. It gained recognition for its creamy flat whites, stylish store layouts, and prices 30% to 40% lower than those of Western chains (CBBC, 2022). Embracing eco-friendliness, they offer a cup of coffee at 10-yuan ($1.50) to customers who bring their own cups. Yulong expressed his intention, stating, "I wanted to get average Chinese consumers to accept coffee" (Che, 2021). Many people in China often perceive coffee as a luxury beverage.

Consumers value high-quality coffee with rich flavours and unique profiles, seeking superior experiences with expertly brewed coffee and knowledgeable baristas. They cater to growing consumer tastes by offering diverse products, customization options, and convenient ordering channels as online and mobile app services. This ensures that customers can access their favourite coffee quickly and conveniently, whether they're on the go or ordering from home.

This shapes market demand for premium, ethically sourced coffee by aligning its offerings with consumer preferences and trends. The growing demand for specialty coffee and the developing coffee culture in China provided them a lucrative opportunity to cater to discerning consumers. Thus, playing a significant role in shaping and driving market demand for premium, sustainable, and ethically sourced coffee products. This resonates with environmentally conscious consumers. The commitment to sustainability and consistent quality has been crucial to its success.

Attracting loyal customers who share its values, the brand differentiation strategy revolves around its emphasis on specialty coffee expertise, effectively distinguishing it from competitors. With the goal of differentiating itself in the market, the company sought to offer a carefully curated range of specialty coffees and build warm and inviting cafe atmospheres that strongly appeal to its target demographic.

CHALLENGES AND FUTURE DEVELOPMENT

Trademark Infringement

A trademark is a mark, symbol, word, phrase, or motto that identifies a company's products (Kelly & Williams, 2019). Amidst its remarkable rise, Manner Coffee faces a significant challenge that threatens its very identity. A trademark infringement issue with Josef Manner, an Austrian confectionery conglomerate, has shadowed the rapid expansion of the Chinese unicorn (Che, 2021).

The Austrian company had registered the "Manner" trademark under a category that includes coffee in China. As a result, China's trademark office has rejected Han's company multiple times when attempting to register the same brand name. This has forced them to operate under the alternative domain wearemanner.com, as the Austrian company already taken the manner.com domain. The existing trademark held by the Austrian company has led legal experts to confirm that if they are using the name, it may be on questionable legal ground. This poses serious risks for as they expand across China and the future international expansion.

Brand Identity Challenges

Not having full legal rights to its core brand name makes it difficult to fully establish its identity as an authentic Chinese coffee brand aiming to make the beverage a cultural mainstay. This poses a serious risk for expanding across China and globally. The primary challenge lies in maintaining a cohesive and recognizable brand identity amidst legal uncertainties. The legal ambiguity around the brand name may raise concerns among current and potential investors about risks to the company's future growth prospects. An in-depth explanation of the brand identity challenges that result from this trademark conflict.

Brand Rebranding

Legal action by the Austrian Manner company may ultimately lead to the forced rebranding and complete name change, resulting in significant costs for the company after years of building brand equity. They have built its brand identity around the Manner Coffee name, which is integral to its marketing, customer loyalty, and overall brand recognition. However, the existing trademark held by the Austrian company, with the same name, jeopardizes this identity and the risk of losing the brand recognition it has worked hard to establish. Consistency is key to branding, and any disruption can confuse customers and weaken brand loyalty.

Consumer Trust and Perception

Consumers associate the "Manner" name with specific qualities such as product quality, service excellence, and a particular aesthetic. A forced name change, or rebranding, can lead to confusion and scepticism among consumers. They might question the legitimacy and stability, which can erode the trust and positive perception that the brand has cultivated. Maintaining consumer trust is crucial, especially in a competitive market like China's rapidly growing coffee sector.

Marketing and Advertising Challenges

The brand name plays a significant role in its marketing strategy. The "Manner" brand is at the centre of promotional materials, digital marketing campaigns, and social media presence. Legal constraints or the need to rebrand would cause a complete overhaul of marketing strategies, materials, and communication channels.

This not only incurs additional costs but also disrupts ongoing marketing efforts, diluting the brand's message and market presence.

Operational and Financial Costs

Rebranding involves significant operational and financial costs. The company would need to redesign its logo, update its packaging, change signage across all stores, and change its digital footprint, including websites and social media profiles. These changes demand substantial investment and time, diverting resources from other crucial areas, such as product development and market expansion.

Competitiveness

In a highly competitive market, brand identity is a critical differentiator. The inability to secure its trademark puts it at a competitive disadvantage. Competitors with strong, protected brand identities can leverage this instability to attract customers. The distraction and resources spent on resolving trademark issues can hinder the ability to innovate and respond swiftly to market demands, further weakening its competitive position.

Future Expansion

As they expand across China, the legal uncertainty surrounding its brand name could pose challenges in new regions. Without a clear and secure trademark, the company faces the constant threat of legal actions, which can impede its growth and expansion plans. This uncertainty can also affect investor confidence, making it difficult to secure funding for future growth initiatives.

The trademark conflict with the Austrian company presents significant brand identity challenges for them. Ensuring a cohesive, recognizable, and trusted brand identity is crucial for the company's continued success in the competitive Chinese coffee market. Resolving this conflict promptly and effectively is essential to maintain consumer trust, support marketing efforts, manage operational costs, and secure a strong competitive position.

While Manner Coffee has not publicly addressed how it plans to resolve this trademark dispute, the company is likely exploring options such as negotiating to purchase the relevant trademark from the Austrian company or finding an alternative brand name it can fully trademark across product categories. As they continue its rapid ascent as a Chinese coffee unicorn, resolving this trademark infringement conflict will be crucial to protecting its brand identity, enabling nationwide expansion, and reassuring investors about its long-term trajectory.

CONCLUSION

Manner Coffee's remarkable journey from a humble specialty coffee chain to a leading brand in China's dynamic coffee market is a testament to its unwavering commitment to quality, sustainability, and innovation. By prioritizing premium coffee, inviting ambiance, and community engagement, the company has carved a niche for itself, captivating coffee enthusiasts and shaping the growing coffee culture in China.

However, the trademark infringement conflict with the Austrian confectionery company poses a significant challenge to Manner Coffee's brand identity, consumer trust, marketing efforts, operational costs, and future expansion plans. Resolving this legal ambiguity is crucial for the company to protect its hard-earned brand recognition, maintain consumer confidence, and secure a strong competitive position in the market.

As Manner Coffee continues its rapid expansion across China, its ability to navigate this trademark dispute strategically, while upholding its core values and commitment to excellence, will determine its long-term success. Whether through negotiating a coexistence agreement, amending its trademark application, or asserting the distinctiveness of its offerings, finding a workable solution to this conflict is paramount.

Despite this obstacle, Manner Coffee's dedication to delivering exceptional coffee experiences, fostering meaningful connections with the community, and embracing sustainable practices has resonated deeply with consumers. By staying true to its vision and continuously innovating, the company has the potential to solidify its position as a leading force in China's burgeoning coffee culture, leaving an indelible mark on the industry's developing landscape.

REFERENCES

CBBC. (2022, January 12). *Will manner coffee conquer Starbucks in China?* China-Britain Business Council. https://www.cbbc.org/news-insights/will-manner-coffee-conquer-starbucks-china

CBinsights. (2024). *Manner stock price, funding, valuation, revenue & financial statements.* CB Insights. https://www.cbinsights.com/company/manner/financials

Che, C. (2021, November 5). The rise of Manner Coffee. *The China Project.* https://thechinaproject.com/2021/11/05/the-rise-of-manner-coffee/

Chu, Y. (2023). Manner Coffees marketing strategies: A review. *Advances in Economics. Management and Political Sciences*, 8(1), 275–279. DOI:10.54254/2754-1169/8/20230325

ECS. (2024). *1.4 billion reasons to sell coffee* [The European Coffee Symposium]. China's Coffee Revolution: Opportunities and Challenges Ahead. https://www.europeancoffeesymposium.com/blog/1-4-billion-reasons-to-sell-coffee

He, Q. (2024). Shanghai pushes China's coffee industry to nearly $40b. *China Daily.* https://www.chinadaily.com.cn/a/202405/01/WS6631eea3a31082fc043c5022.html

Husni, M. A., Nugroho, A. K., Fakhrudin, N., & Sulaiman, T. N. S. (2021). Microencapsulation of ethyl acetate extract from green coffee beans (coffea canephora) by spray drying method. *Indonesian Journal of Pharmacy*, 221–231. DOI:10.22146/ijp.1457

Kelly, M., & Williams, C. (2019). *BUSN11: Introduction to business.* Cengage.

KrASIA. (2023, December 14). *With 1,000 stores established, can Manner Coffee fend off the likes of Starbucks, Luckin, and Cotti to keep growing?* KrASIA. https://kr-asia.com/with-1000-stores-established-can-manner-coffee-fend-off-the-likes-of-starbucks-luckin-and-cotti-to-keep-growing

Ma, W. (2021). *It is rumored online that Manner Coffee will be listed in Hong Kong next year.* IYIOU. https://www.iyiou.com/news/202110131023145

Mordor. (2024). *China coffee—Market share analysis, industry trends & statistics, growth forecasts 2024—2029.* Gire Research. https://www.giiresearch.com/report/moi1404108-china-coffee-market-share-analysis-industry-trends.html

WCP. (World Coffee Portal). (2024, March 22). *China: 1.4 billion reasons to sell coffee.* World Coffee Portal. https://www.worldcoffeeportal.com/Latest/InsightAnalysis/2024/March/China-1-4-billion-reasons-to-sell-coffee

KEY TERMS AND DEFINITIONS

Brand Identity: The visible elements of a brand, such as its name, logo, design, colour schemes, and symbols, that together create a distinctive image in the minds of consumers.

Chinese Unicorns: Privately held startup companies in China that have reached a valuation of over $1 billion. Rapid growth, innovative business models, and significant influence in their respective industries often characterized these companies.

Consumer Trends: The patterns and behaviours observed in the buying habits and preferences of consumers over time, such as cultural shifts, economic changes, technological advancements, and social influences.

Expansion Strategy: A business approach aimed at growing a company's operations, market reach, and overall scale. It involves implementing plans to enter new markets, increase product offerings, acquire new customers, and enhance the company's presence in existing markets.

Investor Confidence: The level of trust and optimism that investors have regarding the stability, performance, and potential for future growth of a particular company, industry, or financial market.

Market Analysis: Evaluating the dynamics, characteristics, and trends of a specific market is to understand its structure, potential, and opportunities. It involves gathering and interpreting data related to consumer behaviour, competitors, economic conditions, and regulatory factors affecting the market.

Operational Challenges: Difficulties or obstacles that organizations face in the day-to-day management and execution of their business activities. These challenges can arise from various factors within the operational framework of a company and typically affect its efficiency, productivity, or ability to meet goals.

Specialty Coffee: High-quality coffee that is distinct in flavour, sourced from specific regions known for producing exceptional beans, and carefully processed to preserve its unique characteristics.

Sustainability Practices: Methods and strategies adopted by businesses and organizations to operate in a way that ensures long-term ecological balance and minimizes environmental impact, which includes reducing waste, conserving energy and water, sourcing materials responsibly, minimizing carbon footprints, and promoting social responsibility.

Trademark Infringement: The unauthorized use of a trademark or service mark on or in connection with goods and/or services in a manner that is likely to cause confusion, deception, or misunderstanding about the source of the goods or services.

Chapter 2
Heytea:
Revolutionizing the Beverage Industry With Innovation and Customer Engagement

Zizhen Wang

http://orcid.org/0000-0001-9968-5553

University College London, UK

EXECUTIVE SUMMARY

This case study delves into the transformative journey of Tuhu Car Care Network, examining its rise to prominence in China's automotive service industry. The purpose is to analyze Tuhu's innovative business model, comprehensive product offerings, and strategic initiatives that have enabled it to capture a significant market share. It explores the company's history, from its inception to its current status as a market leader, highlighting key milestones and challenges faced along the way. The analysis includes a thorough examination of Tuhu's customer profiles, marketing tactics, and a competitive environment. The case profiles MIN Chen, the visionary Chairperson and CEO, whose expertise in software development and data management has helped to shape Tuhu's growth trajectory. By providing a thorough understanding of Tuhu's operational strategies and market positioning, this case offers valuable insights into the dynamics of the automotive service industry in China and the factors contributing to the success of a leading industry player.

DOI: 10.4018/979-8-3693-2921-4.ch002

UNICORN DESCRIPTION

Brief History of the Unicorn

Legend has it that around 2737 BC, Emperor Shen Nung, the father of Chinese medicine and herbalism, sat under a tree as his servant boiled water. While the servant was boiling the water, leaves from a nearby tree, often believed to be a wild tea tree, blew into the pot. Intriguing by the resulting infusion, Emperor Shen Nung decided to taste it. He found the drink refreshing and invigorating, which is how tea was discovered. Although the historical accuracy of this legend is uncertain, it symbolises the ancient origins of tea in Chinese culture. It emphasises the significant role of tea as a beverage with both medicinal and recreational attributes. Tea has since become an integral part of Chinese society, influencing all aspects of Chinese culture, including philosophy, art, and social customs. The legend of Emperor Shen Nung and the discovery of tea is one of the most famous stories in Chinese tea, preserved through oral tradition and various historical documents.

China is a significant producer and consumer of tea and holds a prominent position in the global tea industry. The country has a long history of tea cultivation dating back thousands of years and boasts a rich diversity of tea varieties, including white, green, oolong, and black teas. In addition to being a vital tea producer, tea is deeply ingrained in Chinese culture and social fabric. It plays a central role in social gatherings, rituals, and daily life, contributing to a strong appreciation and cultural tradition of tea throughout the country. Heytea has played a significant role in rejuvenating and innovating Chinese tea culture and has become a leader in China's new tea beverage industry.

Heytea was established by Yunchen Nie (NEO) in 2012 in Jiangmen City, Guangdong Province. Formerly known as Royal Tea, the company focused mainly on 'cheese tea' made with natural raw materials. The unique tea quickly gained popularity, leading Heytea to expand into neighbouring cities such as Zhongshan, Foshan, Dongguan, and Huizhou. In October and December 2015, the company entered the first-tier city markets of Guangzhou and Shenzhen, opening more than 50 stores in Guangdong province. In response to numerous imitation shops and trademark issues, the brand was upgraded to the registered brand 'Heytea' on February 26, 2016. Since then, Heytea has been expanding across China, introducing high-quality teas worldwide and rejuvenating the ancient culture of tea drinking.

Heytea specialises in using natural ingredients and real milk and tea to create innovative beverages. They are known for introducing the first cheese tea, which has revolutionised the tea beverage industry in China. The Very Grape Cheezo is one of their popular products, with over 150 million cups sold since its launch, making it the top choice for consumers for six consecutive years. In November 2018,

Heytea expanded to the overseas market by opening its first shop in Singapore. In July 2021, Heytea secured a record-breaking $500 million financing round, valuing the company at 60 billion yuan. The brand has since expanded to iconic cities in the United Kingdom, Australia, Canada, and the United States, making it the first new tea beverage brand to enter the US market. This expansion has significantly strengthened Heytea's global presence. The company's success was recognised when it was listed in the 2023 Hurun Global Unicorns Ranking on 18 April 2023, with a valuation of RMB 34.5 billion.

According to Heytea's Annual Report for 2023, released on January 4, 2024, Heytea expanded its presence to over 300 cities globally, entering more than 210 new cities. By the end of 2023, Heytea operated over 3,200 retail shops, with over 2,300 being business partnership shops, representing a 280% year-on-year growth in shop scale, making it the fastest-growing brand in the industry. The number of Heytea's memberships grew by 37 million in 2023, with the total number of members surpassing 100 million. Heytea also had over 30,000 social groups, marking it as the first new tea beverage brand with a user base of over 100 million. Over 90% of Heytea shops are located in local high-quality business districts, demonstrating outstanding profitability. In 2024, Heytea aims to achieve three primary goals: to serve the public better, integrate the new tea drink into daily life, and introduce the new tea drink to the global market.

Business Model

The industry in which Heytea operates is the new tea beverage industry, a fast-growing and highly competitive market. It involves using tea concentrate extracted by different methods and adding it to milk, cream, or fresh fruits to make beverages, commonly known as 'milk tea'. This category includes a wide range of tea beverage products such as milk tea, fruit tea, and flower tea. As residents' living standards improve, milk tea has become a fashionable and popular drink. Consumers now demand higher quality tea beverages, prompting investment and financing growth in China's new-style tea beverage industry. According to iiMedia Research (2022), the industry has grown from 1971 to 2023. In recent years, premium tea beverages have been driving growth in the fresh-made tea beverage industry, with consumer demand entering a period of significant growth. The market size of China's new-style tea beverage industry was 184.03 billion yuan in 2020 and surged to 279.59 billion yuan in 2021 after a rapid recovery from the epidemic.

The new tea beverage industry has a straightforward supply chain, low costs, simple formulas, easy access to ingredients, and low entry barriers. The industry has intense competition, with many tea beverage brands entering the market. This has led to increased competition, pushing tea beverage brands to innovate and introduce products with unique features to stand out. Consumer experience is a crucial focus for tea beverage brands, with consumers placing high importance on taste, quality, and service. Consumers seek healthier and higher-quality tea drinks as they become more health conscious. Effective brand marketing is also crucial for tea beverage companies. Innovation and differentiation have become essential strategies for brands to compete in this market.

The market will eventually become less profitable in a competitive environment as more imitators enter the industry. Heytea, as a prominent representative in the tea drink brand industry, actively addresses industry challenges. Heytea focuses on product innovation, brand marketing, and shop design to establish a strong reputation and brand image in the market. Through these efforts, Heytea has distinguished itself in the tea drink industry, attaining a leading position. Research data indicates that Heytea has become the preferred brand among consumers, capturing 58.1% of the market (iiMedia Research, 2022).

Products and Services

As one of the most popular new tea brands, HeyTea always focuses on consumers' needs and offers a wide range of products. The product series includes the Comforting Milk Tea Series, the Freshly Squeezed Fruit Tea Series, which combines fresh fruits with tea; the Handmade Tea Latte Series, which combines the characteristics of tea and coffee; and the Classic Tea Series. The most popular Comforting Milk Tea Series product, Roasted Brown Boba Milk, sold 14,000,000 cups in 2023 (Heytea, 2024). In 2023, HeyTea disclosed its product recipes and ingredients to the public, leading the industry in improving beverage quality. They provided information on the formula ingredients of more than 60 products and the traceability information of more than 70 ingredients, such as natural tea, real fruit, real milk, and natural sugar, from over ten countries and regions worldwide and over 40 cities and counties in over 20 provinces in China. They also made more than 60 authoritative test reports on the nutritional composition of the products available online, setting a new standard for product transparency in the industry. This initiative satisfies consumers' right to know and choose healthy tea consumption and promotes the transparency and healthiness of ingredients in ready-made tea recipes. At the same time, HeyTea promotes the transparency and healthiness of ready-made tea drink ingredients, ushering in the 'ingredient list era' in the new tea drink industry.

Cheese Tea

In 2012, Heytea introduced the first Cheese Milk Cover Tea, using raw leaf tea and mellow cheese instead of creamer powder and tea powder commonly used in the milk tea industry. The brand used high-quality ingredients such as Golden Phoenix Tea from Alishan, Taiwan, King of Jade Tea from North India, Australian imported block cheeses, and European imported fresh milk to create a high-quality milk cover. The series featured a cheese milk cap on top of the tea, adding a rich milky flavour and silky texture to the drink. Heytea's Very Grape Cheezo, introduced in 2018, became the first choice for consumers for six consecutive years, selling more than 150 million cups. Heytea also became the first milk tea brand to add zero-calorie sugar to its drinks, meeting the demand for "both delicious and non-fattening". In addition, Heytea developed a low-fat cheese tea series, reducing the calorie and sugar content of the products by more than 90% and offering customers the option to replace that with an additional RMB 1.

Seasonal Only Drinks

Seasonal, limited drinks are essential in maintaining Heytea's brand novelty and appeal. Different seasons bring different consumer preferences and needs. For example, in the summer, people may seek refreshing drinks to beat the heat, while in winter, they might prefer warmer, nourishing beverages. Heytea's seasonal-only drinks feature unique flavours and recipes tailored to the season, piquing consumers' curiosity and fulfilling their seasonal desires. These limited-edition flavours create a unique selling point for Heytea, and the sense of urgency they create ("if you miss it, you have to wait for another year") drives consumer impulse purchases and anticipation, leading to impressive sales. Furthermore, the marketing strategy around seasonal, limited drinks helps Heytea capture consumer attention, increase brand exposure, and stimulate word-of-mouth. Launching these limited drinks sparks discussions and sharing, contributing to positive social engagement and heightened brand awareness.

Heytea creates seasonal, limited flavours by staying aware of market trends and being innovative. These flavours, which include seasonal fruits, flowers, and plants, are introduced based on specific seasons and festivals. They are made without adding fruit juice jam and are only available for a limited time. A significant characteristic of the brand is the frequent introduction of new products. One popular seasonal fruit tea for 2022 is the "Very Nectarine Plum," which is made using 2,500 tonnes of fresh nectarines and plums (Heytea, 2024).

Customers

According to a report, young people, particularly Generation Z (born between 1995-2009), make up nearly 60% of consumers of new tea drinks, as per iiMedia Research's 2021 data. Heytea focuses on creating a new beverage experience by blending traditional milk tea with a healthy tea culture. The brand primarily targets white-collar and younger workers, offering leisure and beverage products. Heytea takes consumer feedback seriously and continuously innovates to meet customer needs. They customise all tea ingredients to their country of origin and offer a unique taste by incorporating fruits, milk caps, and various tea base combinations. Heytea's success is built on resonating with consumers rather than imposing their brand.

Young People in Generation Z

As a significant consumer group, Generation Z focuses on meeting basic needs and prioritises leisure, entertainment, and personal growth. They are independent thinkers with unique consumption habits and preferences. Heytea's beverage designs are distinctive, incorporating creative decorations, layers, and colour schemes to enhance the visual appeal and provide a more engaging consumption experience. Heytea stays popular among young people by offering innovative designs and regularly introducing new and limited-time drinks, catering to their desire for novelty and innovation.

Heytea frequently introduces cross-border co-branded products, which share common characteristics. These co-brands should have a youthful, fashionable, and high-end image, and their target audience should overlap with Heytea's. This approach allows Heytea to strengthen its brand image and attract its target audience. Cross-border co-branding enhances consumer experiences and product innovation, enriching the brand's dimensionality. These products reinforce Heytea's "Tea of Inspiration" brand positioning, making it more appealing to consumers and attracting those interested in fashion, trends, and new experiences.

Sharing, following new trends, and embracing fashion have become important traits of Generation Z. Their buying habits reveal vital social and emotional needs. For Generation Z, consumption is about more than just the practical value of products. It also involves the symbolic meaning of individuality, community culture, and self-expression that products embody, creating a unique form of 'symbolic consumption'.

When Heytea first started, it positioned itself as a high-end beverage brand. Its pricing, which was among the highest in the industry, gave Heytea the reputation of being 'top-tier', appealing to young people with a certain level of purchasing power. The identity of a 'high-end beverage' was firmly established and became synonymous with top-quality drinks. Having entered the market with a strong positioning and becoming well-known for premium beverages, Heytea has become a social influencer. Its products give consumers something to share and discuss and make them appear more sophisticated, stylish, and trendy, resulting in increased attention, positive feedback, and a more favourable impression of the consumer.

The Generation Z group was seamlessly born into the network era. They are deeply influenced by digital information technology and intelligent mobile terminals. In the network media, marketing new tea drinks, milk tea, and other instant satisfaction is no longer just a drink for the Z generation. It also caters to the trend of seeking recognition of the 'social currency'.

Heytea attaches great importance to the operation of social media accounts. Taking Weibo as an example, Heytea's official Weibo is updated every day. If you send a Weibo about Heytea with Heytea's keywords, it is easy to be liked by the official Heytea account. The fan's comment response rate is very high. Heytea will modestly accept good comments, and if there is a nasty comment, Heytea will be the first to respond to the problem and deal with it. This approach can go a long way in increasing brand favouritism and consumer bonding. In addition, some brands use social media as a medium to share information about discounts and events. However, Heytea chooses to operate content. They post various content, including product promotion, event promotion, fan interaction, and content related to current events and popular culture. This subconsciously influences consumers, turning customers into brand fans and building a strong brand image through social media.

Young Women and Health Seekers

Female consumers account for 68.5% of new tea drink consumers in China (iiMedia Research, 2022). As consumers become more health-conscious, they pursue the health and quality of new tea drinks. To meet the consumer taste and healthy low-fat consumer demand, Heytea, a leading company in the industry, has introduced the concept of "healthier and lower fat." They have developed a low-fat cheese tea series with reduced product calorie and sugar content by more than 90%. Additionally, users can add 1 yuan to replace traditional ingredients. The term 'low-fat' has resonated with young women and health-conscious consumers, providing a new option for those who enjoy milk tea but are concerned about weight gain. Furthermore, consumers can now learn the details of the ingredients and calculate the calorie value of the drinks using the Heytea GO applet.

To ensure the quality of ingredients, Heytea has continuously delved into the upstream tea plantations, orchards, ranches, and factories to oversee the cultivation, production, and manufacturing of ingredients with strict quality standards. They also combine their research and development capabilities to innovate quality ingredients consistently. In 2023, Heytea innovated and launched the industry's first special milk for the new tea drink, enriched with high-quality milk protein (3.8g/100mL), 27% higher than ordinary milk. This upgrade from regular dairy to enriched milk includes publicising the product formula and introducing the 'Heytea Real Tea Standard,' reaffirming the commitment to rejecting flavoured tea and instant tea powder. This move aims to lead the industry into the era of 0-flavored tea in response to consumers' demand for high-quality and healthy tea beverages. To further alleviate consumers' concerns about drinking milk tea, every Heytea shop showcases ingredients, using visible natural ingredients as part of the decoration.

Young White-collar Workers and Students

The leading consumer groups of Heytea are students and young white-collar workers. The consumers' purchasing philosophy is closely related to individual buying power. According to IImedia research data (2022), more than 70% of the new tea drink consumers could accept a unit price ranging from 11 to 20 yuan. Thanks to the brand potential, scale advantage, and accumulation in the supply chain, Heytea has implemented a price adjustment strategy for some of its products without changing the formula, ingredients, and product quality. Among these adjustments, the price of pure tea products has been reduced by RMB 3-5, and the cost of 5 fruit teas has been reduced by RMB 2-3.

Heytea initially set high prices, which led to many young people aspiring to consume their products but finding it challenging due to the high prices. After years of high-priced sales, the brand established its image as a high-end brand. Gradually, Heytea adjusted the prices to be more approachable, which has led to consumers lowering their guard due to increased purchasing power and psychological buildup over the years. This change has significantly increased the possibility of consumers giving in to their desires.

Market Analysis

Original Situation of the Market

New-style tea drinks are a modern take on traditional ready-made tea beverages. They are made with high-quality, fresh ingredients such as raw tea, milk, and fruits and often feature innovative combinations of these ingredients. This results in a range of unique and differentiated products. New-style tea drinks offer a broader selection to consumers and expand the beverage product category. This trend is expected to continue growing in China, with the market projected to reach nearly 200 billion yuan by 2030.

As the Chinese economy strengthens and disposable incomes rise, the demand for premium and personalised consumer products, including new-style tea drinks, is increasing. These drinks effectively cater to the evolving preferences of modern consumers. With their unique offerings, new-style tea drinks are well-positioned to tap into the growing market and meet the demands of consumers looking for upgraded beverage options.

Evolution of the Market Until Today

From 1990 to 1995, China's tea beverage industry was in the era of tea powder mixing. The ingredients were mostly blended with milk tea powder; the price of the products was usually within 10 RMB; the tea shops were mostly street shops, usually located around schools, with minor shop sizes and no tables and chairs; and the consumer groups were typically young people or students. Between 1996 and 2015, China's tea industry entered the era of traditional tea drinks. Using tea dregs as the base of tea, adding creamer and synthetic additives, the unit price of the product is 10-20 RMB; the tea drink shops started to have the style of decoration and design, and most of them were opened in the shopping malls and the surrounding commercial streets; the consumer groups were usually young people for leisure and entertainment; however, it gradually started to focus on the production of the product, and the concept of the product culture was relatively weak.

From 2016 to the present, it has entered the era of new-style tea drinks. In the choice of ingredients, the selection of fresh and high-quality original ingredients, including raw tea, fresh milk, fresh fruit, etc., subverting the taste of traditional pearl milk tea, diversified matching and fusion of tea, milk, fruit, etc.; the price is usually more than 20 yuan; shops are primarily selected in the first and second-tier cities in the main urban areas of the crowded commercial shopping malls, the shops are decorated with a unique style of design and seating area to create a conceptual space with social attributes; the buying group is usually young people with a higher purchasing power and who like to share socially; in terms of brand culture, it pays more attention to brand culture construction, innovatively creates an 'experience + social' conceptual space, and pays more attention to creating differentiation and establishing brand value and competitive advantages. In recent years, the new style of tea drinks, because of its label 'high quality and natural ingredients, standard professional modulation skills and warm customised service', to promote the ready-made tea drinks industry has entered the 3.0 era, that is, the era of boutique tea drinks, the consumer demand has entered a period of golden growth.

As a result of the impact of the epidemic, the number of online orders in the catering industry surged, with the ready-made tea drink industry experiencing the fastest online growth of approximately 744.0% (iiMedia Research, 2022). For the new tea drink industry, from the perspective of the supply side of the enterprise, the sharp decline in customer traffic in offline shops has forced many new tea drink brands to accelerate their shift to online marketing channels, such as third-party takeaway platforms, APP/WeChat apps, etc.; from the perspective of the demand side of the consumption of consumers, consumers could not leave their homes during the epidemic, and could only purchase food and beverages and other consumer goods by way of online delivery, and offline consumption demand was suppressed in the short term, as well as residents' consumption demand during the epidemic was suppressed in the short term. IiMedia Research data show that in 2020, China's new-style tea drinks market size of 184.03 billion yuan, the new-style tea drinks market recovered rapidly after the epidemic, the market size reached 279.59 billion yuan in 2021, and in 2022 exceeded 300 billion yuan.

Competition Analysis

The competitive landscape of China's new-style tea beverage industry can be broadly divided into the southern market, northern market, and central and western market according to geographical distribution. Compared with the northern market (Northeast China, North China, Beijing-Tianjin-Hebei region, Midwest China, etc.), the southern market (Yangtze River Delta, East China, Southwest China, Central China, South China, etc.) has more new tea beverage brands and shops. There are many brands in the new-style tea and beverage industry. According to incomplete statistics, 163 new-style tea and beverage brands are currently in China. Shanghai, Guangzhou, and Beijing have the most extensive new-style tea and beverage brands, with 41, 33, and 28, respectively. The new tea beverage industry is divided into chain and non-chain business modes, of which the chain can be divided into direct mode, franchise mode, and 'direct + franchise'; chain brands in the new tea beverage industry accounted for a significant market share of about 90.8% (iiMedia Research, 2022), of which the majority of the franchise mode, accounting for 67.3% of the total chain brands.

Competition in China's new tea beverage industry is particularly fierce, with the leading competing brands in the directly-managed model being Heytea; ChaYanYueSe, a Modern China Tea Shop brand, founded in Changsha, Hunan Province in 2013, with outlets in Changsha, Changde, Wuhan, Nanjing, and Chongqing, focusing on milk-covered teas and pure teas; NaiXue, a listed brand founded in Shenzhen, Guangdong Province in 2015, covering 70 cities and concentrate on cheese milk-covered fruit tea and cold-brewed tea; and A Little Tea, which was founded in Taiwan in 1994 and focuses on milk tea; Coco, which was also born in Taiwan in 1997 and entered mainland China in 2007; and MiXue, a low-end chain of tea brands founded in 1997. In these, Heytea and NaiXue's tea leading high-end brand and product route, the average unit price is relatively high, basically in the 25 yuan or so, fuelled by capital through a unique, distinctive high-end brand and product marketing approach, in the minds of consumers to firmly occupy the position of the premium image. MiXue has a lower unit price, through the main attack on the sinking market, so that it covers the broadest range of cities and consumer groups and a large number of people, plus a specific brand marketing strategy, also gained a high degree of market attention.

Forecast for this Market

With more diversified consumption scenarios of new-style tea drinks as well as continuous innovation and broadening of categories, consumers' enthusiasm for new-style tea drinks continues to rise, and the market size of China's new-style tea drinks is expected to reach RMB 374.93 billion in 2025 (iiMedia Research, 2022). 24.6% of China's consumers of new-style tea drinks in 2023 said that the consumption frequency would increase and that consumers' demand would continue to rise. In recent years, China has introduced a series of consumer-related policies, laying a good business environment for the innovative development of new business formats, business models, and product forms, thus boosting the substantial rise of many emerging consumer brands. Under favourable consumer-related policies, new-style tea drinks are based on traditional ready-made ones. They are constantly innovated and upgraded in multiple dimensions, such as category and product innovation, supply chain optimisation and upgrading, diversified expansion of business formats, brand value enhancement, technological empowerment, and user experience enhancement.

Firstly, the future development trend of China's new-style tea beverage industry is the innovation and upgrading of categories and products. On the one hand, brands may pay more attention to creating theme concepts, co-branding concepts, health concept products, closely tracking market conditions and changing trends in consumer demand, increasing product R&D efforts, launching new products regularly, and genuinely improving the brand's differentiated competitive advantages from the product dimension; on the other hand, the product category will be extended to layout the coffee track, and the similarity between the ready-to-eat tea drinks and ready-to-wear coffee categories is relatively high. New-style tea drink brands began to enter the coffee track, based on the existing raw material suppliers, product research and development capabilities, business models, marketing channels and other primary accumulation, by drawing on the product structure of the new-style tea drinks, including fruit, coconut milk and other raw and supplementary ingredients for tea drinks and different types of freshly brewed coffee for innovative combinations, breakthroughs in the traditional freshly brewed coffee product structure, to create a rich level of unique flavours coffee, to achieve a new fusion of Chinese tea and western coffee, and to extend the new tea brand into a new 'tea + coffee' brand, to achieve a further expansion of the target customer groups and consumption scenarios.

Secondly, improving the supply chain service levels will also become the industry's future development trend through the supply chain integration and digital empowerment system. The use of digital technology to establish a resource base of upstream channel suppliers, including tea sources, milk sources, fruit sources, etc., and real-time dynamic updates and analysis of advantages and disadvantages, including quality, price, etc., to select high-quality raw and supplementary ingredients, and establish a long-term dynamic relationship with them to improve the bargaining power of procurement. For the critical parts of the supply chain, such as warehousing, logistics, payment, and online, based on the professional support of the industry leader or emerging technology enterprises, including digitalisation, intelligence, and other technologies, to comprehensively improve the ability of integrated supply chain integration and service efficiency.

Thirdly, an omnichannel standardised product and service system should be established from upstream suppliers to downstream shops. From the perspective of the supply side of the enterprise, enterprises continue to drive the development of the new tea beverage industry iteratively through product research and development, systematic integration of the supply chain, the creation of diversified business formats and marketing channels, innovative business models, and digital empowerment. The supply process and all aspects of the supply chain, including ingredients supply, warehousing/logistics, and the corresponding technological tools, all impact the cost of ingredients, supply costs, product quality, and shop operational efficiency. As companies continue to gravitate towards supply chain integration and empowerment through digitalisation, intelligence, and other modern information technology tools, the operational efficiency and profitability of the industry will improve.

Fourthly, marketing channels will be diversified through 'online + offline' full-scene marketing. On the one hand, the new tea drink shops are primarily opened in commercial/shopping centres in the main urban areas of first- and second-tier cities, which can not only successfully gather high-density offline traffic but also provide traffic entrances and media for social communication of the products, to successfully achieve the "free" interpersonal communication effect. On the other hand, in 2019, the number of mobile Internet users in China was 1.32 billion, and the number of takeaway users was 460 million (iiMedia Research, 2022); in the next few years, the number of takeaway users in China will still present a growth trend. As one of the industries that focus on online marketing strategy and has a relatively high degree of online popularity, the large number of Internet users and takeaway users has laid a good user base for its online promotion and sales, thus favouring its online marketing model.

Finally, China's new tea beverage industry will pay more attention to improving brand value and culture to consumers, leading to the 'new Chinese tide' and 'new Chinese style'. With the innovation and iteration of traditional national brands and the emergence of new Chinese brands, Chinese national brands continue to absorb traditional customs and cultures, from the concept and packaging to ingredients, to create a full range of products with craftsmanship quality of the product core, and innovation and integration with the contemporary mainstream culture, in-depth fit with the mainstream values of the modern young people and consumer interest, will gradually become the leading consumer brands in the minds of young people in the Z-generation.

DEVELOPMENT AND STRATEGY

Launch Period and Branding

Before the introduction of Heytea, the milk tea industry had been developed for 30 years, and standardisation was completed very early. Almost all the products on the market were provided with recipes by suppliers, and franchised shops were responsible for selling them. The milk-covered tea, popular in the streets, was made from powder, with a thin taste and weak tea flavour. However, Heytea's predecessor, RoyalTea, insisted on using healthier ingredients, such as freshly brewed tea, fresh fruits, fresh milk and cream for freshly made milk cover, which set a high quality for the product. Heytea, meanwhile, ventured to break away from formulaic traditions and continued to innovate its products, introducing a variety of new flavours and products to satisfy consumers' demand for different tea experiences.

The brand strictly controlled the selection of ingredients and production process to pursue high-quality, natural, and healthy products, which set up the brand image of high-end tea drinks and brought significant influence. Due to the "RoyalTea" trademark registration problem, from 2012 to 2015, a variety of 'RoyalTea' shops sprung up, which also brought a huge problem to the then RoyalTea because everywhere on the market, Royal Tea's brand people did not know which one is authentic, so in 2015 'Royal Tea' at that time spent 700,000 to buy someone else has been registered trademarks, and since then all the shops are renamed to Heytea.

With sensitivity to consumer needs, Heytea is committed to the younger generation of tea as a starting point to create products and brands that inspire the world. Heytea is dedicated to making tea drinking a style and a lifestyle, creating a new Chinese tea drink that is 'youthful, technological, and international'. Although Heytea originated in an alley named Jiangbianli in Jiangmen, Guangdong Province, and is a local brand, the brand mainly focuses on the Scandinavian simplicity style. It takes simplicity as a bridge to connect consumers and the brand, which is the secret of people seeking the joy of life under the pressure of a modern, complicated life. Consumers can see that Heytea's brand image is uniquely designed to successfully appeal to the younger generation through eye-catching logos, packaging design, and shop decoration. Their design focuses on simplicity, style, and distinction. In the design of the brand image, the logo of Heytea is a side face: a person holding a cup of Heytea in his hand, closing his eyes as the drink is about to be brought to his mouth, looking intoxicated. Although the design is simple, it is very memorable, so consumers can see these little characters outlined in black lines and associate them with Heytea.

Start-up and Marketing

In the initial period of Heytea's creation, long queues would always be in front of the tiny shops. It was rumoured that Heytea adopted a unique marketing strategy, employing queuing to create a queue to increase brand awareness and attract customers. This strategy aimed to create the impression that the product was in high demand, popular, and in short supply. Coupled with the 'herd effect' of customers, it greatly stimulated their desire to buy and created a word-of-mouth effect. Especially with the opening of the shop in Shanghai in February 2017, the news reported that some people even lined up for six or seven hours to buy a cup of cheese tea, scalpers speculated nearly 100 yuan a cup, the entire Shanghai and even Jiangsu and Zhejiang, set off a wave of puzzling 'Heytea fever', at the time, Heytea was given the role of 'social currency' - providing the owner with something to talk about and a sense of superiority. The cool brand concept, beautiful space design, unique product taste, and incredible queues all coincided with the rise of the WeChat Moment, making it fashionable for customers to post content about their Heytea via social media, and drinking Heytea became a cool thing to do. The queuing phenomenon at the Shanghai shop triggered national attention, and the spreading path of Heytea, gradually spreading from the previous word-of-mouth to the initiative of multiple catering and lifestyle media, instantly imported a large amount of online traffic to the offline. Many netizens discussed Heytea simultaneously, bringing a very high degree of topic for Heytea, and squeezing into the hotspot three times, earned media saved much money on promotion and expanded the influence of their brand layer by layer.

The regular Heytea shops are mainly white or grey, with simple and generous spatial design, transparent and bright, and high-value shop designs. Each Heytea shop can be redefined by incorporating different elements of design style. The company has also launched various types of shops, from 'Chinese inspired' shops, which are based on a deep understanding of the core spirit of Chinese culture and are created and presented using youthful and modern design techniques, to 'Heytea Black' shops, which are pioneering experiments in exploring the possibilities of the tea drink culture. There are also Heytea Pink shops with a strong sense of fashion, Heytea Lab shops that highlight the concept of spatial design, and Heytea Daydreamer Project shops that seek inspiration from ancient China, among others. The same product core, rich shop types, and diverse product categories continue to refresh the novelty of Heytea and reap the benefits of conversation and popularity. Heytea's IPs are also created with city characteristics to enhance the IP's memory points. In the report, the city refrigerator magnets, popular with consumers and have sparked a unique social culture, were named 'Brand Peripheral Product of the Year' by Heytea. To date, Heytea has launched more than 470 different models and distributed more than 2.1 million fridge magnets (Heytea, 2023). In addition, Heytea has collaborated with several independent illustrators to express the joy of drinking tea through the language of painting, creating a series of original illustrations in line with Heytea's brand philosophy.

Meanwhile, Heytea actively participates in offline activities and cross-border cooperation marketing with other brands and events to expand brand awareness. The cross-border brands include Baileys, Fenty Beauty, Loopy, Fendi, Stanley, Dove, etc. Heytea has cleverly combined the product functions, design aesthetics, cultural connotations, and styles of two brands in the same category or in different categories to make the new product more innovative and attractive than a single brand. Heytea could use these brands to strengthen its brand image and attract the target audience of these brands simultaneously. On the one hand, such cross-border marketing can provide consumers with more diversified experiences, and the richness and innovation of the products can also enhance the brand's stereoscopic degree. On the other hand, through cross-border cooperation, the products and peripherals of Heytea have become more abundant, covering almost all standard items in life: lipstick, clothes, hats, stereos, bags, umbrellas, mobile phone cases, and socks. ...... The peripheral products also deepen the brand positioning of 'Inspired Tea', which is conducive to consumers' better acceptance of the concept. The co-branding with Italian luxury brand FENDI created a new mode of cooperation between new tea drinks and luxury brands for the first time. This cooperation was on the Weibo hit list of hot searches, which significantly promoted brand awareness and stimulated consumers' enthusiasm for purchasing, and the 'FENDI Joy Yellow' products launched during the period set a new record for the sales of Heytea's new products for the third day and the first week. The co-branding of Heytea was closely related to the current hotspots and was promoted on various online apps before the release of the co-branded products, while the design of eye-catching co-branded products; the co-branding of Milk Tea with a high-luxury brand was unprecedented, as most people have curiosity about high luxury as well as a desire to chase it. The co-branding of Heytea and Fendi consolidated the brand positioning of Heytea for middle- to high-income consumers, and reinforced the brand's positioning for middle- and high-income consumers while stimulating their enthusiasm for consumption. For each co-branding collaboration, Heytea creates a new logo based on each co-branding, repeatedly reinforcing the brand's logo while conveying new ideas.

Development Period and Digitalization

Customers are annoyed by milk tea queues, and most of the acceptable queuing time for consumers is within half an hour, while 12.4% of consumers choose never to queue. To solve the queuing problem, in 2018, Heytea developed and launched the 'Heytea GO' mini app; it also launched a membership system and online ordering services through mobile applications, placing an order in advance through the mini app and reminding users of the progress of the order, allowing users to collect the tea as soon as possible when they arrive at the shop, providing a more convenient consumer experience; To avoid on-site queuing customers to take tea customer 'queue jumping' misunderstanding as well as reduce the crowdedness of the shop and customers, recently Heytea launched a tea cabinet in some of the shops on a trial basis, online order and offline customers no longer need to squeeze to the artificial counter to collect the tea, but can be like a delivery box to self-collect, which is greatly conducive to improving the operational efficiency of collecting tea. Heytea's active adoption of digital technology and innovation improves the customer experience and contributes to data analytics and operational efficiency.

The application of digital technology facilitates customers and provides companies with more data and operational flexibility. After Heytea used the applet, the average waiting time for consumers using the applet to order has been shortened by nearly 1/3 compared to before, the repurchase rate has increased by three times, and more than 80% of the shop's orders came from the applet. Using the applet has dramatically improved the operational efficiency of the shops and boosted the sales growth of Heytea shops. At the same time, the emergence of online ordering and takeaway significantly solved the problem of queuing at Heytea. Through technological empowerment, Heytea has cultivated and further consolidated consumers' habits of consuming new tea beverages online. More than 50% of all Heytea consumers choose to place orders online. In 2022, the 'Heytea GO' WeChat mini-programme membership exceeded 63 million people, with more than 13 million new members added yearly (Heytea, 2024). Many users reached through WeChat's mini-programs, which provide Heytea with informative consumption scenarios and behavioural data. These accurate and comprehensive data are of great significance to the product development and shop operation teams in understanding user preferences and needs, calculating order time, and monitoring shop operations. At the same time, Heytea has independently developed and launched seven types of intelligent devices in 3 categories, covering the entire process of shop application scenarios such as ingredient preparation, ingredient management, and tea mixing, which has led to the innovative and scientific development of the supply chain of the new tea beverage and significantly improved the accuracy and efficiency of the shop's product production.

Maturity and Expansion into Overseas Markets

On 10 November 2018, Heytea officially launched in Singapore, opening five shops nationwide. Singapore's food culture is quite diverse as a country that contains multiple races and blends many cultures. The Food and Beverage (F&B) industry is highly active in Singapore. Because of this, Singapore's food and beverage industry has always been in a relatively saturated state of competition, and its development is full of uncertainties, with new shops opening and old shops closing almost every day. In choosing Singapore as its first overseas stop, Heytea considers that although there are many local tea brands in Singapore, the market is highly competitive. However, Singapore is also one of the most internationally recognised countries globally. Taking Singapore as Heytea's first overseas stop is conducive to the brand's entry into the global market.

Moreover, Singapore has many Chinese residents, with solid continuity in distance and culture, and there is a gap in the market for new tea drinks. Heytea adopts the overseas direct cultivation rather than the agency model. For this reason, Heytea has made many efforts in the early stage of going overseas. For example, in the supply chain, Heytea development staff spent several months in advance to conduct market research, testing, and find suitable fruits and dairy products in the local area; in the staff training, two months in advance to bring the entire overseas team to the headquarters in Shenzhen for training, and from Guangzhou to transfer the two senior shop manager resident in Singapore for a year.

In 2023, Heytea accelerated its overseas market layout, opening its first shops in iconic cities in the UK, Australia, Canada, and the US, which received widespread attention. The opening was a hit, with the highest sales volume of a single shop exceeding 3,000 cups in a single day (Heytea, 2024). Among them, with the opening of the New York Broadway shop, Heytea advertised on the significant financial screen in New York's Times Square Midtown, about 300 meters away from the shop, where Heytea's iconic tea-drinking portrait logo was played on a loop. Heytea's New York shop maintains its usual simple design style, with white colour palettes paired with metal. Regarding products, the New York shop menu currently features 16 products in 3 categories, namely fruit tea, buttermilk tea, and tea series. With a price range of $3.99-$7.49 per cup, Heytea has also become the first new tea drink brand to land in the US market, with a youthful and trendy brand image that refreshes the impression of traditional tea drinks in local consumers. For Heytea, opening shops in these developed cities through local franchisees can help it quickly sort out a set of methodologies for dealing with different international markets. At the same time, the primary challenge of going overseas lies in the compliance requirements of each market. In London, for example, most of the ingredients and equipment are shipped from China, but this requires franchisees to have a good understanding of local regulations and policies and the ability to ensure that they are operating in a compliant manner.

Once the shop opens, Heytea must quickly gain experience connecting the supply chain. The menu structure of the first batch of products in Heytea's New York shop has been simplified quite a bit compared to China. Only products with common fruits such as grapes, mango, grapefruit, and lemon are used in the fresh fruit tea. This is one of the major problems faced by ready-made tea drinks going overseas, as they need help maintaining a product and new product introduction frequency comparable to that at domestic markets. Not only fruits but also new tea drink products are highly customised. Heytea is adapting to local conditions and looking for more convenient locally sourced fruits for menu adjustments. For example, the Melbourne shop in Australia adds seasonal kiwi fruit products, and London and Kuala Lumpur add mulberry and strawberry products to their menu. New York's classic succulent grapes have even been changed to red grapes, which is also happening in London shops. Heytea has brought China's new tea drink to more consumers across the country and has used its youthful and trendy brand and products to refresh the impression of traditional tea drinks in the minds of local consumers, bringing China's new tea fragrance to consumers around the globe, and bringing overseas consumers a revolutionary beverage experience of real quality, which has been widely welcomed.

THE PEOPLE BEHIND THE UNICORNS

Yunchen Nie (Neo)

As the founder of Heytea, Yunchen Nie (Neo), born in 1991 in Jiangmen, Guangdong Province, studying at Guangdong Polytechnic of Science and Technology of Humanities, majoring in administrative management, after graduating at the age of 19, Neo started his first business, opened a mobile phone shop, because of the reasons for the location of the shop's business into the bottom. However, Neo still earned the first bucket of gold in his flexible operation through his first business. So, he started the second business - opening a milk tea shop. From the beginning, Neo decided on his milk tea shop's audience, flavour, service, and quality. On the eve of the shop opening, he deliberately spent several months studying milk tea flavouring ratios, drinking no less than 20 cups of milk tea daily to record the taste of different ratios. It is the consensus of many that Heytea's products taste good, which mainly comes from Neo's emphasis on the products. He said in an interview that the three aspects he usually spends the most time on are products, branding, and operation. He does not believe that a product that is not good can be famous. In May 2012, Neo's first milk tea shop, RoyalTea, was opened. Almost all of the first group of employees know how strict Neo is; as long as there is a mistake in the work, they will be harshly rebuked. Under Neo's almost strict management, Heytea's quality was rapidly improved. To enrich the taste of milk tea and reduce the sweetness, Neo added fruity and salty cheeses to the drinks, which not only changed the appearance of the milk tea but also made it taste more flavourful. The new Cheese Milkcap Tea was launched and immediately received an enthusiastic response from consumers. Due to the reason that the trademark could not be registered, Neo decided to abandon 'ROYALTEA' and changed it to 'HEYTEA'.

Heytea on brand building is deservedly the industry's first-class, and this Neo aspect has unique insights. He believes the product is only a starting point to becoming more significant and, eventually, the brand. When there was just one Heytea shop, Neo personally did all the work related to brand building; he has his own unique understanding of brand building and perseverance. To communicate brand positioning to customers, a specific carrier is needed, and in terms of related design, the idea of the Heytea logo came from the ancient Greek and Roman currencies Neo loved as a child. He said, 'All the people on those currencies, whether Alexander, Caesar, or Augustus, have the same face on the side. The funny thing is that you cannot tell who is who because all human beings have pretty much the same side face.' The design of Heytea focuses on simplicity, fashion, and difference, implanting the brand concept of 'cool, inspiration, zen, design'. Neo hopes that Heytea is a more neutral brand because he wants Heytea to win everyone's hearts, and Neo has succeeded in matching Heytea's products with the brand's style of a youthful set of tea drinks.

Firstly, the positioning of the brand should be narrow enough. He believes that the ultimate vision of 'Heytea' is to rejuvenate, internationalise, and internetise tea and the culture behind it, and based on this, make a symbol and brand that transcends culture and geography. Secondly, the brand communication needs to be well carried out and detailed. In one of his speeches, Neo mentioned that brand communication in the Internet era needs good content. However, the content could be more specific, so finding a carrier for better communication is necessary. Promotional materials are carriers, shop space, product packaging, and even the fire hydrant in the shop can also be seen as carriers. He still insists on participating in the final review of all the copywriting and design drawings for the opening of a Heytea shop. Not a single shop, but all of them. Many people who have worked with him are impressed by his meticulousness. The person in charge of the branding and visual centre of Heytea said Neo would check the promotional materials before they went out on the street; not even a single typo, or even a single pixel movement, would be tolerated. Yunchen Nie once said he only cares about the most significant and minor things. The biggest thing is the brand strategy, and the smallest is the details, as small as some banners, decorations, and text details; for Heytea, the pursuit is always BETTER rather than DIFFERENT. So, on the '2020 Shenzhen Creative Wealth 100 List', Yunchen Nie(Neo), who was only 29 years old, became the current youngest billionaire and business legend who started from nothing with his $4.092 billion fortune.

FUTURE PROJECTS

Whether it is traditional milk tea or new drinks represented by fresh fruit and fresh milk tea, tea has always been essential. Consumer demand for tea has always existed, and now there is a trend of placing more and more emphasis on tea. After the market's continuous exploration of tea over the past decade, it has been found that young people have a natural desire for tea and a sense of intimacy. Based on this insight into the market trend, Heytea has formally proposed a 'return to tea' strategy in its 2023 annual report. The tea house (Heytea·Pure) business can be seen as an essential step in the return to tea. Some boutique teahouses have emerged in the market in the past two years. Still, these teahouses mainly aim at the on-site drinking experience, and the consumption scene is relatively concentrated. The tea house proposed "fresh, tea, pure" product characteristics, more focused on providing convenient, quality tea products, which have been widely accepted by the new tea drinking, covering more consumer scenarios to achieve differentiated competition.

The menu of Heytea Tea House shops is different from that of regular Heytea shops, with only four categories: 'Freshly brewed - Ming Milk Tea', 'Freshly brewed - Chinese Tea Latte', 'Freshly brewed - Lemon Tea', and 'Freshly brewed - Pure Tea'. 'Fresh Tea - Pure Tea' demonstrates Heytea's pursuit of quality and flavour. This is not only a respect for traditional tea culture but also a response to the new generation of consumers' tastes and concepts of wellness, showing the brand's market acumen. In terms of design style, it fits the idea of a tea house, draws inspiration from the Song Dynasty tea house and bamboo room, and adopts a modern Chinese minimalist design to create a tea house space with a sense of atmosphere, suitable for both the ancient and contemporary worlds. At the same time, through the pricing of RMB 8-19, the consumption threshold of boutique tea is lowered to the mainstream level of the new tea beverage track and through the efficient delivery of cups to balance the take-away, self-service and in-store experience scenarios. Overall, Tea House is more approachable for the younger groups who want to try tea.

From the market perspective, the tea house business also has the advantage of being 'faster and brighter'. After 2023, a whole year of shop expansion wave, the new tea drink competition into the deep water, the shop model has become a brand competition. The first tea shop has the advantages of being in a small area, having a low cost, and being highly efficient. From the product aspect, the freshly extracted boutique tea category pioneered by Tea House, with milk and tea as the main ingredients, and no fresh fruit raw materials, thus reducing supply chain pressure and shop loss rate; if Tea House forms a certain scale, it could further enhance the advantages of the supply chain's centralised procurement. With the continuous development of the tea beverage market, Heytea faces competition from brands such as Nai Xue and Cha Yan Yue Se. By opening 'Heytea Pure', Heytea is trying to find new growth points and differentiate itself from other brands in the new tea beverage market while maintaining its innovative features.

It is reported that the first shop of Heytea Pure Shanghai will be opened on 6 February 2024, and the Beijing and Shenyang shops have been fenced off and prepared for opening. From another point of view, the tea house business also provides ideas for the innovation of the new tea beverage industry. When Heytea changed the entire traditional milk tea track to create a new tea drink era, the tea house may have led the new tea drink track into a new ecology. In Heytea's view, serving the public has just begun, and there is no end, but it will firmly serve the public in 2024. At the same time, Heytea will further promote the return and manifestation of tea in the new tea drinks and the process of tea drink health. Finally, with the acceleration of globalisation, Heytea will further bring Chinese tea to the world.

CONCLUSION

By collecting and analysing customer data from various digital touchpoints, Heytea gains insights into consumer preferences, behaviours, and trends. This allows them to tailor their marketing efforts, menu offerings, and customer experiences better to meet the needs and expectations of their target audience. In addition, Heytea's explosive growth and standing out in the fierce competition in the industry cannot be separated from a strong brand effect. Yunchen Nie, the founder of Heytea, is a loyal brand believer, and everything he does is centred around the brand. There is a correlation between the speed of shop expansion and the construction of the brand. The brand effect is the use of the brand on the product for the brand user to bring benefits and impact. Heytea's successful brand effect is based on high-quality products, rapid innovation of new products, complete understanding of the needs of consumers, and constant technology empowerment and innovation to serve customers better, supported by excellent marketing and more understanding of young people's operations, such as the use of the official social account to shape the brand image, the use of cross-border co-branding to expand the influence of the use of seasonally limited drinks to meet the curiosity of consumers. With the brand philosophy that product is the starting point, the brand is the core, and operation is the foundation, Heytea has become a unicorn enterprise.

REFERENCES

Heytea. (2024, January 3). *[Heytea Decennial Report]*. Heytea. https://www.heytea .com/

iiMedia. (2022). 2021 *[China New Style Tea Drink Industry Research Report 2021]*. iiMedia. https://www.iresearch.com.cn/

Zhang, Z. (2022). *Analysis of the recent development of the ready-made tea industry in China based on the innovation of Heytea.*, DOI:10.2991/978-94-6463-052-7_168

KEY TERMS AND DEFINITIONS

Brand Image: Brand image refers to the overall cognition, feeling, and impression consumers have of a brand. It is the image and symbol of the brand in the minds of consumers, including the brand's characteristics, values, culture, personality, and other aspects of the comprehensive expression. The essential components of the brand image include the brand logo, brand values, product and service quality, consumer experience, brand reputation, brand culture and brand positioning.

Content Operations: Content operations are the activities of managing, creating, and promoting content on the Internet to achieve the goals of brand marketing, user interaction, and brand image building. Content operations involve planning, creating, distributing, promoting, and analysing content, aiming to attract target audiences, increase brand exposure, increase user engagement, and promote interaction between users and brands.

Cross-Boundary Marketing: Cross-boundary marketing refers to a marketing strategy in which a brand or company combines its products or services with other industries or fields and achieves the objectives of brand promotion, market expansion, and increased sales through cooperation, integration, or innovation.

Customer Profile: A customer profile refers to the detailed description and analysis of the target customer group, including a comprehensive overview of their basic information, interests, behavioural habits, demand characteristics, and other aspects. Customer profiles are derived through collecting and analysing user data, market research, and consumer insights, helping companies better understand their target audience, accurately position themselves in the market, formulate effective marketing strategies, and provide personalised products and services.

Earned Marketing: Earned marketing is a strategy of brand promotion and marketing through consumers' word-of-mouth and sharing their consumption experience. It relies on word-of-mouth and social sharing among consumers rather than traditional advertising channels.

Herd Effect: The herd effect refers to the tendency to follow the behaviour or opinions of the majority of people. In a group, individuals are influenced by the behaviour or opinions of those around them and thus go along with the masses.

Market Barriers: Market barriers are factors and conditions that prevent new firms from entering a particular market or make it difficult for them to compete with existing firms. These factors can be limitations or obstacles from technology, law, economics, branding, resources, etc., that allow companies already in the market to maintain a relative competitive advantage.

Peripheral Products: Peripheral products are derivative or ancillary products associated with a brand, work, IP (intellectual property) or theme. These products are usually based on the elements, characters, storylines, etc., of the brand, work, or IP. They are developed through licensing or cooperation to satisfy consumers' fondness and admiration for a specific brand or theme, and at the same time, provide another profit channel for the brand or IP holder.

Social Currency: A product becomes social currency when it is widely shared and discussed and makes the person who owns it look better and more stylish.

Chapter 3
Hello Trans Tech:
Pioneering Sustainable Mobility in the Shared Economy

Haoyue Yu

Beijing Normal University-Hong Kong Baptist University United International College, China

EXECUTIVE SUMMARY

This case study examines the evolution and strategic initiatives of Hello Trans Tech, a pioneering force in China's shared mobility sector. Founded in 2016 amidst the boom of bike-sharing, Hello Trans Tech quickly emerged as a leader by leveraging innovative technologies and sustainable transportation solutions. The journey from its inception, navigating through phases of market expansion, technological adaptation, and diversification into electric vehicles and intelligent mobility systems. Key aspects include strategic partnerships with Alibaba and Contemporary Amperex Technology, its transition from bike-sharing to a comprehensive mobility platform, and its expansion into Singapore. The study also highlights the leadership of founders Yang Lei and Kaizhu Li, their vision for sustainable urban mobility, and Hello's pioneering efforts in AI-driven optimization and carbon-neutral initiatives. Through this exploration, readers gain insights into how Hello Trans Tech has reshaped urban transportation and positioned itself at the forefront of China's shared economy revolution.

INTRODUCTION

Shanghai Hello Puhui Technology Co., Ltd, a pioneering force in China's sharing economy, was founded in 2016 by Yang Lei. Originally a bike-sharing company in Shanghai, Hello Trans Tech (formerly Hello Bike) is now a travel-sharing and

DOI: 10.4018/979-8-3693-2921-4.ch003

life service platform in China that has developed innovative ways to enhance travel experiences in various cities.

The sharing economy has become a significant trend worldwide, especially in China. In such a competitive landscape, Hello Trans Tech has chosen to conduct efficient operations to survive and expand its market. In 2016, Hello Bike was officially launched; in 2018, Hello Electric Vehicle was introduced; in 2019, Hello Shared Bike was released; and in 2020, Hello Electric Vehicle business was launched. Between 2020 and 2022, Hello underwent a brand upgrade and expanded its commercial offerings to include local community life services.

Over the years, Hello Trans Tech has experienced impressive growth and has diversified its portfolio with micro-mobility solutions. Noteworthy achievements include the Bluetooth road stud parking technology. This technology involves the use of Bluetooth-enabled road studs to assist in parking. These road studs are equipped with Bluetooth technology, allowing them to communicate with vehicles or parking management systems to provide information about available parking spaces. Hello Trans Tech's emphasis on cutting-edge technology and user experience sets it apart from competitors in the market.

The main goal of Hello Trans Tech is to provide a more convenient mode of travel for users in the "last 1 km" of their journey. To achieve this, Hello Trans Tech has established an intelligent decision-making command center that utilizes modern information technologies and algorithms to efficiently deploy operational resources. In addition to providing transportation services, Hello Trans Tech aims to create a community-centered ecosystem that enhances urban living. In 2018, Hello Trans Tech launched a credit-free riding business and also proposed offering the first 15-minute ride free of charge to meet short-term car rental needs. Through effective marketing strategies, the platform has gained over 600 million registered users and expanded its services to 500 major cities nationwide. Users have collectively travelled over 58 billion kilometers, capturing a significant market share (Xinhua New Media, 2024).

Hello Trans Tech advocates for two-wheeled micro-mobility to alleviate strain on current infrastructure and foster a healthier, more vibrant lifestyle for its participants. By promoting the use of bicycles and similar modes of transport, the company contributes to reducing congestion on roads and public transportation systems. Additionally, Hello encourages individuals to engage in physical activity as part of their daily routine. Through these initiatives, Hello Trans Tech is redefining urban transportation and prioritizing its participants' health and vitality.

The more profound benefits promoted by Hello Trans are extensive and far-reaching. Regularly using this infrastructure promotes physical fitness by encouraging physical activity, improving cardiovascular health, increasing muscle strength, and enhancing flexibility. Engaging in active transportation or recreational activities also positively impacts mental well-being, reducing stress levels, alleviating symptoms of anxiety and depression, and improving overall mental well-being. Additionally, by encouraging outdoor activities and reducing reliance on motor vehicles, Hello Trans supports cleaner air quality, leading to better respiratory health and a decreased risk of respiratory diseases. Furthermore, the shared spaces promoted by this initiative foster social connections, reducing feelings of isolation or loneliness, which are crucial for mental health. This initiative addresses immediate transportation needs and contributes to the holistic well-being of individuals and communities alike while relieving pressure on existing infrastructure.

UNICORN DESCRIPTION

Development and Strategy

Initial Growth (2016-2017)

Hello Bike Company was born in 2016 amidst the rise of bike-sharing in China. It aims to transform urban transportation and promote eco-friendly commuting. Despite challenges like deposit refund issues and poor road management, Hello focused on securing funding and building its infrastructure, deploying bikes with smart locks and GPS trackers across urban centers. The company also invested heavily in product R&D, with a team comprising primarily automotive industry veterans. This led to higher R&D expenditure than competitors but resulted in high-quality, comfortable bikes that set Hello apart.

Expansion and Market Penetration (2017-2018)

Hello Bike Company recognized the importance of trust in the competitive bike-sharing market. It transitioned to a credit-based model, eliminating traditional deposits and building a system based on user activity. This approach differed from competitors like Ofo and Mobike and won consumer trust. Despite the increased depreciation costs from heavy investments in bikes and electric vehicles, Hello managed to expand rapidly, thanks to financing from Alibaba. However, the company's over-reliance on bike-sharing for revenue was challenged, prompting a rebranding to Hello a comprehensive travel and lifestyle platform.

Comprehensive Layout of Sustainable Financing (2019)

In 2019, Hello Trans demonstrated its commitment to innovation with over 130 patent applications. The company also expanded into four-wheel transportation services and established a joint venture for electric vehicle battery swapping in partnership with Ant Group and Contemporary Amperex Technology. This move marked a significant expansion from the traditional bike-sharing model, solidifying Hello's position in the shared mobility sector and paving the way for future ventures.

Diversification and Vertical Integration (2020-present)

Today, Hello Trans is a leading player in the shared mobility sector, with a user base exceeding 550 million and a range of services, including cycling, electric vehicles, and ride-sharing. Hello has faced financial losses despite expanding business channels due to high capital investment and rising operating costs. Thus, the decision to go public in 2021 was made to secure financial support. Furthermore, Hello has shown commitment to social responsibility, even during the COVID-19 crisis, by creating jobs and releasing the first carbon-neutral proposal in the shared travel industry to promote sustainable development.

Business Model

Hello Trans Tech is based on the O2O (Online to Offline) structure. They operate a business model centered around fulfilling short-distance, point-to-point travel needs in urban areas. Hello's primary sources of profit are customer leasing income and commercial partnerships on online platforms. Its target customer base requires daily short-distance, timed, and fixed-point travel (Peng, 2023). During the initial stages of company development, users can unlock bikes using a mobile app, paying a fee for the duration of their ride, making it a convenient and eco-friendly way to travel. In response to potential user issues, Hello Trans Tech has also established a practical credit supervision system. Additionally, Hello Trans Tech generates revenue through commissions on car rentals (Peng, 2023).

The key to successful implementation of cost control is not about compromising quality but rather implementing a more comprehensive and systematic approach to cost control. Hello's strategy focuses on simplifying products, maintaining quality, improving operational efficiency, and optimizing design to achieve cost reduction goals, all while emphasizing quality, stability, and strengthening internal control. Instead of exploring other options, Hello has directed its resources toward improving the collection and utilization of intelligent data related to vehicle usage. Hello's intelligent technology significantly reduced operational costs by identifying and controlling big data, minimizing vehicle wear and tear, and timely inspecting and maintaining vehicles to minimize the obsolescence rate.

Hello Trans's technical team, consisting of thousands of engineers, utilizes advanced technology and data analytics methods to support Hello's operations in over 300 cities nationwide. These engineers have developed heat maps and health diagrams to visualize the quantity and condition of vehicles or devices in each area. When the system detects excessive vehicles or inadequate supply in a particular area, it automatically dispatches tasks to maintenance personnel for prompt adjustment.

Hello Brain's intelligent scheduling system employs intelligent delivery and scheduling to effectively alleviate the pressure of the growing demand for shared travel. The system considers urban population density, bicycle distribution, and electric vehicle delivery strategy and dynamically regulates supply and demand through AI calculations. Hello optimizes the allocation of cycle resources through this efficient scheduling system, enhances service levels, and ensures users have a superior service experience.

Products and Services

Hello Trans Tech Share Bike

The Hello Trans Tech sharing bike is the company's first product and has gained a loyal customer base. Most Hellobikes come in white and blue, which enhances the recognition of the Hello brand. Hellobike prioritizes safety and comfort and consistently updates its bikes. The body is made of advanced wear-resistant materials, and the cushion is designed based on ergonomic principles. Hello Trans Tech addresses the growing need for sustainable transportation in urban areas. Consumers can use the Hello Trans Tech mobile app to view a map of bike distribution and navigate to their locations. Bluetooth remote technology eliminates the hassles associated with traditional bike rental systems. This is achieved through dockless designated parking technology, which aims to establish standardized parking areas by locating users' mobile phones and vehicles to determine the return location (HelloRide, n.d.).

Here is how each competitive advantage of Hello Bike:

1. Swappable Battery: Hello Bike's Swappable Battery is revolutionizing electric mobility. The breakthrough swappable battery technology allows for seamless battery change, enabling consumers to extend their ride time without needing to charge. This advantage also highlights the technology's environmental benefits, such as reducing carbon emissions and promoting sustainable transportation options. The high-quality swappable battery provides greater flexibility and convenience for urban commuting and leisurely rides.

2. Braking System: Hello Bike's Durable Drum Brakes ensure safe and smooth stops, emphasizing their durability, reliability, and superior braking performance. The discussion delves into the engineering behind Hello Bike's drum brakes, enhancing braking agility and responsiveness for riders.
3. Hybrid-Parking Technology: To use the system, deploy the beacon in the designated area and set geofencing through Bluetooth positioning technology. The system can intelligently determine the vehicle's parking status utilizing an algorithm.

Hello Carpooling

As Hello Carpooling expands, it is now offering a carpooling service in addition to its existing bike-sharing service, aiming to provide multi-channel shared mobility. This new carpooling service offers a eco-friendly alternative for four-wheeled transportation to complement the current two-wheeler service. The innovative ride-sharing platform seamlessly connects drivers with passengers heading in the same direction, marking a significant advancement in urban transportation solutions. Hello Carpooling's success is attributed to its ability to provide an alternative to traditional taxi services and promote the concept of carpooling. Through the user-friendly mobile app, users can access a variety of vehicles, including Hello e-bikes and bicycles, adding flexibility and convenience to transportation options.

Governments worldwide are placing significant importance on regulating the ride-sharing industry. Hello's carpooling feature is integrated with Alibaba's service, prioritizing passenger safety through cloud-based processes like real-name verification and facial recognition. Hello also collaborates with public security departments to perform background checks on its partner drivers, demonstrating a solid commitment to customer safety.

Hello E-Bike

Electric bikes, also known as e-bikes, are powered by rechargeable batteries and are becoming increasingly popular among people with a growing energy need. Hello Trans Tech offers a modern solution for short-distance travel with its Hello e-bike. Bicycles and e-bikes are designed to be comfortable, environmentally friendly, and easy to ride. Lithium-ion batteries power E-bikes to provide pedal assistance.

Hellotrans deploys and rebalances e-bikes in every city to complement the existing transportation infrastructure.

Regarding market penetration, the shared e-bike industry still has room for growth, and its growth rate is higher than that of the shared bicycle industry. The current number of shared electric bicycles needs to meet the high user demand, and the implementation of relevant policies is helping to accelerate the development of the electric vehicle industry. By promoting cycling as a means of transportation, Hello Trans Tech reduces the strain on current infrastructure and encourages a healthier, more active lifestyle for its users.

Customers

Hello Trans has strategically positioned itself through segmentation and target market selection. It divides its market into urban commuting and scenic leisure riding, catering to different usage scenarios and travel needs. Within urban commuting, Hello Trans further segments markets based on city tiers, targeting first, second, third, and fourth-tier cities. Unlike competitors focusing solely on first-tier cities, Hello concentrates on second and third-tier cities, capitalizing on less intense competition and more significant growth opportunities (Xie & Yan, 2023).

The current age group of Hello Trans users mainly falls within the 26-35 age range. Hello primarily caters to large and medium-sized city residents suffering from severe traffic congestion and lack of public transportation coverage. Consequently, city dwellers are more likely to use shared travel services to address short-distance travel challenges. The percentage of people requiring travel services in first-tier cities is notably higher than in other cities. Additionally, Hello's user base generally exhibits a robust digital awareness and is comfortable using mobile apps for travel planning, booking, and payments. They are enthusiastic about experimenting with new technologies and innovative products and are receptive to using convenient mobile apps to resolve travel-related issues (Xie & Yan, 2023). By consistently introducing new technological advancements and enhancing user experience, Hello can attract more customers and maintain a competitive edge over its rivals.

Hello Trans's customer loyalty is crucial for its future development, as it faces intense competition. Hello Trans's customers will likely be sensitive to price and service quality. They may test out different mobility service providers before deciding based on their experiences and needs. As a result, Hello Trans's customer loyalty may be slightly lower than that of other industries. Therefore, they must consistently improve service quality and enhance user experience to increase customer loyalty (Pang, 2022).

Market Analysis

This section aims to comprehensively analyze Hello Trans's market environment using the PEST model. The PEST model, which stands for Political, Economic, Social, and Technological factors, provides a framework for understanding the macro-environmental factors a company needs to consider in its strategic planning. By analyzing these four dimensions, Hello Trans can better understand the market challenges and opportunities and formulate effective strategies to navigate its business environment.

Political factors have played a significant role in shaping the market environment for Hello Trans. The Chinese government's strong advocacy for low-carbon, environmentally friendly transportation has led to favorable policies that encourage green travel and the development of public transportation. These policies have spurred the growth of the sharing economy, facilitating the robust development of sharing economy enterprises. Two significant policy boosts, the inclusion in the "Green Industry Guidance Catalog" and the introduction of the "Technical Specifications for Electric Bicycle Safety," have directly benefited the electric bike-sharing industry, prompting collaborations with companies like Contemporary Amperex Technology and improving product performance and user experience.

Economic factors have also significantly influenced the market environment. Despite the economic fluctuations caused by the COVID-19 pandemic, China's overall economic development continues to improve, with market consumption and purchasing power gradually increasing. The rise of advanced technologies like artificial intelligence, big data, and cloud computing has ushered in a new phase for industries within the Internet economy, such as platforms and sharing economies. However, these economic changes have also intensified market competition and increased price pressure. In response, Hello Trans has embraced the evolution of the Internet economy, implementing features like in-app payments, customer service, and vehicle location tracking.

Social factors, including urbanization, population mobility, and increased societal awareness of environmental protection and healthy lifestyles, have also impacted the demand for sharing services. Cities with dense populations tend to have a higher demand for bike-sharing, and the increased societal endorsement of concepts such as the sharing economy and green travel has significantly improved public acceptance of bike-sharing and car-pooling services. The benefits of cycling, such as reduced carbon emissions, sustainable cities, preservation of resources, and personal health, have also contributed to the rise in demand for bike-sharing services.

Finally, technological factors have provided additional opportunities. Advances in mobile internet technology have improved bike-sharing user experiences, including mobile app reservations, location services, and online payments. Furthermore, the development of new energy vehicles and intelligent transportation technology has opened up more opportunities for bike-sharing, such as electric bicycles, smart locks, and autonomous driving technology. In conclusion, by understanding and responding to these political, economic, social, and technological factors, Hello Trans can seize market opportunities and address challenges more effectively.

Original Situation of the Market

Bike-sharing services emerged as a response to the pressing need to tackle urban traffic congestion and environmental challenges. The evolution of China's shared bicycle market can be delineated into three historical phases (Zhou, 2023). The initial stage spans from 2007 to 2010, characterized by government initiatives. During this period, prominent cities like Beijing and Hangzhou imported public bikes from foreign countries, integrating them into the urban public transportation system under governmental guidance. Initially, these services operated by strategically placing fixed parking stations throughout cities, enabling users to rent and return bicycles conveniently. However, with technological advancements and shifting consumer demands, the scope of shared mobility has broadened significantly.

When they were first introduced, shared bicycles became extremely popular, leading to many companies entering the market. By the end of 2017, China had seen the rise of at least 23 shared bicycle brands. Introducing shared electric bikes is a significant advancement in shared mobility solutions. These electric bicycles, equipped with battery-powered propulsion systems, provide users with a seamless and efficient mode of transportation. Like traditional bike-sharing services, users can easily access and return electric bikes through user-friendly mobile applications, making urban commuting more flexible (Zhou, 2023).

The shared mobility landscape has become more diverse with the emergence of various alternative transportation options, including shared electric bikes, skateboards, pedal-assist bicycles, and more. These alternatives cater to the growing demand for eco-friendly and convenient urban travel solutions, offering urban residents various commuting choices. Shared mobility services have evolved from the basic bike-sharing concept to include a broader spectrum of transportation options, such as shared electric bikes. The main goal remains consistent: to improve urban mobility, reduce environmental impact, and provide users with enhanced convenience and flexibility in their daily commutes. As shared mobility concepts gain momentum, further innovation is expected to enrich the urban commuting experience, ensuring greater convenience for city residents (Pang, 2022).

Evolution of the Market Until Today

Increased awareness and acceptance of sustainable transportation options are driving the growth of China's bike-sharing market. As concerns about environmental pollution grow and the need for efficient urban mobility solutions increases, bike sharing has become popular among consumers. The accessibility and cost-effectiveness of bike-sharing services have also contributed to their appeal and boosted demand (Zhou, 2023).

In addition, the bike-sharing market has evolved significantly due to technological advancements and changing user demands. The introduction of dockless bike-sharing has provided users with greater flexibility as fixed docking stations no longer constrain them. Technological innovations such as GPS tracking and integration with mobile applications have improved user experiences. Bike-sharing services have expanded globally and become a popular urban travel choice.

In recent years, the market has seen new micro-mobility options, such as electric bicycles and scooters, providing users with more choices. The market offers various services, including Hello Battery Swap and Hello Community. China's policy environment for shared economy development has also become more favorable. The government has been introducing and refining laws and regulations concerning the shared economy, creating a more compliant business environment conducive to innovative development in the sector.

Competition Analysis

The bike-sharing market is highly competitive, with significant players like Meituan, Didi, Lime, Mobike, and Ofo vying for dominance. These companies use various strategies to attract and retain users, including pricing, service quality, and marketing. By the end of 2017, the domestic bike-sharing market had consolidated significantly, resulting in a duopoly between Mobike and Ofo. Meituan acquired Mobike, Didi acquired Bluegogo, and Hello Bicycle secured substantial funding from Alibaba's investment arm. This has further solidified the competitive landscape. The well-funded entities backing most bike-sharing firms indicate that future competition is expected to intensify. Additionally, emerging micro-mobility modes such as e-bikes and bicycles add to the competitive landscape. The ride-hailing sector in China also presents intense competition, with brands like Didi, Autonavi, Cao Cao, and Hello expanding into carpooling services, further intensifying competition in this segment.

Forecast for this Market

The future of the bike-sharing market appears promising and is anticipated to maintain its growth momentum. As urban populations swell and traffic congestion intensifies, micro-mobility solutions such as bike-sharing are expected to become increasingly essential for urban commuting. Although the bike-sharing market may encounter heightened competition and challenges in the upcoming years, it will also present abundant opportunities for growth and development. Consequently, it is crucial for Hello Bike Company to persistently innovate and enhance its services to adapt to market shifts and sustain its competitive edge.

The global move towards shared mobility aligns with the worldwide efforts to achieve "carbon neutrality." With governments and societies globally prioritizing carbon emissions reduction, shared transportation options like bike-sharing are critical in fostering sustainable urban mobility. Furthermore, the growth of bike-sharing services extends beyond addressing transportation needs and generates many job opportunities. From bike maintenance and customer service to executive roles, the bike-sharing industry creates employment in various sectors, contributing to economic growth and stability.

In parallel, the partnership with battery swap suppliers is also noteworthy. China is the largest global light electric vehicle (EV) battery-swapping market. Hello Trans Tech is among the leading providers in this domain, with an estimated deployment of over 1,000 battery swap stations for electric two-wheel vehicles (E2WVs). Looking ahead, companies investing in battery swap infrastructure are broadening their networks to accommodate the growing demand for electric mobility solutions. This expansion is vital for scaling up battery swap services and catering to a more extensive market.

THE PEOPLE BEHIND THE UNICORNS

Founder and CEO: Yang Lei

Yang Lei, the CEO of Hello plays a critical leadership role. As an experienced business leader, his leadership style has been described as firm and pragmatic. He is focused on driving innovation and the continued growth of Hello and has a keen insight into strategic planning and decision-making. According to publicly available information, Yang Lei graduated from Shanghai University of Technology. After graduation, he gained valuable experience in technological innovation and business management while working in computer repair and parts sales in computer malls in Shanghai.

Yang Lei is also a serial entrepreneur and one of the co-founders of Hello. He established Hello in September 2016 and has led its growth over the past few years. Under his leadership, Hello quickly became one of the leading companies in shared mobility. Yang Lei has been recognized for his achievements, being selected for Forbes China's 30 Under 30 Elite list and winning the title of "Young Business Leader of the Year." These accomplishments further highlight his exceptional performance and leadership in the business field, especially in the sharing economy business model.

Co-Founder: Kaizhu Li

Kaizhu Li, one of the co-founders of Hello Travel, boasts a wealth of experience and deep expertise in information technology. He earned his bachelor's degree in Computer Science from Hangzhou Dianzi University in 1997. Subsequently, in 2007, he pursued a master's degree in software engineering from the Software School of Fudan University. From 2005 to 2014, Kaizhu Li served as a Senior Engineer at Ericsson (China) Communications Co., Ltd., focusing on information and communication technology. He then transitioned to Senior R&D Manager at Ctrip in 2014, a major player in travel services. In the subsequent years, from 2015 to 2016, he co-founded Shanghai Jingyao Network Technology Co., Ltd., where he led software development. These diverse experiences have equipped him with a broad skill set and deep insight into technology.

Li Kaizhu held essential positions at Ctrip and Shanghai Jingyao Network Technology Co., LTD throughout his career. While at Ctrip, he was a senior Research and Development Manager, managing the software research and development team. He was actively involved in promoting Hello's technological innovation and product optimization. Additionally, he co-founded Shanghai Jingyao Network Technology Co., LTD with Yang Lei. He was primarily responsible for software research and development, focusing on creating innovative products and solutions in mobility.

FUTURE PROJECTS

Digitalization, Intelligence, and Visualization

Hello Trans Tech is focused on leveraging Artificial Intelligence (AI) to enhance its services and products. The company plans to use AI technology to analyze user travel preferences and behaviors and to provide tailored mobility solutions. This approach, known as "Hello Brain," will help optimize vehicle scheduling, route planning, and real-time dynamic monitoring, improving operational efficiency and customer retention. Additionally, Hello is set to enhance its visualization capabilities to provide users with intuitive and informative travel options. This might include developing interactive maps, data visualization tools, and augmented reality capabilities. With these initiatives, Hello Trans Tech strives to redefine mobility through AI-driven innovation, catering to individual preferences and promoting sustainable growth.

Expansion Into Overseas Markets

As competition intensifies in the domestic market and user demand saturates, Hello Trans Tech plans to expand its business to overseas markets. The company's successful shared mobility platform in China provides a solid foundation for this expansion. Hello's entry into the Singapore market in 2022 marks a significant step in its overseas expansion. With its advanced transportation infrastructure and wide use of digital applications, Singapore is an ideal location for bike-sharing services. Hello aims to establish a strong presence in overseas markets through market research, strategic partnerships, and targeted promotions. This expansion will not only provide more growth opportunities for Hello Trans Tech but also contribute to the development of intelligent transportation in Singapore and beyond. Hello plans to expand overseas markets, seek new growth opportunities and accelerate internationalization.

Sustainable Urban Mobility Initiatives

Hello Trans is responding to the increasing demand for sustainable mobility solutions by implementing carbon neutrality initiatives and partnering with government agencies. The company plans to develop policies and measures to reduce traffic congestion and emissions. This could involve optimizing traffic management, promoting shared electric vehicles, and reducing reliance on traditional fuel vehicles. Moreover, Hello aims to collaborate with the government on intelligent transportation projects. This could include introducing intelligent traffic management systems, such as bright lights and parking systems. These initiatives will help cities realize intelligent traffic, providing data support and decision-making references for the government to address urban transportation challenges.

REFERENCES

HelloRide. (n.d.). *Helloride shared micromobility: World's leading shared E-mobility operator*. HelloRide. https://www.helloride-global.com/

Hou, J. (2022). The evaluation of Hellobike. *Proceedings of the 2022 2nd International Conference on Economic Development and Business Culture (ICEDBC 2022)*, (pp. 1736–1742). Atlantis Press. DOI:10.2991/978-94-6463-036-7_259

Pang, H. W. (2022). *[Factors affecting the precise operation of orderly parking of shared bicycles]*. [Master's thesis, Beijing Jiaotong University].

Peng, F. (2023). *[Research on customer relationship management strategy of Hello Travel platform]*. [Master's thesis, Huazhong Agricultural University].

Wang, J. (2023). The tripartite pattern of sharing bicycles in China: Future development of Hello Bike. Highlights in Business. *Economics and Management*, 11, 125–130. DOI:10.54097/hbem.v11i.7956

Xie, Y., & Yan, L. (2023). "Enterprise strategic risk management of Hello Trans Tech". *Modern Business*, 02, 16–19. DOI:10.14097/j.cnki.5392/2023.02.02

Xinhua New Media. (2024). *Hello releases annual sustainability & ESG report, cumulative carbon reduction exceeds 13.1 million tons*. SH News. http://sh.news.cn/20240606/3df28c748d034b21944145af60d74207/c.html

Zhou, C. (2023). "Current situation and countermeasures of internet shared bicycle operation". *Journal of Jinhua Vocational and Technical College*, 02, 23–29.

KEY TERMS AND DEFINITIONS

Carbon Neutrality: This is the commitment made by Hello Trans Tech to achieve a net-zero carbon footprint. The company works with global efforts to stabilize global warming and promote environmental sustainability.

Community-Centric Ecosystem: This refers to Hello Trans Tech's approach to creating an operational model that focuses on community needs. It aims to not only provide transportation services but also contribute to urban living and community relationships.

Customer Loyalty: This concept aims to reward repeat users and build long-term relationships. It includes membership benefits and personalized service offerings.

Data-Driven Operations: This operation process involves utilizing big data to optimize business strategy, thereby enhancing the objectivity and efficiency of business decision-making.

Growth Flywheel: This is a concept in business strategy where elements such as user needs, service quality, and operational efficiency interact to form a continuous business cycle that drives business expansion and service enhancement.

Micro-Mobility: This term refers to small and convenient transportation methods that provide short-distance travel options within urban environments. The aim is to promote a greener lifestyle.

O2O (Online to Offline) Business Model: This is the core operational structure of Hello Trans Tech, which integrates online platforms with apps to provide services to offline urban users.

Sharing Economy: This is a system based on the sharing of social resources. Hello Trans Tech leverages this system by offering shared mobility solutions such as bikes and carpooling to residents.

User-Centric Design: Hello Trans Tech's approach to product development focuses on user needs to create products and services that are comfortable, safe, and easy to use.

Chapter 4
Zongmu Technology:
Autonomous Driving and Advanced Driver Assistance Systems (ADAS)

Zhuoyue Ji

Beijing Normal University-Hong Kong Baptist University United International College, China

EXECUTIVE SUMMARY

This case study provides an in-depth market analysis of Zongmu Technology, a leading player in autonomous driving and advanced driver assistance systems (ADAS) in China. It explores the evolution of the automobile market from traditional vehicles to new energy vehicles, highlighting the shift from secondary software algorithms to full-stack solutions. The case study investigates Zongmu's strategic position, the competitive environment it operates in, and the difficulties it encounters when competing against major rivals such as Velodyne Lidar and Pony.ai. It also details the company's latest developments, including the introduction of new products like FlashBot and Lightning Bao by Silkworm Bush Robotics. The study delves into Zongmu's complex shareholding structure, strategic partnerships, and future projects, such as comprehensive intelligent driving systems, wireless charging for NEVs, and smart city solutions. Through this comprehensive analysis, the case aims to explain Zongmu Technology's strategies for growth and innovation in the rapidly developing autonomous driving market.

DOI: 10.4018/979-8-3693-2921-4.ch004

INTRODUCTION

Founded in 2013, Zongmu Technology is a leading entity in the era of Automatic Driving (AD) and Advanced Driver Assistance System (ADAS) technologies within China. The company operates with a vision of safe driving and intelligent living, harboring the ambition to transition from assisted to autonomous driving. Although rooted in China, it aims to have a global influence. As a high-tech company, it specializes in the research and development of automotive intelligent assisted driving systems. The founding team comprises seasoned professionals from globally renowned automotive electronic chip manufacturers and automotive tier-1 suppliers. With over 80% of its workforce possessing a postgraduate education or higher, Zongmu Technology has secured several software copyrights and invention patents.

Zongmu Technology has developed a comprehensive industrial chain from basic R&D to mass production and application. Its core business encompasses three major areas - intelligent driving systems (including intelligent sensors), innovative city products and services, and wireless charging. The unique strengths of Zongmu Technology's products and technologies are steadily gaining market recognition. Owing to its superior system capability and unparalleled mass production strength, the company has become one of the first in China to secure a contract for L4-level mass production projects from Original Equipment Manufacturers (OEMs). It has also established mass production partnerships with FAW Hongqi, Changan Automobile, and other leading domestic OEMs.

DESCRIPTION OF ZONGMU TECHNOLOGY

Zongmu Technology's Brief History

Since its inception in 2013, Zongmu Technology has made significant strides in the AD and ADAS sectors. The company's dedication to evolving from assisted to autonomous driving has been a critical driver of its growth and influence within China and globally. Zongmu's commitment to innovation is reflected in its high-tech focus on the research and development of automotive intelligent assisted driving systems. This dedication has led to the company's recognition as one of the Top 50 Innovative Companies in China in Artificial Intelligence and Hardware in 2022 and its inclusion in the 2022 Forbes China's Most Innovative Companies in Artificial

Intelligence and Hardware. Moreover, the company's rapid growth and potential have earned it a spot on the 2023 Hurun Global Unicorn List.

Beyond these achievements, Zongmu Technology has made a name for itself through its partnerships with leading domestic OEMs such as FAW Hongqi and Changan Automobile. These collaborations have bolstered the company's reputation and facilitated the mass production of its innovative products. Looking ahead, Zongmu Technology continues to expand its reach through its wide-ranging industrial chain, encompassing everything from foundational R&D to mass production and application. As it continues to grow, the company remains steadfast in its commitment to safe driving and intelligent living, leveraging its unique strengths to offer innovative products and services increasingly recognized and valued in the market.

Development and Strategy of Zongmu Over the Years

Zongmu Technology, established in 2013, has rapidly evolved into a leading player in China's autonomous driving industry. The company's journey has been marked by numerous milestones, from launching the industry's first hypervisors based on infotainment and surround-view integrated solutions to securing significant funding rounds and forming strategic partnerships. Its continuous innovation in autonomous driving and advanced driver assistance systems (ADAS) has earned it recognition and awards, further solidifying its position in the market. Zongmu's focus on cutting-edge technology and strategic collaborations reflects its commitment to shaping the future of intelligent transportation.

In 2013, Zongmu Technology was established, marking a significant milestone in the autonomous driving industry. The same year, the company launched the industry's first hypervisors based on infotainment and surround-view integrated solutions. Additionally, it signed its first cooperation agreement with Desay SV, China's largest display, radio, and navigation system supplier.

In 2014, Zongmu Technology unveiled the first industry-leading and fully featured surround-view ADAS (Advanced Driver Assistance Systems) solution. The company also earned Outstanding Enterprise in the third China Innovation and Entrepreneurship Competition, underscoring its innovative and entrepreneurial prowess.

In 2015, Zongmu Technology secured tens of millions of yuan in its Series A funding round from Synergetic Innovation Fund. This year, the company also signed an agreement with HSAE, China's largest automotive electronics supplier, to research and develop next-generation 360-degree surround-view ADAS.

In 2016, Zongmu Technology achieved several significant milestones. The company set up a new R&D center in Beijing dedicated to the R&D of autonomous driving systems. It also completed the transformation of its corporate structure, officially registering as a limited liability company. Furthermore, Zongmu Technology partnered with the 3D Image R&D Lab of Tsinghua University. Lastly, the first 2016 Geely Boyue fitted with Zongmu Technology's surround-view ADAS product started mass production.

In 2017, Zongmu Technology launched its self-developed low-speed automated parking assistance product and completed its Series B funding round at RMB 100,000,000, co-led by Legend Capital and Dyee Capital. The company was also successfully listed on the National Equities Exchange and Quotations (NEEQ, the New Third Board).

In 2018, Zongmu Technology won a mass production contract for an automated valet parking system from FAW Group. The company's Xiamen manufacturing center also came into operation for mass production. Also, Zongmu Technology announced a strategic collaboration with Visteon Corporation and completed a several hundred million RMB Series C funding round.

In 2019, Zongmu Technology secured a several hundred-million-yuan Series C+ funding led by Qualcomm Ventures. The company also reached cooperation agreements with Guangzhou Automobile Group Research and Development Center (GAC R&D Center), Chang' an Automobile, and Keytop Parking in automatic parking assistance technology.

In 2020, Zongmu Technology's automatic parking assistance platform development project received the certification of Automotive SPICE Capability Level 2. The company also set up a Southwest Research and Development Center in Chongqing, was shortlisted for the SAIL Award TOP 30, and secured a Series D1 fund from the Japanese Tier 1 supplier Denso.

In 2021, Zongmu Technology's Xiamen factory received IPC QML certification, and the company established strategic partnerships with Horizon Robotics and SemiDrive Technology. The company's NEV wireless charging project started operations in the Beibei area, Chongqing, and it announced the completion of the Series D financing round, which totalled $190 million.

In 2022, Zongmu Technology was awarded the title of "National Specialized and New 'Little Giant' Enterprise". The company's intelligent driving system production base officially started construction in Dongyang, and it released the latest strategies to maintain its leading position in automatic parking assistance. Zongmu Technology also signed a strategic cooperation agreement with PhiGent Robotics and completed a Series E funding round for an amount exceeding RMB 1 billion.

In 2023, Zongmu Technology secured the mass-produced contract of Amphiman3000 for a series of models from Chang'an Automobile and won the "Shanghai Enterprise Technology Center" title. The company also set up a Joint R&D Center for Intelligent Assisted Driving Systems with Tsinghua University and won the first prize in the SAE Science and Technology Award.

Business Model

Zongmu Technology is dedicated to developing perception-based multi-sensor fusion technology in automatic driving. This technology combines high-precision deep learning algorithms, timely localization, and map-building technology to create a high-performance, low-cost, mass-producible software and hardware platform. The goal is to develop products to benefit customers and establish comprehensive automatic driving solutions.

According to a report from Carriage House Polytechnic (2021), Zongmu began as a secondary software algorithm provider. However, it has since grown into a leading supplier with comprehensive research, development, and production capabilities. The company's strength is intelligent driving solutions covering levels L0 to L4. Their Drop'nGo platform provides integrated software algorithms, control units, and intelligent sensor hardware, all tailored to suit specific customer vehicle models.

Another critical area to discuss is Zongmu's dominance in parking solutions. The company's intelligent parking system supports both low-speed and high-speed scenarios. Their L2-level autonomous parking assistance features are already being mass-produced across nearly twenty vehicle models, with annual shipments surpassing 100,000 units. The company is also expanding its focus to include integrated driving and parking solutions.

Zongmu's strategic focus extends beyond parking. The company is working to strengthen its parking solutions while also developing driving assistance and integrated driving solutions. Their Amphiman system supports L2+ level highway NOA (Navigate on Autopilot) and L4 level AVP (Automated Valet Parking). In addition, Zongmu is also involved in the development of sensor hardware. The company provides system solutions and develops intelligent driving-related hardware sensors, including cameras, ultrasonic sensors, and 4D millimeter-wave radar. These sensors have already been used in numerous vehicle models.

It is important to note that the Society of Automotive Engineers (SAE) defines vehicle automation levels from Level 1 to Level 5. Level 1, Driver Assistance, involves the vehicle assisting with some functions while the human driver handles all accelerating, braking, and monitoring of the surrounding environment. For instance, the car might offer steering assistance or acceleration and deceleration support, but not simultaneously.

At Level 2, or Partial Automation, the vehicle can control steering and accelerating/decelerating under specific circumstances. However, the human driver must remain engaged with the driving task and continuously monitor the environment. These vehicles can, for example, keep a car in its lane and adjust its speed based on the presence of other vehicles. Level 3, or Conditional Automation, allows the vehicle to manage all aspects of driving in certain conditions, but the human driver must be ready to take control when the system requests. This means the car can make informed decisions for itself, like overtaking a slow-moving vehicle, but it needs the human as a backup in case the system fails or encounters a situation it cannot handle.

In Level 4, High Automation, the vehicle can handle all driving tasks in certain conditions. If the system fails or encounters a situation it cannot manage, the car can park safely. The human driver may still have the option to control the vehicle manually. Finally, Level 5, or Full Automation, is where the car can handle all driving tasks under all conditions a human driver could manage. No human intervention is required at this level. The vehicle is designed to be entirely autonomous, so the car does not even need pedals, steering wheel, or controls for a human to use.

Lastly, Zongmu is actively working towards expanding its global presence through collaborations with international brands. With research centers in the United States and Germany, the company has partnered with Ford, Mercedes-Benz, and Volvo. The aim is to penetrate foreign automakers' joint ventures and supply chains. While Zongmu's primary source of revenue is from intelligent driving, the company is also exploring the potential of wireless charging for new energy vehicles. Despite its rapid growth, Zongmu is not profitable due to heavy investments in R&D. The company's IPO is intended to raise funds for further research and production of intelligent driving systems.

Zongmu's Core Technologies

Algorithmic Capabilities

Zongmu Technology stands out for its high-precision deep learning algorithms, which demand minimal computational power while delivering accurate and robust results. This is achieved by a nearly 100-fold compression of algorithmic models, which optimises performance on constrained hardware and allows for faster inference and deployment across various platforms. Computational power is critical for customers because it directly impacts the speed and efficiency of a system. In the context of autonomous driving, higher computational power means faster real-time processing of complex algorithms, enabling the vehicle to make quick, accurate decisions. This improves safety, reliability, and overall performance, enhancing the user experience. These characteristics underscore Zongmu's leadership in the field of algorithmic capabilities.

Real-time Location Mapping

Zongmu Technology is dedicated to developing vision-based multi-sensor fusion technology. The company's Simultaneous Localization and Mapping (SLAM) for the surround-view camera system offers a broader range of environment-awareness angles, superior robustness, and precision output. Moreover, it reduces sensor costs, making it more suitable for large-scale mass production. The SLAM forms the core of their surround-view camera system, providing wider environment-awareness angles and higher robustness than traditional systems.

Comprehensive Automated Driving System

Zongmu Technology develops comprehensive automotive-grade automated driving system software and hardware platforms. These include High-Definition (HD) cameras customised for machine vision, 4D high-precision point cloud and object contour outputs, millimetre-wave solutions for 360-degree intelligent environment sensing, and new-generation ultrasonic sensing technologies. The HD cameras, designed for precise machine vision tasks, are the eyes of Zongmu's autonomous driving systems. They capture essential visual data, and the company's algorithms construct detailed 4D point clouds, providing rich spatial information for accurate object detection and tracking.

Advanced Driving Assistance System (ADAS)

The Advanced Driving Assistance System utilises various sensors installed in the car, such as millimeter-wave radar, LiDAR, mono/bi-ocular camera, and satellite navigation. These sensors continuously monitor the surrounding environment while driving, collecting data, recognising static and dynamic objects, and performing detection and tracking. Combined with navigation map data, the system calculates and analyses potential hazards, thereby enhancing the comfort and safety of driving by alerting the driver to possible dangers in advance. The ADAS market has expanded rapidly in recent years, moving from the high-end market to the mid-range segment. Concurrently, several low-tech applications are becoming prevalent in the entry-level passenger car segment, with new and improved sensor technologies opening up fresh opportunities and strategies for system deployment.

Customers

Business To Business

Car manufacturers often collaborate with specialized technology companies like Zongmu for several reasons. Firstly, developing autonomous driving technologies and Advanced Driver Assistance Systems (ADAS) requires specific expertise in artificial intelligence, machine learning, sensor fusion, and computer vision. Car manufacturers may need to gain in-house expertise in these highly specialized fields. By partnering with a company like Zongmu, they can leverage its knowledge and technical proficiency to develop sophisticated autonomous driving systems.

Secondly, technological advancement in the autonomous driving field is rapid. To stay competitive, car manufacturers must continuously innovate and improve their offerings. Collaborating with a technology-focused company like Zongmu allows them to remain at the forefront of technological advancements and incorporate the latest developments into their vehicles. Thirdly, developing autonomous driving systems is a resource-intensive process that requires significant investment in time and money. By partnering with a company like Zongmu, car manufacturers can share the costs and risks of research and development, making it a more economical option. Lastly, regulatory requirements for autonomous vehicles are becoming increasingly stringent. Zongmu's experience in developing automotive-grade software and hardware platforms can help car manufacturers meet these regulatory standards, ensuring the safety and reliability of their autonomous driving systems.

According to Zongmu Technology's annual report, from 2019 to 2021, its cumulative R&D investment was 561-million-yuan, accounting for 155.31% of the company's cumulative operating income (Zongmu, 2021).

Business to Consumers

For end users, the advancements made by companies like Zongmu in autonomous driving and ADAS technologies can significantly enhance their driving experience and lifestyle, mainly for two types of consumers: technophiles and creative thinkers.

Technophiles are always on the lookout for the latest technological developments. They are drawn to the cutting-edge features of autonomous driving, such as self-driving capabilities, automated valet parking, and seamless integration with mobile applications. These features make driving more convenient and align with their desire for a digital, connected lifestyle. The appeal of being at the forefront of technology adoption often makes technophiles early adopters of such innovations.

On the other hand, creative thinkers are attracted to the disruptive potential of smart driving cars. These are not just vehicles with advanced powertrains; they represent a complete reimagining of what a vehicle can be, from design to charging infrastructure. Creative thinkers appreciate products and services that challenge the status quo and offer new ways of doing things. Companies like Zongmu's innovative approach to developing autonomous driving systems can, therefore, appeal to their desire for novelty and disruption.

In both cases, the work of companies like Zongmu plays a crucial role in meeting the diverse needs and preferences of consumers, enhancing their driving experience, shaping the future of transportation, and providing market positioning for car manufacturers.

Market Analysis of ZongMu Technology

Initial State of the Market

Historically, the automobile market was primarily occupied by traditional fuel vehicles. However, with escalating environmental concerns and the swift progression of new energy vehicles, the landscape shifted. Regarding intelligent driving applications, conventional fuel vehicles and the first generation of new energy vehicles were mainly limited to simple high-speed outdoor scenes, such as highway cruising. The industry's initial focus was on secondary software algorithm development. As time progressed, it evolved to become a full-stack provider.

In this context, a secondary software algorithm refers to software designed to process data and make decisions based on that data. In autonomous vehicles, these algorithms might be used to process sensor data (like camera images or radar readings) and decide how the car should respond, such as when to brake, turn, etc.

Over time, the industry evolved into what is known as a full-stack provider. A full-stack provider in the context of autonomous vehicles is a company or entity that offers comprehensive solutions encompassing all necessary components for autonomous driving. This includes the aforementioned software algorithms for decision-making and the hardware components like sensors (cameras, LiDAR, radar, etc.), computing platforms, and the software that integrates all these components. This shift represents an evolution from focusing on one specific system element (the software algorithms) to providing a complete, integrated solution for autonomous driving.

Market Evolution to Present Day

For Chinese consumers, most application scenarios for autonomous driving are in low-speed, complex environments like urban areas. Increasingly, automobile manufacturers and autonomous driving companies have started to focus on developing autonomous driving systems capable of navigating these complex environments. Cars require enhanced assistance functions to improve user experience in these low-speed scenarios. Recognizing this, Zongmu quickly addressed the challenges consumers face in low-speed scenarios after entering the intelligent driving sector.

The autonomous driving market has seen a remarkable surge over the past decade. The industry has grown from experimental prototypes to commercial applications, driven by advancements in sensor technology, regulatory support, and consumer demand for safer, more efficient transportation. Zongmu Technology has established itself as a leading player in this evolving landscape, specializing in autonomous driving solutions and advanced driver assistance systems (ADAS).

Market Evolution

The market has transitioned from focusing on research and development to practical implementation, with companies like Zongmu moving from theoretical concepts to mass production.

Competitor Analysis

Velodyne Lidar is a significant competitor in the field, renowned for its leadership in LiDAR technology and high-resolution sensors for perception and mapping. A SWOT analysis of Velodyne Lidar reveals strengths in its established brand and robust sensor portfolio. However, the company faces weaknesses in the form of costly sensors and competition from emerging players. Opportunities lie in expanding applications beyond automotive, while threats include increasing competition and price pressure. Another notable competitor is Pony.ai, a self-driving startup focusing on robotaxis and autonomous freight delivery. Its strengths include strong partnerships and extensive road testing. However, it has a limited global presence and faces regulatory challenges. The growing ride-hailing market and strategic alliances offer opportunities, while intense competition and safety incidents pose threats.

Zongmu's Positioning and Challenges

Zongmu distinguishes itself by offering end-to-end autonomous driving solutions, from perception to control, and has a strong presence in China's tech ecosystem. Their hardware expertise enhances perception accuracy, particularly in intelligent sensors such as cameras and radar. However, the company faces competition from established players and has a limited international footprint compared to global giants. Strategic partnerships with automakers and tech companies and capitalizing on favorable policies for autonomous driving are part of Zongmu's growth strategy. The company is also expanding into adjacent markets, such as smart cities. Nevertheless, Zongmu faces challenges such as potential technological leapfrogging by rivals, market dynamics influenced by economic shifts, and the need to ensure robust security against cyber threats.

Latest Developments

Introduction of New Products: FlashBot

Tang Rui, the leader of Zongmu Technology, had a strategic plan in response to the unpredictable market. He aims to collaborate more closely with car companies and tech giants such as Huawei, drawing upon the vast opportunities in the market. Since its inception in 2013, Zongmu has been on a mission to become a world-leading AD and ADAS Technology Provider. Over the past 11 years, they have assisted many car manufacturers in achieving mass production of automatic driving. As 2024 began, Tang Rui took on a new role as founder and CEO of Silkworm Bush Robotics, a company dedicated to advancing the mass production of L4 autonomous driving.

According to Tang Rui, Silkworm Bush Robotics will focus on two key areas. The first is to enhance the return on assets through continuous algorithm, software improvement, and innovation. Zongmu Technology and Silkworm Robotics aim to expand the scope of power trading by continuously developing autonomous driving capabilities, reaching more new energy-charging customers, and establishing stronger connections with them through machine learning, data mining, and cooperation with vehicle manufacturers. They plan to introduce new types of value-added services to iterate the software. Secondly, they are creating automotive-grade hardware to ensure affordability and durability. They aim to produce quality-assured products for consumers by cooperating with top-tier supply chain partners and conducting rigorous temperature and ageing tests.

Silkworm Robotics aims to build a resilient mobile energy network by combining autonomous driving and energy storage technologies, promoting energy trading on a larger scale. The rapid development of new energy vehicles influenced the decision to expand into the field of mobile charging robots. According to data released by the China Association of Automobile Manufacturers (CAAM), production and sales of new energy vehicles we reached 9,587,000 and 9,495,000 in 2023, marking a year-on-year growth of 35.8% and 37.9%. The market share reached 31.6%, an increase of 5.9 percentage points from the previous year.

Despite the growth in new energy vehicles, range anxiety and charging anxiety remain significant issues in the industry. Tang Rui states that the average utilization rate of each charging pile is less than 6%. Companies across the industry, including car manufacturers, battery-related companies, and autonomous driving companies, are exploring solutions to address this issue.

Given the industry's current state, although promotional policies for L3-level autonomous driving have been introduced, it is still in the trial phase. Issues such as incomplete mapping of underground parking lots, immature L4-level autonomous driving technology, and unresolved responsibility divisions present challenges. This lack of progress in commercializing high-level automated driving has led companies to seek secondary businesses. Zongmu Technology focuses on low-speed Autonomous Valet Parking (AVP) technology scenarios. Before the large-scale implementation of AVP, FlashBot is expected to be the first to achieve the commercial application of autonomous valet parking in closed parks.

Silkworm Bush Robotics has signed a long-term strategic cooperation agreement with the Electric Housekeeper Group and a strategic cooperation letter of intent with the French Hengtong Group and France Radiance Company.

Introduction of Lightning Bao by Silkworm Robotics

Lightning Bao, introduced by Silkworm Robotics as a new energy robot, has a large capacity of electric energy reserve (104KWH, high power 100KW) and L4-level autonomous driving ability. It can be used as a mobile charging pile and automatically come to the car in any corner of the parking lot (Yisi, 2024). Users can summon Lightning Bao through the Drop'n Go App, which will quickly and automatically come after receiving the order. The Drop'n Go app can monitor the charging process, which provides previously recorded parking location information to help users quickly find their car.

The fusion of autonomous driving and power storage opens up more rechargeable battery applications. In future developments, Lightning Bao will be introduced to more life scenes, such as old cities that cannot be transformed for electric power expansion, open-air concerts to avoid noise from temporary generators, and disaster relief and emergency electricity use. The robot's screen can also be used for advertising, further expanding the profitability of the leading business. As a multi-functional energy robot, Lightning Bao creates various electricity trading modes and value-added businesses, ensuring electricity security and a high return on assets for its owners.

Complex Shareholding Structure and Management of Admiral Technology

Zongmu Technology has a complex and multifaceted financial structure. The company, which has navigated through numerous financing rounds, boasts diverse shareholders, including industry giants such as Xiaomi, Lenovo, Fosun, Qualcomm, and Junlian Capital. This vast and varied shareholder base is a testament to Zongmu Technology's financial strength and these significant players' confidence in its future. However, the company's shareholding structure and management are intricate, reflecting the complexity and dynamism of the modern tech industry.

Zongmu Limited underwent a complete transformation in August 2016, rebranding itself as Zongmu Technology. The revised shareholding structure saw Hong Kong Zongmu, Ningbo Zongmu, Synergy Wo Sheng, and Synergy Innovation holding 53.60%, 26.40%, 10%, and 10% of the shares, respectively. Looking back at its financial history, Zongmu Technology has undergone about ten financing rounds. Its shareholder list includes prominent names such as Xiaomi, Lenovo, Fosun, Qualcomm, and Junlian Capital, making it a veritable gathering of star shareholders.

Before its Initial Public Offering (IPO), Zongmu Technology had 54 shareholders. The actual controller is RUITANG (Chinese name: Tang Rui), whose actions are coordinated with Li Xiaoling (Tang Rui's mother). RUITANG, through Zongmu Technology, owns 100% of Hong Kong Zongmu's equity, indirectly controlling 22.17% of Zongmu Technology's shares. Through the employee shareholding platform Shanghai RUITANG, they hold 100% equity interest in Hong Kong Zongmu Technology, indirectly controlling an additional 22.17% of Zongmu Technology's shares. Shanghai Zongmu and Shanghai Zongmu, under the platform, respectively, hold 1.92% and 1.31% of Zongmu Technology's shares. Li Xiaoling, RUITANG's concert party, is the executive partner of the employee shareholding platform Ningbo Zongmu and Ningbo Tianzhong. She controls 6.35% and 1.56% of Zongmu Technology's shares through these platforms, respectively. Therefore, RUITANG and its concert parties collectively control voting rights corresponding to 33.30% of Zongmu Technology's shares (Chengxiang, 2023).

Junlian Capital, the holding company of Xiuyue Investment, and Legend Holdings, the holding company of Lianrui Frontier, are associated enterprises. They acted in concert on matters relating to Zongmu Science and Technology, holding 9.94% of the shares. Synergy Innovation Fund Management Co., Ltd., the managing partner of Synergy Innovation, has 49% of the equity interest of the managing partner of Synergy Wo Sheng. Synergy Wo Sheng and Synergy Innovation act in concert on matters relating to Zongmu Technology, collectively holding 7.97% of the shares (Yunfan, 2022).

Dongyang Guanding, which holds 6.48% of Zongmu Technology's shares, is another enterprise with a shareholding of 5% or more. Dongyang Guanding is 99.02% owned by Dongyang City State-owned Assets Investment Co., Ltd, the actual controller of which is the State-owned Assets Supervision and Administration Office of the People's Government of Dongyang City. Zhejiang Caitong Capital Investment Co., Ltd, a wholly-owned subsidiary of Caitong Securities, holds the remaining 0.98%.

Notably, Zongmu Technology became Xiaomi's first investment in the intelligent driving industry after the latter's official announcement of car manufacturing. In May 2021, Xiaomi Industry Fund spent approximately 212 million yuan to acquire the relevant shares from the original shareholders of Zongmu Technology for 43.45 yuan/share. It then purchased newly issued shares at a price of RMB 56.48/share. As per the prospectus disclosure, Xiaomi Industrial Fund held approximately 4.73% of Zongmu Technology, becoming its fifth-largest shareholder (Jianping, 2023).

Zongmu Technology and Xiaomi

Amid the burgeoning new energy industry, an increasing number of individuals are shifting their focus to this sector, a move inspired by the decision of Lei Jun. Lei Jun, the founder of Xiaomi and a highly esteemed business magnate in China, is renowned for his sharp market insight and decisive maneuvers. He once declared, "Even pigs can fly if they stand at the gust's mouth," currently, new energy is undeniably that gust. Xiaomi identified autonomous driving as a crucial component of the future automotive landscape. By investing in Zongmu, they are tapping into a company with profound knowledge of ADAS (Advanced Driver Assistance Systems) and autonomous driving solutions. Zongmu's emphasis on hardware such as cameras, radar, and sensors is in harmony with Xiaomi's IoT ecosystem. The collaboration of these two entities can expedite the evolution of intelligent vehicles.

Since the launch of the Xiaomi car project in March 2021, Lei Jun has devoted himself entirely to this new entrepreneurial venture. He pledged to "risk all the reputation I have earned and personally spearhead the team to battle for Xiaomi Auto". Zongmu Technology, recognized as China's premier provider of autonomous driving and advanced driver assistance system technology and products, received an investment of 180 million from Xiaomi. Xiaomi's investment in Zongmu Technology is a strategic move for their automobile layout. On March 30, 2021, Lei Jun officially announced the Xiaomi car project. Lei Jun has recently visited numerous companies for research, including Ningde Times, Changan Automobile, and Wuling Automobile (Jianping, 2023).

THE PEOPLE BEHIND ZONGMU

Rui Tang, the founder and CEO of Zongmu Technology, holds a Master's in Electronic Engineering from Tsinghua University, often regarded as "China's MIT" (Deng, 2011). He has 14 years of experience in R&D and management of automotive electronics and semiconductors in Silicon Valley. His past roles include serving as the software director of Palm Microelectronics and the global senior R&D director of CSR Semiconductor, which Qualcomm later acquired. Tang founded Zongmu Technology (Shanghai) Co. Ltd. in January 2013.

While living in the U.S., Tang recognized that high-speed driving was a significant challenge, whereas parking was less of a concern, given the ample availability of parking spaces both at work and home. However, the need for better assistance functions in low-speed scenarios became apparent in China, where high-speed driving is less daily and low-speed urban driving is more prevalent. This led Zongmu to focus on addressing consumers' pain points in low-speed scenarios after entering the intelligent driving sector.

Surround view ADAS, as Tang describes it, refers to a system that offers more than just 2D/3D panoramic parking. It includes moving object monitoring (MOD), blind spot vehicle detection (BSD), open door warning (DOW), crossroads alarm (CTA), and automatic parking assistance (APA). It can also overlay functions like lane departure warning (LDW) and pedestrian detection (PD).

Before founding Zongmu Technology, Tang spent 14 years in Silicon Valley working in automotive electronics and semiconductor R&D management. His roles included Director of Software at Palm Microelectronics and Global Senior R&D Director at CSR Semiconductor. Between 2010 and 2012, Tang observed global trends indicating the fast-growing potential of the Assisted Driving System (ADAS), particularly the Intelligent Assistance System (IAS). This observation and the realization that China had become the world's largest automotive market led Tang to believe that the next significant growth direction for automotive electronics could be ADAS and autonomous driving. With this in mind, he founded Zongmu Technology in January 2013, deciding to start with surround view ADAS.

Other key members of Zongmu Technology include Fan Wang, Vice President of Zongmu Technology and General Manager of the Intelligent Transportation Division, who is an expert in embedded software and machine learning. Xuyang Li is Vice President and General Manager of the Intelligent Sensor Division of Zongmu Technology. He is an expert in vehicle millimeter-wave radar, ADAS/AD unmanned system sensors, and architecture. Chaozhuo Chen is Vice President, General Manager of Strategy and Marketing at Zongmu Technology and a senior expert in automotive safety.

FUTURE PROJECTS

The future endeavors of Zongmu Technology encompass a more comprehensive intelligent driving system. This includes L4 Autonomous Valet Parking (AVP), Autonomous Parking Assist (APA), a 360-degree Surround View Advanced Driver Assistance System (ADAS), ZATLAS full-stack high-precision maps, and other intelligent travel ecosystem products. Another critical project is developing a wireless charging system for new energy vehicles. This system uses electromagnetic coupling resonance to transfer power from the ground to the car, offering a more intelligent, convenient, and safe alternative to traditional wired charging products. By integrating intelligent driving technology, the system fully leverages its advantages, with APA/AVP enabling automatic positioning and alignment to automate power supply. Zongmu Technology is also working on a Smart City Solution. This project involves the unified management of dynamic data related to the city's road parking business. By leveraging the Internet of Things technology, cloud computing, data mining, and decision analysis, this solution aims to provide government managers with intelligent research and judgment services for urban traffic while making road traffic data accessible for autonomous driving.

REFERENCES

Carriage House Polytechnic. (2021, December 14). *Getting to Know Enterprises | Phase 7, Zongmu Technology*. WeChat Public Platform; Vehicle Engineering College Youth League Branch Media Center. https://www.36kr.com/p/2450960495483008

CEOCLUB. (2018). Zongmu Technology CEO Tang Rui: We Aim to Innovate from 0 to 1. *Technology and Finance*, (07), 43–46.

Chengxiang, Z. (2023, January 19). Zongmu Technology Files for the STAR Market After Losing 785 Million in Three Years. *National Business Daily*.

Jianping, L. (2023, September 28). *Zongmu Technology IPO Terminated: Pre-Investment Valuation of 8 Billion, Xiaomi Junlian Tongchuang is a Shareholder*. 36Krypton. https://www.36kr.com/p/2450960495483008

Yisi, X. (2024, January 22). Autonomous Driving Companies Enter the Field as "Mobile Power Banks" for Cars. *Yicai Daily*.

Yunfan, Z. (2022, December 13). Zongmu Technology's A-Share Autonomous Driving Debut: Braving the Winter of the Race Track. *21st Century Business Herald*.

Zongmu. (2021). *About Zongmu Technology*. Zongmu. https://www.zongmutech.com/our.html

KEY TERMS AND DEFINITIONS

360-Degree Surround View Advanced Driver Assistance System (ADAS): This advanced driver assistance system provides a 360-degree view of the vehicle to help drivers navigate tight parking situations more safely and efficiently. It is also known as a surround-view camera.

Autonomous Parking Assist (APA): This technology helps alleviate the stress and potential damage associated with parking. It uses sensors, radars, and cameras to control specific parking tasks or the entire parking process autonomously. It assists drivers in safely and securely parking their vehicle without causing damage to it or other nearby parked cars.

Autonomous Valet Parking (AVP): This system uses Level 4 autonomous driving technology, which combines vehicle and road-integrated technologies. Sensors such as lasers, radar, and communication devices in parking areas identify and track vehicle and obstacle positions. This information is sent to the vehicle via the 5G network to guide it into a parking spot.

Intelligent Driving: This refers to using advanced sensors, controllers, actuators, communication modules, and other devices to assist or even replace the driver in controlling the vehicle, thereby achieving autonomous driving functions.

L1: This is an auxiliary driving stage where the driver is primarily responsible for operating the vehicle. Depending on the driving environment, the vehicle can provide support for either steering or deceleration.

L2: This is a partially autonomous driving stage, during which the driver can take a short break but needs to be ready to take over manual driving at any moment.

L3: This is a conditional autonomous driving stage. In this stage, the vehicle can perform all driving operations under certain conditions, with the driver providing adaptive responses as required by the system.

L4: This is a highly autonomous driving stage in which the system can perform all driving operations. In suitable driving conditions, the driver can completely let go of the controls.

ZATLAS® (ZongMu Auto Learning Mapping & Service): ZATLAS® is a full-stack, high-precision map product that provides more than just high-precision map data. It also offers embedded map SDKs, navigation map engines, and cloud services. In addition, it includes self-learning crowdsourcing map collection services based on LiDAR and visual solutions.

Chapter 5
UISEE:
Driving Innovation Technology and the Evolution of Autonomous Vehicles

Jingtian Fang

Beijing Normal University-Hong Kong Baptist University United International College, China

EXECUTIVE SUMMARY

This case explores the dynamic landscape of the autonomous driving industry, focusing on UiSee Technology as a prominent player. It examines the competitive strategies, technological advancements, market dynamics, and regulatory influences shaping the sector. UiSee Technology, founded by Ganesha Wu in 2016, emerges as a key innovator in China's autonomous driving market, navigating partnerships with major industry players and expanding its footprint in both passenger and logistics applications. The case delves into UiSee's pivotal role in advancing autonomous vehicle technologies, its strategic collaborations, and the broader implications for the automotive industry's future. It also discusses market forecasts, investment trends, and the developing regulatory framework driving the industry towards the widespread adoption of autonomous driving technologies.

INTRODUCTION

In 2015, driven by the growing trend of artificial intelligence, Wu Gansha, then director of Intel China Research Institute, decided to leave Intel and pioneer in the nascent field of autonomous driving. UISEE was founded in Beijing in 2016 during this technological shift. Since its inception, UISEE has focused on unmanned

DOI: 10.4018/979-8-3693-2921-4.ch005

driving and, in 2019, introduced an unmanned logistics solution for cargo delivery, marking a significant technological milestone. This advancement paved the way for their "full scene, true unmanned, all-weather" autonomous driving technology, facilitating large-scale commercial use.

UISEE has not confined itself to unmanned logistics. It quickly partnered with automotive companies to expand its technology into new areas. UISEE developed the U-Drive intelligent driving platform through continuous research and innovation, utilizing AI drivers to enhance intelligent logistics, personal travel, and public transportation (UISEE, 2024). Over the past few years, UISEE has consistently been at the forefront of the unmanned driving industry, achieving significant strategic and technological breakthroughs. Within two years of its founding, the company won the global Red Dot Design Award. By 2019, UISEE had realized true unmanned operation and completed operational safety tests, achieving a major technological milestone. The company has also maximized the benefits of autonomous driving technology, achieving comprehensive coverage for both manned and unmanned vehicles.

UISEE has received numerous accolades for its patent innovations, including the 20th China Patent Award, Machine Heart's "AI China" Top 30, and the LT China Logistics Technology Award for Innovative Product. Strategically, UISEE has been a pioneer in commercialization, developing a sustainable business model while building technical expertise. The company has successfully partnered with leading industry players and has become one of the world's most successful commercialized unmanned driving companies (American Institute, 2023). UISEE's inclusion in the Hurun Unicorn List in 2022 and the Global Unicorn List in 2023 underscores its robust development trajectory. Looking ahead, UISEE plans to focus on globalization, establishing an international headquarters and research and development center in Hong Kong, which will provide an ideal platform for considering dual listing.

UNICORN DESCRIPTION

Business Model

UISEE is a technology-based enterprise focusing on autonomous driving. Relying on its self-developed U-Drive® intelligent driving platform, UISEE not only provides self-developed autonomous driving devices such as sensors, embedded high-performance servers, and other parts but also offers multi-scene, high-level unmanned driving solutions to vehicle manufacturers, automotive suppliers, and other industrial customers. The aim is to achieve a "full scene, true unmanned, all-weather" automatic driving technology for large-scale landings.

UISEE has a unique market positioning that is distinct from the three main models of the current global autonomous driving industry. It neither builds cars nor operates directly. Instead, it is committed to providing AI driving services for the entire industry and scene, encompassing whole-scene autonomous driving across travel, logistics, and other industries. UISEE views all operators and automakers as ecological partners. The main business segments include 'products and technology' and 'industry solutions'.

The products encompass various uncrewed vehicles, such as Logistics Vehicles, Buses, Light Trucks, Delivery UiBox, Retail UiBox, Patrol Cars, Sweepers, Personal Mobility, and Engineering Technology. The industry solutions mainly include Automotive, Chemical, and Airports scenarios.

As the only autonomous driving company with practical application cases in Chinese airports, UISEE has collaborated with the Hong Kong Airport Authority and the Civil Aviation Department to develop multiple scenarios and test cases. This collaborative effort has involved testing hundreds of thousands of data sets and creating new unmanned driving business cases. UISEE has also contributed to developing several civil aviation industry specifications, lending its expertise to China's unmanned driving standards.

UISEE's business model emphasizes lightweight and flexibility, allowing it to adapt to various business backgrounds and connect urban service ecology with autonomous driving technology. This approach ensures lower operating costs and higher asset turnover. It accelerates the company's road test data collection, algorithm optimization, and product iteration, thereby gaining a competitive advantage in the industry.

UISEE's unique advantage lies in its position at the forefront of unmanned driving technology development. In comparison to other companies at the same level, its distinctive edge is in leading commercial exploration and global strategic positioning. As early as 2017, UISEE Technology initiated cross-border collaboration with Capitaland Group to delve into the commercial operation of autonomous driving. Furthermore, in 2019, the world's first unmanned logistics vehicle operation project was launched at Hong Kong International Airport (UISEE, 2024).

Moreover, the technological development and multi-industry coverage of UISEE's autonomous driving model improve the company's business stability, reduce the risk associated with fluctuations in a single field, and enhance its safety margin and ability to navigate industry cycles (Ifeng et al.).

Product Offers

UISEE offers a diverse portfolio of autonomous driving products and services, categorized into "Products and Technologies" and "Industry Solutions". The product range includes both manned and cargo solutions. The manned solutions feature uncrewed buses and passenger cars with advanced autonomous driving technology. The cargo solutions include a variety of uncrewed logistics vehicles, such as light trucks, UiBox uncrewed distribution vehicles, UiBox uncrewed retail vehicles, and UiBox uncrewed patrol vehicles. Additionally, UISEE offers UiBox unmanned sweepers, further expanding the application of their autonomous technology (UISEE, n.d.).

The company's industry solutions are tailored to specific sectors, including intelligent logistics for the automotive and chemical industries and unmanned driving solutions for the airport sector. UISEE's passenger car technology is marked by its high intelligence-to-price ratio. This results from a focus on creating cost-effective intelligent solutions, ranging from users summoning vehicles from the elevator to the parking lot to automatic valet parking in the city and achieving end-to-end autonomous driving from point to point (UISEE, 2024). UISEE's approach to technology development provides a technical reserve advantage in the industry and emphasizes the need for legal compliance and safe operational experience in developing passenger cars. This aids in creating differentiated L2 products.

UISEE's unmanned logistics solutions outperform traditional automotive logistics in several ways. Traditional logistics often involve high labor costs and challenging management (Securities Daily, 2023). In contrast, UISEE's unmanned logistics are fully integrated, all-weather, and truly unmanned, reducing labor costs and management difficulties. The unified scheduling of the UISEE cloud platform resolves the issue of multiple closed equipment interfaces and facilitates collaborative work. Moreover, the customized data interface integrates various business platforms and prevents data isolation. The unmanned nature of UISEE's logistics transportation reduces personnel contact, offering significant advantages during epidemics (Baidu, n.d.).

Customers

UISEE, operating mainly within a B2B framework, holds a distinctive market position. It is devoted to cultivating partnerships with operators, auto manufacturers, and yards, creating a robust ecosystem. The application of UISEE's technology spans various industries, such as automotive, airport, chemical, mining, port, animal husbandry, breeding, energy, food, and medicine. Its partners include leading automotive brands like China FAW, SAIC Volkswagen, Geely Automobile, Beijing Automobile, and Orient Automobile. Large corporations such as Huawei, China Telecom, China Unicom, China Mobile, and State Grid also collaborate with UISEE (UISEE, n.d.).

UISEE's approach towards its clients is unique. Instead of viewing them simply as customers, the company sees them as partners. This perspective is central to UISEE's business strategy, as it believes that profound understanding and penetration of industry and acquisition of technical know-how can only be achieved through effective collaboration. Thus, UISEE works closely with its partners to innovate and adapt its solutions to specific scenarios, aiming to reduce costs and increase efficiency (The Paper, n.d.).

In practice, UISEE typically delivers incremental, standardized models to its partners. These models are designed for easy replication on a large scale in various settings, such as airports, factories, and parks. This approach necessitates close collaboration with partners in research and development. The company's short-term strategy is to provide autonomous driving technology to its partners as a comprehensive solution (The Paper, n.d.).

Market Analysis

Original Situation of the Market

UISEE is a technology-based enterprise focusing on automatic driving. The market size of the automatic driving industry will continue to maintain the trend of rapid growth, with broad market prospects and development space. According to the data compiled by the Huajing Industrial Research Institute, the market size of China's autonomous driving industry is projected to reach 89.4 billion yuan in 2022. With the continuous progress of technology and the expansion of scenarios, the autonomous driving industry will usher in more business opportunities and market share (Huajing et al. Institute, n.d.).

China has now become the world's largest market for vehicles and mobility services due to the booming development of local and multinational companies. Between 2007 and 2017, the Chinese market grew at an annual rate of 16 per cent, and its share of the global passenger car market increased from 9 per cent in 2007 to 30 per cent in 2017. McKinsey estimates that China will likely become the world's largest market for autonomous driving in the future, generating more than $500 billion in revenue from new vehicle sales and mobility services related to autonomous driving by 2030 (McKinsey Greater China, 2024b).

Political and Regulatory Analysis of the Business Environment

As the trend of unmanned driving becomes increasingly obvious, the Chinese government has begun introducing corresponding policies to remove policy restrictions on intelligent driving and promote the vigorous development of autonomous driving.

The government has established relevant policies for data privacy protection and network security to ensure compliance and safety of intelligent driving vehicles. Additionally, a brilliant driving technology licensing and audit system has been implemented. The government has also implemented a series of incentives to promote the development and application of intelligent driving technology. These incentives include tax breaks, research and development funds, and support for industrial park construction.

Furthermore, the government has collaborated with enterprises and universities to establish research bases and experimental sites. This initiative aims to promote technological innovation and experimental testing and verify technologies' maturity and feasibility in pilot and demonstration projects.

In March 2023, the Ministry of Natural Planning issued the "Guide to the Construction of the Intelligent Vehicle Basic Map Standard System (2023 Edition)" to strengthen the top-level design of the intelligent vehicle basic map standard specifications. This move aims to promote the safe application of geographic information in the autonomous driving industry and establish a dynamic update mechanism for the intelligent vehicle basic map standard system. It provides continuous and strong support for promoting the innovative application of basic map technology for visionary vehicles and the healthy development of the intelligent automobile industry (Liu, 2023).

The government's efforts create a robust environment for developing intelligent driving technology and ensure sustainable development and operation. This also promotes the development of related industrial chains, leading to economic growth and innovation. Overall, the current policy in unmanned driving is geared towards providing incentives to encourage the industry (State Council, 2023).

Economic Analysis of the Business Environment

According to the China Association of Automobile Manufacturers, China's automobile production and sales have grown since 2021. By the first half of 2023, China's automobile production reached 13.248 million units, a year-on-year increase of 9.3 per cent, while its sales reached 13.239 million units, a year-on-year increase of 9.8 per cent. The continuous growth of automobile production and sales means that the intelligent driving market will begin to expand after the popularization of new energy vehicles (China Automotive Industry Association, 2023).

The expansion in demand has attracted companies to enter the field of driverless driving to promote the development and commercialization of intelligent driving technology. With the development of intelligent driving technology, the coordinated growth of the chip, sensor, algorithm, vehicle manufacturing, and other fields also plays a reverse incentive role in the intelligent driving industry. The training and education of relevant talents and the research development and innovation of enterprise technology will play a positive role in the commercialization process and economic benefits of intelligent driving technology (Ministry of Industry and Information Technology of the People's Republic of China, n.d.).

Social Analysis of the Business Environment

The number of auto traffic accidents in China remains high, reaching 171,941 in 2021, resulting in 43,601 deaths, according to the National Bureau of Statistics. However, with the help of intelligent driving, vehicles can effectively communicate and cooperate and recognize road signs, pedestrians, and other obstacles, thus reducing the number of traffic accidents caused by human factors.

In addition, according to the Ministry of Industry and Information Technology data, the number of 5G base stations reached 2.937 million in the first half of 2023, laying a solid foundation for the continuous improvement of communication technology. This allows cars to efficiently obtain real-time traffic information, enabling them to achieve reasonable scheduling between vehicles and optimize traffic flow measures. This, in turn, allows for selecting the optimal driving route and time to reduce vehicle congestion, improve road traffic efficiency, and reduce energy waste and environmental pollution (Institute of Industrial Economics, Chinese Academy of Social Sciences, n.d.).

Technological Analysis of the Business Environment

Since 2020, the number of patent applications for intelligent driving technology in China has been climbing, reaching 1,140 by 2023, an increase of 22.71 per cent year-on-year. With the continuous progress of artificial intelligence and sensor technology, many automakers and technology companies have begun to develop and deploy intelligent driving technology.

First, sensor technology is integral to intelligent driving technology, from vision sensors to radar sensors to Lidar technology. The number of patents for sensor signal processing, sensor resolution, and sensor data fusion is increasing. According to the data, China's Lidar market size is rising year by year. By 2025, the market size of China's radar is expected to reach 4.31 billion US dollars.

Secondly, the autonomous driving algorithm is the core of intelligent driving. The research and innovation of various enterprises in autonomous driving algorithms, such as path planning algorithms, obstacle detection algorithms, and intelligent decision algorithms, are also reflected in patents. The large number of patents for these algorithms reflects the continuous optimization and innovation of intelligent driving technology at the algorithm level (Baiteng, 2023).

Competition Analysis

Understanding the competitive landscape in the autonomous driving industry is crucial. This includes the basic competition pattern, which refers to how companies are competing in this space, the key competitors that are currently leading the market, the barriers to entry that could pose potential competitive threats, and the threats of substitutes, which are alternative technologies or solutions that could replace autonomous driving (Huajing et al. Institute, n.d.).

Rapid growth is observed in the upstream sensor and chip market, which holds significant future potential. According to statistics from Huajing Industry Research Institute, China's sensor market is expected to reach 309.69 billion yuan in 2022, growing at a compound annual rate of 12.26 per cent from 2019 to 2022 (China Economic Information, 2023).

The competition among controller enterprises within the autonomous driving sector is quite diverse. Key players in this market comprise tier-1 suppliers, chip manufacturers, and startups. Tesla, for instance, maintains a significant market share with other major players, including Desay Siwei, Veoneer, Bosch, Ambofu, Freitech, Hongjing Intelligent Driving, and Zhixing Technology. Each of these enterprises has adopted different strategies, leading to various development models in the autonomous driving industry.

Original Equipment Manufacturers (OEMs) employ different entry strategies. Established OEMs often collaborate with traditional tier-1 suppliers and invest in startups specializing in chips and algorithms to enhance their autonomous driving capabilities. Conversely, new car makers prioritize autonomous driving, often developing their chips and algorithms to establish their core competitiveness. Strategic collaborations and joint ventures exist between some OEMs and leading autonomous driving solution companies to create independent, autonomous driving vehicle brands (Institute of Industrial Economics, Chinese Academy of Social Sciences, 2023).

The autonomous driving industry also sees a variety of third-party suppliers. These include traditional automotive electronics tier-1 suppliers like Bosch, internet giants such as Alphabet's WAYMO and Baidu's Apollo, autonomous driving solution integrators like Horizon and Mobileye who focus on self-developed chips, algorithm-leading integrators such as Momenta, and scenario-oriented integrators like Tucson.

OEMs hope to maintain their dominant position in the supply chain during the traditional automotive era. Conversely, autonomous driving enterprises aim for more control and a stronger voice in the supply chain. Consequently, host manufacturers and conventional and emerging suppliers are locked in fierce competition to dominate the supply chain's value chain. Autonomous driving technology has become a focal point in the automotive industry, leading to an intensifying competition landscape and promising future development prospects (Institute of Industrial Economics, Chinese Academy of Social Sciences, n.d.).

Enterprises in the autonomous driving sector are predominantly divided into two camps: domestic and foreign. Domestic companies such as Baidu, Huawei, and Didi have excelled in technology research and development and market promotion, leveraging their local advantages. This contrasts with foreign companies such as Google, Tesla, and Ford, which boast significant expertise in autonomous driving technology.

Due to the involvement of sensors, chips, algorithms, high-precision maps, and other components in autonomous driving technology, enterprises are engaged in intense competition within the industrial chain. With the increasing complexity and integration of current cockpit and intelligent driving functions, few suppliers can fully meet OEMs' needs.

Consequently, most mainstream brands have opted for in-house research within the domain control domain, with enterprises ramping up their investments to drive technological progress. The primary competition lies in technological breakthroughs, with the core of automatic driving technology encompassing perception, planning, and control. Companies are intensifying their research and development efforts to achieve breakthroughs in perception technology, data processing technology, and algorithms. In the future, technology will be a pivotal factor in determining a company's competitiveness.

Recently disclosed data from Enterprise Chacha reveals that the autonomous driving sector has witnessed a surge since 2021. In the first two months, 24 investment and financing events attracted a total investment and financing amount of 17.64 billion yuan. Over the past decade, there have been 376 investment and financing events for autonomous driving projects, with a total disclosed financing amount of nearly 237.75 billion yuan. These figures underscore the increasingly fierce competition in the autonomous driving field (Qichacha, 2023).

However, the competitive threat UISEE poses seems less significant due to high technical barriers and challenges related to high investment, long return cycles, and commercialization issues. Consequently, some small enterprises may need help with financial problems. For instance, Drive.ai, a prominent autonomous driving company once valued at $200 million, encountered financial and technical obstacles and was eventually sold to Apple at a low price. Similarly, Zoox, another autonomous driving company, was sold to Amazon due to a breakdown in its financial chain.

As a result, several self-driving companies have been acquired by car companies. Based on the surviving autonomous driving companies, either an Internet giant platform is backing them, or they are extensively linked to car companies. An innovative business model characterizes the prevailing trend of providing AI driving services for the entire industry and every scenario without manufacturing cars or engaging in direct operations. This entails forming an ecological partnership with all operators and car factories.

Evolution of the Market Until Today

The Society of Automotive Engineers (SAE) has established a classification for driver automation systems. In this new SAE Driver Automation Classification, Levels 1 and 2 (L1 and L2) have been labelled "Driver Support Systems". This means that while the driver receives support from the system, they still maintain control of the vehicle and are responsible for its safety, whether the driver assistance function is active. This category includes autonomous emergency braking, lane departure warning, lane keeping, and Adaptive Cruise Control (ACC) (SAE, n.d.).

In contrast, Levels 3 to 5 (L3-L5) are termed "Automated Driving Systems". Here, the vehicle, not the driver, dominates control once the system is activated. For Level 3, the driver is required to take over the car when the system requests it. However, for Levels 4 and 5, the driver's intervention is unnecessary (SAE et al.).

In 2020, 11 national ministries and commissions, including the National Development and Reform Commission and the Ministry of Industry and Information Technology, jointly released the "Smart Vehicle Innovation and Development Strategy". This strategy outlined several goals:

- The "intelligence" goal: By 2025, the mass production of L3 autonomous driving and the market application of L4 autonomous driving in specific environments will be achieved.
- The "network connectivity" goal: By 2025, Long-Term Evolution Vehicle-to-Everything (LTE-V2X) will achieve regional coverage, 5G Vehicle-to-Everything (5G-V2X) will be applied in some cities and highways, and a high-precision spatiotemporal reference service network will be fully covered.
- The "standard completion" goal: By 2025, a standard intelligent vehicle system will be essentially formed in China (DJ et al.).

In July 2021, the Ministry of Industry and Information Technology issued an opinion on access to intelligent connected vehicle products, setting the stage for the mass production of L3 and L4 autonomous vehicles. Autonomous driving has received strong support from local governments at all levels. Notably, the relevant regulatory system is also evolving. The development of autonomous driving laws and regulations is based on the principle that "the central government sets the program, and local governments implement the pilot", using local pilots as the foundation to promote the formulation of future national laws and regulations (Ministry of Industry and Information Technology of the People's Republic of China, 2024).

Positive market news at the national level is very significant, and consumer trends are equally encouraging. Research by McKinsey's Center for the Future of Mobility shows that Chinese consumers are more receptive to autonomous driving than their counterparts in major European and American countries, demonstrating a higher level of interest and willingness to pay for such features.

On the supply side, a comprehensive local autonomous driving industry chain has begun to form, with companies emerging to develop advanced autonomous driving application scenarios. While it is challenging for innovative enterprises to achieve large-scale commercialization in the short term, the continuous expansion of application scenarios means that China's relevant entrepreneurial teams will likely find more opportunities in the global competition. For instance, UISEE has emerged as a more successful commercial enterprise in this space (Wu Tin et al., 2022).

Forecast for This Market

McKinsey's analysis of historical market data suggests that China is on track to become the world's largest autonomous driving market. They project that 2030 revenues from new car sales and mobility services related to autonomous driving will surpass $500 billion. This serves as a fundamental prediction for the future market size.

The digitalization of cars is expected to lead to cost reductions, thus facilitating the scalability of autonomous driving. McKinsey anticipates an inflexion point for autonomous driving between 2025 and 2027. This is predicted to be the economic equilibrium point where autonomous and human driving costs align. Following this inflexion point, the market demand for autonomous driving is projected to grow steadily (Sharp et al., 2024).

However, the growth in the autonomous driving sector is challenging. Autonomous driving systems' high costs and safety concerns significantly hinder their development. A McKinsey survey of mobility experts revealed that only 27% believed the cost issue would be resolved by 2025. Another 37% predicted resolution between 2025 and 2030, 20% between 2030 and 2034, and 17% after 2035. Similarly, reliability and safety concerns pose a significant hurdle. Only 30% of survey respondents believed these issues would be addressed by 2025; 33% predicted resolution between 2025 and 2029, and 36% not until after 2030 (Insight research report, 2023).

Investment data reveals a strong interest in the autonomous driving sector from capital markets, with a notable concentration of funds in leading projects. In 2021, China's autonomous driving industry experienced a surge in investment. The most attractive areas for investment were complete vehicles, autonomous driving solutions, core hardware components such as chips and radars, and robotaxis services.

Notably, Pony Zhixing secured the most funding, receiving over twice as much as the second-highest funded company, Wenyuan Zhixing. This trend underscores a clear industry effect, with prominent companies continuing to attract significant capital support.

Development and Strategy

UISEE Technology, founded in 2016, has demonstrated its technical prowess and resilience in the market. The company quickly emerged as a leading player in China's autonomous driving industry, and it saw its first wave of start-ups in 2015.

Technology and Design

UISEE Technology was established by Wu Gansha, former president of Intel Research China, and a group of co-founders in Beijing. The company splashed at the 2017 CES exhibition in less than a year, showcasing its "Urban mobile box," a new vehicle category. This innovation won the newly established "Red Dot Design Concept Award" and marked the beginning of the company's journey in autonomous driving. UISEE Technology expanded its innovative city service solution business in 2021, launching unmanned delivery services in Saudi Arabia using its driverless delivery vehicles.

Regarding product development, UISEE Technology was the first to complete the operational test of removing the safety officer in June 2019, a crucial step for the large-scale implementation of autonomous driving. The company also led the mass production of AVP and other autonomous passenger car products in 2020. It was the first to achieve product landing in the AVP automatic valet parking field, delivering the first L4 AVP automatic valet parking product in collaboration with SAIC-GM-Wuling in November 2018 (UISEE, 2024).

UISEE Technology's strategy includes full scene coverage of manned and loaded vehicles. Its unmanned logistics vehicles have been applied at Hong Kong International Airport, Chongqing Bonded Port, Changan Minsheng Logistics, Hunan Airport, and other places (Tecent, 2021). In November 2019, the company launched the regular operation of unmanned logistics in the SAIC-GM-Wuling factory.

Commercialization and Cooperation

UISEE Technology's first driverless debut was at Guangzhou Baiyun Airport in March 2017. By April, the company had partnered with CapitaLand Group to implement driverless shuttle cars in underground parking lots and from 2015 to 2018, this period marked a boom in China's autonomous driving industry, with over 20 start-ups established and news of corporate financing coming in waves (UISEE, 2024).

In the era of uncrewed public transport, UISEE Technology's shuttle buses provided airport ferry services at Guangzhou Baiyun Airport in 2017. By 2019, the company's uncrewed buses were used at the Boao Forum for Asia, and its logistics solution was implemented in the SAIC-GM Wuling Factory area, marking the advent of fully uncrewed logistics vehicles.

In passenger car autonomous driving, UISEE Technology partnered with Dongfeng Motor in 2020 to build an autonomous taxi fleet and establish the most significant autonomous driving demonstration operation fleet in Wuhan. The company's performance increased by 150% that year, and it delivered hundreds of sets of its "AI driver" autonomous driving solutions.

In 2020, several autonomous driving companies, including UISEE Technology, Wenyuan Zhixing, and Didi Autonomous Driving, completed new rounds of financing. UISEE Technology stood out with a total financing amount of over 1 billion yuan, including a strategic capital injection from the CDB Manufacturing Transformation and Upgrading Fund, a national team in the field of investment (36Kr, 2021).

UISEE Technology has collaborated with dozens of leading enterprises in various industries, including automotive, civil aviation airports, and the chemical industry. This has positioned UISEE as one of the world's most commercially successful driverless companies.

THE PEOPLE BEHIND THE UNICORN

Ganesha Wu is the co-founder, chairman, and CEO of UISEE Technology (Beijing) Co., LTD., an autonomous driving company he established in 2016. Before founding UISEE, Wu had a successful career at Intel. He joined Intel in 2000 and, by 2011, was appointed as the chief engineer of Intel China Research Institute. He led the company's long-term strategic planning for big data technology during his tenure.

Wu's educational background includes a master's degree from Fudan University. His early career at Intel focused on Managed Runtime research, where he worked on developing mobile Java systems. By 2005, he transitioned to the role of a research manager in the Programming Systems Lab. Here, he led a team that contributed significantly to Intel's transition from single-core to multi-core/multi-thread products. In 2009, Wu was promoted to Director of the Embedded Software Lab at Intel, where he spearheaded the embedded software innovation. His leadership extended to defining the research directions of 5G communication, intelligent computing, and robotics when he became the director of Intel China Research Institute in 2014.

Wu's vision for the future of transportation is ambitious and forward-thinking. He envisions a future with zero fatalities and congestion, reduced travel and logistics costs, and increased productivity during commutes. Wu believes autonomous driving is a technological revolution that can significantly improve people's livelihood and social efficiency. He argues that sharing autonomous vehicles can make travel more convenient and affordable. Moreover, having been trained over billions of kilometers, autonomous cars can significantly reduce traffic accidents and congestion and even eliminate the need for traffic lights. He believes this will help address issues like traffic jams, accidents, and environmental pollution (Wu, 2023).

REFERENCES

36Kr. (2022, April 12). *The journey of ten thousand miles begins with the landing of the road to the commercialisation of Uishi technology autonomous driving.* 36KR. https://www.36kr.com/p/1695459324366855

Baidu. (n.d.).*() [UISEE Technology (Beijing) Co., LTD].* UISEE Technology (Beijing) Co., LTD. Baidu Baike. https://baike.baidu.com/item/%E9%A9%AD%E5%8A%BF%E7%A7%91%E6%8A%80%EF%BC%88%E5%8C%97%E4%BA%AC%EF%BC%89%E6%9C%89%E9%99%90%E5%85%AC%E5%8F%B8

CSDN. (n.d.). *Honour, UISEE Technology recently won an awards review.* CSDN. https://blog.csdn.net/UISEE2031/article/details/130460487

DJ Research. (n.d.). *Professional real-time research report sharing, industry research report, industry analysis report, brokerage research report, industry think tank.* DJ Research. https://www.djyanbao.com/report/search?channel=360yanjiubaogao&qhclickid=f11092d753085801

Enterprise Check. (n.d.). *Enterprise business information query system_Check the enterprise _ check the boss _ check the risk on the enterprise check!* QCC. https://www.qcc.com/

Future Think Tank. (n.d.). Autonomous driving industry competition pattern and future outlook analysis. https://www.vzkoo.com/read/20240305ea109edebbab09d2d89f077b.html

Huajing Industrial Research Institute. (n.d.). Huajing Industrial Research Institute - focuses on industrial economic intelligence and research in Greater China. https://www.huaon.com/

Ifeng Finance. (n.d.). *UISEE Technology - The future global AI driver covering all models.* Ifeng Finance. https://finance.ifeng.com/c/8PrdFAPWzk9

Liu, Y. (2023). Analysis of the Development Environment of China's Intelligent Driving Industry in 2023 (PEST): Policies remain favourable, and market competition is fierce. https://www.chyxx.com/industry/1153277.html

McKinsey Greater China. (2024, March 13). China may become the world's largest autonomous driving market. *: [McKinsey Future Mobility Research Center: China May Become the World's Largest Autonomous Driving Market].* McKinsey Greater China.

McKinsey Greater China. (2024, March 14). Making science Fiction Reality: Progress and trends in autonomous driving in China. : *[Making Science Fiction Reality: Progress and Trends in Autonomous Driving in China]*. McKinsey Greater China.

Ruiyan World Report Network. (n.d.). https://baogao.ruiyanshijie.com/?tag=360search&actID=home&word=pinpaici5-2&qhclickid=06dd4342f1734eb4

Sohu. (n.d.). *Making science Fiction Reality: Progress and trends in autonomous driving in China.* Sohu. https://www.sohu.com/a/524648166_121207965

Tencent News. (n.d.). Autonomous driving company "UISEE Technology" introduced the national team strategic capital injection and completed more than 1 billion yuan of financing. *Tencent News.* https://new.qq.com/rain/a/20210125A01C3O00

The Paper. (n.d.). Autonomous Driving Insights: Changing roles and challenges for suppliers and OEMs. *The Paper.*https://www.thepaper.cn/newsDetail_forward_23806166

The Paper. (n.d.). [Wired founder] Wu Gansha of UISEE Technology: I hope to change the world's traffic with uncrewed vehicles. *The Paper.* https://www.thepaper.cn/newsDetail_forward_11233736

UISEE. (2022). *Won the second prize in the Beijing Science and Technology Award.* UISEE Award. https://www.uisee.com/en/article91.html

UISEE. (n.d.). Core technology. https://www.uisee.com/core.html

U.I.S.E.E. (n.d.). *IC design industry chain and domestic substitution in-depth research report.* UISEE. https://zhuanlan.zhihu.com/p/421016440

Weixin Official Accounts Platform. (n.d.). *Wu Gansha: Driverless is your yearning for a better life.* Weixin. https://mp.weixin.qq.com/s?__biz=MzA4OTMyNzIzOA==&mid=2650832005&idx=1&sn=d0ba287b71f0599fea4bea8f4def9bbc

Xueqiu. (n.d.). *To help enterprises, scientific research institutions, investment institutions, and other units understand the development trend and future trends of the autonomous driving industry, China Economic Research Institute has launched.* Xueqiu.https://xueqiu.com/1973934190/273329499

Yicai. (n.d.). *What are the barriers to large-scale commercialisation in the field of autonomous driving?* Yicai. https://www.yicai.com/news/101004523.html

KEY TERMS AND DEFINITIONS

ADCU (Autonomous Driving Control Unit): The ADCU is an intelligent computing platform for level 3 to L5 autonomous driving applications. It integrates computationally intensive sensor data processing, sensor fusion work, and control strategy development into one control unit, helping establish a structured and organized vehicle controller network.

Autonomous Vehicles: These are vehicles equipped with artificial intelligence, visual computing technology, radar, monitoring devices, and global positioning systems. These components work in unison, allowing the car to operate automatically and safely without human intervention.

Ecological Partnership: This concept emphasizes creating a mutually beneficial relationship with customers. The goal is to expand the overall market (make the pie more prominent) and form a community that promotes symbiosis, mutual benefit, and regeneration.

Lidar (Light Detection and Ranging): Lidar is a type of sensor that uses laser beams to detect and measure distance, speed, and other information about a target. It emits low-power laser pulses and measures the time it takes for the laser to bounce back from the target or surface.

OEM (Original Equipment Manufacturer): This term refers to the company that assembles a vehicle's parts to create a complete car. Once the car passes the necessary tests, it is shipped for sale to various sales outlets, such as 4S stores.

Sensor: A sensor is a detection device that can sense specific information, such as temperature, light, or motion. It converts this sensed information into an electrical signal or other required output form. This output can then be used for information transmission, processing, storage, display, recording, and control.

Unmanned Driving Algorithm: This refers to machine learning algorithms, such as reinforcement learning, used in autonomous vehicles. These algorithms help vehicles make optimal decisions in complex traffic environments and control their trajectory and speed.

Chapter 6
Keenon Robotics:
Innovating the Future of Commercial Service Robots

Qinghao He

Beijing Normal University-Hong Kong Baptist University United International College, China

EXECUTIVE SUMMARY

This case study delves into the rapid evolution and strategic initiatives of Keenon Robotics, a pioneering force in commercial service robots. Focusing on innovative technologies such as robot as a service (RaaS), Keenon Robotics has revolutionized sectors including catering, healthcare, hospitality, and epidemic management with its diverse range of robots. The case explores Keenon Robotics' journey from its historic breakthroughs in robotic technology to its pivotal role in addressing contemporary challenges like the COVID-19 pandemic through products like the Disinfection Robot M2. It also highlights the strategic expansions into new markets and industries, such as hotels and education, underscoring the company's commitment to technological innovation and societal impact. Through insightful analysis and strategic milestones, the case explains how Keenon Robotics navigates opportunities and challenges in the burgeoning field of service robotics, positioning itself at the forefront of industry transformation.

DOI: 10.4018/979-8-3693-2921-4.ch006

UNICORN DESCRIPTION

Brief History of the Unicorn

Keenon Robotics Co., Ltd. is an artificial intelligence company that provides intelligent unmanned delivery solutions for global enterprises. Founded in 2010, the company has become a trusted business partner in the worldwide market, with a presence in more than 60 countries and serving over 20,000 companies (Keenon Robotics, n.d.). Keenon Robotics has also received numerous high-level achievements, including being named as one of the TOP30 Chinese Artificial Intelligence Robot Companies in 2019, winning the Best Technologies for China's Anti-epidemic in 2020, recognized as one of the TOP Artificial Intelligence Cases in 2019, listed as one of the TOP25 Domestic Robot Companies in 2018, named as one of the Top 100 Private Enterprises in Science and Technology Innovation in 2020, recognized as one of the TOP30 Artificial Intelligence Companies in 2019, and featured in the 2019-2020 Top 100 black technologies in the Chinese market (Keenon Robotics, n.d.).

Currently, the company has developed 16 models of robots and serves customers in a wide range of fields, including catering, healthcare, hotels, venues, business offices, community elderly care, and airports. As a leading company in commercial service robots, Keenon Robotics has won various honors, such as the Hurun Global Unicorn (2021-2023), for three consecutive years and secured first place in the robot direction of the 2019 World Artificial Intelligence Innovation Competition. This has placed Keenon Robotics in the leading position within the intelligent service robot industry (36Kr Research Institute, 2022).

Business Model

Keenon Robotics' products are primarily leased, with the proportion of leasing gradually increasing. To reduce the threshold for downstream customers and enhance the service efficiency and robot repurchase rate, Keenon Robotics has adopted the RaaS business model (Robot as a Service). This model allows users to rent robots and order required services according to their needs rather than purchasing them outright (Keenon Robotics, n.d.). This approach not only eases the burden of hiring employees for merchants but also effectively lowers the usage threshold for downstream customers. As a result, small and medium-sized restaurants that cannot afford the upfront cost of robots can still benefit from the value created by human-machine collaboration. The monthly rental for a catering robot is RMB 3,000, with lease contracts lasting 1-2 years. Founder and CEO Li Tong believes that "The industry will eventually shift towards leasing, and sales are just a short-term, temporary behavior" (Keenon Robotics, 2019). This shift is driven by customers not only requiring tangible and reliable products but also demanding dependable technical support and efficient operational management. Keenon Robotics has a high renewal rate for its leased products and anticipates that this rate will continue to improve.

Product and Services

With over a decade of R&D experience, Keenon Robotics has built a solid technological foundation that sets it apart. Their technological prowess is reflected in their first commercial-grade indoor positioning and navigation system, intelligent safety and obstacle avoidance, and scheduling and collaboration capabilities. These three features are the core of Keenon's smart technology and have contributed to its market-leading position. The company's intelligent technology experience and stable product performance have become unique identifiers. Keenon Robotics has developed four categories of robotic products for various applications: a Dinerbot for catering delivery, a Guiderbot for meeting and greeting, a Disinfection Robot for sanitization, and a Butlerbot for building delivery tasks.

Keenon Robotics stands out in the competitive landscape due to its technical advantages and cost-effectiveness. Unlike many other robots available in the market, the company's robots integrate proximity sensors and ultrasonic radar depth fusion, significantly reducing the cost of hardware and manufacturing. This strategic approach to cost compression has quickly earned Keenon Robotics market recognition for its high value-for-money proposition.

Besides its technical ability, Keenon Robotics has equipped its robots with the most advanced intelligent speech recognition system. This system significantly enhances the robots' capabilities, allowing them to interact more effectively in complex environments and engage in in-depth, free dialogue with users. The result substantially improves the traditionally poor interaction experience other robots offer.

Keenon Robotics' competitive edge extends to its multi-machine collaboration efficiency. Its robots, particularly the DynaSky line, can navigate autonomously for extended periods stably and reliably in complex environments. This capability is essential for effective multi-machine collaboration. Coupled with a unique intelligent scheduling system, the robots can coordinate and schedule multiple machines in an area. This system effectively addresses potential conflicts and congestion that can occur when multiple robots operate in the same area, increasing the efficiency of collaborative work by a hundredfold.

Beyond its technical and operational advantages, Keenon Robotics also excels in user experience. Its robots use high-performance lithium batteries, offering an ultra-long battery life. They can operate continuously for up to 10 hours and automatically recharge, ensuring they meet user needs around the clock.

Keenon Robotics has a diverse customer base and a significant presence in the catering industry. Its DynaSmart robots, which include five catering delivery models, have undergone extensive iterations and have been refined over a long period. Driven by domestic R&D and manufacturing advantages and the potential for cost reduction and efficiency improvements, DynaSmart has used the catering industry as a springboard to penetrate higher-growth sectors.

Today, Keenon Robotics has a strong foothold in the hotel, healthcare, venue, KTV, business office, community pension, and airport sectors, offering various intelligent solutions across these verticals. Customers choose Keenon Robotics for its technological advantages and efficient after-sales service, which includes rapid response times and high-quality support. This comprehensive package helps enterprises complete their digital transformations.

Keenon Robotics has partnered with thousands of catering brands, such as Haidilao, Grandma's, Guangzhou Restaurant, and Quanjude, to deliver intelligent restaurant solutions. It has also established relationships with over 180 hotel brands, including Sofitel, Westin, Hilton, Sheraton, and Marriott, and collaborates extensively with 17 large hotel groups. Keenon Robotics' robots are operational at Aeroporto di Milano-Malpensa and Singapore Changi International Airport in the airport sector. Furthermore, its robots are used in nearly 100 hospitals, including Shanghai National Women's Hospital, Shanghai Huashan Hospital, Shanghai Sixth People's Hospital, and Peking University Third Hospital.

Market Analysis

Before 2019, there were only 26,668 service robot-related companies registered in China. However, the COVID-19 epidemic has created an opportunity for the application of service robots. This trend is driven by normalized epidemic prevention and control, an ageing population, technological advancement, and policy support. As a result, the value of service robots was being further explored, and the industry was quickly moving past the market education stage and entering a golden development period. According to statistics, the number of service robot-related enterprises in China increased by 296% during the three years of 2019-2021, exceeding 100,000 enterprises (Mordor Intelligence, 2024). Many enterprises are entering the market, indicating a wave of industrial development in the service robot sector.

Competition in the service robot industry has shifted from a single technology race to emphasizing product deployment and cultivating sustainable business models (Bhaskar et al., 2020). Leading players in the service robotics sector have achieved a large deployment volume of robot units, and some service robot products have become increasingly mature and stable in terms of usage scenarios. This trend has led to a change in the focus of competition in the industry, from technology-driven competition to the pursuit of successful product deployment and sustainable business models. Market-validated products have helped promote the maturity of business models and the creation of a closed-loop business. Additionally, enterprises achieve sustainable growth only through the scale of product applications and healthy cash flow (IEEE Xplore, 2024).

Service robots have found wide applications in guided tours, delivery, medical care, companionship, and household functions. With the rapid increase in intelligence and personalization of service robots, their potential application areas continue to expand. Presently, commercial service robots, serving functions such as guided reception, distribution, and extermination, are deployed indoors and outdoors in scenarios such as museums, art galleries, exhibition halls, hotels, restaurants, office buildings, schools, and industrial parks to achieve large-scale applications (36Krypton, 2022). Meanwhile, the adoption rate of household robots for companionship and cleaning is steadily increasing. Surgical robots, medical rehabilitation robots, and open-road unmanned delivery robots currently have limited deployment due to high technical barriers, policy constraints, or technical maturity limitations. Still, their future development prospects are promising (Mordor Intelligence, 2024).

In the future, service robots will interact with other intelligent hardware devices, and their application scope will be expanded further. With more diverse and complex application scenarios, service robots are no longer confined to basic operations to replace human labor. Instead, they are deeply involved in the digital transformation wave of downstream application enterprises. They connect and integrate with hardware devices in both household and public scenes, contributing to the advancement of smart homes and industrial digitalization and promoting the wider evolution of society towards intelligent production and lifestyle (Mordor Intelligence, 2024). It is evident that in the future, service robots will have a larger scope for application expansion, ushering in new development opportunities. Building a service robot application ecosystem to create integrated, one-stop digital solutions with other intelligent hardware will become increasingly common. Consequently, the application of service robots will further expand its boundaries (Automate, 2024).

Competitive Analysis

The service robotics market is moderately consolidated, with major players holding significant market share. However, new players are entering the market due to growing demand, leading to increased competition and ultimately fragmenting the market. Vendors use various strategies to strengthen their market position, including product innovation, partnerships, acquisitions, etc. Some of the major players in the market include Daifuku Co. Ltd., Dematic Corp., Swisslog Holding AG, and iRobot Corporation.

In addition to the large technological consortiums entering the market, smaller tech-oriented companies provide robots for specific and already mature markets with tremendous growth potential. For example, in September 2022, Avidbots, a Canada-based robotics company, secured $70 million in Series C funding. The company focuses on developing autonomous cleaning robots and has created Neo 2, a robotic floor cleaner designed for commercial spaces such as warehouses, airports, and shopping centers. Also in September, Jacky's Business Solutions, a leading provider of B2B technology solutions, announced that it is showcasing the latest version of its Temi robotics at the Gitex event. The company launched this new personal assistance robot in the Middle East with a Robot as a Service (RaaS) business model.

Market Forecast

Morder Intelligence forecasts a robust growth trajectory for the service robotics market, which is predicted to burgeon from USD 50.33 billion in 2023 to USD 122.81 billion by 2028. This translates to a CAGR of 19.53% during the 2023-2028 period. The Asia-Pacific region is a significant contributor to this growth, which is one of the fastest-growing areas worldwide. The Asia-Pacific region's accelerated growth is attributed to its large consumer base, which has prompted an increasing demand for service robots, particularly in countries such as China, Japan, South Korea, and India. Evidence of this growth is seen in the sales of professional robots in Asia, which rose by approximately 30% in 2021 (IFR, n.d.).

In parallel with consumer demand, regional governments are also playing pivotal roles in shaping the development of their respective robotics markets. A case in point is India, which is planning substantial investments in military robotics. The country is preparing for the deployment of advanced robotic soldiers in the forthcoming years, a move substantiated by the All India Robotics Association's (AIRA) announcement in January 2022 to commence indigenous manufacturing of defense robots.

Similarly, the Chinese government's ambitious plans for its robotics industry are worth noting. The government has earmarked robotics, artificial intelligence (AI), and automation as priority areas for high-end development, aiming to drive the transformation and upgrading of manufacturing. This initiative is projected to increase the global market share of Chinese-made robots.

Furthermore, demographic changes, especially in major countries like Japan and China, are expected to drive the demand for service robots. According to estimates by UN DESA and China's National Bureau of Statistics (NBSC), the population segment aged 60 and above is expected to grow to approximately 38.81 percent by 2050. This trend is anticipated to catalyze the demand for service robots in these countries.

Development and Strategy

In 2010, founder Tom Li, driven by his passion for robots and his belief in "You got a dream, you got to protect it," established KLM Intelligence with the strategic goal of making intelligent robots the core and providing robot and technology empowerment for various industries in daily life. With this strategic goal in mind, Keenon Robotics was founded. Looking back on 12 years of development, they have experienced the entire process of the commercial service robot industry, from its inception to its rapid growth, from technological gaps to gaining favor from investors, and have witnessed the growth and development of the entire industry.

Breaking Through Technical Boundaries (2010-2016)

After achieving early technological breakthroughs, building supply chains, and testing hundreds of project scenarios, Keenon Robotics has evolved from creating educational robots to service robots. This has opened up much larger markets, focusing on restaurant food delivery robots and leading robots for supermarkets. In 2016, Keenon Robotics developed its first commercially successful service robot, "Peanut," marking the official beginning of the era of intelligent delivery robots (Keenon Robotics, 2023).

An Important Marketing Strategy for KEENON in 2015

Machine learning has had an extensive history, but in 2015, there was a sudden significant advancement that made it commercially viable. This development drew the attention of investors, leading to Keenon Robotics securing its Series A financing six years after its establishment. As commercialization expanded, data gathered from various application scenarios drove continuous improvements in robot intelligence. Service robots are primarily focused on solving data, algorithm, and mobility challenges in complex environments. Therefore, practical experience in real-life scenarios and cost considerations are critical. Li Tong also noted that everyday needs across different industries lead service robotics companies to prioritize core demand scenarios, such as mobile applications, before expanding further. As a result, breaking through to large customers became an important early-stage market strategy for Keenon Robotics. "It's easier to customize standardized products for large customers, who prioritize the input-output ratio and are better at analyzing the cost-effectiveness. When a suitable program is offered, they are more willing to adopt it," said Li Tong (Shanghai Office for Promoting the Construction of Science and Technology Innovation Centre, n.d.).

Rapid Expansion and Product Globalization (2017-2020)

In 2017, Keenon Robotics began rapidly expanding and completed mass production. In 2018, Keenon Robotics was recognized by Haidilao (n.d., a popular restaurant chain in China) for in-depth cooperation, and together, they established the world's first Haidilao smart hotpot restaurant, which brought the catering delivery robot into the public eye through extensive media coverage at home and abroad. The robot has gained recognition in the industry and the market. With steady cultivation, Keenon Robotics has formed a matrix of T1, T2, T5, T6, T8 (Flying Fish), and other delivery robots aimed at meeting the various delivery needs of large, medium, and small-sized restaurants, as well as lobby-type and box-type scenarios, hot pots, local cuisines, Japanese and Korean cuisines, Western food, and other food delivery requirements. The coverage rate of China's top 100 catering brands reaches 65% (KEENON Robotics, n.d.).

Widening of Service Areas and Application Scenarios (2020-2024)

In 2020, when the global epidemic broke out, KLM Intelligence rushed to assist the Hangzhou quarantine point for the first time. Since then, KLM has supported more than 200 unmanned delivery robots to hundreds of hospitals and designated quarantine zones in more than ten provinces and cities, assisting healthcare workers to complete the delivery work in the worst-hit epidemic areas. At the same time, Keenon Robotics has addressed the pain points of the healthcare service industry by releasing the medical delivery robot M1 and the disinfection robot M2, which will help the healthcare scenario achieve intelligent transformation and become an indispensable force in the fight against epidemics with science and technology (Keenon Robotics, n.d.).

In 2021, Keenon Robotics officially entered the hotel industry, further expanding its accumulated experience and advantages in unmanned delivery to the hotel industry by releasing the intelligent delivery robot W3, which further enriches and completes Keenon Robotics's full-scene product matrix. With the extensive development of commercial service robots worldwide, Keenon Robotics has seized the opportunity to "go overseas" to lay out its business earlier. It has opened six business regions in North America, Asia-Pacific, Europe, the Middle East, South America, and Africa, covering more than 60 countries and 600 cities worldwide. Keenon Robotics has also reached in-depth strategic cooperation with international first-tier brands, such as Japan's SoftBank, South Korea's Hyundai, and Saudi Aramco, to jointly promote the commercialization of unmanned delivery robots.

Opportunities and Challenges

Since the epidemic swept the world in 2020, it has gradually changed people's lifestyles, especially affecting the consumption habits of offline commercial scenes. This, coupled with the gradual disappearance of the demographic dividend and the initial completion of the market education of the "no-touch delivery" service, has led to increased recognition of the importance of the word "unmanned" in commercial service robots by more and more industries, directly leading to an explosion in demand (Bhaskar et al., 2020). The initial market education of the "contactless delivery" service has made more and more industries gradually realize the significance of the word "unmanned," which has directly led to an outbreak of demand for commercial service robots. This has brought multiple opportunities and challenges to KELLYLANDS Intelligence (Bhaskar et al., 2020).

At the beginning of the epidemic, Keenon Robotics took the lead in applying commercial service robots to the frontline of the battle against the epidemic. Combining the rich experience and mature technology system of the catering industry with disinfection technology, Keenon Robotics released a brand-new category of commercial service robots - Disinfection Robot M2, which has become a powerful tool for disinfection in many airports, railway stations, and hospitals due to its features of 24/7 autonomy and multiple disinfection modes, proving the advantages of unmanned delivery with practical cases on the ground (KEENON Robotics, n.d.).

Meanwhile, based on the demand of epidemic outbreaks, Keenon Robotics has successfully launched multiple product lines, such as hotel and medical robots, expanding the technology to fight against epidemics to more application scenarios. For example, the hotel industry has an increasingly high demand for delivery, while consumers prefer intelligent and private services. Hotel robots are beginning to become an effective tool for hotels to improve services. Keenon Robotics has seized the market demand and created a digital distribution solution for hotel robots. Through "Robot + Unmanned Container + Cloud Management Platform + IoT System," Keenon's robots are fully connected with the hotel's ladder control module, communication equipment, and ERP system to realize the functions of autonomous ladder delivery and make phone calls to inform the customers. This is done to grasp the needs of the hotel's tenants for delivery and to solve the troubles of the hotel's operators (Keenon Robotics, n.d.).

Keenon Robotics' multi-category strategy allows It to be used in multiple scenarios in different industries. Its intelligent algorithms enable multi-machine collaboration to ensure the smooth operation of multiple Keenon Robotics in hotel scenarios. This multi-scenario intelligent solution is more convenient and effective in assisting the industry's intelligent and digital transformation compared to other single-point solutions (36Krypton, 2022).

THE PEOPLE BEHIND THE UNICORNS

CEO Tong Li

Tong Li, who studied at Huazhong University of Science and Technology in 2002, majored in Electrical Engineering Automation. At that time, he probably never imagined that 20 years later, he would not only find a robotics company but also sell his products at home and abroad. The seed of his love for robotics was planted in his heart from then on, becoming an important starting point for his future dreams, seemingly unintentionally. As a student, Li Tong participated in numerous scientific and technological innovation activities and tournaments with the college teachers, winning top awards such as the Microsoft Embedded Challenge and the first prize in the National Challenge Cup. During these events, Li Tong's interest in robotics grew, and he decided to participate in the Kechuang Shanghai competition in 2023, further confirming his passion for robotics.

Following graduation, Li Tong participated in Microsoft's Robotic Studio project, eventually leading him to Microsoft Research Asia, where he worked on robot operating systems. This experience gave him a deeper understanding of robotics, professional training, and a more intense passion for the field. The wave of artificial intelligence development prompted Li Tong to establish his technology enterprise, KEENON Robotics, in Shanghai in 2010. According to Li Tong, when the "team" entered the robotics industry, they possessed nothing but enthusiasm. In a humble room, several young men in their early twenties dedicated themselves to their work day and night. Li Tong likened his journey to that of Chris Gardner in "The Pursuit of Happyness," where he travelled around the world with a suitcase to conduct business. Similarly, Li Tong and his companions adhered to a firm belief: "You got a dream, you got to protect it!". Over fourteen years, Li Tong transformed from a teenage robotics enthusiast into a successful business leader, and his company has seen significant growth during this time.

FUTURE PROJECTS

Artificial Intelligence education is a key area of focus for Keenon in 2023. At the 6th World Conference on Artificial Intelligence, Keenon Robotics launched a full-link solution that encompasses the popularization of AI education in primary and secondary schools, the integration of the robotics/AI industry with vocational education, school-enterprise cooperation at the undergraduate level, and research topics at scientific research institutes. Keenon Robotics is committed to providing comprehensive educational solutions for primary and secondary schools, vocational colleges, and universities. Its business includes curriculum design, teaching equipment, teacher training, competition activities, certification exams, research and innovation, and other aspects. Through collaboration with schools, Keenon Education aims to enhance teaching quality and promote students' all-round development (Li, n.d.).

Currently, it promotes Keenon Robotics in three main areas:

Curriculum Design and Teaching Equipment: Keenon Education has combined artificial intelligence and robotics to develop innovative course content that enables students to better understand and apply what they have learned. Keenon Robotics has launched several teaching robots, such as the INNOExplorer R&D and innovation teaching robot, the BoundlessPractice deployment testing teaching robot, and the RoboHeart assembly and maintenance teaching robot. These teaching robots can help students carry out practical operations and projects to improve their hands-on skills and problem-solving abilities (China Education Network, 2023).

Teacher Training and Student Competitions: Keenon Education values teacher training and support and provides professional training courses and resources for teachers to use Keenon's teaching methods and tools to improve their teaching effectiveness. Additionally, Keenon Education organizes competitions to encourage students to demonstrate their talent and innovation by participating in competitions (Li, 2023).

Research and Innovation and Certification Exams: Keenon Education encourages teachers and students to actively participate in research and innovation by providing appropriate support and resources. Keenon Education also offers a series of certification exams to assess students' learning outcomes and abilities.

Keenon Education showcased its innovative capabilities and vision in the field of EdTech at the conference. Its teaching robotics products attracted much attention at the conference and are considered a breakthrough in EdTech (China Education Network, 2023). Keenon Education hopes to bring more changes and progress to the education industry through continuous innovation and scientific research while remaining committed to providing high-quality education solutions and promoting the modernization and internationalization of education.

REFERENCES

A3 Robotics. (n.d.). *Association for Advancing Automation.* Automate. https://www.automate.org/robotics

Baidu. (2024). *Kenglang Intelligence CEO Tom Lee: Leave the mechanical things to the robots and let people do more meaningful things.* Bajiaho. https://baijiahao.baidu.com/s?id=1622717804465260603&wfr=spider&for=pc

Baobao. (2020). *Focusing on Unmanned Delivery Robots, "Optimus Intelligence" Receives 200 Million RMB Series B Financing Led by Source Capital.* 36Krypton. https://www.36kr.com/p/1724969369601

Bhaskar, S., Bradley, S., Sakhamuri, S., Moguilner, S., Chattu, V. K., Pandya, S., & Banach, M. (2020). Designing Futuristic Telemedicine Using Artificial Intelligence and Robotics in the COVID-19 Era. *Frontiers in Public Health*, 8, 556789. DOI:10.3389/fpubh.2020.556789 PMID:33224912

China Education Network. (n.d.). *The 2023 World Conference on Artificial Intelligence recently opened. KLM focuses on robotics/artificial intelligence education.* China Education Network. http://www.edu-gov.cn/edu/23510.html

IFR International Federation of Robotics. (n.d.). *IFR presents World Robotics 2021 reports.* IFR. https://ifr.org/ifr-press-releases/news/robot-sales-rise-again

36. Krypton Research Institute. (2022). *China Service Robot Industry Research Report 2022.* 36Krypton. https://www.36kr.com/p/2030626518920196

Lina. (2021). *DynaLang Intelligence Closes $200 Million Series D Funding Round Led by Softbank Vision.* 36Krypton. https://www.36kr.com/p/1397821032561417

Mordor Intelligence. (2024). *Service Robotics Market - Size, Analysis and Companies.* Modor Intelligence. https://www.mordorintelligence.com/zh/industry-reports/service-robotics-market

National Bureau of Statistics of China. (2021). *National Bureau of Statistics of China Yearbook.* National Bureau of Statistics of China. https://www.stats.gov.cn/english/Statisticaldata/yearbook/

PubLink. (n.d.). *After-sales service, creating "zero distance" between customers.* SHB. https://www.shb.ltd/customerCase_49/255.html

Rometty, G. (2018). The era of cognitive business. *Harvard Business Review*, 96(1), 72–81.

Shanghai Office for Promoting the Construction of Science and Technology Innovation Centre. (n.d.). *Kenglang Intelligence Li Tong: "The 'China Smart Manufacturing' we represent is being seen by the world!"* KCB. https://kcb.sh.gov.cn/html/1/168/151/155/3234.html

Xplore, I. E. E. E. (n.d.). Robotics: Science and Systems VII https://ieeexplore.ieee.org/book/6276859

KEY TERMS AND DEFINITIONS

After-Sales Operations and Maintenance (O&M): It encompasses the services offered to customers following the sale of a product. These services include maintenance, warranty assistance, training, and ongoing support. It involves a series of operational and managerial activities conducted after the product has been delivered to ensure its smooth functioning and customer satisfaction.

Artificial Intelligence Industry-Education Convergence: Artificial Intelligence Industry-Education Convergence refers to a model or strategy that combines artificial intelligence technology with industry and education to promote industrial development and talent training. It emphasizes AI technology's close connection and mutually reinforcing role in industrial applications and education and training.

Blue Ocean Markets: Blue Ocean Markets are market segments that are untapped or have fewer competitors, where there is room for opportunities to create new demand, provide unique value, and realize high profits.

Commercial Closed-Loop Construction: Commercial closed-loop construction refers to the construction of a complete circular system in business operations. This system makes the various links of the enterprise interconnected and mutually promoting, forming a closed, continuous cycle of the business model. This circular system covers the whole process of product or service design, production, sales, consumption, and recycling.

Cost Reduction and Efficiency: Cost Reduction and Efficiency refers to an enterprise's behavior or strategy for improving productivity and economic efficiency by reducing costs and increasing efficiency.

Cost-Effectiveness: Cost-effectiveness refers to a situation where a product or service offers relatively high performance, quality, or benefits for a certain price. Simply put, it is a situation in which the performance, quality, or benefits that can be obtained under a certain amount of spending are relatively superior.

Demographic Dividend: Demographic Dividend refers to the advantage of economic growth and development that a country or region obtains due to its demographic characteristics. Typically, the demographic dividend occurs when the demographic structure has a relatively high proportion of people in the working age group (usually 15 to 64 years old) and a relatively low proportion of non-working people who depend on them (e.g., children and the elderly population). This demographic structure contributes to economic growth and development, as an increase in the working population improves labor supply, promotes employment, and creates more monetary value.

Digital Transformation: Digital transformation refers to the use of digital technology and information technology by an organization or enterprise to comprehensively redesign and reshape its business model, processes, operations, and value creation to meet the needs and challenges of the digital era. It involves not only changes at the technical level but also changes in organizational culture, employee skills, and management systems.

Technological Boundaries: Technological boundaries are the dividing lines or boundaries between different technologies or areas of technological applications. These boundaries may be formed due to the characteristics of the technology, the different application areas, or the segregation of related industries.

Chapter 7
Star Charge:
Developing China's Electric Vehicle Charging Landscape

Jiantao He

Beijing Normal University-Hong Kong Baptist University United International College, China

EXECUTIVE SUMMARY

This case study examines Star Charge, a pivotal player in China's electric vehicle (EV) charging infrastructure market. Founded amid ambitious government initiatives to bolster EV adoption, Star Charge rapidly emerged under the visionary leadership of Danwei Shao. The case explores how Star Charge has developed strategically, from its unique crowdfunding approach to its current success, overcoming challenges and taking advantage of opportunities in a competitive industry where State Grid and Special Call are the dominant players. It explores Star Charge's business model, technological advancements in charging stations, and the pivotal role in supporting China's dual carbon goals. The study analyzes future projections, including international expansion strategies and technological innovations such as vehicle-to-grid (V2G) technology. Through this comprehensive analysis, the case illustrates how Star Charge continues to shape the future of sustainable mobility in China and beyond.

DOI: 10.4018/979-8-3693-2921-4.ch007

INTRODUCTION

Brief History of Star Charge

Star Charge, established in 2014, is a Wan Gang New Energy Investment Group subsidiary. In 2016, the company started sharing its progress via its website (https://www.wbstar.com/). Initially, Wan Gang's parent company, Wan Bang, was prominent in the taxi industry and the '4S' automobile sales service shops, a franchise model encompassing sales, spare parts, service, and surveys. Recognising the potential of the new energy car market, Wan Bang established DeHe Charging Station to address the growing need for charging stations as the number of electric vehicles increased. DeHe sold charging stations and provided home installation services. A crowdfunding model strategy was implemented during this period, contributing significantly to DeHe's success.

Star Charge, initially the name of the driver software within DeHe, gained national recognition in 2015 following the National Conference on Charging Facility Promotion organised by the State Council of China in Changzhou. By 2016, it had evolved into an investment and operational brand garnering nationwide attention. As of 2024, Star Charge holds over 400 patents, including those for hardware security protection and OTA software upgrades, and is listed as one of the top 50 companies in China's charging station industry. Star Charge adopted an aggressive strategy upon its establishment: it invested heavily in infrastructure and used crowdfunding to expand. This approach led to the rapid construction of over 1500 charging stations within three months, drawing the attention of the state council and earning Star Charge significant public recognition.

To address the issue of the increasing number of electric vehicles outpacing the speed of charging station construction, Star Charge implemented a private stake-sharing strategy. This strategy integrated private charging stations with the "Star Charge" platform and encouraged owners to offer private stations to the public. However, this model faced challenges due to the charging stations' high maintenance costs, necessitating future improvements.

Business Model

Star Charge mainly makes a profit in these four areas: equipment sales, software services, investment operations, and hosting services. Star Charge has a deep collaboration with OEMs and the real estate industry. Initially, Star Charge always initiates collaborative business programs with shopping malls or hotels. In 2016, Star Charge started to expand, offering a platform for private and corporate charging stations to conduct agent sales to meet the trend. Private cars will become a significant force in the future market. With the improvement of science and technology, the cost of batteries will continue to decrease. The upgrade of safety and performance will make the future charging stations no longer confined to public parking lots under the supervision of security personnel but settled in every family with electric vehicles, making the future charging method more convenient. Furthermore, Star Charge also developed the scale of public charging stations. Until 2024, Star Charge has set up over 450k charging stations in China, becoming one of the primary sources of financial income.

Product and Services

Equipment Sales

In 2016, Star Charge introduced a new selling model, Private Stake Sharing, which involves selling private charging stations to individuals and hotels to expand their business. Star Charge's products can be categorised into two main types: AC charging stations and DC charging stations, which differ significantly in appearance and function. DC charging products are integrated and are used in public parking lots for small cars, while split products are primarily used for large public vehicles or home charging columns for high-power private cars (Lv, 2017). Integrated products are commonly found in particular charging locations such as marinas. Meanwhile, split-type products, which allow one machine to charge 12-gun ports, are generally more common at community or plaza entrances. In addition to traditional charging stations, Star Charge has also introduced new products, including a bi-directional DC charger for OEMs and multiple energy storage solutions.

Software *Services*

After equipment sales, some users require the corporation's software management service. Consumers, such as small and medium-sized investors (regional small-scale operators) and neighbourhood managers, must access detailed information about electrical inflow and outflow in residential areas. Star Charge can initiate the development of the platform for investment operations. Additionally, city operators and government regulatory agencies, unlike neighbourhood managers, require more than a developing management system; they need overall management of the entire city or a specific company. Star Charge can provide them with a mature software service, which has been proven to be a common phenomenon.

Charging Fees

Charging fees vary in different areas, depending on the city's development and the availability of electricity. For instance, in Beijing, for DC charging, the service charge is allowed to be no more than RMB 0.8/kWh. In contrast, in Changzhou, the total price of charging, including the service charge, is not more than RMB 1.45/kWh. In this aspect of the marketing strategy, Star Charge intends to give up part of the benefits by providing coupons to lower the price. Even if the profit is smaller, a low charging fee can attract customers to Star Charge and increase passenger flow.

Hosting Services

The service for OEMs differs in many ways. In one instance, Star Charge collaborates with Mercedes-Benz to establish a Mercedes-Benz supercharging station featuring an elaborate photovoltaic roof and lighting equipment. It offers 3-meter-wide oversized parking spaces and is paved with floor paint, showcasing high-end luxury and low-carbon green attributes. In addition to collaborating with Mercedes-Benz, Star Charge also partners with Volkswagen. Star Charge aids in setting up home charging stations when consumers purchase a car and its accompanying services from Volkswagen. Even in cases where a buyer's environment does not meet the qualifications for building a charging station, Star Charge will provide the buyer with charging service vouchers, which may cover more than 70% of the charging fee. Star Charge will conduct a door-to-door survey of the collaborative automobile brand's offline 4S stores to identify a suitable location for installing the charging service. Additionally, certain automobile brands desire to establish their charging stations to enhance their brand advantage, often achieving this through renting and loaning services from Star Charge at the time of service purchase.

Customers

Star Charge serves a diverse range of customers in the charging station market. Its primary clientele includes Original Equipment Manufacturers (OEMs), both domestic and international, for whom it installs charging ports and offers warranty and upgrade services for the charging stations. The government is another significant customer, providing public spaces and infrastructure for Star Charge. It also funds Star Charge's ventures into dock transportation, supporting the development of large integrated charging stations for electric dock cranes and transport vehicles, thereby contributing to automated terminals. Additionally, private enterprises seeking a well-organized electricity management system are part of Star Charge's customer base. The company offers them a mature platform or collaborates through commissioning operations.

Market Analysis

Charging Station Industry Development Environment

The charging port serves as a base station, similar to the gas stations used for refuelling traditional cars, but for charging new energy vehicles. It can be installed on the wall or the ground, and different charging columns are used based on various vehicle models and voltages. In early 2014, Wan Bang New Energy Group entered the early stage of the charging station industry and experienced rapid growth. From 2015 to 2016, most new charging station companies focused on developing wall-mounted DC chargers. However, another new technology, high-voltage AC equipment, was introduced during this time. The fast-paced development resulted in many new companies exiting the market before 2017. The remaining companies shifted from the traditional competition, which imitated the gas station model, and began exploring new ways to offer services in the industry. The leading players and competitors in this market include Special Call, Star Charge, Trayde, Cloud Charge, and Stat Grid.

Evolution of the Market Until Today

In 2012, the Chinese government introduced a series of national policies to stimulate the charging market. These policies called for the construction of 2000 charging stations and 400,000 charging piles, which spurred the development of numerous new companies specialising in high-level charging stations (China Charging Station Industry Market Prospect and Investment Research Report, 2021). 2014, the National Grid announced its entry into the new energy charging station industry. This was a significant development, as the National Grid is a major player in the energy sector. Also, in 2014, the state issued the "On the New Energy Vehicle Charging Facilities Construction Incentives Notice," which clearly defined incentives for regions that achieved certain milestones in promoting new energy vehicles. This policy strengthened the relationship between charging stations and new energy vehicles.

2015, the Guidelines for the Development of Electric Vehicle Charging Infrastructure (2015-2020) were issued. The guidelines projected the need for more than 4.8 million decentralised charging posts by 2020 to meet the anticipated demand from a rapidly growing number of electric vehicles (China Charging Station Industry Market Prospect and Investment Research Report, 2021). From 2016 to 2019, local governments actively invested in the charging station industry, supporting emerging businesses and accelerating the development and deployment of charging infrastructure. This period has marked a significant expansion in the industry, with a surge in the number of charging stations and piles across the country.

Competition Analysis

In May 2022, the market share composition of China's top five charging station operators, referred to as CR5, was as follows: Star Charge held 19.6%, Telegraph Charge held 19.5%, State Grid held 13.8%, Cloud Fast Charge held 12.5%, and Little Orange Charge held 5% (Jian, 2023).

Special Call, established in 2014, is a significant competitor with over 1200 patents and involvement in more than ten major national scientific research projects. Special Call leads the charging station market with an investment of RMB 11 billion over nine years. The company received the "2022 China New Energy Tech 50" award at ESG2022, organised by Equal Ocean. Special Call's marketing strategy involves collaborations with third parties and implementing complete payment reduction strategies. Besides offering promotional pricing, they also partner with high-traffic commercial centres like supermarkets and hotels to set up charging stations, attracting customers to stop and recharge. Special Call has publicised its 16 core charging safety technologies, earning recognition and praise and solidifying its leading position in the industry.

State Grid, with its subsidiary Nation Grid Electric Vehicle Service Co., is another crucial player in the charging station industry. Established on December 29, 2002, State Grid reported earnings of RMB 3570 billion in 2022 (State Grid Company Limited 2021 annual report, n.d.). The wholly state-owned and centrally managed company has provided nationwide electricity for over two decades. Their main advantage is their extensive grid layout in China, which facilitates the establishment of charging stations. The company also has competitive electricity pricing due to its access to state-supported power stations. Despite its late entry into the market and a reputation less strong than Star Charge and Special Call, Nation Grid has proven its reliability in fundamental equipment, including charging stations and other infrastructure. Unlike Star Charge and Special Call, which achieved positive net profit after years of debt, Nation Grid receives steady government funding, allowing for a broader range of business activities.

Anyue Charging, a Shanghai Automotive Industry (Group) Corporation subsidiary, was founded in October 2015 with a registered capital of 478 million yuan (Shanghai et al., 2024). The company operates in various segments, including charging station sales, supporting installation, public charging station construction and operation, charging advertisement leasing, and intelligent charging platform construction services consulting. In the "2020 First Half of China's Charging Station

Operators TOP10" released by Media Ranking, Anyue Charging was listed among the top ten. The company upholds SAIC Group's core values of meeting user needs, enhancing innovation, integrating global resources, and honouring "people-oriented management." It constantly explores innovative charging station business models, addresses the pain points of charging station enterprises, and establishes a new energy vehicle industry chain ecosystem.

Forecast for this Market

Rapid Development and Supportive Policy Environment

In September 2023, the Chinese government introduced the first policy concerning electricity spot market trading rules. This marked a significant shift in China's focus towards the evolution of the electricity market—the government-backed new technologies, including energy storage, with substantial investment. Meanwhile, high-tech development regions like Guangdong started exploring new markets, such as the spot electric energy and ancillary services market. This move set the pace for the development of the electricity charging industry. The combination of innovation and supportive policies will elevate the charging market.

High Product Similarity and Accelerated Generational Upgrade

With the rise in the adoption of electric vehicles, customers' expectations started to shift. Customers began to demand higher-quality charging posts instead of merely having a charging post. This consumer shift challenged the technological capabilities of charging station companies. Both speed and safety became paramount considerations for customers, prompting companies to upgrade their charging systems and develop core technologies to maintain their market foothold. Companies realised that engaging in price wars was not a sustainable way to profit, as it could lead to a vicious cycle. Instead, they recognised that seeking innovation and reform was the path to progress (Tencent New, 2023). This realisation signalled a watershed moment in the industry, likely leading to market consolidation as companies unable to adapt would be forced to exit.

Overseas Market Potential

American Charging Station Market: The United States, ranking second in the global electric vehicle market, has seen significant government and public support towards the construction and operation of charging stations. Charge Point, the largest charging station operator in the U.S., uses a "charging station construction + APP" business model, effectively combining product and service.

Japanese Charging Station Market: By the end of 2015, the number of public and personal home charging stations in Japan had significantly surpassed that of gas stations. Japan employs the "NCS" business model, a charging service company jointly funded by Toyota, Honda, Nissan, Mitsubishi, and others. The four manufacturers are primarily responsible for installing, operating, and maintaining charging stations in Japan. The charging service network built by NCS includes shopping malls, hotels, parking lots, transportation hubs, etc., which apply to NCS for charging station installation and provide the corresponding installation services.

European Charging Station Market: In 2017, IONITY, a joint venture between BMW, Daimler, Volkswagen, and Ford, was established to build a fast-charging network across Europe. In Europe, car companies are mainly responsible for constructing and operating charging facilities, and they support the operation and development of public charging facilities through subsidies or dividends.

The overseas markets present a more mature revenue model than China's developing electricity exchange and service provision business. Unlike China's limited policies towards the market, overseas markets have more suitable policies and regular selling modes. This generates a more significant price difference and demands higher supply chain quality, including positive and negative electrode materials and even batteries. The shift in the overseas market suggests that domestic industries should increase exports and consider building factories overseas to establish their supply chain. However, challenges such as foreign investment environment, customer preferences, and cultural differences require careful product promotion and responsiveness to market changes for sustainable development.

Emergence of Light Storage Integration

According to the 2023 Digital Energy Annual Report (2023), light storage integration has become increasingly critical in the charging industry. Light storage integration combines photovoltaic power generation, storage, and charging. It offers a new solution to the impact of high-power fast charging on the power grid while maintaining the balance between the input and output of photovoltaic and wind power generation. Europe has led in this field, providing valuable insights for the industry. Regions with many new energy cars and distributed charging stations strongly demand grid-connected photovoltaic distribution and storage. They are responding to the call for renewable energy development through measures like time-of-use electricity price adjustments and the development of virtual power plant businesses, creating profitable opportunities for light storage integration. As successful experiences in these areas are gradually verified, the light storage integration profit model will be more widely promoted and applied. However, challenges persist, such as high installation costs and service efficiency. The payback period for a single photovoltaic charging station with six parking spaces is five to six years. The layout needs to be more balanced, the scene definition more accurate, and the service vehicle less, with higher efficiency. Despite these challenges, photovoltaic charging stations are expected to overcome the hurdles that traditional charging stations have faced, and with the experience gained, they are expected to progress more smoothly.

Development and Strategy

2014 was the time when most of the charging station companies sprang out, and Star Charge, like other companies, joined the market. Different from the companies from scratch, Star Charge's parent company gave it a solid background. Its parent company, Wan Gang New Energy Investment Group, was mainly engaged in car sales. One of its significant assets is Wan Bang Golden Star, the most prominent car dealer in Jiangsu province. Danwei Shao, the current chairman and president of Star Charge, has also worked for the car sales industry for more than ten years, accumulating numerous experiences in sales and the rich human resources of original equipment manufacturers (OEMs). When Star Charge was founded, it chose a radical route: putting much money into building infrastructure and even crowdfunding to push for program expansion, which was later named crowdfunding mode. Although this way is aggressive, especially for a company set up within months and still owes much money, Danwei Shao gives a perfect answer with her far-sighted view. Within three months, Star Charge built more than 1500 charging stations using the "crowdfunding mode," thus solving the nationwide problem of difficulty accessing electricity and land. The "crowdfunding mode" has widely solved social issues, allowing those with money to contribute money and those with land to contribute land, and has attracted the attention of social media. This massive operation gained interest from the state council. Later, in 2015, Vice Premier Ma Kai paid great attention to it after reading the report from journalists and held a national conference on the promotion of charging facilities, calling on everyone to learn from the company. At that time, Star Charge was the only software that managed electronic charging platforms. Probably because of luck, this brave expansion won a wide range of approval. With various reports about the name of the software, Star Charge gradually moved to the public's vision and became a company brand.

Apart from traditional public charging stations and private charging station modes, Star Charge noticed that the shortcomings of charging stations might be problematic to solve regardless of building more and more piles as the speed of increase in the car is far faster than the speed to build charging stations, so they implemented this private stake sharing strategy allowing the binding of private charging stations with the "Star Charge" platform and encouraging piles owners to sell their private pile to the public while the platform shared a transaction with individuals. More individuals and companies began to join the "self-pile sale" program. They cooperated with Star Charge, expanding its "circle of friends". Though Star Charge was a good try, the charge must still receive the expected outcome. The program was soon out of sight as the joint individual still needed to receive the expected income. Moreover, because maintaining the charging stations turned out to be more expensive than individuals can earn, this model continued to improve in the future.

THE PEOPLE BEHIND STAR CHARGE

CEO and Founder of Star Charge: Danwei Shao

Danwei Shao was born on August 28, 1982, in Changzhou, Jiangsu. After graduating from Freie Universität Berlin, Germany, in 2011, she embarked on a career in the new energy field. 2014, she founded the Wanbang New Energy Investment Group Co., Ltd., marking a significant milestone in her professional journey. From June 2011 to June 2014, Danwei served as the director and president of Wanbang Golden Star Vehicle Industry Group. In 2013, she was pivotal in establishing Dehe New Energy Technology Co., LTD, further solidifying her commitment to the new energy field. That same year, she assumed the role of chairman of Wanbang New Energy Investment Group Co., LTD.

Danwei's entrepreneurial spirit and leadership have been recognised by The People's Government of the People's Republic of China, who lauded her as a representative figure of enterprise executives' entrepreneurship, internal incubation entrepreneurship, and secondary entrepreneurship. Her contributions to the industry have earned her multiple awards, including the "2014 China Industry Leader," "Jiangsu New Economy Leader" (awarded by the Jiangsu Business Development Promotion Association), "EY Entrepreneur Award 2020 China," and "Harvard Business Review Business Person of the Year."

FUTURE PROJECTS

Government Collaborations and Infrastructure Development

In February, Wanbang Digital Energy secured a contract with the Hebei Public Security Department to procure and install charging stations and related equipment. Wanbang Digital Energy supplied Star Charge car charging stations, including two

60KW stations and seven 7KW stations. Further, in March 2023, it won another bid for a similar project with Changzhou City Construction Information Facilities Construction Co., LTD, worth 116,242 yuan. These developments highlight Star Charge's ongoing collaboration with local governments for sustainable development.

Star Charge also engages in technical exchanges with local transport bureaus, such as the Huixian Municipal Transportation Bureau, to collect data and upgrade systems. With the bureau's support, Star Charge is revisiting the "public stake" delegation, previously known as the private stake-sharing mode. This involves charging station owners sharing their private stations with the public. Wanbang Digital Energy provides operation and support service packages for these stations, including inspection and maintenance services.

Contributing to Carbon Reduction Goals

Under China's "dual carbon" strategy, new energy vehicles have proliferated, increasing the demand for charging stations. With its years of experience in new energy vehicle charging, Star Charge plays a vital role in promoting the electrification of China's transportation and leading the digitalisation of energy. Star Charge and Star Energy, the two core brands of Wan Gang Digital Energy, focus on reducing transportation and energy emissions, aiding the city in achieving its "low-carbon" and "zero-carbon" goals.

Mobile Energy Network Concept

In 2020, Star Charge introduced the concept of a "mobile energy network" at the Xumu Mountain Conference, proposing a time-free energy interconnection network utilising mobile transportation, energy carriers, replenishing facilities, and communication terminals. This concept was further developed at the 2023 conference, where Star Charge leaders emphasised the importance of creating a charging ecosystem.

Vehicle-to-Grid (V2G) Technology

V2G, or Vehicle-to-Grid, involves the two-way interaction between the grid and electric vehicles, using the latter's energy storage function as a buffer. Star Charge has a comprehensive range of V2G charging stations, boasting the industry's best efficiency, lowest noise, and highest grid compatibility. This technology direction is a vital part of Star Charge's future development.

CONCLUSION

This case discusses the background, development, and future forecast of Star Charge and the charging station market. Star Charge must continue to invest and expand like a snowball to maintain a leading position in the industry. There are many ways to improve sales. For example, Star Charge can leverage its OEM resources and develop supporting services with OEMs. With its current market share advantageous, Star Charge can also seek cooperation with local government platform companies while seizing market opportunities in the real estate market and local operator business.

The company also has some shortcomings. Firstly, Star Charge needs to focus more on talent training and promotion to attract more people to the industry. With intense competition in the charging station market, the demand for talent is increasing significantly. If Star Charge pays attention to talent education or advertising, it could retain human resources for other companies.

Furthermore, if Star Charge wants to expand into the overseas market, innovation in its operational strategy is crucial, as intelligent devices heavily rely on operational data. Compared to the overseas market, which has a more comprehensive policy system, Star Charge should focus on its core competencies, such as the technical content of its charging equipment. With the rise of the electric era, governments are expected to introduce more industry-friendly policies. Before this happens, Star Charge should accurately position itself to capture market share quickly and efficiently.

REFERENCES

China charging station industry market prospect and investment research report. (2021). Electric appliance industry, (12), 13–33.

China Electromechanical Recruitment Network. (2023, February 28). *Hebei Provincial Public Security Department charging pile and related equipment procurement and installation project transaction announcement.* China Electromechanical Recruitment Network. https://caizhao.jdzj.com/purchases/2023-02-28.31592b669f42 4971f973adb4162c7343

Hu, Z. (2024). Sprint IPO Star Charge: Expansion, pressure, transformation. *Zhihu column.* https://zhuanlan.zhihu.com/p/681012997

iiMedia. (2020, August 10). *Top 10 charging pile operators in China in the first half of 2020.* iiMedia. https://www.iimedia.cn/c880/73400.html

Jian, Y. (2023). *Charging pile industry data analysis: Star Charge's market share was 19.6%.* IIMedia. https://www.iimedia.cn/c1061/90253.html

Lv, R. (2017). Charging the Tigers and Roses in operation. *New energy economic and trade observation,* (Z1), 74–75.

Ma, L. (2015). *Interview: Shao Danwei, Chairman of Wanbang New Energy Investment Group Co.* China Government Net. https://www.gov.cn/wenzheng/2015 -09/15/content_2931970.htm

Shanghai SAIC Anyue charging Technology Co. (2024, March 25). *Ltd.-Love enterprise check.* Aiqicha. https://aiqicha.baidu.com/company_detail_83402490651136

State Grid Company Limited 2021 annual report. (n.d.). SH Clearing. https://www .shclearing.com.cn/xxpl/cwbg/nb/202204/t20220429_1048012.html

Tencent News. (2023). Dialogue "Star Charge," glimpse "unique innovation". *Tencent News.* https://new.qq.com/rain/a/20230421A00YNU00

Ye, T. (2023). Shao Danwei: Strengthen the construction of new energy vehicle charging and replacement infrastructure. *Intelligent connected car,* (02), 44–45.

Yin, G. (2012). Read the report and see the change II National Grid: Integrating the concept of social responsibility into strategic goals. *WTO Economic Guide,* (04), 60.

KEY TERMS AND DEFINITIONS

Charging Service Vouchers: These are electronic coupons issued by the charging station companies as a sales promotion strategy.

CR (Concentration Rate): The concentration rate (CR) is a term defined by American economist Bain. When CR is lower than 30%, the market is biased toward competitive markets.

Integration of Optical Storage: This refers to an electronic storage medium that uses a low-power laser beam to record and retrieve digital data, such as Compact Discs or Video Compact Discs. It signifies integrating new technology, which may advance the technical capabilities to a new level.

OEMs: OEM stands for Original Equipment Manufacturers. They typically refer to the industry capable of manufacturing cars. In this case, the OEMs cooperating with Star Charge include Mercedes Benz and Volkswagen.

OTA Software Upgrades: OTA (Over-the-Air) technology refers to wireless upgrades, such as network or Bluetooth. Currently, the most common OTA software upgrades are for applications based on the operating system, including user interface, car map, human-computer interaction interface, and entertainment system updates.

Positive and Negative Electrode Materials: These power supply poles generate voltage when connected to a medium.

Split Products and One-piece Products: One-piece products are complete devices that integrate components like the main body of the charging station, the LCD screen, and the charging cable. Split products separate the charging station from the charging cable and are usually installed on walls or stands.

Transport Bureau: An organization that administers and supervises local traffic and maintains traffic order. In this case, it refers to the Huixian Municipal Transportation Bureau.

Watershed Moment: It represents a phenomenon in which a group divides into different parts due to capability and environmental issues.

Chapter 8
Medlinker:
Innovations at the Forefront of China's Internet Healthcare Market

Yuxin Wang

Beijing Normal University-Hong Kong Baptist University United International College, China

EXECUTIVE SUMMARY

This case study examines Medlinker, a leading figure in China's internet healthcare sector, focusing on its evolution, market strategy, and technological innovations. Founded in 2014 by Dr. Wang Shirui, Medlinker has transformed from a social networking platform for doctors to a comprehensive disease management service integrating AI-driven solutions. The study delves into Medlinker's pioneering role in leveraging MedGPT, China's first large language model for medical applications, and its strategic initiatives to enhance healthcare accessibility and efficiency. It examines Medlinker's way of doing business, competition, and market position in a rapidly growing industry with developing government regulations. Ultimately, the case explores how Medlinker continues to innovate and expand, shaping the future of digital healthcare in China.

INTRODUCTION

Medlinker is a chronic disease management platform based in Chengdu, Sichuan Province. It provides practical and accessible healthcare services to patients by managing a service system around the disease process. This company focuses on

DOI: 10.4018/979-8-3693-2921-4.ch008

both online and offline. Relying on powerful online internet technology to integrate medical resources, they also do offline activities such as charity clinics.

As China's healthcare reform continues to deepen and develop, it has formed more than 18,000 healthcare alliances across the country by the end of 2023. Moreover, the number of two-way referrals has reached an impressive 30,321,700 nationwide (Dong & Li, 2024). In this environment, Medlinker plays a crucial role in streamlining the healthcare process, enhancing its accessibility, and contributing to the overall improvement of the healthcare system. As the number of healthcare alliances and referrals continues to increase, this may also represent an upsurge in demand for digital healthcare solutions, potentially benefiting Medlinker's growth and success.

This case study will examine the development of Medlinker's products and services, the profitability model of the business model, the market environment, and its competitiveness. It will provide an in-depth analysis of the reasons behind Medlinker's success and its contribution and impact on Internet healthcare.

MEDLINKER DESCRIPTION

Brief History of the Medlinker

Medlinker is a company that was founded in 2014 in Chengdu, Sichuan Province. The Medlinker application mainly focuses on social and academic exchanges among doctors. The successive launch of features such as "doctors' groups" quickly created a rich educational platform for doctors. Later, it upgraded to become a doctor's service platform and a whole process of disease management platform. Medlinker became one of the first companies to obtain an Internet hospital license in China. It was also one of the first Internet hospitals in the country to enable online payments through medical insurance.

Medlinker received 3 million RMB in angel round financing from Lianchuang Ceyuan and PreAngel two months after its establishment. It launched the Medlinker APP, which focuses on doctors' social networking and academic exchanges, and introduced several complementary features to create a more content-rich platform. In February 2015, Medlinker received multi-million-dollar Series A financing from Sequoia China. In September of the same year, it received a 40 million Series B financing led by Tencent, followed by Yunfeng Fund.

The release of Medlinker APP4.0 marked the official transformation of Medlinker from a social platform for doctors to a service platform for doctors. It received a series of C-round financing of 400 million RMB, strategically invested by CLP Health Fund, with participation from China Renaissance New Economy Fund and current shareholders Tencent and Sequoia. With the support of strategic investors, Medlinker proliferated.

In 2023, Medlinker began researching medical artificial intelligence standards and launched China's first prominent model-driven AI doctor. Professional associations and organizations recognized the innovative technology and results achieved. They were expected to lead the industry. In the same year, the AIIA Medical Artificial Intelligence Committee was awarded as the deputy leader of the research and evaluation standards. This helped the medical AI industry standards land so that high-quality medical resources and technologies could benefit more patients, grassroots doctors, and medical students.

Medlinker has consistently improved yearly, earning numerous milestone achievements (Medlinker, 2024). These achievements include being named a 2016 Deloitte-Huaxing China Rising Star, receiving the Most Innovative Digital Medical Solution award from HC3i China Digital Medical Network in 2017, joining the first cohort of the Digital Healthcare Innovation Alliance initiated by Tencent in 2019, ranking among Forbes China's Most Innovative Companies in 2019, being recognized as an Excellent Poverty Alleviation Charity Case in 2020 by Global Times & Global Network, being listed on the Top 10 Chinese Medical and Health Model Innovation Enterprises in 2023 by Yiou Health, and appearing on the Hurun Research Institute's Global Unicorn List in 2021 and 2023.

With AI technology's development and widespread adoption, Medlinker launched MedGPT in 2023, which became China's first medical vertical model-driven AI doctor. This groundbreaking innovation earned MedGPT the first prize in the "New Model" category at the China International Digital Economy Expo in the same year. Medlinker's innovative achievements in medical AI also earned the company a spot on the 2023 China Digital Healthcare Industry Vitality Ranking as one of China's Top 10 Healthcare Large Model Innovative Enterprises.

Business Model

A business model describes the core activities of an enterprise and their inter-relationships to enable the creation, delivery, and capture of value (Zott & Amit, 2010; Osterwalder & Pigneur, 2010; Richardson, 2008; Wirtz et al., 2016). The rise and popularity of the mobile internet have made it difficult for the general public to correctly identify the authenticity of information in this age of information explosion. Little is known about the medical industry, making people more susceptible to being fed misinformation. Internet medical platforms, which gather expertise and doctors and screen quality content for users, have gradually become a reliable channel for the general public to acquire medical knowledge.

Doctors are considered the best entry point to the medical industry, and social networking among doctors is the most efficient way to bring them together. While purely social networking among doctors may not generate commercial value, building active user communities through topics and circles can increase user stickiness and attract more platform traffic than other apps. In the early stages, Medlinker's profit was mainly derived from the commercialization of medicine. The company focused on "medicine" in its cash flow and profitability, particularly chronic and special-effective diseases. It also generated profits through patient management and other marketing services, such as connecting doctors on the platform with outpatient services and multi-practice.

In terms of Medlinker's actual behavior, it currently makes money through different channels. In the Medlinker application, Medlinker earns commissions by promoting additional services such as insurance and digital marketing for pharmaceutical companies. Medlinker receives commissions from doctors in tertiary hospitals for outpatient visits to patients in townships and villages and receives traffic generated by patient referrals between hospitals. Medlinker Cloud, on the other hand, is where Medlinker sells its cloud systems to medical institutions to generate revenue. This platform can help medical institutions with information management and other digital intelligence assistance.

In today's world, where traditional marketing methods are limited, the Internet has become the preferred platform for pharmaceutical companies to market their products (Medlinker, 2022). Medlinker, through its years of accumulating excellent doctors and high hospital coverage across China, provides a platform that links pharmaceutical companies with doctors to promote high-quality products and meet the needs of doctors who want to practice at multiple sites and deal with a diverse range of patients (Bao et al., 2022).

According to a recent research report by Euromonitor.com on China's Internet medical content industry (Lin, 2021), there are two main types of Internet medical platforms - content-based and service-based. Content-based platforms focus more on collecting and creating medical content to provide users with comprehensive information about diseases and symptoms. Some platforms also offer preliminary online diagnosis and treatment capabilities. On the other hand, service-based platforms mainly provide health management, chronic disease management, and online diagnosis and treatment. They also offer medical content, but it mostly focuses on health information. Medlinker is a platform that primarily serves doctors. It links doctors' resources with medical institutions, pharmaceutical manufacturers, and commercial insurance companies to enhance doctors' abilities for productization and commercialization. This ultimately becomes Medlinker's actual profit model.

Products and Services

Medlinker Application

Medlinker is a vertical social networking application for doctors. It is designed for doctors to share their professional knowledge, experiences, and profiles or to express their emotions outside of work. The application's primary functions are divided into two parts: real-name communication and anonymous communication.

In the real-name communication section, users can follow or apply to become friends with interested doctors. The information flow in this section comes from two primary sources. The first source is from the social connections of the user's own "doctor circle." The second source is from Medlinker's screening and editing of user-generated content (UGC), such as selected topics and classic cases. With the anonymous forum that opens between midnight and two o'clock, doctors have a reliable platform to talk about their problems and difficulties. They can also discuss objective industry trends. The anonymity of the scene is more conducive to the authentic voice of the doctors' community.

Vertical communities of doctors have flourished abroad, but the domestic vertical community of doctors is still in its early stages. The emergence of the Medlinker application has undoubtedly injected new life into China's Internet medical industry. Additionally, the Medlinker application needs to be more content with the status quo; it has transformed its product strategy through precise positioning. While similar apps are still deepening their social and medical knowledge, Medlinker has already undergone fission in 2016, transforming from a social platform into a service platform and changing "doctor's social life" into "a service for all doctors".

Medlinker Cloud

The official position of this product is to act as a medical management system, which is China's most comprehensive hospital management platform. Its Medlinker HIS software-as-a-service includes three different versions of sub-products: dental version, clinic version, and hospital version. Regardless of which version is used, it has two main features - security and confidentiality- and is easy to operate. This platform can link dental clinics, general practices, and hospitals and manage information for them. By docking with the Medlinker platform, high-quality doctor resources can be gathered to provide strong material security. Moreover, if the partnership or partners have business expansion needs, Medlinker Cloud will fully assist their business layout and brand building.

Medlinker YLT

MedLinker YLT is a platform that offers doctor visits and patient referrals. Experienced and renowned doctors are often located in tertiary hospitals in large cities. At the same time, many township patients usually find it difficult to travel to first-tier towns when they are seriously ill. Through the MedLinker platform, doctors can be contacted and facilitated to provide treatment services to patients in medically backward areas. Moreover, referral is a way for less senior doctors to introduce patients to other doctors based on their knowledge and experience. They do this when they feel that the patient's condition is beyond their ability, and they contact the other doctor through the MedLinker platform to see if they can accept the patient. However, this activity involves transferring patients from the same city or region.

MedGPT

Generative AI is currently leading the new AI boom and showing great potential. In the medical field, MedGPT is the first medical large language model (LLM) in China. As an AI doctor, it can learn and replicate top specialists' diagnoses and treatment experiences, making high-quality medical resources available to everyone. Although LLMs have certain shortcomings in terms of accuracy regarding medical problems, MedGPT addresses this issue. Large language models may give incomplete or even incorrect conclusions during the consultation stage due to insufficient or inaccurate information. In contrast, MedGPT can collect enough information for diagnosis through multiple rounds of questioning before proceeding to diagnosis, thus improving accuracy. According to test results on 30 June 2023, Medlinker's AI doctors can achieve up to 96% consistency assessment with real doctors (Chen, 2021).

Throughout the entire medical treatment process, MedGPT is the first AI tool in China that can provide a comprehensive approach to prevention, diagnosis, treatment, and rehabilitation. This means that MedGPT enables Medlinker Digital Hospital to move away from the 1.0 stage, which is centered on internet medical connections and mainly aims to improve efficiency, and into the 2.0 stage of digital healthcare, which involves the intelligence of the whole process of disease management. When MedGPT designs a treatment plan for a patient, the patient can receive home medication delivery through the Internet hospital. MedGPT then carries out intelligent diagnosis and treatment behaviors such as medication guidance, rehabilitation guidance, and follow-up for patients. By continuously improving the coverage of disease types, MedGPT is one step closer to genuinely realizing medical benefits.

Users

Doctors

Medlinker provides doctors with three primary social, academic, and practical services. Regarding educational services, it is associated with hundreds of media resources, such as JAMA and the Journal of the American Medical Association (JAMA), which authorizes long-term academic cooperation. This is conducive to constructing a knowledge base, combining multiple cases, concentrating a wealth of medical information on one platform, and providing one-stop services from clinical to scientific research.

Medlinker is a fragmented vertical community of doctors regarding social services at its inception. Users are all real-name certified doctors in service who can follow or add friends to the doctors they are interested in and set up their social circle of doctors outside of the hospital on the app. They can also use their fragmented time to conduct academic exchanges.

Interestingly, Medlinker's MedGPT was compared to leading physicians in China in a live-streamed real-world assessment. The evaluation involved 120 real patients and 10 attending physicians at West China Hospital of Sichuan University. The results showed that MedGPT's diagnostic accuracy reached 96%, which is comparable to that of top physicians. This demonstrates the efficiency and usefulness of MedGPT in Clinical Settings, and experts generally recognize MedGPT's ability to ensure medical accuracy and gather information.

Finally, in terms of practical services, since the distribution of medical resources in China is very uneven, the State Council issued the Opinions on Deepening the Reform of the Medical and Health Care System as early as 2009, which advocated for multi-disciplinary practice by doctors. However, in China's capital city of Beijing, for example, the city's multi-practice physician registrations had accumulated less than 10 percent of the total number of physicians by 2015. Through the brokerage platform Medlinker, doctors can realize multi-practice, arranging how and where they practice, such as accepting invitations for online consultations and offline clinics. Medlinker supports practice services other than seeing a doctor (Feng, 2016).

Patients

According to iMedia's 2021 Survey on the Perception of Pain Points in China's Healthcare Industry's Consultation Process, more than 60% of respondents reported that scheduling offline appointments was difficult or impossible. 51.7% and 45.9% of respondents also reported excessive checkups and difficulty in doctor-patient communication during the consultation process. At the end of the consultation, more than 50% of respondents found the payment and medication pickup process cumbersome, and the medical insurance conditions needed to be clarified (iMedia, 2021).

The increasing popularity of the internet has accelerated the growth of mobile medical care, leading to a surge in demand for Internet hospitals among the general public. As one of the first Internet hospitals in China to obtain a license and offer medical insurance payments, Medlinker provides various services to meet current demands, including health knowledge dissemination, online diagnosis, medicine purchases, offline consultation appointments, and chronic disease tracking and management. Patient feedback to Medlinker has also been overwhelmingly positive. One patient who participated in the evaluation said that after making a doctor's appointment through Medlinker, their doctor's visit was very smooth, and the doctor could answer their questions in detail on the platform, greatly improving their medical experience. According to iMedia's "China Mobile Medical User Scale and Forecast 2015-2024," the number of mobile medical users in China has steadily increased, reaching 690 million in 2021 (iMedia, 2021).

Market Analysis

Situation and Evolution of the Internet Medical Market in China

Internet healthcare is a business that leverages Internet technology to provide professional healthcare services. In the Western world, it is commonly known as "telemedicine" or "telehealth"; in China, it is referred to as a combination of the Internet and healthcare, known as Internet medical healthcare. Online platforms have enabled patients to conveniently and quickly obtain medical services, including those for chronic diseases and particular diseases, thus reducing the difficulty or lack of time to see a doctor. Patients can also benefit from the entire management process, from consultation to medication and later recovery. Technological advancements allow patients from almost any geographical area to join the Internet medical platform.

Internet healthcare in China has undergone four stages of development, from its infancy to its current mature model. In 2000, early websites combining the Internet and health, such as Dr. Ding Xiang, began to appear. Internet medical care was mainly based on health popularization and medical knowledge search, needing more substantive services. In 2014, the National Health and Family Planning Commission clarified the content of telemedicine services for the first time, and Internet healthcare began to involve the consultation process. The same year, the Guangdong Provincial Health Commission officially approved the Second People's Hospital of Guangdong Province. They agreed to prepare for the construction of a cyberhospital and built the first cyberhospital in China, i.e., the Guangdong Provincial Cyberhospital, which was officially set up. In 2018, to ensure medical quality and safety, the Opinions of the General Office of the State Council on Promoting the Development of "Internet + Medical and Healthcare" called for further regulation of Internet diagnosis and treatment behaviors. It also clarified the industry standards for Internet healthcare. Online medical services are gradually emerging, but the quality varies.

The outbreak of COVID-19 in 2020 has caused a significant increase in the demand for internet healthcare. This has led many people to recognize the business opportunities presented by internet healthcare. Moreover, the Chinese government has released a series of policies to strengthen information technology to prevent and control epidemics while encouraging internet services. As a result, the number of internet medical products and users has rapidly grown. The internet healthcare market is expanding, and companies are adopting diversified business models such as health insurance and internet hospitals. Consequently, industry regulation has been strengthened to ensure safe and effective practices in the Internet healthcare sector.

Competition Analysis

Medlinker needs to distinguish between direct and indirect competitors when evaluating the competition. Direct competitors who provide the same or similar services to the same customer base directly affect Medlinker's market share. For example, Jingdong's JD Health is a direct competitor of Medlinker. In contrast, indirect competitors, such as Alibaba's Ali Health and Ding Xiang Yuan (DXY), offer different services to the same customer base and indirectly affect Medlinker's market share by influencing users.

Medlinker is a platform that relies primarily on user-generated content (UGC) to create and disseminate information. The company's approach involves creating high-quality content by leveraging the expertise of head users, which is then branded by the official team to promote the content further. Medlinker also offers courses, including expert lectures and conferences, but the organization needs to be more systematic than some of its competitors.

DXY, on the other hand, has a more extended development history than Medlinker and operates mainly on professionally generated content (PGC) supplemented by user-generated content. The company emphasizes systematic and refined open course sections catering to core users with learning needs. In DXY's forum, users' posts form UGC content, which is carefully screened by the official team before being pushed to the homepage for non-core users.

JD Health provides online medical services and retail pharmacies, selling medicines, and Internet hospitals complement each other, similar to Medlinker's online and offline combination model. JD Health poses a significant threat to Medlinker. Finally, Ali Health is a platform operated by Alibaba that enables online trading services for drugs and similar products. However, the platform primarily caters to manufacturers and suppliers, and consumers need more access to the service.

Forecast for Internet Medical Market

In recent years, the Chinese government has issued several policies to meet the growing demand for healthcare in China, which have been conducive to developing Internet hospitals. For example, the General Office of the State Council's Opinion on Promoting the Development of "Internet and Medical Health" encourages qualified third-party organizations to set up Internet information platforms (General Office of the State Council, 2018). The Chinese government has also included eligible "Internet+" medical service fees in the scope of medical insurance payments, set uniform and transparent prices and payment methods, and encouraged designated pharmaceutical organizations to innovate their distribution methods (National et al. Bureau National Health and Health Commission, 2020). These measures have fueled the development of China's internet healthcare market.

According to the "2019-2024 Internet and Medical Market Outlook Research Report" released by China Business Industry Research Institute, the market size of China's internet healthcare industry is predicted to reach RMB419 billion in 2024, after reaching 309.9 billion in 2022. During the outbreak of the epidemic, many hospitals introduced online medical consultation and internet prescribing to prevent cross-infection, and more patients experienced this convenience and efficiency.

In particular, China's relative history of outbreak prevention and control management has fostered Chinese people's habit of using Internet healthcare with increasing trust and acceptance. Taking the online penetration of pharmaceuticals as an example, according to the data of the 2019-2024 Internet + Pharmaceuticals Market Operation Mode Research and Consulting Report released by China Business Industry Research Institute, China's online pharmaceutical retail sales are predicted to increase to 74.5 billion yuan in 2024, after reaching 50.7 billion yuan in 2022. The market size is expected to grow (China Business Industry Research Institute, 2023).

WANG SHIRUI - THE CORE FIGURE OF MEDLINKER

Wang Shirui, the founder and CEO of Medlinker, is an eight-year doctor at West China Stomatological Hospital of Sichuan University and a visiting scholar at Harvard University. In 2013, Wang Shirui, who was a research scholar in the United States, noticed that foreign doctors' groups mainly used particular doctors' exchange platforms such as ResearchGate, Doximity, and Figure1 to communicate. He also observed that these platforms helped foreign doctors to form vertical communities, develop and prosper, and effectively achieve work-life balance.

The following year, while on a plane back to China, Wang Shirui wrote a business plan for a social platform for doctors, which marks the beginning of Medlinker. He acknowledged that Chinese doctors face too much pressure with an overloaded work schedule and are often exhausted from writing papers. Perhaps because of this early realization, instead of choosing to continue working as a doctor, he set up Medlinker, perhaps in an attempt to help more people like himself. In June 2014, Medlinker was founded in Chengdu, Sichuan Province, China. In 2016, Wang Shirui was selected as one of Forbes Asia's "30 Entrepreneurs Under 30". He was also twice selected as one of Fortune's "China's 40 Business Elites Under 40" in 2016 and 2018. He now also serves as CEO of Future Healthcare.

Wang Shirui believes that Medlinker is an Internet hospital, and the core of it is the word "hospital". He thinks that hospitals should mainly focus on caring for the sick. If an Internet medical platform does not prioritize seeing patients but only pursues short-term profits, it will have no value and no future. As CEO, Wang Shirui has a medical background, and he understands that the medical business needs at least three years to start and requires patience. While other companies are rushing to "buy drugs," Medlinker is taking a step-by-step approach to developing severe medical care and actively looking for ways to benefit doctors and patients. Wang Shirui said that regardless of changes in the capital market, Medlinker's focus is on how to extend the life expectancy of all human beings. With doctors' social networking as the entry point and disease and patients as the core, the ultimate goal is to "extend the life of all mankind for one year."

Many old employees have said they would like to accompany Medlinker to the end, regardless of success or failure. Even employees who have left the company often ask about the latest developments at Medlinker. During the development of Medlinker, the original intention of insisting on curing diseases and saving people has remained the same. That wish, which used to be Wang Shirui's, has gradually become the dream of all employees.

FUTURE PROJECT OF MEDLINKER

Medlinker is making significant strides in medical professionalism and is focused on strengthening the fundamental work of medical practice. The company has established the first academic committee in the industry. Expanding its coverage of disease types horizontally is also improving the standardization of services vertically. With the guidance of experts, online management SOPs for each disease type are gradually being developed, making the disease management of Internet medicine more standardized and effective.

Medlinker's core has always been its online platform for disease management. In 2021, Future Healthcare formally merged into Medlinker, making Medlinker's original full-process services more comprehensive. On the one hand, Future Healthcare's offline clinics can complement Medlinker's online disease management. Medlinker's users can complete tests and pick up medication within the Medlinker group. On the other hand, Future Healthcare offers Medlinker the possibility of expanding its departments, such as dentistry, which is highly dependent on offline resource support. Through this integration, online and offline are linked more closely, and Medlinker achieves further closed-loop management.

Furthermore, Medlinker held China's first AI medical conference in 2023 and established the AI medical committee, a significant achievement for society. As medical and AI technology develops, more researchers are entering the field. However, the lack of unified evaluation methods and standards has left the reliability of medical AI unassured. Given Medlinker's achievements in medical big language models, it was awarded the deputy head unit of the Standards and Evaluation Working Group of the Medical Artificial Intelligence Committee in the same year. This has helped to realize the norms and standards of the medical AI industry.

For the company itself, Medlinker will increase its investment in MedGPT to enhance its stability while strengthening its cooperation with healthcare organizations and expanding the scope of AI applications. Medlinker continues to extend invitations to potential partners on its official website, especially companies with multimodal modeling technology. It hopes to provide all patients with more accurate, accessible, and high-quality medical services.

CONCLUSION

In summary, despite facing fierce competition in the market and an ever-changing industry environment, Medlinker has established a strong innovation capability and a robust business model, which have laid the foundation for its sustainable development in the future. With investments from major corporations such as Tencent, Medlinker has continued to launch a diverse range of products and services and has taken a leading position in the market. However, managers must monitor operational management enhancements and policy changes to maintain the company's favorable development trend.

REFERENCES

Amit, R., & Zott, C. (2001). Value creation in E-business. *Strategic Management Journal*, 22(6–7), 493–520. DOI:10.1002/smj.187

Bao, Y., Chen, B., Chen, X., Wang, Q. Y., & Kang, J. (n.d.). *"Data analysis of Chinese Doctor group."* McKinsey Greater China. https://www.mckinsey.com.cn/%E6%95%B0%E8%AF%B4%E5%8C%BB%E7%94%9F%EF%BC%8C%E4%B8%AD%E5%9B%BD%E5%8C%BB%E7%94%9F%E7%BE%A4%E4%BD%93%E7%94%BB%E5%83%8F/

Chen, P. (2023, July 4). *AI,MedGPT96% "China's first medical generative AI milestone, Medlinker MedGPT has over 96% diagnostic consistency with tertiary experts"*. Vbdata. https://www.vbdata.cn/1518918039

China Business Industry Research Institute. (2023, November 14). *2024 "Research Report on market prospect forecast of China's Internet medical industry in 2024"*. Netease. https://www.163.com/dy/article/IJGACK2805198SOQ.html

Dong, R., & Li, H. (2024). *1.8 "A total of more than 18,000 medical alliances of various forms have been established across the country"*. Economic Information Daily. http://dz.jjckb.cn/www/pages/webpage2009/html/2024-03/06/content_96735.htm

Feng, T. (2016, September 13). *"Academicians such as Zhan Qimin and Yang Huanming praised Medlinker as a 'pioneer of doctors' multi-practice"*. Chinadaily. https://caijing.chinadaily.com.cn/finance/2016-09/13/content_26787915.htm

General Office of the State Council. (2018, April 28). *"Opinions of the General Office of the State Council on Promoting the Development of 'Internet + Healthcare'"*. Central People's Government of the People's Republic of China. https://www.gov.cn/zhengce/content/2018-04/28/content_5286645.htm

iiMedia. (2021, November 5). *2021 "China Internet Hospital Industry Development Research Report 2021"*. https://www.iimedia.cn/c400/81955.html

Lin, H. (2021, July). *2021 "China Internet Medical Content Industry Research Report in 2021"*. iyiou. https://www.iyiou.com/research/20210707877

Medlinker. (2022, November 1). *, "Medlinker's Precision Marketing Platform Goes Live, Helping Pharmaceutical Enterprises Transform Digital Marketing"*. Medlinker. https://www.medlinker.com/pc/news/detail/191

Medlinker. (2024). *"Medlinker empowers doctors to improve the efficiency and quality of patient management"*. About Medical Alliance Honors. https://www .medlinker.com/pc/about/honor

National Health and Family Planning Commission. (2014, August 29). *"Opinions of National Health and Family Planning Commission on Promoting telemedicine services in medical institutions"*. National Health Commission. http://www.nhc.gov.cn/

Osterwalder, A., & Pigneur, Y. (2010). *Business model generation: A handbook for visionaries, game changers, and challengers*. Wiley.

Qianji Investment Bank. (2023, September 18). *2023 "2023 Internet medical industry research report"*. https://www.21jingji.com/article/20230918/herald/57dee0449c71 b1ba2ce449391a9e3bc7.html

Richardson, J. (2008). The business model: An integrative framework for strategy execution. *Strategic Change*, 17(5-6), 133–144. DOI:10.1002/jsc.821

Wirtz, B., Pistoia, A., Ullrich, S., & Göttel, V. (2016). Business models: Origin, development and future research perspectives. *Long Range Planning*, 49(1), 36–54. DOI:10.1016/j.lrp.2015.04.001

KEY TERMS AND DEFINITIONS

Generative AI: Generative AI is a type of artificial intelligence that generates original content by learning from large amounts of data using algorithms and models.

Vertical Community: A vertical community is a group of people who share a specific interest or content orientation. This community is usually aimed at a particular target group or range.

HIS: A Health Information System is an IT system offering hospital data collection, integrated management, and information processing services. It utilizes modern means, such as computer technology and network communication technology.

Serious Healthcare: Serious healthcare is the opposite of consumer healthcare. While consumer healthcare emphasizes autonomy, serious healthcare emphasizes professionalism. Professional doctors and healthcare institutions usually provide it.

UGC: User Generated Content (UGC) refers to original content created by users and shared with others over the internet.

PGC: Professional-generated Content (PGC) is high-quality content produced by professional organizations. It is usually guaranteed to meet specific standards.

LLM: A Large Language Model (LLM) is an artificial intelligence algorithm with many parameters. It uses neural network technology to understand and generate human language deeply.

Chapter 9
WeDoctor:
Journey to Leadership in China's Internet Healthcare Industry

Zhenxiang Yuan

Beijing Normal University-Hong Kong Baptist University United International College, China

EXECUTIVE SUMMARY

This case study explores the evolution and strategic growth of WeDoctor, a pioneering force in China's internet healthcare sector. Founded amidst challenges within China's medical regulatory environment, WeDoctor leveraged technological innovation and strategic partnerships to establish itself as a leader. Beginning with an innovative appointment registration platform, WeDoctor navigated regulatory landscapes through local government collaborations, leading to the establishment of China's first Internet hospital. The study details WeDoctor's progression through germination, demonstration, theorization, and diffusion stages, highlighting pivotal strategies such as stakeholder engagement, technological integration, and policy advocacy. WeDoctor's success in gaining regulatory legitimacy and scaling innovative models underscores its role in transforming healthcare delivery through digital solutions, setting benchmarks in internet-based medical services in China.

UNICORN DESCRIPTION

Brief History of the Unicorn

WeDoctor was founded in 2014, and its headquarters are in Hangzhou, China. Established by Liao Jieyuan and others, it is one of the most prominent and most promising unicorns internationally in the digital health sector. Initially focused on

DOI: 10.4018/979-8-3693-2921-4.ch009

providing online appointment scheduling services to streamline hospital processes, WeDoctor later transitioned into the market of Internet hospitals. It established China's first Internet hospital, Wuzhen Internet Hospital, integrating online and offline medical services. Subsequently, WeDoctor embarked on the phase of digital health communities, progressively constructing internet hospitals in various cities and collaborating with major hospitals and grassroots medical institutions to provide standardized medical services and health management for the public.

WeDoctor's core businesses span three significant sectors: digital healthcare, digital medical devices, and digital traditional Chinese medicine. Leveraging an open digital health cloud platform, the company aims to enhance medical service efficiency, reduce medicine distribution costs, optimize medical insurance fund utilization, and advance the development of traditional Chinese medicine, thereby creating a nationally distinctive digital health management system centered around health. Notably, WeDoctor's innovation and uniqueness lie in its closed-loop industrial layout and the openness of its digital health cloud platform. It collaborates with major hospitals, grassroots medical institutions, pharmaceutical enterprises, and insurance companies to build a digital health ecosystem. Additionally, WeDoctor is committed to promoting the development of upstream and downstream fields such as medical artificial intelligence, innovative medical devices, medical education, and new drug research and development.

Thanks to its outstanding products and services, WeDoctor holds a prominent position and influence in the industry, garnering numerous accolades and recognitions, including ranking 105th on the "2023 Global Unicorn List." Furthermore, WeDoctor actively fulfills its corporate social responsibilities. Apart from actively developing its industrial ecosystem and constructing digital health towns, it collaborates with high-quality enterprises and projects to cultivate a virtuous digital health industry ecosystem. Regarding health poverty alleviation, WeDoctor assists impoverished areas in signing up for family doctors and enhancing the professional capabilities of township health centers and village clinics. Amid the global fight against the pandemic, WeDoctor's internet hospital's real-time COVID-19 rescue platform provides online consultations, psychological assistance, follow-ups, medical insurance medication, and epidemic prevention knowledge for users nationwide.

Looking ahead, WeDoctor's development plans include expanding the coverage of digital health communities, promoting the establishment of more Internet hospitals in cities, and providing comprehensive medical treatment and health management services. Furthermore, WeDoctor will continue to drive the development of medical artificial intelligence, innovative medical devices, and other fields while seizing industry opportunities and trends to offer users better digital health solutions.

Business Model

WeDoctor Group's multi-platform integrated service model, with the WeDoctor Internet Hospital platform as the core, provides patients with online outpatient services, remote consultations, two-way referrals, health check-ups, chronic disease management, precise appointments, and other health and medical services. In addition, WeDoctor Group also includes multiple platforms such as the WeDoctor tiered diagnosis and treatment platform, internet general practitioner signing platform, and WeDoctor prescription sharing platform, providing patients with customized health management plans, achieving rational allocation of medical resources, and improving the efficiency and quality of medical services. Committed to building a multi-platform integrated health and medical service ecosystem, WeDoctor Group provides patients with convenient, efficient, and considerate medical experiences. It offers broader career development opportunities for doctors. As of October 2018, WeDoctor has connected more than 2,700 critical hospitals in 30 provinces and cities nationwide, with 260,000 doctors, providing medical guidance and expert consultation services and equipped with professional medical staff to provide medical advice and consultation, free answers to patient questions, and triage services, including recommending hospitals and experts. Thousands of hospital experts serve as the website's expert team, providing targeted consulting services to needy patients.

Product and Services

WeDoctor's products and services are divided into two categories: medical services and health maintenance services.

Regarding medical services, WeDoctor connects hospitals to provide integrated online and offline consultation, diagnosis, and treatment services. Firstly, it offers digital medical consultation and diagnosis services. Users can consult with over 150,000 doctors online via the WeDoctor platform to receive professional diagnoses and advice. Secondly, it provides comprehensive medical and specialized medical services. Users can make offline appointments with specialist doctors through the WeDoctor platform to receive initial consultations and access services such as medical records, online follow-ups, electronic prescriptions, and prescription dispensing. Additionally, WeDoctor offers assisted reproductive services and sales of assisted reproductive devices, providing users with professional consultation and device purchasing services.

Regarding health maintenance services, WeDoctor provides digital chronic disease management services and health management services. Digital chronic disease management services are primarily provided through the acquisition of Tai'an Pharmacy, offering chronic disease management and medication supply services to help patients manage their conditions, provide professional health advice, and deliver medications. Health management services are achieved by introducing digital examination services and expanding into rural markets, providing users with health check-ups and management services to help them maintain their physical well-being. Moreover, WeDoctor is committed to increasing the number of corporate clients and providing them with health management services.

By continuously expanding its service scope and innovating scenarios, WeDoctor meets users' medical and health management needs. For example, it introduced mobile hospital vehicles in Jia County, Henan Province, to provide convenient medical services to patients. WeDoctor also collaborated with Tai'an, Shandong Province, to realize digital management services that can be settled through medical insurance payments. In conclusion, WeDoctor strives to provide comprehensive medical and health maintenance services, enhancing users' experiences in medical care and health management.

Customers

According to statistics, WeDoctor's primary target audience is 30-39 users with a balanced gender ratio. Most of these users have become parents and have an urgent need for medical care. They face challenges such as high medical costs and difficulty accessing healthcare. Internet healthcare can help address these immediate needs. Additionally, as WeDoctor is headquartered in Zhejiang, an economically developed region with relatively abundant medical resources and a concentration of tertiary hospitals, patients and doctors from the Eastern region show more frequent demand than other areas. Although WeDoctor has fewer hospitals in regions such as North China and Northwest China, with the widespread adoption and development of Internet healthcare, users in these areas will gradually accept and use WeDoctor's services.

Market Analysis

Original Situation of the Market

The integration of the internet with the healthcare sector can be traced back to the early 21st century, with the concept of "mobile healthcare" coined by Professor Istepanian Robert of Imperial College London. The 2010 Mobile Summit in the United States defined "Mobile-Healthcare" as providing medical services through mobile medical devices. In China, the development of the healthcare sector has been significantly influenced by government policies. Starting with the healthcare reform in 1985 and culminating in the official inclusion of "Internet Plus" in government reports during the 2015 12th National People's Congress, healthcare system reform has consistently been a focal point of public attention.

With the foundation laid by early 21st-century innovations and government policies fostering growth, the evolution of China's Internet healthcare sector gained significant momentum. Since 2010, the internet healthcare sector has attracted considerable investment. The years 2013-2014 were dubbed the "Internet Healthcare Year" due to factors such as reduced policy barriers, increased market demand, the growth of e-commerce, and advancements in Internet technology, catalyzing reforms in the traditional healthcare sector. Even before 2013, numerous domestic Internet healthcare enterprises had emerged, including platforms like 39 Health Network, Quick Doctor Consultation, and Appointment Booking Network. These enterprises have progressed from their initial stages of inception to startup, then to a trial-and-error phase by 2015, and finally to a phase of systematic integration after 2016. Through gradually improving their platforms, accumulating users, and enhancing market adaptability, these Internet healthcare enterprises have propelled industry development.

The traditional ecological system of the healthcare sector revolves around hospitals as its core. Hospitals serve as the central hub for medical consultation and patient services and facilitate the exchange of information, funds, and materials among related pharmaceutical companies, insurance services, and other service providers. However, the introduction of the Internet has disrupted this traditional unidirectional system, fostering closer information exchange among patients, doctors, hospitals, and healthcare services, thus enhancing channel utilization and accelerating the overall system operation.

Evolution of the Market Until Today

The development of the medical and health industry is crucial for the well-being of both the nation and its people. Currently, China faces new challenges such as industrialization, urbanization, population aging, and changes in disease patterns, ecological environments, and lifestyles. These factors present both new opportunities and challenges for the development of healthcare. In this context, the deep integration of "Internet Plus" with the medical industry has become a reality. Driven by policies and technology, China's Internet Plus healthcare applications have shown diverse and vigorous development trends. These applications play a significant role in alleviating the imbalance of medical resources, facilitating the vertical flow of high-quality medical resources, providing real-time, convenient, and high-quality services for the public, improving the medical experience, and easing doctor-patient conflicts.

In 2015, "Internet Plus" was mentioned for the first time in the government work report, and subsequently, it was highlighted as one of the critical actions in the "Internet Plus" action plan. Since then, the State Council has issued multiple documents explicitly calling for integrating "Internet Plus" with the medical industry. Since 2016, the Chinese government has introduced a series of policies and regulations to promote the healthy development of Internet Plus healthcare actively. Relevant departments such as the National Health Commission, the National Development and Reform Commission, and the Ministry of Human Resources and Social Security have also formulated supporting policies to regulate and promote the development of Internet Plus healthcare. These policies have provided a favorable policy environment and support for developing Internet Plus healthcare.

Technological applications are the driving force behind economic and social development. Under the leadership of the CPC Central Committee and the State Council in recent years, China's construction of population health informatization has made comprehensive and rapid progress. This includes advances in regional information platform construction, medical institution informatization, formulation of health information standards, and establishment of information security systems. These efforts have laid a solid technological foundation for developing Internet Plus healthcare applications. The rapid development of new technologies coupled with the close integration with medical services, such as cloud computing promoting the transition of diagnostic methods from disease medicine to health medicine, the application of Internet of Things devices integrating wearable devices with everyday items, the combination of mobile internet with healthcare enabling real-time information sharing in medical institutions, and the application of big data in health care services, are all changing the mode of medical and health services. With the in-depth application of new technologies such as artificial intelligence, genetic testing, and virtual reality in the medical field, China's medical industry's ecological and service models will be redefined.

Internet Plus Healthcare continuously innovates medical service models, reshaping the healthcare ecosystem. With the support of various levels of health and health data centers and integrated platforms and the utilization of advanced technologies such as cloud computing, big data, and the Internet of Things, residents can complete health consultations and find suitable doctors at home through the network. Continuous monitoring and sharing of data are carried out using mobile applications and wearable devices, and medical diagnoses are assisted through data analysis. Patients can make appointments online, wait remotely, pay for services during consultations, and check reports, thereby improving the medical experience. Establishing tiered diagnosis and treatment platforms, collaborative platforms, regional imaging centers, regional electrocardiography centers, regional pathology centers, regional testing centers, and regional, remote centers have enhanced the service capabilities of grassroots medical institutions. Meanwhile, Internet Plus Healthcare also plays an essential supporting role in public health and pharmaceutical distribution. Through innovative application models, Internet Plus Healthcare is gradually realizing its crucial supporting role in tiered diagnosis and treatment, health management, public health, pharmaceutical distribution, and other aspects.

Internet Plus healthcare is experiencing rapid development globally, with China being one of the key players. The market size of Internet Plus Healthcare in China continues to expand, and investment activities remain active. Internet Plus Healthcare is exploring various profit models, with primary fee targets including users, doctors, hospitals, pharmaceutical companies, insurance companies, and large corporations. The development of Internet Plus healthcare optimizes the existing medical and health system and gives rise to new formats such as Internet hospitals and cloud hospitals. As an emerging model, Internet hospitals can only have lasting vitality when combined with tiered diagnosis, treatment, and cost control objectives.

In conclusion, the prospects for developing Internet Plus healthcare in China are broad. The support of national policies, the consolidation of technological foundations, the continuous innovation of application models, and the flourishing development of the industry have provided a strong push and opportunities for the healthy development of Internet Plus healthcare.

Competition Analysis

The competition in China's internet healthcare market is intense, with a high concentration of top-tier enterprises and clear stratification among competitors, influenced by the companies' backgrounds and internet traffic advantages. Additionally, there are changes in the healthcare industry chain, with the Internet Plus healthcare industry forming a new chain, facilitating the rapid and orderly exchange of customer demand information upstream, midstream, and downstream, leading to more efficient and convenient capital circulation.

The competition in China's Internet healthcare market includes participants falling into five categories. Firstly, traditional pharmaceutical companies like Pien Tze Huang and Yunnan Baiyao are expanding online businesses. Secondly, conventional medical information technology companies like Weining Health and Neusoft Group are actively transforming and developing online healthcare businesses. The third category includes internet companies, such as JD.com, Alibaba, and Baidu, entering the healthcare sector and leveraging their traffic advantages. The fourth category consists of medical and healthcare-related entities, such as insurance funds and pharmaceutical distributors, leveraging the internet to create new business models, as seen in Ping An Good Doctor. The final category comprises new enterprises, such as Chunyu Doctor, WeDoctor, and Zhuojian Technology, providing healthcare services through the Internet.

From another perspective, according to public data from the Hurun Brand List, the competition in China's Internet healthcare industry is stratified. Enterprises can be classified into different tiers based on their valuations. The top-tier enterprises have valuations exceeding 20 billion yuan, mainly represented by traditional pharmaceutical companies such as Pien Tze Huang and Yunnan Baiyao. The second-tier enterprises have valuations exceeding 10 billion yuan, including AliHealth and JD Health, which entered the market leveraging their internet traffic advantages. The third-tier enterprises have valuations below 10 billion yuan, with Ping An Good Doctor being the only one exceeding this mark, while others have relatively lower valuations. Subsequent tiers have even lower valuations, indicating weaker competitiveness.

Forecast for This Market

Looking ahead, the Internet healthcare market holds limitless potential. Emerging information technologies such as artificial intelligence, healthcare big data, and precision medicine are becoming significant drivers of healthcare service development. As a new service model, Internet Plus Healthcare will actively integrate with these new technologies, accelerating the formation of new business formats.

Firstly, the combination of Internet Plus healthcare and artificial intelligence will play a crucial role in clinical auxiliary diagnosis, improving the efficiency of doctors and overcoming limitations in healthcare service resources. With the assistance of artificial intelligence, doctors can make more accurate diagnoses and provide better medical services.

Secondly, combining Internet Plus healthcare and precision medicine will deepen the connotation of personalized services. By integrating extensive data analysis and individual genetic information, more personalized medical solutions and health management recommendations can be provided to patients, enhancing treatment and prevention effectiveness.

Furthermore, integrating Internet Plus healthcare with virtual reality technology will contribute to cultivating medical talent and remote healthcare. Virtual reality technology can provide realistic simulation environments, assisting medical students in low-cost, high-efficiency training and making remote healthcare more tangible and accessible for patients to receive professional medical services.

Finally, Internet Plus healthcare itself will also drive the development of new technologies. As an integrated platform for healthcare big data, Internet Plus Healthcare will provide application scenarios for new technologies and necessary data support for further development, promoting their application in the medical field.

Development and Strategy

Germination Stage

In the early stages of entrepreneurship, WeDoctor faced issues such as the lack of structural relationships and institutional norms in the Internet medical field. However, its founders recognized the gap between China's medical and advanced Western systems. By intensely studying the dynamics of China's medical industry, WeDoctor explored new medical service models suitable for the Chinese context (Chen, 2017). Although the initially envisioned family health management model could not be implemented due to China's medical regulatory environment, continuous exploration led the WeDoctor team to gain profound insights into the Chinese medical industry, clarifying the direction of institutional entrepreneurship based on industry insights.

With the emergence of new technologies, the medical field underwent a "sudden shock" in its institutional structure, leading to the entry of numerous new entities and sparking localized entrepreneurship. Positioned at the edge of this field, WeDoctor rapidly established an efficient appointment registration service platform using its technological advantages and foundation (Meng et al., 2017). By stimulating network effects through subsidies, WeDoctor gained competitive discourse power compared to other institutional entrepreneurs, qualifying for negotiations with local governments. Subsequently, to obtain regulatory legitimacy from the government, WeDoctor adopted a negotiation strategy with local governments, elucidating the economic benefits of innovative solutions while facilitating regulatory oversight and making the risks of the creative solutions manageable.

With competitive discourse power relative to other institutional entrepreneurs and cooperation with local governments, WeDoctor successfully piloted its innovative solutions. Through pilot practices, WeDoctor gained recognition from the central government and became a leader in the internet medical field. Through cooperation with the Tongxiang municipal government, WeDoctor obtained a medical institution practice license and established the first internet hospital in Wuzhen, realizing a full-cycle closed-loop model of online diagnosis and treatment, prescription circulation, online medical insurance payment, and door-to-door drug delivery.

Demonstration Stage

In the initial phase of the demonstration stage of WeDoctor's entrepreneurship, the company established a dominant position in the Internet medical field through negotiations with local governments and piloting innovative solutions (Li & Li, 2021). However, due to the influence of old institutional norms in the field, other stakeholders held biases against Internet medicine compliance and did not recognize WeDoctor's innovative solutions. To gain recognition and support from different stakeholders, WeDoctor invested in constructing relationships with significant stakeholders, resulting in unstable relationships among field members.

Nevertheless, WeDoctor still needed more resources to legitimize its entrepreneurial propositions, which were dispersed among different stakeholders. Consequently, WeDoctor collaborated with hospitals and medical practitioner users, winning partners through resource exchange, activation, and value enhancement strategies. Additionally, WeDoctor leveraged its technological advantages to assist local governments in achieving political performance. This allowed WeDoctor to aggregate the demands of significant stakeholders, forming broad social influence. Based on its scalable, innovative solution output and leading position in the Internet medical field, WeDoctor actively negotiated with the central government, urging the formulation of policies conducive to the development of Internet medicine and presenting policy suggestions to the central government.

With its technological efficiency and widespread influence in Internet medical innovation, WeDoctor successfully promoted the central government's demonstration of regulatory legitimacy for Internet medicine (Xu et al., 2021). As a result, the central government issued a policy document known as "Opinions on Promoting the Development of 'Internet + Medical Health,'" referred to as Document No. 26 within the industry. This document confirmed the legality of Internet medicine and enabled its nationwide promotion.

Theorisation Stage

In the early phase of the theoretical stage of WeDoctor's entrepreneurship, it had already achieved central regulatory legitimacy for internet medicine through innovative practices such as internet hospitals, chronic disease medical alliances, pharmaceutical procurement, and internet + health poverty alleviation (Wei et al., 2023). Stakeholders in the internet medical field began innovative entrepreneurial activities under the guidance of the central government's opinions on internet medicine. WeDoctor had established definite relationships with significant stakeholders, with bidirectional interaction among multiple stakeholders.

At this point, to address the inefficiency of traditional medical services, WeDoctor conducted in-depth analyses, dividing the problem into three aspects: pharmaceuticals, medical services, and medical insurance. It then pursued local innovations in these areas. By providing modular technological solutions, WeDoctor developed three major innovative models: "Internet + Pharmaceuticals," "Internet + Medical Services," and "Internet + Medical Insurance." These innovative models were not merely theoretical but had practical cases supporting them. For example, Sanming WeDoctor progressed in pharmaceutical procurement, Tianjin WeDoctor succeeded in grassroots medical health community construction, and Taian WeDoctor progressed in chronic disease fund management. Moreover, these models were characterized by simplicity and ease of promotion.

To obtain normative legitimacy for innovative models, WeDoctor actively responded to national strategies and emergency needs, participating in poverty alleviation, epidemic prevention, and control activities (Gao et al., 2019). WeDoctor's internet medical innovation models gained recognition and honors at national and industry levels. Through official and mainstream media publicity and government guidance, WeDoctor's innovative models gained recognition of normative legitimacy. For example, the Health Commission recognized Tianjin WeDoctor as one of the top ten new measures for "promoting medical reform and serving the health of the people" (2020), becoming the only internet hospital to receive this honor.

Diffusion Stage

In the diffusion stage, with the central government's clarification of Internet medical regulations and the issuance of responsive policy documents by various regions, other actors have actively promoted innovative models in the Internet medical field, leading to maturation and intensified competition in WeDoctor's field.

To address this issue, WeDoctor adopted various strategic actions. Firstly, WeDoctor expanded innovative models to different scenarios and user bases through platform envelopment and organizational strategies. They provided the most suitable internet medical modules based on user needs. They gradually promoted other modules while replicating innovative models in smart homes, future communities, large groups, regional health communities, and different scenarios. Secondly, WeDoctor employed organizational strategies such as political authority and relationship bridging to penetrate potential customer markets quickly. They leveraged central government policies and endorsements from local government leaders, actively pressuring local government medical reform departments to obtain opportunities for innovative model penetration. Meanwhile, they collaborated with partners with good government relations to gain opportunities to dialogue with local governments, rapidly entering local medical service markets. Finally, WeDoctor built an efficient and convenient business reception system, including online and offline exhibition halls, business reception teams, etc., and constructed an integrated media matrix for internal and external communication, extensively publicizing its internet medical innovation models. Based on the benefits of their innovative models, WeDoctor persuaded potential customers to accept them, accelerating innovation diffusion.

Through these strategic actions, WeDoctor achieved rapid diffusion of innovative models and widespread public acceptance. They successfully embedded innovative models into existing normative systems, promoting the objectification of innovative models and gaining cognitive legitimacy for internet medicine among the public. WeDoctor's innovative models have helped implement centralized procurement schemes in 105 cities in 22 provinces, covering more than 450 million people (We-Doctor, 2024). The WeDoctor app has become an essential software for the public.

THE PEOPLE BEHIND THE UNICORN

Liao Jieyuan is the founder of WeDoctor. His entrepreneurial story stems from his personal experience with medical difficulties (Jiang, 2021). After accumulating rich technical experience at companies like iFlytek, Liao Jieyuan founded WeDoctor in 2010 to revolutionize the Chinese healthcare industry through the internet and technology. However, the establishment of WeDoctor had its challenges. He faced various obstacles within the Chinese healthcare system, including difficulties in hospital cooperation and industry barriers. Nonetheless, with unwavering faith and determination, Liao Jieyuan overcame these obstacles and established WeDoctor's first successful partnership with top medical institutions like Huashan Hospital, gradually expanding its scope of collaboration and garnering recognition from millions of users.

Growing up, Liao Jieyuan was influenced by the spirit of the Communist Revolution and was instilled with the values of serving the people in his hometown, which was a starting point for the Red Army's Long March. This upbringing and regional culture deeply ingrained in him a sense of duty and responsibility. Therefore, after founding Weiyi, he did not forget his original intention but actively explored ways to utilize the internet and medical technology to address healthcare challenges in impoverished rural areas. He established China's first Internet hospital, Wuzhen Internet Hospital, and implemented the "Internet + Healthcare" poverty alleviation project in disadvantaged regions of both central-western and eastern provinces.

Through initiatives such as online appointment services, family doctor signing programs, medical equipment donations, and remote diagnosis and treatment systems, Weiyi elevated medical services in remote areas, enabling impoverished populations to access professional healthcare without leaving their villages. Liao Jieyuan's efforts have been highly recognized by various sectors of society, with his achievements even acknowledged by the Office of the National Poverty Alleviation and Award Selection Committee, making him a role model in poverty alleviation efforts.

FUTURE PROJECTS

In the future, WeDoctor will optimize its plans and development directions on multiple fronts to achieve the vigorous development of Internet + Healthcare (Yuan, 2023).

Firstly, WeDoctor can fully leverage the characteristics of the Internet, combined with information technology, to deeply integrate with medical and health informationization, addressing issues such as uneven distribution of medical resources, lack of information sharing, and poor user experience. This means WeDoctor needs to optimize the allocation of healthcare resources, enhance the efficiency of healthcare resource utilization, achieve healthcare data interoperability, improve user experience, and innovate healthcare services' types and delivery methods (Li et al., 2022).

Secondly, WeDoctor should prioritize healthcare as the core, emphasizing demand-driven and problem-oriented approaches. This means WeDoctor needs to adhere to the essence of healthcare services and the principles of public welfare, focusing on solving practical problems in healthcare services, driving industry upgrades through technological innovation, and continuously exploring innovative applications and service models. Additionally, WeDoctor should prioritize value creation as a core objective. This implies that WeDoctor should focus on rapid development and capital-driven growth and emphasize long-term accumulation and creation of genuine value. WeDoctor must address pain points in healthcare services, find the best ways to integrate with the Internet, and achieve sustainable development.

Finally, WeDoctor needs to embrace a sound ecological mindset. WeDoctor cannot exist in isolation but must integrate with multiple resources to form an Internet-based healthcare ecosystem. WeDoctor must build an open platform to achieve mutual benefits and win-win outcomes for sustainable development.

CONCLUSION

WeDoctor plays a crucial role in China's internet healthcare sector. It has successfully integrated online and offline medical services, establishing exemplary and standardized Internet healthcare models through innovative practices and cooperation with the government. With the rapid development of internet healthcare, WeDoctor's successful experiences provide valuable insights for the industry's future. In the future, WeDoctor should continue prioritizing healthcare services, emphasizing value creation, and ensuring safety and order. Governments should enact policies and regulations conducive to the development of Internet healthcare.

REFERENCES

Chen, X. (2017). Research status and prospects of Internet healthcare. *People's Forum: Academic Frontier, 24*, 40-47+95. DOI:10.16619/j.cnki.rmltxsqy.2017.24.005

Gao, S. Y., Ma, X. H., & Zhang, Y. (2019). Research on the driving factors and driving mechanism of business model innovation of shared medical enterprises: A case study based on WeDoctor. *Lanzhou Journal*, 09, 149–163.

Jiang, T. Y. (2021, July 9). The road of China's digital healthcare from the growth of WeDoctor. *Health Newspaper*, 6.

Li, X. Q., & Li, N. (2021). Research on the business model of Internet hospitals. *Software*, 12, 1–3.

Li, Z. X., Li, W., Guo, X., Han, W., & Wang, H. L. (2022). Research the intelligent service model based on "Internet Plus Medical Care". *China New Communications*, 14, 87–89.

Meng, Q., Yin, X., & Liang, C. (2017). Overview of the current situation and development of "Internet Plus Healthcare" in China. *Chinese Journal of Health Information Management*, 02, 110–118.

WeDoctor. (2024). *WeDoctor-Internet Hospital [Mobile application software]*. Huawei AppGallery. https://appgallery.huawei.com/app/C10193357

Wei, J., Su, Z. H., & Liu, Y. (2023). Research on the entrepreneurial process mechanism of emerging field platform-type enterprises. *Management World*, 09, 158–177. DOI:10.19744/j.cnki.11-1235/f.2023.0113

Xu, H., Zhou, Q., & Yu, C. (2021). Empowerment mechanism of internet platforms under sudden changes: A longitudinal case study of WeDoctor platform. *Research and Development Management*, 01, 149–161. DOI:10.13581/j.cnki.rdm.20201854

Yuan, S. Y. (2023). *Study the profit model and its effects on "Internet Plus" medical health enterprises* [Master's thesis, Chongqing University of Technology]. https://kns.cnki.net/kcms2/article/EXECUTIVE SUMMARY?v=HR7ide6_o4T_JzBSpff75560rNIkr39nFAyjl4qfQWXRvRzPx-yox8TqYaO0C_YEEPErjYhYWSCzgpMEDMyFi-smQzTzrcc4Yc6xz-BN-HKBX0X_4JnQ1VW6RkXMxfQE&uniplatform=NZKPT&language=CHS

KEY TERMS AND DEFINITIONS

Central-Level Bargaining: The process where the central government or relevant authorities negotiate, discuss, and reach consensus with enterprises, institutions, etc., nationwide on the prices of specific affairs or services, aiming to unify and coordinate price levels nationwide, safeguard national interests, and promote economic development.

Hierarchical Diagnosis and Treatment: A management model within the healthcare system where medical resources is allocated to patients according to different levels or tiers, allowing patients to choose suitable medical service institutions based on the severity and urgency of their conditions, thus improving the efficiency of medical resource utilization.

Institutional Entrepreneurship: Refers to innovating and reforming within existing institutional frameworks to address social issues or meet market demands, thereby achieving economic development and social progress.

Local Bargaining: The process where local governments or relevant authorities negotiate, discuss, and reach consensus with enterprises, institutions, etc., on the prices of specific affairs or services, aiming to safeguard local interests and promote economic development.

Platform Enterprise: Enterprises that use internet technology to establish online platforms connecting supply and demand sides, providing various services or products, such as Alibaba, Tencent, etc.

Poverty Alleviation and Eradication: A series of policies and measures adopted by governments and various sectors of society to address poverty issues. These measures aim to improve the production and living conditions of impoverished areas and populations, ultimately achieving poverty alleviation and prosperity.

Shared Platform: A platform established through the Internet or other technological means to facilitate the sharing of resources or services among multiple parties, aiming to optimize resource utilization and enhance efficiency, such as bike-sharing programs, shared office spaces, etc.

Chapter 10
Weilong:
Journey From Regional Delicacy to Global Brand

Zihui Yang

Beijing Normal University-Hong Kong Baptist University United International College, China

EXECUTIVE SUMMARY

This case study explores the rise of Weilong, a leading player in China's spicy snack market, examining its transformation from a regional brand to a national and international powerhouse. Led by CEO Liu Weiping and CFO Peng Hongzhi, Weilong strategically navigated challenges like intense market competition and low brand loyalty through innovative branding, extensive market expansion, and effective cultural promotion. The case details Weilong's journey from localized marketing strategies in Henan province to national prominence, leveraging digital platforms and cultural resonance to engage a youthful consumer base. It highlights key strategies such as product innovation, diversified marketing campaigns, and CSR initiatives, showcasing how Weilong capitalized on China's spicy snack craze while promoting traditional Chinese culture globally. Through meticulous market positioning and operational optimization, Weilong exemplifies effective growth strategies in the dynamic Chinese consumer goods sector.

INTRODUCTION

Weilong Company, located in Luohe, Henan Province, is a modern firm that focuses on producing spicy snacks. The organization aims to promote Chinese culture globally by distributing traditional and delicious food while promoting a healthy lifestyle. The organization also seeks to use digital intelligence and eventually build

DOI: 10.4018/979-8-3693-2921-4.ch010

a prosperous enterprise that offers joy and satisfaction to people. Looking ahead, Weilong aims to be a pivotal player in developing and enhancing industry ecosystems. The company's ethos is rooted in consumer-centricity and innovation, and it is committed to fostering transparency, fairness, and equity within the Weilong ecosystem. This approach is designed to accelerate the growth of the company's exceptional team and empower partners to participate actively in the platform and ecosystem development. In that endeavor, Weilong has proactively addressed public concerns about the cleanliness of its spicy strips production process. By employing a fully automated aseptic manufacturing workshop and having professional photographers document the process, the company effectively showcases the hygiene and modernity of its operations. This strategy has been fruitful, with the photos gaining considerable traction on Weibo and attracting an expanding customer base.

UNICORN DESCRIPTION

Brief History of the Unicorn

Every region has its unique way of catering to its inhabitants. The inception of Weilong can be traced back to the creator's experience in Henan, where the distinct and delightful flavor of beef gluten noodles inspired him. This led to developing Weilong spicy strips, using carefully selected raw ingredients to capture and enhance the unique taste (Liu, 2023). Initially, Weilong was only available in Henan. However, by 2010, the brand had grown significantly and began to leverage celebrity endorsements to boost product sales. Recognizing the potential of e-commerce, Weilong established its online presence on JD.com in 2017, resulting in a substantial increase in product sales online. In 2019, Weilong strategically integrated its online and offline sales channels to reach a broader market. The brand's growth trajectory continued, and by 2022, Weilong was officially listed on the Hong Kong Stock Exchange, enhancing its reputation and corporate value (Weilong, 2021). With the advancement of technology, Weilong has successfully expanded globally. It has secured a leading position in the spicy strip sector, attributed to its effective use of the Internet, continuous innovation, and efficient marketing strategies (Gao, 2015).

Business Model

Weilong is predominantly known for its trendy and casual goods. The company's primary target demographic is the younger generation. Its comprehensive sales strategy encompasses offline stores, online proprietary stores, and online dealer distribution. Weilong actively engages with customers, agents, wholesalers, convenience stores, and online shopping platforms to foster robust relationships. The company is also keen on establishing solid partnerships with manufacturing machinery suppliers, raw material suppliers, and third-party logistics companies (Shen, 2022). Weilong's strategic focus lies in bolstering brand recognition, advancing manufacturing technology, and broadening its product research and development scope. Additionally, the company aims to expand its brand marketing and sales network across multiple channels to reach a wider audience.

Product and Services

Flavored Flour Production

Liu Weiping, the founder of Weilong, initially invented "eel noodles" by adding chili to beef tendon noodles, giving them an eel-like appearance. However, due to transcription difficulties, the name was later changed to "fish sticks" (Jiang, 2023). Owing to its unique spicy flavor, this dish quickly gained popularity and is now commonly called "spicy strips." The enticing blend of tangy, sweet, and salty flavors enhances mood and helps alleviate anxiety and pessimism, providing a calming effect.

The popularity of Weilong's spicy noodles first surged among Henan residents before spreading across the nation. Weilong, specializing in spicy flavors, understands the importance of customer engagement and tailoring its products to suit different tastes across various markets. Over the past two decades, Weilong has extensively researched the preferences of spicy food lovers in other regions. This has allowed the company to offer a wide range of spicy flavors, from spicy, sour, and hot to pungent, catering to varying degrees of spiciness preferred by customers, ranging from mild to intense.

Initially, spicy strips were perceived as "junk food," "unhealthy," and "unclean." Weilong aimed to counteract these stereotypes by emphasizing its products' health benefits and cleanliness, ensuring customers enjoy delicious and safe food. This is achieved by enhancing the manufacturing process to ensure safety, security, and high quality throughout the supply chain (Jiang, 2023). Weilong carefully manages and monitors the sources of raw materials from its suppliers, procuring agricultural items directly from their origin to ensure safety. Strategic partnerships have been formed with premium raw material suppliers, such as COFCO granaries and COFCO oil, to provide a consistent and reliable supply. China National Cereals, Oils and Foodstuffs Corporation is the largest supplier of diversified products and services in China's agricultural products and food industry.

Regarding production technology, Weilong has continually upgraded its equipment to achieve automated manufacturing. The production workshop utilizes five main types of equipment: powder mixing, curing, seasoning, sterilization, and packaging, which includes automatic feeding and packaging to replace manual labor (Jiang, 2023). Customers are highly interested in the processing methods of high-quality raw materials. In 2014, Weilong established a fully automated aseptic production workshop that met 100,000-level cleanliness standards.

This workplace utilized modern automation technology and implemented an intelligent and digital update system. The facility offers a full range of digital inspection technologies that can monitor the operational status of each production line and accurately track capacity-related data. Weilong has recently invested in intelligent manufacturing, incorporating new technologies like robots to enhance production quality and efficiency (Liu, 2023). In 2021, it partnered strategically with Tencent to establish a specialized cloud platform for businesses using its advanced technologies, products, and ecosystem resources. This initiative aims to achieve complete digitalization across production, operations, and management levels, helping companies accelerate their transformation and upgrade processes.

Weilong operates five main production locations that efficiently monitor upstream control in the industrial chain. All production areas are equipped with standardized, clean workshops. By using automated production technology to meticulously oversee each stage, the standardized production facility strictly adheres to on-site procedures to enhance product manufacturing (Liu, 2023). Integrating advanced technology and equipment with traditional flavors has significantly improved product quality, providing customers with strong health assurance.

Weilong adheres to a philosophy of originality and minimal processing, focusing on 0 trans fatty acids and 0 preservatives. They use a non-fried, self-developed extrusion and cooking method to preserve the product's taste and characteristics while prioritizing safety and health (Ding, 2022). The spicy strips are prepared using a non-fried extrusion and cooking technique with flour as the main ingredient, combined with water and approved food additives. They are extruded and cooked at high temperatures to ensure customer safety (Liu, 2023).

Weilong's spicy strips undergo 119 tests, including raw ingredients, manufacturing, and consumer stages. Eighty-five index tests are required for raw material and process testing, while 34 tests are needed for finished product testing. Weilong also uses nitrogen-filled packaging to ensure customers can enjoy the fresh and healthy taste of the product. Weilong's commitment to "assured spicy strips" is evident in its consistent production standards.

Weilong considers food safety and quality to be its top priorities in its operations. The company has identified consumers' concerns about healthy food consumption and has worked on improving its production and processes. As a result, Weilong has stood out in the competitive seasoned noodle products industry and has been consistently moving towards standardization and maturity.

Vegetable Products

The increasing consciousness about health and the shift in consumption patterns have led to a heightened demand for nutritious food. Consumers widely recognize vegetable products as a healthy, nutritious, and convenient meal option. Responding to these market trends, Weilong has stepped up its efforts to research, develop, and market vegetable products. Konjac Shuang, a spicy snack food, is a standout vegetable product that Weilong's research and development team innovated. Known for its Q-elastic silky texture and spicy, aromatic flavor, Konjac Shuang has quickly gained popularity among various consumers. This is particularly true for female customers who appreciate beauty and indulgence and young customers seeking a low-fat, high-fiber diet to meet their strict body management goals. Following the success of Konjac Shuang, they launched the Little Witch Konjac Vegetarian Hairy Belly. This product, part of the Little Witch Konjac Vegetarian Tribe series, is a high-fiber meal that caters to consumers' desire for healthy options and adds variety to its product line (Xin, 2023).

Soy Products

In addition to its vegetable product line, Weilong has expanded its offerings to include various soy products and other items. Among these is the Sichuan spicy soft bean skin, which features tender bean skin and 78° cooked eggs. This product offers a flavorful experience that is rich yet not overly greasy, with the aromatic combination of cumin and sesame seeds enhancing its aroma. The company has also succeeded with its lively braised eggs, selling over 53,490,000 pieces. This food item is soft and sticky, ensuring it is safe to consume without choking, making it suitable for young and elderly consumers. It is high in protein, boasting a Nutrient Reference Value (NRV) of 23%. This makes it an excellent choice for a post-meal snack or a nutritious breakfast.

Weilong's expansion into the soy product market is a strategic move to cater to diverse consumer preferences. The company aims to provide items that appeal to a wide range of consumers, and the quality of these soy products is rigorously monitored to ensure they are free from preservatives and inferior raw materials. The result is a flavorful, high-quality product that meets the growing demand for spicy soy products. This commitment to quality and variety underscores Weilong's dedication to meeting its customers' needs while maintaining the highest standards of product safety and quality (Liu, 2023; Ding, 2022).

Customers

Pupils from Primary to Secondary Education

Pupils from primary to secondary education exhibit a keen ability to analyze food. They prefer uniqueness and creativity over conventional and monotonous structures and value innovation over repetition. Hot strips, offering a spectrum of flavors such as spicy, numbing, sweet, and more, cater to these pupils' desire for taste stimulation. The unique texture and innovative flavor profile of these snacks can captivate the curiosity and interest of pupils. Spicy bars are more cost-effective than other costly snacks, making them an ideal selection for budget-conscious students. Within a school setting, pupils might recommend or share spicy noodles with their peers, fostering a group behavior that encourages exploration of new food experiences and cultivates a liking for spicy noodles as a delightful snack. Numerous small businesses located near schools offer spicy noodles. Pupils frequently buy a pack after school to snack on when bored and to keep their mouths busy, helping to alleviate the stress of a day of studying. Weilong has adapted the packaging of spicy strips from large to compact and changed the theme color from warm hues to basic white to make it easier for children to carry them to school. The new packaging is more visually appealing and convenient for pupils to bring to school and share with friends.

Working Adults

Working adults encounter substantial job stress daily. They form the backbone of society, managing work-related responsibilities and caring for older people and children at home, often leaving home early and returning late. They face pressures from superiors and subordinates, leaving little time for relaxation and pushing them to continue despite work stress. Picking a pack of Weilong hot strips from the store after a meal can be an effective stress reliever (Jiang, 2023). Weilong's spicy Tiao is not just spicy; it combines salty and sweet flavors to boost moods and combat stress and negativity. The rich-tasting spicy strips have a deep emotional value for individuals, satisfying their need for personalized and fresh experiences (Weilong, 2024). Spicy noodles have become common in workplace pantries and are often shared among colleagues. Spicy strips have become more than just regular snacks for those juggling work and family responsibilities. They serve as an effective method to manage their emotions.

Retirees

Contrary to the common belief that older people do not enjoy snacks, Weilong Spicy Tiao is popular among many seniors. One plausible reason is that due to diminished taste perception, elderly individuals often opt for more flavorful food to stimulate their senses. Additionally, as people age, they are likely to face increased life stress, and stimulating food like spicy snacks may help alleviate this stress. It provides emotional satisfaction and enhances their sense of happiness. Eating strongly flavored food can often trigger elderly individuals to recall memories and emotional events from their younger days. This memory association can bring comfort and joy and improve their emotional well-being. Weilong offers spicy noodles and triggers consumers' nostalgia for their youth. The company has redesigned its flagship store in a nostalgic vintage style to attract a broader customer base. This move enhances traditional memory and enjoyment, emotionally resonating with customers and significantly increasing the purchase rate (Gao, 2015).

Market Analysis

Initial Market Conditions

The leisure snack industry in China took root in the 1980s, initially under the control of foreign capital and joint ventures. The market was characterized by a limited range of product types, primarily imported goods such as candy and chocolate. During this era, overseas enterprises were pivotal in educating consumers and fostering industrial development (Eason, 2023). Understanding the snack category involves addressing customer demand. Sweet confections like candy compote offer a sugary delight, while crunchy snacks like potato chips and biscuits cater to those seeking a crisp texture, satisfying customers' taste desires. Specialized markets such as nuts, and meat snacks cater to those searching for nutritional options. Individual taste preferences have driven the emergence of new sectors like hot strips and seasoned vegetable products.

In the 1970s, small workshops in Hunan began to produce a spicy snack with chili pepper as the main ingredient. These snacks, made from paprika and wheat using a unique processing technique, were initially only available in local markets. However, their distinct flavor and texture led to their widespread popularity and distribution nationwide. The rising demand for spicy strips led to numerous companies beginning to produce and market this delicacy. Different regions have distinct industrial technology characteristics and preferences. For instance, Hunan's spicy strips are known for their spicy solid flavor from red oil and chili powder, while Sichuan's spicy strips emphasize spiciness with ingredients like peppercorns. Over time, the spicy strip industry has evolved, leading to the creation of more innovative products.

Market Evolution to Present Day

At present, there are approximately 1,000 spicy strip manufacturers in China. Research suggests that China's spicy strip industry has experienced four development stages: the developing embryonic period (1998-2006), the industry standardization period (2007-2014), the market explosion period (2015-2019), and the brand scale development period (2020-present). In 1998, spicy strips gained popularity in Hunan during the nascent embryonic phase. Before the market was formalized, there was little concentration as most products were localized, and the industry needed standards. 2005, the national spicy strip industry underwent its first restructuring due to a rectification trend. This restructuring marked the transition of the spicy strip market into the industry standardization phase. As industry regulations became more established, the spicy strip market evolved. In 2015, the rise of e-commerce brought significant channel traffic benefits to spicy noodle companies, leading to innovative sales models and increased channel rewards. The e-commerce sector is experiencing tremendous growth, with online and offline retail models expanding. Spicy strip companies are enhancing their growth by leveraging e-commerce traffic advantages. In 2019, the spicy noodle market was valued at 65.1 billion yuan, displaying an annual growth rate of 8.59%. The spicy noodle sector has continued to expand. Currently, with over 1,000 spicy strip manufacturers in China, it is projected that the market size for spicy strips in China will reach approximately 100 billion by 2026. Companies like Weilong have secured a significant market share in the spicy strip industry due to their brand culture, encouraging several retail brands to venture into the spicy strip market.

Competitive Strengths

Appropriately Selected Path

Weilong's triumph can be attributed to the inherent popularity of the spicy dish. Domestic snacks can be categorized into two primary groups based on flavor: "spicy" and "other." Owing to their culinary tradition of using salt and chili peppers for seasoning, Chinese people have a unique fondness for salty and spicy food. Conversely, spicy food consumption can provide pleasure and alleviate stress from a busy lifestyle. Spicy food has been on the rise in major cities in recent years.

Weilong's spicy snack stands out with its "heavy oil," "heavy salt," and "heavy, spicy" flavors, which resonate strongly with Chinese tastes, making it a preferred choice among the Chinese population (Yang, 2024). The preference for spicy flavors in snack purchases has been on the rise among consumers, leading to significant growth in the spicy snack sector that has outpaced the entire market for a prolonged period. Unlike the salty and spicy snack market in the United States, which primarily focuses on puffed snacks, China has six main subcategories of spicy snacks: spicy meat and aquatic products, seasoned noodles (usually spicy strips), spicy vegetable snacks, spicy crispy snacks, spicy roasted seeds and nuts, and spicy tofu snacks.

Seasoned noodle and leisure vegetable products are the industry's two most significant and fastest-growing sub-categories, offering more versatility and growth opportunities. Compared to melon seeds, these two categories can offer a broader range of flavors, such as sweet and spicy, sour and spicy, and varying levels of spiciness. Additionally, spicy strips can produce large and small gluten, extensive and small spicy sticks, spicy slices, and spicy blocks. Leisure vegetable products within these categories can also utilize different vegetable varieties, indicating a more significant growth potential. Weilong's primary products are focused on these two categories and are part of the high-growth elevator track.

Product Differentiation

The spicy snack industry has low entry barriers and many participants. Weilong has excelled in all primary categories simultaneously, surpassing the combined market share of the 2nd to fifth firms. It is crucial to investigate the underlying reasons, given that the product has unique characteristics. Weilong's early renowned product was sweet and spicy strips. Unlike the prevalent salty and spicy items on the market at that time, the addition of sugar to create a lovely and tangy flavor not only tempered the spiciness but also introduced a new appealing element that better aligned with the public's taste preferences (Gan, 2023). This change also increased the product's addictive nature and facilitated the promotion of repeat purchases.

Weilong has expanded its product line with spicy options like large gluten, small gluten, and kiss mouth roast and a new series like "Spicy Mala." The company has improved the flavor and texture of its seasoned noodle products by upgrading ingredients, recipes, and processes. As living conditions and education levels have significantly improved, people are shifting from focusing solely on food taste to a more scientific and nutritious diet. At the same time, there has been a widespread increase in body awareness due to the influence of social media. Weilong's new konjac shuang and wind-eaten kelp offer a healthy, tasty, and low-calorie alternative to traditional spicy strips, often associated with being unhealthy. These new products feature a unique spicy blend (Yang, 2024).

Branding

The spicy strip market poses challenges for snack companies due to the dominance of large industries, the distinctive characteristics of small enterprises, cheap pricing, narrow profit margins, the persistent association with junk food, and weak brand loyalty among consumers. However, these issues are not a concern for Weilong. Weilong's efforts to increase brand awareness align with the transition from a regional to a national brand. The enhancement of the brand image corresponds to subsequent price increases. The rise in brand exposure correlates with reaching consumers nationwide. The expansion of the young customer base corresponds to attracting individuals most inclined to consume snacks.

Before 2010, Weilong primarily focused its marketing efforts on Henan. It used low-cost strategies like posters and colorful campus flags to generate word-of-mouth among customers, mainly targeting students due to limited financial resources. After 2010, Weilong began a phase of national growth, using various marketing techniques to boost its market share. Weilong has demonstrated that the domestic snack industry's fragmented nature can foster major firms' growth. Additionally, sophisticated marketing strategies can elevate local snacks to a high-end status.

Offline Channel Network Focus

Before 2015, Weilong primarily used traditional sales channels such as local shops, wholesale markets, and family-owned stores. This channel's main advantage is its low pricing, proximity to consumers, and convenient purchasing process. However, establishing such channels necessitates the enterprise to engage with provincial agents, who then handle product distribution within their region. Enterprises need more control over terminals and have poor channel revenues. Since 2015, due to improvements in brand image and national strategy promotion, Weilong products have been increasingly available in shopping supermarkets and chain convenience stores. This has attracted more customers and made spicy snacks with ready-to-eat and impulsive consumption characteristics more accessible to consumers, aligning with young consumers' purchasing habits and tendencies.

By the end of 2022, Weilong will have partnered with over 1,847 offline dealers in China, and its goods will be available in more than 143 shopping malls, supermarkets, and chain convenience store operators worldwide (Shi, 2023). Spicy cuisine is a cost-effective and addictive delight that customers in lower-tier cities with lower incomes may purchase in the long run, unlike more fulfilling items like meat. Lower-tier cities have a larger market share and a faster growth rate for spicy snacks than first—and second-tier cities.

Global Marketing

Weilong's delicacy is derived from traditional Chinese noodle products with conventional Chinese cultural characteristics. Recently, the company has been actively exploring the profound cultural significance of the brand, aiming to promote the traditional culture of excellence to the world through the brand strategy. Weilong adheres to the purpose of making people all over the world fall in love with Chinese taste, constantly explores the international market, and strives to let people all over the world feel the taste of traditional Chinese culture (Cai, 2023).

Through an open and inclusive corporate culture and innovative spirit, Weilong has penetrated international markets, entered different countries, and attracted consumers worldwide. Through innovation, technological iteration, and creative marketing campaigns, Weilong Delicacy combines traditional Chinese culture with contemporary marketing principles to showcase the appeal of Chinese culture to a global audience (Cai, 2024). While spreading the excellent traditional Chinese culture, it expands the company's target market and increases the company's revenue.

Weilong's New Year's advertisement appeared in Times Square in New York, aligning with the corporate vision of promoting Chinese flavors to the world, allowing overseas Chinese to experience the essence of Chinese New Year even abroad (Cai, 2024). This made the overseas Chinese feel the care of the motherland during the New Year and allowed foreign friends to feel the warmth of Chinese culture, attracting people's attention. Weilong received high praise for this New Year's event and gained a new batch of consumers.

High-Level CSR

In response to the national energy conservation and emission reduction policy, Weilong vigorously develops the photovoltaic industry, promotes energy conservation and emission reduction, and strives to be environmentally friendly, demonstrating Weilong's sense of social responsibility (Weilong, 2021). In addition to the environment-friendly policy, Weilong actively participates in charity activities. In September 2021, Weilong provided two primary schools in Luliang County, Shanxi Province, with more than 500 poor children in mountainous areas, a large number of signature food – 78-degree braised eggs, which are worth about 460,000 yuan, providing not only breakfast but also kindness and support for the children in mountainous areas. This move demonstrates Weilong's philanthropic activities, their concern for social well-being, and the accelerated development of the poverty-stricken regions (Weilong, 2021).

Forecast for this Market

China ranks as one of the world's leading snack food markets. Owing to the country's traditional food culture, the spicy flavor has garnered widespread popularity among consumers, offering pleasure, stress relief, and satisfaction. This has made it the fastest-growing segment in the snack food industry, with substantial growth potential (Shan, 2023).

The central and local governments have heightened the management of the spicy strip market, leading to the establishment of industry standards and the expansion of the market size. Production technology has improved, resulting in a specialized, high-quality production process. The spicy strip category in China has been experiencing growth in recent years and is anticipated to prosper in the next five years. By 2026, the market size of China's spicy strip is projected to reach approximately 100 billion yuan.

The industry's division of labor predominantly determines the future of the spicy strip business. Various companies in the spicy strip industry are engaged in activities ranging from planting to processing, packaging, and marketing. A larger consumer space has been created in the era of processing, including the development of brands and hot food companies. During the initial phase of the spicy strip industry's growth, the market share of spicy strips was relatively low. However, due to the promotional efforts by various spicy strip brands, the industry's specialization has significantly improved, leading to increased consumer interest in purchasing. The rise of the media has concurrently created opportunities for the spicy strip sector. As the spicy strip sector has evolved, it has begun to engage with digital media technologies. Specifically, adopting promotional technologies has enabled companies to effectively disseminate information about spicy bars and reach a broader audience (Xing, 2022). Companies are projected to see a substantial increase in product demand in 2023.

In the future, technological advancements should be leveraged to update raw materials, ingredients, and methods in the spicy strip business to overcome existing limitations. Firstly, improving the scientific approach, technological advancements, and investing in the contents of raw materials are necessary to address the issue of raw material blending and configuration to produce softer and more flavorful spicy strips. Secondly, the manufacturing process should transition from traditional manual production to sophisticated automated lines to optimize labor impacts, enhance efficiency, and improve quality. The spicy strip industry should innovate new types to expand its market base. Incorporating flavors such as garlic, hemp, and spicy elements in developing spicy strips to cater to diverse tastes and consumers is crucial. For instance, milder options could be suitable for children and elderly consumers. Additionally, aligning with lifestyle marketing trends by introducing modern and fashionable spicy strip products can enhance market competitiveness.

Government agencies have intensified their strict control to elevate industry standards, ensuring the quality and safety of spicy strips while reducing the prevalence of OEM packaging and substandard varieties. The "National Food Safety Standard for Spicy Noodles" issued by state authorities outlines regulations on variety, raw materials, production requirements, and inspection to ensure spicy noodles meet nutritional and production standards, stand out, and capture the market.

THE PEOPLE BEHIND THE UNICORNS

CEO: LIU Weiping

Mr Liu completed his studies in administration management at Southwest University in Chongqing, graduating in July 2017. He brings over two decades of experience in the snack food industry. Mr. Liu, in partnership with Mr. Liu Fuping, co-founded Ping Ping Foods Factory in 2001, serving as the general manager until September 2004. He continued to lead as the director general of Ping Ping Foods from September 2004 to November 2006. Then, he took on the role of general manager of Zhumadian Ping Ping Foods from November 2006 to July 2014. Since 2014, Mr. Liu has been chairman of Weilong Commerce. As the company's CEO, Weiping Liu is responsible for devising and executing the company's strategy, overseeing daily operations, ensuring the attainment of business objectives, and interacting with external stakeholders on the company's behalf.

CFO: PENG Hongzhi

Mr. Peng earned his bachelor's degree in geographical sciences from Hunan University of Science and Technology in Xiangtan, China, in June 2005. He later obtained a master's degree in cartography and geographic information systems from North-east Normal University in Changchun, China, in July 2008. Mr. Peng has over a decade of experience in operational management. His career includes serving as an engineer at Beijing Aoshi Sports Timing Service Co., Ltd. from March 2007 to June 2008 and at the Guangdong Province Digital Guangdong Research Institute from October 2009 to September 2010. He moved on to become the assistant to the general manager of Ping Ping Foods from October 2010 to March 2013 and the deputy general manager of Beijing Dermat Jiekang Technology Development Co., Ltd. from April 2013 to April 2016. He then served as the director and general manager of Shenzhen Qianhai Xiangming Equity Investment Co., Ltd. from May 2016 to May 2019. From June 2019 to February 2023, he primarily managed the finance center, IT center, and other managerial tasks within the company. Since March 2023, his primary responsibilities have been working in the organization's finance and overseas business development center. As the CFO, he oversees the organization's financial management and strategic planning, including financial reporting, cost control, budgeting, fundraising, and investment decisions.

FUTURE DEVELOPMENT AND STRATEGY

Focus on the Younger Generation

As an innovative company, Weilong is proactively integrating itself into youth culture to become a viral sensation among consumers. To gain popularity, it is essential to "let loose and enjoy," as this aligns with the target customers' behavior and is a fundamental principle of the Internet. Weilong excels at effortlessly embracing enjoyment to the point that it becomes irresistible (Yang, 2022). The younger generations, particularly those born after 1985 and 1990, prefer to source information from social media. Since 2013, Weilong Enterprise's marketing team has effectively utilized social media platforms by partnering with popular Weibo influencers to create and share humorous stickers and jokes related to spicy noodles. Weilong companies use this type of advertising, subtly embedded in humor, to penetrate the extensive market. Weilong quickly gained immense popularity in the post-90s subcultural community and developed a strong association with hot noodles. The phrases "Eat spicy noodles to calm down" and "Eat ten packs of spicy noodles angrily" have become popular among many internet users, serving as iconic spicy noodle references that stimulate the public's entertainment sensibilities (Lin, 2022).

For example, to commemorate the 2016 Double 11 promotion, Weilong designed a 60s-themed poster, inducing a nostalgic mood with its design and imagery. Weilong has successfully captured the interest of young people by blending a cross-winded wind with elements of humor and amusement that are popular among today's youth. Creating a mock social phenomenon by imitating vintage films and television shows to evoke nostalgia is an unusual strategy.

Recently, Wei Long has partnered with well-known youth comics, further solidifying its status as an internet sensation. Storm Man has granted Weilong the right to use the copyright of the emoji package. Weilong's personalized items are attached to the large packaging with a prominent label. Each small box will reveal a unique storm expression upon opening. Many people find the collaboration between the two somewhat puzzling (Gao,2022). Why would two seemingly incompatible companies, one being a food company and the other a comic company based on popular humorous elements on the Internet, come together? Upon closer examination, the partnership between these two organizations is a logical fit. Weilong's online presence is renowned for being entertaining and engaging. Consumers who appreciate Weilong products also enjoy entertainment, gaming, and two-dimensional content. The online presence of the storm is potent, and there is a significant overlap between those who consume Weilong and those who enjoy watching the chaos. The collaboration between the two has introduced a new marketing tool and increased the visibility of both parties.

Sustaining Product Innovation

For enterprises, branding, digitalization, and chain operation are gradually becoming the new directions for future development. As a leading brand of snack foods, Weilong Group will continue to target young consumer groups in its future development, fully utilizing its advantages in geography, technology, resources, and so on. It will also continue to strengthen the scale and standardized production safety of spicy strips. Weilong's primary consumer base comprises young individuals. While youth is constant, eternal youth is elusive. Consumer group consciousness and lifestyles evolve, making it a challenge to stay completely in sync with consumer preferences, especially given the new generation's strong sense of identity and emotional connection to brands. This might necessitate starting from the ground up and re-establishing brand appeal. Weilong must perpetually stay in tune with the current trends set by younger generations (Cai, 2022).

To cater to the varied preferences of customers, Weilong can bolster product research, development, and innovation to offer a range of spicy snack foods that are flavorful, healthy, and nutritious. Concurrently, it should monitor emerging culinary trends and customer preferences to adjust its product strategy swiftly.

Expanding Reach and Optimizing Operations

Weilong can enhance its market reach and brand recognition by expanding its online and offline sales channels. This could involve strengthening collaborations with e-commerce platforms and establishing more official flagship stores or cooperative shops. Moreover, setting up offline or franchise outlets could further augment brand impact. As part of its growth strategy, Weilong can also leverage the growing trend of globalization by marketing its products internationally and expanding into other markets. This would require enhancing product quality and safety control, conducting market research, and adapting products to align with various markets' cultures and consumption patterns (Xing, 2022).

In addition to these strategies, improving supply chain management is crucial for Weilong to save costs, increase efficiency, and maintain product quality. This can be achieved by establishing lasting and dependable relationships with suppliers, ensuring a consistent supply of raw materials, and managing costs effectively. Lastly, Weilong can use digital technologies such as big data and artificial intelligence to reinforce data analysis and consumer insights. This would enable the company to achieve precision marketing and personalized services (Gao, 2022). Simultaneously, it could optimize production processes, enhance production efficiency, and realize digital transformation and intelligent manufacturing, further strengthening its position in the market.

REFERENCES

Caijing. (2024, February 16). *From spicy strips to delicious, Weilong Delicious strongly opens a new era of development in 2024*. Sina. https://finance.sina.com.cn/stock/relnews/hk/2024-02-16/doc-inaifksa4442046.shtml

Ding, Z. (2022). Wei Long: Reshaping quality standards. *China Quality Supervision*, (12), 90.

Interface news. (2024, January 12). The next ten years of Chinese snacks. *Interface News*. https://finance.sina.com.cn/jjxw/2024-01-12/doc-inachqhs1822188.shtml

Jiang, C. (2023). Weilong Food: Turning a 50-cent business into billions. *Zhongguancun*, (01), 32–33.

Lin, S. (2022). Analysis of Weilong's marketing strategy. *The China Business Review*, (05), 44–47. DOI:10.19699/j.cnki.issn2096-0298.2022.05.044

Liu, Y. (2023, March 21). Weilong insists on quality first and guards safety on the tip of the tongue. *China Food Safety News*, B03. DOI:10.28737/n.cnki.nspzl.2023.000556

The Beijing News. (2023, December 29). From spicy strips to spicy snacks, Weilong multi-layout puffed snack track what? *The Beijing News*. https://finance.sina.com.cn/jjxw/2023-12-29/doc-imzzsqhx5780830.shtml

The first strand of the spicy strip. (2023, March 2). Weilong Delicious. https://www.shiyetoutiao.cn/article/110193.html

Weilong. (2021). *Weilong Delicious's Photovoltaic power station grid-connected power generation ceremony was successfully held*. Weilong. https://www.weilongshipin.com/en/xinwenjujiao/134.html

Weilong. (2024). *Weilong Spicy Tiao sells well in 40 countries around the world, capturing the preferences of young people and demonstrating brand competitiveness— China Net*. Weilong. http://zjnews.china.com.cn/yuanchuan/2024-03-28/418541.html

Weilong latiao is a unique choice for contemporary young people. (2023, September 7). Zhuan Lan. https://zhuanlan.zhihu.com/p/654842663

What changes has the spicy strip industry experienced, from snacks at the school gate to a hundred billion industry? (2023, May 31). Bajiahao. https://baijiahao.baidu.com/s?id=1767381814629528454&wfr=spider&for=pc

Why does Weilong stand out in the spicy snack industry? (2023, June 13). Sohu. https://business.sohu.com/a/685424521_121123922

Yang, G. (2024, January 29). Competitiveness is the foundation for enterprises to go global. *Henan Business Daily*, A06. DOI:10.28373/n.cnki.nhnsb.2024.000082

Yang, Y. (2019). Weilong Latiao's Internet Celebrity Training Manual. *Business Observation*, (Z1), 60–63.

Yao, F. (2017). Analysis of the rise of Weilong Spicy Tiao from the perspective of strategic management. *Chinese and Foreign Entrepreneurs*, (19), 99.

KEY TERMS AND DEFINITIONS

Brand Culture: It is essentially a company's heart and soul. It encompasses the values that guide all forms of brand communication, how the company engages with customers, and even how it makes hiring decisions. It's the atmosphere a company cultivates to showcase its brand to the market in an effective, consistent, and competitive way.

Brand Impact: It measures the influence a company's advertisements and marketing efforts have on shaping customer attitudes. This influence can be measured across various channels, including digital, traditional, and a mix of both.

Brand Recognition: It is the ability of consumers to identify a specific brand by its attributes compared to other brands. If a brand has high recognition, customers can easily distinguish it from its competitors.

E-commerce: Also known as electronic commerce, this term describes the buying and selling of goods and services over the Internet. This can involve selling to other businesses, businesses selling to consumers, or even consumers selling to different consumers.

Financial Resources: The funds and assets a company uses to support its activities and cover its expenses. Financial resources could include cash, investments, or other assets that can be used to generate income or pay for services.

Product Variety: This term refers to the diverse range of different types or categories of products that a company offers within a specific market. If a company has a high product variety, it means it offers many different kinds of items.

Supply Chain Management: It involves managing the entire process of moving goods and services to and from a company. It covers everything from obtaining raw materials and components to producing goods and delivering the finished products to the end consumer.

Chapter 11
Guoquan Shihui:
Reforming the Prepared Food Market Through Integrated Supply Chain and Digital Innovation

Yiru Wang

Beijing Normal University-Hong Kong Baptist University United International College, China

EXECUTIVE SUMMARY

This case study examines Guo Quan Shi Hui, a prominent player in China's new retail and prepared food market. Founded by Mingchao Yang, Guo Quan Shi Hui revolutionized the hotpot industry through innovative supply chain management and digital integration. Yang's journey from a night market entrepreneur to a billionaire showcases his strategic vision for building a robust logistics system, collaborating with over 266 ODM plants, and implementing cold chain technology for freshness. The case details Guo Quan Shi Hui's expansion from a small retail outlet to a nationwide network of 10,000 stores, leveraging multi-platform marketing strategies, including TikTok, for consumer engagement. It explores the company's franchise model success, online-offline integration, and plans for global expansion. Guo Quan Shi Hui's story underscores its leadership for blending traditional cuisine with modern business practices, setting a benchmark for industry transformation and consumer-centric innovation.

DOI: 10.4018/979-8-3693-2921-4.ch011

DESCRIPTION OF GUO QUAN SHI HUI

Brief History of Guo Quan Shi Hui

Guo Quan Shi Hui, which won the top ten innovative models of Chinese hot pot in 2019, is a grocery store that sells up to 700 kinds of hotpot and barbecue pre-made food and is almost established within 3 kilometers of central residential communities. Guo Quan Shi Hui is developing at an astounding speed. It successfully and quickly went public on November 2nd, 2023, just seven years after its first offline outlet was established in January 2017 in Zhengzhou, Henan province. As of September 26, 2023, Guo Quan Shi Hui has 9,978 retail stores covering 31 provincial-level administrative regions. In addition, Guo Quan Shi Hui has been honored as "2020 Forbes China High Growth Gazelle Enterprise" and "2021 China Unicorn List Top 30 Consumer Unicorns".

Guo Quan Shi Hui implemented a robust strategy to improve its economies of scale and enhance its profitability. By focusing on raising brand awareness, rapidly expanding its reach, and optimizing costs in the early stages, the company laid a strong foundation for success. Later, Guo Quan Shi Hui gained greater control over its products and operations by investing more in the supply chain and collaborating with manufacturers to co-build production lines. This upstream involvement allowed them to streamline processes, ensure quality, and possibly even reduce costs further.

Business Model

Guo Quan Shi Hui adopts a vertical supply chain integration approach that utilizes timely logistics and cross-docking warehouses. The main objective of Guo Quan Shi Hui is to integrate and enhance efficiently its supply chain. In the upstream sector, Guo Quan Shi Hui utilizes cold chain technology and standardized mass production through cooperation with 266 original design manufacturing (ODM) plants. The approach revolves around a single product and a single factory, focusing exclusively on that factory's most crucial product categories. This is done by providing product design data and equipment support, which ensures quality assurance while effectively addressing production constraints in specific regional factories. This approach enables the client brand, Guo Quan Shi Hui, to concentrate more on core technology, services, and brand promotion.

Products

Guo Quan Shi Hui offers up to 700 products to the market, and these abundant categories significantly increase its potential customer base and revenue. They offer a diverse selection of dishes and beverages. Non-vegetarian options include shrimp sliders, lobster balls, beef balls, beef yellow throat, tripe, duck intestine, duck blood, sliced beef, sliced lamb, and blackened chicken rolls. Vegetarian dishes include mushrooms, lettuce, bok choy, scallops, tofu, broad noodles, winter squash, bean sprouts, pumpkin, potatoes, and other vegetables. They also have a range of barbeque food materials like tilapia, octopus whiskers, chicken wings, lamb chop skewers, and fatty intestine skewers.

Additionally, they offer a variety of beverages like hawthorn juice, sea buckthorn juice, kiwi juice, sour plum soup, yellow peach juice, and almond juice. They have one-person meals like rice with shredded pork and bamboo shoots, canned beef and tomato gumbo, spicy beef hotpot, spicy hotpot, and braised beef with rice. For instant meals, they offer pickled fish, spicy crayfish, hand crackers, and brown sugar mochi. They have fresh food options like squid skewers, shrimp, frozen abalone, and sea-caught small yellowtail. Those who prefer Western-style food have sirloin steak, bacon, black pepper beef spaghetti, tomato beef spaghetti, filet mignon, and German grilled sausage. Lastly, they offer snacks like a gift box, desserts, iced gourds, melon seeds, canned yellow peaches, and brown sugar potpourri.

Customers

Guo Quan Shi Hui targets a specific customer segment consisting of individuals who frequently consume hotpots at home and are sensitive to prices and time consumption. Although hotpot is a popular food option in China, the market for consuming hotpot at home is relatively small. This limits the number of potential customers and profitability. For instance, Guo Quan Shi Hui's gross profit is only 45 per cent compared to the Haidilao Hotpot Restaurant chain's 60 per cent (Guoquan Food (Shanghai) Co., Ltd., 2023). However, Guo Quan Shi Hui's higher single sales, longer brand lifecycle, and enhanced customer stickiness make it a competitive option, helping it gain more comprehensive customer loyalty.

Preparing hotpot materials had several issues before implementing Guo Quan Shi Hui. Customers had to choose between small convenience stores nearby or supermarkets far from their homes. On one hand, the main benefit of smaller grocery stores is their proximity. Especially for homemakers and older people, small grocery stores in the neighborhood offer the goods they need quickly and conveniently. However, the most significant disadvantage is that the items offered are limited due to the store's small size. Smaller grocery stores provide few options for complicated meals like hotpot or barbeque.

On the other hand, larger supermarkets offer a wide variety of food materials, and they can provide almost everything that a complicated meal requires. Additionally, the items offered are fresh and of higher quality than those sold at smaller grocery stores. However, the downside of larger supermarkets is that they are often located farther away, which adds to the energy and monetary consumption of homemakers and older people.

Based on the benefits and disadvantages of both the groceries and supermarkets mentioned above, Guo Quan Shi Hui offers the most convenient online and offline purchase and delivery services for people living in areas needing short distances and abundant food materials. This approach successfully eliminates the need for more basic hotpot pre-made food options compared to small supermarkets in the neighborhood and the high time and energy costs associated with travelling to larger supermarkets far from residential areas. Guo Quan Shi Hui's ample food options and convenient and close location are what attracts a large number of potential customers.

MARKET ANALYSIS

Situation of the Market

Hotpot New Retail Market

Let us first acknowledge the new retail market. The most significant difference between the traditional and new retail markets is adding an online platform and big data to improve customers' convenience and comfort. When we stay up late at home, sometimes we may feel a little hungry and crave a burger or a sandwich. Such easy-to-get food is often sold in a store within 500 meters of the house. However, considering the troublesome processes, people usually give up wasting time and energy on such small food. Thus, to solve the delivery service shortage of this kind of short-distance and high-requirement goods like fresh food, a new retail market is created to offer people a more convenient service within 5 kilometers of one store in the neighborhood. It's a beautiful creativity for customers (Wang, 2019).

The experience offered by new retail is updated from previous retail. On the one hand, the last retail relationship between customers and goods is in a straight line. The customers are only in one fixed retail space, choosing the items that have been selected and picked on the selling shelves. This satisfaction largely depends on the retailers' supply, and the shopping scene seems fixed and limited, which cannot provide more choices. On the other hand, the new retail offers a new environment where customers can always stay in the shopping space, whether online or offline. Apart from this, the new form can customize orders depending on the customer's personal preference and need so that they can gain more value through the whole chain of selecting, comparing, shopping, and buying processes.

After experiencing the comprehensive new retail business, current customers also pay more attention to the attached and delivered feelings of other customers regarding the goods. They always communicate with others actively through social media, especially when searching and obtaining information or sharing and commenting on the experience of items.

Meanwhile, this new market and business model is also a win-win situation for suppliers and retailers. Online retailers and shopping platforms no longer have a chance to earn massive revenue with lower advertising and marketing costs, as was possible during the beginning of online commerce. As the market has matured, attracting new customers has become increasingly challenging, and the cost of doing so has risen sharply. For instance, in 2017, the cost of attracting one new customer to an online platform increased to 200 RMB, which is much higher than in the early years (Wang, 2019).

For offline retailers, the growth of online shopping has made it increasingly challenging to run a business offline. Online commerce not only bears fewer costs, like rent fees and utilities, but also sells goods at a lower price to compete with offline retailers and attract more customers. Online and offline retailers now face the challenges of high costs in obtaining new customers, gradually higher running costs, and lower selling prices.

The invention of the new retail market solves this problem. With the help of big online data, offline stores can accurately identify the habits and tendencies of different age and gender groups and deliver the most likely liked goods based on user profiles and segmentation to generate more revenue. This approach combines the online and offline users' consumption habits and provides more ways to analyze customers' behavior and potential consumption. In addition, with quick and convenient delivery services, neighbors in the community can be introduced to the store by word-of-mouth advertising, leading to a continuous increase in new and loyal customers at little cost to the online platform.

Under the new retail business consumer decision process model, customers can comprehensively participate in the entire chain through five processes: need recognition, information search, alternative evaluation, purchase and consumption, and post-purchase processes (Grewal & Levy, 2020).

The first process is needing recognition. Although necessities are essential for survival, people may also desire goods that are not strictly necessary to satisfy themselves physically and mentally. For example, a hotpot may be one of the most desired meals when having a social dinner with friends or family in cold winter.

The second process is information search. When individuals look for their preferred items, they turn to external online platforms such as the official website, e-commerce sites, and social media. Besides, they also search for internal, already-known information. Online advertising promotion allows for quick and efficient searches, which can not only leave a good memory in potential customers' internal minds but also help merchants leverage consumer data to identify individual interests and potential shopping requirements.

The third process is alternative evaluation. Apart from traditional methods such as listening to staff recommendations and trying on items in offline stores, consumers can also make choices based on others' shares on social media. Therefore, in the new retail era, the brand's reputation on social media becomes crucial for marketing. On the other hand, even offline stores, businesses leverage emerging technologies to enhance the in-store experience, such as using VR technology for simulated try-ons.

The fourth process is purchase and consumption. The integration of online and offline channels has peaked in the purchasing process. Retailers are breaking down the separation between online and offline channels, utilizing a dual-channel approach to drive traffic and facilitate cross-selling. For instance, online membership systems regularly release exclusive coupons for offline use, while offline stores encourage customers to scan QR codes to utilize online membership system points. This approach is exemplified by "Hema Fresh" as well. By allowing consumers at offline stores to place orders online, subsequently fulfilled by the store with home delivery, significant time savings and efficiency improvements have been achieved for consumers. Customers can choose the delivery approach according to individual preferences and urgency. Mostly, Guo Quan Shi Hui customers prefer instant delivery services to obtain food materials quickly. It is to be noted that mobile payment has significantly enhanced the convenience of transactions. Payments can be swiftly completed by scanning QR codes or utilizing facial recognition, eliminating the need for waiting in queues and the spatial constraints of offline payments. For instance, after purchasing from Guo Quan Shi Hui's online store, entering the payment password promptly completes the transaction.

The fifth process is the post-sale process. It involves returning or exchanging products and encompasses feedback from merchants on consumers' user experience. Sharing user experience on social media helps potential consumers acquire information and stimulates improvements in the products and services offered by businesses to a certain extent. This leads to more precise consumer positioning for merchants, facilitating repeat purchases of existing customers and expanding new customer groups.

In addition, against this backdrop, many enterprises have entered this new retail market during the COVID-19 epidemic. People have gotten used to making meals at home, and the demand for in-home hotpots has risen rapidly. This brings us to the prepared dishes market.

Prepared Dishes Market

As mentioned above, changes in consumption patterns due to the epidemic and the increasing popularity of prepared dishes among young single individuals are becoming more prevalent. Let us understand the meaning of prepared dishes. Generally, prepared dishes are made from livestock and fresh food, undergo many steps, such as cutting and picking, and are provided to customers as ready-to-eat semi-finished or finished dishes. Due to the demanding storage requirements, almost all prepared dishes need an integrated supply chain and cold-chain transportation.

Prepared dishes are a familiar invention, unlike the new retail market. There are several reasons why the prepared dishes market is becoming increasingly popular. Changes in consumption concepts and the potential to earn huge profits drive its development. There are ample upstream suppliers of agricultural products and small food processing suppliers for prepared dish suppliers, but they are small in size. Downstream consumers, especially customers, are also highly dependent on prepared dishes. As a result, prepared dish suppliers have strong bargaining power throughout the entire supply chain, which helps them attain higher gross margins. For example, among Guo Lian's products, a leading enterprise of the aquatic prepared dishes listing company, the gross margin of primary aquatic prepared dishes is significantly higher than others, up to 45 per cent in its online commerce channel (Zhang et al., 2024).

Additionally, there is significant policy support for the prepared dishes market. In March 2023, the "Opinions of the Central Committee of the Communist Party of China and the State Council on Doing a Good Job of Comprehensively Promoting the Key Work of Rural Revitalization in 2023" first mentioned prepared dishes and explicitly stated the need to nurture and develop the prepared dishes industry (Zhang, 2023). Therefore, with policy support and leading enterprises, the prepared dishes industry has broadened the scope for further development and industrial expansion.

However, considering the current beginning stage, several regulatory problems must be addressed. Firstly, the uneven development within the industry means that no powerful leading enterprises exist as a model. Consequently, production regulations and employees' qualifications should be supervised more. This problem chain creates a huge trust deficit among customers about the qualification of prepared dishes and their corresponding insurance, significantly affecting the further development of the prepared dishes industry.

Evolution of the Market Until Today

With the rise of takeaways, the demand for prepared dishes has significantly increased. According to Zhong et al., the market size for the prepared dishes industry reached 415 billion in 2022, representing a growth rate of 32.4%. With this upward trend, it is estimated that the industry size will reach RMB510 billion in 2023 and 1072 billion in 2026.

In the business-to-business (B2B) sector, using prepared dishes can help lower costs and improve efficiency for companies. For instance, the cost of food preparation for a highly purchased noodle dish in takeout is around 7 RMB when prepared by the business, while the cost of buying prepared dishes is around 9 RMB. Although the cost of food materials occupies 47% and increases to 60%, considering the much lower labor cost and greatly improved efficiency, the gross profit will significantly increase. This change enhances business people's enthusiasm for prepared dishes (Yan & Guo, 2024).

However, as the prepared dishes industry develops, many safety and regulation problems are becoming more highly debated, particularly in school canteens. In September 2023, a video of students' lunches made from prepared dishes caused significant protests on popular social media. The parents of the students found that the lunches delivered to their children needed to be faster, of better quality, and tasteless. They were concerned that the long-term consumption of such lunches, made from pre-prepared vegetables, would negatively impact their children's health. Compared to fresh produce, prepared dishes seem more unsafe. This video led to many parents opposing the appearance of prepared dishes in school canteens (Zhong et al., 2023).

In response to people's concerns about the quality and standardized regulations of prepared dishes, 25 provincial governments across the country have introduced their documents and local standards related to the high-quality development of prepared dishes. Despite these efforts, there are still numerous problems that need to be addressed in the future, including the low participation of government departments in setting standards across the country, the limited space for setting regulations due to the variety of prepared dishes, the shortage of professional talent and supervisory staff, and the current lack of benchmarking with international standards (Zhang et al., 2024).

Competition Analysis

Haidilao

Haidilao is a well-known Chinese hot pot chain restaurant famous for providing high-quality ingredients and a unique service experience. Customers dining at Haidilao can enjoy carefully selected ingredients, including premium meats, fresh seafood, and various fresh vegetables. In addition to delicious food, Haidilao is acclaimed for its distinctive services, such as providing warm blankets and complimentary fruit platters to customers. Haidilao also enhances customer experience through technological innovations, such as offering iPads for entertainment in waiting areas and providing nail services to waiting customers. The company continuously strives to elevate the overall dining experience for its customers (Iimedia, 2019).

Haidilao has a robust supply chain, and almost all its hotpot condiments are provided by its subsidiary corporations, Yi Hai and Shu Hai Enterprises. These two enterprises also provide up to 80 kinds of food materials for customers, unique to Haidilao, regarding recipes, processing methods, and presentation. The menu is updated regularly, including the rotation of old dishes and the introduction of new ones. In addition to newly officially created dishes, popular dishes made by customers based on Haidilao dishes have also been adopted into the regular menu.

The most competitive aspect of Guo Quan Shi Hui is its takeaway service. Haidilao's takeaway service offers a variety of ready-to-eat hotpot dishes and corresponding minor ingredients. Customers have the option to choose individual dishes or opt for set meals. Once a dish is selected, delivery is typically completed within 30-40 minutes, handled exclusively by Haidilao staff. The delivery team delivers the food and sets up the table for the customer upon arrival. Additionally, customers can opt (with an additional charge) to include a pot and hotplate, as well as regular plates and cutlery (instead of disposable ones), all arranged and served by the delivery staff.

Moreover, Haidilao Delivery has recently been introduced on HungryMou, a widely used third-party food delivery platform, offering a new mini hotpot delivery option. Reservations for Haidilao's takeout service can be conveniently made through the dedicated takeaway hotline, WeChat public account, the Haidilao app, and various prominent third-party online food and beverage delivery platforms in China.

Another competitive business between Haidilao and Guo Quan Shi Hui is integrating and managing the whole supply chain. In 2007, Shu Hai gained independence from Haidilao, focusing on delivering comprehensive supply chain hosting services to diverse establishments. By 2011, it officially established its venture, expanding its clientele beyond its parent company, Haidilao, to include a broad spectrum of food and beverage enterprises, even extending to 7-11 convenience stores. Guo Quan Shu Hai's primary focus is providing comprehensive food supply chain solutions to many restaurant chains and retail clients, encompassing services such as net food production, food research and development, centralized kitchens, warehousing, logistics, and more. The overarching integration of the supply chain is one of Guo Quan Shi Hui's strengths. (Te, 2022).

Xia Bu Xia Bu

Targeting the "one person, one pot" approach, the small hot pot brand Xia Bu combines bar-style dining with traditional hot pot. The brand insists on providing convenient, fast, and value-for-money hot pot service with its convenient, quick, and cost-effective positioning. Xia Bu Xia Bu creates a cost-effective dining experience with a per capita consumption of 40 RMB using the "one person, one pot" split-meal hot pot approach (Zheshang, 2023).

There are two competition categories between Xia Bu and Guo Quan Shi Hui. The first category is takeaway services. Unlike Haidilao and Guo Quan Shi Hui, Xia Bu Xia Bu's takeaway products contain fresh raw hotpot materials like meat and vegetables and the cooked, ready-to-eat hot pot set for one person. This dramatically increases the convenience of customers who are busy or too lazy to cook the hotpot. Because of this advantage, many workers prefer Xia Bu over the other two brands, even on weekends.

The second competition between Xia Bu Xia Bu and Guo Quan Shi Hui is their logistic systems and supply chain management. The implementation of a three-tier logistics system by Xia Bu Xia Bu aims to achieve cost control through leverage of scale advantages. The company has established a distribution structure comprising a national warehouse, regional warehouses, and operation centers. The national and North China regional warehouses are strategically located in Beijing. Operation centers are directly linked to stores for the collection and division of store orders. They dynamically strategy the most efficient distribution routes based on distribution radius, costs, and order demand, optimizing distribution costs and efficiency. As the store count expands, the radial capacity of the operation centers increases, facilitating cost control through the benefits of scale (Xu, 2023).

The specific model is as follows: Xia Bu has established a logistics production center in Beijing/Shanghai dedicated to the production of hotpot soup. The three-tier distribution network ensures the efficient supply of ingredients to stores nationwide, facilitated by a flexible distribution mechanism. Aligned with high-quality upstream channels, the company has implemented a three-tier distribution network for warehousing and transportation. The primary warehouse in Beijing manages the storage and distribution of core materials from the central kitchen. In contrast, secondary and tertiary warehouses handle ingredient turnover in regional and specific areas. Unlike conventional warehousing and logistics systems, Xia Bu Xia Bu's three-tier distribution network demonstrates high flexibility, allowing suppliers and distribution centers, under certain conditions, to deliver directly to restaurants. This approach helps avoid ingredient losses associated with cumbersome supply chain mechanisms (Minsheng Security, 2023).

In response to the trend of digitization and informatization in the catering industry, Xia Bu is actively upgrading its supply chain by implementing information technology. Significant efforts are being made to enhance information construction in logistics, transportation, and digital supervision systems. This includes adopting a Transportation Management System (TMS), GPS monitoring system, and vehicle temperature monitoring system. These measures aim to guarantee the punctuality and efficiency of logistics and transportation, thereby effectively securing the stability of cold chain logistics and minimising ingredient losses. The focus is on ensuring the strength of the cold chain logistics and reducing the likelihood of food loss (Minsheng, 2023).

Market Perspectives

Urgent action is required to solve existing issues and avoid potential challenges, address the public's negative perception of the prepared dishes industry, and promote its continued growth.

The first step is to establish unified country regulations governing the prepared dishes industry's production, transportation, supervision, and marketing process. Furthermore, the relevant departments should strengthen the study and comparison of food regulatory standards at home and abroad, benchmarking against the highest international standards and continuously updating and improving the relevant, comprehensive system.

After setting robust standards, the second step is strengthening regulatory agency enforcement patterns. Food safety monitoring of prepared dishes should rely on something other than unannounced and reactive enforcement. Regulators should take the initiative to identify problems and regularize enforcement actions. Also, when receiving reports from the public, they should be the first to receive feedback, launch investigations, and carry out corrective actions.

Apart from the above, the third step is integrating resources, encouraging enterprises to maximize their advantages and promote the development of the entire industry. Given the fragmented market for prepared dishes, the construction of standards at all levels of the prepared vegetable industry should be accelerated. The current situation of prepared vegetables should be accurately classified before adopting different levels of the standard system, promoting the further development of the prepared vegetable industry in the direction of standardization, industrialization, and normalization.

In conclusion, the prepared dishes industry has entered a development spurt under the influence of both the business and customer sides. Takeaway demand, the ageing population, and profit squeeze have led to a strong demand for pre-prepared dishes (Yan & Guo, 2024). Then, from the degree of processing, China's prepared dishes industry is still dominated by ready-to-heat and ready-to-cook products. Regarding consumption concentration, customer-oriented prepared dishes will focus on the first and second-tier cities, especially in Beijing, Shanghai, Guangzhou, Shenzhen, and nearby cities (Zhong et al., 2023). Finally, China's prepared dishes industry has not formed a competitive market. The industry has low product barriers and lacks national standards, resulting in a highly decentralized industry pattern. Leading and benchmarking enterprises in prepared dishes need to be improved. Therefore, there is an urgent need to learn from foreign experience and establish a united national standard to address the existing problems (Zhang et al., 2024).

Development and Strategy

Guo Quan Shi Hui is rapidly developing at a surprising speed. It successfully went public on November 2nd, 2023, just seven years after its first offline outlet was established in January 2017 in Zhengzhou, Henan province. Such excellent development is based on three main business strategies: relying on franchising for expansion, constructing a digital supply chain management and a powerful logistics system, and using a multi-platform layout for online channels.

As of September 26, 2023, Guo Quan Shi Hui has successfully established almost 10,000 retail stores within six years of its creation. Out of these stores, only six are managed directly by Guo Quan Shi Hui, while the rest are franchised stores, accounting for 99.9% of the first-mover advantage. While this vast number of franchised stores has helped Guo Quan Shi Hui occupy the market rapidly, it is not necessarily the best way to build the brand, as the quality of food materials cannot always be strictly guaranteed.

However, the large percentage of franchised stores has its advantages. Franchisees must pay a fixed franchise fee of 20,000 RMB per store, making franchise revenue the mainstay of Guo Quan Shi Hui's revenue. In 2022, revenue from sales to franchisees accounted for 91.75% of total product sales and 90.29% of total operating income (Zhao, 2023). Franchisees usually complete payment before Guo Quan Shi Hui delivers products, which helps maintain a good cash flow situation for the company. Moreover, Guo Quan Shi Hui focuses on expanding in county and township markets, with 71.2% of its outlets outside first-tier cities.

Digital Supply Chain Management

Guo Quan Shi Hui uses the model of "upstream ODM plant + downstream store opening" to build a powerful logistics system and hold the robust management of the supply chain. In the upstream process, Guo Quan Shi Hui employs cold chain technology and standardized mass raw materials production by collaborating with 266 Original Design Manufacturing (ODM) plants. This strategy revolves around a singular product and a specific factory, concentrating on the most critical product categories of that particular factory. By providing product design data and equipment support, this approach ensures quality assurance while effectively addressing production constraints in specific regional factories. Consequently, the client brand, Guo Quan Shi Hui, can focus more on core technology, services, and brand promotion.

In the downstream phase, products are delivered to outlets through cold chain technology to ensure the nutrition and freshness of the ingredients, through the supply chain logistics management to the stores, transportation, and cross-docking warehouse management for customers placing orders in online stores, food and corresponding cookware are swiftly delivered.

Guo Quan Shi Hui also follows the principle of building warehouses before opening stores to ensure the rapid delivery of cold chain warehouses and deep cooperation with 266 ODM factories. The mode of collaboration is a single primary product, single factory, and only the core categories of the factory are selected for cooperation, which can guarantee quality and effectively respond to product production limitations in specific regional factories.

Guo Quan Shi Hui attaches great importance to integrating the supply chain and logistic systems. It creates a business model combining the integrated supply chain, the franchising stores, and the customers through online and offline logistic systems to establish integrated production and selling processes.

From the front to the back end of the entire business process for IT systematization and standardization of operations, Guo Quan Shi Hui built its warehouse to maintain the flow of goods and brand sinking. While selling ingredients to franchisees, in response to the situation of uneven quality, they standardized and regulated the management of franchised stores by improving their digital and information control capabilities.

The Multi-Platform Layout of Online Channels

Diversifying its online presence, marketing, and promotional strategies to boost sales, Guo Quan Shi Hui employs a multi-platform approach. Its online channels include a dedicated pot circle APP and minor programs and platforms like Mei Tuan, Hungry, and TikTok. The proprietary platform of Guo Quan Shi Hui leverages consumer data to recommend product combinations, which enhances sales. TikTok's life service terminal engages in live broadcasting and short-video marketing, enabling consumers to place orders through embedded links. By the end of April 2023, over 8,000 company stores had successfully sold products through TikTok (Zhao, 2023).

Furthermore, Guo Quan Shi Hui's marketing initiatives extend to platforms like CCTV and others, coupled with offline billboards. Additionally, stores organize online and in-store promotions during events such as the "517" food festival, general food festivals, and the "Double Eleven" festival, contributing to the growth of sales (Zhao, 2023).

THE PEOPLE BEHIND GUO QUAN SHI HUI

In 2022, Mingchao Yang, the founder of Guo Quan Shi Hui, debuted on the Hurun Hundred Rich List with a net worth exceeding 5 billion yuan. Originally from Luyi County in the east of Henan Province, known as the "hometown of Laozi," Mingchao Yang graduated from Zhengzhou University. He left his government job in 2006 and embarked on an entrepreneurial journey starting from a night market, where he initially sold beer, seafood, and other items (Yan, 2023).

The Previous Startup Experience

Yang opened "Black Wife," Zhengzhou's largest open-air night market, where the signature dish, "screw prawns," gained popularity and became a legend. In 2013, Mingchao Yang continued to innovate in the hot pot industry and introduced a small bench bar-style hot pot concept featuring the unique experience of "eating hot pot in a bar." Within a year, Little Bench expanded to 80 locations, creating a sensation in Zhengzhou with up to 1,000 stations.

Recognizing the challenges of a scattered and inefficient supply chain in the upstream hotpot market, Mingchao Yang founded Guo Quan Shi Hui Supply Chain Management Co. in 2015 to provide ingredient services for hotpot restaurants. The small bench brand gradually transitioned into a micro-supply chain pot circle, presenting an opportunity for transformation. In 2017, Guo Quan Shi Hui opened its first retail store in Zhengzhou, positioning itself as a hot pot ingredients supermarket.

An exciting story involves Mingchao Yang and Zhujie Li, a significant investor. In mid-2018, Yang joined an entrepreneurial training camp to learn about investing. Through discussions with mentors, he recognised the industry's untapped potential and secured early investments from several mentors. At that time, the Pot Circle food hui stores numbered only 200 but expanded rapidly after that. One of the mentors was Zhujie Li, the founding partner of Bu Bu Venture Capital.

Unique Perspectives

Mingchao Yang has unique perspectives on the challenges encountered during the development of Guo Quan Shi Hui. During his speech at the New Consumer Brand Industry Summit, the founder of Guo Quan Shi Hui expressed his primary concern: "My greatest worry is that the staff of Guo Quan Shi Hui might lose patience and struggle with loneliness." Despite the apparent vulnerability in the boss's expression, it reflects an underlying determination.

According to Yang, "Consumption is an ever-evolving industry. Some of today's new brands lack not innovation but endurance." With this resilience, Mingchao Yang invested six years and successfully expanded into the city with the assistance of franchisees. Securing comedian Yunpeng Yue as an endorser, the brand transformed from obscurity to an industry leader. While venturing into the competitive market, Mingchao Yang garnered support from star investors such as IDG, Sanquan, Wumi, Maotai, and others. He emphasizes, "Competitiveness lies not in the quantity of innovations but in enduring loneliness and dedication to a single objective." Mingchao Yang possesses unique insights into business models, revealing that he spent five years building infrastructure.

Amid the pandemic, Mingchao Yang introduced the concept of "eating hot pot at home," rapidly opening 3,000 stores in just nine months. Relying on fresh products to attract consumers, Guo Quan Shi Hui positioned pre-prepared dishes as quick-cooking options, aiming to bring the essence of Chinese cuisine to households within a five-minute dinner range. Guo Quan Shi Hui boasts 10,000 stores, with registered members exceeding 22 million and an annual order volume exceeding 100 million (Han, 2023).

FUTURE PROJECT

Expand and Deepen Omni-Channel Sales Network

Guo Quan Shi Hui aims to enhance and broaden its comprehensive sales network to establish direct connections with consumers, according to Zhao (2023). The strategy involves opening additional stores in provincial capitals and municipalities to increase market penetration in existing regions and explore new areas, gradually extending to townships. The plan includes establishing Black Pearl stores in critical locations like Beijing, Shanghai, Hong Kong, and Macau, focusing on high-end ingredients. Expansion into overseas markets such as Indonesia, the Philippines, and the Singapore-Malaysia-Thailand region is also on the agenda, emphasizing the development and sale of locally favored ingredients.

Integrating online and offline channels is a key focus, with efforts to enhance existing online sales platforms to overcome physical retail space constraints. Online platforms will recommend tailored product combinations based on consumer purchasing habits, encouraging offline customers to place orders online. This integration aims to mutually empower online and offline channels mutually, ultimately driving sales growth.

The initiative encourages franchisees to open more stores and cultivates business-oriented franchisees. Support is provided to control costs, including offering cost and profitability analysis to franchisees and streamlining the procurement process. The optimization of the internal training system, "Guoquan Academy," and the establishment of an organization for franchisees and store managers facilitate the sharing of management experiences (Zhao, 2023).

Expansion of Product Categories

Plans also include expanding product categories to cater to diverse consumer scenarios, such as camping and solo dining. This involves actively diversifying product categories and introducing fruits, snacks, beverages, and alcoholic beverages. These additions align with specific consumption scenarios like camping, living room snacks, fruit snacks, and one-person meals (Zhao, 2023). An ingredient product preparation center is envisioned to offer a broader range of ready-to-eat meal kits. This center aims to meet the demand for regional flavor segments and further support the next-day delivery business.

Strengthen R&D and Supply Capabilities

They are strengthening their R&D capabilities and expanding their product range. To enhance its R&D and innovation capabilities, the company plans to establish additional R&D centers and maintain collaborations with upstream suppliers. Continuous adjustments to the production process based on consumer feedback will develop new products, including high-end ball sliders, shrimp sliders, seafood items, and local snacks.

Continued Vertical Integration of the Supply Chain

Guo Quan Shi Hui intends to deepen its "single product, single factory" strategy for core products, such as beef and mutton ball sliders and bases, while further integrating upstream resources. The company will also continue cultivating new brands, exemplified by Seven Tomatoes, a tomato hotpot base brand developed in collaboration with Chen Ming Foods (Zhao, 2023).

Strengthen Digitalization Capabilities in Operations

The initiative involves enhancing visual production management and implementing digital monitoring. This includes establishing a procurement and fulfilment management platform to synchronise inventory turnover data. Store sales data will inform upstream production decisions and adjust product development and production strategies.

Guo Quan Shi Hui aims to further optimize the centralized purchasing system for franchisees, providing them with intelligent functions such as product recommendations, settlement reconciliation, and inventory management. The optimization of intelligent store profitability analysis is planned to assist franchisees in enhancing performance and management efficiency. Deploying intelligent video monitoring equipment and a self-developed cash register system will enable comprehensive digital management for franchisees.

The company plans to connect different systems, launch self-developed systems for centralized management, and achieve the digital integration of business, financial, and supply chain management systems. Guo Quan Shi Hui intends to expand membership groups and optimize membership benefit plans through precise marketing. Enhancing consumer behavior analysis capabilities will facilitate the delivery of the most suitable marketing, services, and products (Zhao, 2023).

CONCLUSION

In conclusion, Guo Quan Shi Hui is a new retail and prepared food market unicorn. Although it faces challenges such as ensuring food safety and providing insurance, it has already achieved remarkable success in just seven years. This business model is a prime example for other similar businesses to explore and emulate in the new retail and prepared food market.

REFERENCES

Grewal, D., & Levy, M. (2020). *Marketing* (7th ed.). McGraw-Hill Education.

Guan, W. (n.d.). *53,,50,IPO53-year-old boss sells hotpot ingredients, opens nearly 10,000 stores, worth $5 billion, sprints to IPO*. cyzone. https://m.cyzone.cn/article/739918.html

Guoquan. (2024). *Guoquan Shihui brand advantages—Guoquan Shihui Hot Pot BBQ ingredients supermarket*. ZZHQSH. https://www.zzgqsh.com/website/advantage

Han, W. J. (2023, April 8). IPO,100Moutai invested in hot pot supermarket to IPO, valuation of more than 10 billion]. *Foodaily*. https://www.foodaily.com/articles/32383

Iimedia. (2019). *: 2019H1Ai media research report: 2019H1 submarine operation status and industry trends research report*. iiMedia. https://www.iimedia.cn/c1000/65350.html

Security, M. (2023, March 30). *2023 , Gluttony Research Report 2023 Twenty-four years of deep plowing into the restaurant industry, diversified operations to create industry leaders*. Xue Qiu. https://www.vzkoo.com/read/20230330cb177433bf45bed668310ae5.html

Shang, Z. Z. Q. (Ed.). (2023). *[Gluttony in-depth report: reorganisation and start again, fresh clothes and angry horse teenagers]*. Maverick Research. https://www.hangyan.co/reports/3040103611704018909

Tang, H. Y. (2018, February 6). *"" [The way to win for retailers in the era of "new retail."]* PwC. https://www.strategyand.pwc.com/cn/zh/reports-and-studies/2018/new-retail-era.html

Te, Y. T. (2022). *[Supply chain of Haidilao]*. Zhihu. https://www.zhihu.com/tardis/zm/art/412681115?source_id=1003

Wang, H. (2019, December 6). *??What is "New Retail"? What are the key points?* Zhihu. https://www.zhihu.com/question/52950329/answer/179975491

Xu, G. H. (2023, March 17). *[Gluttony Research Report: Kicking into gear, re-starting the road to growth.]* Xue Qiu. https://xueqiu.com/9508834377/244728717

Yan, M. H. (2023, October 12). *: [Yang Mingchao: A Boss Who Lets Moutai Back Him Up]*. China Financial Online (CFO), a financial newsletter. http://mp.cnfol.com/31441/article/1697101223-141111304.html

Yan, X. Q., & Guo, L. L. (2024). Exploring the Dilemma of Food Safety Supervision and Legal Regulation of Prepared Dishes. *Preservation and Processing, 24*(01), 64–69.

Zhang, L., Zhou, F., & Zhou, C. F. (2024). .Bottleneck Constraints and Path Choice of China's Prefabricated Vegetable Industry in the Perspective of High-Quality Development. *Shipin Yu Fajiao Gongye*, 1(11). doi:10.13995/j.cnki.11-1802/ts.037771

Zhang, Q. L. (2023). SOR-SEM. [Analysis of Consumption Trends and Influence Mechanisms of Prepared Vegetables Based on SOR-SEM Modeling.]. *Operations and Management, 1*(12). doi:10.16517/j.cnki.cn12-1034/f.20230712.005

Zhao, Y. N. (2023, October 17). , *[Pot Circle Food Prospectus Sorting Eat-at-home meal leader, scale operation first breakout].* DFCFW. https://pdf.dfcfw.com/pdf/ H3_AP202310221602714879_1.pdf?1697983474000.pdf

Zhong, J., Sun, L. J., Li, H. Q., Cai, Y. H., Guan, R., & Tian, Q. (2023). [Research Progress, Problems and Suggestions of Prefabricated Vegetable Standard System in China]. *Preservation and Processing, 1*(11). https://link.cnki.net/urlid/12.1330 .S.20231025.1323.002

KEY TERMS AND DEFINITIONS

Brand Image: This is like brand reputation. When people mention the brand name, what first comes to mind is the brand image left by that person.

Business to Business (B2B): This means that the supplier and the receiver are enterprises rather than a single customer.

Business to Customer (B2C): This means that the supplier is the business enterprise, but the customer represents the single customer rather than the business enterprise.

New Retail Market: Combining big data technology, online platforms, and offline stores to give customers convenient participation through the purchase process.

Omni-Channel: An omni-channel sales network refers to a multi-channel approach to sales that provides customers with a seamless shopping experience across various channels, such as brick-and-mortar stores, online platforms, mobile apps, social media, and more. The critical aspect of omni-channel sales is integrating and synchronizing all these channels to ensure consistency in product availability, pricing, promotions, and customer service.

Original Design Manufacture: (ODM): For one specific factory, it just concentrates on one of the most critical product categories. Guo Quan Shi Hui provides product design data and equipment support to the ODM plant. This approach ensures quality assurance while effectively addressing production constraints in specific regional factories.

Product Promotion: In this situation, promotion is the same as advertisement. It means the way and method of advertising the production, such as TV, social media apps, etc.

Supply Chain: This refers to the process from the manufacturer's part to customers, including production, packaging, delivering, and marketing.

Vertical Integration: Vertical integration occurs when one enterprise invests in the upstream and downstream businesses and forms a complete supply chain.

Chapter 12
Jiuxian:
Revolutionizing Liquor Distribution in China Through Omnichannel Innovation

Ziyi Li

Beijing Normal University-Hong Kong Baptist University United International College, China

EXECUTIVE SUMMARY

This case study examines Jiuxian's transformative journey within China's competitive liquor distribution industry, focusing on its innovative strategies and evolution into an omnichannel powerhouse. Founded in 2009 by Hao Hongfeng, Jiuxian capitalised on the burgeoning e-commerce landscape, pioneering online liquor retailing in a market traditionally dominated by offline channels. Through strategic partnerships and aggressive expansion, Jiuxian established itself as a leader, leveraging its online platform and a nationwide network of offline stores branded as "Jiuxian International Wine & Spirit Centre." The case explores Jiuxian's adaptation to market shifts, including its embrace of new retail concepts and integration of live-streaming commerce to engage a younger consumer base. Despite challenges like financial setbacks and IPO delays, Jiuxian's resilience and strategic vision have positioned it at the forefront of China's liquor retail sector, setting a benchmark for omnichannel excellence and market innovation.

DOI: 10.4018/979-8-3693-2921-4.ch012

UNICORN DESCRIPTION

Brief History of the Unicorn

Jiuxian Network Technology Co., Ltd (hereinafter referred to as "Jiuxian"), China's leading integrated liquor e-commerce service company, is an omnichannel, full-category retailer and service provider of alcoholic beverages with brand operation as its core. Jiuxian.com, an online B2C platform, was established by Jiuxian in Shanxi province, China, in March 2009. Subsequently, after finding that the local e-commerce environment of Shanxi was not conducive to its operations, Jiuxian moved its headquarters to Beijing in May 2010, with a brand value of 66.539 million RMB.

In July 2011, Jiuxian was selected as one of the top fifty dark horse companies with the most investment value in China by "Entrepreneur" magazine. In November 2011, the company completed the Series B financing of 80 million RMB, jointly invested by Sequoia Capital and Oriental Fuhai Capital. The Tianjin subsidiary was established in December 2013. In the Tmall Double Eleven event in November 2014, Jiuxian.com ranked first in Tmall's alcohol sales rankings. In June 2015, Jiuxian and COFCO W&W International Co., Ltd. announced a strategic partnership to promote the development of China's imported wine market. In November 2016, Jiuxian.com achieved a 30% increase in Double Eleven orders through multi-platform linkage.

In March 2017, the strategic cooperation with Rémy Cointreau Group was upgraded again. Jiuxian became its most crucial e-commerce strategic partner for domestic alcohol products in all e-commerce channels. In March 2018, the Ministry of Science and Technology released the 2017 China Unicorn List, and Jiuxian became the only company in the alcohol industry to be on the list. In August 2019, Jiuxian's brand value was RMB 26.116 billion, ranking first in China's liquor distribution. In September 2020, Jiuxian ranked first for the fifth consecutive year in the Huazun Cup China's liquor distribution industry with a revenue of RMB 32.541 billion. In December of the same year, Jiuxian ranked among the top 500 global unicorn companies for two consecutive years and was awarded the honorary title of "Reliable Liquor Project Demonstration Enterprise" by the China Liquor Distribution Association.

The early stages of pioneering often involve experiencing uncertainties, leading to a less smooth development path than it may appear for Jiuxian. Throughout its journey in financing, product sales, and market share competition, Jiuxian has faced both opportunities and challenges. Transitioning from traditional online B2C to integrating online and offline channels, Jiuxian established its own offline sales network to achieve an O2O model. It has achieved omnichannel development by combining technology and collaborating with other liquor brands.

Jiuxian has established in-depth cooperation with more than 500 domestic and foreign liquor enterprises. The company sells more than 50,000 kinds of liquor, mainly in the online and offline omnichannel sales business of international and domestic famous brands and imported excellent brands and other liquor commodities. After many years of rapid development, Jiuxian has nearly 2,000 employees and over 1,500 offline stores. It is the largest liquor e-commerce retail platform in China.

Business Model

Jiuxian is an omnichannel alcoholic beverage retailer and service provider that offers online and offline products and services. Relying on its online platform "Jiuxian.com", offline brand chains "Jiuxian International Wine & Spirit Centre", "Jiu Kuai Dao", and other channels (Jiuxian, 2021), the company has deep cooperation with domestic and foreign famous wine enterprises in the areas of liquor procurement and sales, product development, brand cooperation, and promotion, etc., to develop the O2O strategy and promote the development of multi-branding strategy of channel brands, product brands, and service business (Jiuxian, 2023).

Unlike traditional alcoholic beverage retailers, Jiuxian adopts a hybrid business model, integrating online and offline channels. In 2009, Jiuxian entered the liquor Internet retail industry. In 2017, the company formally built a robust management model of a branded retail chain, realising the deep integration of omnichannel liquor retail online and offline (Jiuxian, 2021).

In the traditional liquor circulation chain, due to the many intermediate links, the extended supply chain, and the lack of branded chain retail platforms, end-consumers products often have gone through layers and layers of price increases. Counterfeiting has long plagued consumers due to the market's mixed and confusing nature (Financial Sharp Eye, 2021). Therefore, consumers have attached increasing importance to channel brands, and several leading liquor retailers with branding effects have also been spawned to create their channels. For example, Jiuxian created O2O channels, such as "Jiuxian International Liquor City" and "Jiu Kuai Dao", which changed the business serving from online to offline.

As one of the earliest enterprises to enter the alcohol e-commerce industry, Jiuxian empowers the industry chain through Internet technology, innovates the traditional alcohol distribution business, and deeply integrates the online and offline omni-channel plus omni-category operation mode, effectively solving consumers' pain points when purchasing alcohol products.

Product and Services

Channel Brands

Regarding channel brands, the company covers Jiuxian's online platform, third-party online retail platforms such as Tmall and JD, live broadcasting platforms such as TikTok, and offline brand chains. It retains the original distribution channels under the brand agency mode and has steadily realised omnichannel operation in the development over the years. The company continues to improve the brand awareness and recognition of its channels. Since 2017, Jiuxian has been actively expanding its offline brand chain business under a robust management model. It has gradually set up two types of offline chain stores through franchising: "Jiuxian International Wine & Spirit Centre" and "Jiu Kuai Dao". These have developed rapidly with small city stores, big city small stores, and different investment promotion strategies. The offline brand chain channel has emerged as a significant sales channel for the company. In 2020, it generated a sales revenue of 8228.53 million RMB; in the first half of 2021, it achieved a sales revenue of 54469.75 million RMB (Jiuxian, 2021).

Jiuxian provides a comprehensive range of marketing services, including product display and brand promotion to brands and other wine merchants, with the help of its online platform and omnichannel marketing and promotion system. The company collects brand and product promotion fees for these services. For merchants who set up their shops on Jiuxian's online platform, the company charges platform usage fees and transaction commissions, such as merchant service fees, at a certain percentage of the transaction amount. In the case of Jiuxian's offline chain shops, the company provides brand authorisation, business systems, and training services to improve the management level and profitability of the shops and collects brand usage fees.

Product Brands

Regarding product branding, Jiuxian's product branding business can be categorised into flow products and exclusive products. Flow liquor products are standard products famous domestic and foreign liquor companies sell. Jiuxian is not involved in the design and development of these products, such as well-known products including Moutai, Wuliangye, Jiannanchun, Luzhou Laojiao, Diaoyutai, Guotai, Remy Martin, Pernod Ricard, Diageo, and so on.

Jiuxian works closely with well-known domestic and international wine enterprises to provide customers with high-quality, cost-effective products and cooperates intensely with upstream wine enterprises. Jiuxian has created a series of own-brand and co-promoted exclusive products by integrating upstream and downstream resources. Private label and co-promoted products mainly include the "Rongda Sauce

Wine" series, "Zhuangzang" Sauce Wine series, "Montres Cavaliers" wine series from France, "Dingo Tree" wine series from Australia, and "Dolce Vita" wine series from Spain, as well as the Luzhou Laojiao "Sanrenxuan" and "Wuliangye" which have been developed in cooperation with renowned wine companies.

Service Business

Leveraging years of experience in liquor retail, the company introduced the "Jiu Zhen Kuai" express delivery service in the second half of 2018. This service caters to the immediate consumption needs of colleagues' gatherings, family gatherings, and other occasions. Under the "Jiu Zhen Kuai" model, the company's branded chain stores are equipped with uniformly branded delivery vehicles and software systems. Users can place orders through the Jiuxian App and third-party delivery platforms like Meituan and Ele. Me. Online orders are then transferred to the nearest "Jiuxian International Liquor City" or "Jiu Kuai Dao" store, which completes the delivery.

The company empowers offline stores with online traffic, and these cooperative stores also serve as "front-end city warehouses" for Jiuxian, fulfilling consumers' demands for timeliness and achieving deep integration and complementary advantages between online and offline channels. In 2019, the company's "Jiu Zhen Kuai" service brought in orders worth over 33 million RMB for offline stores. By the first half of 2021, the service had already brought in order amounts exceeding the total sales for the entire year of 2019, reflecting the rapid growth of the business.

Customers

Segmentation and Target Market

Jiuxian's main consumer groups include mid-range and high-end customers. With the rapid development of the internet, consumer demographics constantly change, requiring e-commerce companies to monitor market trends and accurately target their consumer groups. Jiuxian's consumer group positioning can be mainly analysed from geographic and demographic segmentation (Wang, 2014).

Geographically, Jiuxian's potential consumers can be classified into two categories: first, those residing in economically developed areas and major coastal cities like Beijing, Shanghai, Shenzhen, Guangzhou, and Tianjin; second, those living in relatively developed areas with convenient transportation, including cities like Jinan, Qingdao, Dalian, Chengdu, and Nanjing.

Demographically, Jiuxian's future consumer base mainly consists of post-80s and post-90s young people who are familiar with the internet, have relatively high incomes, are proficient in internet usage, and are relatively prosperous. Additionally, many university students and recent graduates just entering the workforce are significant consumers of Jiuxian.

Importance of the Products and Services for Customers

According to the analysis of Jiuxian's consumer base, young people are the primary consumer group in cities with convenient transportation and economic development. They mainly include business and management professionals, new entrants to the workforce, and college students, with work-related socialising being a core scenario for them. In these situations, alcohol is often used for gifting, banquets, and socialising, highlighting its significant social aspect.

The demographic of the 80s and 90s, who are familiar with the internet, prefer online shopping. Jiuxian provides convenient shopping and cost-effective products for professionals. Those in higher positions in the workforce tend to pursue higher quality and class in alcohol consumption. Meanwhile, post-95 newcomers usually explore alcohol options below 500 RMB, especially products below 300 RMB, as they actively engage in work and maintain good relationships with colleagues and clients through social gatherings.

As for the demographic born between 1985 and 1994, facing a plateau in their career development, they turn to alcohol to relieve work and life pressures. They prioritise alcohol quality over brand value, seeking more cost-effective options. With over 5,000 types of alcohol, ranging from high-end to budget-friendly, and direct collaboration with distilleries, Jiuxian ensures product quality and meets the diverse needs of consumers of different ages, professions, and scenarios, providing reassurance for consumers to purchase and enjoy.

Market Analysis

Original Situation of the Market

The initial environment of the liquor industry was less favourable than it is today. Take the example of Baijiu (rice wine), where sales soared from less than 35 billion RMB in 1990 to 426.5 billion RMB in 2012. However, this significant increase in sales was primarily due to the industry's relative monopoly and frequent artificial price increases by manufacturers. Over the past decade, major domestic liquor brands have consistently raised prices at an average annual rate of over 10%. The development of China's liquor industry has been moving towards a closed and highly pathological direction, driven by grey demands such as corruption and gift-giving between officials and corporate executives (TMI & CADA, 2023). This development has been disconnected from the market and needs to reflect the genuine demands of many consumers for liquor products.

In addition, due to the lengthy distribution process and the need for a reliable anti-counterfeiting and traceability system, the Chinese liquor market has long been flooded with counterfeit liquor. It takes a long time for consumers to trust and purchase authentic products (Wang, 2014). Consumers tend to rely on the qualifications and trustworthiness of authorised retailers, such as liquor speciality stores, for their purchases. However, these speciality stores are often independently operated by individual merchants with limited credit qualifications. This shows that the central issue in the Chinese liquor market is the lack of reliable large-chain brands that can assure consumers.

Evolution of the Market Until Today

Those who deviate from the basic rules of industry development will eventually return to fundamental principles. The development of the liquor industry is no exception. Since the second half of 2012, under the comprehensive impact of policies such as national liquor bans, strict inspections on official consumption, prohibition of drunk driving, and prohibition of price monopolies, the liquor industry in China has been stimulated, leading to the development of liquor retail (Chen, 2017). As a result, the distribution model dominated by offline sales in the Baijiu industry began to change, and the overall trend toward online retailing accelerated.

In the meantime, the scale of online liquor retailing has grown significantly, and online liquor sales have also rapidly developed towards specialisation. Overall, the proportion of e-commerce platforms in liquor circulation has increased yearly. From 2013 to 2018, the proportion of e-commerce platforms rose from 1.1% to 11.5% (TMI & CADA, 2023). Although the industry was affected by the COVID-19 pandemic from 2020 to 2022, the fundamental trend of stable and positive development has not changed. Since the end of 2022, with the adjustment of national epidemic prevention and control policies, consumer scenes have gradually recovered, and the market environment has improved.

Liquor e-commerce platforms mainly operate under the B2C model, centred around online platforms such as Tmall and JD, while also incorporating the B2B model, connecting upstream and downstream distributors and corporate clients. As China's online consumer base becomes increasingly youthful, the B2C model, which directly targets consumers, has advantages in terms of quality and service. With the increasing number of internet users and high penetration rates of online shopping, the online penetration rate of liquor sales is expected to continue to increase. According to statistics from the China Internet Development Status Survey (2023), as of June 2023, China's internet user base reached 1.079 billion, with an internet penetration rate of 76.4%, providing a solid consumer foundation for the development of the e-commerce industry.

In recent years, new sales channels and promotion platforms, such as live streaming and short videos, have emerged. Data from Byte Dance's TikTok platform revealed that 2023 searches for Baijiu-related keywords increased by 128.02% compared to the same period last year.

Competition Analysis

The competition among enterprises represents a comprehensive strength resulting from the interaction between external and internal factors. The liquor industry has transitioned from exaggerated to squeezed growth, leading to intense price wars and prevalent industry mergers and acquisitions.

1919.com has a strong reputation and extensive offline coverage in the market due to its O2O model and fast delivery service, allowing it to quickly meet the immediate needs of consumers. Jiubil.com, on the other hand, focuses on community chain stores, offering a convenient and affordable shopping experience with a 30-minute delivery service and membership system. In contrast, Jiuxian excels in brand promotion, supply chain management, and technological innovation to compete with 1919.com's efficient distribution and Jiubil.com's liquor coverage, further enhancing its market competitiveness.

There is competition between online liquor B2C and traditional sales channels, where each side leverages its advantages to attract consumers. Competition among B2C websites in the same industry mainly focuses on pricing and complementary services. The website with the lower prices gains a significant advantage. Moreover, there is competition among B2C websites for liquor consumers. Large-scale platforms such as Tmall and JD utilise their user base, warehousing logistics, and extensive product coverage to provide comprehensive commercial services to consumers. On the other hand, websites like Jiuxian attract users through precise differentiation positioning, refined market targeting, and unique brand-added value. Their main advantage lies in offering products with solid professionalism, complementarity, compatibility, and competitive prices.

China's liquor industry has transitioned from rapid growth driven by production capacity to a phase where production volume has stabilised. The next round of industry growth will be driven by the consumption upgrade, focusing on mid to high-end liquor consumption. With liquor production stabilising, companies in the industry need to focus on refined operations to keep a competitive edge.

Forecast for This Market

Since 2018, the liquor e-commerce sector has utilised online resources to focus on comprehensive market deployment and drive offline new retail business development. By integrating online and offline resources and leveraging supply chain, data, and operational advantages, liquor e-commerce platforms have actively expanded cooperation with offline stores, deepening consumer awareness of retail platforms.

During the continuous development of liquor retail enterprises, integrating online and offline channels has gradually expanded the consumer base and enhanced competitiveness within the industry. The increasing consumer awareness of retail platforms has prompted more liquor companies to collaborate and introduce a broader range of products. In this context, chain brands have gained more robust market advantages due to their extensive channel distribution and regional layout.

As chain brands continue integrating and implementing standardised management and refined operations, their increased market share drives many industry enterprises to innovate and reform. In this trend, more companies are committed to building their own product brands by establishing their production bases or partnering with suitable manufacturers for production, swiftly expanding their sales networks. This trend has become a global development trend in the retail industry, demonstrating vibrant growth prospects (Jiuxian, 2021).

DEVELOPMENT AND STRATEGY

Founding Jiuxian

Jiuxian is the largest operator of B2C liquor websites in China and commands a 50% share of online Baijiu sales in the country, holding an absolute leading position in the industry. However, the company and its management team started from humble beginnings to achieve this height. In March 2001, the founder, Hao Hongfeng and his founding team began their entrepreneurial journey by representing offline liquor brands. In 2009, they established the vertical e-commerce brand Jiuxian, thus entering the online retail of liquor. At that time, not to mention O2O, "e-commerce" itself was a fresh term in the liquor industry. The only reference points for liquor e-commerce were "Yemaijiu" and "Jiumei Wang," both founded in 2008. It was in May 2010 that Jiuxian moved to Beijing, marking the beginning of its e-commerce journey. Purchasing traffic, building a nationwide logistics network, and competing for users with low prices - all these marked a departure from traditional retail for this company.

Offering One-Stop Marketing Services

In the traditional channels, the distribution cost of liquor, especially Baijiu, typically accounts for around 50% or even more of the selling price. There are generally four channel levels: primary distributors, provincial distributors, city-level distributors, and retailers between liquor companies and consumers. The gross margin for each channel level is usually around 15%. Markups vary in hotels and supermarkets, ranging from 20% to 50% and reaching 40% to 100% in hotels. Small-scale retailers have limited markup capabilities and often rely on selling counterfeit products to make a living.

On the other hand, Jiuxian's business model is relatively simple: it directly purchases liquor from upstream liquor companies and sells directly to the market downstream. This approach allows Jiuxian to offer much lower prices than traditional channel terminals, even with a 15% gross margin. It can also eliminate problems such as counterfeiting and price hikes in the circulation process of liquor products. While Jiuxian's model is straightforward, the high threshold of the liquor industry makes it challenging to obtain support from upstream liquor companies and secure the highest-level distributor qualifications. However, Hao Hongfeng's experience in the wine industry has brought many conveniences to Jiuxian. Leveraging his resources accumulated as a traditional liquor distributor, most of Jiuxian's suppliers provide products at the highest distributor level prices, which are 20% to 30% lower than market prices for similar products.

Many liquor companies understand that e-commerce is a significant trend. Still, it is only feasible for some distilleries to create an e-commerce website due to various constraints in marketing, logistics, and other aspects. For instance, Maotai ventured into e-commerce in 2010, but due to logistics issues, the business format outweighed the substance (Financial Sharp Eye, 2021). Jiuxian can bring sales volume to large liquor companies and even more to small ones. It offers end-to-end services from brand promotion, marketing, sales, logistics, payment processing, and direct market feedback. It is a nationwide sales platform. In May 2011, Jiuxian became the exclusive e-commerce agent for Henan Dukang Liquor. The same cooperative return was given by Yibin Dream of Red Mansions Liquor Industry (Li, 2016). Gradually, Jiuxian explored the B2B model and developed it pretty well. Jiuxian has signed strategic cooperation agreements with over 100 well-known liquor companies, supplying products directly to Jiuxian at the highest distributor prices. The cooperation includes nearly the top 30 brands in the domestic Baijiu industry, including Maotai, Zhangyu, and others (Chen, 2013).

Innovation of Patterns and Format

With a team boasting seasoned expertise and deep industry backgrounds, Jiuxian has developed a keen market sense for the liquor distribution industry, enabling the company to continuously innovate its business models and keep pace with industry trends. Facing an increasingly youthful liquor market, Jiuxian continuously innovates in brand promotion and channels, consolidating its advantages in the online liquor retail business. Presently, Jiuxian has established its own online sales platform with its official website and mobile app while also opening official flagship stores on third-party online channels such as Tmall, JD, TikTok, and Kuaishou (Jiuxian, 2021), achieving full coverage of online channels to meet the consumption habits of different demographics.

Starting in April 2012, Jiuxian has successfully collaborated with Dangdang. com, Koobee, YHD.com, and other e-commerce platforms, operating their liquor channels exclusively. In addition to these platforms, Koobee, QQ Wanggou, Suning. com, Newegg, and JD have all reached cooperation agreements with Jiuxian.com.

Using the e-commerce platform, Jiuxian achieved tens of millions in sales during the "Double Eleven Promotion" in 2011, surpassing 61 million RMB in 2012. Sales through platform e-commerce channels account for 40% of Jiuxian's total sales. Offering discounts is a return mechanism for e-commerce users and demonstrates the e-commerce format's challenge to traditional business ecosystems. Meanwhile, to meet liquor consumers' increasingly diverse and personalised demands, Jiuxian continues to expand cooperation with well-known liquor companies domestically and internationally, ensuring its advantage in operating a full range of products. The slogan "Buy authentic liquor, go to Jiuxian.com" is gradually becoming well-known.

Moreover, Jiuxian also actively advocates liquor "new retail". Starting in 2014, it attempted to empower offline stores online and gradually formed a "brand chain" retail system with a robust management model. Currently, Jiuxian's offline brand chain stores are spread across the country. As of the end of June 2021, the company's offline chain stores have reached 1,009, covering 31 provinces and municipalities nationwide. Relying on widely distributed offline stores, Jiuxian achieves rapid delivery in 19 minutes, meeting the timely demands of liquor consumers for the last mile. The Jiuxian brand chain retail system integrates 30 million online registered members into offline stores, continuously improving service quality through the "online ordering, offline delivery" and "online traffic drainage, offline experience" model.

In 2020, live-streaming e-commerce became famous overnight, becoming a new track for various e-commerce platforms. Jiuxian quickly entered the fray, laying out on mainstream short video platforms such as TikTok, creating IPs, opening stores, and incubating KOLs. On the TikTok platform, Jiuxian has formed an IP matrix centred around "Jiuxian.com's Fly Brother", "Jiu Gongege", and "Jiuxian.com's Official Flagship Store", with a total fan base exceeding 10 million. During the 2023 Tmall Double Eleven, the anchor "Jiuxian Liang Ge" achieved a live transaction volume of 480 million RMB.

IPO

After experiencing rapid growth over five years of operations, Jiuxian has gained the favour of numerous renowned investment institutions. Since its inception, Jiuxian has undergone ten rounds of financing, accumulating billions of dollars in total funding. According to the prospectus released in 2021, Jiuxian secured approximately $200 million in its first round of funding in April 2011, followed by a joint investment of $50 million from Sequoia Capital and Eastern Fortune Capital in November of the same year. In August 2012, Jiuxian received its third round of investment totalling $200 million from multiple funds, including Beijing Woyan Capital. This funding aimed to enhance service quality and logistics quality and build its in-house logistics team (Jiuxian, 2021). With its unique value proposition and competitive system, this e-commerce company, founded in November 2009, succeeded in the fiercely competitive liquor market in just four years.

Despite securing significant funding in its early stages, Jiuxian also experienced considerable losses. According to data disclosed during its listing on the New Third Board in 2015, the company incurred losses of over 600 million RMB in just two years, 2013 and 2014, with an additional loss of 250 million RMB in the first half of 2016 (Jiuxian, 2021). Due to repeated delays in disclosing its 2016 financial report, Jiuxian was classified as having a "risk of delisting" by the New Third Board in June 2017, after which the company applied for delisting voluntarily. Subsequently, the company underwent another round of financing in December 2017.

In 2021, Jiuxian submitted its prospectus, officially embarking on the path to IPO. However, despite submitting prospectuses frequently, Jiuxian has yet to go public (Chen, 2022) successfully. On January 26, 2022, the Shenzhen Stock Exchange suspended the IPO review of Jiuxian due to an investigation launched by the China Securities Regulatory Commission into Beijing-based Jindu Law Firm. On March 31, 2022, the IPO review of Jiuxian was again suspended by the Shenzhen Stock Exchange due to expired financial information requiring supplementary submission. Three months later, Jiuxian applied to withdraw its IPO application, leading to the Shenzhen Stock Exchange's decision to terminate the review of its initial public offering. This has marked the failure of Jiuxian's listing on the A-share main board.

Expanding Into Offline Retail

In 2017, Jiuxian began expanding its offline retail channels by establishing "Jiuxian International Wine & Spirit Centre", and its financial condition gradually improved. During this process, the proportion of offline sales for Jiuxian also increased, and its traditional identity as a vertical "website" became increasingly diluted. Subsequent prospectuses showed that from 2018 to 2020, Jiuxian's operating revenues were 2.207 billion RMB, 2.997 billion RMB, and 3.717 billion RMB, respectively, with net profits attributable to shareholders being 28.5565 million RMB, 81.6617 million RMB, and 182 million RMB.

As Jiuxian transitioned into the new retail sector, the increasing proportion of offline sales represented its evolution towards becoming a comprehensive platform. According to Jiuxian's previously released prospectus, from 2018 to 2020, its online channels accounted for 62.9%, 57.5%, and 59.8%, respectively, with traditional online revenues decreasing if excluding live streaming channels, while the number of conventional stores exceeded a thousand. The current proportion of revenues between Jiuxian's online and offline channels is "nearly equal". Another visible trend is that traditional e-commerce platforms and manufacturing companies focus on "new retail". Hao Hongfeng believes that Jiuxian expanded its O2O business too quickly in the past without sufficient accumulation. At that time, no enterprise in the industry is focusing solely on the O2O model. The enterprises are all transitioning to new retail. Therefore, "Jiu Kuai Dao" also needed to transform into new retail.

At this stage, Jiuxian has also made a large-scale transition into "new retail," announcing plans to expand its offline presence with nearly 10,000 "Jiuxian International Wine & Spirit Centre" within the next five years. Initially, Jiuxian opened almost 50 offline "Jiuxian International Wine & Spirit Centre" in Beijing, Shanghai, Guangzhou, Tianjin, Urumqi, Shandong, and Hebei, with an average store area exceeding 300 square meters each. To promote the rapid development of its new retail business, Jiuxian has established a dedicated team of nearly 200 people responsible for integrating upstream liquor resources. In 2018, Jiuxian began focusing on developing its offline chain brands and promoting store expansion through various store models. By the end of 2020, the number of "Jiuxian International Wine & Spirit Centre" had reached 549. Jiuxian's offline revenue has also rapidly increased after implementing these business strategies, growing from 290 million RMB in 2018 to 890 million RMB in 2020, accounting for 24% of Jiuxian's total revenue.

The leaders of Jiuxian also realise that the ability of traditional vertical e-commerce to transform the industry is limited. In an interview with reporters, Jiuxian's chairman, Hao Hongfeng, revealed multiple formats in China's liquor retail industry, including liquor convenience stores, chain stores, liquor e-commerce, and new retail, but traditional models still account for over 90%. This realisation differs entirely from Jiuxian's ambitious goal during its initial establishment, which aimed to capture 5% of the liquor sales market.

THE PEOPLE BEHIND THE UNICORN

Founder and Chairman of the Board: Hao Hongfeng

When discussing the contributors of Jiuxian, one person must be mentioned: Hao Hongfeng. Hao Hongfeng, hailing from Hebei Province, is the founder and chairman of the board of Jiuxian. Today, the success of Jiuxian owes a great deal to the effective leadership of its board of directors, Hao Hongfeng. Before founding Jiuxian.com, Hao Hongfeng had nearly ten years of experience in liquor sales representation. With a dream of achieving 10 billion RMB, he considered various paths, but they all posed significant challenges. It was not until 2009, during his MBA studies at Tsinghua University, where he encountered an e-commerce course, that he saw the market potential in the liquor B2C industry (Zhao, 2017). Consequently, he decided to channel all the resources he had accumulated in the traditional sector into online development, ultimately founding Jiuxian.

Hao Hongfeng stated that amidst the flourishing development of e-commerce, the liquor e-commerce sector was a blank slate at the time. He saw it as the most significant opportunity he had encountered in the past few years, analogous to how coal mining and real estate were lucrative ventures a decade ago. Initially, Hao Hongfeng held a dismissive attitude towards e-commerce, considering it something only children would do, not a pursuit for mature entrepreneurs. However, he later realised the vast potential of this market. He noted that while traditional industries could only cover a 5-kilometer radius with a single store, e-commerce could reach customers across China and globally with just one store (Yang, 2023).

Initially, Hao Hongfeng was indifferent towards the O2O model. At that time, let alone O2O, e-commerce itself was a novel concept in the liquor industry, with "Yemaijiu" and "Jiumeiwang", founded in 2008, were the only reference points. Hao Hongfeng's primary concern was, in a seller's market with tightly controlled distribution and pricing systems, who would sell liquor online at low prices? As Shanxi's largest local liquor distributor, Hao Hongfeng's mindset was already forward-thinking. He believed that leveraging e-commerce could expand his business into broader markets.

Consequently, he embarked on a second entrepreneurial journey with Jiuxian.com, albeit facing considerable pressure. With tens of millions of RMB in funding, Hao Hongfeng travelled to Sichuan hoping to establish partnerships with some distilleries but found it challenging (Zhao, 2017). For large distilleries, orders worth tens of millions were too insignificant, and some distributors viewed Jiuxian, intending to sell liquor online at low prices, as a "foe" and resisted cooperation.

Understanding that traditional methods were inadequate, Hao Hongfeng pushed boundaries to secure the first breakthrough for liquor e-commerce. When distilleries refused to cooperate, he utilised his resources to procure goods from major distributors. He also purchased liquor, storing some high-end products and selling them online at discounted prices under the guise of "old stock" to attract attention. Simultaneously, he firmly upheld the pricing of the distillery's "signature products," ensuring that they provided products exclusively for online sales, thus maintaining profit margins and distinguishing them from offline products.

FUTURE PROJECTS

Overall Development Strategy and Goals

Jiuxian plans to leverage and maximise its existing advantages in product supply chain, research and development, consumer operations, and brand management. By fully utilising technology and logistics services, it aims to accelerate the integration of global upstream supply chains and downstream consumer scenes. Adhering to the culture of "a group of people, a lifetime, only doing one thing" with focus and professionalism, the company will continue cultivating the liquor market deeply and establishing itself as the leading brand in liquor retailing.

Further Expansion of Offline Chain Stores

Offline brand chain stores are among the most critical channels for companies to reach consumers directly. During the reporting period, Jiuxian has already established nearly a thousand stores. However, the domestic liquor consumption market is vast, and there is still significant room for growth in the number of stores (TIM & CADA, 2023). The company will emphasise both scale and quality. It will vigorously develop offline brand chain stores and continue strengthening the management of existing "Jiu Kuai Dao" and "Jiuxian International Liquor City". By improving its operational efficiency, it aims to achieve dual growth in transaction revenue and brand reputation, accumulate liquor retail data, and promote the branding upgrade of the liquor retail industry. The company plans to open thousands of "Jiuxian International Liquor City" and "Jiu Kuai Dao" stores nationwide. It intends to achieve nationwide coverage under a strong management and quality control model (Jiuxian, 2021).

Development of Channel Brands and Product Brands

The company is an omnichannel liquor retailer and service provider that strongly emphasises its brand. Its development is driven by the coordinated operation of the "authentic and fast" channel brand and the "high cost-performance ratio" liquor specialised product brand (Jiuxian, 2021). The company aims to increase the influence of channel brands such as Jiuxian.com and Jiuxian International Liquor City. It also plans to develop its product brands to shape its corporate brand image, increase brand awareness and premium capabilities, strengthen its capital market value, and develop branding in the liquor retail industry (Jiuxian, 2023). Internally, the company will implement brand operation strategies, focus on brand promotion, actively implement corporate brand strategies, enhance the premium capability of the corporate brand, and establish Jiuxian as a leading digital service platform for liquor retailing in China. This will provide consumers with trustworthy channels and purchasable products.

Strengthening Talent Development and Organizational Construction

The talent team is the foundation for maintaining an enterprise's stability and development (Li, 2016). Companies that have succeeded in various industries attach great importance to talent introduction, cultivation, and management. Jiuxian will continue to promote its team construction strategy, adopt scientific methods for selecting, cultivating, retaining, and utilising talents, and cooperate with the company's rapid development. The aim is to provide sufficient talent support for the rapid expansion of business and the continuous enhancement of brand value.

CONCLUSION

The success of Jiuxian is not accidental. The founding team has been deeply involved in the liquor industry for 20 years, accumulating rich market data and target customer segmentation information. They entered the vertical B2C field from scratch and innovatively collaborated with distilleries. They have demonstrated significant innovation and business capabilities by developing a multi-brand strategy encompassing channel brands, product brands, and service businesses. Thanks to the team's unique insights into the market, innovative business models, and effective leadership, Jiuxian has smoothly transitioned from B2C to B2B and O2O, becoming the omnichannel layout company for alcohol in China. It has emerged as a unicorn in the fiercely competitive market and holds a significant position in the liquor market.

This is the result of Jiuxian's peaceful evolution and contribution to the omnichannel revolution, which has profoundly impacted the entire Chinese economy.

REFERENCES

Chen, X. M., & Xu, H. Y. (2017). Strategic cost management in the start-up and growth period of China's e-commerce enterprises: A case study of Jiuxian.com. *Finance & Accounting Monthly*, (31), 82–87. DOI:10.19641/j.cnki.42-1290/f.2017.31.018

Chen, Z. X. (2022). [Jiuxian.com's IPO has not been bid, so who will become the "second share" of liquor circulation?] *Huaxia Wine News*, A06. DOI:10.28390/n.cnki.nhxjb.2022.000367

CNNIC. (2023). *The 51st statistical report on China's Internet development*. CNNIC. https://www.cnnic.com.cn/IDR/ReportDownloads/202307/P020230707514088128694.pdf

Financial Sharp Eye. (2021). *[Jiuxian.com, which sprinted to the market, burned more than a billion dollars, false publicity, and sold fake wine]*. Zhihu. https://zhuanlan.zhihu.com/p/371770835

Jiuxian. (2021). *[IPO prospectus]*. Huatai United Securities Co., Ltd. https://pdf.dfcfw.com/pdf/H2_AN202109291519304688_1.pdf

Jiuxian. (2023). *Company description*. Jiuxian.com. https://help.jiuxian.com/view-0-105.htm

Li, B. (2016). [1919 & Jiuxian: The Coopetition and Cooperation of Liquor E-commerce]. *China Business News*, C07.

TMI & CADA. (2023). *2023 white paper on consumption in China's liquor industry* [White paper]. TMI. https://file.tencentads.com/web/pdf/index/f90b46878551cdba

Wang, C. M. (2014). *Research the wine b2c website for vertical development strategy – take the example of jiuxian.com*. [Unpublished doctoral dissertation. Tianjin University of Commerce. Tianjin].

Yang, M. H. (2022). Behind Jiuxian.com's "off-grid", the first generation of e-commerce has accelerated its transformation. *Huaxia Wine News*, A06. DOI:10.28390/n.cnki.nhxjb.2022.000248

Yang, M. H. (2023). [Instant retail reshapes the trillion-dollar market of the wine industry]. *Huaxia Wine News*. A08.

Yunjiu. (2018). 5. [In two years, 5 Jiuxian International Wine & Spirit Centre stores have been opened, and what is the store's profit?] *Business Culture*, (16), pp. 78–80.

Zhao, B. H. (2017). [Hao Hongfeng, Chairman of Jiuxian: The liquor industry is transitioning from the marketing era to explosive products]. *North Daily*, B03.

KEY TERMS AND DEFINITIONS

B2B: Business to business. It is the transactions and trades between companies or institutions.

B2C: This is business to customer. It is also known as a retail business, and it involves directly selling products and services to consumers.

Channel brands: After production, goods are transported through logistics to various channels, such as distributors, wholesalers, retailers, etc., and finally reach the end consumers. In e-commerce, platforms like Taobao, JD, etc., are considered channel brands.

Demographic Segmentation: Group the consumers based on objective characteristics like age, gender, and education.

Exclusive Products: Distributors in the region exclusively sell products from a particular manufacturer and are not allowed to sell any other manufacturer's goods.

Flow Products: Refer to standardised products sold by well-known domestic and international liquor companies. The company does not participate in the design and development of the products.

Geographic Segmentation: Group the consumers based on where they live.

O2O: Online to Offline. By integrating offline commerce with the Internet, the Internet serves as the front end for offline transactions. This allows offline services to attract customers and enable consumers to screen services online.

Vertical E-Commerce: This refers to an e-commerce model that focuses on deepening operations within a specific industry or niche market. Products on the website fall under the same category of goods.

Chapter 13
Wenheyou:
Reviving and Preserving Changsha's Culinary Heritage

Ke Chen

Beijing Normal University-Hong Kong Baptist University United International College, China

EXECUTIVE SUMMARY

This case study explores Wenheyou, a pioneering culinary brand in Changsha, China, founded by Wen Bin. Positioned at the intersection of nostalgia-driven consumption and urban cultural preservation, Wenheyou exemplifies a strategic blend of culinary innovation and emotional engagement. Targeting young consumers, particularly post-80s and post-90s, Wenheyou revives Changsha's cultural memories through themed dining complexes like Super Wenheyou, integrating local specialties and immersive historical settings. The case delves into Wen Bin's entrepreneurial journey, from humble beginnings with a skewer stall to establishing Asia's largest lobster restaurant and expanding into multi-floor cultural hubs. Through detailed analysis of Wenheyou's market positioning, operational strategies, and community engagement initiatives, the study illustrates how Wenheyou has transformed into a symbol of Changsha's cultural identity, fostering deep consumer connections and contributing to local cultural revitalization efforts.

INTRODUCTION

As the pace of society quickens and the future becomes more uncertain, increasing life pressures can lead to negative emotions such as panic and anxiety. To counteract these feelings, individuals often seek nostalgia, a trend gaining traction across economic, social, and cultural domains. This has led to a growing number

DOI: 10.4018/979-8-3693-2921-4.ch013

of spaces that evoke a sense of nostalgia through visual imagery, offering a refuge from modern anxieties (Wang, 2023). Furthermore, introducing nostalgia into the consumer world has led to a boom in nostalgic consumption. Businesses have also taken advantage of the psychological characteristics of consumers by adopting nostalgic marketing strategies to cater to consumer demand for product promotion and brand building (Chen et al., 2023).

Wenheyou is a restaurant chain that began in 2016 as the Hunan Wenheyou Cultural Industry Development Group. Wenheyou operates a catering-themed cultural tourism business complex across China from Changsha. Today, Wenheyou has become a cultural industry group with catering as its core focus. It is dedicated to researching traditional folklore catering culture, discovering regional folk snacks, blending them with contemporary culture, and creating the "Wenheyou catering model." Its portfolio includes several brands such as Wenheyou Old Changsha Deep Fryer, Wenheyou Old Changsha Lobster House, Wenheyou Big Sausage, Wenheyou Stinky Tofu, māmāchá, Wenheyou Old Changsha Takeaway, and more.

Its commitment is to provide its consumers with personalized, diverse, and high-quality culinary products and services. Although initially rooted in the culinary landscape, Wenheyou quickly transformed into Changsha's most experiential and stylish dining brand, weaving together the rich tapestry of traditional Hunan culture. Wenheyou exemplifies the success of a brand that goes beyond culinary offerings to become a cultural and nostalgic icon.

UNICORN DESCRIPTION

Brief History of the Unicorn

Changsha has two tourist food streets - "Pozi Street" and "Taiping Street". As a veritable old street, Pozi Street is often the first stop for tourists to taste food after visiting Changsha. In this culinary environment, Wenheyou's founder, Wen Bin, started "Sharp Pork Ribs", a small skewer stand on Pozi Street in Changsha in 2010 with only 5,000 RMB in start-up capital. Three months later, his daily revenue reached 3,000 to 4,000 yuan. His success is attributed to strong brand awareness. 2010, there was no IP concept, but Wen Bin used one-fifth of the start-up capital to create a signboard. At the same time, the launch of fried ribs as the primary model, which fits the current pop-up practice concept, increased the skewer stall's popularity. Finally, in the product's differentiation, he developed many new varieties of deep-fried ribs, meatballs, sauces, and so on.

In 2011, after working with a new partner, they opened a 10-square-meter Old Changsha Deep-Fried House, and Wen Bin's entrepreneurial journey went from a stall to a store. As the business expanded, in the winter of 2012, Wen Bin pursued his success by opening the first "Old Changsha Lobster House". Subsequently, from 2015 onwards, Wen Bin's business map expanded rapidly, step by step, with the success of the lobster house, large sausage, deep-fried society, stinky tofu, and other brands and independent stores. The cumulative revenue in 2015 exceeded 100 million yuan. In the first half of 2018, Wenheyou Group developed to open a large store of nearly 5,000 square meters in the Changsha Hisense Plaza.

After Wenheyou opened for business, it was loved by many consumers, with an average queuing time of 3 hours and an average daily turnover rate of 8.5 times, leading to the "Wenheyou Effect" in Changsha. In 2019, Changsha Wenheyou was expanded by two floors to 20,000 square meters and renamed Super Wenheyou. "Super Wenheyou" highlights the old Changsha market culture of the 80s and 90s. Since its opening, Super Wenheyou has seen over 10,000 visitors per day. These tourists primarily visit Super Wenheyou to immerse themselves in the rich cultural heritage of old Changsha, which suggests that the appeal of Super Wenheyou itself to local consumers is relatively low (Canyinjie, 2021). The same year, Wenheyou Old Changsha Lobster House won the Red Dot: Best of the Best Design of the Year award at the German Red Dot Design Awards 2019 (Changsha Evening News, 2019).

In July 2020, after two years of preparation, "Super Wenheyou" opened in Guangzhou Taigu Hui. Compared with the overwhelming praise in Changsha, Guangzhou citizens had mixed reactions. However, it still drew a lot of attention and became a hot topic of discussion in the catering industry. The popularity of "Wenheyou" is mainly due to its nostalgic 80 and 90 Changsha old civic culture decoration, which inherits the civic culture and retains the atmosphere of the hustle and bustle (Luo, 2022). As of April 2021, the company boasted a valuation of $1.55 billion. In October 2022, Wenheyou earned the title "New Consumer Rising Star Brand", according to the Changsha New Consumption Research Institute (Xiong, 2022). By April 2023, the company achieved an impressive valuation of 105 billion RMB, securing a position in the 2023 Global Unicorn List at 705th place (HuRun Research Institute, 2023).

Product, Services, and Cultural Experience

"Crooked" spatial layout, dilapidated old buildings, tiny and messy street food stores. For a modernized provincial capital city that pursues neatness and uniformity, Wenheyou, located in Hisense Plaza on Xiangjiang Middle Road, Tianxin District,

Changsha City, Hunan Province, appears to be particularly "alternative" and "incongruous". The 20,000-square-meter space is located in a modern shopping mall, and Wenheyou was set in the 1980s, with the layout and decoration of the space initially reproducing scenes from the streets of Changsha in the 1980s. Here, small and straightforward stores are scattered; whether selling sausages or cold noodles, all have retained their most primitive state, with stores selling Changsha's local street food. Even the signboard is hand-written on an irregular wooden board. Inside, one feels as if one has "traveled" back in time to the streets of Changsha in the 1980s, and a sense of intimacy arises (Mai, 2020).

The brand's success lies in integrating diverse elements, from traditional cuisine to cultural artifacts, to create a comprehensive experience. Super Wenheyou, in addition to offering marketplace cuisine and an 80's 80-themed marketplace culture scene, also features branded businesses such as a bookstore and G.I. Joe's Laughing Factory. Apart from gourmet food and beautiful photos, the latter offers photo studios, video parlors, hairdressers, video game studios, dance halls, wholesale stores, hardware stores, marriage agencies, and more. Diversified businesses allow customers to have various cultural experiences, enhance the sense of customer experience, extend playtime, and promote consumption. Furthermore, many of the furnishings in the store are "real" and come from thrift markets or residents' old objects. Each object carries its Each has a unique story, and together, they tell the story of the city during that era. These old and storied objects are likelier to evoke fragments of consumers' memories, deepening their impact on the brand (Luo, 2022).

Super Wenheyou incorporates local cultural elements in its space design and introduces art and cultural businesses in its operations. This is one of the reasons why Wenheyou can attract many consumers to its brick-and-mortar restaurant experience. Wenheyou introduces bookstores, the Laughing Factory, art galleries, and more, and organizes cultural exhibitions, such as dialect exhibitions, which further enhance the cultural atmosphere. Additionally, Wenheyou has set up a team to open an art gallery in Super Wenheyou at Hisense Plaza, creating 4-6 local cultural exhibition designs and producing peripheral products yearly. Although the art gallery does not bring direct economic benefits to Wenheyou, it helps to establish Wenheyou's brand image and enhance its cultural atmosphere and overall experience (Chen & Li, 2021).

Customers

Wenheyou's main target audience could be divided into two age groups: 35-45-year-olds who see the 80s and 90s as their childhood or adolescence, who have their feelings and a certain amount of spending power, and who are willing to spend money on products that evoke nostalgia and emotions. Secondly, there are 18-35-year-olds who are curious to explore the 80s and 90s and are interested in popular brands.

Under the influence of nostalgia, young consumers become curious about the past and reminisce about their childhood memories. On the other hand, the middle-aged and old-aged groups who have experienced changes over time seek to revisit nostalgic spaces to find memories of the past and enjoy nostalgic food. Under the influence of nostalgia, restaurants can connect the emotions of several generations and become a symbol of an era. Some brand marketers use nostalgia to establish a strong relationship between consumers and the brand, increasing brand loyalty among consumers (Chen et al., 2023).

Market Analysis

Original Situation of the Market

Changsha is considered one of the most prosperous cities in China, particularly in terms of the nighttime economy. According to the Changsha Municipal Data Resource Management Bureau's report, nighttime entertainment consumption between January and June 2020 accounted for 69.4% of all-day entertainment consumption, and nighttime consumers increased by more than 49% annually. Furthermore, Changsha has a long-standing tradition of emphasizing cultural consumption, and its citizens have developed a consumption habit that values material and spiritual enjoyment and cultural experience as an integral part of daily life. These concepts and norms are rooted in Hunan cultural genes that emphasize initiative, action, openness to change, truth-seeking, utility, and the media's role in cultivating Changsha's consumption ecosystem. Moreover, Changsha was selected as one of the first national pilot cities for expanding cultural consumption in 2016, and the local government has since implemented measures such as government purchases and cultural benefits to boost the city's cultural consumption further and stimulate Changsha's cultural tourism.

According to the "Report on the Impact of China's Urban Night Economy (2020)", nighttime consumption in the leading cities of the domestic nighttime economy has accounted for more than 50% of all-day consumption. In December 2019, the Implementation Opinions on Accelerating the Development of the Nighttime Economy issued by the General Office of the Changsha Municipal Government made it clear that to create a "24-hour city," Changsha would spend three years on promoting the development of the nighttime economy. The plan involves the creation of several characteristic nighttime consumption neighborhoods, nighttime economy carriers, and nighttime economy scenes. To this end, Changsha's Tianxin District Bureau of Commerce has partnered with the Meituan Dianping Group to create a "24-hour city" (Hongwang, 2019).

As urban modernization accelerates, the traditional culture of many cities has gradually decreased, falling into the predicament of a thousand cities. However, in recent years, Super Wenheyou has helped Changsha to overcome this trend and has become an essential attraction for Changsha's cultural and nighttime economy consumption. This attraction is dedicated to the protection and inheritance of Changsha's urban culture. Super Wenheyou is not only a carrier of old Changsha's urban memory but also carries Changsha's consumer culture gene. As an integral part of Hunan's cultural genes, Changsha's marketplace culture enables foreign consumers to experience Hunan culture through artistic and tourism consumption. At the same time, it awakens Changsha locals to remember life in old Changsha and establishes a regional identity (Fu & Wang, 2021).

Super Wenheyou has established an urban cultural space that combines catering, culture, and tourism, providing a comprehensive solution to expand the urban nighttime economy while promoting cultural and tourism consumption. This innovative approach has yielded positive results. Following the successful launch of Changsha Super Wenheyou and Guangzhou Wenheyou in July 2020, Shenzhen Wenheyou opened its doors in April 2021. On the opening day, April 2, it attracted a queue of 50,000 people, causing a significant social impact (Securities Times, 2021).

Evolution of the Market Until Today

The socio-economic pattern is transforming from a service economy to an experience economy. In the era of the experience economy, traditional nighttime economic modes such as late-night snacks and leisure sightseeing can no longer adapt to the consumption needs of the night-time market. Under the multi-layer penetration of immersive experience elements into industrial development, the "catering + social + cultural" model has emerged as a new path to boost nighttime cultural tourism consumption. For example, the Yokohama Ramen Museum in Japan is an immersive interactive experience complex built on the theme of ramen culture. It is equipped with many cultural experience devices and social interaction platforms. Consumers can experience making their ramen and interact with staff dressed in costumes of that era. The museum also showcases multiple scenes of life in the olden days, such as post offices, bookstores, cinemas, kiosks, and clinics, putting people into the urban living environment of the Showa era in Japan. By combining these scenes, people can immerse themselves in the urban living environment of Japan's Showa Era.

On the contrary, many old domestic restaurants are facing a crisis. Beijing's famous gourmet enterprise, Quanjude, which used to be a must-visit nighttime consumption place for foreign consumers in Beijing for a long time, is now entering the era of an experienced economy. However, with a single food consumption model, high prices, and a lack of cultural consumption experience, a hundred-year-old roast duck store,

Quanjude, now fell off the altar. From 2017 to 2019, Quanjude's operating income decreased from 1.861 billion yuan to 1.777 billion yuan and 1.566 billion yuan. The net profit also showed a downward trend, 1.36 billion yuan, and 1.566 billion yuan, respectively, and the net profit of 1.3 billion yuan. The market capitalization has shrunk by over half (He, 2021).

In the era of experience economy, consumer demand has gradually transitioned from superficial sensory experience to the pursuit of deep experience of spirit and identity. The requirements for the scene have also risen from the one-dimensional visual, auditory, gustatory, olfactory, and tactile enjoyment to the three-dimensional spatial scene experience of physical and mental immersion, meaningful connection, and cultural identity resonance. According to "Experiential Marketing" written by Bird Schmitt, product marketing in the era of the experience economy should put customers' experience first, and consumer experience consists of five kinds of experiences: Sense, Feel, Think, Act, and Relate (Schmitt, 1999).

The immersion, cultural identity, and spatial consumption characteristics of Super Wenheyou make it a new paradigm of cultural tourism consumption and a new landmark of urban culture in the era of the experienced economy. It offers consumers a unique cultural experience that activates their identity. Cultural identity experience is a cognitive process that involves exploring and confirming one's identity. This process is related to sensory, emotional, and thinking experiences and is mainly reflected in the following aspects: action experience and association experience. Super Wenheyou offers consumers a distinctive cultural experience, showcasing its unique charm.

Super Wenheyou uses immersive scenes as a channel and urban cultural memories as a basis to facilitate consumers' emotional interaction and cultural identification. The key to achieving this is creating scenes imbued with urban cultural memories. According to German scholar Jan Assmann, cultural memory is inherited through external symbols, and it connects the experiences of each cultural subject with the world of meaning they inhabit together. Based on this experience, individuals can shape their identity through the symbols of identity that materialize in the world they belong to. Super Wenheyou is an immersive consumption place and an experiential space for storing urban cultural memory. When consumers from different backgrounds and identities visit this cultural space, they can feel the city's cultural memory, experience the common attributes of the ethnic group, and then generate a sense of identity. This sense of identity arises from the retrospection of the dying emotions and memories in the post-industrial city, which leads to cultural homogeneity. The existence of cultural symbols and memories prompts consumers to sublimate their feelings and extend them to the depth of the experience level.

DEVELOPMENT AND STRATEGY

Wenheyou focuses on the city's nostalgia-driven consumption. By using exterior design, they create a culture that reflects the urbanization process that has been going on since China's reform and opening up. With young consumers looking for urban imprints, the main focus of consumption is the vintage generation. The theme of 80 years of urban culture is chosen, and the era theme, color tone, lighting, and other design elements are used to activate the emotional interaction between consumers and the dining space. This nostalgic theme-based dining complex design differs from the high-tech futuristic catering space that neglects human nature design. It emphasizes the emotional belonging of consumers and activates the nostalgic psychology of consumers from three aspects: customer segmentation, demand excavation, and value proposition. It restores and re-designs the past life scene with the background of the current era (Shandong University Cultural Industry Key Laboratory, 2021).

From a customer segmentation perspective, Wenheyou has been targeting the young generation of post-80s and post-90s since the beginning of their skewer stall. On the one hand, this generation grew up in a time of rapid economic growth and environmental changes, and many are far from their hometowns. They have memories of their lives in the last century, and Changsha Wenheyou's preservation of the old city can provide them with a nostalgic experience. On the other hand, young people are increasingly becoming the primary audience for dining out. They value individualism and may have a weaker sense of family, which leads them to eat out more frequently, making them a key consumer group for Changsha Wenheyou's catering industry. Furthermore, the younger generation prefers more convenient ways of socializing and acquiring information, which allows Changsha Wenheyou to create a "pop-up" product quickly, thereby achieving higher traffic creation and driving consumption (Luo, 2022).

Wenheyou's team conducted regular seminars by going to the street markets to conduct research. They believe that the loss of urban culture has the most direct impact on small businesses. Many old brands and crafts grown in the city are slowly disappearing, and the city's culture faces extinction. In this situation, catering, as a direct expression of urban memory, can attract young consumers to explore cultural memories through food. Furthermore, after conducting long-term research on various consumer groups, Wenheyou has positioned its brand price between 100 and 150 RMB per meal, focusing on the post-80s and post-90s consumer groups. This positioning was developed by the Shandong University Cultural Industry Key Laboratory in 2021.

Wenheyou team's value proposition delivery starts from the hidden needs of merchants and users. It is committed to making Wenheyou a part of the city infrastructure to realize a win-win situation for all parties. Firstly, it emphasizes the value of users by not only introducing various food categories and setting up entertainment venues such as art museums and billiard rooms. This provides consumers with an integrated experience of sports, entertainment, and food, capturing the consumption preferences of young people. Secondly, it emphasizes the value of merchants by adopting the "cooperation + direct operation" model. Wenheyou bears store decoration, infrastructure, and fixed costs, while the merchants bear Wenheyou's fixed costs. At the initial stage of cooperation with introduced merchants, Wenheyou only determines the target turnover, and Wenheyou only participates in the share of the overage portion. Thirdly, it emphasizes discovering the value of the city. Wenheyou positions itself as the excavator of each city's culture and explores local cuisines while actively promoting local characteristics through various channels to promote the city's construction.

Taking "Super Wenheyou" as an example, Wenheyou entered into strategic cooperation with Tangrenshen in 2018 to set up the first Wenheyou Hisense Plaza store, which focuses on the lobster category. It also invites local small stores with specialties to move in and boost the late-night snack economy. The seven-floor store is decorated with old objects, marketing the atmosphere of the streets and alleys of old Changsha in the 1980s. 2019, it was upgraded to Super Wenheyou, known as the "Museum of Old Changsha Culture". Changsha Super Wenheyou, as a sub-brand of Wenheyou, aims to promote Hunan culture. Using this as a template, Wenheyou has opened Super Wenheyou in Guangzhou and Shenzhen, abandoning the traditional ribbon-cutting ceremony on the opening day and organizing Cantonese dialect exhibitions to interpret the culture of Guangdong and Hong Kong. This has helped Wenheyou quickly integrate with the local market culture (Shandong University Cultural Industry Key Laboratory, 2021).

Therefore, Super Wenheyou focuses on "experience marketing" for consumers. For example, its WeChat public account frequently promotes interactive activities such as the "Super Friends Program," which records stories between customers and Wenheyou, and "Sharing Love Stories in Wenheyou on Tanabata Festival," to establish and strengthen relationships with customers. During holidays, the company assigns staff specific roles in interacting with consumers. It launches diverse theme activities such as "Super New Year's Day Carnival Retro Disco Party" and "June 1st Searching for Hidden Trigger Points". Additionally, it collaborates with the media to produce value-driven Wenheyou IP add-on products, such as participating in the production of the documentary "My Changsha" and organizing an exhibition of images of the city's wells and humanities.

This has enabled Changsha Wenheyou to establish itself as the guardian of Changsha's urban cultural inheritance and transform Changsha's urban culture into a bridge between the enterprise and the city. As a result, the brand has become an embodiment of Changsha's tourism attributes. Furthermore, Changsha Wenheyou has delved deeper into local specialties by taking Changsha's long-established brands as the core of its catering IP. The brand has explored local reputable stores, little-known stores with collectively representative business places in Changsha's old city, and daily spaces with memories of life. In doing so, Changsha Wenheyou has ultimately formed a composite form of business that meets young people's demand for offline experiential consumption and stimulates their desire to consume and share. Based on this, Changsha Wenheyou's marketing will expand its consumer influence further (Luo, 2022).

THE PEOPLE BEHIND THE UNICORN

Unicorn Founder Wen Bin

Wen Bin, formerly known as Wen Yanran, was born in 1987 and is native to Changsha. After graduation, Wen Bin was under immense pressure to make ends meet. He took a job at a store, but his income remained unstable. During these challenging times, Wen Bin sought solace in frequent visits to a barbecue stall. His situation prompted the stall owner to intervene, urging him to reconsider his priorities and focus on making a living more efficiently. This wake-up call prompted Wen Bin to realize the gravity of his situation and inspired him to face the challenges that life presented to him. Determined to turn things around, he pursued a new career path.

Wen is not your typical business owner at first glance. He describes himself as a hard worker, a good street vendor, and the owner of Asia's largest lobster restaurant, affectionately known as the "Changsha Mango" (Ai & Shi, 2022). According to Weng Donghua, co-founder of Wenheyou, "Wen Bin is a very lonely person." Wen Bin had a difficult childhood growing up in a family that was not well-off. He moved countless times through the streets of Changsha, often staying with relatives more than a dozen times alone. This lack of security at an early age partly shaped Wen Bin's relatively introverted personality and gave him a particular obsession with achieving something.

Wen Bin, the founder of Wenheyou, had worked in various occupations, such as waiting tables and cell phone customer service, before starting his own business. In 2010, he decided to venture into the food industry, offering fried food that he knew how to prepare best, and the people of Changsha loved that. At just 22 years old, he quit his job as a car salesman and set up a fried skewer stand on Pozi Street in Changsha (Shi Mei Kan Changsha, 2020). Wen Bin started his business because he recognized the potential financial benefits of setting up a stall. At the beginning of his company, he set a small goal: make the stall earn 3,000 yuan daily. This was close to the monthly salary of an ordinary citizen in Changsha at that time. Therefore, from the beginning of his business, Wen Bin had an almost obsessive and strict demand on himself (Wen & Liao, 2016).

Wen Bin has repeatedly shared his early business journey with the public. He started with a capital of 5,000 yuan and would only sleep four hours a day. Wen Bin's stall was open for 12 hours, from 4:00 pm to 4:00 am, and he managed everything from purchasing and preparing food to cooking and entertaining customers. At 22, he set up his first stall; at 23, he opened a deep-frying store; and at 24, he started the Old Changsha Lobster House. His next venture was the first Super Wenheyou, which he founded at 30. Wen Bin's success can be attributed to his excellent storytelling skills in business. As mentioned earlier, at the beginning, he spent almost one thousand yuan out of his five thousand to craft a sign and create his first IP, Sharp Pork Ribs. The sign on the store read "Old Changsha Deep-Fried House". The style of the black letters on the white background was reminiscent of a vintage plaque from a "People's Commune Canteen". This unique product and branding strategy quickly helped him generate his first bucket of money, as no one had ever done the "barbecue ribs" category before.

Despite the store's small size, it featured a big pot, clay stove, four square tables, and nostalgic decor. The shop launched deep-fried products that were real, sufficient, and affordable, which helped him win a reputation for quality and loyal customers. This helped him stand out in a highly competitive industry where quality was often sacrificed for the sake of competition. During this exploration stage, the enterprise developed a preliminary concept of the brand centered around innovation and renewal. Looking back, these core driving forces allowed Wenheyou to rise above the fierce competition in the restaurant industry and quickly become a leading player.

He was born and raised on Pozi Street, where he sells pork ribs. He says he wants to take the neighborhood he grew up in and turn it into a restaurant with 'more attitude'. Whether it's a lobster restaurant or a super Wenheyou, he's looking to develop Pozi Street into a business model. The Wenheyou team has created an immersive urban space like a movie set. They use old objects to present the story of 'Old Changsha'. In an interview, Wen Bin confessed that 'innovation cannot be done without subjectivity'. Wenheyou owes its success to Wen Bin's profound market insight and brand-building strategy. By innovating products and creating a consumer space with regional cultural characteristics, Wenheyou satisfies consumers' pursuit of food and touches their nostalgia. Additionally, Wen Bin's unique understanding of brand storytelling sets Wenheyou apart from its competitors, making it an iconic brand representing not only food but also the civic culture of Changsha.

CONCLUSION

The Wenheyou community in Changsha is a unique blend of traditions, childhood memories, and flavors. It is based on the concept of Super Wenheyou. When people visit Super Wenheyou in Hisense Plaza today, they experience more than just a restaurant, attraction, or museum of old things. It is a 7-story, 20,000-square-meter business space where visitors can savor traditional Changsha food like crayfish and sugar-oil poi. The space features black-and-white TV sets broadcasting old documentaries, radios playing news from the past, and various amenities such as street food stalls, bookstores, theatres, grocery stores, and foot-washing stores, all reminiscent of Changsha's civic area in the 1980s. Wenheyou is a bustling and intimate place that evokes emotional connections and relaxation. Over the past decade, it has become a culinary city with cultural significance and a distinctively "Changsha flavor".

REFERENCES

Ai, J., & Shi, D. (2022). ,Wenheyou: Escaping the troubles of Changsha. *Business School*, (05), 48–51.

Canyinjie. (2021). *With a valuation of tens of billions and a rumored listing, is Wenheyou's value worthy of being China's No. 1 Catering Media?* Canyinjie. http://int.canyinj.com/index.php?m=home&c=View&a=index&aid=249

Cao, J. Y. (2020, June 23). ——Wenheyou [The Crowd-Pulling Popularity King]. *New Hunan·Daxiangcai News*. https://m.voc.com.cn/xhn/news/202006/14651666.html

Changsha Evening News. (2019, November 4). *""["Wenheyou" wins Germany's Red Dot Design Award.]* ICWSB. https://www.icswb.com/h/152/20191104/627699.html

Changsha Municipal Data Resource Management Bureau. (2020, October 28). 2020 analysis report on the night economy data of Changsha City. *WeChat Official Account: Changsha Releases*. https://mp.weixin.qq.com/s/zq7LerZth9_aPIH5DAJ-ZA

Chen, G. E., & Li, J. X. (2021). ""——Research on "Internet Celebrity" Consumption Space in the Internet Era: A Case Study of Changsha Super Wenheyou. In *Urban Design Towards High-Quality Development: Proceedings of the 2021 China Urban Planning Annual Conference (07 Urban Design)* (pp. 1210-1220). School of Architecture, Southeast University. https://doi.org/DOI:10.26914/c.cnkihy.2021.026600

China Hunan Province Political Consultative Conference. (2022, June 28). *! "" [Boosting the Hunan Cuisine Industry from Billions to Trillions! Provincial Political Consultative Conference Continues to Focus and Contribute Wisdom to "Creating a Great Table of Hunan Dishes."]* Political Consultative Conference Media. https://www.hunanzx.gov.cn/hnzx/wzsyszx/zxdt/202206/t20220628_26527415.html

Fu, C., & Wang, Y. (2021). —— [Research on urban night-time cultural and tourism consumption space from the perspective of the scene: A perspective based on the cultural scene of Changsha Super Wenheyou]. *Journal of Wuhan University (Philosophy & Social Sciences)*, 74(6), 58–70. DOI:10.14086/j.cnki.wujss.2021.06.006

Fu, C., & Zhong, S. (2014). —— [Research on the construction of regional cultural tourism themes from the perspective of cultural identity experience: A case study of the Hexi Corridor]. *Journal of Wuhan University (Philosophy & Social Sciences)*, 67(1).

He, Y. (2021, April 25). *20202.62 [Quanjude faces a massive loss of nearly three years of profit in one year, with a 2020 deficit of 262 million yuan].* China Business Network. http://www.zgswcn.com/article/202104/20210425153451141.html

Hongwang. (2019, December 25). *[Changsha Pozi Street and Taiping Street become the first national "Must-Eat Streets" recognized by Dianping]*. SOHU. https://m.sohu.com/a/362638374_100180399

HuRun Research Institute. (2023, April 18). *2023 Global Unicorn List*. HuRun. https://www.hurun.net/zh-CN/Info/Detail?num=PH71LJQJPANH

iMedia. (2024). *The poor boy, whom his ex-girlfriend abandoned, became a student of Jack Ma and opened three stores with a valuation of 10 billion*. iMedia. https://min.news/en/entertainment/722bc88fc8d6d4fb5135872cfc33ac71.html

Luo, M. (2022). *[Reevaluation of the value of Changsha Wen He You from the perspective of urban renewal practices]* [Master's thesis, Hunan University]. https://link.cnki.net/doi/10.27135/d.cnki.ghudu.2022.003410

Mai, J. H. (2020). " [The rebellion of Wenheyou]. *Splendor*, (10), 56–58.

QCC. (n.d.). Hunan Wenheyu Cultural Industry Development Group Co., Ltd. *QCC*. https://www.qcc.com/firm/cfd3bfb144580a8b8112a1a6633d37a2.html

Schmitt, B. (1999). Experiential marketing. *Journal of Marketing Management*, 15.

Securities Times. (2021, April 2). *five , [Over 50,000 people queue up, and Shenzhen Wen He You goes viral]*. WeChat Official Account: Securities Times. https://mp.weixin.qq.com/s/n3JG-MOYkP55o8JbeSlPVSQ

Shandong University Cultural Industry Key Laboratory. (2021, May 7). *"" [Marketing Model Research on the "Wenheyou Phenomenon" in the Context of Internet Celebrity Economy]*. CS Lab. http://www.cslab.sdu.edu.cn/info/1078/2416.htm

Shi Mei Kan Changsha. (2020, May 14). *[A decade of innovation: How Changsha's Wen He You moved from street stall to the world stage]*. Xingchen Online. https://news.changsha.cn/cslb/html/111874/20200514/78683.shtml

Wen, N., & Liao, Q. (2016, July 20). : [Wen Bin: Even with a street stall, I aim to create a brand]. *Hongwang*. https://hn.rednet.cn/c/2016/07/20/4039241.htm

Xiong, Y. (2022, November 1). *2022(), [2022 China (Changsha) New Consumption City Summit inaugurated, establishing the Changsha New Consumption Research Institute]*. Huasheng Online. https://hunan.voc.com.cn/article/202211/202211010711551222.html

KEY TERMS AND DEFINITIONS

Brand Awareness: It is the familiarity of consumers with a particular product or service.

Cultural Landscape: This is a term used in geography, ecology, and heritage studies to describe a symbiosis of human activity and the environment. As defined by the World Heritage Committee, it is "cultural properties that represent the combined works of nature and of man.

Experience Economy: An experience economy sells memorable experiences to customers.

Intellectual Property (IP): It refers to creations of the mind, such as inventions, literary and artistic works, designs, symbols, names, and images used in commerce.

Nighttime Economy: It is a series of activities and experiences tied to entertainment and nighttime socialization, stressing its social aspects.

Nostalgia: It is a feeling of sadness mixed with pleasure and affection when you think of happy times in the past.

Nostalgia Consumption: It is a social and cultural trend that could be described as the act of consuming goods that elicit memories from the past. It is associated with a feeling of nostalgia.

Chapter 14
Beisen:
Transforming Human Capital Management

Liu Yuan

University of Warwick, UK

EXECUTIVE SUMMARY

This case study examines Beisen Holdings Limited's evolution as a pioneer in China's Human Capital Management (HCM) industry. Beginning with its inception in 2002, Beisen strategically embraced cloud computing and advanced AI technologies to offer integrated HCM solutions. The study traces Beisen's transition from software as a service (SaaS) to platform as a service (PaaS), culminating in the development of iTalent X—a comprehensive HCM platform. Key innovations include AI-driven recruitment, talent management, and performance analytics tools, which have reshaped HR practices for over 6,000 enterprises, including 70% of the Fortune 500 in China. Through detailed analysis of market dynamics, technological advancements, and socio-economic effects like the pandemic and demographic shifts, the case underscores Beisen's leadership and its transformative impact on the HCM landscape.

INTRODUCTION

Beisen Holdings Limited is an innovator in China's Human Capital Management (HCM) sector. Since its establishment in 2002, the company has been revolutionizing human resource management with its innovative cloud-based solutions. In 2015, Beisen shifted from a Software-as-a-Service (SaaS) model to a Platform-as-a-Service (PaaS) model, solidifying its position as an industry leader. The company's successful IPO in 2023 showcased its growth, resilience, and market dominance, with RMB 750.9 million in revenues and a client base of over 6,000 organizations,

DOI: 10.4018/979-8-3693-2921-4.ch014

including 70% of China's Fortune 500 companies. This document delves into Beisen's strategic journey, charting its progress from early challenges to achieving unicorn status in the HR industry, focusing on its innovations in integrating cloud and AI technologies. The paper also discusses Beisen's influence on HR practices, its adaptation to a changing market, and its significant role in shaping the future of work in China. Furthermore, it sheds light on how Beisen thrived in the complex world of HR technology, emphasizing its dedication to technological excellence and customer-centric solutions in the transformation of HR management.

Introduction

Beisen Holdings Limited was established in 2002 and is dedicated to the Human Resource Management (HRM) industry. Since its inception, Beisen has been committed to developing and providing innovative Human Capital Management (HCM) solutions to help businesses optimize talent management and development. Beisen has won many awards during its development. In 2019, the Ministry of Industry and Information Technology of China evaluated Beisen as one of China's top 20 Internet growth enterprises. In August 2021, Beisen was awarded the "Best Growth To B Enterprise Service" in the 2021 iResearch Awards. The same year, Beisen was listed in the "Forbes China Technology 50". On April 18, 2023, Beisen was ranked 597th on the 2023-Hurun Global Unicorn List with an enterprise valuation of RMB 13 billion.

With the advancement of cloud computing technology, Beisen launched cloud services for HR management in 2010 and transitioned from a Software as a Service (SaaS) model to a Platform as a Service (PaaS) model in 2015, marking a significant shift in technology and service models. Introducing Beisen's cloud services and PaaS model allowed it to offer more flexible and integrated HCM solutions. Through this model, Beisen could provide customized services to enterprises and integrate various SaaS software on its platform, covering the entire process for employees from onboarding to offboarding, including AI interviews, intelligent check-in, onboarding guidance, and performance tracking. The PaaS product, Beisen iTalent X, aims to provide customised services to enterprises through PaaS as the underlying logic. Moreover, Beisen offers AI and BI (Business Intelligence) intelligent decision-making analysis to assist corporate leaders in making informed decisions and understanding employee efficiency. In 2020, Beisen released a comprehensive, all-in-one cloud-based HCM solution, becoming the only Chinese company to build a unified and open PaaS infrastructure. This event further solidified Beisen's HCM industry leadership, showcasing its technological innovation and service integration capability.

The successful IPO in Hong Kong in 2023 recognized the company's growth and market position and marked a new chapter in Beisen's development. The IPO success provided Beisen with the financial support to further expand its business scale, strengthen technological research and development, and extend its market reach, allowing the company to maintain a leading position in the fiercely competitive market and continue to provide high-quality HCM solutions to its customers. According to the reality of the FY2023 financial report, Beisen's total employees reached 2,085, and the group's total revenue was RMB750.9 million, of which the subscription revenue from cloud-based HCM solutions was RMB537.3 million, accounting for 71.5 per cent of the total revenue. Its total assets amounted to RMB1,870.8 million, of which non-current assets amounted to RMB199.8 million and current assets amounted to RMB1,671.0 million. Additionally, Beisen has helped more than 6,000 medium-sized and large enterprises improve their business, including 70% of the Fortune 500 companies in China and completed many successful business cases in the HCM industry, such as helping Shanghai Volkswagen Automotive Co., Ltd. build a campus recruitment platform, creating an AI interview system, assisting Mengniu Dairy Group in managing 40,000 employees, and cooperating with Tencent Meeting to develop a new video interview mode (Beisen Holdings Limited, 2023).

Based on Beisen's official website, the IDC industry report for 2016-2023 reveals that Beisen has held the first place in China's HR SaaS market share for eight years and has been the leader in the three significant sub-markets of Core HR, Performance Management, and Recruitment Management. By 2023, over 1 billion users had checked in through this system, the cloud database had processed over 120 million resumes and arranged more than 7 million interviews. After product iterations, its main products reached 17 kinds, and in recent years, new products like AI Family, SenGPT, and Beisen Inspiring were launched.

EVOLUTION OF BEISEN

Early Stage: Entering the Internet, Becoming an Industry Benchmark

In 2002, Ji Weiguo, the current general manager of Beisen, and his high school friend Wang Zhaohui, the chairman of Beisen, collaborated to establish their own business. Despite Wang Zhaohui's plans to pursue a career in pharmaceutical chemistry, he chose to forego that path to join Ji Weiguo in the human resources industry after learning about his friend's venture (interview with General Manager Ji Weiguo). At that time, China's human resources market was still in its early stages, providing ample opportunities for development (interview with General Manager Ji Weiguo).

When Beisen first started, its target customers were university students, and the initial product was software designed to assist students in gathering and organizing recruitment information (interview with General Manager Ji Weiguo). However, the receptiveness of university students to Internet products was low, leading Ji Weiguo and Wang Zhaohui to shift their focus. They then attempted to promote the software to university teachers; however, the teachers found that it increased their workload instead of streamlining it (interview with General Manager Ji Weiguo). Later, they targeted universities as potential clients but found that the small number of universities in China at the time necessitated a broader scope of the market share (interview with General Manager Ji Weiguo).

Nevertheless, in 2003, while promoting their products, a teacher from Qinghua suggested that the products could be sold on the Internet. This crucial suggestion brought about one of the most significant innovations in the history of Beisen - abandoning the software and providing services over the Internet. They embraced this valuable suggestion, recognizing the internet human resources market as a largely untapped opportunity. With numerous companies reaching out, eager to offer talent assessment services to aid in selecting suitable candidates, the enterprise rapidly moved beyond its initial survival phase. This transformation's success inspired Ji Weiguo to realize that most innovations in enterprise products originated from customer suggestions. He understood that true enterprise innovation should align with customer demand and market needs. From this initial breakthrough, Beisen's journey of innovation has continued unabated.

This insight influenced Beisen's approach to innovation and established a solid foundation for the company's future successful innovations. Initially, Beisen's offerings were rooted in traditional talent assessment systems like the California Psychological Inventory (CPI) and the Edwardian Personal Preference Inventory (EPP). In 2005, Ji Weiguo introduced an innovative approach to better cater to customer needs: deconstructing these tests and merging multiple sets of questionnaires into a single, customizable module. This innovation allowed customers to tailor the combination of tests to their specific requirements. Furthermore, the system was designed to generate the most pertinent test outcomes for managers, enabling the parallel comparison of multi-dimensional assessment results. The product also featured built-in templates for frequently sought-after roles, including sales professionals, teachers, and others.

Beisen developed its competency assessment test system to guarantee the product's professionalism. After consulting with experts who accepted the innovative test template's practicality and credibility, Beisen launched it into the market to let its performance be judged by real-world demand. The product turned out to be a tremendous success. Between 2006 and 2008, it experienced rapid growth, and by

2008, Beisen had become a leading name in talent assessment, securing an almost monopolistic stance in the Chinese market.

The success in the evaluation domain firmly established the direction for Beisen's product development strategy, emphasizing the principle of "combination". Reflecting on Beisen's evolution from SaaS to PaaS, which achieved the integration of their offerings, it is clear that their business philosophy and the transformative shift in evaluation methods initiated in 2005 are inseparable. Throughout its development, Beisen has always prioritized crafting intuitive interfaces within each system module. By deeply understanding customer needs, they adeptly assemble these components, ensuring they meet their clients' specific, customized requirements. This approach underscores Beisen's commitment to innovation and customer satisfaction.

Rising Period: Launch of iTalent and the Emergence of the HCM industry

The evolution of Beisen Holdings Limited, under the leadership of Ji Weiguo, exemplifies a proactive and forward-thinking approach in the rapidly evolving HCM industry. Initially gaining traction with its leading assessment products, Beisen, under Ji's stewardship, did not rest on its laurels. Through rigorous business practices and market feedback, the company identified critical limitations in its offerings. While their assessment tools were practical, they needed to meet the comprehensive needs of clients who sought a deeper understanding and management of their employees. This gap prompted a pivotal strategic shift marking Beisen's second major transformation.

Understanding the need for a more holistic approach to HCM, Ji Weiguo and his team pivoted from focusing exclusively on assessment tools to developing an integrated management system. This strategic redirection was not merely an expansion of services but a fundamental reimagining of Beisen's role in the HR tech landscape. The new integrated system encompassed modules for recruitment, onboarding, performance management, payroll management, and more, aiming to offer a one-stop solution for all HCM-related challenges. This approach aligned with the trends in international markets, with a growing preference for comprehensive HCM solutions over standalone products.

In 2009, Beisen embarked on a project that culminated in the launch of China's first talent management cloud computing platform, iTalent, in 2010. This platform represented a significant leap forward for Beisen and the HCM industry in China. However, the innovative nature of iTalent meant that initial market reception was tepid, as the concept of a cloud-based HCM platform still needed to be developed and somewhat misunderstood among potential clients.

The global HCM landscape witnessed a paradigm shift in 2011 when Success-Factors, an American company with 4,000 customers, was acquired by SAP for $3 billion. This acquisition underscored the immense value and potential of HCM software solutions, serving as a worldwide wake-up call to the industry. Following this, other major players like IBM and Oracle made similar moves, acquiring Kenexa and Taleo. These acquisitions signaled a growing recognition of the strategic importance of HCM systems in driving organizational success.

After global developments, Beisen's strategic pivot and foresight began to resonate more firmly within the Chinese market. Competitors and potential clients started to acknowledge the critical role of comprehensive HCM solutions in achieving business efficiency and talent optimization. Beisen's iTalent platform, with its innovative cloud-based approach, positioned the company at the forefront of this industry transformation, enabling it to tap into the vast potential of the HCM market. This period marked a significant turning point for Beisen as it transitioned from a market challenger to a leading force in China's HCM industry, setting new standards for innovation and comprehensive talent management solutions. Crisis: Uncertain Market, Beisen at a Crossroad

Despite Beisen's preparedness and innovative iTalent platform, the company faced unexpected difficulties that severely tested its resilience and adaptability in the competitive market. In an ambitious move to expand its user base, Beisen, inspired by Qihoo 360's success with a "free product model," offered its products for free in mid-2011. This strategy aimed to attract users by providing them with no-cost access to the system's personnel management functions, hoping to monetize the accumulated traffic eventually. However, this approach yielded different anticipated results, leading to a reevaluation of Beisen's business strategy.

In 2012, Beisen focused on developing a product specifically designed for small and medium-sized enterprises (SMEs) to recover and realign their market position. This new product was conceived to be both user-friendly and economically priced, aiming to penetrate the market quickly through a competitive pricing strategy. Beisen's objective was to quickly achieve a high sales volume, thereby securing a steady cash flow to stabilize the company. Despite these strategic adjustments, the launch of the new product encountered significant challenges, failing to meet market expectations.

A critical issue arose from the customization of services; the sales team occasionally overstated the capabilities of Beisen's products, leading to a mismatch between customer expectations and the actual performance and functionality of the deployed solutions. This disconnect resulted in customer dissatisfaction, as the products frequently needed to address the unique challenges faced by the businesses. The accumulation of such instances precipitated a period of intense difficulty for

Beisen, significantly impacting its financial health and pushing the company into a dire cash crisis.

Reflecting on this tumultuous period, Ji Weiguo, the CEO of Beisen, candidly shared the gravity of the situation. The company found itself in an unforeseen financial predicament, necessitating the sale of assets to manage the liquidity shortfall. The financial strain was so acute that there was a moment when Beisen faced the possibility of being unable to fulfil its payroll obligations for a month. This critical juncture represented a significant low point for Beisen, challenging its survival and forcing the company to reevaluate its strategies and operational approach to face the crisis.

The trials faced by Beisen underscore the unpredictable nature of business, the importance of adaptability and strategic flexibility, and the need to align product offerings closely with market needs and customer expectations. This experience also highlights the critical role of effective communication and realistic promises in maintaining customer trust and satisfaction.

Overcoming Challenges: The Journey From SaaS to PaaS Upgrade

In this predicament, Beisen finally decided to adjust the target customers again. Organizations often deal with more complex personnel management processes and commonly face communication, file sharing, and talent management issues. These issues sometimes require the development of new IT systems to address them. However, this solution model brings with it many potential problems. For example, if the system interfaces of different IT systems need to be better designed, it can easily lead to system incompatibility. Second, data between systems often need to be fixed. From the perspective of employee workflow, frequent switching between different software can significantly reduce work efficiency. Moreover, the more systems used, the longer the employee training time required. This affects immediate productivity and adds to the operational environment's overall complexity, making it more challenging to maintain high efficiency and effectively manage and execute tasks.

In an interview, Mr. Wang Zhaohui noted, "HR managers have very high expectations for the operational experience, interactivity, and user-friendliness of their work systems. The inconvenience of constantly switching between different modules would be especially driving them crazy!" This insight underscored the necessity for Beisen to develop a comprehensive, integrated digital HCM product tailored to the specific needs of medium and large-sized enterprises, aiming to enhance the efficiency and effectiveness of their HR management processes. Indeed, innovation needs to be based on solid ground, and Beisen conducted an in-depth investigation of this strategy. In 2014, Beisen's founder, Wang Zhaohui, personally led a team to the United States to do market research. After understanding the business models, operating conditions, customer relationships, and other aspects of more than ten similar companies, they discovered that US HCM enterprises have a favorable market environment and a loyal customer base among upper-market segments, namely medium to large enterprises. Consequently, Beisen decided to focus on the upper market, aiming for product development and research, emphasizing block integration and integrated services as the product's selling points.

In 2016, Beisen embarked on a new strategic direction to create an "integrated cloud-based HCM system" to provide comprehensive support for employees throughout the entire lifecycle, from onboarding to departure, within the HR software era. The development and refinement of this product consumed nearly three years for Beisen, during which the company's marketing and sales activities were significantly scaled back. During these challenging times, Beisen faced slow financing, impeded expansion efforts, and severe internal friction. Zhaohui reflects on that period as three years filled with fear and anxiety.

In 2019, Beisen achieved a milestone with the launch of iTalent X, a new product that effectively addressed the longstanding incompatibility issue between various modules within enterprise systems. Users and employees can now access all necessary software through a single portal, streamlining operations and enhancing efficiency. External evaluations praised Beisen's integration strategy as being at least three years ahead of its competition. Furthermore, the pandemic's push towards remote work amplified the demand for online office solutions, prompting many companies to customize Beisen's services to coordinate their remote operations better. As a result, Beisen saw a significant increase in customer orders, doubling in the first quarter of 2020, marking the beginning of a promising upward trend.

The product has seen positive market acceptance, evidenced by Beisen's revenue growth from CNY 382 million to CNY 750 million over the five years from 2019 to 2023. This growth reflects an increase in revenue and a gradual expansion in market share, showcasing the product and the company's growing influence in the industry.

Summarising the development in the era of integration, Beisen strategically evolved through three main pillars: Firstly, targeting medium to large enterprises, specifically those with over 500 employees; secondly, offering cloud computing services on a subscription basis, utilizing a low-code platform for service delivery; and thirdly, implementing an integrated approach to human resources management, covering the entire employee lifecycle from onboarding to departure.

Beisen's success can be attributed to its sharp market insights and clear understanding. Rather than chasing short-term market shares and trends, Beisen focused on accurately identifying and addressing customer needs. From its inception in 2002 to its successful listing in 2023, what might seem like a straightforward business mindset has supported Beisen in achieving numerous accomplishments. This approach underscores the importance of strategic market positioning and the ability to fulfil and anticipate customer demands in achieving long-term success.

MAIN PRODUCT AND TECHNOLOGY

Beisen With AI

The launch of ChatGPT-3 by OpenAI in 2020 and its subsequent enhancements, leading to versions 3.5 and 4.0 by April 2023, have set a new benchmark in the capabilities of artificial intelligence in natural language processing. This breakthrough has ignited a global fascination with AI, propelling it to the forefront of innovation across various sectors. In this wave of technological evolution, the notion of AI+ has emerged, symbolizing a new frontier of competitive advantage and opportunities for digital enterprises poised for future success.

Recognizing this trend, Beisen strategically introduced the AI Family product line in 2020, positioning it firmly as an indispensable asset for the HR ecosystem. This suite of tools is designed to cater to the nuanced needs of three primary stakeholders within any organization: HR managers, the executive management team, and employees at large. Beisen's AI Family seeks to redefine the role of AI in the workplace, envisioning it not just as a tool for operational efficiency but as a strategic advisor and a supportive companion, thereby enhancing workplace satisfaction and productivity.

At its core, Beisen's AI Family integrates cutting-edge artificial intelligence technologies such as Natural Language Processing (NLP), Machine Learning (ML), and Big Data analytics. These technologies empower the product line with diverse capabilities, including sophisticated text and image analysis and comprehensive talent data analytics. By harnessing the power of multiple databases and leveraging open-source models like ChatGLM2, coupled with vector model databases, Beisen showcases its commitment to technological openness and integration. This strategic approach enables Beisen to effectively utilize external technological advancements to fuel its innovation, ensuring it remains at the bleeding edge of AI application in HR.

The AI Family product line is distinguished by its multifunctionality, providing services such as automated job description generation, creation of recruitment posters, and even the personal leadership coach, Mr. Sen. These features signify Beisen's dedication to harnessing AI for enhancing the recruitment process, employee engagement, and leadership development. With such a broad array of functions, the AI Family product line is a testament to Beisen's innovative spirit and foresight in anticipating the evolving needs of the modern workplace.

As businesses evolve in the complexities of the digital age, increasing uncertainty in business environments, and rapid development of digital technologies, adopting and integrating AI-based solutions like Beisen's AI Family product line is becoming increasingly crucial. Beisen's initiative aligns with the global shift towards more agile and intelligent HR management practices and underscores the company's role as a pioneer in integrating AI technology to foster a more efficient, satisfying, and interconnected workplace.

In summary, Beisen's AI Family product line epitomizes the company's strategic response to the burgeoning AI+ era, demonstrating its capability and vision in leveraging artificial intelligence to meet the comprehensive needs of HR professionals, managers, and employees. This initiative reflects Beisen's ongoing commitment to innovation and excellence in human resource management, setting a new standard for applying AI to enhance workplace dynamics. This approach allows the company to leverage external resources to accelerate its technological development effectively. The current features include a range of capabilities designed to enable HR teams to enhance their operations.

INTELLIGENT RECRUITMENT SERVICES FOR THE HR DEPARTMENT

AI Can Help HR Staff in Many Ways

Leveraging its established text and image analysis capabilities, Beisen's AI Family rapidly generates job descriptions (JDs) and work position posters. This feature's maturity is rooted in over two decades of human capital management (HCM) experience, backed by a vast database that ensures the reliability and detail of images and JDs, thus effectively attracting candidates. Moreover, Beisen introduces a new AI customer service robot by harnessing the ChatGPT-2 open-source model alongside its database. It efficiently handles candidates' inquiries and provides 24/7 online responses with accurate and detailed information. This advancement signifies a pivotal stride in enhancing the recruitment process, offering seamless interaction and support for prospective candidates.

Building upon this technological foundation, Beisen facilitates rapid analysis of candidates' resumes to construct AI talent profiles directly, integrating various aspects such as assessment, interview, and test results. Through platform preprocessing of data, feature extraction, and talent assessment, calculations are swiftly completed via the cloud, leveraging extensive data to present detailed candidate profiles. This innovative approach streamlines the recruitment pipeline, transforming vast data into actionable insights, enabling a more effective and efficient matching process between candidates and job openings.

Further enhancing its HR technology suite, establishing a talent database on the cloud service platform enables swift talent identification amidst extensive databases, providing insights and intelligent candidate recommendations. Advanced security technologies and measures ensure data security for both the enterprise and its employees, including data encryption, access control, and identity authentication, in compliance with relevant data protection laws and regulations. This ensures that the sensitive data handled during the recruitment process is safeguarded, maintaining trust and integrity within the system.

In a complementary manner, Beisen's activation of AI Flash Interview optimizes interview efficiency. Candidates are provided with a set of questions, followed by two minutes of preparation time before answering through video recording. Utilizing Natural Language Understanding (NLU) technology, the system comprehends interviewees' language and responses, analyzing their language proficiency, professional knowledge, and logical thinking. Emotion analysis assesses non-verbal cues such as tone and pace, aiding in evaluating candidates' emotional state and confidence level. This high level of analytical depth offers a nuanced understanding of a candidate's potential, far beyond what traditional interviews could capture.

These developments contribute to a holistic approach to modern HR management underpinned by AI technology. By streamlining the recruitment process, enhancing data security, and providing deep insights into candidates' abilities and potential, Beisen is optimizing HR processes and shaping the future of work. By integrating advanced AI technologies, Beisen sets new standards for efficiency and effectiveness in talent acquisition and management, marking a significant evolution in human capital management.

Assist Managers in Data Analysis

Assisting managers in data analysis involves several vital functions. Firstly, it entails providing timely alerts for abnormal data while analyzing the overall situation of the company team. This aids managers in promptly identifying and addressing any adverse data anomalies, thus preventing potential risks before they escalate. Furthermore, it generates comprehensive data reports encompassing vital information such as total personnel count, budget execution, per capita cost, etc. These reports serve as valuable tools for the company in constructing a modern management model that prioritizes informed decision-making and strategic planning.

Additionally, it offers People Analytics services to assist businesses in gathering diverse employee data, including performance metrics, behavioral patterns, feedback insights, and development trajectories. This data is stored securely in a cloud-based database, ensuring accessibility and scalability. The collected data is processed using advanced Beisen AI models to generate detailed employee profiles, personalized recommendations and actionable insights. Importantly, this data undergoes continuous real-time updates facilitated by stream data processing technologies, enabling managers to stay abreast of evolving employee dynamics and trends.

By seamlessly integrating these data analysis capabilities into managerial practices, businesses can unlock more profound insights into workforce dynamics, enhance decision-making processes, and ultimately drive organizational success.

Help Staff in Boosting Efficiency and Advancing Careers

Beisen's AI assistant is pivotal in assisting employees with career planning by leveraging cutting-edge technologies such as Natural Language Processing (NLP), Machine Learning (ML), and Big Data analysis. Integrating these advanced tools offers comprehensive support within the workplace environment. Drawing from employees' work performance, skills, and career aspirations, coupled with market trend analysis, the AI assistant can provide tailored recommendations for career development paths and essential skill training. Moreover, it employs a personalized recommendation system to suggest relevant online courses and training materials based on employees' specific development goals and learning behaviors, fostering continuous personal growth and professional advancement.

Furthermore, Beisen's AI assistant is instrumental in alleviating employee burdens and enhancing work efficiency through real-time analysis of work performance data. Providing timely feedback and improvement suggestions in performance management and daily task automation empowers employees to identify their strengths and areas for growth. The AI assistant can detect employees' mental health issues and offer valuable stress management advice. Furthermore, it streamlines workflow processes by automating repetitive tasks such as scheduling meetings and managing emails. These features underscore Beisen's commitment to leveraging AI technology to support employees' career development and work-life balance, facilitating mutual growth for individuals and organizations.

Beisen With Cloud Computer

Cloud computing refers to the integrated development and commercialization of advanced information technologies in distributed computing, parallel computing, grid computing, network storage, and large-scale data warehousing. The following main features characterize it. (Wang et al, 2016):

a. **Sharing:** Cloud computing technologies facilitate data access, exchange, and sharing, accessible to anyone, anytime, and anywhere. Unlike conventional information technologies, cloud computing fosters teamwork and enables the sharing of manufacturing resources across enterprises.
b. **Flexibility:** Users can request services and access manufacturing resources from any location and anytime using various personal assistant devices (PADs) or computing terminals.
c. **Pay-as-you-go:** Cloud computing allocates manufacturing or service resources based on users' demands, allowing users to pay for the platform or services based on the allocated resources without any wastage.
d. **Low cost:** Large-scale enterprises can build their cloud-based systems and optimize system utilization to reduce the cost of their information systems.

Through an examination across four dimensions, it becomes evident that the technological paradigm of AI cloud computing has attained a significant level of maturity. Its commercial viability has garnered recognition and adoption among enterprises and academia alike. For Beisen, this technological advancement represents the cornerstone and technical standard of its overarching "integrated" business concept. As previously articulated, the integration-driven reforms have not only facilitated Beisen's resilience during challenging periods but have also underscored its prowess in maintaining a competitive edge through core technological innovations. This study endeavors to elucidate Beisen's integrated product portfolio, offering insights into Beisen's technological rationale in the contemporary era and the pivotal role that cloud computing plays in the talent management market. The case studies presented herein draw from client testimonials on the official Beisen website.

Integrated Recruitment System: Digitization of Recruitment

Recruitment involves multiple stages, including resume screening, written tests, talent assessments, interviews, etc. Before the invention or commercialization of cloud computing, this process required a considerable workforce. Each stage involved dedicated personnel to handle data and required communication with other stakeholders to ensure successful data transmission. "Under the application of cloud computing, what used to take a month for talent recruitment now only takes a week," responded the recruitment director of 360 Group (a well-known Chinese internet conglomerate) - a client of Beisen.

Beisen achieves this by digitizing recruiter data. Firstly, resumes are screened and categorized using keywords. After the screening, automatic notifications for written tests are sent to candidates' emails. Then, interviews are automatically scheduled with project managers based on the requirements provided by the business department and the candidates' preferences. All these processes are handled through cloud-based processors, enabling architectural analysis and classification processing. Business managers no longer need to constantly monitor the recruitment system, eliminating interruptions from incoming resume emails and allowing them to focus on recruitment tasks steadily.

Integrated Performance Management: Digitization of Project Data

The Beisen Performance Management System is an advanced tool designed to revolutionize how companies approach their performance management strategies. With its inception, the system brings a robust platform that caters to the nuanced demands of modern enterprises, aiming for a blend of goal orientation, process efficiency, and tangible results. This software is distinguished by its adaptability. It offers flexible process configurations, customizable assessment forms, and a rich indicator library, ensuring a tailored fit for any organization's diverse performance management requirements. Delving deeper, the system empowers project managers and employees to set precise Objectives and Key Results (OKRs). Leveraging a sophisticated cloud-based database goes beyond goal-setting; it compares these OKRs with historical data and benchmarks against successful outcomes in other enterprises. This comparative analysis facilitates a dual approach, incorporating both quantitative metrics and qualitative insights, to chart out effective OKR implementation pathways. This feature is invaluable for management teams seeking to understand the complexities of contemporary management landscapes.

Furthermore, the system enhances operational visibility through real-time task-tracking functionalities, elevating the management process by automating the generation of insightful daily and weekly reports. This continuous monitoring extends to evaluating the project's progress and the performance of individual team members, fostering a culture of accountability and continuous improvement. It synthesizes evaluations and feedback at strategic intervals, translating them into actionable improvement suggestions. This holistic approach not only streamlines performance assessment but also significantly contributes to the strategic decision-making process, thereby optimizing organizational performance and driving success.

Integrated Agile Talent Management: Digitization of Employees

To facilitate management oversight of employees, Beisen utilizes cloud computing to integrate salary, attendance, performance, and employee analysis on a single platform. For each employee, Beisen's cloud computing system initially establishes a digital document containing a range of data, such as interview results, project status, weekly work hours, and number of leaves taken. Moreover, data can be transferred between different systems. For instance, during project allocation, project supervisors can use data on project completion rates, project experience, and other metrics to select the most suitable employees. During salary calculations, the system integrates attendance records with the quality of completed projects and leadership evaluations to provide specific salary recommendations. In the attendance phase, employees' attendance is continuously updated in real-time, providing project managers with feedback on project progress and identifying outstanding employees through OKR reporting.

The rapid development of Beisen's products demonstrates its keen grasp of market trends and its continuous launch of new products to maintain a competitive edge. Beisen has already seized a significant position in the current market, and its success is a microcosm of the Chinese HCM market. This success is not solely attributed to Beisen's innovative products and services but is also closely intertwined with the broader market landscape and evolving business needs. Beisen's ability to adapt and evolve in response to these dynamics has played a pivotal role in its ascent.

Furthermore, Beisen's success underscores the importance of human capital management (HCM) solutions in China's corporate landscape. As businesses increasingly recognize the strategic value of effective talent management, demand for sophisticated HCM software solutions has surged. Beisen's rapid growth reflects its ability to effectively address these evolving market demands and position itself as a leader in the industry.

INSIGHTS FROM BEISEN ON THE CHINESE HCM MARKET

This section investigates the development status and future challenges of China's digitized human resources management market from social impact, technological advancement, and market dynamics. It specifically explores the long-term effects of the pandemic on labor mobility, the emerging work concept shifts in the Z-generation workforce, the impact of the ageing population on the labor market, as well as the application and driving role of technologies such as cloud computing, big data, and artificial intelligence in the field of human resources management. Additionally, the article points out the growing trend of flexible employment models and their demands for digitalization.

Social Dimension

The Impact of the Pandemic

In 2022, China emerged as a success story in controlling the pandemic, showcasing remarkable resilience in the face of a global crisis. However, the aftermath of this achievement has cast a long shadow over various industries, with the personnel management sector enduring significant repercussions. The pandemic's pervasive impact is multifaceted, extending beyond immediate health concerns to alter the fundamental dynamics of the workforce and employment landscapes. An insightful report by iResearch Consulting in 2022 sheds light on these challenges, revealing how the pandemic has fundamentally disrupted labor mobility, leading to a pronounced shortage of available workforce. This disruption stems from stringent restrictions and lockdowns, which, while effectively curbing the virus spread, inadvertently hampered the free flow of labor across regions and industries (iResearch Consulting, 2022).

Moreover, the prolonged pandemic, characterized by two years of intermittent lockdowns, has financially strained many businesses. The report highlights a consequential issue: Organizations, tiny and medium-sized enterprises (SMEs) grappling with depleted cash reserves find themselves in a precarious position, needing help to afford the costs of recruiting new employees. This financial vulnerability underscores a more profound economic challenge as companies struggle to rebound and scale their operations in the post-pandemic era. The resultant scarcity of job opportunities has further exacerbated the situation, leading to a tightening job market where recruiting difficulties loom large. This phenomenon is particularly acute in China's talent market, where labor demand and supply dynamics have been significantly altered. The pandemic has not only affected the availability of jobs but also reshaped employer expectations and job seekers' preferences, leading to a mismatch in the labor market. Consequently, companies reevaluate their talent acquisition strategies while job seekers adjust their career aspirations and priorities in response to the evolving economic and social landscape.

The lingering effects of the pandemic on China's HCM (HCM) industry underscore a period of adjustment and transformation. As businesses experience these challenges, there is a growing emphasis on adopting more flexible, innovative approaches to personnel management and recruitment. The industry is at a crossroads, with the potential to redefine workforce management practices, embracing remote work, digital transformation, and employee well-being as cornerstones of the new normal in the post-pandemic world.

Changing Work Attitudes Among Chinese Youth in the Z Generation Era

With the advancement of the times, young people from Generation Z (typically born between 1995 and 2010) are entering the labor market, leading to gradual changes in the talent market environment. Firstly, there has been a significant increase in demand for digitalization. According to research by Janssen and Carradini on Generation Z workers, emerging users of the Z generation are more inclined to use personal smartphones and smart devices for business communication, with a rise in social media usage. In contrast, using voice calls and emails has sharply declined(Janssen & Carradini, 2021). Furthermore, they primarily receive external information through the internet, social media, and job-seeking websites, such as corporate WeChat Official Accounts and online platforms like Boss Zhipin APP. Therefore, companies must establish a positive online presence and develop HCM software platforms for effective internet-based personnel management.

Moreover, users from Generation Z often harbor unrealistic and idealistic perceptions of the work environment, necessitating employers to manage their workplace expectations effectively (Schroth, 2019). Their work demands exceed those solely focused on high wages or salaries. Interests and spare time have become essential considerations in career choices, as some individuals prioritise factors such as self-fulfillment, alignment of work with hobbies and interests, and achieving a balance between life and work in their job selection process. To meet the needs of these Generation Z employees, companies need to utilize human resources digitization to achieve rapid job matching.

Challenges of Population Aging

According to the National Development Report on Elderly Care Development for the Year 2022 released by the Ministry of Civil Affairs by the end of 2023, the elderly population in China has reached significant proportions. Specifically, individuals aged 60 and above account for 19.8% of the total population, while those aged 65 and above comprise 14.9% (Civil Affairs Bureau of China, 2023). Furthermore, as the competition for skilled workers intensifies, organizations must differentiate themselves as employers of choice by offering attractive benefits packages, opportunities for career advancement, and a supportive work environment. By investing in employee well-being and professional development, businesses can attract top talent and foster loyalty and retention.

In essence, while the ageing population presents challenges for labor supply and human resources management, it also presents opportunities for innovation and adaptation. By embracing diversity, investing in talent development, and implementing forward-thinking strategies, businesses can manage the demographic shift and emerge more robust in the face of change.

Technology Dimension

The enterprise's flexible employment management model represents a paradigm shift in modern human resource strategies designed to navigate the complexities of today's volatile market landscape and the evolving nature of work environments. This innovative approach to HR management empowers organizations to dynamically adjust workforce parameters—such as working hours, locations, and contractual arrangements—to align more closely with fluctuating business demands. Notably, tech giants like Tencent are at the forefront of this movement, offering their employees unprecedented flexibility to tailor their working schedules around personal preferences and job requirements. This flexibility might include starting the workday earlier or compressing the workweek to extend the weekend, promoting work-life balance and enhancing job satisfaction.

As businesses grapple with increasing market uncertainty and the rapid advancement of digital technologies, adopting flexible employment practices is gaining traction. This trend reflects a shift from rigid, traditional employment frameworks to more adaptable human resource configurations. Such flexibility is instrumental in fostering organizational agility, enabling companies to respond more effectively to various potential challenges and risk factors. While initial uptake of flexible employment was more pronounced in labor-intensive sectors—where roles are generally characterized by lower skill requirements and higher substitutability—the demand for such practices is expanding into more specialized, professional fields, including IT and other technical domains.

The growing preference for flexible employment models also catalyzes a parallel demand for digitalisation, particularly in recruitment and workforce management. The digital transformation of these processes is essential for effectively administrating a flexibly employed workforce, encompassing aspects such as compensation, time tracking, performance evaluation, employee development, and swift staffing solutions. As flexible employment practices continue penetrating various industry sectors deeper, the imperative for digitalized HR management systems becomes increasingly pronounced. Companies are thus investing in technology-driven solutions that can streamline and optimize the management of a fluid and diverse workforce, highlighting a significant evolution in corporate human resource strategies aimed at harnessing the full potential of digital innovation to support flexible work arrangements.

Economic Dimension

The impact of China's economic growth targets on HR services indicates a growing demand for such services as companies seek to manage the complexities of talent acquisition and workforce management in an expanding job market. The drive for around 5% GDP growth for 2023 is anticipated to generate more job opportunities, necessitating effective recruitment strategies and comprehensive workforce management solutions. This expansion is supported by technological advancements, with companies adopting cloud-based HR management systems, AI, big data for recruitment, and e-learning platforms for training, showcasing the critical role of technology in transforming HR practices in China.

Moreover, the labor market dynamics in China are changing, with unemployment challenges driven by automation and a growing population juxtaposed against the rise in demand for tech-savvy employees in new job sectors such as IT, data analysis, and AI. These sectors require highly skilled workers and offer better wages and job security. Responding to these challenges includes government initiatives to retrain displaced workers and promote new industries, indicating a proactive approach to fostering a resilient and adaptable workforce. The HR service industry itself is becoming "smarter" with the acceleration of digitalization, further emphasized by the establishment of HR service industrial parks in major Chinese cities. These parks not only facilitate talent-job matching and full employment but also promote innovation and high-quality development within the HR service industry. The adoption of Big Data technology and the China Talent Index exemplify the use of information technology to advance HR service industry digitalization, offering insights into talent development trends and aiding in policy and planning.

As China continues to speed up its digital development, the HR service industry stands at the forefront of this transition, leveraging technological advancements to enhance service delivery, improve efficiency, and meet the evolving needs of businesses and the workforce. The focus on digitalization, alongside the proactive strategies to address labor market challenges and the emphasis on innovative HR solutions, underlines the considerable growth potential of the Chinese HCM market in the coming years.

CONCLUSION

Beisen Holdings Limited, established in 2002, has become a leading company in the Human Capital Management (HCM) industry, primarily due to its pioneering integrated cloud HCM solutions. Initially focusing on providing innovative HR solutions, Beisen embraced cloud computing technology in 2010 and transitioned to a Platform as a Service (PaaS) model in 2015. This strategic shift allowed Beisen to offer more flexible and integrated HCM solutions, encompassing the entire employee lifecycle. Beisen's PaaS product, iTalent X, and the introduction of AI and BI for intelligent decision-making underscore its commitment to technological innovation and customization to meet corporate needs. The company's successful IPO in Hong Kong in 2023 marked a significant milestone, affirming its market position and enabling further expansion. Financially, Beisen reported a total revenue of RMB 750.9 million in FY2023, with cloud-based HCM solutions accounting for 71.5%. It has served over 6000 medium-sized and large enterprises, including 70% of the Fortune 500 companies in China.

Beisen's leadership in the HR SaaS market in China is well-documented, securing the top position for eight consecutive years. Its products have processed over 120 million resumes and facilitated over 7 million interviews, demonstrating its significant impact on the HR industry. The report also chronicles Beisen's evolution, highlighting the initial challenges and strategic pivots that defined its journey. The company's shift from a focus on talent assessment to a broader integrated management system, iTalent, and the eventual development of iTalent X showcase its ability to innovate and adapt to market needs. This evolution from SaaS to PaaS and the incorporation of cloud computing and AI technologies have been pivotal in Beisen's growth and market leadership.

Beisen's product offerings, including its AI Family line, leverage advanced technologies like NLP, ML, and Big Data analytics to provide comprehensive solutions for HR managers, corporate leaders, and employees. This includes intelligent recruitment services, AI talent profiles, talent databases, employee career development and efficiency improvement support. The integration of cloud computing has enabled Beisen to offer solutions that significantly enhance HR management processes, making them more efficient and cost-effective. This technological advancement underpins Beisen's integrated approach to talent management, illustrating its commitment to innovation and customer satisfaction. Furthermore, the report discusses the broader context of the HCM software market in China, exploring the impact of social changes, technological advancements, and market dynamics on HR management. It highlights the challenges posed by the pandemic, changing work attitudes among Generation Z, and the implications of an ageing population for the labor market.

In summary, Beisen's success is attributed to its clear understanding of market needs and commitment to providing innovative and integrated HCM solutions. Its strategic focus on leveraging cloud computing and AI technologies and its adaptability to market changes positions Beisen as a leader in China's HCM industry. The company's journey from its inception to becoming a Chinese unicorn in the HR tech space demonstrates its resilience, innovative spirit, and the strategic vision of its leadership.

REFERENCES

Beisen Holdings Limited. (2023). *Beisen 2023 financial reports [Financial reports].* Beisen Holdings Limited. https://ir-upload.realxen.net/iis/9669/uploads/iis/2023/10827405-0.PDF

Chen, X. (2016). Trial and error in Hokusen. Twenty-first Century. *Business Review*, 12, 52–53.

Civil Affairs Bureau of China. (2023). *2022 China National Aging Development Report.* Civil Affairs Bureau of China.

Cong, L., & Wu, Q. (2014). Talent management enters the era of a cloud computing platform—Interview with Ji Weiguo, Co-founder of Beisen Assessment. *China Human Resource Development*, 90–97. DOI:10.16471/j.cnki.11-2822/c.2014.12.020

Hurun Research Institute. (2023, April 18). *Hurun Report 2023 Global Unicorn List.* Hurun Research Institute. https://www.hurun.net/zh-CN/Info/Detail?num=PH71LJQJPANH

iResearch Consulting. (2021). *iResearch Awards [2021 iResearch Awards Gold Award-winning Companies Announced].* iResearch Consulting.

iResearch Consulting. (2022). *Research Report on Digitalization of Human Resources in China*, 557–615. iResearch Consulting.

Janssen, D., & Carradini, S. (2021). Generation Z workplace communication habits and expectations. *IEEE Transactions on Professional Communication*, 64(2), 137–153. DOI:10.1109/TPC.2021.3069288

Ministry of Industry and Information Technology Information Center. (2019). *2019 China's Top 100 Internet Enterprises Development Report.* Ministry of Industry and Information Technology Center.

Sina Website. (2021). *"50" HR SaaS [Beisen was listed in the Forbes China Enterprise Technology Top 50, all-in-one HR SaaS was praised].* SINA. https://client.sina.com.cn/2021-12-08/doc-ikyakumx2790566.shtml

Wang, X. L., Wang, L., Bi, Z., Li, Y. Y., & Xu, Y. (2016). Cloud computing in human resource management (HRM) system for small and medium enterprises (SMEs). *International Journal of Advanced Manufacturing Technology*, 84(1–4), 485–496. DOI:10.1007/s00170-016-8493-8

Yipai, H. (2021). [Beisen Progress Rapid]. *21*, (08), 72-73.

Yipai, H., & Qi, Z. (2022). HR SaaS [A new way to use HR SaaS]. 21(03). *21st Century Business Review*(03), 46-48.

KEY TERMS AND DEFINITIONS

Artificial Intelligence (AI): A branch of computer science that aims to create intelligent machines capable of performing tasks that typically require human intelligence.

Human Capital Management (HCM): Focusing on the value of people in the organization, HCM is similar to HRM but places more emphasis on the value and development of employees.

Human Resource Management (HRM): Refers to activities such as planning, recruiting, training, evaluating, and managing compensation for human resources in an organization to achieve business and employee goals.

Machine Learning (ML): A branch of artificial intelligence that involves improving computer system performance through analysis and learning from data. Machine learning encompasses algorithm design and data processing and is used for tasks like prediction and classification.

Natural Language Processing (NLP): A branch of artificial intelligence that deals with the interaction between computers and human natural languages. It includes tasks like language understanding and language generation and is applied in translation, speech recognition, text analysis, and more.

Natural Language Understanding (NLU): A subfield of natural language processing that involves machines' understanding of human language, including semantic analysis and sentiment analysis.

Platform-as-a-Service (PaaS): A cloud computing service model that provides developers with a platform on which they can develop, deploy, and manage applications.

Small and Medium-Sized Enterprises (SMEs): Smaller businesses typically defined by metrics such as the number of employees or revenue. SMEs play an important role in the economy, characterized by flexibility and innovation.

Software-as-a-Service (SaaS): A cloud computing service model in which users use software applications on-demand over the Internet. The SaaS provider maintains and updates the software, and the user does not have to manage the underlying infrastructure and platform.

Chapter 15
Yuanqi Forest:
Navigating Growth in China's Health Drinks Market

Enyi Zhang

Beijing Normal University-Hong Kong Baptist University United International College, China

EXECUTIVE SUMMARY

This case study examines how Genki Forest has grown and changed its strategy in the competitive health drinks market in China. Founded with a vision to offer healthier beverage alternatives, Genki Forest capitalized on rising consumer demand for natural, low-sugar beverages by innovating with unique flavors and leveraging digital marketing channels. The case delves into Genki Forest's early challenges in product sourcing and its subsequent growth through effective branding, product diversification, and e-commerce expansion. Analyzing competitive pressures from established players and emerging brands, the study examines Genki Forest's strategies to maintain market leadership, including sustainability initiatives and international expansion ambitions. Through a comprehensive exploration of its development phases, market positioning, and outlook, this case provides insights into navigating the complexities of consumer-driven markets and achieving sustained growth in the beverage industry.

DOI: 10.4018/979-8-3693-2921-4.ch015

UNICORN DESCRIPTION

Brief History of Yuanqi Forest (Beijing) Food Technology Group Co., Ltd.

Established in 2016 in China, Yuanqi Senin, also known as Genki Forest or Yuanqi Forest, is a unicorn beverage brand that offers a range of drinks, including sparkling water and milk tea. These beverages have quickly become a hit with Chinese consumers, propelling Yuanqi Forest to widespread popularity and making it one of China's most prominent startup success stories (Yuanqi Forest, 2024). The company has received numerous awards, including the National High-tech Enterprise Award, the 2020 China Integrity Brand Award, and the 2020 Poverty Alleviation Excellence Award. Furthermore, its products are now available in over 40 countries, including the United States and Australia (Yuanqi Forest, 2024).

In 2023, Yuanqi Forest was recognized on the "2023 Global Challenger Brand List" by Eatbigfish, a significant achievement as the only Chinese brand to make the list that year. This honor underscores their innovative approach and growing global presence (Yuanqi Forest, 2023). The company's marketing strategy emphasizes the "0 sugar, 0 calories, 0 fat" aspect of their drinks, which, combined with their modern marketing techniques, has resonated with young consumers. This has led to impressive revenue growth from 2018 to 2021, with increases of 300%, 200%, 307%, and 260%, respectively, marking the company as a rising star in the beverage industry (Xu & Zhang, 2023).

Yuanqi Forest has demonstrated a rapid pace of growth since its inception. In 2016, they established the Genki Forest R&D Centre. By 2020, they were the top-selling beverage brand at the Tmall 618 Shopping Festival, a major annual shopping event in China akin to Black Friday in the U.S. As of November 2020, the company's products were available in over 40 countries, including the United States, Australia, New Zealand, Japan, and Singapore. In December 2021, Yuanqi Forest was listed as a unicorn company valued at 95 billion yuan. The company has continued to innovate, launching products like natural soft mineral water in 2021 and a variety of sparkling waters in 2022. Yuanqi Forest has carved out a significant share of China's beverage market in less than a decade.

The brand has also gained significant public attention for its achievements and initiatives. In February 2022, the company announced partnerships with three Olympic gold medalists, Xu Mengtao, Valley Ailing, and Su Yiming, which led to a surge in online interest in the brand. In April 2022, as part of their response to the COVID-19 pandemic, Yuanqi Forest donated 460,000 boxes of beverages to critical institutions in various provinces and cities, including Shanghai and Jilin. In June 2022, the company partnered with the Communist Youth League on a program to support disadvantaged youth. By May 2023, Yuanqi Forest had also collaborated with Capital Normal University to establish a "labour education" model, demonstrating their commitment to fostering the growth of young students and fulfilling their social responsibilities.

Business Model

Yuanqi Forest, also known as Genki Forest, is a Chinese beverage brand that has gained substantial popularity since its founding in 2016. The company has made a name for itself by focusing on the tastes and preferences of younger consumers. It has achieved this by incorporating innovative product designs and using effective marketing strategies, such as partnering with famous figures like athletes and utilizing social media and entertainment platforms for promotion. This approach has enabled Yuanqi Forest to stand out in a crowded market.

The company operates under an "asset-light, marketing-heavy" model, meaning it invests significantly in marketing and distribution while keeping physical assets to a minimum. Furthermore, Yuanqi Forest embraces digital transformation, using data chaining and operational automation to boost efficiency and responsiveness to market trends. They also leverage artificial intelligence and other advanced technologies to improve business operations.

Interestingly, Yuanqi Forest does not manufacture its products. Instead, it relies on Original Equipment Manufacturer (OEM) factories for production. This approach allows the company to focus on its core competencies, such as product innovation, brand operation, and digital marketing. The products are manufactured in factories in critical markets, such as Beijing, Tianjin, Hebei, the Yangtze River Delta, and the Pearl River Delta, ensuring efficient delivery and comprehensive market coverage.

Yuanqi Forest's journey to success had its challenges. Initially, the company invested 5 million yuan to develop its first batch of products. However, these products have not reached the market due to taste issues. Instead, they were destroyed, costing the company an additional 1 million yuan. Despite this setback, the company persevered, investing tens of millions of yuan more until it was satisfied with its product.

According to Euromonitor data, sales of traditional carbonated beverages, like Coke and Sprite, grew at a sluggish rate of 0.7% annually from 2008 to 2018, with negative growth recorded from 2015 to 2018 (Xu & Zhang, 2023). Yuanqi Forest seized this opportunity to innovate within the carbonated beverage sector, developing a range of sugar-free sparkling water products that addressed the drawbacks of traditional carbonated beverages.

As consumers become increasingly health-conscious, there is a growing demand for natural, low-sugar beverages. High-sugar drinks are often linked to weight gain and an increased risk of diseases like diabetes. Recognizing this shift in consumer preferences, Yuanqi Forest positioned its products as "0 sugar, 0 fat, 0 calorie" beverages, appealing to health-conscious consumers. This focus on health and wellness aligns with a broader global trend towards healthier living, where people are becoming more aware of the impact of their dietary choices on their health and the environment (Chang, 2020).

Yuanqi Forest's success can be attributed to its innovative strategy. While sugar-free sparkling water was not new, Yuanqi Forest elevated the product to a new level. Their market research revealed that most mainstream carbonated beverages were old brands that did not resonate with younger consumers, particularly the "Z generation" (Xu & Zhang, 2023). These consumers found high-sugar carbonated beverages unhealthy and low-sugar sparkling water unpalatable. Furthermore, the high price of existing sugar-free sparkling water products, like Paris Water, was a barrier for young consumers.

In response to these insights, Yuanqi Forest rejuvenated its brand, developed healthier formulas, and diversified its flavors. They connected with young consumers, making them feel that Yuanqi Forest was a brand made for them. The company also pioneered using erythritol, a natural ingredient with low calories and a refreshing taste, in their formula. Despite its high cost, Yuanqi Forest chose erythritol over artificial sweeteners, commonly used in the industry.

Furthermore, Yuanqi Forest invested 5.5 billion yuan to build an aseptic production line, a first in the carbonated beverage industry. This allowed their sparkling water products to be produced without chemical preservatives (Xu & Zhang, 2023). From zero sugar to zero preservatives, Yuanqi Forest has created a healthy and tasty beverage, setting itself apart in the industry.

Products Portfolio

Yuanqi Forest possesses a comprehensive portfolio of beverages that cater to a wide array of tastes and dietary preferences, helping it appeal to a diverse consumer base and reinforce its standing in the beverage industry. The company's products extend beyond its well-known sugar-free sparkling water, featuring a broad selection of tea drinks, functional beverages, plant-based milk substitutes, and coffee drinks.

Initially, the brand offered a variety of sparkling water drinks, each infused with different natural fruit flavors. These beverages serve as a healthier substitute for traditional soft drinks without any added sugars or artificial ingredients. Customers can choose popular flavors like lychee, peach, and lemon, reflecting the brand's dedication to natural, tasty refreshments. Furthermore, Yuanqi Forest's tea drinks are another highlight of their product line. They offer a range of beverages brewed from high-quality tea leaves sourced from various regions. These light and flavorful drinks, including famous green, black, and oolong teas, are a favorite among those seeking a refreshing natural beverage.

The company also caters to health-conscious consumers with a selection of functional beverages. These drinks are enriched with vitamins, minerals, and herbal extracts to support health and wellness. The range includes collagen drinks, immune-boosting drinks, and energy-boosting beverages. Moreover, acknowledging the growing demand for dairy-free alternatives, Yuanqi Forest offers a selection of plant-based milk substitutes. Made from ingredients such as almonds, coconut, and oats, these beverages are an excellent choice for those who are lactose intolerant or follow a vegan diet. The brand provides coffee lovers with a range of coffee drinks that includes cold brew and ready-to-drink options. These beverages, brewed from premium coffee beans, cater to those who seek convenience without compromising on the taste and quality of their coffee.

In its commitment to promoting healthier beverage options, Yuanqi Forest offers a series of zero-calorie drinks. Free from sugar and artificial sweeteners, these drinks are a guilt-free choice for those looking to reduce their calorie intake but still enjoy a tasty beverage, making them an excellent choice for diet-conscious consumers. The brand also keeps its product range exciting by regularly introducing limited-edition flavors. These unique flavors, often inspired by seasonal ingredients or popular trends, add a new dimension to the brand's lineup and enhance the customer experience.

Moreover, Yuanqi Forest collaborates with various artists, designers, and brands to launch special edition packaging and flavors. These collaborations bring a creative and unique touch to the brand's products and appeal to collectors and fans of both Yuanqi Forest and the collaborators. Collaborations with famous artists, for instance, can attract a large fan base, thereby driving product sales. In addition to its diverse product range, Yuanqi Forest also offers various services, providing customers with many choices. The more popular services will be discussed in the subsequent sections.

Services Overview

Yuanqi Forest's services extend beyond selling beverages. They focus on providing a seamless, integrated experience for customers across multiple platforms. This omni-channel approach allows the brand to meet the needs of modern consumers who expect flexibility, convenience, and consistency, regardless of whether they interact with the brand online or in-store.

The brand operates an online shop, providing a convenient platform for customers to explore its extensive product range and purchase from the comfort of their homes. This online presence ensures that customers can access Yuanqi Forest's products regardless of location and deliver their favorite drinks straight to their doorsteps.

Yuanqi Forest offers an early subscription service to enhance convenience further. This allows customers to receive their favorite beverages regularly without needing constant re-ordering. The service caters to the average consumer who enjoys the brand's drinks and the enthusiast who wants to avoid running out.

Yuanqi Forest also runs regular promotions and offers product discounts through various channels, including its website, social media platforms, and partner retailers. These promotions provide customers with savings and incentivize them to try new flavors or stock up on their favorite drinks. Yuanqi Forest also has a customer rewards program to reward loyal customers. Customers can earn points on their purchases, which can be redeemed for discounts, free products, or exclusive items. This program encourages repeat purchases and fosters community among the brand's fans.

Yuanqi Forest runs interactive marketing campaigns such as social media contests, giveaways, and influencer partnerships to engage its customer base further. These initiatives help to build brand awareness and create excitement around new product launches. For instance, the brand has developed interactive mini-games that allow customers to win points and redeem gifts, a strategy that has resonated well with its audience. Product sampling events are another critical component of Yuanqi Forest's service offering. By organizing these events at various locations, such as supermarkets and gyms, the brand allows consumers to try its drinks before they commit to a purchase. This strategy lets consumers experience the product's quality and flavor firsthand and helps convert them into loyal customers.

Lastly, Yuanqi Forest values customer feedback and actively engages with its audience through social media, surveys, and customer service channels. By considering customer preferences and addressing their concerns, the brand continually refines its products and services to better serve its target market.

In conclusion, Yuanqi Forest's comprehensive range of services, coupled with its diverse product portfolio, enables the brand to meet the evolving demands of its customers. Yuanqi Forest has established itself as a leading player in the Chinese beverage market by focusing on natural ingredients, low-calorie formulas, and unique flavors. Its online shop, subscription services, promotions, and engaging marketing campaigns continue to attract and retain customers who appreciate the brand's commitment to delivering tasty and nutritious beverages.

Customers

Genki Forest is a well-known brand that offers a variety of healthy, natural beverages such as sparkling water, tea, and juice drinks. The brand has gained popularity among health-conscious consumers who value wholesome ingredients and unique flavors. To better understand Genki Forest's target market, it is crucial to analyze the various customer segments that the brand serves and examine why its products and services can fulfil the needs of these customer segments.

Health-Conscious Consumers

One of Genki Forest's main customer segments is health-conscious individuals actively looking for beverages that are tasty and beneficial to their health. These consumers prioritize products with natural ingredients, no artificial additives, and low sugar levels. Genki Forest's beverages stand out to this group because they use high-quality, natural ingredients such as fruit extracts, green tea, and mineral water, which are all known for their health benefits. The brand's commitment to nutrition and transparency in labelling appeals to health-conscious consumers concerned about what they eat and how it affects their overall health.

Millennials and Generation Z

It is important to remember that millennials and Generation Z consumers are an important customer segment for Genki Forest. These consumers are attracted to brands that reflect a modern and stylish lifestyle. They are often trendsetters and appreciate Genki Forest's innovative flavors and elegant packaging design. For this younger demographic, the brand's products represent a fresh and exciting alternative in the beverage market, offering a healthier option to sugary sodas and artificial beverages. With an emphasis on natural ingredients and unique flavors, Genki Forest resonates with millennials and Generation Z, who are looking for products that are not only healthy but also visually appealing, creating potentially shareable content on social media platforms such as Instagram (Genki Forest, 2021).

Busy Professional

Busy professionals who are constantly on the go and wear multiple hats are another vital customer segment for Genki Forest, such as lawyers, doctors, etc. These individuals often value convenience and are looking for products that are not only healthy but also Instagram-worthy. They need quick, nutritious beverages that fit their busy schedules when they do not have time to eat. Genki Forest's ready-to-drink beverages are convenient for busy professionals who want to stay hydrated and energized throughout the day without compromising taste and quality. The brand's range of beverages, including sparkling water and functional teas, caters to busy professionals looking for a refreshing, satisfying drink to take on their fast-paced lives.

Fitness Enthusiasts

Fitness enthusiasts and athletes are an important customer segment for the company, as they constantly seek products that support their active and healthy lifestyles (Genki Forest, 2022). These customers are interested in beverages that provide hydration, energy, and supplements after exercise. Genki Forest's beverages, such as sports drinks and electrolyte water, are designed to meet the needs of fitness enthusiasts by providing hydration and nutrients that aid in post-exercise recovery. As demonstrated in its ingredient list, the brand's focus on natural ingredients and functional benefits appeals to this customer segment, which prioritizes products that enhance their performance and support their fitness goals (Genki Forest, 2022).

Environmentally Conscious Consumers

Finally, environmentally conscious consumers are a growing customer segment for Genki Forest. These consumers seek sustainable and environmentally friendly options when purchasing beverages. Genki Forest's commitment to sustainability, such as using recyclable packaging materials and reducing carbon emissions in the manufacturing process, appeals to these consumers. The brand's efforts to minimize its ecological footprint resonate with this segment of consumers, who prioritize brands committed to environmental stewardship and take an active role in social responsibility.

Genki Forest has successfully identified and targeted multiple customer segments that align with its brand values and products. By catering to health-conscious consumers, Millennials, Generation Z, busy professionals, fitness enthusiasts, and environmentally conscious individuals, the brand has created a diverse customer base that values its commitment to quality, innovation, and sustainability. With a focus on natural ingredients, unique flavors, convenience, and environmentally friendly practices, Genki Forest has positioned itself as the trusted brand of choice for health and satisfaction-seeking consumers looking for beverages that align with their lifestyle and values.

Market Analysis

Original Situation of the Market

According to the National Bureau of Statistics (NBS, 2019), domestic final consumption expenditure accounts for approximately 57.8 per cent of economic growth. This is coupled with a notable increase in domestic productivity levels and sustained robust domestic demand, indicating a substantial long-term growth potential. As consumers born in the 80s and 90s increasingly become the primary consumers, the demand and market potential for beverages are progressively expanding. Pertinent sales data indicates a persistent rise in consumer demand for various beverage products.

Despite the growth of the beverage market, there has been a considerable shift in the consumer goods category. The traditional market share of fruit and vegetable juices is contracting, while functional beverages, tea drinks, and health drinks exhibit a promising development trend. Statistics reveal an increasing prevalence of diabetes in China, prompting individuals to be more health-conscious. As a result, many consumers consciously reduce their consumption of high-sugar foods, indirectly boosting the demand for sugar-free beverages. This has led to the progressive emergence of the "health, nature" era into the public consciousness (Wang, 2021).

The demographic for beverage consumption is increasingly skewing towards younger consumers. Even though companies can keep introducing new products through technological innovation, creating enduringly popular products is challenging. Expert analysis indicates that the life cycle of new beverage products is shortening, and the survival rate is decreasing. The survival rate of new beverage products has dropped from 10% to 5% (Wang, 2021).

Operating within the healthy beverage sector, Genki Forest offers consumers zero-sugar, natural, and low-calorie beverages. The company emerged when the trend towards healthier beverages gained momentum due to rising consumer health consciousness. The market was moderate in size, with the health-conscious consumer segment seeking alternatives to traditional sugar-laden drinks. Genki Forest positioned itself as a brand providing innovative and healthier beverage choices.

Evolution of the Market Until Today

The health drinks market has experienced significant growth and expansion over time. As mentioned above, Consumers are becoming more health and wellness-conscious, leading to a surge in demand for natural, low-sugar and functional beverages. Genuine Forest has capitalized on this trend through its unique product and marketing strategies, gaining popularity and market share. The company has expanded its product lines, distribution channels and market reach to cater to a broader audience.

Over the past few years, Yuanqi Forest's marketing channels have mainly consisted of traditional and modern ones. Traditional channels include large and medium-sized supermarket outlets and convenience stores, while modern channels are focused on social networks.

At the start-up stage, the company first established a marketing strategy focusing on traditional channels and took the lead in spreading out in large and medium-sized cities. In China's capital city of Beijing, for example, Yuanqi Forest chose to focus on convenience stores, which are more popular with younger users, including chains of superior size and volume, such as Convenience Store and Family Store (Zhang & Liu, 2022). In addition, Yuanqi Forest is slowly spreading the consumer trend pioneered in big cities to third and fourth-tier cities, gaining rapid expansion in offline channels.

To enhance brand heat, Yuanqi Forest fully uses modern channels to play the powerful appeal and influence of new media. Through the paid promotion of Xiao-hongshu, it took the lead in quickly harvesting a group of key opinion leaders of the netizen group. Coupled with the platform's unique consumer culture and the chain of trust between fans, it is easier to achieve the effect of proliferation on a large scale (Zhang & Liu, 2022).

In addition, Yuanqi Forest also fully uses the "live with goods" Internet trend, and China's well-known beauty blogger Li Jiaqi and other very hot with goods anchor cooperation; frequent sponsorship of popular variety shows, and employing celebrity spokesmen to put online and offline advertising in a short period to greatly enhance the product's sales and achieve the breakout of pop-up products.

Competition Analysis

In the market for health beverages, Genki Forest confronts competition from long-standing brands and new market players. This competition may come from other companies offering zero-sugar or low-calorie drinks and traditional beverage companies introducing their healthy product lines. Genki Forest's primary competitors might have comparable product portfolios, pricing strategies, distribution networks, and marketing approaches. For instance, competitors might entice consumers with lower-priced products or a more comprehensive range of services. If a competitor prices the same 500ml drink at $5 and Genki Forest sells it at $5.50, consumers might opt for something other than Genki Forest, given the identical flavor and volume.

Currently, the primary challengers to Genki Forest include new products from Coca-Cola, the reduced sugar sparkling water drink "Xi Xiao Bao" from the milk tea brand Xi Cha, and over ten other products. Despite having the first-mover advantage of ultra-high traffic, the introduction of original birthday drinks is also making a considerable impact in the face of the domestic beverage giants' pursuit.

Genki Forest cannot leverage the existing convenience store channel advantage when venturing into markets beyond first and second-tier cities due to the lack of brand chain convenience store layouts in these regions. Moreover, consumers in these emerging markets, where the pace of life is slower and income levels are relatively lower, are more price-sensitive. Genki Forest's sparkling water might have a weak appeal, and traditional drinks may retain many loyal customers (Cooper, 2023).

Furthermore, Genki Forest's asset operation model, to some extent, intensifies the instability of the supply chain. The key to maintaining a fast-selling trajectory is to have a comprehensive supply chain and production system belonging to the enterprise (Zhang, 2022). Genki Forest employs the factory model because OEM production is less risk-resistant, potentially leading to uncontrollable production processes and quality, exacerbating the supply side's fluctuations and instability. When competing with leading beverage companies, Genki Forest's supply disadvantage may become more pronounced (Cooper, 2023).

Additionally, in recent years, the recurring issues with beverage product quality have gradually led to a crisis of consumer trust in non-traditional brands. If a company cannot deeply penetrate the core of the supply chain to guarantee product quality and safety, it might struggle to ensure the brand's long-term development.

Forecast for this Market

The health drinks market is expected to continue expanding as we move ahead due to the ongoing health and wellness trend. A growing consumer demand for natural, lower-sugar beverages presents an opportunity for companies like Genki Forest to thrive. Genki Forest can differentiate itself through innovation, product quality, brand image, and customer engagement to stand out in the increasingly competitive market. Conforming to consumer preferences and adapting to market dynamics is essential to maintaining flexibility and convenience.

DEVELOPMENT AND STRATEGY

Vision and Outlook

At the company's inception, the founders discerned a market void for healthier beverage alternatives catering to health-aware consumers. They drew inspiration from the triumph of other US and European beverage startups, which emphasized natural ingredients and innovative flavors. The team sought to distinguish themselves by establishing a brand that provided healthier choices and embodied a minimalist, modern aesthetic that would appeal to China's youthful urban consumers. Nevertheless, one of their preliminary challenges was sourcing high-quality natural ingredients at a large scale. Being a startup, Genki Forest needed more sourcing capabilities and supplier relationships than larger beverage enterprises possess. The founders leveraged their network and industry connections to address this issue and form successful partnerships with reliable suppliers.

Product Development and Innovation

Genki Forest's signature product is a range of sparkling water beverages that offer a variety of unique flavors like White Peach Oolong Tea and Lemon Coconut. The company committed significant resources to product development, experimenting with diverse recipes and flavors to craft drinks that would stand out in a saturated market. They conducted thorough market research and consumer surveys to identify flavor trends and preferences of their target demographic. A key innovation that sets Genki Forest apart is their use of natural sweeteners like erythritol instead of conventional sugar. This choice was motivated by a dedication to health and wellness and to cater to the growing consumer base shifting away from sugary drinks. However, achieving the right sweetness balance without sacrificing taste presented a challenge. The team worked relentlessly to fine-tune the recipes to perfect the flavor blend for each product.

Branding and Marketing

As a relatively obscure brand in a competitive market, Genki Forest faced the task of building brand recognition and a devoted customer base. The company implemented a multi-faceted marketing strategy, prioritizing digital channels, mainly social media and e-commerce platforms. They employed influential partnerships and online campaigns to generate excitement about their products and drive traffic to their online store. A unique facet of Genki Forest's marketing approach is the focus on storytelling and brand narrative. The founders appreciate the potency of connecting with consumers emotionally and have developed a brand image that underscores wellness and authenticity.

E-Commerce Expansion

Genki Forest identified the potential of e-commerce in China early on as a crucial growth and popularity catalyst. The company invested heavily in establishing a robust online presence through platforms like Tmall and JD.com and its direct sales website. This has allowed them to reach a broader audience beyond their physical retail stores and rapidly escalate sales. However, scaling up e-commerce operations also posed several challenges, particularly regarding logistical security and timely fulfilment. Genki Forest had to refine its supply chain and distribution network to meet the escalating product demand. The most significant issue was the competition they faced from other beverage brands for market share, which mandated them to persistently innovate and stay at the forefront in terms of product diversification and marketing strategies.

International Expansion of the Market

Following Genki Forest's success in the Chinese market, the company aimed to expand internationally and establish a global presence. They began exploring opportunities in markets such as Southeast Asia, Europe, and the United States, with an increasing demand for healthy beverages. The company's founders were ambitious to leave their imprint on the global stage and compete with the established beverage giants.

THE PEOPLE BEHIND YUANQI FOREST

Benson Tang is the founder of Yuanqi Forest. Global Entrepreneur Magazine named him one of the top 40 business elites under 40 in 2010. General Secretary Hu Jintao received him on the 90th anniversary of founding the Youth League in 2012 as a representative of outstanding youth. In addition to founding a beverage company in 2015, he furthered his efforts to break through the market of developed countries with his self-developed game CLASH OF KINGS. It took sixth place in the North American bestseller list, becoming the highest-ranking game in the history of internationalization of Chinese games with the highest flow of water, thus expanding the boundaries of Chinese games once again.

FUTURE PROJECTS

As a beverage brand distinguished for offering innovative and healthy products, Genki Forest consistently anticipates future trends and consumer preferences to maintain its market lead.

Broadening Product Lines

Genki Forest might broaden its product portfolio to cater to more diverse consumer tastes and requirements. This could involve introducing new flavors, such as unusual fruit combinations or distinct herbal infusions, considering the Chinese's unique fondness for herbs and traditional Chinese medicine. This strategy could cater to customers seeking a varied selection of beverages. Additionally, the brand could investigate the creation of functional beverages, such as energy-enhancing drinks or beverages with added health benefits, to satisfy the growing consumer demand for beverages that offer more than just hydration.

Sustainable Packaging

With global environmental concerns escalating, Genki Forest could prioritize sustainable packaging solutions to decrease its carbon footprint and appeal to environmentally aware consumers. This could entail transitioning to biodegradable or recyclable materials or adopting innovative packaging designs that reduce waste. By adopting a proactive stance towards sustainability, Genki Forest can manifest its commitment to environmental preservation, actively participate in social responsibility, and distinguish itself in a competitive marketplace.

E-Commerce and Online Sales

In the wake of the rise of online shopping and digital advertising, Genki Forest might invest in fortifying its e-commerce capabilities and digital marketing strategy. This could involve launching an easy-to-navigate online store, partnering with popular e-commerce platforms to extend its reach, and utilizing the expansive reach of social media to advertise its products. Genki Forest can engage a more diverse audience of varying age groups or profiles, interact directly with customers, and gather invaluable insights to guide product development and marketing strategies by bolstering its online presence.

Global Expansion

Genki Forest might consider global expansion opportunities to cultivate new markets and establish itself as a recognizable international brand. This could involve penetrating new regions with a high demand for healthy beverages, forming strategic partnerships with local distributors or retailers, and adapting products to align with different cultural preferences. By establishing subsidiaries overseas, Genki Forest can diversify its revenue sources, enhance brand awareness, and emerge as a global health drink industry leader.

REFERENCES

Chang, Y. (2020). Research on the marketing strategy of burgeoning sugar-free beverages: Taking Yuanqi Forest as an example. *E3S Web of Conferences*. e3s. DOI:10.1051/e3sconf/202021802002

Cooper, B. (2023). *Challengers to Watch 2023: Genki Forest*. BizCommunity. www .bizcommunity.com

iMedia. (2024). *Yuanqi Forest deepens cooperation with Fenxiang Sales: Using data to connect businesses to drive decision-making*. iMedia. https://min.news/en/economy/d97291f425e4b78e19e83f0fa89d9452.html

iNEWS. (2023). *Tang Binsen: Before the success of Yuanqi Forest, I had a "Ten Billion Dollar Lesson" [Interview]*. iNews. https://inf.news/en/economy/b46674018582 5621db468760de59c973.html

Ren, Z., & Xin, X. (2022). Analysing the word-of-mouth marketing strategy of Netflix products based on the 5T theory - Taking "Genki Forest" as an example. *Modern Marketing*, 18, 67–69. DOI:10.19932/j.cnki.22-1256/F.2022.06.067

Wang, C. (2021). Yuanqi Forest will own Netflix's ready-to-drink coffee brand, Never Coffee. *Food Safety Magazine*, 7-15.

Xu, Y., & Zhang, A. (2023). *Yuanqi Forest: Beverage Market Breaker*. Business Management. DOI:10.3969/j.issn.1003-2320.2023.02.018

Yuanqi Forest. (2023). *2023 Global Challenger Brand List*. Yuanqi. https://www .yuanqiForest.com/news/86

Yuanqi Forest. (2024). *About us*. Yuanqi Forest. https://www.yuanqiForest.com/about/recommend

Zhang, S. (2022). *SWOT Analysis and Recommendations for Genki Forest - The Case of Soda Sparkling Water*. CHN. DOI:10.13939/j.cnki.zgsc.2022.02.128

Zhang, T., & Liu, L. (2022). *Research on brand innovation of Yuanqi Forest*. Co-operative Economy and Technology. DOI:10.3969/j.issn.1672-190X.2022.06.038

KEY TERMS AND DEFINITIONS

Generation Z: Generation Z, or Gen Z, refers to individuals born from the mid-1990s to the early 2010s. This generation matured during the digital age, with smartphones, social media, and immediate communication as fundamental parts of their lives. Generation Z is known for being independent, entrepreneurial, and diverse. Societal shifts, such as the growing awareness of social justice issues and environmental concerns, have also influenced them.

Millennials: Millennials, also recognized as Generation Y, typically pertain to individuals born between the early 1980s and mid-1990s. This generation experienced the emergence of technology, social media, and globalization. Millennials are often depicted as tech-savvy, diverse, and socially aware. They have been molded by events such as 9/11, the Great Recession, and technological advancements.

OEM Production: OEM, an acronym for Original Equipment Manufacturer, denotes a process where a company manufactures a product that is subsequently sold to another company, which retails it under its brand name. In OEM production, the manufacturer constructs the product according to the specifications or designs provided by the buyer. This allows the purchaser to market the product as their own, bypassing the need to invest in manufacturing. OEM production is prevalent in the electronics, automotive, and consumer goods sectors.

Xiaohongshu: Xiaohongshu is a popular social media platform in China, akin to Instagram.

Chapter 16
Weride:
Pioneering Autonomous Driving Innovation and Global Expansion

Shuyi Feng

Beijing Normal University-Hong Kong Baptist University United International College, China

EXECUTIVE SUMMARY

The case study explores WeRide, a leading innovator in autonomous driving technology, tracing its journey from inception to becoming a global powerhouse in the autonomous vehicle industry. Founded by Xu Han, WeRide has strategically positioned itself through significant investments, strategic partnerships with global giants like Renault-Nissan-Mitsubishi Alliance, and continuous technological advancements. The case examines WeRide's growth strategies, including product diversification into Robotaxis, Robobuses, and Robovans, as well as its expansion into international markets with operations spanning 26 cities globally. Highlighting key figures such as Xu Han and Hua Zhong, the study delves into their pivotal roles in driving WeRide's technological evolution and market dominance. It discusses prospects, including upcoming technologies like WeRide Sensor Suite 5.2 and strategic alliances with major travel platforms. WeRide's journey highlights their dedication to revolutionizing transportation through advanced self-driving technology and valuable international collaborations.

INTRODUCTION TO WERIDE

WeRide is a Chinese company that specializes in developing autonomous driving technology. They are creating self-driving cars to make transportation safer and more efficient. Their technology is already being tested in several cities, paving

DOI: 10.4018/979-8-3693-2921-4.ch016

the way for a future where cars can drive themselves. Currently, WeRide's products have been upgraded and developed in Guangzhou and have also been developed and expanded in other cities in China, such as Nanjing, Beijing, Suzhou, Wuxi, Shenzhen, and Zhengzhou. At the same time, WeRide is gradually developing new markets overseas.

Since its establishment in December 2017, WeRide has quickly grown into a formidable player in the autonomous vehicle industry, with Guangzhou serving as its global headquarters. The company's rapid progression from unmanned driver testing to launching China's first L4-level autonomous driving operation in less than two years is a testament to its innovative prowess. WeRide introduced the nation's first robotaxi commercial operation service, an exclusive offering that has since evolved into a fully public robotaxi operation. In 2019, WeRide's robotaxi service catered to 4,683 individuals, averaging over 270 rides daily without any safety incidents (IT Information, 2019).

In the wake of the 2020 epidemic, WeRide's autonomous vehicles played a crucial role in Guangzhou, particularly in areas under strict quarantine measures. WeRide's robobusses and robotaxis were deployed in the sealed Liwan District to transport essential supplies, ensuring the delivery of necessary goods and express packages. These autonomous vehicles also facilitated the distribution of fresh fruits and vegetables in collaboration with relevant departments. The use of driverless cars for supply delivery during the epidemic ensured zero human contact, mitigating the risk of cross-infection and aiding in preventing the new coronavirus spread. Leveraging perceptual positioning technology, these driverless vehicles could locate and complete accurate distribution around the clock, thereby enhancing transportation efficiency.

Brief History of WeRide

In April 2017, Jingchi Technology was founded in Silicon Valley, U.S. The first open-road autonomous test was completed 81 days later. In December of that year, the company sensed Guangzhou's growth potential and relocated its worldwide headquarters to this city, the capital of the Guangdong province. The company changed its name to WeRide.

In 2018, WeRide secured backing from the Guangzhou Municipal Government to establish the inaugural domestic L4-level autonomous driving normalized operation within a designated zone on Guangzhou Bio Island. L4-level autonomous driving refers to a highly advanced stage of autonomous vehicle technology where the vehicle can operate without human intervention under certain conditions. In L4 autonomy, the vehicle can handle all aspects of driving in specific environments or situations, such as highway driving or urban areas, without input from a human driver. However, L4 autonomy is limited to predefined operational domains, and human intervention may still be required in certain situations or environments outside these domains. The same year, the company collaborated with Guangzhou Automobile to develop an uncrewed self-driving vehicle. It started self-driving tests, achieving tunnel crossing under the river and safe driving in stormy weather. In November 2018, the company partnered with Guangzhou Baiyun to launch the first L4 self-driving taxi (Wang, 2021).

In 2019, many core technical experts joined the company's technical research and development and engineering management team, launched the "WeRide One" general algorithm for autonomous driving, achieved all-day, all-scene coverage of unmanned autonomous driving operation scenarios, and set up the WeRide Robo-Taxi (Wenyuan Yuexing) Joint Venture with Baiyun Taxi and Science City Group to carry out urban open road test rides and driverless taxi services, covering the core urban open roads in Guangzhou's Huangpu District and Development Zone (WeRide, 2022).

In 2020, WeRide obtained a remote testing license from Smart Internet and cooperated with Gaode, which holds big data on traffic demographics and traffic. The Gaode taxi platform went live with WeRide's Robotaxi service. The first passenger research report on driverless taxis in China, released by the Institute of Transportation Studies at Tsinghua University, showed that WeRide's self-driving taxis did not have any active liability accidents (Wang, 2021). At the end of the year, the company received a strategic investment of US$200 million from Yutong Group, a large commercial vehicle company, to focus on developing commercial self-driving vehicles and intelligent mobility.

In 2021, WeRide developed a self-driving micro-circulation minibus and collaborated with Guangzhou Public Transport Group Sanqi to operate self-driving buses, providing citizens with convenient, innovative bus services in specific areas. In the same year, WeRide acquired China's leading self-driving freight startup, Maketsu Technology, enhancing its R&D strength. WeRide also cooperated strategically with two upstream and downstream enterprises, namely Jiangling Motors and Zhongtong Express, to push forward intelligent freight transport in the city. Additionally, WeRide released China's first L4-level self-driving freight vehicle (Wei, 2022). In the same year, WeRide was granted a self-driving license by the State of California in the United States, and a self-driving taxi service in the United Arab Emirates will soon be launched, bringing a new travel experience to residents and tourists.

In 2022, WeRide, together with WoSai Technology and Suteng Poly, developed hardware and software to upgrade its technology from automotive-grade semi-solid-state LiDAR (I.e. et al., a remote sensing method used in many fields to measure distances) to automotive-grade solid-state LiDAR. They also released a new-generation universal technology platform for automated driving technology called WeRide One. In the same year, WeRide collaborated with automotive technology service provider Bosch to develop a new-generation automated enhancement sensor suite, WeRide SS 5.0. Furthermore, WeRide launched a mass-produced full robosweeper and conducted open road tests in Guangzhou.

In 2023, WeRide attended the 7th Future Investment Initiative Summit held in Riyadh, the capital of Saudi Arabia, and provided the only self-driving dynamic demonstration and minibus test ride service at the summit. WeRide also received written notification that it had been awarded the Singapore Land Transport Authority's Driverless Vehicle Level 1 Public Road Test License and Driverless Vehicle Level 1 Public Path Test License for Special Areas. With this, WeRide has become the world's first and only technology company to hold four autonomous driving licenses in China, the United States, the United Arab Emirates, and Singapore simultaneously (People's Public Transport, 2024).

Business Model

WeRide is a leading L4 driverless technology company in China, guided by the corporate culture values of "GRIT", representing Grow Together, Result Driven, Innovation, and Team Work. Pursuing business partnerships, attracting scientific and technological leaders, establishing research teams, and driving technological innovation are ongoing objectives for WeRide. Its primary focus is providing technological solutions to automotive firms, articulated as the business model of "1 platform + 3 major scenarios + 5 major products." The "One platform" refers to WeRide One, the company's primary general technology platform for autonomous driving. It encompasses full-stack autonomous driving software algorithms, flexible and adaptable modular hardware solutions, and a powerful and reliable cloud architecture platform. WeRide One enables the company to meet diverse autonomous driving needs in urban scenarios across several models.

WeRide's involvement in autonomous driving spans three major categories: passenger travel, bus transportation, and freight commercial use, showcasing the company's extensive presence and application in the field. The company's five major products include self-driving minibusses, self-driving freight trucks, self-driving taxis, self-driving sanitation vehicles, and advanced intelligent driving goods, forming a versatile portfolio of autonomous driving solutions to cater to various client demands. WeRide has seamlessly integrated technological research and development with commercial operation, creating a distinct profit model. Furthermore, the company leverages the "Iron triangle" model, partnering with automakers, Tier 1 suppliers, and travel service platforms to expand its market share and enhance profitability. More than 20 million kilometers in autonomous driving mileage have been accumulated through WeRide's R&D, testing, and autonomous driving operations conducted in over 26 cities worldwide (Huxiu Technology, 2023).

WeRide's product matrix has helped the company establish strong technical barriers. By using a modular integrated design approach, WeRide developed the LCS (Lidar Camera System) Lidar camera system. This approach allows for standardizing parts, easier stock facilitation, and streamlining of supply chain management. The company also offers variously shaped sensor kits that work with the same set of perception algorithms, saving time during software and hardware improvements and enhancing product competitiveness. Additionally, WeRide provides distributed machine-learning platforms and fully automated solutions for data processing and acquisition through local and worldwide data centers. This platform can support massive fleets of test activities in multiple locations simultaneously to obtain closed-loop data and ensure efficient operation. WeRide benefits from significant technical support from this big data processing capability, allowing continuous optimization of the automatic driving system and enhancement of the product's performance (Li, 2021).

WeRide has created a sustainable cash flow for the company through diversified revenue sources, efficient supply chain management, and continuous technological innovation. The company's diversified autonomous driving solutions and services have brought in varied sources of revenue and reduced operating risks. The use of modular integrated design and component standardization has helped to reduce the cost and time investment of supply chain management, thereby increasing the company's profitability. WeRide is committed to ongoing technological innovation and investment in research and development in the field of autonomous driving. This continuous improvement enhances the competitiveness and performance of products, positioning the company as a leader in the industry and attracting more customers, which in turn provides stability to its cash flow (Li, 2021).

Product and Services

Overview

WeRide stands at the forefront of autonomous driving technology thanks to its exceptional research team and deep technical expertise. The team's capabilities span vital areas such as automatic driving algorithms and sensor fusion, and they possess numerous independent intellectual property rights and core technologies. The company has also forged strategic partnerships with industry leaders such as Gould, Bosch, GAC Group, Mitsubishi, and others. These alliances provide WeRide with access to their partners' experience, technology, and financial support and open up a broader market for their autonomous driving technology.

WeRide's vehicles have proprietary software and driverless technology, including a self-driving sensor suite. This technology helps to reduce driver fatigue, lower accident rates, and improve vehicle safety, giving their products a competitive edge in the market. Furthermore, the company's experience in project implementation is another strength. WeRide has successfully rolled out projects like Robotaxi and Robovan in various locations, gaining invaluable hands-on experience that bolsters their ability to expand into other cities and countries. Then, to cater to a wide range of customers, WeRide offers a variety of driving capabilities and programs aligned with the unique uses and demands of different vehicle models. This approach allows them to serve a diverse customer base (WeRide, 2022).

WeRide's growth is further facilitated by supportive national policies and local initiatives promoting the autonomous driving industry. The rapid development of new infrastructure, such as 5G networks, Internet of Things (IoT), artificial intelligence, and computing power, provides a favorable environment for WeRide to collaborate with suitable tech leaders and high-tech companies (WeRide, 2022).

In the competitive landscape, WeRide differentiates itself with its self-driving products that cater to various scenarios, such as passenger travel and freight transport. This versatility sets them apart from competitors like Baidu and Pony Smart, which primarily focus on specific fields. Furthermore, WeRide has developed two unique technologies: WeRide Go, a mobile app, and WeRide One, a comprehensive tech platform for automated driving. These platforms, which include advanced software algorithms and hardware solutions, give WeRide an edge in urban automated driving (Mark, 2022).

Robotaxi

Robotaxi is the first autonomous product developed by WeRide, designed to offer affordable and reliable driverless travel services. In a partnership with the Guangzhou Municipal Government and Guangzhou Municipal Public Transportation Group Baiyun Company, WeRide launched the first L4 robotaxi in November 2018. A year later, in August 2019, WeRide, Baiyun Taxi, and Science City Group formed the self-driving taxi company Wenyuan Yuexing. This partnership quickly led to the acquisition of China's first driverless license in Guangzhou. By December, WeRide became the first company to successfully deploy a robotaxi fleet in a tier-one city, providing travel services with self-driving technology. In February 2020, in collaboration with Tsinghua University's Institute of Transportation Research, WeRide released China's first self-driving taxi operation report. In June, it partnered with the Gaode platform to launch a public robotaxi service. In 2021, WeRide expanded its services to Abu Dhabi, UAE, where it was well-received by the local community (Zhong, 2021; Guo, 2021; Qiming et al., 2020; Uncle et al., 2019).

WeRide's Robotaxi boasts several strengths. Its development time and efficiency are impressive, reaching the fourth stage of autonomous driving development in just two years. This rapid progress brings it close to the current top level globally (Zhong, 2021). The "WeRide one" general algorithm for autonomous driving allows the Robotaxi to adapt to various road conditions, including highways, tunnels, rush hour traffic, nighttime conditions, and rainy and cloudy weather (Guo, 2021). The company also demonstrates strong regionalization, localization, and openness of operations. WeRide's Robotaxi taxi software, WeRide Go, is integrated with the Yangchengtong APP, a significant travel software for Guangzhou citizens, and cooperates with the Gaode taxi platform (Qiming et al., 2020).

Users can easily book the Robotaxi service through the WeRide Go App. This convenient method of booking and traveling offers users great convenience and reduces the time spent waiting and searching for transportation. Additionally, robotaxis provide comfortable and efficient self-driving travel services. Once inside the car, users simply need to fasten their seat belts and tap the "Go" button on the screen to enjoy the convenient experience of automatic driving. This allows users to focus on enjoying the trip rather than worrying about driving and navigation. WeRide is the first company to launch Robotaxi products and charging operation services in China. They have operated Robotaxi for over 1,400 days without any active safety liability accidents, demonstrating their excellent safety performance (Zhong, 2021).

Robotaxi presents opportunities for external financial and technical support from the world's largest automobile alliance, Renault Nissan Mitsubishi Automobile Alliance, which invested 30 million US dollars in WeRide (Uncle et al., 2019). China's focus on Artificial Intelligence as a development strategy, coupled with the strong support of the local government of Guangzhou for robotaxi services, creates a favorable regulatory environment (Uncle et al., 2019). WeRide's partnerships with well-known companies, such as Gaode, expand the customer demographic and drive future business development (Zhong, 2021).

Robobus

The Robobus is the world's first fully uncrewed, self-driving minibus that can be mass-produced on a large scale. Equipped with WeRide's proprietary hardware and software solutions, the Robobus has no steering wheel, accelerator, or brake. It offers a cockpit-less design, providing passengers with a spacious and comfortable riding experience. The Robobus supports V2X technology and can reach a maximum speed of 40 km/h. Robobus services are available to the public both domestically and internationally and have been well-received. In Guangzhou, to facilitate public travel at night, the night shift line of Biological Island Line 1 and Line 2 will also be put into operation, becoming the first autonomous night bus line in the country, further enhancing the convenience of the service (Wang, 2021).

Safety is a vital strength of the Robobus. Passengers must remain seated and buckled up throughout the journey, and alarms will sound if these rules are not followed (E cars, 2024). The Safety and Security Centre monitors every operational Robobus to ensure passenger safety. Additionally, WeRide has purchased liability insurance for every passenger on board. The Robobus also boasts a high-end driverless design, equipped with multi-module sensors like LIDAR, HD camera, blind spot LIDAR, and millimeter-wave radar to efficiently handle complex urban traffic situations (E cars, 2024). Opportunities for the Robobus include its positive reputation gained from pilot projects in various locations and its novelty as a symbol of future technology, which attracts passengers curious about new travel options.

Robovan

In September 2021, WeRide collaborated with Jiangling Motors and Zhongtong Express to launch China's first L4-class self-driving pure electric Robovan. This vehicle, designed for inter-city freight transport, is equipped with WeRide's self-driving solution and uses the BEV model of Jiangling Light Bus. The Robovan is set to be tested and commercially piloted in China Express's same-city freight transport scenario (Xu, 2021).

The Robovan is designed to operate 24/7 in various urban traffic scenarios, including urban villages, city centers, highways, tunnels, and bridges, regardless of time and weather constraints. This ensures transportation efficiency by reducing workforce costs, planning routes efficiently, and minimizing fuel consumption. Its lightweight and flexible design is advantageous for same-city freight transport. The Robovan can provide 7X24 hours of continuous transportation thanks to its digital management platform, which also increases the level of automation in urban logistics, making shipping and receiving items easier and faster for clients. The Robovan's completely redundant chassis ensures the vehicle's hardware is secure and dependable. WeRide has implemented a robust quality control system to conduct stringent testing and assessment of vehicles, guaranteeing that every Robovan can satisfy elevated safety standards (WeRide, 2022).

Opportunities for Robovan include a strategic partnership with Jiangling Motors and China Express, which guarantees the sales of cargo trucks and helps establish a solid partnership with China Express (Qi, 2021). China Express will assist in screening and confirming Robovan's self-driving pilot routes. This partnership will allow WeRide to utilize China Express's rich road experience to improve Robovan's performance and produce better products (Xu, 2021).

Robosweeper

WeRide's Robosweeper is China's first front-loaded, mass-produced, fully self-driving sanitation vehicle. This vehicle can reach a maximum speed of 40km/h and has a cockpit-less design that allows for maximum rubbish storage, with a water storage capacity of up to two tons. The Robosweeper uses an all-electric model, saving fuel costs and reducing operation costs. It can replace sanitation workers for urban cleaning and perform various urban sanitation operations such as road sweeping, sprinkling and dust reduction, spraying and extermination, etc. The Robosweeper can also assist cities in coping with special public health events like the COVID-19 pandemic, achieving the zero-touch completion of the designated area elimination.

Opportunities for the Robosweeper include the high safety risks and poor working conditions in sanitation services, which can affect workers' health. The Robosweeper can effectively isolate the contact between people and the harsh environment. As the aging trend intensifies and the sanitation industry faces difficulties in recruiting and retaining workers, driverless sanitation vehicles can reduce the need for a workforce and solve the pain point problem. The rapid development of urbanization has led to a surge in roads that need to be swept and cleaned, and purely manual work can no longer effectively solve the problem of road sweeping. New public health problems also put forward unmanned new demands for urban governance.

Wepilot (A High-Level Intelligent Driving Solution)

WeRide and Bosch, the world's largest Tier1, have collaboratively developed a high-level intelligent driving solution based on infrastructure, toolchain, and big data algorithms. This solution, which can be installed in a wide range of vehicles, provides advanced driving aid in the presence of a driver, ensuring safe and reliable assisted driving. WeRide intends to apply this solution to the front-loaded mass production and marketable application of L2+/L3 intelligent driving products for passenger cars, expanding the market competitiveness of automated driving products (Yang et al., 2019).

The Bosch Group, known for its innovative and cutting-edge technology products and solutions, is the world's No. 1 automotive technology supplier. Automotive and Intelligent Transportation Technology is the largest business segment of the Bosch Group, accounting for more than half of the Group's total sales. WeRide's strategic cooperation with the Bosch Group allows it to learn from Bosch's mature business model and R&D experience. Leveraging Bosch's market recognition can increase WeRide's reputation in the industry and attract more investors. Bosch China's high-level intelligent driving solution is tailor-made for the Chinese market by Bosch Intelligent Driving and Control Division China, which includes critical technology elements such as sensors, computing platforms, software applications, and cloud services, as well as a scalable architecture for the future (Chen & Chen, 2022).

WeRide Go

WeRide Go is a mobile app independently developed by WeRide. It integrates robotaxi and robobus services, allowing passengers to call a robotaxi in the designated operation area, check the location of the robobus, and predict the arrival time according to their travel needs. This provides a new, more convenient, safe, and intelligent driving experience. WeRide Go coordinates all the company's driverless products that provide travel services, offering customers the convenience of hailing a car. The app's clear and straightforward interface provides intuitive guidance for passengers. It is more convenient than hailing a car on the Gaode map, saving energy and time when searching for driverless car options within the app.

Customers

General Public: Individuals Aged 18-50 Years Old

People within the age range of 18-50 years old are typically more open to embracing innovative technologies due to their prolonged exposure to the digital world. This demographic group is more likely to trust and utilize autonomous travel solutions than older generations. Moreover, these individuals travel more frequently than younger children or adolescents, making them a primary target for autonomous vehicle services (Wan & Liu, 2024). The demand for autonomous travel from this demographic is primarily for commuting and leisure, which can be effectively satisfied by WeRide's Robotaxi and Robobus services. These services meet their travel needs and cater to their curiosity and interest in exploring the realm of autonomous driving.

Governmental Organizations: Urban Administration

Government departments, particularly those involved with urban administration and public health, require efficient and cost-effective solutions for urban sanitation management. WeRide's Robosweeper offers a solution to this need. It is capable of autonomous street sweeping and can operate 24/7, reducing labor costs and enhancing cleaning efficiency (Qi, 2021). This innovative solution aligns with the needs of these departments to enhance operational efficiency and maintain cleanliness standards in urban areas.

Corporate Sector: Logistics and Freight Companies

Many companies, especially those in the logistics and freight industry, rely heavily on trucks to transport goods between different locations. The demand for truck drivers in these businesses is high. WeRide's Robovan offers an autonomous solution that meets basic transport needs and reduces the cost of hiring truck drivers, thus promoting a more rational allocation of corporate resources. Furthermore, truck drivers working at night are often susceptible to fatigue, leading to potential accidents that can delay deliveries, tarnish the company's reputation, and, in severe cases, endanger lives (Liu, 2021). Autonomous freight vehicles like Robovan can operate continuously in various weather conditions, effectively mitigating these risks.

Market Analysis

The Original Condition of the Market for Driverless Cars

In the 1970s, developed countries took the lead in researching driverless cars. In the subsequent three to four decades, numerous automobile manufacturing producers have also started to lay their groundwork in the field of driverless cars. In October 2015, Tesla launched Autopilot, a semi-autonomous driving system, the first commercially available self-driving program. In addition, Google is the representative of the new technology force, and many startups have also entered the field of uncrewed vehicles, most of them adopting the "one-step" technology development route, that is, the direct development of L4-level uncrewed vehicles.

Research on driverless cars in China started relatively late, in the 1980s. Tsinghua University and other top universities began to research and develop driverless cars under the funding of the Ministry of National Defense and the National Plan. In 1992, the National University of Defense Technology developed China's first driverless car, officially opening the track of autonomous driving in China. In the 21st century, some automakers and high-tech companies have launched self-driving products and services under their corporate umbrellas and have continued to improve their functionality through repeated testing (Academic Headlines, 2018). Since 2014, driverless technology and road test development have become even more rapid. Driverless cars gradually move from the lab to the road and are beginning to be tested and operated in real-world traffic environments.

Market Development So Far

The development of driverless cars has surpassed market expectations. With the advancement of intelligent Internet technology and the widespread usage of 5G networks, major Internet companies have also entered the driverless car industry. Driverless technology is a scenario application of automatic driving and intelligent services, and there is still plenty of room for its development to achieve accurate unmanned automatic driving (Qi, 2021). Currently, widely publicized driverless taxis have a "safety officer" in the driver's seat. This safety officer does not control the steering wheel but addresses any unexpected situations the algorithm might not account for, ensuring that the automatic driving system can promptly handle any issues with other vehicles (Liu, 2020).

Similarly, ferries and lorries can operate on prescribed routes without drivers in some ports, enterprises, and plants. However, supervisors are still present, and the entire process of unmanned driving is yet to be possible. With the current level of technology, there is still a considerable distance to be covered before driverless vehicles can be used on open roads.

Competitive Analysis

WeRide operates in a complex and multifaceted autonomous driving industry that involves a variety of suppliers, including those for sensors, chips, radar, and software development. To mitigate the bargaining risk and ensure a stable supply chain, WeRide has formed strategic partnerships with key suppliers. For instance, in 2022, WeRide and Bosch, a leading automotive Tier 1 supplier, collaborated on the development of intelligent driving software, thereby enhancing WeRide's supply chain security.

In the autonomous driving market, consumers have relatively low bargaining power. Autonomous vehicles are high-tech products that require substantial R&D and production costs, which leaves little room for price negotiations. Moreover, consumers are generally receptive to the emerging technology of autonomous vehicles, indicating a significant market demand potential (Guo, 2021).

Despite its high technological threshold and capital investment requirements, the autonomous driving industry is attracting an increasing number of companies. These potential entrants could come from traditional automotive industries, tech giants, or startups (Bogumil et al., 2018). With innovative technologies, robust capital, and aggressive market strategies, these new entrants threaten WeRide's market position.

Substitutes for WeRide's services, such as traditional human-crewed vehicles, shared bikes, and car-sharing services, also present challenges. Car sharing, in particular, has seen rapid growth in recent years, aided by government initiatives

(Wei, 2022). As autonomous driving technology is still maturing, some consumers may prefer traditional modes of transportation.

The autonomous vehicle industry is nascent but has already drawn interest from major tech companies and automakers like Ford, Toyota, Google, and Tesla. With their robust R&D capabilities, strategic business layouts, and partnerships, these companies pose significant competition to WeRide (Liu, 2020). For instance, Yihang Technology offers more affordable robotaxi services, while companies like Baidu and Google have larger vehicle fleets, more recognizable brand images, and more robust capital. To thrive in this competitive landscape, WeRide must increase its investment in R&D and continue to expand its market cooperation channels.

Investment and Growth Strategy

Throughout its initial stages and growth period, WeRide navigated a phase of high consumption characterized by significant investment and modest returns. This phase was crucial for technology accumulation and market positioning, setting the stage for potential exponential growth. WeRide secured multiple rounds of financing, including Pre-A round financing of USD 57 million, strategic investment from the Renault-Nissan-Mitsubishi Alliance, and subsequent funding rounds amounting to nearly USD 400 million from various investors. This financial empowerment has facilitated the transition of WeRide's autonomous driving products from fixed-point trials to operational services and industrialization (Wang, 2020).

Innovation and Technological Advancement Strategy

WeRide has prioritized disruptive technologies and innovative products since its inception to secure lasting competitive advantages. The company's technology suite has undergone continuous upgrades, including WeRide Smart Suite 3.0, WeRide Sensor Suite 4.0, WeRide SS 5.0, and WeRide Sensor Suite 5.1. The latest generation of WeRide Smart Suite 5.1 has received the ASPICE CL2 certification from UL Solutions, a globally renowned certification body, indicating that WeRide's software development quality aligns with international standards. This recognition serves as an endorsement of WeRide's automatic driving middleware, paving the way for the company's autonomous driving technology's scaling up and mass production (Zheng et al., 2018; Bai, 2024).

Product Expansion and Collaboration Strategy

Leveraging robust technology platforms and hardware-software integration, WeRide has expedited its self-driving products' deployment and commercial application. The company's diverse product range includes Robotaxi, Robobus, Robovan, and Robosweeper Wepilot. Collaborations with the Renault-Nissan-Mitsubishi Alliance, Yutong Group, Bosch, and GAC Group have enabled WeRide to offer a variety of services, such as online taxis, on-demand buses, intra-city freight transport, and intelligent sanitation. WeRide operates in 26 cities globally and has accumulated approximately 25 million kilometers of autonomous driving mileage (Zheng et al., 2018). WeRide's accolades include a ranking in the "2023 Global Unicorn List" and being named one of the "2023 Forbes China - Top 30 Global Brands Going Overseas" (Hurun, 2023). In 2021, WeRide acquired autonomous trucking company Maki Technology, further broadening its offering and enriching its operational landscape (Wang, 2021). These strategic moves, coupled with a new round of financing, have positioned WeRide for the mass production of autonomous vehicles and rapid development in the autonomous driving industry.

THE PEOPLE BEHIND THE UNICORN

Xu Han (CEO of WeRide)

Xu Han, the founder and CEO of WeRide, is also an adjunct professor at the South China University of Technology. Renowned for his expertise in computer vision and machine learning technologies, he has been instrumental in the evolution and commercialization of autonomous driving technologies. Before establishing WeRide, Xu Han served as a tenured professor and doctoral supervisor at the University of Missouri, USA, and later as Chief Scientist of Baidu's Autonomous Driving Division in 2016. Here, he led the Perception, Simulation, Sensing, and Hardware teams, contributing to developing DeepSpeech2, a speech recognition system recognized as one of the top 10 technology breakthroughs of 2016 by MIT Tech Review. In 2017, he co-founded Jingchi Technology, the predecessor of WeRide, with Jin Wang, a former Senior Vice President of Baidu. Upon succeeding Jin Wang as the CEO of WeRide in February 2018, Xu Han has guided WeRide's steady growth from a startup, implementing strategic decisions that have accelerated the company's development.

WeRide's strong development strategy and plan are a result of Xu Han's leadership. He focuses on propelling the organization forward by integrating technical research and development with commercial applications. In order to achieve rapid growth, he has overseen the company's expansion into new business areas and market segments. Xu Han possesses a solid academic background and extensive experience in autonomous driving research and development. Under his guidance, WeRide has made significant advances in autonomous driving technology research and development, such as successfully crossing a river tunnel and achieving 5G remote-controlled automated driving. These technical advancements have greatly enhanced WeRide's competitive position and laid a strong foundation for the company's commercial operations. Thanks to Xu Han's dynamic leadership, WeRide has emerged as a global leader in the commercial deployment of autonomous driving technology. For example, receiving a commercial pilot permit in Yizhuang, Beijing, allowing WeRide to launch Robotaxi services, marks a major milestone in the commercialization of its advanced autonomous driving technology (Sina Finance, 2024).

Throughout his career, Xu Han has led numerous research projects, securing 11 funded projects totaling over $7 million. His teams have also won several international computer vision competition awards, including recognition from the ImageNet International Object Detection Competition and the International Computer Vision Action Recognition Competition. Xu Han has contributed to various international magazines and journals, and currently serves as an associate editor for the Journal of Multimedia and an expert for the NSF review committee.

Hua Zhong (Vice President of WeRide)

Hua Zhong, formerly the vice president of WeRide, managed Guangzhou Jingqi Technology Co. before that. He has extensive experience from his time at Google and Siemens Research, as well as being one of the earliest members of Microsoft Research Asia. During his time at Microsoft Research Asia, he oversaw the research and development of computer vision, graphics, and machine learning algorithms. Hua Zhong holds a Ph.D. in Computer Science from Carnegie Mellon University, graduating from the esteemed Robotics Institute established by Professor Takeo Kanade, a member of both US Academies. He has been awarded 9 US patents, which have contributed to his ability to lead WeRide's research and development team in making significant breakthroughs in autonomous driving technology. The autonomous driving technologies he co-developed, such as WeRide Smart Suite 3.0, have notably improved WeRide's Robotaxi fleet operations (Tian, 2021).

Hua Zhong places a high value on team building and talent training, implementing the "veteran" with "novice" model at WeRide to ensure new members receive quality growth. He has established two criteria for talent selection: extensive experience and expertise in a specific field, and exceptional engineering ability. This emphasis has resulted in WeRide having a high-quality science and technology research and development team. In addition, Hua Zhong holds a Ph.D. in Computer Science from Carnegie Mellon University, graduating from the renowned Robotics Institute founded by Professor Takeo Kanade. The institute is a member of two American Academies of Sciences, and Hua Zhong has obtained nine US patents, reflected not only his technical expertise but also contributing valuable intellectual property to WeRide (Maimai, 2019).

FUTURE PROJECTS

WeRide is committed to establishing a strategic triad of collaboration with automobile manufacturers and platform providers. The company already enjoys strong partnerships with renowned global car companies like the Renault-Nissan-Mitsubishi Alliance and plans to expand these alliances further. Future strategies include opening new financing avenues, forging agreements with additional car manufacturers, and attracting top-tier talent in artificial intelligence, algorithms, and computing to join WeRide's research and development team. Together, they aim to pioneer advanced autonomous driving technologies, such as the upcoming WeRide Sensor Suite 5.2 and 5.3, and to introduce new autonomous vehicle models (Zhong, 2021).

As driverless technology moves towards commercialization, major travel platforms are increasingly seeking partnerships with autonomous driving companies. WeRide has already established collaborations with Gaode Travel and Ruqi Travel and plans to extend these partnerships to more travel platforms. This will enable WeRide to offer autonomous driving services and solutions to other major cities across China and countries or regions with a high level of autonomous driving maturity.

In addition to its existing product array, WeRide is developing new autonomous products, including intelligent driving trucks and engineering vehicles. These additions will diversify its product line and cater to a broader range of public needs. Moreover, WeRide is working on a more sophisticated intelligent network system that leverages advanced artificial intelligence and communication technology. This system will interconnect elements such as roads, transport infrastructure, and vehicles, facilitating more efficient and intelligent traffic and travel.

WeRide currently holds autonomous driving licenses in China, the United States, and the United Arab Emirates, among other countries. The company plans to continue its market expansion and negotiate collaborations with more governments. This will enable WeRide to offer convenient autonomous driving services to users in more countries, including emerging markets like Brazil, Spain, and Russia (Han, 2019).

CONCLUSION

In the rapidly advancing world of science and technology, unmanned automatic driving technology is becoming increasingly integrated into our daily lives, making it a focal point in the realm of science and technology. WeRide has established a strong global presence with its state-of-the-art autonomous driving technology and diverse product range. From autonomous taxis to advanced intelligent driving systems, WeRide's products not only showcase its comprehensive approach to autonomous driving technology, but also demonstrate its technical prowess in various application scenarios.

A new era of driverless technology evolution is on the horizon, and the widespread adoption of this technology will greatly benefit special groups such as the elderly, children, and the disabled, facilitating easier travel and integration into society. However, the development of driverless technology also presents urgent needs for infrastructure and policy solutions. This significant transformation requires collaborative efforts from research and development organizations, technology companies, operating companies, governments, and financial institutions to embrace the change for a better future (Zhong, 2021).

REFERENCES

Academic Headlines. (2018, July 27). *Historical changes in the development of autonomous driving from the 1970s to the present.* Baidu. https://baijiahao.baidu .com/s?id=1607101656119496661&wfr=spider&for=pc

Bai, M. (2024, March 6). *WeRide's self-developed autonomous driving middleware receives ISO 26262 ASIL-D functional safety product certification.* Sohu. https:// sports.sohu.com/a/762272100_120159294

Bakhmutov, S., Saykin, A., Endachev, D., Evgrafov, V., Shagurin, A., Kulikov, I., & Fedoseev, K. (2018). Prospects of development of land driverless trucks. *IOP Conference Series. Materials Science and Engineering*, 315, 1. DOI:10.1088/1757-899X/315/1/012001

Bogumil, V., & Vlasov, V. (2018). Analysis of the main risks in developing and implementing uncrewed vehicles for urban passenger transport. *Transportation Research Procedia*, 36, 63–67. DOI:10.1016/j.trpro.2018.12.044

Chen, B. (2020). *Exploration of China's car-sharing development strategy based on SWOT analysis. Journal of Chongqing Jiaotong University.* Social Science Edition.

Chen, L., & Chen, D. (2022, May 25). *WeRide receives strategic investment from doctorate holders and conducts intelligent driving software development jointly.* Baidu. https://baijiahao.baidu.com/s?id=1733763700373840579&wfr=baike

Fan, Z. (2020). Prospecting unlimited possibilities for future traveling in the era of smart connected cars. *Smart Connected Vehicles*, 6, 53–55.

Guo, W. (2021). *Driverless taxis are edging closer from manned tests to eliminating safety officers.* Smart Connected Cars.

Han, X. (2019). Progress and outlook of L4-level autonomous driving. *Intelligent Networked Vehicles.*

Hurun. (2023). *Hurun global unicorn list.* Hurun. https://www.hurun.net/en-US/ Rank/HsRankDetails?pagetype=unicorn

Huxiu technology. (2023, September 4). *WeRide focuses on innovative business models and accelerates the implementation of autonomous driving technology.* Dongchedi. https://www.dongchedi.com/article/7274776701589094973

IT information. (2019, December 8). Xueqiu. https://xucqiu.com/8175691790/ 137009115

Li, L. (2021, March 3). *Behind the mass production of automatic driving before loading, the breaking work of Wen Yuan knows the line*. Sohu. https://www.sohu.com/a/453812593_99919085

Liu, J. (2020). The driverless era accelerates. *Economic Journal*.

Lu, Z. (2021, September 9). *WeRide enters the freight field and launches L4 autonomous light passenger vehicles in cooperation with Jiangling and Zhongtong*. Sina. https://finance.sina.com.cn/tech/2021-09-09/doc-iktzscyx3258444.shtml

Maimai. (2019, March 1). *WeRide SVP Hua Zhong: Engineers are the people who solve problems*. Maimai. https://maimai.cn/article/detail?fid=1146584014&efid=cS3KDTyj0vQDhAxdXKbcmw

People's Public Transport. (2024). International News. People's. *Public Transport (Berlin)*, 1, 90.

Qi, C. (2021). *Research on the current situation and development trend of car sharing*. Automobile Maintenance and Repair.

Qiming Venture Partners. (2020, April 22). *WeRide: Robotaxi brings autonomous driving to the masses*. Sohu. https://www.sohu.com/a/390071500_313637

Sina Finance. (2024, April 25). *Xu Han: Change human travel with unmanned driving*. Baidu. https://baijiahao.baidu.com/s?id=1797315237395513217&wfr=spider&for=pc

Tian, Z. (2021, June 17). *17 "former" Microsoft people have achieved another Whampoa Military Academy for China's automatic driving*. Lepiphone. https://www.leiphone.com/category/transportation/LeSYLRm3ozHsR0yZ.html

Uncle Cars Talk Cars. (2019, December 13). *Why did autonomous taxis choose WeRide?* Zhihu. https://zhuanlan.zhihu.com/p/97253961

Viewpoint Institutions. (2023, November 20). *WeRide approved the launch of commercial autonomous driving mobility services in Beijing*. Wangyi. https://www.163.com/dy/article/IK015R7U0519D45U.html

Wan, L., & Liu, J. (2024). Analysis of consumer acceptance of driverless internet taxi - Based on UTAUT2 theoretical model paradigm. *Business and Economic Review*, 5, 80–83.

Wang, X. (2020). *The unmanned taxi race: Ambitions, bottlenecks and counterattacks*. China Entrepreneur.

Wang, X. (2021). *WeRide dances with self-driving giants*. China Entrepreneur.

Wei, L. (2022). *The commercialization of uncrewed sanitation vehicles speeds up to increase quality.* Intelligent Networked Vehicles.

WeRide. (2022). *WeRide Inc. environmental social and governance report.* WeRide. https://d2s675kp4ttxrq.cloudfront.net/uploads/We_Ride_Inc_2022_Environmental _Social_and_Governance_Report_EN_c474448943.pdf?updated_at=2023-09 -08T06:29:25.000Z

Xu, J. (2021, September 9). *WeRide officially entered the unmanned freight transportation field and cooperated strategically with Jiangling and Zhongtong.* Tencent. https://new.qq.com/rain/a/20210909A071UZ00

Yang, X., Lu, S., Zhou, M., Tian, Z., & Tan, W. (2019). GPS attitude measurement with a baseline-constrained optimization algorithm for the unpiloted car. *Wireless Networks.* DOI:10.1007/s11276-019-02062-y

Zheng, Y., Bao, H., & Xu, C. (2018). A method for improved pedestrian gesture recognition in self-driving cars. *Australian Journal of Mechanical Engineering,* 16(sup1), 78–85. DOI:10.1080/1448837X.2018.1545476

Zhong, H. (2021). *Robotaxi's scaled-down operational system on the ground.* Intelligent Networked Vehicles.

KEY TERMS AND DEFINITIONS

Big Data: A kind of data accumulation, which is large and complex.

Brand image: Refers to the public or its customers' perception or impression of a company.

Intelligent Logistics: A modern logistics model that leverages advanced technology and artificial intelligence to enhance the efficiency and effectiveness of logistics operations.

Intelligent Travel: Involves the real-time collection, analysis, and application of traffic information through artificial intelligence technology, aiming to improve travel efficiency and experience.

IoT: The Internet of Things (IoT) refers to the network of physical devices, vehicles, appliances, and other items embedded with sensors, software, and connectivity, which enables these objects to connect and exchange data over the Internet.

L2: This level of autonomous driving, also known as Level 2, signifies that the vehicle has certain automated functions, such as adaptive cruise control and self-parking. Although the vehicle can handle some tasks, the driver must keep their hands off the controls but remain alert and ready to take over at any moment.

L3: Level 3 autonomous driving means the vehicle can handle some driving tasks under certain conditions, but the driver must be prepared to take control when the system requests it. This level is also known as "conditional automation."

L4: Level 4, or "high automation," refers to fully autonomous vehicles that can perform all driving tasks under certain conditions without requiring a driver to intervene.

R&D investment: Research and development investment.

Robosweeper: These are autonomous sanitation vehicles designed to clean streets or facilities without human intervention.

Robovan: This term refers to autonomous lorries or delivery vans capable of driving themselves.

Tier 1: A Tier 1 supplier is a company that supplies parts or systems directly to the original equipment manufacturer (OEM), which in this context is the car factory.

V2X: Vehicle-to-everything (V2X) communication allows a vehicle to share information with any entity that may affect it, such as infrastructure, other vehicles, or even pedestrians.

Chapter 17
Tuhu:
Changing China's Automotive Aftermarket

Chenyu Wu

Beijing Normal University-Hong Kong Baptist University United International College, China

EXECUTIVE SUMMARY

This case study explores the development and strategic growth of Tuhu Vehicle Co., Ltd., a leading player in China's automotive aftermarket, under the leadership of MIN Chen. It provides a comprehensive analysis of Chen's extensive background in software development, data management, and the automotive service sector, highlighting his pivotal role in transforming Tuhu from a tire-changing service to a diversified O2O one-stop automobile repair and maintenance company. The case delves into Tuhu's innovative approaches, including the implementation of standardized services, the creation of industry alliances, and the launch of an open product platform. It examines Tuhu's strategic expansion, its successful IPO on the Hong Kong Stock Exchange, and its forward-looking initiatives in the new energy vehicle market. By analyzing Tuhu's business model, supply chain revolutions, and market positioning, this case provides insights into the company's unique development path, operational resilience, and its impact on China's auto aftermarket industry.

DOI: 10.4018/979-8-3693-2921-4.ch017

UNICORN DESCRIPTION

Background of the Company

Tuhu Car Care Network, a prominent player in the automotive sector, was established in 2011, initially focusing on tyre sales. The company adopted a cooperative partnership model to build its performance infrastructure. Tuhu established its first logistics centre the following year, beginning a significant expansion. By 2013, the company had partnered with over 4,000 stores across China and diversified its services to include automotive maintenance, oil sales, and chassis part sales. The year 2014 marked a significant milestone for the company with the launch of the Tuhu Car Care App, an innovative platform designed to transform how customers manage their vehicle maintenance.

As Tuhu continued to innovate and expand, it launched a one-stop auto parts business in 2015 and introduced the industry's first tyre insurance service. The following year saw the establishment of the Tuhu Car Care Factory Store, which helped the company become China's largest tyre retailer. In 2017, Tuhu diversified further by launching an auto beauty business and providing SAAS solutions for its brand partners. The company's growth continued unabated in 2018, with the launch of China's first front-end distribution centre and becoming the nation's largest motor oil retailer. In 2019, Tuhu introduced the "one item, one code" traceability system, ensuring transparency and accountability across its supply chain.

2020 was challenging due to the global COVID-19 pandemic; however, Tuhu responded by setting up an emergency rescue service team. By 2021, the company had exceeded 20 million trading customers, and its annual sales had crossed the tens of billions of dollars mark. In 2022, Tuhu became China's largest car retailer and third-party service provider for power battery and charging pile maintenance. The following year, Tuhu's registered users surpassed 100 million, and the world's most giant automated third-party tyre warehouse became operational, further solidifying Tuhu's position as a leader in the automotive sector.

Business Model

Tuhu Inc. is China's leading online and offline integrated automotive service platform. With a customer-centric model and a streamlined supply chain, it provides a digital and on-demand service experience that directly meets vehicle owners' diverse product and service needs. Tuhu aims to create an automotive service platform comprised of vehicle owners, suppliers, automotive service stores, and other participants. The Tuhu platform can serve most passenger car models on sale in China, meeting a full range of automotive service needs from tyre and chassis parts replacement to car maintenance, repairs, and car grooming. The main focus is on tyres, oil, car maintenance, car grooming, and car products, providing customers with online booking and offline installation of the car maintenance method.

Product and Services

Tuhu offers car owners a comprehensive suite of services, encompassing various aspects such as tyre and chassis parts, car maintenance and repair, car beauty, and car accessories. These services are complemented with installation assistance, ensuring a seamless customer experience. Beyond serving car owners, Tuhu extends its expertise to all platform participants, offering advertising services and SaaS solutions tailored to different business needs.

Among its broad range of services, Tuhu's tyre and chassis parts distribution business stands out, providing a one-stop installation service. This business integrates online and offline channels to deliver parts and complete car maintenance services, enhancing accessibility and convenience for customers. In addition to serving its network of stores, Tuhu has established an auto parts trading platform, "Auto Parts Dragon," to cater to the procurement needs of auto service stores outside its network. Auto Parts Dragon offers two distinct services: instant procurement and aggregation. These services streamline the sourcing process for auto parts, making it easier for businesses to meet their specific needs.

Customers

According to the company's prospectus, on December 31, 2022, the company had 95.5 million registered users for its flagship app, "Tuhu Car Care", and online interface. By 2022, the company had 16.5 million transactional users, a 12.0% increase from 14.8 million in the same period in 2021. The average monthly active users of Tuhu Car Care reached 9.0 million by 2022.

In a 2023 study by YOUJIA (YOUJIA, 2023), the user demographics of Tuhu's platform were primarily mature and male. Users between the ages of 31-35 made up the most significant portion at 33.47%, followed by those aged 36-40 at 24.32%. Overall, users over 30 represented 80.39% of the total user base (YOUJIA, 2023). Males were the dominant users, comprising 83.69% of the total, while females accounted for only 16.31%. This data suggests that younger and older groups are less likely to be involved in car purchasing and maintenance, with the 31-40 age bracket showing higher car ownership and greater demand for car maintenance. This could be attributed to the higher accumulated wealth and more significant care needs of individuals and families within this age group compared to other age groups.

COMPANY DEVELOPMENT ANALYSIS

Unicorn Market Description

Market Analysis

Before analysing Tuhu, it is necessary to have a macro understanding of the situation of China's automotive market. According to the Ministry of Public Security statistics, the number of motor vehicles in 2023 reached 435 million, of which 336 million were cars. 24.56 million cars were newly registered, and the number of new registrations has exceeded 20 million for ten consecutive years. There are 94 cities in the country with more than one million cars on their roads. The number of new energy vehicles reached 20.41 million. (Ministry of Public Security, 2024). It can be seen that China's car ownership has been in a stage of rapid growth, and the car service market is also booming.

The automotive service market, including automotive maintenance, decoration, audio, safety, electronics, modification, rescue, used car services, etc., is developing in the direction of integration, branding, and internationalisation. China's colossal car ownership has generated a significant demand for diversified services such as repair and maintenance, automobile beauty, automobile insurance, and automobile supplies. This demand is especially prominent for the two significant businesses of maintenance and insurance, which are essential for automobiles. In addition, with the slowdown in the growth rate of automobile sales, in-depth development and excavation of the value of the aftermarket industry has become the focus of market development, and the attention of China's automobile aftermarket has been further enhanced.

According to the definition of the American Automotive Aftermarket Industry Association (AAIA, n.d.), the so-called "automotive aftermarket" refers to "the marketplace for the repair and maintenance of automobiles and the trading of automotive parts, accessories, and materials needed to service and repair those automobiles after they have been sold." The automotive aftermarket encompasses automobile maintenance, repair, and maintenance service enterprises, distributors, and manufacturers of automobile spare parts, automobile supplies, and materials, as well as the corresponding financial, insurance, and other service systems.

Evolution of the Market Until Today

In his research, Prof. Dai from Harbin University of Commerce delineates the evolution of China's automotive aftermarket into four distinct stages (Dai, 2010). The initial stage, spanning from 1990 to 1996, saw the birth of the automotive aftermarket, primarily serving vehicles of governmental units. This was followed by a period of rapid development from 1997 to 2006, where the services were targeted mainly at government vehicles, with private cars forming a secondary market. 2007 to 2010 marked a reshuffling and reorganisation phase, during which the service targets were evenly distributed between governmental and private vehicles. The current stage, beginning in 2011, has been characterised by steady growth, with the focus shifting predominantly towards private cars. This period has seen the emergence of 2-3 leading stores in each region, the parallel development of branded quick repair and warranty stores alongside 4S Automobile Sales Service Shops, and the entry of foreign auto service chain giants into the Chinese market (Youjia, 2023). The local "aftermarket + Internet" e-commerce model has also gradually developed, attracting capital and intensifying competition. A 2023 iiMedia survey revealed that 95.91% of car users had utilised online car maintenance services, and 93.97% of consumers were highly willing to continue doing so (iiMedia, 2023).

Analysis of the Current Automotive Aftermarket Situation

In the early 1930s, the automobile beauty and maintenance industry began to take off in developed countries such as Britain and the United States, and the embryonic form of the automobile aftermarket started to emerge. After the Second World War, the economy's recovery led to the rapid development of the automobile industry. Concurrently, this also spurred the growth of the car beauty and maintenance industry. The car detailing and maintenance industry rose in the 1990s in China. With the increase in car ownership, particularly private car ownership, the car beauty and maintenance industry began to gain recognition among car owners. The concept of car maintenance and care, focusing on seven-part maintenance and three-part repair, gradually gained acceptance among most car owners. Today, the automobile aftermarket in our country has begun to take shape. It is projected that the scale of China's auto aftermarket industry will reach 1.21 trillion yuan in 2022. With the continuous growth in automobile production and sales, the ageing of automobiles, and the ongoing active second-hand car trading market, it is anticipated that consumers will have a more robust demand for automobile maintenance and repair in the future, thus driving further growth in the scale of the automobile aftermarket industry.

The Chinese automotive aftermarket industry can be further subdivided into several key segments. The first of these is the car rental industry. As of the end of 2021, there were 262 million privately owned cars in China, and 444 million people held driving licenses. Interestingly, 182 million license holders did not own a car, which had increased by 4% from the previous year. This growing demographic of license holders without vehicles is expected to become the leading potential user group for the car leasing market (Prospective Industry Research Institute, 2023). As an emerging transport service industry in China, car leasing plays a crucial role in meeting people's personalised travel and business needs and safeguarding major social activities, forming an essential part of the comprehensive transportation system (Baidu, n.d.).

The second segment is the automotive supplies industry. Tmall Auto (2022), a leading car seller in China, has reported that the main consumption scenarios in China's automotive products market include comfortable driving, intelligent driving, film modification, travelling, and car protection. The market offers a wide range of products and has seen substantial production growth, indicating good potential for future development.

Lastly, the new energy vehicle charging and swapping infrastructure industry forms a crucial segment. The DC charging pile currently dominates the public charging infrastructure in China, while the AC charging pile is primarily used for private charging. In 2021, the market size of China's new energy vehicle charging piles was approximately 44.728 billion yuan. Tuhu launched a power battery and pile maintenance business in 2021 that aligns with these developments. By 2022, the company became China's largest third-party service provider of power battery and pile maintenance, demonstrating its adaptability to the evolving market trends.

While China's automotive aftermarket industry has made significant strides, it still faces several challenges and needs to catch up to its counterparts in developed countries. Although relatively mature, the industry chain presents a comprehensive landscape with representative enterprises and service models across the upstream, midstream, and downstream sectors (Prospective Industry Research Institute, 2023). The upstream sector primarily comprises automobile manufacturers like BYD, NIO, SAIC, and Yutong Bus, as well as automobile sales manufacturers such as Zhong-sheng Group, Li Xing Hang Automobile, and China Grand Automobile Service. The midstream sector includes car rental enterprises like CAR Inc., automotive supplies enterprises like Delian Group and Kuster, car maintenance and repair enterprises like Tuhu Car and Tmall Car, and auto finance companies like SAIC-GM Auto Finance and Volkswagen Auto Finance.

The industry also receives robust support from national policies (China Academic Journal Electronic Publishing House, 2023). Various national departments, including the National Ministry of Transportation, Development and Reform Commission, Ministry of Industry and Information Technology, Bureau of Energy, Automobile Repair Industry Association, and others, have issued policies promoting the diversified development of the aftermarket (Guanyantianxia, 2022). These policies cover everything from upstream to downstream, laying a solid foundation for maximising the industry's potential.

However, the industry also has its shortcomings. Zhang Yanfang (2021) points out that the industry's business maturity needs to be improved, as indicated by the small proportion of services. In mature foreign automobile markets, accessories make up 39% of sales, manufacturers 21%, retail 7%, and services 33%. In contrast, the domestic automobile market in China sees accessories accounting for 37%, manufacturers 43%, retail 8%, and services only 12%. This data suggests domestic automobile sales are over-represented in manufacturing and under-represented in service. While whole car and parts sales align with international standards, the automotive service market has significant room for growth (CACC, 2010). The industry's professional quality is also low (Kuangwei,2016). The low percentage of automotive aftermarket industry services, the mediocre level of specialisation of automobile service enterprises, the low technical level of employees, and managers' lack of solid management tools all indicate substantial room for progress.

Competition Analysis

When conducting a market analysis of Tuhu's competition, this study primarily utilizes SWOT analysis. This method enables a comprehensive, systematic, and accurate assessment of the research object's situation, formulating development strategies, plans, and countermeasures based on the study's results. It's important to note that the author is not a professional market research practitioner, so the following analysis conclusions are primarily based on personal knowledge and academic materials sourced from the Internet.

Business Environment Overview

Tuhu has several key strengths in its operations. It has a high market penetration and high profit margins, supported by its value-added business (Baidu.com). The company has attracted small single auto repair stores to join its platform, leveraging its strong brand influence and technology, which is mature in forward-looking industry prediction, data analysis, and store operation technology. Financially, Tuhu is stable and has adequate working capital. Its revenues and gross profit margins have been consistently improving over the years, and as of the first half of 2023, its net cash flow from operating activities reached 700 million yuan. Tuhu's corporate image is also strong, with high customer satisfaction rates and awards for corporate social responsibility (Sohu, 2023c). With a vast market share and cost advantage, Tuhu has established itself as a leader in the industry. Lastly, the company provides high-quality, differentiated services to different customer groups, ensuring customer satisfaction and loyalty.

Despite its strengths, Tuhu also has some weaknesses. Its platform management is somewhat disorganised, as reflected in the high number of complaints on the Black Cat complaint platform (2022). These complaints range from product adaptation errors to false advertising and substandard oil. This disarray in management has led to a lack of trust among customers and franchisees, reflecting poorly on Tuhu's technology and integrity (Sohu, 2023b).

There are several opportunities for Tuhu in the external environment. For instance, industrial stimulus policies have been promoting the development of new energy vehicles, which presents a new chance for Tuhu to expand its services to cover fuel and new energy vehicles. This change would require Tuhu to adapt its parts procurement and maintenance services to cater to new energy vehicles (Hao, 2023).

However, Tuhu also faces several threats. Price wars initiated by competitors could squeeze Tuhu out of the market. For instance, JD.com has been selling its cars at prices 5% lower than its peers. Global incidents, such as the COVID-19 pandemic, have disrupted the supply chain of the automobile industry, leading to higher procurement costs and a potential decrease in demand for automobile products. Lastly, the growth of competitive firms and the increase in substitutes threaten Tuhu(Qpzone, 2022). The company faces competition from several brands in the car repair and maintenance field, and there are numerous competitors in each segment of the automotive aftermarket internet products.

Development and Strategy

Original Business Operation Concept

In 2011, Chen Min, founder of Tuhu, chose to enter the automobile market with tyres and established the Tuhu car service network. The decision to focus on tyres as consumer acceptance primarily drove the entry point. Many car owners in China have about three-year-old vehicles, and their awareness of maintenance and accessories could be much higher. In the aftermarket, auto parts and maintenance are products and technical services with low transparency (Enfodesk, 2016). However, several post-market enterprises were established simultaneously, and Tuhu company faced significant competitive pressure. Chen Min aimed to overturn the traditional 4S shop monopoly of automobile repair and maintenance and sought to combine the Internet to build an online and offline company. This was undoubtedly a groundbreaking and provocative idea at the time, but Chen Min successfully executed it.

Tuhu developed its process to provide customers with the option of "online reservation + offline installation." Customers can purchase Tuhu's goods and services online through the website, telephone, WeChat, major e-commerce platforms, and other channels. Offline, Tuhu has over 1,200 co-installed stores, with service capacity covering 266 cities in 19 provinces (Song, 2016). Tuhu has established numerous distribution and storage centres across the country to carry out centralised procurement, achieve a flat supply chain, and control the turnaround time from 15 days to one month to optimise the efficiency of the entire supply chain(Bai, 2018). In this case, the O2O* platform and the supply chain can be precious to users. It reduces costs, increases service price transparency, and provides users with various cost-effective product choices (Adams, 2021).

Multi-Faceted Brand Strategy Coordination and Cooperation

From the official website of Tuhu, it can be seen that Tuhu has strategic cooperation with many enterprises in the automobile industry. In 2020, Tuhu and major shareholders Tencent and ExxonMobil set up a joint venture to establish a digital car maintenance company using the "S2B2C" model (Lantu, 2023). In 2022, 3M and Tuhu jointly launched the 3M Pro Care Zhuorui series of auto maintenance products to broaden the product matrix. The same year, global filter leaders Mann + Hummel and Tuhu jointly released the first customised filter product line, "Gold Label." At the end of the same year, UFI Group and Tuhu reached strategic cooperation in the fields of new energy vehicle filtration systems and thermal management technology by leveraging their respective advantages (Tu, 2022).

It can be seen that Tuhu not only firmly grasps the automobile aftermarket maintenance and maintenance industry with a high market share but also pays more attention to horizontally and vertically expanding business channels and product lines. Tuhu is involved in almost all parts of the field, which reflects its multi-dimensional brand development strategy and extensive coordination and cooperation with peers.

Continuous Capital Empowerment

Tuhu Company has consistently sought financing and listing opportunities in the past ten years since its establishment. From 2012 to 2021, the company has undertaken 16 financing rounds, amounting to nearly 10 billion yuan. Notable investors in Tuhu include Tencent, Baidu, Sequoia Capital, Hillhouse Capital, Bosch Group, and other globally renowned venture capital firms (Sohu, 2023a). These investors' continuous and substantial capital injections have been pivotal to Tuhu's development.

Drawing from various investment theories, including equity investment application theory, venture capital theory, and equity valuation theory, in competitive markets with numerous innovative enterprises, companies with original technology, rapid business growth, healthy cash flow, and significant market share are more likely to gain favour from policymakers and market investors. Considering Tuhu Company's revenue and cash flow performance over the years, it has successfully achieved its stage goals and met the income requirements of its shareholders (Xinhua Finance, 2022). Therefore, this is one of the most significant reasons for Tuhu's survival and dominant position in the automotive O2O post-market sector.

THE PEOPLE BEHIND THE UNICORNS

MIN Chen

Chen, the Chairman of the Board, Chief Executive Officer, and Executive Director of Tuhu Vehicle Co., Ltd., has an extensive background in software development, data management, and the automotive service market. His experience spans over 18 years in software and data and over 11 years in the automotive service sector, focusing on business data analysis. His professional journey includes roles at notable firms such as Shanghai Yingdao Trading Co., Ltd., Shanghai Yidao Network Technology Co., Ltd., Baixing.com Co., Ltd., CMG (China) Network Co., Ltd., Hewlett-Packard, and Shanghai Minimally Invasive Software Co., Ltd. His tenure at Tuhu began on July 1, 2019. Under Chen's leadership, Tuhu evolved from a simple tire-changing service to operating offline physical stores, adopting a franchising model and providing store management and logistics support (Shanghai Observer, 2020). Chen's philosophy is focused on profitability and industry development, with a clear understanding of the company's target market and service offerings. Chen's cautious approach to innovation has led to two significant supply chain revolutions in China's auto aftermarket, positioning Tuhu as an industry leader (Amber, 2023). He emphasises product quality, transparency, and standardised services. Tuhu initiated the "Honest Service Alliance of Aftermarket Industry" to improve the industry's standards, collaborating with renowned brands like Jingdong Car Care, Tmall Car Care, Continental AG, and ExxonMobil. Furthermore, Chen launched the industry's first service standard open product platform, which includes a technical service guarantee platform, a manufacturer product service platform, and a service standard system evaluation platform. His innovative "Internet +" industrial chain system has streamlined Tuhu's operations from the customer and supply chain ends

300

to the store management ends, enhancing the industry's efficiency (Feng, 2015). Today, Tuhu operates 39 regional distribution centres and 267 front-end distribution centres nationwide, with logistics solutions covering more than 300 cities in China.

FUTURE PROJECTS

From 0 to over 5000 factory stores, Tuhu has spent seven years building the most significant auto maintenance and maintenance chain in China, covering more than 300 prefecture-level cities and nearly 2,000 franchise stores in the sinking market, covering more than 97% of towns and provinces in China. On September 26, 2023, Tuhu Car Co., LTD. successfully landed on the Hong Kong Stock Exchange. The IPO was priced at HK $28 per share, raising a net capital of about HK $1.081 billion and a market value of more than HK $20 billion. In the past 12 years since its establishment, Tuhu has gone public in the auto aftermarket track and has become the leader in China's auto aftermarket.

There is a Chinese saying that "The Times make heroes". In the current era of global traditional energy mining contraction and vigorous development of new energy, Tuhu is making every effort to create products and services suitable for new energy vehicles. In 2022, the number of new-energy passenger vehicles in China reached 12.6 million, accounting for 4.6% of the total number of passenger vehicles. By 2027, the penetration rate of new energy passenger vehicle ownership in total passenger vehicle ownership is expected to reach 20.5%. As an automobile service platform, Tuhu needs to explore the new market space to develop intelligent new energy vehicles to solve the problem of new consumer demand. Unlike traditional fuel vehicles, the primary maintenance items of new energy vehicles come from power batteries, driving motors, and electronic control systems. Although the structure is less complex than that of fuel vehicles, the new energy maintenance market has problems such as a smaller distribution of maintenance outlets, an insufficient supply of parts, and inconsistent maintenance standards. To cope with the test brought by the new energy vehicle era, Tuhu company stated in the prospectus that it would use 20% of the IPO funds to invest in future new energy vehicle service-related services. In this way, the layout of new energy vehicles after the market business can be seen. It can be seen that the Tuhu car is for the attention of the new energy vehicle layout. Although Tuhu has been successfully listed, it is only a beginning. According to the China Securities Website, citing Tuhu officials, referring to listed auto service companies in the United States, the stock prices of listed auto service companies in the United States, such as AutoZone, O'Reilly, and GPC, have risen steadily in the past ten years, especially since 2020. Some have even doubled in value. As the first Hong Kong-listed company in the independent auto after-sales service market, Tuhu still has a lot of room for development.

CONCLUSION

Unicorn enterprises, typified by a relatively young history, high valuation, and significant potential for growth, serve as important indicators of a country or region's innovation capabilities and ecology. In exploring the development of Chinese unicorns, Tuhu Company was selected as a representative case study. While having a late start, China's auto aftermarket is characterised by many enterprises and intense competition. The question arises: how has Tuhu managed to stand out? An examination of Tuhu's development process, business model, and operations, followed by a SWOT analysis from the perspectives of customer groups, market, and original business model, provides insights into Tuhu's unique development path.

Tuhu's operational condition is robust, with stable cash flow and a steadily improving gross margin index. Although there are slight year-to-year fluctuations, the overall trend remains upward. This solid operational state lays a strong foundation for Tuhu's financing efforts. Tuhu's development path is original and challenging to replicate. The company has consistently seized opportunities at the turning points of each era. For instance, it actively embraced the Internet to reduce costs for car owners and established logistics centres nationwide to stimulate the logistics industry. These strategic moves successfully transformed Tuhu from a tire-selling company into a diversified O2O one-stop automobile repair and maintenance company.

Tuhu operates across numerous industries, ensuring reliable product quality and maintaining a positive customer reputation. Moreover, Tuhu has established strategic partnerships with several well-known domestic and international automotive aftermarket brands. These factors collectively provide Tuhu with a strong foothold in the market and contribute to its status as a leading player in the industry (Zhao, 2023).

REFERENCES

Adams, H. (2021, October 8). Online-to-Offline (O2O): Commerce definition and trends. *Investopedia*. https://www.investopedia.com/terms/o/onlinetooffline -commerce.asp

Amber. (2023, March 7). Dismantling Tuhu car: The last stand of the industry's top students. *The Paper*. https://m.thepaper.cn/baijiahao_16955522

Bai, J. (2018). Research the business model of Chinese auto aftermarket e-commerce platform enterprises. Take Tuhu as an example. *Economic Forum*.

Dai, B.B. (2010). Research on the current situation and development trend of the aftermarket in China. *Economic Research Guide, 21*.

Enfodesk. (2016). Special research report on e-commerce in China's auto aftermarket in the first half of 2016. *Auto Maintenance & Repair, 12*.

Feng, S.S. (2015). *Tuhu: Deep in O2O*. Chief Financial Officer.

Guanyantianxia. (2022, October 14). *Analysis of the advantages and disadvantages of the aftermarket industry in our country: The market scale is expanding, and the service level needs to be improved.* 360doc.com. http://www.360doc.com/content/ 12/0121/07/13672581_1051684870.shtml

Hao, X.C. (2023). Tuhu Car Maintenance - The growth path of an automotive aftermarket leader. *Academic Journal of Management and Social Sciences, 2*(1).

Lantu. (2023). Tuhu car digital practice - Leveraging technology to drive the new transformation of automotive aftermarket service. *Zhang Jiang Technology Review, 4*.

Ministry of Public Security. (2024, January 11). *The number of motor vehicles in China reached 435 million, with 523 million drivers, and the number of new energy vehicles exceeded 20 million.* Ministry of Public Security. https://www.gov.cn/ lianbo/bumen/202401/content_6925362.htm

Qpzone. (2022, January 12). *In 2022, China's auto aftermarket faced three pain points.* Qpzone. http://www.qpzone.com.cn/Wap/hynews/10735.html

Shanghai Observer. (2020, July 21). The new generation of Internet: The impression of Chen Min, the founder of Tuhu Car. *Shanghai Observer*. https://sghservices .shobserver.com/html/baijiahao/2020/07/21/227493.html

Sohu. (2023, April 10). *Tuhu updated its prospectus, Tencent, Pleasure Capital, and Sequoia Capital as shareholders, and monthly active users reached 9 million.* Sohu. https://www.sohu.com/a/665128256_100157908

Sohu. (2023, August 31). *When the world auto industry comes to the "Great Age of China", Tuhu car is the result: The business of an independent car service market leader.* Sohu. https://news.sohu.com/a/716612257_585920

Sohu. (2023, June 15). *Behind the "Tuhu Eight steps": Doing a good job in technology and service standardisation is the basis for improving user satisfaction.* Sohu. https://www.sohu.com/a/685616764_118560

Song, J.T. (2016). How does Tuhu become a car O2O market survivor? *Innovation, 86.*

Tu, J.J. (2022). UFI Group signed a strategic cooperation agreement with Tuhu. *Auto Maintenance & Repair.*

Xinhua Finance. (2022, September 7). *Tuhu Car's "burning cash model" encountered a bottleneck: Revenue declined, and the number of cooperative stores decreased by 6,302.* Baidu. https://baijiahao.baidu.com/s?id=1743265642732411071&wfr=spider&for=pc

Youjia. (2023, September 25). *Analysis of competitive products in the aftermarket: Ping An Good car owner, DCar, and Tuhu Car maintenance.* Youjia. https://www.yoojia.com/ask/17-11763544949897401698.html

Zhao, A.L. (2023). How do unicorn enterprises stay innovative? *China's Foreign Trade, 08.*

KEY TERMS AND DEFINITIONS

Celebrity Endorsement: It refers to the practice of engaging well-known personalities to promote a company's products or services. It's a marketing strategy used to expand brand awareness and influence.

Continuous Capital Empowerment: This refers to securing regular and substantial financial investments to fuel a company's growth and development. It involves attracting strategic and financial investors through various rounds of financing.

Following the Trend of the Times: This concept refers to an organisation's ability to align its development and strategies with the evolution of its operating environment, leveraging market trends and technological advancements for growth and innovation.

Multi-Faceted Brand Strategy Coordination and Cooperation: It: refers to the strategic partnerships and collaborations a company establishes with other brands. It involves expanding business channels and product lines horizontally and vertically, thus diversifying the company's offerings.

Original Business Operation Concept: This term refers to introducing unique and disruptive business practices or models that challenge traditional methods. It often involves leveraging new technologies and innovative strategies to gain a competitive advantage.

Solid User Base: This term refers to a substantial and loyal group of customers or users a company has built over time. Innovative marketing strategies, effective communication, and customer-centric business models often achieve it.

Time-Appropriate Marketing Techniques: This term refers to using relevant marketing strategies that resonate with current consumer demographics and trends. It often involves understanding shifting consumer behaviour and preferences and tailoring marketing initiatives accordingly.

Well-Established Industry Chain and High Product Quality: This term highlights the importance of a comprehensive and efficient supply chain and a commitment to high-quality products or services. It involves creating an ecosystem that includes customers, suppliers, and other stakeholders, which promotes a virtuous cycle of service provision and growth.

Chapter 18
Bytedance:
Innovating Global Technology and Navigating Strategic Challenges

Wei Min

*Beijing Normal University-Hong Kong Baptist University United International
College, China*

EXECUTIVE SUMMARY

*This case study delves into ByteDance, a pioneering force in global technology led
by visionary founder Zhang Yiming and CEO Shou Zi Chew. It explores ByteDance's
journey from its inception, driven by innovative AI technologies and a global expansion strategy, to becoming a dominant player in social media with platforms
like TikTok. The case examines ByteDance's multifaceted approach, including its
development of the MegaScale AI system for large-scale language model training
and its strategies for navigating complex data sovereignty issues across international
markets. It also analyzes ByteDance's competitive landscape, encompassing key
rivals in social media, AI development, e-commerce, and cloud services. Moreover,
the case scrutinizes ByteDance's leadership strategies, emphasizing its efforts in
user data privacy compliance and global regulatory challenges. Through these
insights, the case offers a comprehensive view of ByteDance's evolution, strategic
initiatives, and the broader implications for the tech industry.*

EXECUTIVE SUMMARY

ByteDance is a leading name in the global technology sector that has **revolutionized** digital content consumption with its AI-driven platform, which **personalized**
user experiences. Founded by Zhang Yiming in 2012, the company originated with
"Toutiao" (Today's Headlines), a news aggregation platform, and has expanded to

DOI: 10.4018/979-8-3693-2921-4.ch018

create "Douyin/TikTok," a short video-sharing sensation that has captivated a global audience. This case study provides an in-depth analysis of ByteDance's strategic growth, its innovative approach to market penetration, and developing a diverse product portfolio that includes social media, education technology, and office collaboration tools. It will explore ByteDance's commercial ecosystem, compare its vertical products with competitive offerings in the industry, and discuss how the company maintains its edge in a dynamic and highly regulated global landscape. The narrative will reveal the exciting facts behind ByteDance's rise to prominence, its impact on the digital economy, and its challenges in upholding user privacy and data security amidst rapid expansion.

DEVELOPMENT OF THE COMPANY

ByteDance Description

ByteDance is a Chinese internet technology company founded by Zhang Yiming in 2012. The company is known for its strategic focus on creative content sharing and applying artificial intelligence technology to information distribution. With over 150,000 employees based out of nearly 120 cities globally (ByteDance, 2023), ByteDance started its journey with "Toutiao," a news aggregation platform that uses algorithmic recommendations to provide personalized news content to users. Later, the company launched "Douyin" - a platform that combines music, short videos, and social elements. It quickly succeeded in the Chinese market and later evolved into the international version, TikTok. At the same time, most people recognize ByteDance for its hit app TikTok, which boasts over 3 billion global downloads in 2021 (Chen & Ma, 2022).

ByteDance's development has been characterized by rapid iteration and market understanding. The company has continuously introduced new products and services, such as "Dali Education" in the education technology sector and "Feishu" (Lark), an office collaboration tool, demonstrating its innovative capabilities and diversified development strategies. ByteDance has also expanded its presence in emerging technologies through acquisitions and investments, such as acquiring Pico, a VR headset and platform developer.

ByteDance's mission is to drive the creation, distribution, and exchange of information through technology, creating user value. The company is committed to optimizing user experience using artificial intelligence and machine learning technologies, achieving commercial value and social impact through precise advertising placements, content recommendations, and enhanced user engagement. ByteDance's vision is to build a global, diversified digital content ecosystem that provides users with rich, engaging, and valuable content experiences. ByteDance has always prioritized internationalization and has launched its popular local apps with equivalent international versions. The company's global monthly active users exceeded 1.5 billion by the end of 2019, with operations in 150 countries and regions and supporting 75 languages.

ByteDance's Current Business Model Overview

Core Strategy

ByteDance employs an innovative and algorithm-driven approach to market penetration. It uses a data-driven optimization strategy by deeply analyzing user behavior data. This approach enables ByteDance to understand user needs better and deliver personalized and intelligent user experiences to enhance user retention. Integrating artificial intelligence and machine learning technologies allows ByteDance to continuously optimize its products and services, offering users a personalized and tailored experience. This data-driven innovation is evident in TikTok's recommendation algorithms, Lemon8's content creation incentives, and Coze's interactive language model.

ByteDance places significant emphasis on User-Generated Content (UGC) and interactivity, transforming users into content creators and consumers on the platform. This strategy encourages deeper user engagement, enhances user stickiness, and propels the platform's growth. The core tenet of ByteDance's business model lies in a content and community-driven approach, strategically attracting and retaining users by providing rich content and interactive community features. This strategy is evident in TikTok's short video content, Lemon8's community interactions, and Coze's language model interactions.

Revenue Generation Model Through Advertising and Social E-Commerce

ByteDance primarily generates revenue through advertising and social e-commerce. By leveraging advanced algorithms, ByteDance can provide highly targeted advertisements, which enhances advertisers' effectiveness. Additionally, social e-commerce contributes to ByteDance's diversified sources of income. The company leverages its extensive user base and the influence of its social media platforms to generate revenue through advertising and collaborations with brands and e-commerce platforms. Both TikTok and Lemon8 derive income through advertising and brand partnerships, while Coze may explore revenue generation through premium services or corporate collaborations.

ByteDance's Product Mix

ByteDance is a company that has curated a diversified product portfolio, encompassing various products such as TikTok, Lemon8, Coze, Toutiao, and Feishu. This varied product offering has enabled ByteDance to expand its business across multiple market segments and cater to diverse user preferences, enhancing its market coverage.
ByteDance's Portfolio includes:

- ByteDance's flagship product, TikTok, has garnered a substantial global user base through its distinctive short video format. The platform is a stage for creative expression and utilizes an algorithmic recommendation system to ensure users discover and engage with content aligned with their interests.
- Toutiao is a news aggregation platform that provides personalized news feeds to meet users' demand for real-time information. It employs artificial intelligence technologies to curate news content tailored to users' reading habits and preferences, making it an essential news source for many.
- Lemon8 is a content creation application that encourages user-generated content by offering tools and incentives that foster user engagement and community vibrancy. This platform has enabled many users to showcase their creativity and gain recognition for their work.
- Feishu is an office collaboration tool that provides a comprehensive suite of productivity features, including document collaboration, instant messaging, and video conferencing. It enhances team efficiency and communication, making it crucial for businesses and organizations.
- Finally, Coze represents ByteDance's foray into AI-driven conversational interfaces as a large language model product. It aims to provide interactive and intelligent dialogues, potentially revolutionizing how users interact with AI systems for various purposes, such as customer service, education, or entertainment.

ByteDance's products demonstrate its prowess in technological innovation and reflect the company's approach to solidifying its market position by meeting user needs and providing personalized experiences. These products leverage technological innovation and user engagement strategies to facilitate ByteDance's global expansion and market leadership. Through these offerings, ByteDance has established a robust user base worldwide and continues to drive the diversification and internationalization of its business.

Business Model for Each Application

TikTok

TikTok, which is ByteDance's flagship product, has revolutionized the short video format and has become a cornerstone of the company's global presence. Its business model is multifaceted, primarily focusing on advertising revenue, which is boosted by its unique algorithmic recommendation system. Brands leverage the platform's vast user base and high engagement rates to reach a targeted audience through various ad formats, including in-feed ads, branded challenges, and influencer partnerships. These advertisements are highly effective due to TikTok's sophisticated algorithm, which analyses user behavior to deliver personalized content and ads, thus increasing the likelihood of user interaction and conversion.

In addition to advertising, TikTok has explored other revenue streams, such as in-app purchases, live streaming, and social e-commerce. Users can purchase virtual gifts for live streamers, which can then be converted into real currency. Social e-commerce initiatives, where influencers can promote products directly through the app, have also shown growth potential, particularly in markets like China, where Douyin has integrated this feature. TikTok plays a crucial role in ByteDance's broader ecosystem as it serves as a gateway for user acquisition and retention, which is essential for the company's other products and services.

The platform's popularity and user data provide valuable insights that ByteDance can use to refine its algorithms and tailor its offerings across its entire product line. Moreover, TikTok's influence extends beyond its platform. It has become a cultural phenomenon that shapes trends and influences user behavior across various digital platforms. This cultural impact enhances ByteDance's brand equity and positions the company as a leader in the digital content space.

Toutiao

Toutiao is another pivotal component of ByteDance's digital ecosystem, and it has crafted a sophisticated news recommendation system that caters to its users' diverse and dynamic needs. Its recommendation system for personalized news is a refined blend of machine learning, user profiling, and content analysis, designed to provide users with a tailored news experience that is not only engaging but also safe and high-quality. The platform's continuous evolution in response to user behaviour and content trends underscores its position as a leader in the digital news landscape.

This multi-dimensional system integrates content features, user characteristics, and contextual elements to deliver a personalized news experience. The Toutiao recommendation engine is designed to predict user satisfaction with content. It considers three key dimensions: content attributes, user features, and environmental factors. Content analysis involves extracting features from various content types, such as text, images, videos, and user-generated content (UGC). User features encompass interests, demographics, and implicit interests derived from models. Environmental factors account for the user's context, such as location and time, which can shift information preferences.

Toutiao utilizes a comprehensive set of user tags, including interests, demographics, and location, to refine its recommendation algorithm. These tags are continuously updated through batch processing and real-time streaming systems, ensuring user profiles remain current and relevant. The platform's user tag system is designed to filter noise, penalize hot topics, apply time decay, and adjust for unclicked content, enhancing recommendations' accuracy and relevance. The effectiveness of Toutiao's recommendation system is assessed through a robust evaluation framework that considers both short-term and long-term indicators. The platform employs A/B testing to rigorously measure the impact of algorithmic changes, ensuring that improvements lead to positive outcomes for users, content creators, and advertisers alike.

Toutiao prioritizes content safety, employing a dedicated review team and advanced AI models to identify and filter inappropriate content. The platform's commitment to quality extends to its low-quality content detection, which includes mechanisms for identifying fake news, clickbait, and low-quality content. This commitment to content safety and quality is a testament to Toutiao's role as an industry leader.

Lemon8

Lemon8, part of ByteDance's portfolio, empowers users with easy-to-use content creation tools and incentives for engagement. Lemon8 is a lifestyle app that resembles a combination of Instagram and Pinterest. It is visually oriented and allows users to share various content, such as recipes, outfits, travel guides, etc. Popular categories on Lemon8 include fashion, make-up, skincare, travel, health and wellness, fitness, and food. This makes Lemon8 an ideal platform for brands in these industries to showcase their products visually and engagingly.

The platform fosters a vibrant community through features like commenting and liking, enhancing user retention. Integrated with ByteDance's ecosystem, Lemon8 facilitates cross-platform content sharing. Challenges include maintaining content quality and addressing privacy concerns. Overall, Lemon8 exemplifies ByteDance's dedication to fostering creativity and community.

Feishu (Lark)

Feishu, marketed as Lark in international markets, is ByteDance's office collaboration tool. It offers a comprehensive suite tailored to bolster team productivity and communication. This platform is a testament to ByteDance's strategic expansion into the business services sector, providing a unified environment for document collaboration, instant messaging, and video conferencing.

Feishu's suite of productivity features is designed to cater to the diverse needs of modern enterprises. The platform's document collaboration tools enable teams to collaborate on shared documents, facilitating real-time editing and version control. Instant messaging services ensure rapid information exchange, while video conferencing capabilities bridge the gap between remote team members, simulating the immediacy of in-person interactions.

The platform's architecture is engineered to streamline team dynamics and communication channels. By integrating task management and scheduling tools, Feishu enhances project coordination and accountability. This cohesive approach to collaboration minimizes the friction associated with transitioning between multiple applications, fostering a more efficient and cohesive team environment.

Feishu's integration within ByteDance's broader business ecosystem underscores the company's commitment to providing a holistic digital experience. It complements ByteDance's consumer-facing products, such as TikTok and Toutiao, by extending the company's technological prowess into the corporate sphere. This strategic placement allows Feishu to tap into the growing demand for sophisticated collaboration tools in the global market.

Coze

Coze, ByteDance's large language models, marks a significant step in the company's exploration of AI-driven conversational interfaces. This product is designed to facilitate interactive and intelligent dialogues, signifying a potential paradigm shift in user interactions with AI systems across a spectrum of applications, including customer service, education, and entertainment. Coze's primary objective is to enhance user engagement through natural language processing (NLP) capabilities, which allow for more nuanced and contextually aware conversations. By leveraging advanced AI, the platform can understand and respond to user queries with a level of sophistication that mimics human-like interactions, thereby improving user experience and satisfaction.

Coze's versatility extends beyond traditional chatbot functionalities. In customer service, it can provide personalized support, understand complex user issues, and offer tailored solutions. It can be an interactive learning companion in education, adapting to the learner's pace and style. Coze can engage users in creative storytelling or trivia for entertainment, offering a novel form of AI-powered leisure. Coze's development reflects ByteDance's commitment to innovation in AI conversational technology. The product's potential to revolutionize user interactions lies in its ability to learn from each conversation, continuously refining its understanding and response mechanisms. This learning capability positions Coze as a dynamic tool that can evolve alongside its users' needs and preferences.

As part of ByteDance's diverse product lineup, Coze complements existing services by introducing a new dimension of AI-driven user interaction. Its integration could lead to synergistic effects, enhancing the overall user experience across ByteDance's platforms and opening up new revenue streams through innovative AI applications.

Conclusion

In conclusion, ByteDance's strategic approach with its suite of products—TikTok, Toutiao, Lemon8, Feishu (Lark), and Coze—aims to establish a cohesive ecosystem that promotes user engagement, content creation, and collaboration. The personalized and interactive environment ensures that ByteDance's offerings remain cutting-edge in the rapidly evolving digital content landscape. A commitment to continuous innovation and responsiveness to user preferences underpins this ecosystem. However, in the user privacy and data security era, ByteDance must constantly focus on privacy protection measures and maintain transparency regarding data practices. This focus is essential given the heightened regulatory scrutiny and is a critical factor in building trust with both users and regulatory bodies.

Competitive Environment

In the rapidly evolving landscape of the short-form video industry, ByteDance stands as a formidable competitor, with TikTok at the forefront. A dynamic interplay of market trends, technological advancements, and regulatory challenges characterizes the company's competitive environment.

Market Trends and Technological Advancements

The short-form video market has witnessed exponential growth driven by the increasing demand for quick, engaging content. TikTok's success can be attributed to its ability to capture the zeitgeist by offering a platform for creative expression and entertainment that resonates with a global audience. Integrating advanced algorithms allows TikTok to deliver personalised content, enhancing user engagement and retention. This technological edge has been a critical factor in ByteDance's ability to maintain a competitive advantage.

ByteDance faces stiff competition from established social media giants and emerging players in the short-form video space. Meta (formerly Facebook), with its introduction of Reels, and Tencent, with WeChat's short video platform, are direct competitors leveraging their existing user bases to challenge TikTok's market share. These competitors replicate TikTok's format and innovate to capture user attention and ad revenue.

In addition, uncertainty clouds the future of TikTok in the United States following the recent passage of a bill by the House of Representatives. The legislation raises the possibility of a ban on the top-rated video app (He, 2024). Regulatory scrutiny has become a significant factor in ByteDance's competitive environment. The company has faced fines and investigations over data privacy concerns, particularly regarding collecting personal data from minors. The fluctuating regulatory landscape, especially in international markets, threatens ByteDance's operations. For instance, the temporary ban on TikTok downloads in the United States under the Trump administration and the ongoing regulatory changes in China have directly impacted ByteDance's business strategy and market positioning.

In response to these competitive pressures, ByteDance has been strategic in its market expansions and product development. The company's diversification into new industries, such as healthcare, reflects a proactive approach to leveraging its technological capabilities and user base. Additionally, ByteDance's focus on localization and cultural adaptation in international markets has been crucial in overcoming the "liability of 'Chineseness'" and establishing a robust global presence.

The competitive environment for ByteDance is set to become even more complex as the industry continues to grow and mature. The company's ability to innovate, adapt to regulatory changes, and maintain user trust will be critical to its success. As ByteDance navigates these challenges, its strategic decisions and market responses will be closely watched by industry observers and competitors. For inclusion in an English-language business case analysis book, this analysis provides a comprehensive overview of ByteDance's competitive standing, highlighting the company's strengths in user engagement and technological innovation while acknowledging the challenges posed by regulatory hurdles and competitive pressures. The narrative underscores the importance of strategic agility and the need for ByteDance to continually evolve its business model to remain at the forefront of the digital content revolution.

ByteDance's Strategic Positioning and Competitions

The digital landscape is characterized by rapid innovation and shifts in user behavior, with ByteDance's TikTok emerging as a leader in the short-form video content space. The company's success is based on its ability to adapt to technological trends and the fast-paced cultural demands of the digital age. However, as the market expands, ByteDance must navigate a complex, competitive environment that includes established players and emerging challengers across various digital sectors.

While ByteDance's primary focus has been content creation and social media, the company's competitive environment extends to other digital services, including search, e-commerce, messaging, and cloud computing. Each of these sectors has its competitors, each with unique strengths and strategies that could impact ByteDance's market position. The transition from a macro perspective to a more granular analysis of specific competitors is essential to understanding the multifaceted nature of the competitive landscape.

As ByteDance evaluates its competitors, it is crucial to differentiate between direct rivals, such as TikTok's competition with Instagram Reels and Snapchat, and indirect competitors, such as Google's YouTube and Tencent's WeChat. Direct competitors immediately threaten ByteDance's user engagement and market share. In contrast, indirect competitors may influence user preferences and behavior in ways that could indirectly affect ByteDance's business model.

In this competitive environment, ByteDance must consider not only the immediate market share but also the long-term implications of technological advancements, regulatory changes, and shifts in user behavior. The company's strategic positioning must account for the potential disruptions that could arise from these competitors and the opportunities for collaboration and innovation that could emerge from the dynamic digital ecosystem.

ByteDance's competitive advantage lies in its ability to innovate and adapt quickly to user needs. However, this advantage is dynamic and must be continuously nurtured in the face of evolving market dynamics. The company's strategic focus on AI-driven content recommendations, user engagement, and global expansion is a testament to its commitment to staying ahead in the competitive race. Although still relatively small, the percentage of adults in the United States who report regularly obtaining news from TikTok has increased significantly from 3 per cent in 2020 to 14 per cent between September 25 and October 1, 2023, the last time the survey was conducted, according to a study conducted by the Pew Research Center involving over 8,800 adults (Fleck, 2024).

Competitors

ByteDance's success is supported by a multifaceted strategy around leveraging data. This strategy includes a profound understanding of user engagement, strategic market share acquisition, and the ability to generate significant advertising revenue. It indicates that the company has deep insight into consumer behavior and preferences and prowess in leveraging technological innovation, particularly in artificial intelligence for content recommendation, to maintain a competitive edge. However, any direct or indirect competitors sharing the same strategy revolving around leveraging data could threaten ByteDance's evolution. Therefore, a threat evaluation of ByteDance's main competitors is necessary.

In Social Media and Short Video Platforms

- **Facebook (Instagram, Reels)**: Instagram's Reels is a direct competitor to TikTok, leveraging Facebook's vast user base and resources. The integration of Reels within Instagram's existing social media framework poses a significant threat to TikTok's market share, as it offers a familiar platform for users to engage with short videos.
- **Snap Inc. (Snapchat)**: Snapchat appeals to a younger demographic, and its unique features, such as brief content, differentiate it from other platforms. While it may not directly threaten TikTok's user base, it remains a strong player in the multimedia content space.

In Search Engine

- **Baidu**: As a leading search engine in China, Baidu's diversified services could compete with ByteDance's offerings in information aggregation and user data collection. Baidu's AI capabilities also present a technological challenge.
- **Google**: Google's dominance in global search and its suite of online tools could influence user behavior and preferences, indirectly affecting ByteDance's user engagement strategies.

In E-Commerce

- **Alibaba Group (Taobao, Tmall)**: Alibaba's e-commerce platforms are not direct competitors to ByteDance's content-focused services. However, Alibaba's expansion into digital media and entertainment could overlap with ByteDance's interests, particularly in China.

- **JD.com**: Similar to Alibaba, JD.com's e-commerce focus does not directly compete with TikTok. However, its technological advancements and user data could be leveraged to influence the digital content landscape.

In Messaging and Communication

- **WeChat (Tencent)**: WeChat's widespread use in China and its integration of various services, including payment and social media, could challenge ByteDance's user engagement and retention strategies. Tencent's potential to expand its content offerings poses a strategic threat.
- **WhatsApp (Facebook)**: WhatsApp's global reach and messaging capabilities do not directly compete with TikTok's video focus. However, Facebook's ownership and potential integration with Instagram's Reels could create a more comprehensive social media ecosystem that ByteDance needs to consider.

In Content Creation and Consumption

- **YouTube (Google)**: YouTube's vast video library and creator community present a significant challenge to TikTok, as it offers a more established platform for content creators and advertisers. YouTube's recent focus on short-form content could directly compete with TikTok's user base.
- **Netflix**: While Netflix's streaming service is not a direct competitor to TikTok, its influence on content consumption patterns and user preferences could affect ByteDance's content strategy.

In Cloud Services

- **Alibaba Cloud**: Alibaba Cloud's growth in cloud computing services does not directly compete with ByteDance's content platforms. However, its technological advancements and data capabilities could influence the digital media landscape.
- **Amazon Web Services (AWS)**: AWS's global leadership in cloud services could indirectly affect ByteDance by enabling competitors to scale their services and innovate more rapidly.

In Artificial Intelligence

- **SenseTime**: SenseTime's expertise in AI, particularly in computer vision and deep learning, could lead to technological advancements that challenge ByteDance's AI-driven content recommendation systems.
- **OpenAI**: OpenAI's focus on general AI could lead to breakthroughs that impact the entire tech industry, including ByteDance's operations. The potential for AI to enhance user experience and content creation is a double-edged sword for ByteDance.

FUTURE DEVELOPMENT

MegaScale: ByteDance's AI System for Efficient Large Language Model Training

Thanks to its multifaceted approach, ByteDance has achieved remarkable success with its newly developed MegaScale AI system for efficient, ample language model training. The company has developed an innovative system architecture that involves a massive AI cluster of tens of thousands of GPUs, which underpins its capability in large-scale distributed computing and AI model training (Jiang et al., 2024). ByteDance's collaborative approach to designing algorithms and system components ensures a synergy that enhances overall performance. The system's robustness is further bolstered by its extensive fault tolerance and automated recovery mechanisms, which maintain stability during large-scale training tasks. Moreover, algorithmic optimizations, such as parallel transformer blocks and the LAMB optimizer, improve training efficiency without sacrificing accuracy. Additionally, the MegaScale system employs mixed parallelism strategies to maximize the overlap of communication and computation, leading to more efficient resource utilization.

The system also incorporates efficient operators and data pipeline optimization to reduce idle time and enhance data transfer efficiency. Network performance is optimized through custom network topologies and performance tuning, which are crucial for effective GPU communication. ByteDance's expertise in data center network design is evident in its efforts to manage congestion and adjust retransmit timeout settings. The company is committed to sharing its technological achievements, as evidenced by its open sourcing-of specific system components, which fosters community development. ByteDance's multifaceted approach contributes to its ability to train large language models with high efficiency and stability at unprecedented scales.

Data Sovereignty Issues

In today's advanced digital era, data has become crucial for corporations, especially for global tech conglomerates such as ByteDance. TikTok, the famous short video application under ByteDance's umbrella, follows a data management strategy that enhances user experience and raises significant concerns about privacy, national security, and compliance with international regulations. This has been a source of controversy. Critics argue that TikTok collects an extensive range of data points, including information on user location, internet addresses, keyboard input patterns, and device types, among other things, which may exceed user expectations on the extent and usage of their data. Moreover, despite ByteDance's claim that they do not share data with the Chinese government, the practicality of these promises still needs to be solved.

ByteDance also faces the challenge of complying with various data protection policies across different jurisdictions (Kesan & Shah, 2013; Schwartz, 2013). In the US, TikTok is required to adhere to laws such as the Children's Online Privacy Protection Act (COPPA) and the General Data Protection Regulation (GDPR), which emphasize transparency and the protection of user privacy during the collection, storage, and processing of user data (Kesan & Shah, 2013). In China, ByteDance falls under the Cybersecurity Law, which mandates companies operating in China to provide user data to the Chinese government upon request, raising global concerns about data security (Zhou et al., 2016).

ByteDance's Strategy for Global Privacy Compliance and User Trust

To address concerns regarding data privacy, ByteDance has implemented a data localization methodology. The company claims that American user data is exclusively stored on servers in the USA and Singapore, a strategy designed to keep the stored data free of Chinese legal implications and minimize the likelihood of the Chinese government accessing the data. However, the real-world effectiveness of this approach and its ability to dispel user and regulatory concerns is still a subject of ongoing debate.

Transparency and the user's control over their data play a pivotal role in ByteDance's data management methodology. TikTok has taken steps to explain its data collection and usage policies to its users through informative blog posts and periodic updates to its privacy policy. TikTok also empowers users with control over their data and privacy settings. These initiatives aim to build user trust in the platform and educate users about data privacy issues.

Regarding its international collaborative efforts and regulatory compliance, ByteDance's potential partnership with American corporations like Oracle and Walmart shows the company's adaptability in addressing the data security requirements imposed by the American government. Such collaborations propose using cloud services from American companies for the storage and processing of American user data, along with the assurance of data management adhering to American data protection standards. However, ByteDance still needs to navigate the global viability of this collaborative model and reconcile opposing legal mandates from different countries.

ByteDance's localization strategy involves storing user data on servers in the user's region instead of remote or international servers, providing several key benefits. Data localization helps ByteDance comply with countries' regulations about data storage, avoiding violations of crucial rules such as the General Data Protection Regulation (GDPR) in Europe and China's Cybersecurity Law. Localized data storage means that a user's data is less likely to cross international borders, reducing the risk of data being stolen or misused during transfer and providing better protection for user privacy. Data localization also improves data security. Because the data is stored where users are located, it can decrease the likelihood of hacker attacks and make responding to data breaches more immediate. ByteDance's actions in respecting user privacy could increase users' trust in the platform, leading to more positive perceptions of their products.

BYTEANCE LEADERSHIP

Zhang Yiming

From Zhang Yiming's perspective, ByteDance's journey has been characterized by a steadfast commitment to innovation and a global outlook (Bergen, 2018). In 2012, Zhang identified a gap in the Chinese smartphone market, where users needed help accessing relevant information amidst a sea of advertisements. He envisioned a solution that leveraged artificial intelligence to deliver personalized content, a vision that initially faced scepticism from venture capitalists (Reuters, 2020). However, despite the initial challenges, Zhang persevered, securing investment from Susquehanna International Group and launching ByteDance's flagship product, the Toutiao news app.

One distinctive aspect of Zhang's approach was his focus on global expansion from the outset (Zhu, 2020). While many Chinese tech CEOs concentrated on domestic growth, Zhang targeted international markets, recognizing the potential for ByteDance's products beyond China's borders. This strategy was evident in the launch of ByteDance's workplace productivity app, Lark, aimed at American, European, and Japanese markets rather than being confined to China.

Zhang's management style amalgamated Western and Chinese influences (Spence, 2019). Drawing inspiration from US tech companies like Google, he fostered a culture of transparency and egalitarianism within ByteDance, evident in practices such as bimonthly town hall meetings and discouraging formal titles like "boss" or "CEO."

ByteDance's breakout moment came with the launch of TikTok (Douyin in China) in 2016, quickly gaining popularity among millennials worldwide. This success was further bolstered by acquiring Musical.ly, demonstrating Zhang's acumen in identifying synergistic opportunities to strengthen ByteDance's position in the global market.

However, the challenge facing ByteDance lies in monetizing its substantial audience and popularity. The company is expanding its advertising sales operations, mainly focusing on its Toutiao platform. Despite its high costs, many marketers are drawn to ByteDance due to its extensive reach and engaged user base, with some even diverting spending from competitors like Tencent (BBC, 2021). ByteDance has shifted towards handling most of its advertising sales internally, a move noted by industry experts like Kenneth Tan from Mindshare China. However, brands remain cautious due to regulatory concerns, especially given the uncertainty surrounding Beijing's censorship policies. Recent app shutdowns, including a popular joke-sharing app in April, highlight the potential risks for brand collaboration with ByteDance (Fuller & Maheshwari, 2023).

Despite these challenges, Zhang's leadership has propelled ByteDance to unprecedented success (Bergen, 2018), with the company achieving a valuation of $75 billion by late 2018 and amassing over a billion monthly users across its mobile apps. However, the journey has not been without its complexities, underscoring the intricacies of navigating the intersection of technology, politics, and global markets.

Shou Zi Chew

Shou Zi Chew's career is a journey marked by achievements and transformations. Since graduating from University College London in 2006, he joined Goldman Sachs, where he spent two years as a banker in London, laying a solid foundation for his subsequent ventures into business investment (Fried, 2015). Subsequently, he joined DST Global, a venture capital firm led by Yuri Milner. At DST Global, Shou Zi Chew led investments in well-known internet companies such as JD.com, Alibaba, and Xiaomi, becoming one of the early investors in ByteDance in 2013.

2015, Shou Zi Chew joined Xiaomi Corporation as Chief Financial Officer, playing a crucial role in the company's financial strategy and global expansion (Dou, 2015). He was promoted to President of Xiaomi's international business in 2019, expanding his influence in the worldwide technology industry. In March 2021, Shou Zi Chew joined ByteDance as Chief Financial Officer, later assuming the position of CEO of TikTok, succeeding Kevin Mayer, who left the ByteDance subsidiary after just three months. This transition significantly elevated Shou Zi Chew's role and responsibilities within ByteDance, highlighting his importance within the company (Reuters, 2021). Shou Zi Chew testified before the United States Congress in the same month, discussing efforts to ban TikTok through legislation. In January 2024, he testified again, this time before the Senate Judiciary Committee, focusing on legislation regarding child internet safety (Brice & Shepardson, 2024). These testimonies underscore his expertise in handling international legal and regulatory issues and demonstrate his leadership in representing ByteDance and TikTok globally (Ashley et al., 2023).

In addition, Shou Zi Chew served as the honorary chairman of the 2024 Met Gala, a role closely associated with TikTok as the event's main sponsor (Chin, 2024). This further demonstrates his influence in the cultural and entertainment sectors and how he integrates business with culture to add more value and impact to the TikTok brand under ByteDance. Shou Zi Chew's career showcases his exceptional leadership in the global business and technology sectors and his adaptability and strategic vision in a constantly changing international landscape. With his continued development at ByteDance and TikTok, his future undoubtedly holds both challenges and opportunities.

REFERENCES

Bergen, L. Y. C., & M. (2018, October 1). The unknown 35-year-old behind the world's most valuable startup. *The Sydney Morning Herald*. https://www.smh.com.au/business/companies/104b-goliath-the-unknown-35-year-old-behind-the-world-s-most-valuable-startup-20181001-p5072r.html

Brice, M., & Shepardson, D. (2024, February 1). *Tech CEOs said, "You have blood on your hands" at US Senate child safety hearing.* REUTERS. https://www.reuters.com/technology/meta-tiktok-x-ceos-face-tough-questions-child-safety-us-senate-hearing-2024-01-31/

ByteDance. (2021, May 20). *TikTok's co-founder will step down as chief executive.* BBC News. https://www.bbc.com/news/business-57181225

ByteDance. (2023). *Inspire creativity and enrich life.* ByteDance. https://www.bytedance.com/en/

Ceci, L. (2024). *TikTok—Statistics & facts.* Statista. https://www.statista.com/topics/6077/tiktok/

Chen, R., & Ma, R. (2022, February 24). How ByteDance became the world's most valuable startup. *Harvard Business Review*. https://hbr.org/2022/02/how-bytedance-became-the-worlds-most-valuable-startup

Dou, E. (2015). Shou Zi Chew joins Xiaomi as CFO. *WSJ*. https://www.wsj.com/articles/shou-zi-chew-joins-xiaomi-as-cfo-1435719748

Fleck, A. (2024, March 14). More Americans turn to TikTok for news. *Statista Daily Data*. https://www.statista.com/chart/31905/us-adults-who-regularly-get-news-from-tiktok

Fried, I. (2015, July 1). *Xiaomi taps DST investment partner Shou Zi Chew to be CFO.* Vox. https://www.vox.com/2015/7/1/11564020/xiaomi-taps-dst-investment-partner-shou-zi-chew-to-be-cfo

Fuller, T., & Maheshwari, S. (2023, May 12). Ex-ByteDance executive accuses the company of "lawlessness." *The New York Times*. https://www.nytimes.com/2023/05/12/technology/tiktok-bytedance-lawsuit-china.html

He, L. (2024, March 18). *Analysis: Wait, is TikTok Chinese?* CNN. https://www.cnn.com/2024/03/18/tech/tiktok-bytedance-china-ownership-intl-hnk/index.html

Jiang, Z., Lin, H., Zhong, Y., Huang, Q., Chen, Y., Zhang, Z., & Ye, J. (2024). *MegaScale: Scaling large language model training to more than 10,000 GPUs.* arXiv preprint arXiv:2402.15627.

Kesan, J. P., & Shah, R. C. (2013). Setting software defaults: Perspectives from the law, computer science, and behavioural economics. *The Notre Dame Law Review*, 82, 583.

Maluleke, A. M. (2023, January 10). TikTok CEO Shou Zi Chew meets with EU Commission vice-president. *SABC News.* https://www.sabcnews.com/sabcnews/tiktok-ceo-shou-zi-chew-meets-with-eu-commission-vice-president/

Reuters. (2020, September 5). *TikTok troubles narrow gap between Beijing and ByteDance founder Zhang Yiming.* Reuters. https://www.reuters.com/article/us-usa-tiktok-bytedance-insight-idUSKBN25W0EM

Reuters. (2021, March 26). *TikTok owner ByteDance hires CFO in a step towards IPO.* Reuters. https://web.archive.org/web/20210326005416/https://www.reuters.com/article/us-bytedance-moves-xiaomi-idUSKBN2BG1JK

Schwartz, P. M. (2013). The EU-US privacy collision: A turn to institutions and procedures. *Harvard Law Review*, 126, 1966.

Spence, P. (2019). *ByteDance cannot outrun Beijing's shadow.* Foreign Policy. https://foreignpolicy.com/2019/01/16/bytedance-cant-outrun-beijings-shadow/

Zhou, B., Pei, H., & Wenyin, L. (2016). *The function cognition and implementation suggestions of network security legislation.* DEStech Transactions on Computer Science and Engineering.

Zhu, Y. Y. Julie. (2020, March 13). *Zhang Yiming, founder of TikTok owner ByteDance, gears up for the global stage.* Reuters. https://www.reuters.com/article/us-china-bytedance-ceo-idUSKBN21014Y

KEY TERMS AND DEFINITIONS

Competitive Dynamics: It encompasses the interactions and effects between different market competitors, including their strategic decisions, changes in market share, product innovation, price competition, and marketing activities.

Content Recommendation: The technology tailors content recommendations to individual users based on browsing history, preferences, and real-time behavior. Using advanced algorithms, personalized content display ensures that users receive relevant and engaging content.

Data Localization: It is the practice of storing and processing data within the same country or region where it is generated. This is often done to comply with local data protection regulations, enhance data security, and reduce the latency in data transmission.

Data Sovereignty: It refers to the rights and controls individuals, organizations, or nations have over the data they generate or possess. This includes data collection, processing, storage, and sharing decisions, as well as privacy, security, and regulatory compliance considerations.

Diversified Product Portfolio: This strategy refers to a company's broad range of products and services spanning multiple market segments, product categories, or industries. It helps the company **diversify risks and increase revenue sources.**

Social E-Commerce: It is a business model that combines social media and e-commerce, leveraging the power of social media to promote online purchases and sales. This typically involves a combination of user-generated content, social networking interaction, and online shopping to increase user engagement and sales conversion rates.

Social Media: It encompasses online platforms that facilitate the sharing of ideas, opinions, and information among users. These platforms, such as social networks, blogs, and forums, foster interactive communication and community engagement, promoting connections and collaborations.

UGC (User-Generated Content): It refers to content created and published by users rather than professional content creators. This includes blog posts, social media updates, videos, comments, and other forms of online interactive content.

Chapter 19
Xiaohongshu:
Modernizing Social Commerce in China's Digital Landscape

Zhixuan Yu

EDHEC Business School, France

EXECUTIVE SUMMARY

This case study explores the evolution and strategic trajectory of Xiaohongshu, a pioneering social commerce platform in China. Founded in 2013 by Miranda Qu and Charlwin Mao, Xiaohongshu has redefined consumer engagement by seamlessly integrating social media with e-commerce functionalities. Initially conceived as an online guide for Chinese shoppers abroad, the platform quickly developed into a vibrant community where users share product recommendations, reviews, and lifestyle insights. Xiaohongshu's strategic pivot on social commerce in 2014 marked a significant milestone, enabling direct product purchases within its app and fostering a dynamic ecosystem of user-generated content. The case examines Xiaohongshu's growth trajectory, challenges such as counterfeit goods, and strategic initiatives, including influencer marketing and blockchain integration. With a focus on expanding its user base, enhancing e-commerce capabilities, and exploring emerging technologies like Web3, Xiaohongshu continues to shape the future of digital commerce in China's competitive market landscape.

INTRODUCTION

Xiaohongshu affectionately referred to as Little Red Book emerged in 2013 as a visionary social commerce platform in Shanghai, China. Often heralded as "China's Instagram," it seamlessly integrates social media and e-commerce, epitomized by its in-app shopping interface, RED Mall. With a substantial valuation of $20 billion

DOI: 10.4018/979-8-3693-2921-4.ch019

and robust financial backing totaling $917.50 million, Xiaohongshu has firmly established itself as a vital link connecting Chinese consumers with global brands.

At its core, Xiaohongshu's business model is a symbiotic fusion of social media and e-commerce. Users actively contribute to the platform's vibrant community by sharing videos, photos, and reviews, creating a tapestry of lifestyle-centric content. After building the trust of customers, Xiaohongshu developed strategic partnerships and collaborations with domestic brands, which have been pivotal in enhancing its appeal to consumers. Initially designed for cross-border e-commerce, Xiaohongshu bridges the gap between Chinese consumers and international merchants, successfully balancing driving sales and attracting new customers. Strategically targeting the "SHE Economy," it celebrates and caters to women's rising social status and consumption power. Word-of-mouth marketing further propels the platform's success, with influencers and bloggers playing a pivotal role. Integration with major platforms like WeChat and Weibo enhances social connectivity, while the intuitive RED Mall facilitates a seamless in-app shopping experience.

DESCRIPTION OF XIAOHONGSHU

Brief History of Xiaohongshu

Xiaohongshu is a China-based social media and e-commerce platform (Xiaohongshu Official Website, n.d.). It was founded in 2013 by Miranda Qu and Charlwin Mao as an online tour guide for Chinese shoppers. The platform allowed users to review products and share their shopping experiences. In 2014, the founders shifted their focus to connecting Chinese consumers with global retailers and established their cross-border e-commerce platform (Xiao, Guo, Yu, & Liu, 2019). By 2015, Xiaohongshu had set up warehouses in Shenzhen, Guangdong, and Zhengzhou, Henan. Xiaohongshu has been developing "perfectly" over time.

The platform has seen significant growth since its foundation. As of 2020, Xiaohongshu has over 1,000 employees, with headquarters in Shanghai, an R&D center in Wuhan, and another office base in Beijing. It had exceeded 100 million monthly active users in 2020. Daily active users grew from 20 million to 40 million in 2021, and monthly active users doubled to 200 million in the same period (Xiaohongshu, 2022).

Xiaohongshu has achieved several milestones. In August 2014, it launched its e-commerce business. In January 2016, it recognized the importance of big data and AI and started to use machine learning to distribute its increasingly diverse content. By May 2017, it had over 50 million users and nearly CN ¥10 billion in sales, making it one of the world's largest community e-commerce platforms. Its international logistics system, REDelivery, went into service during the same month. In June 2018, Xiaohongshu completed Series D financing, valued at over $3 billion. "Inspire Lives" was set up in June 2019 as Xiaohongshu's mission.

The platform has also received several recognitions. In 2021, Xiaohongshu held its first WILL Awards to recognize promising young Chinese brands that resonate with consumers and represent the future of consumption in China. A total of 320 brands were shortlisted for the 11 awards (Xiaohongshu, 2001). Xiaohongshu has become the go-to platform for effective recommendation marketing, with food and clothing brands being the most active industry in May 2023. It is recognized as a leading lifestyle platform that has incubated the rise of new consumer trends and witnessed the growth of emerging brands (Xiaohongshu, 2022).

Business Model

Xiaohongshu is a unique social commerce platform in China, operating like a combination of Instagram and Amazon. On the platform, users can share photos, videos, posts, and tags linked to e-commerce listings.

The business model had roughly changed over time. First, Xiaohongshu was more like a serving guide where people wrote their comments on anything around them. Later, in 2014, it moved to share communities and used MVP products to verify the product positioning of users' core needs for sharing. After accumulating user behavior data and maturing the community, Xiaohongshu developed e-commerce and profited from data growth in transaction volume.

Xiaohongshu's business model is heavily focused on User-Generated Content (UGC) (ACOLINK LTD, 2018). Over 70% of all content on Xiaohongshu is user-generated. This authenticity is at the core of Xiaohongshu's content, which users have come to trust. When customers discover an exciting product from user posts, they can click through to the product page to make their purchases and post reviews after using the product. This differentiates Xiaohongshu from traditional e-commerce platforms such as Taobao or JD and other social media platforms such as Weibo (Li, 2023).

The platform also uses Key Opinion Leaders (KOLs) and influencers who inform consumers about brands (Chi, 2021). These influencers sometimes have large fan bases and key knowledge within certain industries, such as cosmetics. They can impact product sales by posting positive or negative reviews.

By focusing on search conversion and live-streaming sales, Xiaohongshu caters to its core demographic's shopping needs and cultivates shopping habits among a broader user base. This evolution from a community-focused platform to a dynamic e-commerce powerhouse underscores Xiaohongshu's adaptability and growth in the digital era.

Customers

The platform initially served as a secure space for female users seeking to share their fashion outfits and skincare routines. Over time, it transformed into a bustling "consumer decision-making" platform where predominantly women shared reviews, recommendations, and sought advice. Xiaohongshu caters primarily to young, cosmopolitan, and trendsetting women in China. Based on the demographics of Xiaohongshu users, 70% of the customers are female, 72% of users were born after 1990, 39% of users are 18-24 years old, 50% of users are from 1- and 2-tiers and 63% of users are white-collar workers (VEROT, 2023a).

Primary users can be classified into six different groups based on the latest data on Xiaohongshu user profiles in 2022 (Https://Www.octoplusmedia.com/, 2023):

1. Generation Z: These individuals are highly social, keeping up with the latest trends, gaming online, achieving educational milestones, and participating in competitive sports. They're interested in socializing, staying up-to-date with trends, gaming, learning, and sports.
2. Urban Trendsetters: This group is all about fashion, personal image, independent thinking, and expressing their opinions. They are fashion-conscious, mindful of their image, value independent thought, and aren't afraid to voice their opinions.
3. Exquisite Moms: These moms prioritize quality of life, pay attention to their appearance, indulge in luxury goods, and invest in skincare. They emphasize quality living, care for their appearance, enjoy luxury items, and invest in skincare products.
4. Emerging White Collars: Financially independent and enthusiastic about their careers, they are energetic and keen on showcasing their individuality. They are economically independent, passionate about their work, and full of energy and value, expressing their uniqueness.
5. Singles with High Income: Self-sufficient financially, this group seeks enjoyment, values quality, and tends towards moderate consumption. They are economically independent, prioritize enjoyment, seek quality experiences, and prefer a more moderate level of consumption.
6. Pleasure Seekers: They value entertainment and hobbies, seek out experiential consumption, and prioritize enjoyment above all. They prioritize entertainment, indulge in their hobbies, actively seek out experiences, and find joy in their activities.

Xiaohongshu has been an online hub for high-value, high-influence, and high-activity people in China (CHERNAVINA, 2022). The platform predominantly attracts young female users from major cities, who exhibit significant purchasing power and influence. This demographic presents substantial market potential, making Xiaohongshu a crucial platform for brands targeting this audience.

Product and Services

Xiaohongshu is sharing high-value content as a product for customers. Throughout 2021, Xiaohongshu experienced a notable surge in content creation, totaling approximately 360 million posts. The majority of this content revolves around food, beauty, and entertainment, with 33.686 million, 26.956 million, and 20.342 million posts, respectively, collectively comprising 23% of the total posts.

These figures correspond with the platform's primarily female user base, highlighting Xiaohongshu's prowess in facilitating product recommendations and nurturing a communal atmosphere.

There are some statistics on Xiaohongshu content:

- 360 million posts were generated on Xiaohongshu in 2021;
- 21% of all posts were sponsored (2.361 million);
- 32% month-on-month increase in the number of posts in the gaming category;
- 75% of Gen Z users bought a luxury product they found on the platform.

In 2022, Xiaohongshu, a prominent social commerce platform, exhibited diverse consumption trends across various content categories. Food and beauty content emerged as significant players, constituting 17% of the platform's total accounts. The platform witnessed a staggering volume of user-generated content, with approximately 360 million notes generated over the year. Food, beauty, and entertainment categories accounted for the highest volume, comprising 23% of the total. This trend aligns with the platform's predominantly female user base, reflecting Red's emphasis on product seeding and community engagement. Food-related posts, constituting 9% of the market, were dominated by tutorials, explorations, and sharing experiences, while beauty posts, at 7%, focused on tutorials, recommendations, and makeup sharing.

Additionally, notable growth was observed in gaming, pets, education, mothers and children, and home furnishing. Gaming content, in particular, experienced a remarkable surge, with a month-on-month increase of 31.9% in the past six months, indicating a rising interest in female-oriented, couple-oriented, and multiplayer online games. Similarly, pet-related content witnessed a substantial month-on-month growth of 22.4%, reflecting the increasing importance of pets in young people's lives and their emotional well-being.

Home improvement and renovation content emerged as another significant trend, driven by the post-90s generation's growing interest in creating refined living spaces (Guo, 2022). With 11.278 million notes/posts in 2021, this category experienced a surge in promoted notes, reaching 21% of all notes. The popularity of home-related content peaked in April 2021, underscoring young consumers' desire for a better quality of life. Decoration styles such as Nordic, French, and American garnered the highest interaction volume, indicating consumer preferences for natural and elegant aesthetics.

Furthermore, categories like pet supplies, medical and health, technology, and digital witnessed notable growth, reflecting evolving consumer needs and interests. The pet supplies category saw a tripled growth in the number of notes, indicating a burgeoning interest in pet-related products and services. Similarly, medical and health content gained traction, significantly increasing user-generated content and highlighting a growing emphasis on health and wellness. Technology and digital content also attracted high user engagement, driven by user-generated content and spontaneous traffic.

Xiaohongshu's consumption trends in 2022 underscored the platform's dynamic nature and ability to adapt to changing consumer preferences. It thrives on authentic user-generated content, mainly reviews and recommendations, which are pivotal in fostering community trust and aiding product discovery. Moreover, there is a noticeable uptick in content focused on health, wellness, and sustainability, reflecting users' increasing interest in holistic well-being. Short-form video content, such as tutorials and product demos, has also gained immense popularity due to its ability to deliver quick and visually appealing information. Alongside these trends, there is a growing preference for localized and niche content catering to specific interests and communities, enhancing user personalization.

Future trends in Xiaohongshu are expected to revolve around technological advancements and heightened social consciousness. Augmented Reality (AR) and Virtual Try-Ons are poised to revolutionize the shopping experience, driving engagement by allowing users to try products virtually. Moreover, content will likely surge, promoting sustainable products and ethical consumption practices as users become more environmentally conscious. Additionally, enhanced community engagement through new features for building communities and fostering user interaction will strengthen trust and camaraderie among Xiaohongshu users. Staying abreast of these evolving trends will enable brands and content creators to adapt their strategies accordingly, ensuring they resonate with user expectations and maximize their presence on Xiaohongshu.

Market Analysis

Original Situation of Xiaohongshu Market

Xiaohongshu initially targeted young, urban, and fashion-forward women in China. The platform served as a space for users to share fashion ensembles and skincare regimens.

With its visually captivating content and insightful product reviews, Xiaohongshu quickly expanded its reach and attracted global brands. It boasts a vibrant community of over 140,000 brands (Xiaohongshu, 2022), predominantly catering to females aged 18 to 35 (ACOLINK LTD, 2018). Users actively participate by exchanging style inspiration and discovering premium foreign brands not readily available in China.

Renowned for user-generated content, Xiaohongshu is a go-to destination for fashion, beauty, and lifestyle recommendations and reviews. The inclusion of RED Mall, an online marketplace offering international products exclusively to Chinese consumers, further enhances its appeal to foreign businesses eyeing the lucrative Chinese market (Goh, 2023).

Understanding the demographics and behaviors of Xiaohongshu users is pivotal for foreign brands seeking to thrive on the platform (Pemarathna, 2019). Most users belong to the post-90s generation, residing in urban areas and prioritizing quality. They enthusiastically share and explore product insights, particularly for foreign brands. Predominantly concentrated in first and second-tier cities, these users actively contribute user-generated content and engage in community discussions (Hastam, 2024). Notably, females constitute a significant portion, comprising 88.8% of the user base, and are avid consumers of lifestyle, beauty, and fashion products. Moreover, with 80% of users under 30, younger demographics gravitate towards the platform's social features, forming interconnected communities based on shared interests.

Evolution of the Market Until Today

Xiaohongshu has undergone a remarkable transformation since its establishment in 2013. Initially conceived as a platform for women to share fashion and skincare content, it quickly evolved into a hub for consumer decision-making, where users exchanged reviews, recommendations, and sought advice. Its innovative fusion of social media and e-commerce proved to be a winning formula (Safdar, 2023). The app allows users to explore lifestyle content and make direct purchases. This distinctive combination addressed a market need and propelled Xiaohongshu to rapid success.

By 2023, Xiaohongshu boasted nearly 200 million monthly active users, predominantly females seeking shopping advice and product reviews from fellow users. With a valuation surpassing $3 billion in 2023, the platform derived 80% of its revenue from advertising and the remaining 20% from its integrated e-commerce marketplace. China's booming e-commerce sector, projected to reach $175 billion by 2024, positioned Xiaohongshu as one of the fastest-growing social commerce platforms, with over 300 million users. This presents significant opportunities for international brands to tap into China's market potential and establish a strong presence (Zhao, 2023).

Xiaohongshu's strategic focus on search conversion and live-streaming sales caters to the shopping needs of its core demographic while expanding its user base. This transition from a community-centric platform to a dynamic e-commerce giant underscores its adaptability and success in the digital age. As of October 2022, nearly one-third of Xiaohongshu's user base resided in new tier-1 cities and beyond in China. Recognized as the most valuable e-commerce and direct-to-consumer unicorn globally, Xiaohongshu boasted a staggering valuation of approximately $20 billion as of October 2022.

Competition Analysis

Xiaohongshu is Like Instagram and Amazon, But With its Specific Features.

In contrast to Instagram's focus primarily on visual content, Xiaohongshu transcends mere photo and video sharing. While Instagram often treats captions as secondary, Xiaohongshu places equal, if not greater, emphasis on textual content (Zhong, 2022). Users share reviews, recommendations, and lifestyle insights, where text is pivotal in offering valuable insights and evoking aspiration. This orientation towards textual content aligns with the preferences of Chinese users and fosters a more decadent array of content and interaction possibilities (Flexi Classes, 2021).

Unlike Amazon, which predominantly functions as an online marketplace, Xiaohongshu provides a more socially integrated shopping experience. By seamlessly blending user-generated content with e-commerce functionality, Xiaohongshu enables users to explore lifestyle content while directly purchasing recommended products within the app. This unique fusion of content sharing and online shopping addresses a distinct need in the digital landscape, contributing significantly to Xiaohongshu's rapid growth.

Xiaohongshu also distinguishes itself from other social media platforms in China through its unique fusion of user-generated content, inspirational content, and community engagement. Unlike platforms such as WeChat, Douyin (TikTok), and Taobao, which dominate the social media landscape in China, Xiaohongshu has carved out a specialized niche by prioritizing lifestyle content and e-commerce opportunities (VEROT, 2023b). It transcends aesthetic appeal and hashtags, serving as a dynamic space where users actively explore and share new brands, products, concepts, and ways of life.

One of Xiaohongshu's standout features is its integrated shopping interface, which enables users to browse, search seamlessly, and purchase products without leaving the app. For many users across China, Xiaohongshu has become the go-to destination, effectively replacing traditional search engines. This significance is amplified by the limitations imposed on accessing platforms like Google and the challenges faced by Baidu, China's leading search engine, due to issues such as ad fraud.

Xiaohongshu vs. WeChat

WeChat, renowned as an all-encompassing super app, offers many features ranging from messaging to financial services. Boasting a colossal user base exceeding 1.26 billion monthly active users, WeChat dominates the Chinese digital landscape (Statista, 2023). Conversely, Xiaohongshu is a social commerce platform focusing on lifestyle and shopping experiences. Although Xiaohongshu's user base is comparatively smaller, surpassing 100 million monthly active users, its community is notably engaged. Over 70% of the content on Xiaohongshu is user-generated, fostering an authentic environment that users have grown to trust implicitly.

Xiaohongshu vs. Douyin

Douyin, popularly known as TikTok outside of China, has garnered immense popularity as a short-form video app, amassing a staggering 743 million monthly active users. With a primary demographic skewing towards younger users, particularly those under 26 years old, Douyin captivates audiences with its entertaining video content. In contrast, Xiaohongshu is a lifestyle and shopping platform primarily targeting young urban women. While Douyin specializes in bite-sized, engaging videos, Xiaohongshu distinguishes itself through comprehensive user-generated content, detailed product reviews, and insightful shopping recommendations (China Marketing Agency, 2023).

Xiaohongshu vs. Taobao

Taobao, a stalwart in the e-commerce realm under Alibaba's umbrella, boasts extensive products and sellers, cementing its status as a premier online shopping destination in China. Conversely, Xiaohongshu carves its niche as a social commerce platform, intertwining user-generated content with e-commerce functionalities. Users on Xiaohongshu can seamlessly navigate through product discoveries, share personalized recommendations and insights, and make purchases directly within the app.

This distinction sets Xiaohongshu apart from conventional e-commerce platforms like Taobao, as it prioritizes holistic lifestyle experiences over mere transactional interactions. Notably, Taobao recognized the value of Xiaohongshu's user-generated content, evident in its integration with Xiaohongshu's product description pages, further solidifying Xiaohongshu's influence in the digital marketplace.

Forecast for the Market

The future of Xiaohongshu looks promising. By 2023, the platform has garnered nearly 200 million monthly active users, predominantly females seeking shopping insights and user-generated content from fellow Xiaohongshu users sharing product recommendations and reviews. Valued at over $3 billion, Xiaohongshu's revenue stream primarily derives from advertising, constituting 80% of its total revenue, while the remaining 20% stems from its integrated e-commerce platform.

Anticipated to reach 200 million monthly active users in China by September 2023, Xiaohongshu remains particularly popular among young female consumers residing in top-tier cities according to Statista (Statista, n.d.). Its strategy resonates well with the preferences of modern Chinese consumers, who prioritize social validation and community engagement throughout their shopping experiences.

Compared to other e-commerce and content platforms, Xiaohongshu boasts the highest micro-influencers share (Statista, n.d.). Despite their modest follower counts, these critical opinion consumers are esteemed for their authenticity, passion, and expertise within niche industries. Notably, cosmetics, fashion, and food emerge as the most prevalent sectors covered by Xiaohongshu influencers. With steady growth projected in both user base and revenue, Xiaohongshu is poised for a promising trajectory in the market.

Development and Strategy

Founding and Initial Concept (2013)

Xiaohongshu was conceived in 2013 by founders Miranda Qu and Charlwin Mao, initially serving as an online tour guide tailored for Chinese shoppers. This innovative platform allowed users to review products and share their shopping journeys and experiences within a vibrant community. The initial concept was to create an online tour guide for Chinese shoppers, providing a platform for users to review products and share their shopping experiences. The initial slogan was "Find good things abroad". This pioneering concept filled a crucial gap in the market, empowering female shoppers to exchange insights, recommendations, and reviews for the first time.

During the initial phase, Chinese consumers faced a notable challenge stemming from their limited understanding of products purchased overseas, compounded by complex tax return policies in various countries, fluctuations in the exchange rates of the Chinese currency (RMB), and China's overall economic growth (Fu, 2022). While many saw overseas travel as an opportunity to access quality goods at reasonable prices, they often needed help to grasp the details of their purchasing products (Xiao, Guo, Yu, & Liu, 2019). In response to this challenge, Xiaohongshu emerged as a solution, conceived and launched as a platform dedicated to facilitating user-generated content centered on sharing shopping experiences and product reviews. This innovative approach cultivated a dynamic community environment where users actively participated in discovering and disseminating new brands, products, lifestyle trends, and ideas. Over time, Xiaohongshu evolved significantly, broadening its focus to encompass diverse content categories such as lifestyle, fashion, beauty, travel, and more, thus providing users with a comprehensive platform for creative expression and community engagement (Wang, Huang, & Liu-Lastres, 2022).

Transition to Social Commerce (2014)

In 2014, Xiaohongshu underwent a significant transformation, transitioning into a social commerce platform. This strategic pivot aimed to bridge Chinese consumers with global retailers and lay the groundwork for its cross-border e-commerce platform (Xiao, Guo, Yu, & Liu, 2019). This strategic shift marked a significant milestone in Xiaohongshu's evolution, seamlessly integrating social media elements with robust e-commerce functionalities, enhancing the overall user experience.

During its transition, Xiaohongshu encountered various challenges. Integrating social media features with e-commerce functionality posed a significant hurdle, as the platform needed to enable users to seamlessly discover, discuss, and purchase products directly through the platform. Moreover, maintaining user-generated content while incorporating e-commerce was essential, considering that authenticity is fundamental to Xiaohongshu's content, and the trust users place in it. To overcome these challenges, Xiaohongshu concentrated on integrating social content with e-commerce functionality, allowing users to explore products, read reviews, and make purchases within the app. This seamless integration facilitated swift purchases without requiring users to leave the app, thanks to saved mobile payment and shipping information. Additionally, Xiaohongshu expanded its offerings to include cross-border e-commerce, enabling users to access and purchase products not readily available in China (Www.chinafy.com, 2023). This emphasis on global discovery set Xiaohongshu apart from other domestic platforms.

User Growth and Expansion (2015-Present)

Since its inception, Xiaohongshu has experienced exponential growth and expansion. From its launch in December 2013, the platform took 1,644 days to reach 100 million users. By January 2019, the number of registered users had exceeded 200 million. By 2020, the platform boasted an impressive user base, with over 450 million registered users. By 2023, Xiaohongshu boasted nearly 200 million monthly active users. Most of these users were females seeking shopping notes and user-generated content from fellow Xiaohongshu users, particularly recommendations and product reviews. Beyond the confines of urban China, Xiaohongshu's influence extended to regions with thriving Chinese diaspora communities, including Singapore, Malaysia, and the United States. This widespread adoption underscored its universal appeal and global relevance.

During this phase, Xiaohongshu encountered significant challenges, with one of the most prominent being the escalating cost of acquiring new users. To mitigate this issue, the platform shifted its focus towards enhancing user retention strategies, mainly targeting younger users under 18 years old, who were found to be most prone to leaving the platform. Implementing tailored advertising campaigns and leveraging influencer marketing initiatives emerged as potential solutions to attract new users and maintain the engagement of existing ones.

Additionally, Xiaohongshu grappled with the pervasive issue of counterfeit goods proliferating on its platform, posing a threat to its reputation and legal standing. To tackle this challenge effectively, the platform explored integrating digital technologies, such as blockchain, to authenticate the genuineness of products sold. Collaborating with brands to establish certification marks as indicators of authenticity could further reassure users of the legitimacy of products available on Xiaohongshu.

Amidst these challenges, notable events underscored Xiaohongshu's significance in the Chinese consumer market. The platform received visits from State Council Premier Li Keqiang in September 2015 and Vice Premier of the State Council Wang Yang in 2016, signifying its remarkable success and influence within the industry.

THE PEOPLE BEHIND XIAOHONGSHU

Miranda Qu serves as the co-founder and current President of Xiaohongshu. She co-established the company in 2013 alongside Charlwin Mao. Before venturing into Xiaohongshu, Qu amassed experience in marketing while working for Bertelsmann.

Her educational background includes studies at Beijing Foreign Studies University (Forbes, n.d.-b).

Qu's astute market insights and deep understanding of user behavior have driven Xiaohongshu's exponential growth. She has propelled Xiaohongshu beyond its predecessors' functionalities, transforming it into a dynamic e-commerce ecosystem. This evolution has garnered attention from luxury brands, leading to lucrative partnerships with renowned names like Tiffany & Co, Christian Dior, and L'Oréal.

Qu's achievements have been recognized on numerous occasions. In May 2019, she was honored among the 100 Most Creative People in Business by Fast Company (The Business of Fashion, n.d.). In February 2018, Forbes China also named her one of the 25 Rising Businesswomen of the Year. As of March 2024, her real-time net worth is $1.3 billion. Mao assumes the CEO role at Xiaohongshu, co-founding the company alongside Miranda Qu. Mao's contributions have been integral to shaping the company's strategic direction and overseeing its overall expansion.

Charlwin Mao

Charlwin Mao, also known as Mao Wenchao, is the co-founder and incumbent CEO of Xiaohongshu (CompassList, n.d.). Before co-founding Xiaohongshu, Mao gained valuable experience at Bain Consulting and Bain Capital. He pursued his academic endeavors in mechanical engineering at Shanghai Jiao Tong University and later obtained an MBA from Stanford University in 2011(Forbes, n.d.-a).

An enthusiastic globetrotter, Mao has explored over twenty countries, enriching his perspectives with diverse cultural experiences. Currently, in his early 30s, he distinguishes himself from the historical figure Chairman Mao despite sharing a surname.

Mao's strategic leadership and keen oversight have played a pivotal role in steering the company's trajectory. With a profound understanding of the market landscape and a knack for innovation, he has propelled Xiaohongshu to emerge as one of the swiftest-growing social commerce platforms in the industry (Crunchbase, 2024).

Under Qu's and Mao's leadership, Xiaohongshu has experienced remarkable growth, boasting over 200 million monthly active users. Qu and Mao hold an estimated 10% ownership stake in the company. They introduced a pioneering fusion of social media and e-commerce, allowing users to discover product recommendations and reviews before purchasing directly on the platform. This innovative approach resonated with users, addressing a crucial need in the digital sphere and propelling Xiaohongshu's rapid growth. Notably, Xiaohongshu achieved a valuation of $20 billion following a funding round in November 2021, attracting investments from major players such as Tencent and Alibaba.

FUTURE PROJECTS

Xiaohongshu's comprehensive vision for the future is marked by a strategic road-map encompassing several key areas, each aimed at driving growth and fostering innovation. One of the most significant elements of this strategy is the company's commitment to expanding its user base. Initially, Xiaohongshu gained popularity among young, urban females residing in top-tier cities. However, the platform is extending its reach to include a more diverse demographic, even attracting more male users. This strategic expansion is pivotal to Xiaohongshu's sustained growth and is crucial to securing its long-term viability.

Another crucial aspect of Xiaohongshu's strategy is enhancing its e-commerce integration. As it stands, advertising forms the lion's share of the platform's revenue, at 80%, with the remaining 20% coming from its integrated online marketplace (Liu, 2023). By optimizing this marketplace, Xiaohongshu aims to increase its e-commerce revenue, which aligns with the global trend of social commerce, which sees social media platforms integrating shopping functionalities seamlessly.

Furthermore, Xiaohongshu highly emphasises improving its user-generated content, particularly content that offers recommendations and reviews in the realms of fashion, beauty, and lifestyle. The company believes encouraging more user participation in content creation and sharing is critical to maintaining the platform's authenticity and trustworthiness. These elements are vital in fostering user engagement and loyalty.

In addition to these strategies, Xiaohongshu is keen to explore emerging trends and technologies. The company's investment in a US-based startup developing a blockchain-based Web3 internet platform is a testament to this. This strategic move underscores Xiaohongshu's commitment to innovation and showcases its readiness to embrace new trends shaping the digital landscape.

Xiaohongshu is also eyeing new market opportunities, particularly in the fitness, fashion, and beauty sectors. The company recognizes the significant growth potential in these areas. It is poised to leverage these trends to attract a broader user base and forge partnerships with brands keen on tapping into these lucrative markets.

Lastly, rumors are circulating that Xiaohongshu might be considering a public listing in Hong Kong, potentially in the latter half of 2024. If this comes to fruition, it could provide additional funding to support Xiaohongshu's ambitious development plans, bolster its expansion, and cement its position as a leading player in the social commerce sphere.

In summary, Xiaohongshu's future development strategy is both diverse and comprehensive. By focusing on user base expansion, e-commerce integration enhancement, user-generated content improvement, exploration of emerging technologies, leveraging new market opportunities, and a potential public listing, Xiaohongshu demonstrates its adaptability and foresight, ensuring its continued growth and success in the years to come.

CONCLUSION

In conclusion, Xiaohongshu has truly distinguished itself as a pioneering force in social commerce within China's digital landscape. Founded in 2013 by Miranda Qu and Charlwin Mao, the platform's seamless integration of social media and e-commerce functionalities has revolutionized users' engagement with brands and products.

Xiaohongshu's visionary approach to social commerce has met and exceeded market expectations, evidenced by its remarkable growth and development trajectory. With nearly 200 million monthly active users and a valuation surpassing $3 billion as of 2023, Xiaohongshu has solidified its position as a leader in the industry.

Despite encountering challenges such as the proliferation of counterfeit goods and escalating user acquisition costs, Xiaohongshu has remained resilient and adaptable. Leveraging strategies like targeted advertising, influencer marketing, and innovative blockchain solutions, the platform has effectively tackled these obstacles head-on, further fortifying its market position.

Looking towards the future, Xiaohongshu is poised for continued expansion and innovation. Its strategic roadmap includes ambitious initiatives such as broadening its user base, enhancing e-commerce integration, refining user-generated content, exploring cutting-edge technologies like Web3 and blockchain, tapping into emerging market opportunities in fitness, fashion, and beauty, and potentially pursuing a public listing.

The remarkable journey of Xiaohongshu serves as a compelling case study, offering invaluable insights into the evolution of social commerce dynamics within China. Moreover, it underscores the transformative potential of user-generated content in driving growth and fostering innovation within the e-commerce landscape. As businesses and researchers seek to understand and navigate the interplay between social media, e-commerce, and consumer behavior, Xiaohongshu is a beacon of inspiration and learning.

REFERENCES

ACOLINK, LTD. (2018, September 25). *Little Red Book (XiaoHongShu) paves the way for China's new social consumer culture*. ACOLINK, LTD. https://acolink .com/news/2018/little-red-book-ecommerce-social-consumer-culture

Charlie Mao: Founder. (n.d.). Forbes. https://www.forbes.com/profile/charlwin-mao/

Charlwin Mao (Mao Wenchao). (n.d.). CompassList. https://www.compasslist.com/ founders/charlwin-mao-mao-wenchao

Chernavina, K. (2022, June 29). *2021-2022 Xiaohongshu/RED user trends*. HI-COM. https://www.hicom-asia.com/2022-xiaohongshu-red-user-trends-and-statistics/

Chi, R. (2021, June 9). Jump on the rise of Xiaohongshu, China's fastest-growing social media marketing platform. *The Drum*. https://www.thedrum.com/opinion/ 2021/06/09/jump-the-rise-xiaohongshu-china-s-fastest-growing-social-media -marketing-platform

Chine Marketing Agency. (2023, November 23). *From WeChat to Douyin: Navigating Chinese Social Media Landscape*. Do Matters. https://www.domatters.com/ most-popular-chinese-social-media-platforms/

Crunchbase. (2024). *Charlie Mao*. CrunchBase. https://www.crunchbase.com/ person/charlwin-mao-wenchao

Flexi Classes. (2021, January 12). *Xiaohongshu Vs Instagram | What is ? Should You Get It?* Flexi Classes. https://flexiclasses.com/xiaohongshu-vs-instagram/

Forbes. (n.d.). *Qu Miranda*. Forbes. https://www.forbes.com/profile/qu-miranda/

Fu, Z. (2022, August 19). *The rise of Xiaohongshu: the little red's big ambition*. PingWest. https://en.pingwest.com/a/10594

Goh, I. (2023, January 11). You Probably Didn't Know These 10 Facts About Xiaohongshu. *Goody Feed*. https://goodyfeed.com/xiaohongshu/

Guo, J. (2022). The postfeminist entrepreneurial self and the platformisation of labour: A case study of yesheng female lifestyle bloggers on xiaohongshu. *Global Media and China*, 7(3), 205943642210958. DOI:10.1177/20594364221095896

Hastam, J. (2024, February 29). *What is Xiaohongshu? Marketing Guide for Brands*. Nativex. https://www.nativex.com/en/blog/exploring-xiaohongshu-chinas-answer -to-instagram/

Li, M. (2023, December 8). *Insight Magazine | Xiaohongshu: A Social Commerce Platform You Cannot Miss*. Amcham-Shanghai.org. https://www.amcham-shanghai.org/en/article/insight-magazine-xiaohongshu-social-commerce-platform-you-cannot-miss

Liu, Y. (2023). Analysis of Xiaohongshu's Internet Marketing Strategy. *BCP Business & Management*, 43, 110–116. DOI:10.54691/bcpbm.v43i.4629

Octoplusmedia. (2023, June 20). *What is the Audience Profile of Xiaohongshu (RED) Users? A Demographic Breakdown Across Various Industries*. Octoplus Media. https://www.octoplusmedia.com/what-is-the-audience-profile-of-xiaohongshu-red-users-a-demographic-breakdown-across-various-industries/

Pemarathna, R. (2019). *Impact of Xiaohongshu on Its User Based and Society: A Review*. ResearchGate. https://www.researchgate.net/publication/333974009_Impact_of_Xiaohongshu_on_Its_User_Based_and_Society_A_Review

Safdar, M. (2023, April 2). *The Rise of Social Commerce: Opportunities and Challenges for Brands*. Hannan Muhammad. https://hannanit.com/2023/04/02/the-rise-of-social-commerce-opportunities-and-challenges-for-brands/

Statista. (2023, February 17). *China: Most Popular Social Media Platforms 2018*. Statista. https://www.statista.com/statistics/250546/leading-social-network-sites-in-china/

Statista. (n.d.). *China: most active industries in Xiaohongshu recommendation marketing 2023*. Statista. https://www.statista.com/statistics/1412241/china-recommendation-marketing-by-industries-on-xiaohongshu/

The Business of Fashion. (n.d.). *Miranda Qu | BoF 500 | The People Shaping the Global Fashion Industry*. The Business of Fashion. https://www.businessoffashion.com/community/people/miranda-qu

Verot, O. (2023, September 21). *Xiaohongshu Statistics and Trends For The Upcoming Years - Marketing China*. GMA. https://marketingtochina.com/xiaohongshu-statistics-and-trends/

Verot, O. (2023, August 10). *How Do Different Generations Use Chinese Social Media Platforms? - Marketing China*. GMA. https://marketingtochina.com/how-do-different-generations-use-chinese-social-media-platforms/

Wang, Z., Huang, W.-J., & Liu-Lastres, B. (2022). Impact of user-generated travel posts on travel decisions: A comparative study on Weibo and Xiaohongshu. *Annals of Tourism Research Empirical Insights*, 3(2), 100064. DOI:10.1016/j.annale.2022.100064

343

Xiao, L., Guo, F., Yu, F., & Liu, S. (2019). The Effects of Online Shopping Context Cues on Consumers' Purchase Intention for Cross-Border E-Commerce Sustainability. *Sustainability (Basel)*, 11(10), 2777. DOI:10.3390/su11102777

Xiaohongshu. (2001, September 15). Xiaohongshu debuts the WILL Awards to recognise extraordinary up-and-coming Chinese brands. *PR Newswire*. Www.prnewswire .com. https://www.prnewswire.com/news-releases/xiaohongshu-debuts-will-awards -to-recognize-extraordinary-up-and-coming-chinese-brands-301377677.html

Xiaohongshu. (2022, November 11). Xiaohongshu invites top brands to share insights into China's Gen Z consumers during CIIE. *PR Newswire*. Www.prnewswire .com. https://www.prnewswire.com/news-releases/xiaohongshu-invites-top-brands -to-share-insights-into-chinas-gen-z-consumers-during-ciie-301675472.html

Zhao, L. (2023, October 11). *Analysis: Why Brands Are Flocking To China Instagram Rival Xiaohongshu*. Provoke Media. https://www.provokemedia.com/long-reads/ article/analysis-why-brands-are-flocking-to-china-instagram-rival-xiaohongshu

Zhong, Y. (2022, March 10). How the Chinese version of Instagram is outgrowing Instagram. *Medium*. https://uxdesign.cc/how-the-chinese-version-of-instagram-is -becoming-much-more-than-instagram-61eb70e89b54

KEY TERMS AND DEFINITIONS

Blockchain: A digital ledger technology that records cryptocurrency transactions transparently and immutable.

Critical Opinion Consumers (KOCs): Influential figures within a platform community whose opinions wield significant influence over product sales, whether through positive endorsements or negative reviews.

Cross-Border E-commerce: Online commerce that involves the sale of goods across international borders, a domain Xiaohongshu entered by establishing its cross-border e-commerce platform in 2014.

Daily Active Users (DAU): The number of unique users interacting within a platform within 24 hours provides insights into daily user engagement levels.

Douyin: Known internationally as TikTok, it's a popular short-form video application celebrated for its broad reach and user engagement.

Monthly Active Users (MAU): They represent the count of distinct users engaging with a platform within a 30-day period. They serve as a vital metric for assessing user engagement and platform popularity.

Public Listing: The process of offering shares of a private company to the public through an Initial Public Offering (IPO), enabling investment from external shareholders.

Social Commerce: A fusion of social media and e-commerce, enabling users to explore, discuss, and purchase products seamlessly within a single platform.

Taobao: A cornerstone of China's online shopping landscape, Taobao is a leading e-commerce platform under the Alibaba Group umbrella.

User-Generated Content (UGC): Content crafted and shared by users on an online platform, encompassing product reviews, recommendations, and lifestyle insights, among others, as exemplified on Xiaohongshu.

Web3: An envisioned decentralized internet framework powered by blockchain technology, promising greater autonomy and transparency in online interactions.

WeChat: An all-encompassing super app integrating various services from messaging to financial transactions, ranking among China's most prominent social media platforms.

Chapter 20
Ximalaya FM:
Empowering the Sound Economy and the Evolution of China's Audio Industry

Danyu Luo

Beijing Normal University-Hong Kong Baptist University United International College, China

EXECUTIVE SUMMARY

This case study explores the dynamic evolution of China's audio economy industry, focusing on technological advancements, market trends, and key players, such as Ximalaya. With a historical perspective, it traces the industry's growth through distinct eras, from early audiobooks to the current era dominated by mobile internet and specialized audio services. Market data from AI Media Consulting underscores the industry's exponential growth, driven by factors like the increased demand for online learning and knowledge payment. Detailed demographic insights highlight the user composition and providing a comprehensive understanding of consumer behaviors and preferences. Central to this narrative is the pivotal role of Jianjun Yu, founder of Ximalaya, whose entrepreneurial journey and strategic vision have shaped the platform's prominence in delivering high-quality audio content. As the industry navigates developing media consumption habits and technological advancements, this case study offers valuable insights into the future trajectories of China's vibrant audio economy landscape.

DOI: 10.4018/979-8-3693-2921-4.ch020

INTRODUCTION

Brief History of the Unicorn

Ximalaya FM (Shanghai et al.) is a professional audio-sharing platform that provides users with tens of millions of audio such as audiobooks, audiobooks, children's bedtime stories, comedy sketches, ghost stories, and more. Users can access Ximalaya's free content anytime, anywhere, without paying for any in the Ximalaya app in the "Anytime, anywhere, listen to what I want to listen to" section, which can be accessed through the Ximalaya app.

It was founded in August 2012. Its app was launched in March 2013, and within six months, it attracted ten million users. Offering free audio content, Ximalaya FM's registered users exceeded 5 million by May 2014. In June 2016, Ximalaya launched its first paid program, "Speak Well," and expanded its user base. Ximalaya continued to attract users and monetize its traffic by launching the 123 Knowledge Carnival in 2016 and the 66 Membership Day in 2017 to increase membership and traffic realization (Wen, 2022). According to Ximalaya's official data, the festival attracted 3.42 million new members and generated 61.14 million yuan in new consumption, expanding the platform payment rate (Ximalaya Open Platform, n.d.).

In April 2018, Ximalaya introduced an extensive membership system to expand its audience and reduce the cost of audiobook access for users. However, during this period, Ximalaya faced a bottleneck in traffic realization. In late 2018, Ximalaya FM introduced new add-on products such as speakers, furniture, and other items to enhance the user's listening experience. In February 2019, Ximalaya launched the Fun Dubbing Zone, allowing users to participate in dubbing contests with their favorite celebrities. This move has contributed to increased traffic and revenue for Ximalaya, helping to overcome challenges and propel the platform's growth through fan engagement.

Currently, Ximalaya FM offers 328 types of audio content, including finance, music, news, business, novels, and automobiles, among others. They hold a leading market share of over 70% in the audio copyright market, making it the most prominent industry. They have a significant advantage in terms of user base and user activity in the audio economy industry. Additionally, Ximalaya FM has released the "2023 Ximalayan Chinese Podcast Ecological Report," stating that the platform will have over 220 million Chinese podcast listeners in 2023 and will be the only certified podcast hosting platform for Apple podcasts in mainland China.

In the third quarter of 2023, they reached an average of 345 million monthly active users (Ximalaya Open Platform, n.d.).

Business Model

Ximalaya FM is a pioneer in the industry, utilizing the PUGC (Professional User Generated Content) model. This model combines the PGC (professional scholar-generated content) and UGC (ordinary user-generated content) models. It involves professional and self-published media individuals collaborating to create and distribute content through the internet. The aim is to produce content with both professional depth and user originality and breadth (Wen, 2022).

The platform offers audio products such as audiobooks, podcasts, and blogs tailored to various users. Its main content producers are individual anchors, MCNs (Multi-Channel Networks), and creators with their fan base. This diverse approach to content production has enabled Ximalaya to expand the breadth and depth of its knowledge domain, providing a platform for content creators to showcase their talent and realize their value. Furthermore, Ximalaya offers a creation help center for content producers, promoting the sustainability of content production to a certain extent.

Users, self-publishers, and third-party brands benefit significantly from the Pugc business model. Users can meet their needs by purchasing paid knowledge, while self-publishers can earn additional income through live broadcasting or by collaborating with third-party brands, broadening the scope of publicity. Ximalaya's profit model includes fan economy revenue, advertising revenue, and e-commerce revenue, which will be discussed in more detail later in the article (Zhou, 2021).

PRODUCTS AND SERVICES

Product Type

Audiobook Channel

The Audiobook channel is one of the leading businesses of Ximalaya FM and one of the earliest ventures in which Ximalaya was involved. Half of Ximalaya's traffic is generated by the audiobook channel, and the total listening time of the audiobook channel accounts for 60% of the total listening time of the platform's users (Zhou, 2021). As of March 13, 2024, the top audiobook, "The Audible Purple Lapel", had been played 1.16 billion times. Ximalaya holds the audiobook copyrights for 70% of the bestsellers in the market, the audiobook adaptation rights for 85% of online literature, and has 6,600+ audiobooks of bestsellers in the original English version (Ximalaya, 2024).

The audiobook channel is divided into categories to offer various options for users with different interests. Currently, audiobooks provide a variety of channels, including suspense, informative articles, favorite stories, spiritual content, historical accounts, business topics, original English books, and more. The options include single broadcast, double broadcast, multi-play, and radio drama. Additionally, male and female narrators cater to users of different genders. Furthermore, audiobooks are extensively categorised by plot, romance, characters, genre, background, and label, making it easier for users to select the type of audiobook they want. According to Ximalaya's 2020 Peak List, the content categories have grown from 328 to 393 (Ximalaya Open Platform, n.d.).

Live Streaming

Ximalaya FM introduced a live broadcasting service in 2017. It earns a share of revenue from the live-streaming service by selling virtual gifts to users. The platform's live broadcasting user base has increased. In 2020, Ximalaya launched the Spring Life Plan to support live broadcasting, investing 1 billion in traffic while nurturing grassroots anchors. The audiobook channel gradually improves using the "live broadcasting + recording" development trend, referred to as the amphibious trend. "Amphibious" development enables Ximalayan audiobook anchors to expand their reach, making audio live broadcasts a unique "private domain" for audiobook anchors, enhancing fan loyalty, and opening new income streams.

The Ximalaya "2023 Live Annual Ceremony" competition results further illustrate this trend: 50% of the top ten anchors are "amphibious anchors". It is reported that Ximalaya has over 15,000 "amphibious" anchors who engage in live audio and audiobook recording and broadcasting. During the live broadcast, listeners can communicate with the anchor. Their rewards for their favourite anchor increase the anchor's source of income by enhancing user engagement. According to the data at the end of 2022, Ximalaya's live broadcast anchor start time increased by 185% year-on-year. By the third quarter of 2023, Ximalaya Interactive Entertainment's Business (live broadcast) monthly activity increased by 36.8% year-on-year (Ximalaya, n.d.).

Derivative Products

Ximalaya FM has expanded its channels from mobile devices to in-car, home smart speakers, and third-party platforms by building an IoT service platform. Through cooperation with more than 70 Chinese car manufacturers, Ximalaya provides in-car mobile audio services through pre-installed devices. In addition,

Ximalaya has also partnered with brands such as Xiaomi to develop smart speakers and other related devices.

Product Application Scenario

Audio content can be enjoyed in various situations, as described in the scenarios below:

Commuting: In busy commuting scenes, the younger generation finds it challenging to focus on visual content. Compared to video, audio offers a more convenient and user-friendly experience. People can listen to blogs or other audio content using headphones, providing entertainment or knowledge without impacting their commute, whether walking or riding.

Driving: It's essential to focus on the road when driving. It's advisable to listen to short audio content like podcasts and audiobooks. These formats allow drivers to stay engaged without getting distracted for extended periods, thus enhancing safety on the road.

Sports: When engaged in activities like running and other sports, visuals take a backseat while audio becomes vital. Since watching videos is not feasible during these pursuits, many people listen to audio content, which allows them to stay tuned in while exercising and helps relieve boredom.

Housework: Many individuals choose to multitask while doing household chores, with audiobooks or blogs playing in the background. Whether cooking, doing laundry, washing dishes, or mopping floors, listening to audio content can alleviate the monotony and boredom of housework.

Accompanying: With the growing concern about children's eyesight, the learning style is shifting towards listening to audio content. To preserve eyesight, many parents prefer to listen to picture books with their children rather than watching traditional animated content.

Customers

Ximalaya FM's user base primarily comprises urban, working-class individuals between 31 and 40. These users are predominantly male, with a higher education and income level. They have diverse interests spanning culture, history, science and technology, music, and more, and place a premium on quality and service.

The gender distribution of Ximalaya's user base leans slightly towards males, who make up around 55% of the total users. In comparison, females account for approximately 45%, per the "2020 Analysis of China's Audio Industry Ecological Development." Furthermore, Ximalaya's users are primarily concentrated in first- and second-tier cities. The "2020 China Online Audio Industry Research Report" by

Ai Rui Consulting reveals that about 55% of Ximalaya's users are from these urban areas. More specifically, 52.6% are from first-tier or new first-tier cities, 20.7% from second-tier cities, and 19.1% from third-tier cities. Regarding age demographics, users between 31 and 40 are the largest group, accounting for 58.7% of Ximalaya's user base. Meanwhile, younger users under 30 years old make up 32.4% (Ai Media Consulting, 2023). The occupational profile of Ximalaya's users is diverse, but they primarily consist of salaried professionals, including white-collar workers such as teachers and civil servants. These users have various interests, including literature, music, business, and history.

When it comes to the motivations behind using online audio services, a survey by AiMedia Consulting found that most users seek relaxation and entertainment (Ai Media Consulting, 2023). Other significant reasons include emotional relief, passing time, and alleviating loneliness. Ximalaya's content, both from the PUGC and UGC models, aligns with these user needs. The PUGC model content, produced by professional media personnel and field experts, offers listeners leisure, knowledge acquisition, and emotional relief. Likewise, the UGC model, which essentially involves content from ordinary users, provides a platform for these users to share their knowledge and experiences, providing listeners with a diverse range of content for entertainment and time-passing. Lastly, Ximalaya's live social product caters to users seeking social interaction and companionship, fulfilling their needs to alleviate loneliness and find empathy. This platform also provides an opportunity for the hosts to generate revenue.

Market Overview

Market Evolution Overview

The audio economy industry, which centers around sound, is an expansive field encompassing sound creation, dissemination, technology, and usage. This industry revolves around consumer behavior related to sound, with typical products including recorded audiobooks, personal audio IPs, and audio blogs.

Hardware Dissemination Era (1994-2000)

Audiobooks primarily characterized this era of the audio economy. The 1990s saw the introduction of audiobooks to China, with the content mainly composed of classic masterpieces. A significant milestone was reached in 1994 with the publication of the first independently recorded audiobooks, namely, the "Chinese Masterpieces Half Hour Series" and the "World Masterpieces Half Hour Series."

Website Dissemination Era (2000-2012)

The advent and growth of the internet and related technologies ushered in a new era for the audio economy. In 2003, China's first audiobook website, Hongda Ether Culture Development Co., Ltd., was established, offering users the convenience of online and offline audiobook consumption. This development revolutionized the channels through which audiobooks could reach customers and elevated the communication medium.

Mobile Dissemination Era (2012-Present)

The proliferation of mobile internet technology and the ubiquity of smartphone applications marked the next phase of the audio economy industry. This era saw the industry transcend website boundaries to offer mobile audio services. This includes specialized audiobook services, such as those provided by Oxygen Listening, and comprehensive audio services offered by apps like Ximalaya FM and Dragonfly FM. These developments indicate a gradual shift in the audio economy industry towards specialization, diversification, and high-quality production.

Market Environment Analysis

The increasing significance of audio applications in everyday life, driven by changing consumer behaviors, is also highlighted. This analysis aims to comprehensively understand the opportunities and challenges within China's audio economy.

The audio economy industry in China is experiencing a unique dynamic, characterized by the coexistence of strong state support and regulatory oversight. On February 24, 2021, the State Administration of Radio, Film, and Television (SARFT) released the Notice on the Release of Digital Copyright Management Standard System for Distribution of Audio and Visual Content (General Office of State Administration of Radio and Television, 2021). This aimed to standardize the construction and operation of digital copyright management systems. Furthermore, the report from the 19th National Congress of the Communist Party of China (CPC) underscored the importance of cultural construction in the new era of socialism with Chinese characteristics, signaling further support for the industry. Despite this backing, the industry also faces regulatory policies concerning copyright protection. This balance of support and regulation fosters a robust development environment for the audio economy industry.

Economic indicators also point to a favorable climate for the industry's growth. In 2023, the gross domestic product (GDP) reached 1.26 trillion yuan, a 5.2% increase from the previous year. Concurrently, the per capita disposable income rose by a nominal 6.3% to 39,218 yuan. Notably, expenditure on education, culture, and recreation increased by 17.6% to 2,904 yuan, accounting for 10.8% of per capita consumption (National Bureau of Statistics, n.d.). These trends suggest a promising outlook for the audio economy industry.

Furthermore, The role of audio-related applications in everyday life is becoming increasingly prominent. As education levels rise, so does the demand for knowledge. The recent pandemic has amplified this trend, necessitating widespread internet use for work and study. Finally, technological advancements, particularly in 5G, AI, and IoT, have significantly enhanced audio quality and expanded its application scenarios to include cars, smart speakers, and more. The evolution of digital multimedia technology, coupled with the rise of short videos, has facilitated the digitization of the audio economy industry. This progression is likely to stimulate further growth in the industry.

Market Size and Forecast

The data from Ai Media Consulting reveals a consistent upward trend in China's audio economy industry. In 2022, the sector achieved a market size of 381.66 billion yuan, while the knowledge payment market reached 112.65 billion yuan. This surge represents a remarkable 70-fold increase compared to the figures in 2015. Furthermore, projections suggest a potential escalation to 280.88 billion yuan in the market size by 2025 (Ai Media Consulting, 2023).

Despite the gradual normalization of the pandemic, the enthusiasm for online learning, augmented during the pandemic, continues unabated. This trend has fostered a habit of knowledge payment among users. According to predictions from Ai Media Consulting, the number of paid knowledge users is expected to surpass 570 million in 2023 and increase to 640 million by 2025, indicating a stable growth trend over the next few years (Ai Media Consulting, 2023).

DEVELOPMENT AND STRATEGY

This section will provide an overview of Ximalayan FM's evolution, challenges, and solutions before adopting the PUGC strategy.

Strategy Iteration Process

UGC Strategy

Ximalaya FM initially adopted the Ugc (ordinary user-generated content) model, a common strategy for content production in the initial stages of Internet platforms. UGC is characterized by original content from ordinary users and relies on pan-intellectual content produced by users based on their personal experiences. the UGC strategy broadened the platform's knowledge domain, enriched its content, and made vertical deepening of its content offerings possible. Meanwhile, since the creators are mainly ordinary users, the production cost is relatively low, which helps attract traffic and generate revenue.

Ximalaya's UGC producers come from diverse occupations, such as teachers, entrepreneurs, and white-collar workers, providing more than 70% of audio products for Ximalaya. The UGC strategy has laid a strong foundation for Ximalaya's user accumulation. The populist approach of the creators brings listeners closer to the anchors, promoting interaction and meeting their social needs.

The UGC strategy faces challenges. The lack of professional production capacity leads to low quality audio programs, making it difficult to meet consumer demand for high-quality products. Additionally, UGC has inherent shortcomings in terms of copyright protection, as producers have weak awareness of copyright leading to frequent infringements. Also, inappropriate advertising implementation affects the user's listening experience. Analysis shows that advertising implantation can last up to 6 minutes, significantly reducing the degree of listener goodwill (Sun, 2021).

PUGC Strategy

Ximalaya FM recognized the limitations of the UGC strategy and introduced the PUGC strategy. This approach combines the strengths of professionally generated content (PGC) and UGC. The PUGC model involves both professional media and self-publishing individuals, enhancing the professionalism of the content while maintaining diversity.

Under the PUGC strategy, Ximalaya's revenue sources are primarily divided into three categories: fan economy income, advertising income, and e-commerce income. Fan economy revenue is generated mainly through UGC programs that attract traffic, and the platform uses extensive data analysis to recommend paid programs that users may be interested in. This cultivates their listening habits and encourages them to join the VIP membership. Revenue from membership, paid programs, and live streaming constitute the major components of the fan economy.

Advertising revenue is another significant source of income. Ximalaya innovates the advertisement operation mode and places advertisements accurately using big data. The advertisements on Ximalaya are divided into three categories: display, audio, and soft implantation. Lastly, e-commerce revenue is derived from selling blog-related products like smart speakers and storytelling machines. As Ximalaya's scale expands and the ear economy scales up, e-commerce revenue has gradually formed Ximalaya's third-largest source of income.

Differentiation

Market Dominance

In the landscape of the audio economy, Ximalaya FM has established itself as a formidable leader, outperforming competitors in both market size and financial performance. The company reported impressive figures in 2021, with revenues reaching 5.856 billion yuan and net profit standing at 3.163 billion yuan. These statistics underscore Ximalaya FM's robust position in the market (Zhou, 2021).

Contrastingly, rival platforms like Lychee FM and Dragonfly FM trail behind. Lychee FM's financial performance in 2021 saw a net revenue of 2.12 billion yuan, a 41% increase year-on-year. Furthermore, the company attained a net profit of 8.92 million in the fourth quarter, marking its first-ever GAAP profit. Despite these strides, Lychee FM's financial figures remain dwarfed by those of Ximalaya FM (Ai Media Consulting, 2023).

The unique situation of Dragonfly FM is due to its lack of plans to go public, so there is no information available about its profitability. However, data from Ai Media Polaris shows that Dragonfly FM ranks third in terms of monthly active users. In the first quarter of the previous year, Dragonfly FM reported 22.64 million monthly users, which is about one-third of Ximalaya FM's user base for the same period (Ai Media Consulting, 2023). This demonstrates the dominant position of Ximalaya FM in the audio content market. Also, below are the comparative advantages of Ximalaya and other companies, as well as the reasons for these advantages.

Build Copyright Barriers to Get More Loyal Users

The popularity of an audio platform largely depends on the demand for exclusive content, the availability of exclusive copyrights, user traffic, and user engagement. Ximalaya has strategically positioned itself by securing exclusive cooperation with

Tencent's digital reading platform, Reading Group, to adapt literary works and other content for audio. This has allowed Ximalaya to obtain audio adaptation rights to various famous literary works, enhancing its traffic and user engagement. Additionally, Ximalaya has secured exclusive copyright partnerships with significant entities such as China Publishing, CITIC Publishing Group, and Shanghai Translation Publishing House. As a result, Ximalaya now owns the audio copyrights of 70% of the bestsellers in the market and the audio adaptation rights of 85% of online literature (Ximalaya Open Platform, n.d.). This places Ximalaya ahead of its competitors in terms of copyright ownership, such as Dragonfly FM and Lychee FM. As of 2021, Dragonfly FM has the rights to 20,000 audiobooks, while Ximalaya FM has the rights to 57,184 audiobooks that far outnumber Dragonfly FM (Zhong, 2022).

Leveraging the PUGC Gain Comparative Advantage

To maintain and expand its dominance in the audio economy industry, Ximalaya FM has embraced the PUGC model of content production. This strategy aims to balance breadth and depth in content creation, catering to users' diverse preferences and demands for quality content.

The traditional UGC (User-Generated Content) model offers a broad spectrum of content but often needs more depth. Conversely, the PUGC model enhances content depth considerably, aligning with users' expectations for high-quality content. Ximalaya FM, therefore, employs a combination of both UGC and PGC (Professionally Generated Content) models to remain competitive. The UGC model draws in traffic by offering a wide variety of content, while the PGC model focuses on creating premium audio content to retain users and enhance engagement.

In the audio economy industry, the quality of content is a critical factor in retaining users. Ximalaya FM leverages the skills of professional media creators who join through the PGC model and grassroots creators who bring their fan traffic. These contributors utilize their content creation skills and technical abilities to produce the audience's desired content, Ximalaya FM has gained a large number of loyal users.

Contrastingly, Lychee FM, another player in the audio economy industry, has shifted its focus away from this sector. Data shows that in the third quarter of 2021, Lychee FM's total revenue was 505 million yuan, but podcast advertisements and other revenues only accounted for 4.05 million yuan. Audio entertainment revenues made up 99.2% of the total revenue. This trend continued into the second quarter of 2022, with entertainment business revenues constituting over 99% (Ani Ni, 2020). Meanwhile, Lychee FM is mostly UGC content, with varying quality, making it harder to retain users. Dragonfly FM, like Ximalaya FM, uses the PUGC model but places more emphasis on PGC. this approach prioritizes content depth. However, Ximalaya FM's focus on UGC gives it a significant advantage in terms of the breadth and diversity of its content ecosystem, lowering content production costs and expanding user engagement and the diversity of content on the platform, giving it a comparative advantage.

Good User Experience and Retention

Compared to Dragonfly FM, Ximalaya FM's app design is more detailed and clear, which helps to help users find the products they need. For example, in the core business audiobook channel, the two companies present different app designs, as observed as of 14 March 2024

Ximalaya categorizes audiobooks not only based on topic and completion status, but also further breaks down audiobook content into multiple dimensions such as plot, romance, characters, style, and background. Additionally, it enhances the discoverability of content through a tagging system. On the other hand, Dragonfly FM only classifies audiobooks according to theme, completion status, and member privileges without detailed content classification. The detailed classification method adopted by Ximalaya FM not only improves the convenience for users in searching and selecting content, but also effectively enhances user engagement by meeting personalized and diversified content needs. For example, Ximalaya FM provides an app with easy navigation, rich content, and personalized recommendations, which has helped in retaining existing users and attracting new ones. This focus on user experience has contributed to Ximalaya's leading position in the audio economy industry.

Ximalaya Profit Model is More Diversified to Reduce Business Risks

Ximalaya FM has maintained its competitive edge in the market thanks to its diversified profit model. While platforms like Dragonfly FM focus mainly on audio content, Ximalaya FM has expanded its revenue sources through derivative products and live broadcasting services. This approach not only stabilizes earnings but also reduces operational risk. In comparison to competitors like Litchi FM, which has ventured into the entertainment industry, Ximalaya FM boasts a broader business scope and a more diversified profit model. It covers traditional audio services and extends into entertainment, automotive, and other fields, creating a comprehensive audio ecosystem. This comprehensive business layout has significantly boosted Ximalaya FM's market competitiveness and helped it maintain a leading position. Diversifying profit models also supports the sustainable development of Ximalaya FM and mitigates the risks associated with depending too heavily on a single business.

Risks and Solution

Increased Competition and Market Saturation in the Industry

The current competitive landscape of the audio economy industry shows a high degree of marketization and saturation. In addition to the traditional giants in the industry, many internet giants have also chosen to enter the audio economy industry. With the increase in the number of enterprises in the industry, Ximalaya FM is facing unprecedented competitive pressure. Internet giants such as Tencent, ByteDance, etc., not only have huge capital but also possess strong product innovation and technological innovation abilities. Therefore, in the face of this increasingly fierce market environment, Ximalaya FM must continue to innovate, constantly optimize its products and services, and strengthen its brand building in order to maintain its position as the industry leader.

Changes in User Demand for Audio Content

In the context of the increasing demand for high-quality audio content due to the upgrading of consumption habits, users are seeking not only information but also valuable knowledge. Consequently, it is essential for Ximalaya FM to consistently engage in in-depth content production, enhance the professionalism and innovation of content, and meet users' expectations for superior audio content. Additionally, the platform should focus on the technical quality of audio production by enhancing Ximalaya's creation center, providing guidance for audio production for aspiring producers, and monitoring the work of professionals to ensure quality and deliver an enhanced listening experience for users.

The Low User Payment Rate

Ximalaya FM is a prominent player in the domestic audio industry, but it is challenged by the low willingness of users to pay for content. CEO Yu Jianjun identified that the lack of habit in consuming audio content is the main reason for this issue. He mentioned that for online audio users, free content is the norm, with paid content only forming a small portion of the platform's offerings. According to the prospectus, Ximalaya's average monthly active paying users for 2021, 2022, and 2023 were approximately 14.9 million, 15.7 million, and 15.8 million respectively. However, the growth in monthly active paying users slowed significantly in 2023. Additionally, the payment rate for Ximalaya mobile's average monthly active paying users was 12.9%, 12.9%, and 11.9% from 2021 to 2023, showing a slight decrease in 2023. The revenue from paid programs is crucial for Ximalaya, so it is essential for the platform to diversify its business models and enhance the quality of content to motivate users to pay, ensuring the sustainability of its business model.

THE PEOPLE BEHIND XIMALAYA FM

Jianjun Yu: Founder of Ximalaya

Yu Jianjun, the founder of Ximalaya, is a prominent figure in the audio economy industry. His entrepreneurial journey began in 2001 when he and a group of friends established the Shanghai Jetto Software Company. Their collective expertise led to the creating of products that garnered acclaim from users both domestically and internationally. However, after four successful years, Yu embarked on a new venture. In 2012, Yu turned his attention to the burgeoning mobile audio sector. He invested considerable time and effort in research, culminating in the Ximalaya software launch. The platform quickly gained traction among users, marking a significant milestone in Yu's career.

Yu has often emphasized the role of technology in self-improvement, stating, "Empowerment by technology, to become a better you." He believes that a company's core values should reflect not only the aspirations of its founders but also the desires of its users, employees, and other stakeholders. This philosophy has guided Ximalaya in prioritizing customer needs. As of March 2024, Yu has been actively working on expanding Ximalaya's copyright portfolio. He visited the Qingdao Publishing Group to foster a deeper partnership between the two entities.

Looking to the future, Ximalaya FM, under Yu's leadership, has produced a vast array of high-quality audio content, securing its position as a leader in the sound economy industry. However, the market landscape constantly evolves, with several digital platforms introducing podcast zones and making inroads into the audiobook market. This shift has seen many prominent podcast anchors, such as those from Dragonfly FM, gradually exit the market, with many podcast authors transitioning to short video platforms. Despite these changes, Yu remains committed to steering Ximalaya FM toward continued success.

REFERENCES

An, W. (n.d.). *[Annual GDP growth of 5.2% year-on-year in 2023]*. CN Gov. https://www.gov.cn/yaowen/liebiao/202401/content_6926714.html

Chun, D. (2016, October 20). *[Ximalaya FM business model: Creating a multi-dimensional "ear economy" with "UGC+PGC+Social Scene]*.http://www.jiamengpinglun.com/34996

Consulting, A. M. (2023). *[China Sound Economy Digital Application Development Trend Report 2022]*. iiMedia. https://www.iimedia.cn/c400/91728.html

Consulting, A. M. (2023). *[Chinese Knowledge Payment Industry Status and Development Outlook Report 2023]*. iiMedia. https://www.iimedia.cn/c400/92443.html

Finance, W. H. (2021, September 15). [Behind Ximalaya's return to Hong Kong, the "merits" and "demerits" of 12.46 million UGC creators]. 36KR. https://www.36kr.com/p/1398444289997575

General Office of State Administration of Radio and Television. (2021). *[Notice of the General Office of the State Administration of Radio, Film and Television on releasing the digital copyright management standard system for distributing audio and video content]*. General Office of State Administration of Radio and Television. https://www.gov.cn/zhengce/zhengceku/2021-02-24/content_5588584.htm

Hang, H. C. (n.d.). *[Industry Research Databases]*. Hang Cha. https://www.hanghangcha.com/pdf.html

Hua Jing Intelligence Network. (n.d.). *[An immense talent demand gap and voice training emerge in the analysis of the development status and trends of China's sound economy industry in 2022]*. Huaon. https://www.huaon.com/channel/trend/878350.html

Luo, X. Y., & Wang, N. N..(2024). *[Research on the development strategy of audio publishing platform based on user experience -- taking Ximalaya FM as an example. Digital publishing research]*. Digital publishing research (01),16-24.

Luohuan. (2021). *[Ximalaya FM platform operation strategy research"(Dissertation, Zhongnan University of Economics and Law)*. CNKI. https://link.cnki.net/doi/10.27660/d.cnki.gzczu.2021.000824doi:10.27660/d.cnki.gzczu.2021.000824

Luyun. (2020). [Revenue recognition and measurement analysis of knowledge payment platform: A case study of Ximalaya FM]. *Business accounting*, (21), 52-56.

National Bureau of Statistics. (n.d.-a). *[The situation of residents' income and consumption expenditure in 2023]*. NBS. https://www.stats.gov.cn/sj/zxfb/202401/t20240116_1946622.html DOI:10.14097/j.cnki.5392/2018.20.043

Ni, A. (2020, July 10). *[Ximalaya, why is it leading the online audio market?]*. WoshipM. https://www.woshipm.com/evaluating/4077639.html/comment-page-1

Operations, L. (2023, May 17). *[Product Analysis | Ximalaya FM - The King Who Deserves the Name]*. iYunYing. https://www.iyunying.org/pm/257572.html

Platform, X. O. (n.d.). *[Join the Ximalaya open platform and connect the world with voice!]*. Ximalaya. https://open.ximalaya.com/doc/detailQuickStart?categoryId=21&articleId=43# Zhang

Pro, I. (2022, March 30). *[Sound economy is challenging to make money: Ximalaya's three breakthroughs in the Hong Kong Stock Exchange with a loss of 5.1 billion yuan a year]*. 36KR. https://36kr.com/p/1677147148428549

TMTPost. (n.d.). *[After the wind, can the three audio giants still fight? Litchi, Dragonfly and Ximalaya status analysis]*. TMT Post. https://www.tmtpost.com/6256669.html

Wang, J., Wang, Y., & Jin, Y. (2021). *Marketing and Future of Mobile Audio Apps - case study of the Ximalaya FM*.

Wang, S. (2022). *The Current Situation, Dilemma and Way Out of the Auditory Transmission of Online Novels—The Example of Ximalaya FM*.

Wangyi. (2024, April 28). *[Subscription services prop up half of the revenue, Ximalaya paying users pay lower rates]*. Wangyi. https://www.163.com/dy/article/J0T9D11Q0553YQCC.html

Wen, H. (2022). *[Research on the business model of knowledge payment platform under the background of Internet]*. CNKI. https://link.cnki.net/doi/10.26962/d.cnki.gbjwu.2022.001066doi:10.26962/d.cnki.gbjwu.2022.001066

Ximalaya Marketing Model Problems and Countermeasures Research. (2023a, May 20). *[Ximalaya marketing model problems and countermeasures research]*. Ximalaya Marketing Model Problems and Countermeasures Research. https://www.sbvv.cn/chachong/142302.html

Zhong, J. (2022). *[Ximalayan business model, implications for the rise of the online audio industry]*. China Daily website. https://caijing.chinadaily.com.cn/a/202204/14/WS6257d741a3101c3ee7ad07ab.html

Zhou, E. (2021). *[The research report on the operation strategy of the Ximalaya FM audiobook channel]*. Nanjing University. https://link.cnki.net/doi/10.27235/d .cnki.gnjiu.2021.000550

KEY TERMS AND DEFINITIONS

Core Competitiveness: It refers to the unique resources and strategies that give a business a competitive edge over others. This includes the way resources are allocated and integrated within the company.

Fan Economy: This term describes the monetizing practices built upon the relationship between fans (followers) and the entities they support, such as celebrities or brands.

PGC (Professionally Generated Content): This pertains to professionally produced content, typically characterized by in-depth discussions and a focus on specific subject matter.

Product Usage Scenarios: These are specific situations in which a product is used, often defined by factors such as the user's environment, geographical location, time, physical posture, age, and other relevant characteristics.

PUGC (Professional and User-Generated Content): This is a blend of PGC and UGC, where content creators on a platform include both professional media personnel and independent media creators. This amalgamation allows for a more comprehensive and in-depth exploration of content.

UGC (User-Generated Content): It refers to content created and shared by users via an online platform, often made available to other users.

User Stickiness: It refers to the degree of a user's loyalty, trust, and positive experiences with a brand or product, which often influences their repeat usage.

Chapter 21
Mafengwo:
From Travel Community to Global Tourism Powerhouse

Zhuoxi Jiang

Beijing Normal University-Hong Kong Baptist University United International College, China

EXECUTIVE SUMMARY

This case study explores the transformative journey of Mafengwo, a leading travel platform in China, from 2015 to the present. It examines Mafengwo's strategic shift from a community-based model to a comprehensive travel service platform, focusing on its commercialization efforts and expansion into transaction-based revenue streams. The narrative highlights the visionary leadership of co-founders Chen Gang and Lv Gang, who leveraged extensive data research and strategic foresight to position Mafengwo as a global travel consumer guide. The case delves into the company's innovative use of the Youyun SaaS system to enhance productivity and flexibility for travel agencies and its efforts to capitalize on the "new golden decade of freedom" in tourism. It outlines Mafengwo's launch of "new tourism methods" and its comprehensive community upgrade to meet personalized travel demands. The case concludes with an overview of Mafengwo's plans to integrate AI travel tools, underscoring the company's commitment to leveraging big data for personalized scaling in the tourism industry.

UNICORN DESCRIPTION

In January 2006, the Mafengwo website was officially launched (Mafengwo, 2024). At that time, Mafengwo was just a platform for travel enthusiasts to share travel notes and strategies and engage in Q&A without any commercial nature. In

DOI: 10.4018/979-8-3693-2921-4.ch021

March 2010, Mafengwo officially began operating as a company (Mafengwo, 2024). Furthermore, it is a free travel transaction and service platform based on personalized travel strategy information. It involves user-shared User Generated Content (UGC) such as guides, travelogues, Q&A, and domestic and foreign destination reviews. It also provides travel products such as hotels and transportation.

Business Model

Mafengwo's business model can be briefly described as a "content + transaction" model, big data engine, and tourism industry Internet built earlier than other companies in the tourism industry.

The business model of Mafengwo is different from that of traditional online travel agencies and online ticketing service companies. Mafengwo's unique "content + transaction" model not only helps users bridge information inequality, solve travel problems, and make informed consumption choices but also shares significant traffic with partners through the "content entrance" of the guide. This helps tourism enterprises obtain accurate traffic and orders while saving on high marketing costs and jointly provides consumers with the most cost-effective travel products. Ultimately, it achieves the goals of users, partner enterprises, and the Mafengwo platform, creating a win-win situation for all three parties.

Mafengwo is a representative mobile internet company that has evolved from the IT to the DT (Data Technology) era. Mafengwo's big data engine assists in efficiently matching users, information, and products. Accurate user-profiles and personalized recommendations for thousands of people and faces enable every consumer with different needs to find suitable travel information and products quickly. Based on the product gene (social network service) of Mafengwo Social Network Service (SNS), it has established its own user data research center to analyze and organize registered user data. It regularly publishes user behavior, free travel, and outbound tourism data reports and systematically analyses the behavior preferences of free travel users on PC and mobile devices. Based on these data, Mafengwo collaborates with global suppliers to carry out user reverse customization and sales, also known as the Customer to Business (C2B) model, of free travel products and collaborates with suppliers to optimize and reconstruct free travel products.

Meanwhile, Mafengwo has started to apply AI to its business model. AI-powered personalization is unique because it combines sophisticated algorithms, contextual understanding, real-time adaptation, cross-platform integration, content-based recommendations, and continuous learning to deliver highly personalized and relevant travel experiences for its users.

Product and Services

In addition to the products or services described below, Mafengwo will apply updated technologies to these services and products in 2024—for example, AI technology. Mafengwo's extraordinary combination of user-generated content, AI-powered personalization, comprehensive travel services, trendy appeal, and innovative initiatives position it as a leader in the travel industry, catering to the needs and preferences of modern travelers in China and beyond.

Travel Guides

This is the most essential service that Mafengwo provides. The primary purpose for most users using Mafengwo is to prepare for travel and seek travel experiences and guides from other travelers. The Mafengwo homepage divides tourism types into three main categories: local tours, free trips, and group tours. By using the search box on the homepage, travelers can quickly find the destinations they are interested in. The Mafengwo platform covers over 60,000 tourist destinations worldwide for independent travelers, including most destinations globally (China Digital Marketing Agency in Hong Kong, n.d.). A wide range of travel destinations and comprehensive travel guides can greatly assist travelers in planning their itineraries. These guides are written mainly by experienced travelers, making them more authentic and better able to understand the actual needs of each traveler, thereby assisting each traveler more effectively.

The well-organized travel guides allow users to obtain the information they need quickly. Furthermore, the guides include many high-quality photos and are rich in content. They can help users break through information barriers, resolve travel issues, and make better consumption choices. However, some guides' creators are travel agents or enterprise merchants, not real travelers. They promote themselves heavily and can mislead guests, presenting a reality that may differ from actual experiences, leading to potential disappointment. Some travel bloggers receive advertising fees from merchants; therefore, the actual situations at attractions, hotels, and restaurants may need to align with what the bloggers advertise, potentially causing users to fall into pitfalls.

Hotel-Booking

Like other OTA platforms, Mafengwo also provides hotel booking services to users. Mafengwo has an independent hotel booking platform that supports price comparison across the entire network, with relatively complete functions. Users can enter information such as destination, check-in date, check-out date, and room requirements on the Mafengwo booking service platform. The system will filter out suitable hotel options based on the user's needs. Users can compare the selected hotels through the functions provided by the platform. These comparisons include price, location, rating, etc., to help users make the best choice. In addition, Mafengwo's hotel booking service can also help hotel merchants make profits. By sharing users' needs with cooperating tourism enterprises through big data, Mafengwo can help these cooperating tourism enterprises obtain accurate demands and orders, saving high marketing costs. Furthermore, travelers can be provided with the most cost-effective travel products.

Customized Travel Services

Mafengwo can provide personalized travel services to users. Users only need to fill in the number of travelers, budget, and choose the services they need, including route design, hotel and restaurant reservations, food recommendations, charter services, and tickets, leave their contact information, and finally have a specialist contact them. Whether you are travelling alone, with friends, with family, on a honeymoon, on a graduation trip, or for company team building, Mafengwo will customize suitable travel plans according to the customers' needs. The needs of every tourist are diverse, and personalized travel services are beneficial for every traveler to have a suitable travel experience. This is a unique service as most online travel agencies (OTAs) do not provide it.

Customers

The customers of Mafengwo are undoubtedly travel enthusiasts. According to the data from the Baidu Index over the past year, most of Mafengwo's users come from Guangdong, Beijing, and Shanghai. In terms of age, users under the age of 19 account for about 2.7%, users aged 20-29 account for about 32.43%, users aged 30-39 account for about 35.14%, users aged 40-49 account for about 13.51%, and users aged 50 and above account for about 16.22% (Baidu Index, n.d.). These data demonstrate that Mafengwo's customers mainly come from first-tier big cities with a strong acceptance of information and good economic conditions. Furthermore, with the rise of the economy in China's second and third-tier cities, Mafengwo will also have great potential in these areas.

The customers of Mafengwo can be divided into two groups:

Travelers Who Want to Travel and Need to Plan Their Travels – Travelers with the time and desire to travel may become interested in a specific destination by browsing the travel guides shared by other netizens on Mafengwo's homepage. Additionally, travelers with travel plans can easily plan their destinations by browsing the guide travelogues shared on Mafengwo's website. After determining the travel destination, they can plan their route, hotels, cuisine, scenic spot tickets, and transportation using the travel guides shared by other netizens on Mafengwo's homepage.

Travelers With Itinerary Sharing Needs – Mafengwo's itinerary-sharing function can meet the needs of travelers willing to share their itinerary. On the homepage of their account, every tourist can record their itinerary during their trip and share their travel notes after the journey ends. Tourists with a strong need for sharing can share food, drink, play guides, beautiful photos taken during their itinerary, and their own itinerary and life. It demonstrates one's attitude towards life and helps other tourists who need travel guides. These tourists can achieve self-worth and satisfaction during the sharing process.

Market Analysis

Original Situation of the Market

In 2010, Mafengwo was established as a company. China's tourism industry has recovered significantly and maintained rapid growth throughout the year. According to the 2010 China Tourism Industry Statistics Bulletin released by the National Tourism Administration of China in 2012, China received approximately 130 million inbound tourists and achieved international tourism (foreign exchange) revenue of approximately 45.8 billion US dollars. This marked an increase of about 6% and about 16%, respectively, compared to the previous year. The number of domestic tourists was about 2.1 billion, with a revenue of about 1258 billion yuan, marking an increase of about 11% and about 24%, respectively, compared to the previous year. The number of Chinese citizens leaving the country reached about 57.39 million, marking an increase of about 20% compared to last year. The total revenue of the tourism industry was about 2 trillion yuan, marking an increase of about 22% compared to last year. As people's demand for tourism continues to increase, the demand for OTAs such as Mafengwo is growing synchronously.

Furthermore, the free market dominated by Mafengwo is also flourishing. According to Mafengwo's 2022 travel data report, among travel consumers, 89% of users prefer "peripheral travel", 79% prefer "self-driving travel", 77% enjoy experiencing "light outdoor", and 38% choose "summer escape" self-driving travel (The Economic Observer, 2023). The tourism industry can continue to develop, while Mafengwo-led free travel will also flourish. As a tourism platform in China with a strong voice in freedom of movement, Mafengwo will help more and more tourists, and its market will continue to develop better and better.

Evolution of the Market Until Today

Major travel platforms have shifted their focus to smaller, more granular travel products and personalized experiences. The transformation of the demand for tourism in Generation Z is evident in the fact that they no longer visit traditional tourist attractions as before, and more and more young people's approach to travel has changed from merely visiting places to experiencing them. Since 2021, as the demand for tourism in Generation Z continues to evolve, tourism platforms have been encouraged to remain sensitive and innovative in providing enjoyable travel experiences.

This shift in consumer demand signifies a transformation in the tourism industry market. For example, the change in tourism consumption concepts has led to a significant shift in how young people perceive accommodations, leading to the rapid development of the homestay economy. Nowadays, accommodations are no longer just a place to stay; they are seen as an integral part of the travel experience, with higher expectations. Homestays, offering facilities and services comparable to traditional hotels and unique styles that traditional hotels lack, are increasingly attracting young people. In 2022, the trend of quality-oriented consumption of homestays among young people has become more evident, with a 9.1% increase in the proportion of homestays priced between 1000 yuan and 2000 yuan and a 4.6% increase in the proportion of homestays priced over 2000 yuan (Mafengwo, 2018). This indicates they are willing to pay for the high-quality facilities and services, personalized design, and unique experiences homestays provide. The demand for tourism in Generation Z is constantly evolving, and the diverse range of travel options available on the Mafengwo platform can provide valuable reference points for young people.

Competition Analysis and Comparison With Other OTA Platforms

In this case, Ctrip is an example of another OTA platform. As a representative OTA platform, Ctrip is located in the first tier of the online tourism industry, with a leading market share and can be selected as a benchmark for comparing other travel products. Ctrip earns commission profits through transactions and by providing high-quality services. Therefore, the corresponding product prices will also be higher, targeting business travelers and high consumption groups, generally those with stable incomes. Ctrip Travel's service offers hotel booking, flight booking, tourism vacation, business travel management, and tourism consulting. The advantages of Ctrip Travel lie in its large business scale, leading technology, and standardized system. At the beginning of its operation, Ctrip Travel invested a lot in advertisements to attract customers. After years of continuous operation, Ctrip relies on excellent services to retain users, and users gradually trust Ctrip.

On the other hand, Mafengwo is a platform characterized by "content+transaction", providing users with rich travel products through search engines and big data to meet their personalized needs. The UGC database has also brought many sticky users to the platform. Mafengwo Travel's service offers a travel guide, free travel, a self-service travel guide, and a social sharing platform for travel. As free travel gradually becomes the mainstream mode of travel, although these two OTAs have slightly different positioning, there is a significant overlap in user group characteristics and a clear competitive trend in the free travel market. The advantages of Mafengwo Tourism lie in the accumulation of years of tourism big data and high user stickiness. Some users have been sharing their travel guides, exciting stories, and photos on Mafengwo, gradually accumulating a certain number of fans or travelers with common interests, becoming increasingly inseparable from the Mafengwo platform.

Regarding recommending popular routes, both Ctrip and Mafengwo offer popular routes in the itinerary section. They indicate the number of travel days and attractions, as well as the popularity of the route. Ctrip uses the number of people, while Mafengwo uses percentages to help users make quick decisions. Ctrip also has a filtering function, allowing users to quickly match routes that meet their own needs, including destinations and themes, to improve the user experience and meet the efficiency requirements of Ctrip's business travel users. In terms of formulating and modifying routes, after entering the route details page, Ctrip supports adding routes to the itinerary and modifying them, including editing the order of tourist attractions and hotels, adding food, and meeting the diverse needs of users to enhance the user experience. However, Mafengwo only supports collecting routes, which could be more conducive to users planning routes. Both platforms provide map mode, allowing users to have a more intuitive understanding of the location and route of scenic spots.

Forecast for This Market

Since 2023, with the gradual improvement of the epidemic, Chinese tourists have been gradually returning to the tourism market, and the Chinese tourism industry has been steadily improving. During the three years of the epidemic, the product supply, user travel preferences, travel booking behavior, and tourism market environment in the travel industry has significantly changed.

In the first quarter of 2023, the revenue of China's domestic tourism industry reached 1.3 trillion yuan, representing a year-on-year increase of 69.5%, indicating a solid recovery momentum (The Paper, 2023). In the same period, the number of domestic tourists reached 12.16 million, marking a year-on-year increase of 46.5%

and has recovered to 81.8% in the same period in 2019 (The Paper, 2023). The number of people travelling during the Spring Festival and Qingming Festival in 2023 increased by 308 million and 93 million, respectively, showing a significant year-on-year increase (The Paper, 2023). The demand for holiday travel among residents continues to be released.

In March 2023, 74.9% of users obtained travel information through short videos, and approximately 63% of users obtained travel information through online travel platforms (The Paper, 2023). These data indicate significant changes in how users obtain tourism information, with short videos becoming the most crucial entry point for tourism information acquisition. In the same month, 95.3% of users chose to book online travel tickets and hotels, 84.9% decided to book tickets and hotels on direct sales platforms, and 6.9% chose to book tickets and hotels on short video platforms (The Paper, 2023). OTA and direct sales platforms are still the primary channels for users to make travel reservations, but short video platforms are beginning to emerge for travel reservations. In March 2023, the number of users who made travel bookings through short video platforms increased by 229.9% year-on-year, and short video platform travel bookings are quietly squeezing the market of OTA platforms (The Paper, 2023). It can be seen that OTA is easily replaced if it does not create products and services that are difficult for competitors in the market to imitate.

Development and Strategy

Traveler's Content Community: From 2006 to 2012

In 2006, Mr. Gang Chen and Mr. Gang Lv (co-founders) set their sights on the still chaotic online travel market and spent RMB 2,000 on the launch of the Hornet's Nest forum. For the past six years, it has been positioned as "China's largest travel agency area" (Mafengwo, 2024). During this time, Mafengwo's most important function was to write travelogues.

The company was officially founded in 2010 (Mafengwo, 2024). At the beginning of its commercialization, it relied solely on advertisements to make money, with advertising revenue accounting for the bulk of its profit model. At that time, the major players in the travel industry were still focused on another battlefield, and Ctrip had few rivals in China's online travel industry. Online travel's primary focus was booking air tickets and hotels, which were standard categories, and the users were mainly business travelers.

Leisure and vacation-oriented tourism was still a luxury for Chinese people, and the public's perception of "tourism" was limited to following a tour group to famous mountains and rivers and taking pictures in front of old cities and temples. The market for independent travel, as opposed to group tours, was still in its infancy, and a few travelers with considerable economic means and knowledge had begun to try buying a ticket to an unfamiliar place to explore unknown customs and geographic features. These people, who were the first to start travelling independently, needed a platform to exchange information and collect memories.

Mafengwo became their earliest platform for sharing travel information. Through years of fine-tuning its operation, Mafengwo has accumulated a core user base of independent travelers and a large number of authentic travelogues, guides, Q&A, reviews, and other content produced by them. These contents have become the primary asset in the hands of Mafengwo. The community primarily produces user-generated content and remains an essential resource for Mafengwo.

From Content Company to Data Company: From 2012 to 2014

Mr. Lv Gang, co-founder and COO of Mafengwo, stated that before 2012, Mafengwo had been focused on building a community where everyone could write travelogues. Since travelogues played a crucial role in decision-making, effectively acquiring and sharing users' travel experiences was seen as the key to success. As a result, Mafengwo was fully committed to making users appreciate the beauty of writing and experience the joy of creating travelogues. The company was determined to achieve this without even considering how to make money for a second (Phoenix News, 2017).

The year 2012 marked a turning point for Mafengwo. Capitalizing on the mobile Internet boom, after years of accumulation and maturation, Mafengwo experienced its first major transformation. In 2012, with more than 4 million registered users, Mafengwo announced its transition from a community-based operation to a data-driven company. This marked Mafengwo's first self-evolution. After accumulating a vast amount of content, rather than rushing to monetize it, Mafengwo dedicated more resources and energy to leverage big data in structuring the extensive content on the platform and enhancing the efficiency of accessing and utilizing this content. Although this meticulous work received less attention than some trendy concepts, it was pivotal.

Externally, there were no overt changes during this phase of Mafengwo. The name, logo, and core community content remained the same. However, the internal transformation was radical. Through extensive data analysis, Mafengwo identified its young user group. Through semantic analysis of content and data mining, Mafengwo organized travel information, making travelogues and guides more accessible and easier to find. These changes led to a more open approach, friendlier to new users and more accommodating to inexperienced travelers (Phoenix News, 2017).

Another critical task for Mafengwo in these three years is to lay out the mobile terminal in advance. The rapid development of the mobile Internet has rapidly shifted the online travel market traffic from one web page on the PC side to the apps on cell phones. The island effect of apps has provided fertile ground for Mafengwo to enter the transaction field. In the era of webpages, users can quickly jump away from one website and go to other websites to make transactions. However, each app has become an island and a massive transaction obstacle in the app era. Users are more inclined to solve problems with the same app.

Mr. Lv Gang said in an interview that from 2012 to 2014, Mafengwo began to digitize and structure content, and 60% of Mafengwo's positions were related to technology. Every user always wants to summarize the essence of other people's travel notes to complete more efficient travel. They have to look through many travel notes, but they need help to make a clear summary. At this time, we need to help them do something. We have structured the entire content and generated many scenic spots, restaurants, hotels, etc. These data are straightforward and are only one step away from consumption (Phoenix News, 2017).

Positioning The Freelance Travel Trade Market: From 2015 to 2017

In 2015, Mafengwo reached a turning point with a significant increase in the user scale. This prompted the company to embark on commercialization exploration, leading it toward becoming a unicorn. During this time, Mafengwo rebranded from a "community" to a "platform". It also ventured into transactions, aiming to generate more revenue through increased transactions. Mafengwo introduced the concept of a "free travel service platform", signifying its ambition to establish itself as a universal and international brand.

From 2018 to now, Mafengwo has shifted its focus towards becoming a global travel consumer guide. This move signifies a transition from a content community to a stage where it influences consumer decision-making. The customer base has expanded to include community users who share travel experiences and seek tips and travelers who plan itineraries, make travel-related decisions, and book products.

Chen Gang, co-founder and CEO of Mafengwo, considers this brand shift a milestone in transforming China's traditional and modern tourism industry. On the demand side, there is a noticeable shift towards decentralized and diversified travel preferences, with a preference for personalized and non-standard travel products. Simultaneously, travel product suppliers have begun adapting to these changes on the supply side. Mafengwo aims to provide travelers with smaller, more tailored travel products to meet their evolving needs.

Mafengwo accurately predicted the rise of the free-travel market and strategically positioned itself in this market by entering the transaction field. These shifts solidified the "content + transaction" pattern for Mafengwo. In 2017, Mafengwo's total Gross Merchandise Volume (GMV) reached $10 billion, with advertising revenue accounting for only $250 million, solidifying travel product transactions as the primary source of revenue growth.

THE PEOPLE BEHIND THE UNICORN

Chen Gang

Mr. Chen is the CEO and co-founder of Mafengwo. He is from Yunnan Province, Guizhou City. He graduated from Chengdu University of Information Technology with a major in Communication Engineering. He entered the Internet industry in 2001 and served in Sohu and Sina for nine years, starting in 2002 (Maigoo Travel Website, n.d.). In 2010, he left Sina and established Mafengwo with his friend Lv Gang (Maigoo Travel Website, n.d.). While at Sohu, Chen Gang was primarily responsible for ample data research, which became pivotal to Mafengwo's later data operations. He applied his experience in Sohu's extensive data operations and analysis and his understanding of Weibo's core technologies to the creation of Mafengwo. Additionally, Mr. Chen's foresight and strategic thinking played crucial roles in the development of Mafengwo. While most tourism companies used travel guides as tools, Mr. Chen transformed travel guides into data, believing that the efficiency of using guide content is far less than that of using data and that using data can improve the quality of guide content.

Simultaneously, Mr. Chen Gang has been dedicated to developing the tourism industry in his hometown. As a leading domestic tourism enterprise and a popular travel app for the younger generation in China, Mafengwo possesses a substantial user base and high-quality supply chain resources. Using these advantages effectively to promote the development of tourism industrialization in his hometown has always been a priority for Mr. Chen Gang.

In 2022, Mafengwo established its domestic headquarters in Guiyang (Lai, 2023). This year, Mafengwo also conducted a joint training course with the Guizhou Provincial Department of Culture and Tourism to enhance the province's tourism promotion and publicity capabilities. This included multiple rounds of training for more than 100 cadres of the cultural and tourism bureau, marketing managers of over 300 scenic spots, and managers of vacation hotels and travel agencies in the province, focusing on creating popular tourist attractions, comprehensive online marketing, constructing online tourism assets, designing innovative gameplay, and creating short videos (Lai, 2023). In July of the same year, in collaboration with dozens of local managers, Mafengwo launched the trendy activity brand "Please board on weekends" in Guizhou and made its debut in Guiyang, providing local young people with a "new gameplay" space comparable to that of first-tier cities.

Lv Gang

Mr. Lv is the COO and co-founder of Mafengwo. Like Mr. Chen Gang, he is a former employee of Sina. His extensive experience in SNS data integration and commercial operations, gained during his tenure at Sina, has enabled him and his colleagues to develop an online tourism business system based on a free travel service platform for Mafengwo. This system brings precise users and orders to the tourism industry partners. Since 2013, he has accurately predicted and overseen the commercialization of free travel, traffic, advertising, and other businesses centered around hotels, resulting in many orders.

FUTURE PROJECTS

Leveraging the Youyun SaaS System

The Youyun SaaS system, independently innovated by Mafengwo, covers various functions from supply chain to content creation, product design, itinerary management, sales customer service, order management, financial management, etc. The data of each link is precipitated and circulated in the system. With just one system, travel agencies can achieve all operations of "product design - order generation - group order arrangement - contract signing - fund receipt and payment." It can also provide one-stop supervision of travel agency landing services, flexible employment during off-peak seasons, and supply chain financial support, among many other services. Zhao Qing, Product Director of Mafengwo's "Youyun" platform, said, "Since its inception, the Youyun system has been aimed at building a new tourism ecosystem. Within the ecosystem, Mafengwo is more like a "hematopoietic center", relying on its own "content + transaction" advantages and digital capabilities to export customers and industrial resources to partners continuously."

The Youyun SaaS system has been applied to some travel agencies and received well. The person in charge of a travel agency said at the exhibition site that in the process of using the "Youyun SaaS system", the most prominent feeling is that it dramatically liberates productivity - "Almost all the work can be done through the 'Youyun SaaS system', which makes our office and labor more flexible, without having to be confined to this side of the office; human efficiency has also made a qualitative leap. The 'Youyun SaaS system' complete, which makes our office and labor more flexible, do not have to be confined to the office of this side of the world; human efficiency has also made a qualitative leap, and we have the same workforce can undertake the original two to three times the amount of business, the staff are more motivated, the company has the possibility of being bigger and stronger." The Youyun SaaS system will be applied to more travel products and help more partners.

Seize the Opportunity of the "Golden Decade of New Free Travel"

On the 8th of 2023, at the Earth Discoverer Conference, the founder and CEO of Mafengwo publicly announced that China is about to usher in a "new golden decade of freedom". During this period, the consumption of young people in tourism has exploded, and the strong demand for tourism has forced the reform and upgrading of tourism supply, creating a new period of opportunity for the tourism industry. Mafengwo will seize this opportunity to complete a comprehensive iteration.

Mafengwo's team spent over two years figuring out "What is the personalized tourism demand in the eyes of young people?" During this period, they not only conducted research on a large number of young users but also held multiple offline activities. Through continuous observation, speculation, and a research summary, they finally refined a new gameplay formula: Personalized needs = Segmented Audience x Destination x Interests and Gameplay x Experience of Massive Tourists.

Launch 'New Tourism Methods' and Updated Communities

At the 2023 Earth Discoverer Conference on December 8th, Chen Gang, the founder and CEO of Mafengwo, stated that the 'new tourism method' content has been extracted explicitly from core content such as the North Star strategy and strategy group. Each destination has a strategy expert from Mafengwo to organize a detailed 'new tourism method' map, updated in real-time according to trends. More importantly, Mafengwo has matched the services and products for the tourism method map through a brand-new supply chain, forming a one-stop travel service loop that integrates planning and booking, helping consumers achieve the ultimate experience.

The Mafengwo community is also undergoing a comprehensive upgrade around the "new tourism method". In response to the renewed demand for personalized tourism, the best response formula is to provide different communication platforms for the new tourism method for different segmented groups. For example, for the Z generation 'new youth' who look forward to socializing and advocating freedom, Mafengwo introduces many new urban weekend gameplay and provides opportunities to find travel partners. For "new middle-class families" who prefer light luxury tourism and focus on emotional value, a series of segmented vertical new tourism methods, including long-distance travel and parent-child travel, are provided. For experienced travelers who value profound experiences and cultural values, Mafengwo continues to deepen its exploration of outbound travel content, design various novel overseas experience routes, and launch activities to send them back to a new world. The 'new tourism method' community ecosystem created based on different groups and circles will better meet personalized travel needs.

"New tourism method" has also become a favorable lever for marketing. Mafengwo's marketing aims to help destinations and brands find the right people, produce the right content and then spread it to more people. The community and this year's upgraded strategy group are the first steps for Mafengwo in finding precise marketing audiences. The so-called 'right content' refers to the ultimate exploration and even creation of destination experiences driven by the 'new tourism method' and the creation of new themed products, triggering IP linkage, allowing users to see, buy, feel, and then spread to more suitable people.

Mafengwo Soon to Launch AI Travel Tools

At the 2023 Earth Discoverer Conference on December 8th, Chen Gang, the founder and CEO of Mafengwo, disclosed the development progress of the Mafengwo AI project in detail for the first time. He stated that the company has deeply cooperated with General Motors' leading large model enterprises, and the related achievements will be released in 2024 (The Paper, 2023).

The main reason why Chen Gang is so confident is that Mafengwo holds the critical weapon in shaping tourism AI - comprehensive tourism primary big data. On the one hand, Mafengwo has sufficient big data on tourism content, which has accumulated over a decade. On the other hand, this big data is high-quality structured data that can be searched, maintained, and tracked, enabling AI big models to quickly and accurately understand the user behavior represented by the data. With the support of AI models, it will help the tourism industry achieve the goal of personalized scaling.

REFERENCES

Baidu Index. (n.d.). *[Mafengwo Travel - Crowd Portrait.]* Baidu Index. https://index .baidu.com/v2/main/index.html#/crowd/

China Digital Marketing Agency in Hong Kong. (n.d.). *Mafengwo Guide.* Alarice. https://alarice.com.hk/mafengwo-guide/

Lai, Y. (2023, January 13). *[Two Sessions Connection: Chen Gang, Founder and CEO of Mafengwo Tourism Network: This data city will grow into a world-changing enterprise].* Contemporary Pioneer Website. http://www.ddcpc.cn/detail/d_guizhou/ 11515116071350.html

Mafengwo. (2018, February 26). *[The Evolution of Mafengwo: From New Wave Travel Agency Area to National Tourism Brand].* Magengwo. https://m.mafengwo .cn/travel-news/1424122.html?ivk_sa=1024320u

Mafengwo. (2024). *[About Mafengwo – Mafengwo].* Mafenwo. https://www .mafengwo.cn/s/about.html

Maigoo Travel Website. (n.d.). [Introduction of Chen Gang – Co-founder of Mafeng-wo Tourism Network]. *Maigoo.* https://www.maigoo.com/mingren/19768.html

Phoenix News. (2017, December 30). [Interview with Lv Gang from Mafengwo: I believe the world rewards courage more than wisdom.] *Pheonix.* https://news.ifeng .com/c/7fa2Op7pUYj

The Economic Observer. (2023, December 14). [What does Mafengwo rely on to survive in the "New Golden Decade of Free Travel"?] *The Economic Observer.* https://mp.weixin.qq.com/s?__biz=MjM5OTExMjYwMA==&mid=2670192453 &idx=5&sn=df3910ba5a3baf0d3aa4e019d32f028a

The Paper. (2023, May 2). [Report on the Recovery Trends of China's Tourism In-dustry in 2023]. *The Paper.* https://www.thepaper.cn/newsDetail_forward_22926623

KEY TERMS AND DEFINITIONS

C2B (Consumer to Business): This is a new business model in the era of the Internet economy. C2B is centered on the consumer, where the consumer is in charge and contributes value. This model is conducive to creating a more time-saving, labor-saving, and cost-effective trading channel for consumers and businesses.

Content + Transaction: The content refers to travelogues and guides created by users on the Mafengwo platform, as well as official user travel reports and data published by Mafengwo. Transaction refers to the value trading services Mafengwo provides, such as hotel reservations and ticket booking services.

Generation Z: Refers to the new generation, usually born between 1995 and 2009, who were seamlessly connected to the network information age at birth and are more influenced by digital information technology, instant messaging devices, and smartphone products.

Marketing Is a Strategic Management Activity: The essence of marketing is the exchange of value between customers and the company. In this process, customers receive the products or services they want, and the company earns profits.

OTA (Online Travel Agency): Tourism providers provide products and services online. Tourism consumers can book products or services from tourism service providers through the Internet and make online or offline payments. This means that each tourism entity can conduct product marketing or sales online.

Social Network Service (SNS): It is a service based on the development of the Internet. For example, Mafengwo's social network services include sharing travel strategies among users, mutual answering of travel questions among users, and hotel reservation services.

User-Generated Content (UGC): Everyone can publish content on the platform based on user-generated content, starting from user needs. After the system or manual review, it can be displayed for more people. For example, Mafengwo's Q&A community, Zhihu's Q&A community, Douban, Weibo, WeChat's WeChat Moments, and TikTok all contain many UGC content.

Chapter 22
Kuaikan Manhua:
Empowering China's Digital Comics Landscape

Hailin Wang

University of Manchester, UK

EXECUTIVE SUMMARY

This case study examines Kuaikan Manhua, a prominent player in China's digital comics industry, focusing on its strategic evolution and entrepreneurial journey under the leadership of founder Annie Chen. Beginning with a mission to foster a vibrant Gen Z content community, Kuaikan Manhua employed an "intellectual property plus community" strategy, leveraging AI and big data to enhance content creation and user engagement. The study highlights key initiatives, such as IP development, community integration through the Community World platform, and international expansion efforts, like the Columbus Plan. It also explores challenges, including regulatory constraints and shifting market dynamics, offering insights into Kuaikan Manhua's resilience and innovation in navigating these obstacles. Through this analysis, the case underscores Kuaikan Manhua's pivotal role in shaping China's digital comics landscape and provides strategic lessons for businesses operating in dynamic and competitive digital content markets.

EXECUTIVE SUMMARY

Since its launch in 2014, Kuaikan Manhua has become one of China's fastest-progressing comic applications. It fosters a vibrant community of comic enthusiasts, providing forums, social features, and interactive elements that encourage user participation and collaboration. Its business scope has expanded to various fields, such as cartoons, games and derivative products. Through the operation strategy of

DOI: 10.4018/979-8-3693-2921-4.ch022

"intellectual property plus community", multi-marketing methods, and the double audits of human and artificial intelligence, Kuaikan Manhua has created a differentiated path for the Chinese female Gen Z entertainment market. In addition, Kuaikan Manhua has formed strategic partnerships with authors, organizations, and platforms in other regions to introduce high-quality foreign comics to the platform. Kuaikan Manhua has become a universal comic platform. However, compared with the well-developed animation industry in Japan and Korea, China's animation industry still has a long way to go. How to develop in the future is worth thinking about.

DESCRIPTION OF KUAIKAN MANHUA

Brief History of Kuaikan Manhua

In 2014, the online cartoonist Annie Chen released a cartoon about her entrepreneurial experience on Weibo named Sorry, I am Only Living a 1% Life. This received a large number of retweets and became an instant hit. This also announced the establishment of Kuaikan Manhua. As a new generation of Chinese online content community and original electronic comic entertainment platform, Kuaikan Manhua has quickly occupied a place in the highly competitive Chinese electronic comic entertainment platform since its inception. Not long after Kuaikan Manhua was launched, it got the most significant number of downloads on the smartphone application shop's total free list. In December of 2017, the market valuation of Kuaikan Manhua reached $12.5 billion. In 2018, Kuaikan Manhua was named the most popular application for the 00s (Zheng, 2019). As of 2021, the total number of users of Kuaikan Manhua exceeds 340 million, with nearly 50 million monthly active users (Kuaikan Manhua official website). Among them, more than 85 per cent of the application users are Generation Z. Currently, Kuaikan Manhua has more than 100,000 creators and more than 10,000 comics, with a market share of more than half of the Chinese comic market (Zheng, 2019). Kuaikan Manhua's community, Kuaikan Community, has more than 250,000 interest hashtags. About 400 of these tags have over 100 million views. Up to now, Kuaikan Manhua has received six rounds of financing.

Business Model

In the early stage of the establishment of Kuaikan Manhua, to occupy more markets, Kuaikan Manhua adopted a differentiated competitive strategy, i.e., it tended to occupy the female comic market and captured many new users. Subsequently, the business strategy of "intellectual property plus community" (Kuaikan Manhua official website) has enabled Kuaikan Manhua further expanded its influence in the comic user community. Due to shared interests, much user-generated content related to comics, games, cosplay, and so on was generated, forming a community culture. Since then, Kuaikan Manhua has upgraded from a comic reading platform to a Gen Z Anime and Manga culture creation platform. Kuaikan Manhua innovatively used submissions and audit mechanisms that combined artificial intelligence and manual review to create original intellectual property. This measure vigorously protects original comics and provides them with traffic. In the internationalization process of Kuaikan Manhua, Kuaikan Manhua has laid out more than 70 cooperative overseas platforms to achieve coverage of nearly 200 countries and regions worldwide. Launching the Columbus Plan (Kuaikan Manhua's official website) helped Kuaikan Manhua further establish overseas distribution and self-construction channels.

In 2023, to further meet the commercialization needs of Kuaikan Manhua in the post-epidemic era, Kuaikan Manhua launched a new business model - COS Marketing, which combines Consumer, Occasion and Shop. This model aims to carry out the entire chain marketing of user, scene, and shop to achieve the goal of "increasing the number and loyalty of young users, content recommendation and activities to attract traffic, and in-site purchasing behavior". In this model, the Consumers are mainly China's Generation Z, which consumes the content and products of Kuaikan Manhua. Occasion refers to Kuaikan's five marketing scenarios: the platform scenario, the activity scenario, the scene of watching anime and manga, the secondary creation scenario, and the private domain scenario. Shop refers to the mall function in Kuaikan Manhua, which reduces the loss of users.

Products and Services

From the very beginning of its establishment, Kuaikan Manhua has advocated that "comics are an attitude towards life" (Kuaikan Manhua's official website), hoping to bring happiness and motivation to users through comics. After several years of refinement and development, Kuaikan Manhua provided consumers comprehensive products and services. First, the platform provides users with many high-quality Chinese original domestic and foreign high-definition full-color comics. Moreover, most of them are free of charge for readers. The representative works of Kuaikan Manhua include Thumping Heart, Sweet Bite, Generation Queen, What You Are Looking For is What Your Heart Desire and so on. Kuaikan Manhua also cooperated with authors and organizations in Japan and Korea to introduce many high-quality Japanese and Korean comics to enrich the diversity of works on its platform. Secondly, Kuaikan Manhua actively promotes the animation and climatization of popular intellectual properties and has made specific achievements. The comic film Take My Brother Away grossed RMB400 million, becoming a dark horse in the industry. The TV series Chenqingling, based on the original story of the Modaozushi, a virtual Chinese fantasy novel, reached 10 billion views 2020 across the platform. Then, the platform also has pop-ups and community interaction functions, creating a good atmosphere for the anime and manga culture community. Kuaikan Manhua encourages users to interact with each other while reading, and it has become a trendy cultural place for Chinese Generation Z.

Target Customers

Most of the primary users of Kuaikan Manhua are Chinese Generation Z, with a large proportion of women users, including office workers and students. Most of them are highly educated and have some financial strength. Compared with consumers in other industries, they have a higher desire for expression and are more willing to pay for what they like. Moreover, they have a higher awareness of copyright, and they are willing to pay for originality. In addition, the country's rising power has triggered a widespread recognition of Chinese traditional culture. Also, the revival of the Chinese national trend has led to consumers' preference for original Chinese works.

China's Generation Z is the generation born in the information age. Due to the impact of more information and the popularity of mobile reading, Gen Z has its own values and is eager to express itself. Moreover, circle culture and interesting groups are popular among Gen Z. They need a platform where they can communicate with their peers and build their own persona with what they buy.

China's Generation Z was born in China's entertainment development era. They are generally well-educated and independent-minded. With China's rapid economic growth, they have the right to dispose of a certain amount of money and have a strong sense of independent consumption. Most consumers also have a strong sense of copyright. Buying pirated copies is an act that is looked down upon. They are willing to pay for genuine copies and take the initiative to report piracy when they encounter it. In addition, consumer experience is another aspect they focus on. More than the quantity of consumption, Generation Z focuses on the self-satisfaction they get when consuming and only pays for things they like (Wancaishe, 2023).

Born in the era of China's rising national power, Generation Z has a strong sense of patriotism and national pride. They have a strong sense of inclusiveness and support for national products (Iresearch, 2022). They recognize and seek after the national trend culture for its unique identification. Generation Z promotes the national trend culture as a popular fashion for pioneering youth. At the same time, they are also keen to socialize and share on the internet and are more susceptible to the influence of key opinion leaders. The fan's economy has also become stronger under their drive. For crucial opinion leaders or idols, they love, Gen Z can buy the goods they have recommended, and they will even recommend them to others.

The target users of Kuaikan Manhua can be divided into three categories: comic readers, derivative product consumers, and content creators. These three identities can overlap with each other. Comics Readers generally browse, recharge and evaluate the works on the Kuaikan Manhua application. Some would like to communicate and interact with comic authors and other users. Then, Derivative Product Consumers will be recommended comics, derivative products, etc., by Kuaikan Manhua based on big data. They also like to place orders for their favorite products. Finally, Content Creators can be divided into officially generated and user-generated content. Official-generated content creators mainly create comics and earn revenue, and user-generated content creators focus on communicating with their peers and secondary creation.

Some Examples of User Profiles

Lynn is a 20-year-old female undergraduate student. She is usually free and enjoys watching comics and anime. When on holiday, she often attends comic exhibitions and authors' book signing parties, so she has met a group of friends who share the same hobbies. She never skimps money on the intellectual property of her favorite works and derivative products, such as laser tickets and posters. At the first moment of the sale, she would place orders on time to grab them at the online mall.

Zhao is a 24-year-old professional manga artist. She is still a newcomer to the comic industry. By chance, her comic serialized on Kuaikan Manhua was signed and successfully joined the Columbus Plan, gaining great traffic support and copyright protection. Recently, her comic was made into a film and released, which was a box office hit. In the future, she hopes her work can be promoted overseas.

Chen is a 29-year-old office worker based in Shanghai. She is also a fan of anime and manga culture. On weekends, she likes to relax by playing games on her mobile phone and reading comics serialized in Kuaikan Manhua. She is also a secondary creation writer and cosplayer. She often posts her works and photos of cosplay to the community, which has gained her many followers and likes.

Market Analysis: Evolution of the Market Until Today

Opportunities

Political Factors: China's State Policies Boost Comic Industry – China has been focusing on supporting the cultural industry. In 2005, the government proposed broadcasting domestic animation at night during prime time. In 2008, the government issued several opinions on supporting the development of China's animation industry, proposing to support national originality (Iresearch, 2018). 2012, China implemented preferential tax policies and tax reductions for the animation industry. Then, in 2017, the government promoted the animation and game exhibition. They also decided to promote the marketisation, internationalization and professionalization of key cultural industry exhibitions, support the creation, production and promotion of original cartoons, and cultivate national cartoon creativity and brands (Iresearch, 2019). In 2018, the Ministry of Culture's "Twelfth Five-Year Plan for the Development of the National Cartoon Industry" proposed to build famous cartoon brands and improve industrial financing policies.

Economic Factors: Changes in Residents' Consumption Structure – With China's economic development, residents' consumption ability has gradually increased, and the consumption structure has been upgraded. According to a survey conducted by Iresearch, the entertainment consumption of China's Generation Z accounts for 28.9% of the total consumption expenditure, with an average of more than 1.6 hours spent on online entertainment daily (Iresearch, 2018). Residents' demand for consumption is gradually increasing. The growth of quality content platforms and entertainment is imperative. Online communication platforms have become one of the most critical channels for people to engage in entertainment consumption.

Social Factors: Increased Awareness of Copyright – In recent years, China has increased its efforts to protect the intellectual property rights of original works. China has introduced several laws and regulations to protect intellectual property rights, including the Law on the Protection of Intellectual Property Rights, the Regulations on Collective Management of Copyright, and the Trademark Law. The Chinese government has also set up campaigns to combat piracy and infringement. These actions have strongly protected intellectual property rights within China's entertainment industry and further promoted its development.

Technological Factors: Big Data Technology Advancement – In the age of information technology, utilizing users' fragmented time is the key for applications to capture users. China's data technology continues to evolve toward maturity. Big data can effectively collect and analyze users' reading and consumption habits and recommend content matching their preferences. Even artificial intelligence can launch targeted operation strategies based on content-related data. Furthermore, the ease of control and accessibility of new media technologies has led to media empowerment for the general audience. Every user can participate in and interact to create text on the platform. Users can also utilize the platform for free content creation and maintain their own communities. Every creator has the opportunity to publish their work on the web through the internet. The brand's applications can also be promoted through social media.

Cultural Factors: The Popularity of Anime and Manga Culture – With worldwide cultural exchanges, various cultures are widely spread. China's anime and manga culture industry has entered an explosive period. In 2020, the overall market size of China's animation industry reached 100 billion RMB, with an annual growth rate of 32.7% (Research, 2021). The anime and manga market has gradually transformed into a content-oriented and intellectual property derivative industry, pulling in both directions.

Drawbacks

Political Factors: China's animation industry is slow-moving and unregulated. Compared with neighboring countries such as Japan and South Korea, where the animation industry is well developed, China's animation industry still needs some help. Nowadays, the number of high-quality original cartoon authors in China could be much higher. Some need more drawing skills, and some need help to tell a good story. Then, most comic publishers need more experienced editors. As a publisher, the inability to give professional guidance significantly impacts the development of comics. In addition, the main audience of Chinese comics is primarily primary and secondary school students. They favor a more consistent style, which may impact the creation of the Chinese comics industry. Moreover, China has strict regulations on the aspects of the creative sector involving young people, with laws introduced to regulate creative content, daily activity, etc.

Market Factors: Evolving External Competitors – With the increasing demand for entertainment from China's Generation Z, more and more comic applications, such as Bilibili and Yuewen Group, have emerged. Bilibili's pop-up culture facilitates real-time viewer communication, enhancing their experience and interactivity. It is worth noting that Bilibili has entered into cooperation with several Japanese companies, introducing exclusive Chinese serialization rights for a large number of Japanese comics and bringing in a large fan base. In addition, Bilibili has gradually focused on the intellectual property development of Chinese comics in recent years. It has gained an edge in original Chinese comics and promotion, becoming an essential member of the global comics industry.

Analysis of the Competition

Youyaoqi Original Cartoon Dream Factory: Founded in 2006, the Youyaoqi website was initially just a platform for domestic comic enthusiasts to communicate with each other. In 2014, with the Youyaoqi Comic application launched, it became a domestic internet platform focusing on supporting China's original comics. It was also China's only and the largest purely original comic website. Unfortunately, in

2022, the Youyaoqi Comic application announced the closure of its servers. They mainly conducted business through user-paid rewards and advertisements. Youyaoqi Comic application has launched a monthly ticket revenue scheme. Readers became members to get monthly tickets to reward their favorite works; the top works on the list would be rewarded with a certain amount of money.

Migu Anime: Migu Anime was launched in 2014 and operated by China Yidong Mobile Group. Migu Anime focuses on Internet ACGN (Animation, Comics, Games, light Novels, Original Videos) content operation. Its services include content production and distribution, intellectual property sales, channel operation and promotion, e-commerce and capital operation to create a comprehensive new culture and entertainment industry ecology. In 2017, Migu Anime was renamed as Migu Circle. Its business was expanded to include anime, games, and short videos, among other aspects.

Tencent Animation: Tencent Animation, launched in 2012 and affiliated with Tencent, is a globally renowned interactive entertainment brand (Song, 2021). Tencent Animation owns the exclusive rights to many high-quality and well-known overseas comics. The drawing style of Tencent Animation favors the adventure and fantasy genre. Works on the application's homepage are categorized by gender and specific content (Ao, 2020). Moreover, there are also popular recommendations. Tencent Animation vigorously supports Chinese domestic original animation, integrating film, television, animation, games and other directions according to its pan-entertainment strategy. Tencent Group also use Tencent Animation as the core of content to help creators access the Tencent resource system.

DEVELOPMENT STRATEGY

Product Life Cycle Theory

Product life cycle refers to the entire movement process of a product from the time it is ready to enter the market until it is eliminated and withdrawn from the market, which is determined by the production cycle of demand and technology. This process needs to identify, anticipate and develop strategies for effective implementation (Day, 1981). The whole cycle is generally divided into five stages, including the period of introduction, growth, maturity, and decline (Chen, 2019). In the introduction period of the product, the new product has just entered the market. Consumers have yet to learn much about the product, and only a few people willing to try something new will buy it. In the growth period of the product, consumers become familiar with the product. The market expands further; consumers also increase, and profits proliferate. In the product maturity period, the market demand tends to be saturated. There are few potential customers. Sales growth is slow until it turns down, marking the product into the maturity period. In this stage, competition gradually intensifies. The product promotion costs increase. In the decline period of the product, with the emergence of new products or substitutes, the customer's consumption habits have changed to other products. Sales and profitability of the original product decline rapidly.

Product Introduction Period of Kuaikan Manhua

During the product introduction period, Kuaikan Manhua attracted the first batch of users through its differentiated positioning and online and offline promotion, so it successfully increased its popularity. The year 2015 was an explosive period for Chinese comics. The emergence of Kuaikan Manhua caters to the trend in the Chinese comic industry. Due to the rapid development of the Internet, vertical comics have a larger sub-scope, unlimited reading direction, and are more suitable for mobile phone users to read. Hence, they gradually replaced the former popular comic pages. To adapt to users' mobile use and fragmented reading habits, vertical comics have become the leading content form of Kuaikan Manhua. The simple and convenient layout of the applications reduces the difficulty of reading. In 2015, China's comic industry witnessed the emergence of several new players, including Tencent Animation, which primarily targeted male consumers. However, this left a gap in the market for female comic enthusiasts, as their needs were not being met. Kuaikan Manhua stepped in to bridge this gap. It launched a series of women's comics featuring genres such as mansion love stories and youth on campus, catering to the interests of Gen Z women and creating a new track in the industry.

Kuaikan Manhua, a newly launched online comic platform, used a combination of online and offline marketing strategies to expand its user base and increase its popularity rapidly. To attract more users, the Kuaikan Manhua team used social media platforms. It leveraged the popularity of the founder online cartoonist Annie Chen's discussion on Weibo to generate discussions and retweets, which attracted many original users to the platform. The team also signed many new cartoonists and released their works through the cartoonists' social media accounts, which have a large fan base, to attract more users to the platform. To further boost the popularity of Kuaikan Manhua, the platform organized offline book signing sessions, allowing users to meet and communicate with their favorite famous writers. Fans needed to purchase tickets in the shop of Kuaikan Manhua application to attend. This marketing strategy promoted emotional exchange between fans and authors and increased fans' stickiness with the Kuaikan application, improving its popularity and influence.

Product Growth Period of Kuaikan Manhua

Through previous marketing strategies, Kuaikan Manhua has successfully shared the Chinese comic market and gained many original users. To further establish a good brand image, Kuaikan Manhua starts with content, user experience, and marketing. Firstly, Kuaikan Manhua insisted on retail and originality, emphasizing providing users with high-definition and high-quality comic resources. During this period, Kuaikan Manhua continued to sign many high-quality works by authors, launch original comics, tailor-made marketing programs for them, and provide traffic support. Its self-created works, such as Take My Brother Away and Plastic Surgery Game, gained colossal traffic.

Kuaikan Manhua is an application that focuses on providing a seamless user experience. The application regularly adds new features through updates to enhance the user's experience. The application uses big data to recommend personalized works on the homepage based on the reader's chosen gender, which can be switched and refreshed with a single click. When readers try to decide what to read, the application recommends recent popular comics by entering the homepage hotlist.

In 2016, Kuaikan Manhua launched an author community called V Community to promote interaction between readers and authors. This community allows readers to like and write comments to their favorite authors, and authors can also share their daily lives to bring them closer to readers or set up tag topics for their works. Kuaikan Manhua has also invested heavily in marketing by using various platforms such as WeChat Moment ads and sponsoring entertainment programs that are popular among young people. The platform has successfully broken barriers and emerged as a leading platform in China's comic industry, attracting more users.

Product Maturity of Kuaikan Manhua

During the maturity period, Kuaikan Manhua adopted the development strategy of "intellectual property plus community." The company aimed to build a Chinese Gen Z content community and original intellectual property platform. They created an interest-based anime and manga culture community atmosphere and developed the entire comic industry chain. To achieve this, Kuaikan Manhua focused on developing the intellectual property of existing works and invested heavily in developing potential authors to create high-quality content. The company also acquired new copyrights from existing famous authors. Kuaikan Manhua used technology to promote author content creation, analyze work data, and use artificial intelligence to guide topic selection and content to help authors seize market trends.

To enhance the reader's experience, Kuaikan Manhua's big data algorithms helped readers find their favorite works. The personalized content recommendation feature recommended works based on reading preferences and showed different covers and promotional texts of the same work to other readers. Additionally, Kuaikan Manhua collaborated with Chinese domestic and foreign production organizations to produce quality work jointly. Furthermore, Kuaikan Manhua upgraded the original V community and launched the community World. Every user can apply to become a certified creator to freely publish content on it as long as they meet specific standards. The community also added dubbing, live broadcasting, and other content, creating various interest communities. Over time, the community of Kuaikan Manhua gradually developed into a social and user-social content, with user-generated content becoming more apparent.

THE PEOPLE BEHIND KUAIKAN MANHUA

Annie Chen, the founder and CEO of Kuaikan Manhua, was born in 1992 in Guangdong Province, China. Annie had a passion for drawing from a young age, but reality denied it. Her low-income family circumstances and the discouragement from people around her led her to give up her dream (Luo, 2020). However, in her second year of university, when her father was involved in a severe car accident, Annie tried to pick up her childhood hobby to earn money for the family. She borrowed money to buy a digital drawing board and started hand-drawing comics. Later, she registered as Great Annie on Weibo to publish her works. Most of her comics were drawn from her own life. Annie's delicate strokes and unique drawing style gained much attention from netizens. In 2012, she published her first illustrated book, Nima: This is College. In 2013, she created a comic intellectual property named Annie and Wang Xiaoming, based on her love story with her boyfriend. This comic went on to win the Animation Golden Dragon Award, one of China's most influential awards.

Annie Chen successfully achieved the one per cent chance that was denied to her as a child. However, her dream is much bigger than this. She aims to create a platform that provides more value and assistance for cartoonists. Thus, upon nearing graduation, she decided to establish an animation company. Despite facing the challenge of insufficient funds, Annie Chen persevered and visited numerous investors. After many rejections, she finally secured the start-up capital. However, she faced technical problems because no resources were available then. To find help, she used a rather unconventional method. She searched for technicians on social media QQ and added contacts to find the support she needed. Eventually, in 2014, Kuaikan Manhua was released despite facing heavy pressure.

Annie Chen, now a famous comic artist, shared a new comic on her Weibo account titled "Sorry, I Only Live a 1% Life" to promote her work. This inspiring comic tells the story of her rebirth from a problematic situation and focuses on themes of perseverance and achieving one's dreams. The comic quickly resonated with many netizens, gaining over 400,000 retweets, 200 million readers, and more than 90,000 comments. It also caught the attention of numerous celebrities who retweeted it. As a result, the Kuaikan Manhua application saw a significant increase in users and attracted millions of dollars in financing. (Chen, 2021)

Kuaikan Manhua faced a new stage of development, but this brought about many questions. Some netizens raised concerns that Annie Chen was exploiting the emotions of others for marketing purposes, while others questioned the copyright of Kuaikan Manhua. The negative sentiment on the internet led to reduced licensed content, which dealt a severe blow to Kuaikan Manhuas, which were still in their infancy. However, Annie Chen responded proactively by taking down unauthorized works and compensating the affected parties. She also implemented stricter management policies for original comics and cultivated a large pool of talented original comics authors. These efforts ensured that Kuaikan Manhua continued to develop and thrive despite its challenges.

FUTURE PROJECTS

Although Kuaikan Manhua has emerged as a leading player in China's comic industry, specific weaknesses must be addressed. Firstly, as previously mentioned, the comic industry in China is still in its early stages, with an underdeveloped industry chain and a need for more policy support and regulation. Kuaikan Manhua needs to put more effort into exploring this market. Additionally, the current tight regulations on youth entertainment in China's entertainment industry have also impacted the development of Kuaikan Manhua's application, such as restrictions on underage top-ups and the initiation of the youth mode. Some parents have expressed dissatisfaction with the time-limited member top-up activities within Kuaikan Manhua. Kuaikan Manhua's youth mode has been criticized for artificially and actively regulating the amount of time and duration that teenagers can use the application. It is considered a form of false propaganda and induced consumption.

On the other hand, Kuaikan Manhua's existing operational model has been criticized. Korean comics have gradually replaced Chinese national comics as the mainstream content on Kuaikan Manhua. Many comics have serious homogenization, with no novelty or attraction. To cater to traffic and meet young people's consumption preferences, many new works on Kuaikan Manhua tend to be entertaining, and the content is mixed, including many chapters with adult content. The drawing style of the comics was more delicate than initially, and finding good works is becoming increasingly more challenging.

Furthermore, in terms of revenue, many users would like to change the membership model. They are required to recharge every month, but they still need to buy the virtual currency KK coins to read new chapters. Even the price of these coins is costly. Moreover, the purchased chapters have a time limit for reading, and users must pay again if they want to read them after the expiration date.

Kuaikan Manhua is the leading unicorn enterprise in China's vertical comic content track, which faces the challenge of balancing content and cost. The company has been working to escape the commercial dilemma the entire comic industry faces. In 2021, it officially launched the Columbus Plan, signaling the launch of Kuaikan Manhua's internationalization strategy. Through this strategy, the company aims to create a global distribution system and expand from China to the world.

Before this, Kuaikan Manhua had accumulated 101 works in Europe, America, Japan, South Korea, Southeast Asia, and other regions, costing nearly 100 million yuan. Some of their works, such as "Giantess Also Want to Fall in Love" and "Sweet Bite," have marked overseas revenue as one million yuan. To further develop its international presence, Kuaikan Manhua has established an overseas division and is developing a global version of the application, with content and platform going overseas. The company has also collaborated with the American graphic novel platform Tapas to target the American market.

In 2022, Kuaikan Manhua plans to build its channels to promote more high-quality works to the primary target markets worldwide and penetrate various small language markets. The company will also launch the comic shopping mall Goods Club on the application, selling various popular comic intellectual property. Additionally, Kuaikan Manhua is looking for unique and high-quality selling points for each comic, and a large number of comic intellectual properties have been successfully incubated, such as "Modaozushi" and "Take My Brother Away," which have been adapted into films and sold well at the box office.

In the era of streaming media, Kuaikan Manhua faces the challenge of adapting to an ever-changing new environment while inheriting the characteristics of the past. However, at the 2023 Kuaikan Manhua Carnival Comic Show, Annie Chen expressed optimism, saying, "We still have a chance."

CONCLUSION

Kuaikan Manhua's success can be attributed to strategic initiatives, creative endeavors, technological innovations, and a solid commitment to serving its community of users, creators, and partners. By continually evolving and adapting to meet the changing needs of its audience, Kuaikan Manhua remains at the forefront of China's digital comics industry. These features have a particular reference value for the existing comic platforms in China.

Chinese comic platforms should pay attention to the culture of different circles and adopt key opinion leaders and key opinion consumer marketing to enhance users' experience. In the fan economy, stars are an essential part. When operating through the fan economy, brands should consider how to combine the image of the star and the product, find common points, promote interaction between fans and stars, and boost consumption.

Chinese comic platforms should be adept at integrating mainstream forms of communication to expand their reach and attract more users. In the era of streaming media, various new communication media and communication methods have emerged. Brands should learn to integrate multi-media advantages, such as graphics, games, videos, communities, etc., to create a communication matrix and provide a smoother all-round experience. Platforms should actively look for unique selling points for their products and create their own business models to increase user outlets and communicate well.

The users of China's animation industry have gradually expanded, not only the previous vertical depth of the Anime and Manga culture crowd but also many Anime and Manga cultures. Chinese cartoon platforms should pay attention to the intellectual property value of Chinese cartoon work and guide more users to participate in depth. In the social era, the comic platform should combine comics and reality and pull in the distance between products and users through social-emotional marketing. In addition, the platform should also innovate marketing methods, using methods that are more suitable for young people's habits, triggering resonance.

Chinese comic platforms should focus on developing traditional Chinese culture and actively undertake social responsibility while engaging with users in depth and interacting effectively. By combining excellent traditional Chinese culture with published comics, they can further extend intellectual property content and increase the economic and cultural value of marketing.

REFERENCES

Chen, R. (2021). Annie Chen: Industrialising comics. *China Entrepreneur*, (04), 55-57+54.

Chen, S. (2019). *The Product Life Cycle and Product Design*.

Day, G. (1981). The Product Life Cycle: Analysis and Applications Issues. *Journal of Marketing*, 45(4), 60–67. DOI:10.1177/002224298104500408

iResearch. (2019). *White Paper on the Marketing Value of the Anime and Manga Culture Crowd*. iResearch. https://report.iresearch.cn/report_pdf.aspx?id=3496

iResearch. (2021). *China's Anime and Manga Industry Research Report*. iResearch. https://report.iresearch.cn/report_pdf.aspx?id=3865

iResearch. (2022). *Iresearch: The Tide of China Tradition*. iResearch. https://report.iresearch.cn/report_pdf.aspx?id=3940

iResearch. (2018). *Research Report on China's Animation Industry*. iResearch. https://report.iresearch.cn/report_pdf.aspx?id=3309

Lei, A. (2020). Comparative study on short video function of animation apps: A case study of "Kuaikan Manhua" and "Tencent Animation". *New Media Research*, (09), 35–37.

Rodan. (2020). Delivering Chinese Culture and Chinese Spirit in Comics - Remembering Annie Chen, Founder and CEO of Kuaikan Manhua. *Business Culture*, (35), 5-7+4+130.

Song, H. (2021). Research on the development of web comics in China. *Art Review*, (09), 183–185.

Wancaishe. (2023). *Generation Z Consumer Trend Insight Report 2023*.

Yao, Z. (2020). Analysing the marketing strategy of Kuaikan Manhua based on the 4I principles of network integration. *Theatre House*, (09), 210+212.

Zheng, R. (2019). Exploration of the development strategy of China's comic app under the trend of pan-entertainment—Take the example of Kuaikan Manhua. *Audiovisual*, (08), 173–174.

Zhou, H., & Liu, Q. (2018). Exploration of Multidimensional Communication Strategy in the Internet Comic Industry—Taking Kuaikan Manhua as an example. *Today Media*, (03), 22–24.

KEY TERMS AND DEFINITIONS

Anime and Manga Culture: Anime and Manga culture is a subculture that includes two-dimensional images, animation, comics, games, and other works. It is a form of virtual world derived from human fantasies and independent of mainstream culture.

Circle Culture: Circle culture is a subculture formed by a group of people with similar preferences. Each circle has its own unique culture, values, and opinion leaders.

Community: A community refers to a group of people who share common interests and engage in discussions and activities related to those interests. In the context of comics, a community is a social platform for users to share their own manga or reviews of works related to their respective topics of interest.

Content Marketing: Brands use content to attract and impress users and help them understand the brand and its products. This marketing method aims to create interest and engagement without necessarily trying to make sales conversions. This type of marketing is often used on social media platforms.

Cross-Border Co-Branding: This type of marketing is based on the commonalities between different industries, products, and consumers. Brands integrate various elements to win consumers' favor or establish a good brand image.

Cultural Industry: The cultural sector refers to the business of creating and distributing cultural products and services. It includes industries such as publishing, film, music, and gaming.

Intellectual Property Rights (IP): Intellectual property rights are the legal rights that protect the creations of individuals or companies. It includes copyrights, trademarks, and patents.

Membership Marketing: Brands create membership systems, rights and benefits, and pricing strategies to provide new product experiences and services, promote member consumption and enhance member loyalty.

Secondary Creation: Secondary creation is re-creating a work based on an existing project. It can take many forms, including imitation, adaptation, citation, and exploitation. Secondary creations can be commercial or non-commercial, including animation, comics, plays, games, films, television programs, and novels.

User Relationship: A brand actively builds positive relationships with its users to achieve a specific goal. This relationship-building confirms the product's value proposition and complements the channel. It's also a crucial factor that influences core resources and revenue streams.

Vertical Comics: Vertical comics are a type of comic strip, usually in a vertical format. It typically combines text and graphics in a four-panel manga style and can have a more extended storyline with changing frames.

Chapter 23
Keep:
Transforming Fitness Through Innovation and Integration

Xintong Yu

Beijing Normal University-Hong Kong Baptist University United International College, China

EXECUTIVE SUMMARY

This case study explores Keep, a pioneering company in the Chinese fitness industry known for its innovative approach to blending technology with fitness solutions. Founded by Wang Ning, Keep revolutionized home fitness during the COVID-19 pandemic by introducing interactive live classes and expanding its digital offerings. The study examines Keep's strategic adaptations amid market challenges, such as shifting from offline gyms to collaborative ventures with traditional fitness centers. It highlights Keep's successful integration of gamification and virtual events to enhance user engagement and retention. The case also delves into Wang Ning's entrepreneurial journey, emphasizing his vision to democratize access to fitness through accessible, tech-driven solutions. Through rigorous analysis of Keep's business strategies, technological innovations, and market positioning, this case study provides insights into the dynamics of digital transformation in the fitness sector and its implications for future industry trends.

DOI: 10.4018/979-8-3693-2921-4.ch023

UNICORN DESCRIPTION

Brief History of Keep

Keep was founded in 2014 and officially launched the Keep mobile app in 2015, providing proprietary structured fitness courses. Benefiting from the internet sports and fitness boom, Keep App's usage coverage grew rapidly. In 2015, Keep was named the App of the Year by the App Store and was pre-installed in all Apple retail stores. By 2016, the platform had grown to 10 million monthly active users. In the same year, Keep launched the "Dream Playground" initiative and successfully established playgrounds in numerous primary schools across Qinghai, Xinjiang, Shaanxi, and other regions as part of its commitment to public welfare (Zhang, 2016).

In 2018, the company was upgraded to a sports science and technology ecological company. The operation model expanded from a single content and product output to selling intelligent fitness equipment and supporting sports products. At the same time, it launched a member subscription system to explore a full range of business models. In 2019, it managed to reach 1 million users. During the same year, Keep won the 2019 Responsible Brand Award for its continuous efforts in public welfare and its continuous delivery of the positive energy of "making the world move" (Ikanchai, 2019).

Since the outbreak of the pandemic in 2020, home fitness has taken off, and companies have launched interactive live classes to further increase monthly active users. The average monthly user exceeded 3.5 million by 2022. The company was officially listed on July 12, 2023 (Xie, 2022).

Business Model

Keep is a sports social software equipped with function modules such as a mall, community, personal fitness record, diet guidance, intelligent fitness equipment, and offline sports project experience (Xing, 2019). It is committed to providing fitness enthusiasts with quality online fitness instruction courses to help them achieve their fitness goals, offering comprehensive fitness solutions, and continuously exploring the fitness vertical field.

Its business model consists of three steps. The first step is to accumulate users and improve the essential functions of the product and service. The second step is to explore ways to monetize, such as e-commerce, membership, and offline gyms. Finally, Keep focuses on increasing the content of live classes and professional user-generated content to cope with the competition of fitness content traffic.

All of its business expansion and product iterations are aimed at cultivating user loyalty to the brand and improving user stickiness. The value of sports is transformed into shopping value, and the sports scene is transformed into a consumption scene without a trace. Through continuous exploration and innovation, Keep strives to achieve full coverage and in-depth excavation of sports scenes, sports services, and sports supporting facilities. Keep constantly building its brand power and raising the industry's ceiling, thereby obtaining more excellent space for enterprise development (Yao & Tan, 2022).

Product and Services

Fitness Content

The primary component of the platform is online fitness content. Currently, six categories of fitness courses are available: yoga, running, KIT, walking, and cycling. Sports and fitness enthusiasts can acquire various fitness skills and fundamental fitness knowledge through the Keep APP video courses (Xing, 2019). Fitness courses are categorized according to equipment, movement characteristics, and venue limitations to cater to diverse sport's needs. They also vary in difficulty, duration, and intensity to help users achieve different fitness goals. Keep also uses artificial intelligence algorithms to develop AI virtual coaches and create content such as fat-burning exercises and dances (Liu, 2023). The revenue for this business segment primarily comes from user membership subscriptions and online paid content.

Fitness Communication Community

The second is the fitness communication community of Keep APP. Keep provides various tools to simplify users' recording and posting processes, producing pictures with user statistics and a structure for fitness classes. Users can follow other Keepers, including fitness masters and trainers, and communicate with them through comments and instant messages. Keep analyzing users' past behavior and interactions through artificial intelligence and recommend sectors they are more interested in (Gao, 2022). Users can find their main concern content in the subdivided community section, share fitness experiences, and communicate with other fitness enthusiasts to obtain more scientific and practical fitness methods (Xing, 2019). At the same time, this improves users' fitness enthusiasm and helps them form good fitness habits. In addition, interactive activities between community members will make the community more attractive to members, generate a sense of belonging to the community, and increase user stickiness (Zhang, 2019).

Mall Segment

The third segment is the mall segment, which is also one of the essential channels to achieve online profit. It is subdivided into four product categories: light food meal replacement, sports equipment, men's and women's clothing, and sports life. The light meal replacement series mainly provides a scientific diet for users to exercise, such as sandwiches and salads. Keep recommends customized meal plans, total calorie intake, and diet analysis based on the user's health goals (Xing, 2019).

Sports equipment aims to provide users with various portable and intelligent fitness equipment, such as spinning bikes and treadmills. Spinning bikes have a realistic riding function, which uses the riding data recorded by the spinning bike and the first-person perspective of the riding video to simulate riding in different scenarios and increase the user's sense of experience in the exercise process. Treadmill products are characterized by muscular power and durability. When the user combines a running course on the platform, the Keep treadmill can automatically change the user's speed according to the course goal. Keep provides assisted voice guidance and visual performance analysis after workouts to motivate positive feedback (Xing, 2019).

The reason why it is difficult to adhere to fitness is that users often need help to see the results directly in a short period of time. Timely feedback after each exercise to quantify the results can effectively encourage users to obtain satisfaction with fitness to achieve the goal of adhering to fitness (Gao, 2022). The men's and women's clothing category includes sports clothing such as sports coats and sports T-shirts. The sports life category includes fitness-related products, including schoolbags, kettles, and turbans. Most of the profit methods of these products are accompanied by the course content. They use users' trust in Keep training courses and the convenience of self-operated platforms to attract users to consume on their e-commerce platforms (Xing, 2019).

Fitness Management Tool Service

The fourth service is the fitness management tool. Keep building fitness profiles for users free of charge. Each user has a data center that records the user's sports data, body data, health data, and other information to create a weekly sports report. This report visually displays the user's fitness progress. The Keep app conducts preliminary exercise ability tests on users to help them set fitness goals. Additionally, Keep provides users with real-time positioning, designs sports routes, records sports data, and offers other functions through free outdoor activity tools, popular among running, hiking, and cycling enthusiasts (Liu, 2023).

Offline Events and Keepland Gym

Finally, the offline service section mainly includes fun sports experience activities and Keepland Gym. Based on the Keep online fitness content, Keepland provides users with rich and exciting scenario-based training courses, connecting online user behavior and offline fitness experience (Liu, 2023). Various fun sports experience activities, including surfing and marathon activities, inspire contemporary young people and set off a new wave of naturalistic sports.

Analysis of Competition

The major participants in the domestic online fitness market are divided into four categories: The first is Internet hardware enterprises represented by Xiaomi, Huawei, and Apple, which are cross-border intelligent fitness hardware and software to create an intelligent fitness ecosystem. The second is Internet sports technology enterprises represented by Keep, which have expanded from the online platform to fitness hardware and offline fitness. The third is the comprehensive content platform enterprises represented by Tiktok, Kuaishou and B station enter the market with fitness videos, activate traffic through user-created content, and then realize cash by carrying goods. The fourth is smart device suppliers, represented by FITURE, who enter the market through intelligent fitness hardware and penetrate the family life scene.

In comparison to Xiaomi, Huawei, Apple, and other international intelligent fitness Internet hardware companies, Keep focuses on fitness and has high brand recognition, which results in users having more trust in its professionalism. And compared to comprehensive content platform companies such as TikTok, Kuaishou, and B station, Keep has three advantages. Firstly, Keep's course content is more professional and concise. Unlike B station and TikTok, where punch card analysis and course content are mixed, Keep's content area is more organized and tailored for amateur fitness enthusiasts, providing course classification and calorie consumption data, making it easier for users to choose suitable content for their training. Additionally, Keep's fitness bloggers update their content frequently, provide diverse content, and often include course difficulty ratings, object labels, and heat consumption details, highlighting professionalism. Second, Keep offers functionality and sociability, creating a sense of fitness atmosphere and satisfaction through its vertical community and features like punching in and the same city circle model, which is lacking in comprehensive content platforms. Lastly, Keep has incentive programs and a higher standard for coaches. Unlike comprehensive video content platforms where anyone can post content, Keep's course content is certified by official masters, ensuring professionalism and uniqueness (Xu, 2022).

Furthermore, in the networked sports technology sector, Codoon and Zepp Life share similar essential functions with Keep, including recording functions for running, fitness, walking, and cycling, as well as community features. Codoon positions itself as an intelligent sports platform, a professional equipment shopping guide, and a content community, offering a national sports ecosystem and enhancing social attributes through online events and city activities based on recorded data. On the other hand, Zepp Life positions its product as an intelligent sports platform that focuses on providing accurate sports data. The application is more inclined towards pairing with Zepp Life smart devices for precise sports and health data recording, and it does not offer a commercial mall platform. Compared to Codoon and Zepp Life, Keep offers more comprehensive functions and broader business scope, making it more attractive to customers. Additionally, Keep's diversified operation, combining online and offline, can enhance its influence in the sports and fitness software market and contribute to the establishment of a well-known fitness brand (CSDN, 2020).

Customers

As the dynamics of our daily lives continue to change, the need for convenient and effective fitness solutions becomes increasingly apparent across various age groups and lifestyles. Recognizing this diverse need, Keep has curated platforms to cater to the specific requirements of different demographics.

College students, known for their youthful energy and active social lives, often seek to enhance their appearance through fitness. However, financial constraints may limit their access to professional fitness guidance. Keep's online fitness content platform addresses this by providing access to professional video guidance, allowing them to acquire fitness knowledge and save on time and costs systematically. Furthermore, the platform's communication community facilitates student interaction, helping them find like-minded fitness partners.

For 25-35-year-old office workers who grapple with long work hours, minimal physical activity, and irregular eating habits, Keep's online platforms offer short yet efficient training sessions and office stretching exercises designed to fit seamlessly into their daily routines and help alleviate stress. Lastly, prioritizing physical health becomes increasingly important for company executives aged 35-50. With a focus on personalized exercise programs, Keep helps these individuals monitor their health status and exercise progress, effectively adapting to their needs and lifestyle.

Market Analysis

Original Situation of the Market

The online fitness industry, which encompasses various sectors that offer fitness guidance, training programs, health management, and other fitness experiences through internet platforms or technologies, is characterized by convenience, personalization, interactivity, and affordability, which disrupts the traditional fitness model and caters to consumers' needs for convenient, efficient, personalized, and cost-effective fitness solutions (Doc88.com, n.d.). The resurgence of national interest in sports and fitness can be attributed to the successful hosting of the 2008 Beijing Olympic Games. Concurrently, the gradual introduction of smartphones into the Chinese market led to the industry taking shape in the early 2010s. At this stage, the sports fitness app industry was in its nascent phase, with limited applications and relatively basic functionalities primarily focused on recording users' sports data.

Rapid Growth Period

The market experienced rapid growth from 2013 to 2018, during which many apps, such as Keep and Codoon, were launched, leading to intense competition among users. The product functionality gradually improved, and the business model primarily focused on the online model (Xu, 2022).

The first reason for the market's rapid development during this period was the rapid emergence of new technology and the widespread application of Internet technology. In 2013, China entered a new era of mobile internet with the combination of 4G signal and WiFi technology with intelligent terminals for information access. This background provided enterprises in this market with diverse and extensive communication channels, paving the way for further development of the sports fitness software industry (Xing, 2019).

The second reason is the state's promotion of the national fitness plan, elevating national fitness to a strategic level. The government issued relevant policy documents to encourage public participation in national fitness, creating a favorable policy environment for developing sports fitness apps. The Notice of The State Council on Printing and Distributing the National Fitness Plan (2016-2020) emphasized using diversified technologies to build a new era of national fitness and developing a fitness platform through network information technology (Li, 2023). Simultaneously, the public's demand for scientific and professional fitness guidance and physical exercise venues grew with the national fitness craze.

Thirdly, the development concept of Internet + sports provided a new solution for mass sports and fitness, making sports and fitness apps the top choice for sports enthusiasts and individuals with fitness needs. People could use sports fitness apps at any time for specialized and scientific sports training at the location of their choice, free from the restrictions of private education course arrangements and activity locations (Xing, 2019).

Since 2019, the market has gradually matured, with the core users of various software stabilizing and overall industry user numbers growing steadily. Some small and medium-sized enterprises have exited the market, and the remaining enterprises continually improve product functions and services to compete for more outstanding market share. Additionally, the impact of government policies, such as home isolation during the 2020 epidemic, led to the closure of many offline gyms. This, in turn, increased the demand for home fitness, leading to a surge in users and a market share increase of 11.4% in 2020-2021 (Li, 2022).

Forecast for this Market

User Scale and Forecast.

China's fitness population is projected to continue expanding, from 303 million in 2021 to 416 million in 2026, with a compound annual growth rate of 6.5%. The future growth of the fitness market will mainly be attributed to the online fitness market. The yearly average monthly active users of online fitness members and fitness content increased from approximately 1.4 million in 2016 to 138 million in 2021 and are expected to reach 238 million by 2026, representing a CAGR of 11.6% from 2021 to 2026. Additionally, up to 87% of online fitness users are fitness enthusiasts who have paid for offline fitness services within a year, indicating that offline fitness enthusiasts are transitioning to online platforms. With the gradual shift of offline fitness enthusiasts to online platforms and the continuous increase in active online fitness users, the future growth of China's fitness market is anticipated to come mainly from the online fitness market. China's online fitness market accounted for 47% of the country's overall fitness market in 2021 and is expected to grow at a CAGR of 19.3% from 2021 to 2026, significantly higher than the offline fitness market growth rate of 7% during the same period. The online fitness market is projected to represent 60.6% of the overall market 2026 (Han, 2021).

Market Size and Forecast

The current digital trend in China's fitness industry is evident, driven by the increasing shift of users towards online fitness methods. With the augmentation of factors such as the burgeoning availability of professional content for online fitness, China's online fitness market is poised for continued expansion. China's online fitness market is expected to grow to 896.5 billion yuan by 2026, with a compound annual growth rate (CAGR) of 19.3% from 2021 to 2026. The online fitness market in China encompasses revenue from online fitness memberships and fitness content and the online sales of innovative fitness equipment, fitness gear, and health food. Online health food constitutes the primary contributor, accounting for 53% of the online fitness market. However, it is expected that, with the swift development of other market segments, the market contribution of online health food will decrease to 41% by 2026. Although online fitness memberships and classes had a later start, they are projected to exhibit the fastest growth, with a CAGR of 30.8% by 2026 (Han, 2022).

Development and Strategy

Completing the Market Breakthrough

Before the establishment of Keep, there was an apparent mismatch between supply and demand in China's fitness market. On the demand side, people with body and health problems experienced a sharp increase in the demand for expanding exercise and fitness options. However, on the supply side, standardized fitness resources were scarce, and fitness content needed to be more cohesive. Offline gyms, private education, and other channels were costly (Liu, 2023).

The Keep App was launched in 2015, focusing on the concept of "Internet + fitness", integrating fragmented fitness information and providing proprietary structured fitness courses. Keep App significantly reduced the fitness threshold and quickly filled the gap in the online fitness market (Liu, 2023). Initially, the Keep team focused on vertical social media platforms that attracted the attention of millions of users, including Baidu Post Bar, WeChat fitness mutual aid groups, Douban Fitness Group, etc. They accumulated many fans by serializing exercise and fitness experiences on these platforms over a long period.

Simultaneously, the Keep team also planned and organized chief experience officer recruitment activities, inviting core users to prioritize the experience to cultivate seed users (Xing, 2019). The app grew from an initial beta of 4,000 to 2 million online users within three months of its launch. 2015 the platform had 1 million monthly active users (Xie, 2023). With the rapid growth of China's online fitness market, Keep continued to expand the content library, continuously update and iterate, optimize the user experience, and expand the user groups covered. In 2016, Keep had an average of 10 million monthly active users (Liu, 2023).

Customer Retention Issues

Keep, an online fitness app, faces challenges in retaining customers. The majority of its users are beginners with limited fitness and exercise knowledge. While Keep currently offers professional fitness instruction videos and at-home weight training, it struggles to cater to the evolving needs of users as they progress from beginners to fitness enthusiasts. As users advance in their fitness journey, they often seek additional resources such as fitness equipment, gyms, and private lessons, leading them to transition to traditional gym settings. This is primarily due to Keep's limitations in providing a comprehensive range of fitness content that caters to the diverse needs of its users. To address this issue, Keep is considering solutions such as establishing offline gyms and hosting virtual events.

Explore the Way of Commercial Realization

2018 Keep adopted a commercialization strategy and transitioned into a sports technology ecological company. Keep released Keepland, intelligent fitness equipment, and supporting sports products, focusing on product expansion and scene extension. In the same year, Keep launched a membership subscription program. The "Smart hardware + membership subscription" approach enhances the user experience and integrates sports data online, establishing an effective sports feedback mechanism that improves user stickiness and activity simultaneously (Liu, 2023).

In 2019, Keep officially set the development direction to provide users with a "one-stop solution" for "eating, wearing, and practicing" to cover more life scenes for sports enthusiasts. Keep initiated cross-border cooperation with multiple brands and introduced the "KPartner" plan to integrate high-quality ecosystem resources and enhance user stickability. By 2019, the number of subscribers had reached 1 million (Liu, 2023).

Header IP and Platform Cooperation Mode

Keep has signed up several well-known exercise and fitness bloggers, such as Pamela. In 2020, Keep officially opened the cooperation with Pamela, and the number of followers of its account exceeded 100,000 on the day it was settled. In 2021, Pamela made her world live debut on Keep, attracting much attention. In 2022, it will upgrade its cooperation model. Both parties jointly create exclusive membership courses based on users' sports needs and exercise pain points to provide users with more detailed and practical exercise courses. This model enhances the stickiness and value of the platform to users and increases the number of members who subscribe (Xie, 2023).

A New Experience Combining Sports and Games

Keep is actively exploring gamification features. In 2020, Keep is set to launch live classes. Group competitions and rankings in live classes can simulate a real-time, face-to-face competitive environment and improve user participation. To address the issue of the tedious exercise process, the gamification function is first introduced in live classes to reduce users' resistance to sports, upgrade the user experience, and attract more users to join the Keep ecosystem. In 2021, Keep and SNK jointly launched the world's first Boxing Emperor 97 co-branded course, "sports + games," aimed at enhancing interest and stimulating users' desire for sports through action design, vision, and hearing aspects. As a result, user interaction with content increases, unlocking a better sports experience (Liu, 2023).

Epidemic Outbreak, Content, and Service Upgrades

The epidemic has stimulated the popularity of home fitness, and the content and services have been further upgraded in 2020. Home exercise has become a new trend. During the epidemic containment period, Keep keenly seized the opportunities of home fitness, took the lead in launching interactive live classes, and jointly launched the "Whole Network Live Sports Class Schedule" with a comprehensive consideration of practicality, entertainment, and interaction, covering more user groups and driving the further increase of active users of the platform (Liu, 2023). After gaining many home fitness users through online live broadcasting in 2020, Keep continues to launch high-quality fitness content and services. In 2021, Keep introduced "Temperament Ballet," "Hot Sweat Yoga," and "Fat Burning Party," three boutique IP courses entirely focusing on the fitness needs of female users (Liu, 2023).

The Viral Effect of Virtual Events

In 2018, Keep launched a series of virtual sports events requiring users to register for running activities by paying for them and completing them within a specific time frame to obtain medals, certificates, and other products. In December 2021, Keep collaborated with Japan's Sanrio company to launch the "Yugui Dog" online running activity. Users shared their participation videos and showcased the event medals on social platforms. The videos quickly gained traction among young people and on social media. Keep Medals expanded its popularity circle, attracting over 400,000 users to pay and participate. Since the launch of this virtual event, Keep has experienced its first explosive joint IP event. Within the first 10 minutes of opening for new registrations, "Yugui Dog" attracted over 200,000 registered users, with over 100,000 of them being paid registered users (Xie, 2023). As a result, Keep has increased its investment in IP cross-border cooperation, and the company's online payment revenue in the first quarter of 2022 increased by over 700% year-on-year.

Business Adjustment Under the Impact of the Epidemic

Keep has also encountered difficulties in the process of development. In 2018, Keep opened its first offline store in Beijing and then continued to open stores one after another. However, offline gyms are asset-heavy businesses with significant investments and little income. Fitness clubs have already occupied market share due to their scale advantages, making it difficult for Keepland to make profits in the short term. Furthermore, the epidemic in 2020 has also impacted the development of offline stores, leading Keep to close offline stores one after another. Subsequently, Keep changed its strategic direction and planned to cooperate with traditional gyms to reduce corporate costs. Keep plans to reduce prices by 40%-50% compared to Keepland and re-launch "preferred gyms" in 2022. Presently, Keepland has nine self-owned stores and ten cooperative stores.

After years of development, Keep adheres to the "Internet + fitness" model and has become a representative brand in the domestic sports field. Keep has developed a comprehensive fitness solution and gradually established an ecological closed loop combining hardware and software, fully covering online and offline aspects, forming a new sports ecology.

THE PEOPLE BEHIND KEEP

Wang Ning

Wang Ning, the founder of Keep, graduated from Beijing Information Science and Technology University with a major in computer science. He currently holds the positions of Executive Director, Chairman, and Chief Executive Officer of Keep Corporation. He is responsible for the company's overall strategy, business development, and management (Yao & Tan, 2022). During high school, Wang Ning aspired to start a business and gain more experience in society. Consequently, when he entered university, he actively sought out internship opportunities. Before establishing Keep, he completed internships at several companies. His experience at the APe counselling company had the most significant impact on him, where he was involved in product research, job interviews, and managing interns (Yang & Chen, 2020). This experience proved valuable in laying the foundation for Keep.

The birth of Keep is closely tied to Wang Ning's weight loss journey. Once weighing 180 pounds, he successfully shed the excess weight to achieve a healthier weight of 130 pounds. As a student facing financial constraints, he crafted a successful weight-loss program by gathering information from the internet. This led to him becoming a well-known weight-loss authority among his peers. His friends sought advice from him, revealing the lack of accessible solutions to various fitness-related questions many people face (Yang & Chen, 2020). This realization prompted the creation of Keep to help individuals address their fitness-related challenges. Wang Ning proposed a business model for the development of Keep, which has garnered continuous financial support and lays the foundation for Keep's eventual success and growth. Wang Ning has stated on many occasions that the vision of Keep is to be the "Google" of the sports and fitness industry - just as people Google when they want to search something, they will "Keep" it when they want to exercise and focus on fitness.

Peng Wei

Peng Wei, the founder of Keep, graduated from Tianjin University of Commerce with a major in applied psychology. Currently, he serves as the Executive Director of Keep and Vice President of the Online Operations Division, where he is responsible for leading and managing the online platform division of Keep (Xie, 2023). Before joining the Keep team, he worked as a product manager at APe counseling company, gaining valuable experience in product design. He possesses unique insights and understanding, particularly in the evolution process of Keep products from 0 to 1 to 100 (Yao & Tan, 2022).

FUTURE PROJECTS

The first is accumulation. Keep plans to expand the reachable market by appealing to users of different age groups, interest areas and locations. It strives to achieve market sinking and continues to expand the user base. The second is Innovation. Keep will continue to invest in developing innovation and diversified platform content. At the same time, it will attract more internal coaches and key opinion leaders to settle in. The third is Interaction. Keep encouraging content creators to interact more with users, and plan to form a synergy effect with third-party products through products to enrich products and attract more users. The fourth is research and development. Keep will continue strengthening technological innovation and investing in artificial intelligence and other technologies to provide users with more personalized fitness content products. The fifth is value. Keep committed to further strengthening the brand value through online and offline marketing. At the same time, it will strive to improve user experience and increase user engagement and satisfaction. Finally, is realization. Continue to strengthen the realization capacity and explore other realization channels. Moreover, it is expected to convert more users into subscription members (Yao & Tan, 2022).

REFERENCES

CSDN. (2020, September 7). *[Competitive Product Analysis Report: How Can Keep Make Sports More]*. CSDN. https://wenku.csdn.net/doc/5qt3z9xd4k

Han, X. C. (2021, April 20). *[Online Fitness: A gym at home]*. Zhongtai Securities. https://pdf.dfcfw.com/pdf/H3_AP202204271561920041_1.pdf?1651069207000.pdf

Ikanchai. (2019). *Keep won the 2019 Responsible Brand award, delivering a new way of healthy living through internet technology express chopping network*. Ikanchai. http://news.ikanchai.com/2020/0115/332495.shtml

Li, W. G. (2023). [Keep APP Research on the Development Strategy of Fitness APP Based on PEST Analysis Paradigm——Taking Keep APP as an Example]. *Contemporary Sports Science and Technology*, 13(3). DOI:10.16655/j.cnki.2095-2813.2209-1579-3569

Lin, H. S., & Wang, Y. B. (2023). Research on the Current Situation and Development Strategy of Keep Fitness Software Sports Marketing. *Sports Boutique*, 42(02), 51–53.

Liu, Z. W. (2023, December 28). *[China's largest online fitness platform, deep cultivation of online fitness to form a diversified realization]*. Doc88. https://www.doc88.com/p-95929899267358.html

Wu, A. H. (2022). *Big Data Boosts the Development of China Fitness Industry - Take Keep App as an Example*. Shandong University., DOI:10.2991/978-94-6463-036-7_144

Xie, L. Y. (2023, December 3). *[In-depth discussion: Can Keep's unique business model run through?]*. Topsperity Securities. https://pdf.dfcfw.com/pdf/H3_AP202312041613226542_1.pdf

Xing, W. Y. (2019). *[Research on the development strategy of sports fitness APP under the background of "Internet +]*. Yanshan University. DOI:10.27440/d.cnki.gysdu.2019.001044

Xu, M. J. (2022, March 31). *[How to View the Model of Online Fitness Platform?]* Sinolink Securities. https://pdf.dfcfw.com/pdf/H3_AP202204011556478581_1.pdf?1648818722000.pdf

Yang, W. M., & Chen, M. Z. (2020). *[Keep: The entrepreneurial road of fitness "little white"]*. *Tsinghua Management Review*, 03, 104–111.

Yao, L., & Tan, R. Q. (2021, April 20). *[KEEP in-depth report: Sports + technology first stock, content + consumption dual drive]*. Sealand Securities. https://pdf.dfcfw .com/pdf/H3_AP202204211560651758_1.pdf?1650558366000.pdf

Zhang, S. (2016). "Dream Sports Ground" Charity Plan 6 Years: Multiple playgrounds launched in remote areas. *China News*. https://m.chinanews.com/wap/detail/zw/sh/ 2021/06-01/9490405.shtml

KEY TERMS AND DEFINITIONS

Brand Awareness: It refers to how value consumers identify and remember a company's business and products. The higher a company's brand awareness, the more familiar your audience will be with your logo, message, and product.

CAGR: (Compound Annual Growth Rate): An investment's annual growth rate over a specific period.

Interactivity: This concept means that through an interactive Internet platform, users can obtain relevant information and services and communicate and interact with other users or platforms, generating more ideas and demands.

Key Opinion Leader: This term refers to a person who possesses accurate product information and is accepted or trusted by a relevant group, significantly influencing the group's purchasing behavior.

Professional User-Generated Content: This model of content creation refers to content created by professionals with deep knowledge of a field, typically of high quality and professionalism.

Product Iteration: It refers to continuously improving a product through several small-scale enhancements and updates to adapt to changes in market demand, technological development, and user feedback.

Synergy Effect: It refers to the overall impact of different links, stages, and aspects of enterprise production, marketing, and management when the same resources are used together.

User Stickiness: It refers to the degree of dependence and re-consumption expectation formed by the combination of a user's loyalty, trust, and positive experience with a brand or product.

Chapter 24
Yuanfudao:
Transforming China's K12 Online Education Landscape

Jiarui Yang

Beijing Normal University-Hong Kong Baptist University United International College, China

EXECUTIVE SUMMARY

This case study explores the transformative journey of Yuanfudao within China's dynamic K12 online education sector. Founded by Li Yong in 2012, it initially struggled with its business model centred around their question bank. Overcoming early challenges, they pivoted to capitalize on the burgeoning demand for online live courses, launching Fenbigongkao and subsequently integrating AI-driven solutions like Ape Search and Zebra AI. As the market evolved, they navigated regulatory changes and competitive pressures, adapting strategies to align with national educational policies and shifting consumer preference. The case examines key milestones such as strategic partnerships with Xinhua Publishing House and the launch of the Ape Learning Machine, highlighting their innovative approach to enhancing learning outcomes through technology. Analysing the growth trajectory, technological advancements, and strategic initiatives, the case offers insights into the broader implications of digital transformation in education and their role in shaping the future of K12 online learning in China.

DOI: 10.4018/979-8-3693-2921-4.ch024

UNICORN DESCRIPTION

Brief History of the Unicorn

Launched by Ape Tutor, a subsidiary of Beijing Zhenguanyu Technology Company Limited (affiliated with Chalk.com), towards the end of 2014, Yuanfudao is an online tutoring application catering to K-12 subjects. Yuanfudao's primary service offering is live tutoring courses, capitalizing on fragmented time to deliver online learning during semester, winter, and summer breaks, as well as a plethora of thematic classes. The company provides courses covering all elementary and secondary school subjects Through its online education products, namely Yuanfudao, Ape Search, Yuantiku, Ape Oral Calculation, and Zebra AI Lessons. Yuanfudao is the first online education unicorn company in the K-12 domain in China (spanning pre-school to 12 years of compulsory education), and it is ranked at the top among global ed-tech unicorn companies. This achievement marks the first time a Chinese e-tech firm has been placed at the forefront of global e-tech unicorns (Yuanfudao n.d.).

In 2019, Yuanfudao garnered recognition as one of the "2019 Forbes China's Most Innovative Companies". On December 16 of the same year, Yuanfudao and Ape Search, Ape Troubleshooting, Ape Oral Calculation, and Zebra English were included in the first batch of education apps for the record. The company further elevated its status on July 13, 2020, when Yuanfudao Online Education was announced as the official sponsor of the Beijing 2022 Winter Olympics and Winter Paralympics (Interface News n.d.). Furthermore, in early 2020, it was chosen for the "CCTV Brand Strengthening Project" and became a special partner of the 2020 CCTV Spring Festival Gala (Snowball, n.d.).

The onset of 2020 brought regulatory changes in China's education sector, challenging companies such as Yuanfudao. Strict regulations on after-school education, including restrictions on tutoring hours and a prohibition on certain types of tutoring during weekends and holidays, have notably affected the business models of online education platforms. However, Yuanfudao's incorporation of artificial intelligence into their curriculum enables them to offer personalized learning experiences, interactive content, and immediate feedback, thereby enhancing student engagement and learning outcomes. Moreover, their diversification into science education opens up a potentially profitable market segment while decreasing the regulatory risk associated with the traditional tutoring industry. This strategic manoeuvre broadens its market reach and consolidates its standing as a leader in China's online education landscape (TechNode, 2023).

Business Model

Yuanfudao, an online K12 education platform, primarily operates a dual-teacher classroom model, blending "online live lectures + tutoring on the ground". The health of this business is determined by its revenue, which can be analyzed using the Gross Merchandise Volume (GMV) model: GMV = number of users * conversion rate * customer unit price. An increase in any of these three key indicators—number of users, conversion rate, and customer unit price—directly boosts the business's revenue (36 Krypton, 2024).

Yuanfudao employs a dual strategy of paid advertising and organic word-of-mouth referrals to increase the number of users. The platform invests in paid advertising on popular TV programs and public spaces like subways and elevators, building a subconscious brand impression. Collaborations with well-known personalities like Yu Qiuyu and Zhou Guoping further drive traffic to the platform and enhance the brand's influence. Simultaneously, Yuanfudao leverages its suite of learning tools, such as Ape Mouth Math and Ape Search, to improve the efficiency of parents' tutoring and homework correction efforts. By providing parents with free real-time data on their children's learning progress, Yuanfudao encourages word-of-mouth referrals, attracting new users to the platform (Education.com, n.d.).

Once users are drawn to the platform, Yuanfudao utilizes several strategies to improve its conversion rate. The platform offers trial classes and limited-time vouchers at preferential prices, allowing parents to sample the service at a lower cost. These low-priced experience classes, accompanied by live lectures and real-time student interaction, fully embody the value of the course, reducing the cost of trial and error for parents. Additionally, Yuanfudao's courses, priced between 700-1000 yuan on average, offer a more comprehensive cost-performance ratio compared to expensive offline tutoring classes. The platform also provides flexible class transfer and refund policies, and round-the-clock online customer service, all of which help eliminate user purchasing concerns and encourage parents to commit to a purchase (Bianews, n.d.).

Yuanfudao increases the customer unit price by encouraging users to purchase multiple courses simultaneously and maintaining a high renewal rate. The platform's differentiated pricing for different course subjects and activities like "buy two subjects, get the third free" effectively promote the purchase of multiple courses at once. Furthermore, a high renewal rate, which stood at over 80% in 2019 according to CCTV.com, also contributes to an increase in the customer unit price (36 Krypton, 2021).

In 2020, the online education industry experienced significant growth due to the pandemic. However, stricter market regulations in 2021 led to increased compliance costs and a withdrawal of capital. In response to these changes, Yuanfudao adjusted its business model, focusing on K12 education and product development based on core learning scenarios. The platform continues to attract users through advertising and word-of-mouth, converting them into regular-priced classes through low-priced experiential classes. Yuanfudao also launched an AI-based science education program, diversifying its business and proactively responding to regulatory updates (Runwise, 2022).

Products and Services

Product Portfolio

Yuanfudao offers a diverse portfolio of online education products that cater to various educational needs, such as online tutoring, intelligent exercises, and problem analysis. Here is an overview of Yuanfudao's primary offerings:

- The Yuanfudao app is a comprehensive online tutoring platform that offers instruction for all subjects at the elementary, middle, and high school levels. It serves as the main hub for Yuanfudao's online education services (Sina Mobile, 2020).
- The Xiaoyuansouti APP is a homework question-and-answer tool for primary and secondary school students. It provides a platform for students to seek assistance with their homework, fostering a supportive learning environment (Sina Mobile, 2021).
- The Yuantiku APP is a focused tool for primary and secondary school students, specifically designed for practising math. This app provides a platform for students to brush up on their math skills, reinforcing their classroom learning (Sina Education; 2019).
- The Xiaoyuankousuan APP is a mobile practice and correction tool that supports various question types, including oral calculation, vertical calculation, unit conversion, multiple choice, judgment, application, and fill-in-the-blanks. This app offers students a flexible and comprehensive practice platform (New Beijing News, 2020).
- The Zebra AI Lesson APP is a specialised program for children aged 2-8 that focuses on thinking and language learning. This app uses advanced AI techniques to provide young children with engaging and practical language learning experiences (HuffPost, 2020).

In addition to these education-focused products, Yuanfudao has developed an AI-powered UI design tool called Motiff. Leveraging their expertise in AI, honed through collaborations with prestigious Chinese universities, Yuanfudao aims to tap into the growing demand for advanced design tools with Motiff. This represents a strategic expansion beyond their core focus in education (Foresight Industry Research Institute, n.d.).

For online tutoring, parents' expectations from online education platforms include high-quality teachers, a scientific teaching system to ensure teaching quality, personalized teaching, and suitable timing. Students look for engaging and enlightening courses, systematic knowledge acquisition, practice reinforcement, real-time tutoring, and review of challenging topics (National Bureau of Statistics, n.d.).

Yuanfudao has a professional teaching and research team that systematically designs the curriculum by subject and grade, ensuring the curriculum's integrity and relevance. Yuanfudao also maintains a domestic K-12 learning behavior database of 10 billion, with 7.4 billion instances of students' question-answering behavior data and 28.4 billion topic search data. This extensive data analysis ensures the course design's relevance and focus (China Education Online, n.d.).

In the "dual-teacher mode" of live online teaching, most lecturers are highly educated individuals from prestigious universities like Tsinghua University and Peking University. With an average of over four years of teaching experience and an acceptance rate of less than 1%, these lecturers have undergone a stringent selection process to ensure their qualifications and teaching proficiency. The class teacher supervises tutors and answers questions, providing real-time tracking of the learning situation. This approach ensures excellent in-class content and practical post-class application, leading to student learning conversion and continuous order renewal (Sohu, n.d.).

Yuanfudao's teaching method is based on immersive learning design with real-time interaction to enhance student focus. The course content is delivered using a combination of animations, video demonstrations, and other methods. Small incentives, such as trading gold coins for learning tools, are used to boost student enthusiasm. This diverse and engaging course interaction design encourages students to participate more actively, enhancing their enjoyment and experience.

Yuanfudao's class director provides timely learning reports throughout the child's learning process. On one hand, teachers can use these reports to help students overcome challenges. On the other hand, the learning reports allow parents to monitor their child's progress, providing a quantitative basis for assessing the course's effectiveness and informing decisions about order renewals (Easemob, n.d.).

Yuanfudao offers a range of learning tools to enhance the efficiency of parents and students in learning and tutoring, including Ape Search, Ape Mental Math, and other online education products. These provide users with diverse intelligent education services, such as online classes, intelligent exercises, and problem analysis, helping students complete the learning cycle systematically and highly efficiently (China Science and Technology Information, 2019).

Competitive Environment

Regarding competition, Zuoyebang, which translates to "Homework Help" in English, is a prominent player in China's online education sector. Founded in 2015, the company started as a homework-help app that used AI technology to answer students' questions. Over the years, Zuoyebang has evolved into a comprehensive online tutoring platform offering live-streamed lessons and other educational resources for kindergarten through twelfth-grade students. The platform's user-friendly design and accessible pricing have made it a popular choice for millions of students across China (Bizinnolab, n.d.).

Yuanfudao and Zuoyebang were initially launched as primary tools for question search but they have evolved into comprehensive educational platform products. Their development timelines, growth trajectories, and business models share striking similarities, positioning them as direct competitors. The ensuing analysis focuses on these two products, shedding light on their growth paths and business models (The Paper, n.d.).

Yuanfudao's entire course system is priced at a relatively high range. The company places a significant emphasis on brand promotion and has a robust capacity to secure funding. Their promotional efforts include collaborations with CCTV's "Let's Speak" and Jiangsu Satellite Television's "Strongest Brain". Moreover, Yuanfudao has earned the distinction of being the official sponsor of the Beijing 2022 Winter Olympics and Winter Paralympics. In 2020, Yuanfudao secured funding in two consecutive rounds, amassing a substantial cash reserve. This financial backing fuels an aggressive strategy and enables the diversification of its product offerings. However, it is worth noting that Yuanfudao's customer acquisition costs are the highest among its competitors (Snowball, n.d.).

Conversely, Zuoyebang's overall course pricing is relatively low. The company's founders have technical backgrounds, and the core team hails from well-known domestic and international internet companies, providing Zuoyebang with a more advantageous technical foundation. Overall, Zuoyebang holds the most extensive user base and traffic advantage, resulting in the lowest comprehensive customer acquisition costs (36 Krypton, 2024).

Both brands occupy the leading positions in the industry, attracting substantial attention and support from the capital market. Both Yuanfudao and Zuoyebang have been successful in securing significant amounts of funding. Yuanfudao, being established earlier, has secured more funding, giving it a temporary edge in capital valuation. However, this has not translated into a significant leadership advantage, suggesting the competition between the two companies will continue (Tencent News, n.d.).

Customers

Engaging with K12 online education involves students, parents, and teachers. This discussion explores the specific needs of parents and students and how teachers and platforms address these needs:

Students

K12 education spans elementary, middle, and high school, each stage having unique student needs. Elementary school students need engaging and lively lessons that stimulate their interest in learning, foster independent learning habits, and enhance their understanding of basic knowledge. Junior high school students must identify learning gaps and continue consolidating basic knowledge. They must also learn problem-solving strategies and techniques to improve their midterm examination performance. High school students primarily need to prepare for college entrance examinations. Due to the course's complexity, they must learn problem-solving strategies and techniques, engage in extensive practice, and receive real-time tutoring and review of challenging and essential topics (Tencent News, n.d.).

Parents

Due to societal, economic, and cultural factors, parents are a significant customer group in the K12 online education sector, particularly in China. Education is highly valued and considered a primary pathway to upward social mobility in Chinese society. Parents often see their children's academic success as a reflection of their success, so they invest heavily in their children's education. This investment is financial and involves significant time and emotional commitment (National Bureau of Statistics, n.d.).

The competitive nature of the Chinese education system, exemplified by the high-stakes Gaokao (college entrance exam), further amplifies parents' involvement in their children's education. Parents seek high-quality educational resources to give their children an edge in this competitive environment. Online education platforms cater to this demand by providing diverse, high-quality, and convenient learning resources. Finally, the rise of the middle class in China has led to increased disposable income allocated to children's education. Parents are willing to pay for premium educational services, making them a substantial customer group for K12 online education platforms. Therefore, parents, driven by a desire for their children's academic success and social mobility, are a significant customer group for K12 online education in China (HuffPost, 2020).

Teachers

Teachers are central to the K12 online education ecosystem, and their need for the services provided by online education companies is multifaceted. Teachers require robust platforms to deliver lessons effectively in a digital teaching environment. These platforms, like those provided by online education companies, offer tools and resources that help teachers adapt their teaching methods to the online format, enhancing their ability to engage students and convey complex concepts. Additionally, online education companies provide teachers with a broader reach, allowing them to connect with students beyond their immediate location. This expanded reach can lead to more excellent job opportunities and income potential (Sina Mobile, 2021).

Furthermore, these companies offer support systems for teachers, including training in online teaching methodologies, technical support, and resources for curriculum development. This support can enhance teachers' professional development and teaching effectiveness. Lastly, online education platforms provide teachers with tools for tracking student progress, facilitating personalized education, and communicating with parents. These tools enable teachers to meet individual student's needs more effectively and keep parents informed about their children's progress (China Education Online, n.d.).

Market Analysis

Original Situation of the Market

The K12 online education industry, to which Yuanfudao belongs, encapsulates the comprehensive educational structure from kindergarten to twelfth grade. This term has become a standard reference for primary education. The industry was characterized by five main features: high potential with rapid growth, low market concentration, a separation between consumers and decision-makers, a discrepancy between ideals and reality, and a tension between scale and experience (Bizinnolab, n.d.).

There were numerous market players in the K12 online education field, and from 2018 onwards, institutions with some level of brand recognition and market influence were classified according to their original attributes. These fell into three categories: tool product incubation, internet giant incubation, and offline teaching and training institution incubation. Initially, tool product incubators like Yuanfudao and Zuoyebang focused on business learning tools. As their businesses developed, they converted the user traffic from their learning tools into online live courses. This strategy reduced customer acquisition costs, improved efficiency, and created a closed-loop learning system.

On the other hand, offline teaching and training organizations were initially positioned for traditional offline education with a relatively stable profit model. However, these businesses also transitioned online with the rise of online education. While their course products were mature and complete, their transformation could have been timelier, leading to slower development than online brands like Yuanfudao and Zuoyebang. Internet giant incubation involved industry giants like Tencent, Penguin Tutoring, and Qingbei Online School entering the K12 online education market. They leveraged social traffic advantages to target users and divert traffic to their new business areas. However, due to a lack of industry accumulation, they faced potential challenges, including a lack of high-quality content and technical support (Runwise, 2022).

Evolution of the Market Until Today

China's domestic K12 online education industry has grown significantly in recent years, with the capital market showing optimism and support. The current penetration rate of K12 extracurricular tutoring is around 22%, making the market size about 400 billion yuan. In terms of spending, China's K12 education market reached 254.9 billion yuan, with a per capita spend of 5121 yuan/year. Tutoring institutions accounted for 21% of this, and online education comprised 18%. Around 40% of K12 parents spent more than 5000 yuan per year on their children's extracurricular learning, with 15% investing tens of thousands of yuan. First-tier cities became the primary focus of the K12 online education industry, with cities like Beijing, Guangzhou, and Shenzhen accounting for a large proportion of national expenditure. The industry also saw a shift in the market players, with adult education companies like New Oriental and Hujiang Online School transitioning to K12 due to the high renewal rate. This transition led to heightened competition within the industry (36 Krypton, 2021).

Analysis of the Macro Environment

Macro factors often influence the education sector. The K12 education market is vast, and it is challenging to meet its demands solely through government efforts. Currently, the government encourages market forces, especially the burgeoning online education sector, to participate. Policies like the "national key support for high-tech fields" and "the thirteenth five-year plan for national education development" explicitly back this sector. Recently, the government has introduced a series of policies for internet education. These aim to leverage the Internet and other information technology tools to serve the entire education and teaching process, propelling intelligent education's innovative evolution and creating an "Internet +

education" support service platform that charts the course for Internet education development (Foresight Industry Research Institute, n.d.).

The current national K12 public schools have approximately 100 million primary school students, 43 million middle school students, and 23 million high school students. This pool of 160 million students forms the potential user base for the K12 education industry, offering a theoretical user lifecycle of up to 12 years. Furthermore, the number of new 6-year-olds from 2017 to 2023 has been steadily increasing, signifying the vast potential of the K12 education market. The national birth policy adjustments have also led to a surge in the number of school-age children post-2012, thereby expanding the potential user base for the K12 education industry (National Bureau of Statistics, n.d.).

The wealth disparity in China is significant, and parents' concerns about social mobility extend to their children's education. According to China Education Network data from 2022, the average acceptance rates for China's junior and senior high schools are 57% and 59.6%, respectively. Only a quarter of the educated population can successfully progress to undergraduate school at K12 (China Education Online, n.d.).

China's undergraduate ratio is low compared to that of developed countries like the United States, Japan, and Germany. Consequently, extracurricular tutoring has become an efficient tool for improving grades, and many parents have become long-term consumers in the K12 education market. Additionally, the 2020 pandemic has limited many offline learning activities, which has undoubtedly catalyzed the swift growth of online education. Then, the ongoing advancement of science and technology provides more room for K12 online education to grow. The evolution of China's video cloud service industry in recent years has offered low-cost, efficient video services for online teaching, particularly with interactive live cloud services enhancing live teaching (Easemob, n.d.).

Finally, the constant innovation and iteration of big data and processing technology, the application of science and technology to enhance the learning experience, the stimulation of learning interest, and the cultivation of scientific learning habits have allowed students to access quality educational resources more conveniently. With the improvement of network infrastructure, the prevalence of mobile internet, the construction of online platforms, the development of online tools and content, the supply of marketing/management SAAS, the implementation of artificial intelligence technology, and the recruitment and training of teachers, the emergence and maturity of these technologies provide market opportunities for the development and growth of the K12 education market.

Forecast for the Market

The government has progressively introduced relevant laws and regulations for K12 out-of-school training institutions, continually refining these rules. Online education has also been brought under regulatory purview, necessitating further standardization. More rigorous regulatory measures for offline out-of-school tutoring institutions will inevitably raise the entry threshold, signaling the end of the era of intense competition and rampant growth. Resources will likely concentrate on entities that demonstrate high regulatory compliance and professionalism. Despite the tightening regulatory measures, the state still promotes the development of online education. The K12 online education sector holds immense potential. How to adapt to policy developments and enhance competitiveness are both opportunities and challenges that Yuanfudao faces.

The K12 online tutoring industry faces many opportunities and challenges in the post-pandemic era. From an educational perspective, online education will disrupt traditional education models, fostering the integration of online and offline development and establishing a healthy interactive pattern. It will also guide the shift in the education paradigm from "teaching" to "learning," providing crucial support for establishing a lifelong learning system. Economically, online education will become a significant component of the new industry and model, infusing fresh momentum to create new economic growth points and the high-quality development of the economy in the digital era (Tencent News, n.d.).

DEVELOPMENT AND STRATEGY

Product Testing Phase (2013-2014)

During its inception in 2012, Yuanfudao primarily operated on a business model revolving around its product, Yuantiku. This involved developing and selling the product to target customers with revenues generated from these sales. Core resources included an R&D team and a question bank algorithm. However, this model had significant issues. For instance, while students appreciated Yuantiku, their parents were reluctant to pay for it due to concerns about students' reliance on it. Moreover, collecting and organizing a question bank required extensive data accumulation, leading to high costs. Consequently, despite the product's initial success, it did not form a commercially viable loop (Sina Education, 2019).

In 2014, Yuanfudao segmented its operations, creating Fenbigongkao. This was designed for exam preparation, using paid video live courses, and it quickly generated revenue. This success gave Yuanfudao the confidence to reevaluate its entry into the online education market. In the same year, Yuanfudao established an AI lab to develop a new product, Ape Search. This product focuses on photo recognition technology, crucial for students searching for questions and answers online. The recognition rate of various handwritten questions improved significantly, from 60% to 95%. The team continued to iterate on the product, adding explanation videos after discovering that 55% of students sought explanations after finding answers (New Beijing News, 2020).

Business Model Exploration (2015-2016)

In 2015, Yuanfudao started exploring online education models, focusing on matching students with teachers. However, while transactions were made, the re-purchase rate was low due to issues with teacher quality control and low match rates between teachers and students. Yuanfudao concluded that the platform model was not suitable for online education. In 2016, Yuanfudao made a significant transformation. It stopped using part-time teachers, recruited full-time teachers, and shifted from a platform model to operating independently. The company focused on designing teaching products that catered to students' attention spans and reducing systematic course training costs.

The Growth of Zebra AI (Post-2018)

Zebra AI, introduced by Yuanfudao in 2017, has significantly bolstered the company's revenue stream, quickly ascending to the second-largest contributor. This sophisticated AI platform has demonstrated the viability of online education models and established a replicable blueprint for other online educational offerings. Its rapid development and success within a mere two-year span underscore AI's transformative potential in education. The platform's robust performance across multiple product service stages has set it apart from competitors, contributing to Yuanfudao's increased valuation in the capital market. Zebra AI's success story underscores Yuanfudao's commitment to leveraging cutting-edge technology to enhance educational outcomes (China Science and Technology Information, 2019).

Responding to Challenging Upgrades (2020-2022)

In the face of challenging upgrades from 2020 to 2022, Yuanfudao exhibited remarkable resilience and adaptability. The company navigated through China's rapidly evolving educational landscape, which was marked by increasing regulatory scrutiny and shifting market dynamics. In response to the Chinese government's new policy to reduce student workload and prohibit weekend tutoring, Yuanfudao pivoted its business model. It launched an AI-based science education program, ensuring compliance with regulations while continuing to offer high-quality educational services. This strategic move safeguarded Yuanfudao's business and demonstrated its commitment to aligning with national educational objectives and promoting a balanced learning environment for students (The Paper, n.d.).

Accelerating the Layout of Education Transformation (After 2023)

Yuanfudao continued to expand its offerings in the education field. In May, it launched its flagship product, Ape Learning Machine, in the intelligent hardware field. The product, designed for primary and secondary school students, focused on integrated learning and practice. Additionally, Yuanfudao formed a strategic partnership with Xinhua Publishing House to explore primary and secondary school teaching aids. It also established the Youth Science Exploration Fund to support the "Extraordinarily Abnormal Children's Testing System". These actions marked Yuanfudao's entry into the intelligent hardware track and accelerated its layout in the quality and teaching and learning tracks (Bizinnolab, n.d.).

THE PEOPLE BEHIND THE UNICORN

The core group that established Yuanfudao comprises four individuals: Li Yong, Li Xin, Guo Changzun, and Shuaike. The essential characteristic of the original Yuanfudao founding team is that it holistically encompasses the four primary competitive facets: strategy, product, technology, and promotion.

Li Yong

Li Yong, the founder and CEO of Yuanfudao and former president of the NetEase Portal Division, graduated from the Department of Journalism in 1996. Six years after his graduation, in 2002, Li Yong authored a book titled "The Most Important Thing I Have Ever Seen". Reflecting on his initial career as a professional journalist, Li Yong discusses his transition from focusing on government macro-control to micro-mechanisms at the enterprise's specific level. Around 2005, the "competition for talents" between China's traditional and new Internet media frequently made headlines. Traditional media professionals began transitioning to Internet media. During this period, Li Yong joined NetEase as Vice President/Editor-in-Chief and by 2010 he was promoted to president of NetEase's portal business unit (Tencent News, n.d.).

In 2012, Li Yong departed from NetEase to start his venture. His first product was "Chalk.com". In 2013, he launched the online intelligent question bank Yuantiku, and in 2014, he began focusing on the k12 field. The result of this transformation was successful, and by 2015, Li Yong's team secured tens of millions of dollars in D-round financing, making the company a leader in the K12 track. Li Yong's broad vision, deep thinking, and judgment have propelled Yuanfudao Online Education to become an international business company.

Li Xin

Li Xin, co-founder and vice president of Chalk.com and Ape Tutor, previously served as the General Manager of Marketing of NetEase Portal Division. As a partner of Yuanfudao, he also heads the marketing department. Li Xin, with his years of experience as a financial reporter, understands the mindset of the capital market: rapid company growth ensures easy financing. In Yuanfudao, Li Xin is responsible for securing financing and managing expenditures. He firmly believes that education will undergo a digital transformation to make learning more efficient. In his view, technology's most significant contribution to education is its ability to provide targeted explanations and training based on each student's shortcomings and give real-time feedback (China Education Online, n.d.).

Guo Changzhen

Guo Changzhen, co-founder and product technology director of Chalk.com and ApeQuiz, previously served as the editor-in-chief of NetEase's technology channel. In 2013, he co-founded the company with CEO Li Yong and proposed recruiting a high-precision talent team to concentrate on artificial intelligence. Guo Changzhen's learning and accumulation in science and technology provided a robust technological foundation for the later development of Yuanfudao.

Shuaike

Shuaike graduated from Jiangsu University in 2006 and worked in the marketing and sales departments at Colgate, a Fortune 500 company. Two years later, he joined NetEase and witnessed the portal website's media transformation, serving in different roles from a reporter to the youngest editor-in-chief in the company's history. In 2012, he left the company to co-found Yuanfudao. Shuaike's rational market judgment has significantly contributed to Yuanfudao's marketing, brand-building, and user growth.

CONCLUSION

We are observing a transformative era in China's online education with the rise of Yuanfudao. By fusing state-of-the-art technology with groundbreaking pedagogical paradigms, Yuanfudao has successfully challenged the boundaries of traditional education, offering students a more adaptable and personalized learning environment. Its rapid commercial growth not only underscores the vast educational possibilities of technology but also paints a vivid portrait of China's swiftly burgeoning online education market. With the aid of technology, educational access extends beyond traditional classrooms; Yuanfudao's triumph illustrates that it can now penetrate thousands of homes. The increasing prevalence of intelligent tutoring and personalized learning ensures that every student can avail of tailored educational services. This company is successful and a trailblazer in China's educational evolution. On the whole, the emergence of Yuanfudao presents us with a captivating business case and a glimpse into the future potential of education. As technology and education intertwine, we may anticipate more significant innovation opportunities and an expanded platform for nurturing a more creative and well-rounded new generation of talent.

REFERENCES

36Krypton. (2021, January 5). *2020, The Year of Gains and Losses in the Education Industry*. 36Kr. https://36kr.com/p/1040939156160646

36Krypton. (2024, January 16). 2023 Head Education Company Transformation Review: The business landscape blossoms, and technology becomes an essential driver of transformation. 36Kr. https://36kr.com/p/2606033145526913

Big news. (n.d.). The year of Yuanfudao: rediscovering the rhythm. *Big News*. https://www.bianews.com/news/details?id=179070

Bizinnolab. (n.d.). *Jack's Column | The 2020 Epidemic: Yuanfudao's Business Model: Is Online Education Ready?* Bizinnolab. https://www.bizinnolab.com/h-nd-41.html

China Education Online. (n.d.). *Ministry of Education: China's higher education gross enrollment rate will reach 59.6% by 2022*. China Education Online. https://news.eol.cn/meeting/202303/t20230323_2331956.shtml

China Science and Technology Information. (2019). *The State of K12 China*.

Easemob. (n.d.). *AI+Education is not as optimistic as it seems*. EaseMob. https://www.easemob.com/news/4264

Education.com. (n.d.). *2023 Education Industry Insight|Add, subtract, multiply and divide to answer the "2023" questionnaire*. Education.com. https://www.jiaoyujie365.com/N/1510.html

Foresight Industry Research Institute. (n.d.). *China Online Education Industry Market Status, Segmentation, and Development Trend Analysis in 2021 Further Sinking Trend is Obvious*. Foresight Industry Research Institute. https://bg.qianzhan.com/report/detail/300/211011-e5f2ee29.html

HuffPost. (2020, December 15). The $15.5 Billion Giant Yuanfudao: The Underlying Capabilities Behind Crazy Growth. *Huffington Post*. https://www.huxiu.com/article/400201.html

Interface News. (n.d.). Yuanfudao Becomes the Official Sponsor of the Beijing 2022 Winter Olympics. *Interface news*. https://www.jiemian.com/article/4664407.html

Li, X. (2021). China's education companies diversify their businesses after regulatory updates. *Beijing Review*. https://www.bjreview.com/Special_Reports/2022/NPC_CPPCC_Sessions_2022/Economy/202203/t20220303_800277655.html

National Bureau of Statistics. (n.d.). *Income and Consumption Expenditure of the Population in 2023*. National Bureau of Statistics. https://www.stats.gov.cn/

New Beijing News. (2020, March 31). Good News, No End. *New Bejing News.* https://www.bjnews.com.cn/edu/2020/03/31/711118.html

Runwise. (2022, July 6). *Yuanfudao Product Analysis\In-depth analysis of the growth logic of online education platform.* Runwise. https://runwise.co/digital-growth/63943.html

Sina Education. (2019, January 13). *Yuanfudao joins forces with The Strongest Brain for a full strategic partnership to synchronise and push customised lessons.* Sina Education. https://edu.sina.com.cn/l/2019-01-13/doc-ihqfskcn6781910.shtml

Sina Mobile. (2020, October 22). *The first place of the global education technology unicorn came Yuanfudao, who announced the completion of 2.2 billion U.S. dollars in financing.* SINA. https://finance.sina.cn/tech/2020-10-22/detail-iiznctkc7014466.d.html?fromtech=1

Sina Mobile. (2021, January 4). *"Super" Yuanfudao, now online.* SINA. SINA. https://finance.sina.cn/tech/2021-01-04/detail-iiznezxt0432396.d.html?fromtech=1&from=wap

Snowball. (n.d.). *K12 Education Industry Development Prospect Research: forecast market size of about 400 billion yuan.* Xueqiu. https://xueqiu.com/9569737096/266323310

Snowball. (n.d.). *Online Education Institution Ads Land on Spring Festival Gala Wen.* Xueqiu. https://xueqiu.com/7423950559/140050028

Sohu. (n.d.). *Behind the $10 billion Yuanfudao, founder Li Yong's entrepreneurial story is Li Yong.* Sohu. https://m.sohu.com/a/54123652_172472/?pvid=000115_3w_a&spm=smmt.mt-it.fd-d.3.1603943415501QIJMZ9R

Sohu.com. (n.d.). *Interview with Guo Changzun of Yuanfudao: "AI+Education" is not as optimistic as imagined.* Sohu. https://www.sohu.com/a/242185243_350699

TechNode. (2023, April 23). *Tencent-backed Yuanfudao will launch an AI-powered design tool.* TechNode. https://technode.com/2023/04/23/tencent-backed-yuanfudao-to-launch-ai-powered-design-tool/

Tencent News. (n.d.). *Yuanfudao founder Li Yong steps down as Beijing Stranger, its Chalk Technology sprints to IPO.* Tencent News. https://new.qq.com/rain/a/20221201A03OTD00

Tencent News. (n.d.). *Yuanfudao is valued at $15.5 billion and leaps to the top of global education unicorn companies*. Tencent News. https://new.qq.com/rain/a/20201022A0C9N600

The Paper. (n.d.). Yuanfudao completed a new $1 billion round of financing, led by Tall Capital and Tencent's participation. *The Paper*. https://www.thepaper.cn/newsDetail_forward_6768070

Yuanfudao. (n.d.). *Yuanfudao, online education technology leader*. Yuanfudao. https://m.yuanfudao.com/

KEY TERMS AND DEFINITIONS

Comprehensive Subject Coverage: This means that Yuanfudao offers help in a wide variety of subjects, like science, math, and English. It is like having a one-stop shop for all your academic needs.

Deep Learning: This is a type of machine learning in which computers are trained to think like a human brain. They can process a lot of data and learn to recognize complex patterns. It is used in things like image recognition and speech recognition to make computers smarter.

Educational Technology: This refers to all new tech, like computers and the Internet, to improve learning. It uses digital tools and techniques to make lessons more engaging and effective.

Intelligent Algorithm: This is a set of computer instructions that can make sense of data independently. It can decide what to do next or offer personalized services because it can learn and adapt.

Interactive Instruction: This is a teaching method that gets students really involved. Instead of just listening to a teacher, students ask questions, participate in discussions, and work together. It makes learning more fun and helps students understand better.

K12 Education: This refers to all the schooling from kindergarten (the 'K') through 12th grade. All the learning happens from when you are a little kid to when you are about to graduate high school.

Online Education: This is like taking a class but instead of sitting in a physical classroom, you use your computer or phone. You can learn from anywhere, and the lessons can be shared with people worldwide.

Online Tutoring: This is like having a private teacher, but the lessons are done over the internet. You can use a computer or phone to get one-on-one help from a tutor anytime.

Personalized Learning: This is a teaching method in which the lessons are tailored to fit each student's unique needs and learning styles. It's like having a custom-made education.

Chapter 25
Zuoyebang:
Pioneering the Future of Intelligent Education Hardware

Sijing Zhou

Beijing Normal University-Hong Kong Baptist University United International College, China

EXECUTIVE SUMMARY

This case study examines Zuoyebang's strategic evolution from an online education platform to a leader in intelligent education hardware amidst transformative industry shifts and regulatory challenges in China. Founded by Hou Jianbin in 2015 as a spinoff from Baidu, Zuoyebang initially focused on providing K12 students with homework assistance. Overcoming industry crises and regulatory changes, the company pivoted towards developing AI-powered learning devices, leveraging its extensive data resources and market insights. The case details Zuoyebang's strategic decisions, including extensive financing rounds, workforce expansion to over 30,000 employees, and the launch of successful intelligent hardware products. It also explores future directions, such as expanding offline sales channels and continuous product innovation, highlighting Zuoyebang's adaptation to market demands and technological advancements in the education sector.

UNICORN DESCRIPTION

Brief History of the Unicorn

Established in 2015, Zuoyebang is a leading online education platform in China, providing comprehensive learning assistance services for K-12 students. The company initially gained traction as a photo-based homework help app, leveraging

DOI: 10.4018/979-8-3693-2921-4.ch025

Baidu's user base and traffic to expand rapidly. Over the years, it has developed various learning tools, including live classes, classical literature assistance, and essay searches. By 2020, Zuoyebang had achieved significant milestones, with over 800 million activated user devices and a monthly active user count of 170 million.

Despite facing challenges due to the "double reduction" policy in 2021, which scaled down the activity of private learning companies in China, Zuoyebang has continued to innovate. In 2022, it ventured into the learning hardware field and launched five new products, including learning pens, smartwatches, AI learning desks, electronic vocabulary cards, and teaching printers. This move showcased its vital product research and development capabilities and helped it secure the title "Most Popular Smart Education Product" at the 2022 China New Economy Industry Annual Summit.

In addition to its commercial success, Zuoyebang is also committed to social responsibility. Through its "Qianfan Public Welfare Program," the company helps millions of underprivileged students access quality educational resources, underscoring its positive impact and social recognition in the education sector.

Zuoyebang's business model has evolved in response to user demands and policy changes. Initially, it operated as a subsidiary of Baidu Zhidao and attracted users through its online Q&A platform. The company then transitioned to an instant photo-based homework assistance tool and introduced a free feature, marking the application of big data and artificial intelligence in education. As its user base grew, Zuoyebang monetized its traffic through live online courses, an online marketplace, and VIP services. Implementing the "double reduction" policy prompted another strategic shift, with the company moving into the learning hardware market and forming a "1+N+X" intelligent education ecosystem centered around the Smart Learning System.

Product and Services

Zuoyebang APP

Zuoyebang APP, the core product of Zuoyebang, is a full-featured online education software that helps students solve various learning problems and provides multiple tutoring tools. Photo Search is the earliest feature introduced by Zuoyebang, which uses advanced picture and voice recognition technology to provide users with accurate question search services. Users only need to take a picture or input the question using voice, and they can get a detailed solution process. The size of Zuoyebang's question bank has reached a staggering 660 million questions (Zuoyebang, 2023).

Subsequently, Zuoyebang has continued to expand its range of learning services to establish itself as a one-stop learning tutoring solution. Zuoyebang has introduced services such as live classes for homework help, one-on-one tutoring, VIP videos explaining topics, and added learning widgets such as essay and word search. Zuoyebang has a matrix of self-developed learning tools that meet students' independent learning needs at the k12 education stage. With the advantage of Baidu's traffic and the launch of the photo search function, Zuoyebang has rapidly accumulated many users and maintained an absolute competitive advantage in similar products.

Zuoyebang Oral Calculation

The Zuoyebang Oral Calculator combines an extensive data question bank and AI technology to provide parents and teachers with online homework checking, correction practice, class management, and other functions. Parents can quickly receive feedback and answers to students' assignments through the homework-checking function, improving communication efficiency between parents and teachers. Additionally, Zuoyebang's practice function includes an error book feature, which saves students' errors in real time and can intelligently generate questions based on those errors to help improve students' calculation skills. Simultaneously, teachers can create classes, assign exercises in the app, and monitor students' exercise results in real-time. The Zuoyebang Oral Calculator aims to provide students with personalized tutoring and practice support to improve learning efficiency while making it convenient for parents and teachers to facilitate students' overall development.

Zuoyebang Intelligent Hardware

Zuoyebang Intelligent Hardware is a critical component of Zuoyebang's education ecosystem. Leveraging its vast repository of over 10 billion school data and advanced AIGC (Artificial Intelligence in General Curriculum) technology, Zuoyebang has developed a comprehensive range of highly effective learning companion products for various subjects, school ages, and learning scenarios. This product matrix follows a 1+N+X model, which consists of a Smart Learning System (1), multiple learning scenarios (N), and diverse learning products (X).

Zuoyebang's intelligent hardware is the underlying software capability, functioning like a smart operating system that powers the entire ecosystem. It enables seamless integration and interconnection among intelligent learning products, creating a cohesive, intelligent education environment. These learning products include learning printers, vocabulary cards, smart desks and chairs, all-subject learning pens, learning tablets, and smartwatches, among others.

The intelligent hardware series Zuoyebang offers reflects its ability to extend educational advantages to traditional hardware categories. For instance, the Zuoyebang AI study table goes beyond the conventional study desk by integrating AI technology. It provides comprehensive intelligent support for children studying at home, incorporating features such as fingertip word search, timing focus, voice assistant, and schedule reminders. The Zuoyebang study watch, equipped with self-developed OCR technology, allows users to look up words and translate them anytime, anywhere. Moreover, the watch includes a word memorization function, where specific words are pushed to the user's attention each time they lift their wrist, enhancing memory retention.

The Zuoyebang learning machine employs OCR (Optical et al.), NLP (Natural et al.) technology, and knowledge mapping capabilities to enable automatic homework correction. It identifies correct or incorrect answers, recommends video explanations, and provides additional exercises based on specific knowledge points. Zuoyebang has accumulated over 200 patents in OCR, voice recognition, image recognition, and homework correction.

Additionally, Zuoyebang's educational hardware brand has pioneered the domestic error printer market, becoming China's best-selling error printer brand. The Meow machine error printer utilizes thermal printing technology, eliminating the need for ink cartridges and allowing for fast printing. This design avoids common issues traditional printers face, such as frequent ink cartridge replacements and leakage. The Meow Machine incorporates a question bank with over 660 million questions and offers a compact size, simple operation, and remote printing capabilities. Recognizing traditional printers' limitations in size, complex operation processes, and high maintenance costs, Zuoyebang has also introduced various home-learning printer models. Despite a slowdown in the global consumer electronics market in 2022, the overall intelligent learning machine market is up 55%, with Zuoyebang's Meow Meow Error Printer up more than 600% last year (Li, 2023).

Another original educational smart hardware category from Zuoyebang is the electronic word card. It features an e-ink screen design and leverages the Ebbinghaus forgetting curve to enhance students' word memorization. In the face of intense competition, Zuoyebang continually updates its electronic word card products, which now support nine languages, include a pronunciation function, and offer a vast built-in thesaurus. The introduction of the Meow Meow Machine has expanded the concept of memory and has redefined traditional knowledge cards' boundaries.

Zuoyebang Parent Edition

Zuoyebang's Parent Edition is software designed to empower parents to understand their children's learning progress better and provide timely assistance. This software enables parents to access and review their children's homework completion status, test scores, and other relevant information at their convenience to facilitate effective monitoring of their children's academic performance. Furthermore, the Parent Edition offers a communication platform facilitating direct interaction between parents and teachers. This feature enables parents to stay informed about their children's performance in school and collaborate with teachers to develop appropriate learning plans.

Besides monitoring their child's learning, Zuoyebang's Parent Edition incorporates several other valuable features. For instance, it includes a family education zone that recommends suitable educational resources and learning methodologies based on each child's needs. This feature alleviates parents' concerns about finding appropriate learning materials and facilitates a more comfortable tutoring experience. Moreover, the Parent Edition also provides interactive functions that encourage parent-child engagement during study sessions, fostering a positive and enjoyable learning environment.

Customers

Students

In the context of China's exam-oriented education, students are burdened with a large amount of challenging after-school homework. According to iiMedia Research (2019), during the school year, 50.0% of primary and secondary school students spend 3 to 4 hours a day completing their homework, and 38.7% of them can finish their homework within 3 hours. During holidays, most primary and secondary school pupils spend less than five hours a day on homework assigned by their school, with 44.6% of pupils completing it in three hours and 43.1% needing between three and five hours. Schools that cannot personalize teaching content for individual students may hinder effective learning despite the students' efforts.

Zuoyebang effectively assists students in clarifying their thoughts and finding the correct answers through features such as photo search and VIP video explanations. Simultaneously, Zuoyebang conducts targeted teaching research and curriculum development based on previously accumulated user data, enhancing students' learning efficiency and academic performance by efficiently and scientifically tailoring teaching to their needs.

Parents

With society's rapid development and various real-life pressures, contemporary parents generally experience educational anxiety. However, due to limited time and energy, some parents may lack the necessary knowledge to tutor their children in schoolwork, leading to conflicts during homework assistance. As a result, many parents delegate their children's schoolwork to school teachers or after-school tutoring organizations, which may not have real-time access to their children's learning progress and could impose a financial burden on the family.

Zuoyebang offers a comprehensive online course system to meet all K12 students' needs and tailor suitable tutoring classes based on individual learning conditions. Additionally, parents can monitor their children's progress at any time through the public number. Zuoyebang also provides a learning report function, allowing parents to fully understand their children's learning status anytime and from anywhere.

Market Analysis

Since implementing the double-decrease policy, Zuoyebang has shifted its main development focus to the learning hardware market. This section will analyze the K12 learning hardware market.

Policy Driven

In recent years, the state has issued a series of relevant planning and guidance documents to encourage the promotion of education information and the development of the intelligent hardware market and products. In March 2021, the Ministry of Education issued the "Working Points of the Department of Science, Technology and Informatization of the Ministry of Education in 2021," which explicitly requires promoting the development of "Internet + Education" and constructing a high-quality education support system.

In 2021, the "Double Reduction Policy" will also give the domestic student tablet PC market a more significant opportunity for development. Since the "Double Reduction Policy" struck hard at the education and training industry and cracked down on capitalization operations, it has firmly pushed China's traditional education and training industry to carry out large-scale reform and transformation. Many famous enterprises engaged in education and training, including K12 businesses, both domestic and international, have massively laid off employees and closed down the related courses and training business, which has set off a massive wave of business transformation. Several K12 companies, including New Oriental, Zuoyebang, and

Gao Tu Classroom, are struggling to transform and survive under the declining trend of the capital market.

Under the "double-reducing" policy, subject content training is strictly limited. Still, the demand of students and parents for high-quality education remains unchanged, which triggered a shift in the supply side of education services. After the "Double Reduction" policy, subject content training such as large classes, dual-teacher courses, and 1V1 courses are challenging to continue. In contrast, educational intelligence hardware has the advantages of efficiently integrating resources and improving learning efficiency. Its tool attributes have been further highlighted, which can alleviate the educational anxiety of parents and students to a certain extent (iResearch, 2022).

The above policies show that the state attaches increasing importance to the development of education informatization. This also provides a good political environment for educational intelligent hardware products represented by intelligent learning machines (intelligent student tablets) and brings more development opportunities and convenience.

Economy Driven

China's economic environment under the new situation is favorable for developing the educational intelligent hardware market. Firstly, it is reflected in the rapid increase of per capita consumption ability and consumption level brought about by the improvement of the overall income level of the people in China, which provides the necessary foundation for the rapid development of the education intelligent hardware industry. According to the data of the National Bureau of Statistics (2024), the per capita disposable income of the residents of China in 2023 was RMB 39,218, an increase of 6.3% year-on-year, while the per capita consumption expenditure was RMB 26,796, a rise of 9.2% year-on-year. Improving China's per capita consumption ability and consumption level provides an excellent economic environment for developing China's educational intelligent hardware industry.

Secondly, although people's consumption, such as daily life and entertainment, is generally reduced due to the current downward economic situation, investment in education and self-learning enhancement has increased. This includes the consumption of the majority of secondary school student parent groups in student education innovative hardware. According to the research data of Iresearch Consulting (2022), most student-parent consumers' demand and consumption budget for educational innovative hardware is increasing rather than decreasing. More than 30% of student-parent consumers will increase their spending on educational innovative hardware from 16.3% to 29.5% in the future. Overall, against the backdrop of the epidemic and the downgrading of consumption, parents of secondary school students still maintain a positive attitude towards educational intelligent hardware products.

Technology Driven

The rapid development of artificial intelligence-related technologies has contributed to the swift expansion and accelerated scale of the market for intelligent hardware in education. China's voice recognition and interaction, OCR, data mining, machine learning, knowledge mapping, and other artificial intelligence technologies are becoming increasingly sophisticated and mature. They are gradually being applied to the field of education. Additionally, China's advanced communication technologies, such as 5G and Wi-Fi 6, are constantly being upgraded to improve the scale and speed of data transmission, making the data of AI education applications more stable and smoother (Wang & Zheng, 2021).

Regarding hardware manufacturing technology and capability, China is the world's largest electronic hardware producer, with a well-established and mature electronic components production and manufacturing system. Electronic hardware production and manufacturing capacity can meet the market demand for various educational hardware, laying a solid foundation for the rapid development of intelligent educational equipment. Regarding soft power, China's education industry has more mature educational resources and content development capabilities. In the recent development of online education, the technical research and development capabilities and application management systems related to educational intelligent hardware have also become more mature. Mobile internet course live broadcasting and recording, online classroom Q&A, thoughtful assessment, and other education-related software technologies are constantly evolving and updating.

The current education transformation requires intelligent educational hardware as a carrier, but it also demands a wealth of digital resources and related software technology research and development capabilities. With mature hardware manufacturing technology capabilities and software R&D capabilities, the intelligent hardware education market has a bright future.

Market Overview

According to Morgan Stanley Industry Data (2023), the domestic smart learning devices market size is expected to reach RMB 48 billion in 2023, reflecting a 20% growth from 2022. By 2026, the market size of domestic smart learning devices is projected to reach 106 billion yuan. With the influence of national policies and the advancement of information technology, more enterprises are entering the education intelligent hardware track, leading to continued product and service developments in this field. Intelligent education hardware has transitioned from a technology product to a consumer product, with stable growth in the traditional education intelligent hardware market size, the rapid expansion of the new intelligent hardware market, and a steady increase in the overall market size.

In terms of competition analysis, the size of the learning machine market continues to expand due to the increased penetration rate, and technology-based companies like iFLYTEK are gradually displacing traditional end-user companies. Educational tablets have been a niche and stable market in the past, with the industry growing for 30 years but with a low penetration rate of around 3% (Liu, 2023). Before integrating AI technology in education tablet devices, the leading players in the industry were traditional brands such as BBK and Dushulang. However, with the continuous integration of AI technology in education scenarios, the market landscape has undergone significant changes, and companies with AI technology advantages like iFLYTEK and BBK have capitalized on the changing industry dynamics, with companies such as BBK, Haojixing, and rapidly gaining market share.

Development and Strategy

Expanding the "Q&A Community" Function

Before January 21, 2015 (before version V4.0), the core of the entire platform was focused on improving the "Q&A community." During this period, Zuoyebang only facilitated students posting questions online and waiting for responses from netizens or asking teachers one-on-one questions, with teachers providing professional video answers. Simultaneously, students could answer other people's questions online and earn virtual coins. With a specific social attribute, these business functions are interactive and easily attract users. However, there were also numerous issues, such as unclear photos hindering question answering, the indeterminate response time for posted questions, and a lack of regulation in the forum, leading to varying post quality. Zuoyebang's initial forum interaction mode significantly contributed to its specific activity indicators, such as daily and monthly activity.

Around the "Learning Tools," Capture the Market

From January 2015 to July 2016, between versions V4.0.0 and V6.22, Zuoyebang shifted its focus to tools development. During this period, competitors such as "Ape Search" and "Scholar" launched photo search functions, leading to intense competition and homogenization in the market. Leveraging Baidu's search technology and data resources, Zuoyebang introduced the photo search function and added essay search, word search, and other user-friendly tools. Zuoyebang later started offering composition materials, tutorial videos, winter holiday homework answers, and other services to quickly capture the search market and expand its user base, gradually evolving into a comprehensive learning tool. According to Baidu search index data for Zuoyebang from January to May 2015, after these strategic moves, the number of active users surged at the end of February (end of the winter holidays) and remained consistently high. This indicates a significant improvement in Zuoyebang's user traffic and user engagement at that time.

Expanding the Business Matrix

After July 2016, Zuoyebang achieved many ultra-low-cost conversions of end-to-end traffic through its leading position in tools and technology (Zhou et al., 2021). Since then, Zuoyebang has expanded its business matrix from tools to teachers' answers and course tutoring, with increasingly warm services and gradually improving user experience. Zuoyebang is further building and strengthening the barrier of the "K12 online education comprehensive platform".

Zuoyebang has continued to optimize and expand its functions. For example, in terms of learning tools, it has added an ancient language assistant tool, a calculator for solving equations, a video explanation for searching questions, and one-on-one video explanations. It has also adjusted and optimized the layout of the page, composition search, word search, ancient language assistant, and other learning tools for the home page. This series of actions further consolidates and develops Zuoyebang's dominant position in learning tools.

At the same time, Zuoyebang has done much research to find new business growth points, gradually focusing on live online courses. For example, Zuoyebang added the "one lesson" business and then upgraded "one lesson" to "Zuoyebang live lessons", making it its core business development. In 2019, Zuoyebang switched Homework Help from the "one-on-one" model to live classes for large groups, building a matrix with large classes as the core and tools as support. During this period, Zuoyebang built a healthy profit model by continuously expanding its business scope, seeking product differentiation and gradually becoming a unicorn enterprise in its niche field.

Embracing Smart Education Hardware After the Double-Decrease

As the online education industry opened up new businesses that were difficult to profit from in the nearly saturated homogeneous business, it hoped to gain more users through large-scale advertising and marketing, which led to chaos. Therefore, in 2021, the regulator overhauled the online education industry. The regulators pointed out common problems in the online education industry, including chaotic management, false propaganda, price fraud, and other general chaos. They stressed that "arbitrary capitalizations of education and training institutions is strictly prohibited". Ape tutoring, Zuoyebang, New Oriental, and others have been imposed a top fine.

For Zuoyebang, the policy level is more prominent. The "double reduction" policy pointed out that online training institutions shall not provide and disseminate "photo search" and other inert students' thinking ability, affecting students' independent thinking, contrary to the laws of education and teaching inadequate learning methods to photo search as the core function of Zuoyebang into a development crisis.

Subsequently, Zuoyebang chose to change the track and invested in research and development of intelligent learning hardware products. Compared with other companies in this track, although Zuoyebang is less than the hardware facilities R&D foundation, Zuoyebang has accumulated more than 660 million question banks and ten billion accumulations of learning over nearly ten years, covering 90% of the domestic primary and secondary school students' learning data; the overall extensive data capability is in the leading position in the industry (Wang, 2024). Zuoyebang hopes to connect learning scenarios, learning methods, and learning tools by leveraging its extensive data capability. Based on this, Zuoyebang's team profoundly understands the difficulties and pain points students face in all aspects and scenarios of learning and assists students in different scenarios through a matrix of innovative, AI-algorithmic, and accurate software and hardware products.

On 23 August 2022, Zuoyebang held a conference, announcing the launch of the "Smart Learning" intelligent system and three intelligent learning products to create a "1+N+X" intelligent education ecology, opening a new stage of intelligent learning products. Zuoyebang released three products, such as AI study table and study watch, and focused on the core system of "Smart Learning" to support its hardware ecology, which marks that Zuoyebang has initially gained a firm foothold in the learning hardware market and survived the transition crisis. From a tool product to a former online class, and now focusing on entering the hardware field, Zuoyebang has long been focused on the construction of core scientific and technological capabilities and the precipitation of educational data so that Zuoyebang can still come up with a unique competitiveness to meet the test of the market when switching to the hardware track.

In 2023, Zuoyebang's study machine, in 618 and double eleven periods, won the study machine category, new sales of a double champion, and became the first sales of the fast-hand e-learning office category. Zuoyebang's smart desk, all-subject learning pen, learning printer, wrong question printer, electronic word card, and other products also led the sales on several e-commerce platforms (Wang, 2024).

THE PEOPLE BEHIND THE UNICORNS

Hou Jianbin

Hou Jianbin is the founder and CEO of Zuoyebang, and he is considered the soul of the company. He was born in 1982 and earned his master's degree from Peking University in 2004. Right after graduation, he joined Baidu and became the head of Baidu's knowledge search system in 2012. In early 2014, Hou Jianbin recognized the need for student homework help, which led to the incubation of the Zuoyebang project.

Initially, Hou used this new internet project solely as a tool for homework help. However, through subsequent operations, he realized that Zuoyebang, as a tutoring tool, needed to thoroughly meet the users' needs. Drawing from his extensive experience in Baidu, he believed integrating knowledge content into homework help would better serve user needs. Consequently, at the end of 2014, Hou Jianbin decided to spin off Zuoyebang from Baidu.

In June 2015, Zuoyebang was formally spun off from Baidu, and a new company, Small Boat to the Sea Educational Science and Technology Co. Ltd., was established, with Hou Jianbin assuming the CEO role. Under his leadership, Zuoyebang has evolved from a learning tool into a comprehensive online education platform, offering convenient services to many K12 users in China.

From 2016 to the end of 2020, Zuoyebang completed seven financing rounds, totaling over 3 billion US dollars. The company now boasts a diverse workforce of over 30,000 employees and serves more than 170 million monthly users, positioning itself as a leading brand in primary and secondary school online education.

When Zuoyebang encountered an industry crisis, Hou Jianbin pivoted the company's development trajectory towards deep investment in the intelligent hardware market. Leveraging existing advantages, the company focused on empowering hardware product development. As of 2023, Zuoyebang's intelligent hardware products are leading in sales across multiple e-commerce platforms.

FUTURE PROJECTS

Expand the Sales Channels and Sales Methods

Currently, Zuoyebang's hardware products are mainly sold on major e-commerce platforms. In the future, Zuoyebang will expand sales channels and set up more offline experience shops. Compared to mobile phones, tablets, and other intelligent products, it is difficult for users to deeply understand whether the product suits their needs through the introduction of the details page. The former is more transparent regarding configuration and functionality and requires little experience or research to place an order. The offline channel lets users experience the product face-to-face and make the final purchase decision.

According to the information collected by Zuoyebang, users in most cities are more inclined to use offline methods to obtain information, experience products, and give feedback on repairs. Zuoyebang is currently setting up positions in major cities, which will be divided into counters, brand image shops, and after-sales service shops. Zuoyebang prefers to call these positions rather than shops, hoping they will carry out more brand promotion, brand experience, after-sales service, user maintenance, and service roles rather than focusing solely on sales. Zuoyebang aims to build a closer relationship with consumers through offline methods and improve the shopping experience.

Continuous Product Iteration

Zuoyebang Education Hardware will adhere to the "education + technology" strategy, continuously iterating on existing products and conducting ongoing research and development to broaden the existing categories. AI intelligence has become a development hotspot, and many education companies are promoting their "AI learning system." However, due to the lack of actual learning data support, most of the products on the market cannot meet users' needs, resulting in low user recognition (Zhong, 2023).

Contrastingly, Zuoyebang, with its ten years of experience in the k12 education market, has accumulated more than 10 billion levels of big data on learning conditions and created an intelligent engine that enhances traditional learning hardware. In the future, Zuoyebang will adhere to a long-term perspective to find the development focus point and continually explore the value of AI. We will also focus on the microfeelings of learners, pay extreme attention to students' needs and experiences, and improve product capability at the product service level.

REFERENCES

iimedia. (2019, April 8). *[Analysis of the burden of primary and secondary school workload report: nearly 30% of students learning pressure, more than 50% in the holidays have extracurricular tutoring classes]*. AiMedia.com. https://www.iimedia.cn/c460/64040.html

36Kr. (2023, February 6).*[6 Things to Watch on the Education Smart Hardware Track in 2023]*. 36 Krypton. https://36kr.com/p/2119647329831299

Iresearch. (2022, September). *[China Education Smart Hardware Market and User Insights Report 2022 Report. Research]*. Cn. https://report.iresearch.cn/report_pdf.aspx?id=4069

Li Jing. (2023, February 20). Zuoyebang's hardware success. Economic Observer, p. 004. DOI:10.28421/n.cnki.njjgc.2023.000279

Liu, Q. (2023, July 13). *[AI Education Industry Research (I): Bullish on Smart Education, Education Informatisation and AI Talent Training]*. Data.eastmoney.com. https://data.eastmoney.com/report/zw_industry.jshtml?infocode=AP202307131592237453

Ministry of Education of the People's Republic of China. (2021, March 9). 2021. *Notice on issuing the 2021 Work Points of the Department of Science, Technology and Informatisation of the Ministry of Education.* Government Portal of the Ministry of Education of the People's Republic of China. http://www.moe.gov.cn/s78/A16/tongzhi/202103/t20210319_520941.html

Office for National Statistics. (2024, January 17). *2023. [Income and Consumer Expenditure of the Population in 2023]*. Office for National Statistics. Www.stats.gov.cn. https://www.stats.gov.cn/sj/zxfb/202401/t20240116_1946622.html

Wang, Q. (2024, February 28). *[Deep ploughing into education and technology The underlying logic of Zuoyebang's hardware outbreak. Finance]*. Finance China. https://finance.china.com.cn/roll/20240228/6086294.shtml

Wang, Y., & Zheng, Y. (2021). Intelligent educational products: constructing a new ecology of intelligent education based on AI. *Open Education Research*, 27(6), 9.

Zhou, Y., Chen, T., & Yang, L. (2021). [Research on the Development Status and Trend of High School Online Education--Taking Zuoyebang as an Example]. *, 18*, 127–129. DOI:10.19699/j.cnki.issn2096-0298.2021.18.127

KEY TERMS AND DEFINITIONS

AIGC Technology: AIGC, also known as Generative AI, is a new type of content creation after Professional-generated Content (PGC) and User-generated Content (UGC), which can create new forms of digital content generation and interaction in the areas of dialogue, storytelling, image, video, and music production. Music production, etc., to create new forms of digital content generation and interaction.

Double Deduction: The term "double reduction" refers to the need to effectively reduce the excessive burden of homework and out-of-school training for students at the compulsory education level in China's education sector.

Exam-Oriented Education: Exam-oriented education is the essence of China's current education system. It is usually regarded as an education system mainly aimed at improving students' ability to take tests. It places great importance on test scores, memorization, and problem-solving, which are different concepts of quality education. It is the only education system that prevailed in East Asia and Europe in the Middle Ages and modern times.

IFLYTEK: IFLYTEK Ltd. is a software enterprise specializing in intelligent speech and speech technology research, software and chip product development, and speech information services. Its technological advantage allows its in-learning hardware products to have a high market share in the educational hardware market.

K12 Education: K-12 education is the collective term for primary education in the United States. The "K" in "K12" stands for kindergarten, and the "12" stands for 12th grade (equivalent to senior year in China). "K-12" refers to education from kindergarten to grade 12 and is used internationally as a generic term for the primary education stage.

OCR Technology: Optical Character Recognition (OCR) is also known as text recognition or text extraction. With machine learning-based OCR technology, printed or handwritten text can be extracted from images such as posters, road signs, product labels, and documents such as articles, reports, forms, and invoices. Text is typically extracted as words, lines of text, and paragraphs or blocks of text to obtain an electronic version of the scanned text. This feature eliminates or significantly reduces the need for manual data entry.

Product Matrix: A product matrix is a tool for analyzing and managing a company's product portfolio. It helps companies understand the structure, competitiveness, and direction of their product portfolio by categorizing and organizing the characteristics and positioning of their products across different dimensions. Typical dimensions include product lines/families, market segments, product life cycle stages, and product positioning.

Q&A Community: A Question-and-Answer Community (Q&A Community) is an online platform or social media site designed to allow users to ask questions and have them answered and discussed by other users. It provides an interactive environment for users to share knowledge, seek help, solve problems, and exchange ideas.

Chapter 26
Poizon:
Redefining Fashion E-commerce Through Quality, Community, and Innovation

Zhuoyuan Li

Beijing Normal University-Hong Kong Baptist University United International College, China

EXECUTIVE SUMMARY

This case study examines Poizon, a leading fashion e-commerce platform in China, renowned for its innovative approach to catering to young consumers' demands for authenticity, community engagement, and trend-setting products. Founded by Yang Bing in 2015, Poizon has rapidly established itself as a prominent player in the competitive market by integrating e-commerce with social elements, ensuring product authenticity through robust identification services, and fostering a vibrant community of fashion enthusiasts. The case explores Poizon's strategic initiatives, including its unique business model, technological innovations such as AR try-ons, and community-driven marketing strategies. It also assesses Poizon's competitors, the difficulties of sustaining growth in a competitive market, and the potential opportunities for changing consumer preferences and market dynamics.

INTRODUCTION

Poizon is a cutting-edge e-commerce platform specializing in the secondary market for limited-edition streetwear and sneakers. It intersects multiple industries, such as E-Commerce, Fashion, Information Technology, and Retail. Poizon was the pioneer website that offered limited-edition shoes designed by mainstream fashion

DOI: 10.4018/979-8-3693-2921-4.ch026

designers, including Kanye West, Louis Vuitton, and Raf Simons. The platform primarily caters to young consumers, providing global services for acquiring trend-driven merchandise. Founded by Yang Bing in 2015, Poizon maintains its headquarters in Shanghai, China. It has raised 53.05 million through two funding rounds from four investors, including Hupu, Pluscapital, and DST. In April 2019, the valuation of Poizon stood at approximately 1.00 billion yuan.

UNICORN DESCRIPTION

Brief History of the Unicorn

In July 2015, the app "Du", incubated by Hupu, was officially launched. Its English name is Poizon because " Du " means "poison" in Chinese. Poizon mainly provides users with information exchange and sneaker identification services. As its influence continues to expand, the user base is gradually stabilizing. In September 2016, Poizon launched its live-streaming function and officially joined the live KOL community. The live KOL community refers to the community in which live broadcasting is the main form, and the Key Opinion Leader (KOL) plays a core role. In such communities, Key Opinion Leaders interact with viewers in real-time through live streaming, sharing expertise, experience, and insights, and promoting related products or services. This allowed Poizon to gain more active users and increase its influence.

In August 2017, Poizon transformed into an e-commerce platform, jumping from a trendy community platform to an authoritative authentic goods trading platform. It took the lead in adopting the "Consumer to Business to Consumer" business model and created a new transaction model of "first identification and then delivery", thus achieving the rapid development of goods (Song, 2017). In 2018, Poizon obtained angel round financing from Hupu, and its app downloads rose rapidly in the second half of the year, with daily downloads stabilizing at more than 50,000. In 2019, Poizon successfully attracted a pre-A round of financing from Puz Capital, Gaorong Capital, and Red Shirt Capital China and a round of funding from DST Global. With a post-investment valuation of over $1 billion, Poizon is among the most high-profile unlisted unicorns (Yue, 2023).

By 2020, the Chinese name of Poizon was officially changed from the "Du" app to the "Dewu" app. This marked a shift towards fully developing the entire category, evolving from a single sneaker e-commerce platform to a trend-focused online shopping community. The rapid rise of Poizon can be primarily attributed to its innovative transaction services, which attracted many users and laid a solid foundation for early market expansion. Reflecting on its entire development trajectory, the launch of transaction services in 2017 was undoubtedly a turning point in Poizon's rapid growth. Despite being affected by external factors such as the pandemic in recent years, Poizon has maintained its hiring demand. In 2021, Poizon received numerous awards, including the InfoQ 2021 "Most Attractive Employer Brand," "Most Loved by Technology Executives," "Most Loved by Developers," "Learning Organization," and "Most Employee Happiness Enterprise" (Li, 2021).

In 2022, the Poizon IPv6 project was selected as an excellent case of IPv6 deployment and application by the Central Network Information Administration (Lei, 2022). Several achievements from the "Poizon Security White Paper" were chosen as excellent examples of improvement in national information and communication service perception. In 2023, the information security engineer of Poizon App was honored with the title of "China's Young Good Netizens" by the Central Committee of the Communist Youth League and the Central Network Information Office. This is the highest award for young individuals under the age of 35 in the national Internet field and recognizes the Poizon technical team's achievements in information security and network security. Finally, on December 29, 2023, the Poizon App received the People's Net "Ingenuity Service Award" for its outstanding contributions to ensuring quality consumption. It was also recognized as an excellent case at the People's Net "2023 National Consumption Conference" (Yue, 2023).

Business Model

Poizon focuses on the downstream of the supply chain, especially the sales link, and belongs to the tertiary industry. Its business model is a social e-commerce model, which can be summarized as a dual business model combining e-commerce and social platforms.

Initially, users sell or buy used sneakers on the platform and ensure the quality and authenticity of the goods through the identification service provided by Poizon (Wang, 2021). After successfully building a second-hand sneaker trading platform, Poizon gradually expanded to a full range of fashion goods, including clothing, accessories, watches, beauty products, and event tickets. At the same time, more and more brand suppliers choose to enter the Poizon app and directly provide first-hand supplies for Poizon. This has changed the mode of goods supply from consumers providing second-hand goods to a combination of consumers providing second-hand goods and brands directly supplying goods.

With the development of the business, Poizon gradually increased social functions, such as live broadcasts, trim videos, private messages, and more, forming a unique network community atmosphere. Users can share their treadwear and shoe experiences on the platform and interact with other enthusiasts, enhancing user engagement and activity. This also provides users with more product information to help them make better purchase decisions (Wang & Zhu, 2023). Today, Poizon has transformed from a single sneaker e-commerce platform into a comprehensive fashion online shopping community.

In the operation of e-commerce, Poizon adopts the "C2B2C" transaction model, which combines consumer-to-business (C2B) and business-to-consumer (B2C) transactions. This means that goods flow from brand suppliers or individual sellers to merchants (Poizon platform) and end consumers. Buyers place orders through the app, and individual sellers send the goods to Poizon for identification. Poizon ensures that the goods are genuine and then sends them to the buyer (Xv, 2022). The delivery of goods is entirely Poizon's responsibility. This "first identification and then delivery" transaction model provides buyers with genuine product protection and reduces transaction risks. With more brands cooperating with Poizon and supplying goods directly, Poizon's future transaction model is potentially a combination of C2B2C and B2C.

In operating the social platform, Poizon integrates the interactive functions of the social platform into the e-commerce platform and introduces media functions such as matching sharing, live broadcasting, and trim videos to help customers obtain more product information and fashion trends. Poizon also launched social activities such as "matching challenges" and "daily punch" to facilitate interaction between customers and the brand and other customers, increasing the online community's interest and interaction, engaging existing users, and attracting new users.

Product and Services

Poizon sells various goods, covering almost every aspect of young consumers' daily lives. At the same time, Poizon provides strict product identification services, transportation tracking services, personalized recommendations for different customers, and access to multiple social platforms (Du, 2023). These goods and services provide users with a unique and exciting shopping experience.

C2B2C Model

Poizon is an e-commerce platform that facilitates direct trade between sellers and buyers. Sellers are allowed to post product information, while buyers can explore and make purchases. Poizon's offerings are broad and cater to the tastes of young consumers, focusing on novel and fashionable styles. This makes it a preferred choice over platforms like Vipshop, which may not align as closely with the aesthetic preferences of the younger demographic.

The unique business model of Poizon, known as C2B2C, optimizes market resource allocation and reduces resource waste by directly connecting supply and demand (Xv, 2022). This model also includes the first identification after delivery to ensure the quality of goods. This is a distinguishing feature compared to the Shihuo app, where the identification service is separate from purchasing goods. With Poizon, customers buy the identification service simultaneously with the goods, enjoying the identification service before receiving the goods. This guarantees that goods sold on the platform have higher quality assurance than other e-commerce platforms (Wu, 2021).

Poizon also specialises in the supply of rare and limited commodities. The platform has attracted a large user base interested in buying and selling trendy goods. This, coupled with regular collaborations with major brands to launch limited product sales, helps to meet consumers' demand for unique and scarce goods. An example is the availability of limited-edition sneakers sold out on Nike's official website, which can be found on Poizon. This breadth of cooperative brands and diverse range of goods makes Poizon highly competitive in this field.

The packaging provided by Poizon is another aspect that sets it apart from other e-commerce platforms. Instead of the conventional plastic bag packaging, Poizon uses a unique blue carton secured with black tape bearing the brand logo. This packaging is aesthetically pleasing and functional, helping prevent loss and damage to goods during transit. The packaging also serves as a representation of the brand's unique culture.

Regarding logistics, Poizon outsources to third-party providers and collaborates with various express companies to offer fast services such as "next day" delivery. Tencent Maps allows customers to monitor the location of their goods in real-time, reducing the chance of loss. This system shortens delivery times compared to other platforms like Taobao. The C2B2C model also allows Poizon to reduce warehousing costs as there is no need to build large warehouses for goods storage. This is a significant advantage over platforms like Jingdong, which require extensive inventory warehouses to meet bulk demand.

Pricing on Poizon is typically more affordable than in physical stores due to the direct connection of supply and demand, reducing the cost of intermediate links. Additionally, Poizon uses artificial intelligence and big data technology to provide personalized recommendations and services. By analyzing user behavior and preferences, the platform enhances the shopping experience and aids customers in making better purchasing decisions.

Finally, Poizon has incorporated blockchain technology to ensure the security and transparency of transactions. Every transaction detail is recorded, preventing any tampering or forgery of transaction data. This enhances user trust and improves transaction security, making trades on Poizon more secure and transparent than other platforms like Idle Fish.

Leveraging Online Community

Poizon has successfully established an active online community centered around fashion culture. This community serves as a platform for users to share their fashion wear, discuss trending styles, and post about recent purchases. The interactive nature of the community allows users to connect with like-minded individuals, sharing experiences and insights. It also enables users to keep abreast of fashion trends and learn more about product details, thereby aiding them in making better shopping decisions (Mao, 2021).

Poizon integrates a commodity trading platform, unlike other social platforms, offering customers an immediate "I want it, I get it" experience. This quick response to customer needs sets Poizon apart from its counterparts. Moreover, compared to other e-commerce platforms, Poizon's social network platform is more focused on trend culture. Users can find an abundance of content and information related to trendy goods.

The platform also offers a richer social experience than platforms like Taobao Buyer Show by providing features like live streaming, short videos, and options to like and comment. These interactive functions enhance customer engagement, improve customer stickiness, increase customer activity, and continuously expand the customer base. In addition to fostering a vibrant community, Poizon leverages artificial intelligence and big data technology to offer a personalized recommendation service. The platform can provide customers with tailored recommendations and services by analyzing user behavior and preferences. This elevates the shopping experience and uncovers more business opportunities for goods (Lai et al., 2023).

Customers

Poizon offers an array of products and services that cater to the needs of today's discerning consumers. Firstly, Poizon boasts a diverse inventory in fashion goods sales, encompassing limited edition, co-branded, and other highly sought-after items. Notably, some of these rare commodities are exclusively available through Poizon, attracting consumers who seek unique purchases unavailable on different platforms. Secondly, Poizon maintains strict commodity identification services, ensuring the authenticity and quality of its offerings. These services are particularly crucial for limited-edition rare goods prone to counterfeiting. Consumers are willing to invest more in these genuine goods, valuing the protection of their rights.

Furthermore, Poizon functions as a community exchange platform, facilitating the sharing of fashion insights and styling tips among its users. This aspect enhances consumers' access to fashion information and inspiration and simplifies locating and purchasing desired items. Additionally, Poizon prioritizes consumer efficiency, offering favorable prices and flexible purchasing methods. This includes various preferential activities, such as flash delivery and coupon offers, tailored to meet younger consumers' price sensitivity and convenience preferences. Given the fast-paced nature of trendy goods, Poizon ensures prompt delivery, minimizing the risk of obsolescence. Its seamless shopping process, expedited delivery, and comprehensive after-sales service collectively enhance the consumer's overall shopping experience, addressing their demands for efficiency and satisfaction.

Poizon primarily targets young individuals aged between 16 and 35 who have a keen interest in fashion culture and value personal style and fashionable expression (Wang, 2021). These consumers, who usually reside in first- and second-tier cities, are known for their willingness to experiment with new trends and invest time and money in fashion items such as shoes, clothing, and accessories. They are conscious of their external image and have substantial purchasing power.

One of the critical demands of this target market is the desire for emerging trend goods. These consumers seek to express their individuality and taste through fashionable items. Poizon leverages its expansive supply channels to cater to this demand and offer a diverse selection of fashion goods, satisfying their need for fashion elements and personal expression. Another significant demand of these consumers is the pursuit of limited edition and rare goods. This stems from their unique aesthetic preferences and the desire to showcase their purchasing capability. Poizon collaborates with various brands to launch limited-release events, addressing consumers' desire for uniqueness and scarcity.

Quality assurance is also a critical concern for these consumers. They prioritize the authenticity and quality of their purchases. Poizon addresses this demand through stringent commodity identification procedures and a robust logistics supervision system, ensuring the reliability and quality of the goods sold on the platform. In addition, the target market also seeks opportunities for social interaction centered around fashion. They enjoy sharing fashion ideas and dressing skills with like-minded individuals. Poizon has integrated community functions into its platform to meet this need, allowing consumers to post news, exchange ideas, and fulfil their social interaction needs.

Finally, young consumers are typically price-sensitive and value the convenience of their shopping experience. They seek quality goods at competitive prices and prefer a straightforward, hassle-free purchasing process. Poizon accommodates this demand by offering various purchasing methods and promotional activities, such as lightning-fast delivery and coupons, ensuring both price concessions and purchase convenience. In summary, these demands primarily stem from young consumers' passion for fashion and trends and their consideration of quality, social interaction, and overall shopping experience. By adequately addressing these needs, Poizon has managed to win the trust and loyalty of its young consumer base.

Following Fashion Trends

Poizon is a prominent figure in the fashion industry, keeping a keen eye on the fluctuating fashion market. It initially established itself as an e-commerce platform, leveraging its expertise in identification services and the innovative c2b2c business model. Subsequently, with the ascendancy of social media, Poizon transformed into a social hub, fostering online trend communities.

The fashion industry, linked to the media, combines information and manufacturing seamlessly. Primarily, the fashion market is renowned for its dynamism. Trends and fashion evolve swiftly, shaped by shifting seasons, cultures, societal patterns, and consumer tastes (Shen & Zhang, 2020). Consequently, the fashion and trend market experiences a comparatively brief product lifecycle, necessitating constant updates and iterations to cater to evolving consumer demands. Poizon's C2B2C model fits this dynamic, facilitating direct product transactions while omitting the manufacturing stage. This approach reduces the costs associated with mass production and enhances the efficiency of updates and iterations.

Secondly, the fashion market thrives on innovation. Consumers, with their mutable, intricate, and singular aesthetic appetites, seek fashion items to showcase their personalities and articulate their attitudes. Consequently, the merchandise within the fashion and trend market often exudes a unique design sensibility and incorporates innovative elements aimed at satisfying consumers' diverse aesthetic aspirations. By consistently broadening its collaborations with brand suppliers, Poizon enhances its procurement avenues, thus accelerating the influx of the latest products to cater to consumer demands.

In addition, the fashion market is deeply ingrained with interactivity and sociality. Fashion is a vital component of social interactions, as individuals wear and accessories to express their aesthetic preferences, forge friendships with those who share similar aesthetics, and foster a sense of belonging (Sun & Xv, 2022). This underscores the pivotal role social media and online platforms play in the fashion market. Leveraging this aspect of the fashion market, Poizon cultivates trend communities by establishing online interactive platforms (Shen & Zhang, 2020). This facilitates consumers' swift access to the latest fashion trends and their understanding of emerging design motifs and popular elements. Concurrently, it is a conduit for interaction and communication between brands, designers, and consumers. This heightened level of participation not only enhances consumers' sense of engagement and satisfaction but also ensures that the products offered by the platform are more aligned with market demands, further propelling the growth of the e-commerce platform.

Furthermore, the fashion industry is significantly influenced by the trend towards globalization. As international exchanges and cultural integration intensify, fashion elements and trends from diverse countries and regions merge, creating a multifaceted fashion and trend market. In recent years, the emergence of numerous domestically and internationally designer brands has garnered increasing consumer attention. In response, Poizon strives to broaden its purchase range, extending from China to the global arena and introducing the "overseas delivery" service to offer consumers a more comprehensive array of choices.

Rapid fluctuations and intense competition mark the fashion market. Poizon must monitor market shifts, develop agile strategic responses, and continuously refine its business models to uphold its competitive edge. Within the fashion industry, Poizon specializes in the trading of fashion goods. Notably, as its name suggests, the "trend" market primarily targets young consumers, with its offerings appealing to and in high demand among the younger demographic.

Predominantly, fashion goods cater to individuals aged 16 to 35, a segment whose desire for personalized expression and fashionable attire has steadily grown alongside economic prosperity and improving living standards. Especially post-pandemic, with factories resuming entire operations and the international supply chain gradually recuperating, the supply-demand dynamics of trend items have constantly been bolstered, driving the market size to expand significantly. Concurrently, the ongoing innovation in digital media technology has breathed fresh life into the fashion industry. This facilitates the accelerated exchange of international information and substantially enhances the dissemination speed of fashion culture. Such an economic landscape and technological backdrop provide Chinese youth with a vast array of fashion choices, further propelling the prosperity and development of the trend commodity market.

Forecast for This Market

The trend in the consumption market is gradually exhibiting more distinctive characteristics such as personalization, quality, and phantomization. The trend of personalized consumption is rising, particularly among young consumers who are now market leaders and seek more than essential functions. With economic growth and better living standards, they prefer products that reflect their unique tastes. Big data supports personalized consumption by offering tailored product recommendations, and consumers are shunning standardized goods in favor of personalized options. For example, Poizon's Augmented Reality fitting room, which uses AR technology, allows consumers to try on clothes virtually, enhancing the personalized shopping experience(Sun et al., 2023).

Consumers are increasingly valuing quality and are willing to pay for top-notch products. Poizon's authentication feature is being praised and imitated by competitors. To meet consumers' quality demands and protect consumers, Poizon must improve authentication and strengthen supervision. Platformization is transforming sales models, shifting from offline to online and towards platform-based operations. For instance, once bought offline, limited-edition sneakers are now sold online through Poizon. This is achieved through collaborations with brands and offers convenient, efficient purchases. This model aligns with fashion's social attributes, paving the way for future large-scale online shopping platforms integrating shopping with socializing.

Business Environment Analysis

In the dynamic and fast-paced world of e-commerce fashion, staying attuned to the business environment is crucial for platforms like Poizon. To navigate the industry's complexities, respond to changes effectively, and maintain a competitive edge, Poizon must keep a pulse on many external factors that could impact its operations and strategic planning. This is where a PESTEL analysis, which stands for Political, Economic, Social, Technological, Environmental, and Legal factors, becomes an invaluable tool. Poizon must thoroughly understand the macro-environmental factors that could influence its performance. This broader perspective can help Poizon anticipate potential challenges and opportunities, adapt to shifts in the external environment, and, ultimately, drive sustainable growth and success in the e-commerce fashion industry.

Political factors play a significant role in Poizon's operations. As the e-commerce industry expands, the government has increased its oversight of such platforms. This necessitates Poizon's constant vigilance and adaptation to evolving policies and regulations. Furthermore, recent fiscal policies aimed at stimulating consumer spending have driven the growth of online shopping. National commendations for quality goods, supported by policies, have brightened their prospects. However, changes in international trade, such as tariff adjustments or trade barriers, could disrupt supply chains and increase costs for imported goods, thereby affecting Poizon's pricing and competitiveness in the B2C segment.

From an economic perspective, the recovery of the economy and the rise in consumer incomes have led to an increase in consumers' pursuit of trend culture and purchasing power. This offers significant market potential for Poizon. The surplus inventory caused by the pandemic has led more suppliers to collaborate with Poizon for sales. The overall economic situation also influences consumers' willingness to spend, directly impacting goods sales. For instance, the pandemic significantly affected sales.

Social factors also significantly impact Poizon's operations. The emergence of trend culture, driven by digital media, provides a favorable social environment for Poizon's growth. The Poizon App, with its blend of shopping and social features, caters to changing social habits, fulfilling users' desire for social interaction during shopping. The quest for individuality and fashion among young people positions the Poizon App as an ideal platform for their expressions and trend pursuits.

Technological advancements, including AI and big data, strongly support the Poizon App, enhancing user understanding, experience, and service quality. This ensures the optimal distribution of supply and demand resources, maximizing the platform's benefits. Meanwhile, the continuous improvement of network security ensures the safety of user information and transactions, protecting data privacy.

Legal factors are crucial for Poizon, especially given its focus on selling trendy goods. Intellectual property protection is paramount, ensuring non-infringement to avoid legal disputes. Protecting consumer rights is a core responsibility, guaranteeing product quality, post-purchase care, and safeguarding legitimate interests.

Environmental factors are becoming increasingly important as awareness of environmental issues grows. Sustainable development is essential for businesses, and implementing environmentally friendly practices in supply chains and packaging promotes green consumption. Recognizing regional differences in fashion acceptance and shopping habits, Poizon customized marketing strategies to cater to diverse consumer needs.

Market Competition

The Poizon platform is currently facing the challenge of fierce market competition and limited user growth. Due to consumer demand and rapid technological innovation, Poizon platform needs to compete with other large mainstream e-commerce platforms to protect its market share. In the fashion commodity market, Poizon is facing competition from various sources. Apart from traditional offline physical shopping stores, there are other online platforms such as Smart Goods, Nice App, Taobao, Jingdong, and more. At the same time, the limited product range has also become an important factor limiting Poizon's appeal to consumers. However, Poizon has successfully stood out in the market through its precise market positioning and unique operating model, attracting the attention and love of a large number of young consumers.

Poizon's competitors can be divided into similar trend e-commerce platforms and large integrated e-commerce platforms. Let's take a closer look at Poizon's main competitors.

First, in the category of similar trend e-commerce platforms, there are Nice and Knowing Goods. Nice and Poizon are identical in their positioning and operating model; both focused on fashion goods sales and community building. Nice's advantage lies in its early market entry, which has accumulated a specific user base and brand awareness. However, Poizon has gradually gained a dominant position in the market with a broader variety of products, stricter quality control (including free identification services), and a more active community interaction model, combining e-commerce and social platforms.

Knowing Goods is another trendy e-commerce platform that competes with Poizon. It focuses on the authenticity of goods identification and quality assurance and shares a certain competitive relationship with Poizon regarding the quality of goods. However, Poizon offers a wider variety of goods and is more active in community construction. It not only focuses on fashion wear and sharing but also live broadcasts, lotteries, and more, attracting the attention of more young users.

Second, there are large-scale integrated e-commerce platforms such as Taobao or Jingdong. As China's largest comprehensive e-commerce platform, Taobao boasts a vast user base and a complete e-commerce ecosystem. Numerous fashionable goods are available on Taobao, and the pricing is relatively flexible, creating competitive pressure for Poizon. However, by focusing on the trend field and providing more professional product recommendations, quality assurance, and more active community interaction, Poizon has successfully attracted many young users who pursue individuality and fashion.

Jingdong, another large integrated e-commerce platform, also has a presence in trendy e-commerce. Jingdong possesses certain advantages in terms of commodity quality, logistics distribution, and other aspects, and it shares a competitive relationship with Poizon regarding quality and service. However, Poizon has maintained its leading position in the market by profoundly understanding the trend culture and implementing an operational strategy that is more relevant to young users.

Moreover, in competition with large e-commerce platforms, Poizon rarely engages in commercial traffic. So, one of the most significant differences between Poizon and other traffic platforms is that it is based on something other than the flow realization of advertising mode. In the Internet industry, one of the monetization channels for many traffic platforms is to make money by setting up app advertising spaces and displaying advertisements placed by advertisers. Taobao and JD.com, for example, often advertise on subways and billboards.

However, Poizon uses quantitative technology to collect and analyze data to evaluate consumers' preferences and prioritize what consumers are interested in. Poizon also cooperates with the brand and will provide the brand with free on-site marketing and promotion resources. At the same time, the brand can offer some exclusive rights and interests to Poizon, such as launching new products on Poizon, offering exclusive product lotteries, or participating in anniversary celebrations.

THE PEOPLE BEHIND THE UNICORN

With his innovative spirit, Yang Bing, a dynamic young entrepreneur, has transformed Hupu and Poizon into market leaders. His journey inspires young entrepreneurs to pursue their dreams. Yang Bing also steered Poizon to fulfil social responsibilities, donate to schools, and, in crises, promote positive values among entrepreneurs.

Yang Bing was born in 1985 in Ji'an, Jiangxi, and graduated from Shanghai Jiao Tong University. He is the founder and CEO of Poizon App, chairman of Xifang Information, and co-founder of Hupu Sports. While still in college, he co-founded Hupu Sports with partners and was the co-founder and president. This early venture into entrepreneurship was notably successful in meeting the youth's passion for sports. Hupu delves into sports events' brand and cultural potential and is now a leading sports event service provider in China. In 2015, Yang Bing embarked on a new entrepreneurial journey by founding Poizon App. Recognizing the youth's pursuit of a quality lifestyle and beauty, he positioned the Poizon App as a platform that combines authentic fashion e-commerce and a fashion life community aimed at helping users acquire beautiful things. Under Yang Bing's leadership, Poizon App rapidly grew into the world's largest fashion e-commerce platform and China's top fashion culture community, where youth engage in daily fashion buying and sharing. Yang Bing's ideas and spirit have made Poizon popular among the youth. He also places great value on corporate culture, emphasizing "truth-seeking" as its core, which supports the company's daily operations. Poizon pioneered a new service model to ensure authenticity, making substantial investments in personnel, technology, and inspection systems (Sun & Xv, 2022). As a result, it boasts the world's first and most extensive commodity research and identification team, database, and national lab, all of which Chinese youth love.

FUTURE PROJECTS

Poizon's current positioning is "a leading new generation of trend online shopping community", and its goal is to become "a new generation of quality lifestyle platform"(Zhou, 2022). In order to realize this vision, it is necessary to optimize the operating model around brand incubation, digital technology application and promotion, and one-stop service construction, as well as realize the near-expansion of goods categories and service groups.

In recent years, China's young consumers have shown a growing interest in domestic brands and products with Chinese traditional style and culture, known as Guochao. Around 2020, national fashion brands were supported to boost supply. Factories capitalized on this trend, quickly launching national fashion clothing with lower prices, and some brands grew rapidly. Many national brands reported high online sales due to vertical product flow and favorable conditions. Poizon App hosts a "National Tide Design Competition" to promote Chinese culture and support young designers, fostering creativity and vitality for China's original design and Guochao brands. Poizon is a key platform for brand incubation, while Guochao has driven Poizon's goods category expansion, which can help Poizon better serve and expand the main consumer groups.

In addition, Poizon will apply high-tech to digital new consumption, developing technologies for online shopping like AR try-ons, 3D displays, etc. This will help consumers intuitively feel products' size, characteristics, and wear effect, finding favorites faster (Zhang & Peng, 2022). Poizon App's future AR upgrade will innovate technologically and visually, leading the industry in fit, stability, and authenticity, simulating real try-on experiences. Poizon will also improve its trend commodity model database and digital services to optimize consumer experience.

REFERENCES

Du, C. (2023). Analysis of the current situation and operation path of social content e-commerce under the new media background. *National Circulation Economy*, 13, 24–27. DOI:10.16834/j.cnki.issn1009-5292.2023.13.016

Lai, L., Wan, B., & Li, Y. (2023). Scene, interaction, and consumption: The power characteristics and realisation mechanism of online shopping platforms—A "Dewu APP" case study. *Media Forum*, (08), 38-40.

Lei, X. (2022). China Inspection Forms Joint Identification Research Team with Depwu. *China Quality Milestone Journey*, 11, 50–52.

Li, X. (2021, September 16). Identify first, then ship: Dewu App's quality online shopping stimulates consumption potential. *China Consumer News, 007.*

Mao, Q. (2021). Research on the interaction mechanism of trend-related platforms from the perspective of interaction ritual chains: A case study of Depwu App. *Journal of News Research Guidance*, 18, 57–59.

Shen, J., & Zhang, Y. (2020). Research on platform innovation in the value chain of internet trend items: A case study of Dewu App. *China Economic & Trade Guide (Middle)*, 08, 111–113.

Song, Z. (2017). Exploring the development of e-commerce from C2C to C2B2C in the context of consumption upgrading. *Commercial Economic Research*, (14), 66–68.

Sun, H., & Xu, J. (2022). Research on the business model of platform enterprises under the background of the digital economy: A case study of Dewu APP. *Open Management*, (04), 19–24. DOI:10.16517/j.cnki.cn12-1034/f.20211231.001

Sun, X., Feng, Z., Zhou, X., Kong, Y., & Zhao, Q. (2023). Analysis of AR technology empowerment path under the background of new e-commerce formats. [First Half of the Month]. *Modern Marketing*, 08, 92–94. DOI:10.19921/j.cnki.1009-2994.2023-08-0092-030

Wang, M. (2021). Analysis of network marketing strategies in China's sneaker market: A case study of Depwu App. *Western Leather*, 03, 38–39.

Wang, Q., & Zhu, J. (2023). Research on the impact of the accurate push of commodity information on consumers' online shopping behaviour on e-commerce platforms. *Office Automation*, 11, 23–26.

Wang, S. (2021). Depwu App: We are committed to meeting the enthusiasm of young people. [Marketing Edition]. *Sales & Marketing*, 02, 23–25.

Wu, R. (2021). Research on developing new e-commerce platforms under the C2B2C model: A case study of Dewu App. *Hebei Enterprise*, 11, 54–56. DOI:10.19885/j.cnki.hbqy.2021.11.013

Yue, P. (2023). "Identify first, then ship" carries quality trust. The "Dewu" service trademark was selected as one of China's top ten trademark protection cases. *China Quality Walk*, (05), 70–71.

Yue, P. (2023). Robust quality, emphasis on quality, excellent experience: Dewu App injects youth vitality into boosting consumption. *China Quality Walk*, (03), 64–67.

Zhang, Y., & Peng, L. (2022). Competitiveness analysis of the trend e-commerce platform Poizon APP under the C2B2C model. *Open Management*, 10, 46–51. DOI:10.16517/j.cnki.cn12-1034/f.20220426.001

Zhou, J. (2022). Development strategy research of the Poizon APP based on SWOT analysis. *Economic Research Guide*, 18, 44–46.

KEY TERMS AND DEFINITIONS

E-Commerce Platform: An e-commerce platform is an online platform that enables businesses or individuals to showcase, sell, trade, and pay for goods and services over the Internet.

Emerging Trend Goods: These refer to newly emerging goods in the market that are widely consumed by consumers and show a growing trend.

Jingdong: Jingdong is a leading integrated e-commerce platform in China, offering millions of quality products, including home appliances, digital products, clothing, and food. It is known for its quality assurance, affordable prices, and fast delivery.

Nice App: It is a community and resale platform focused on sneakers, fashion, and lifestyle.

Shihuo: Shihuo is a Chinese e-commerce platform focusing on authentic shopping decisions. It provides users with recommendations for authentic stores and discount information across various e-commerce platforms, covering shoes, clothing, beauty, digital goods, and other categories. Shihuo also provides physical identification and after-sales protection services.

Taobao: Taobao is a comprehensive Chinese e-commerce platform with many products and millions of registered users. On the platform, consumers can browse, search, and purchase goods across categories such as clothing, home, and digital products, enjoying a convenient shopping experience within a safe trading environment.

Vipshop: Vipshop is an e-commerce platform that sells branded discount goods in China. It offers "selected brands + deep discounts + flash sales" to provide users with high-quality goods in various categories, including clothing, beauty, mother and child, and home.

Web Community: A web community is an internet-based platform that allows people to communicate and interact around shared interests, topics, or goals. These platforms often include forums, social media groups, post bars, and blogs, enabling users to share information, exchange ideas, and make connections.

Chapter 27
Zhuan Zhuan:
Pioneering Sustainability in Second-Hand E-Commerce

Pan Zuo

Beijing Normal University-Hong Kong Baptist University United International College, China

EXECUTIVE SUMMARY

This case study examines Zhuan Zhuan, a prominent second-hand e-commerce platform in China, focusing on its development, sustainability initiatives, strategic partnerships, and prospects. Founded under the leadership of Yao Jinbo from 58 Group, Zhuan Zhuan has strategically positioned itself in the circular economy by facilitating the trade of idle goods to reduce carbon emissions and promote sustainable consumption. Rigorous quality control measures, extensive user engagement via Tencent's WeChat, and partnerships enhancing logistical and financial capabilities underscored the platform's success. Zhuan Zhuan's plans include deeper integration with Tencent for user acquisition and trust-building, expanding product categories to include larger appliances, and leveraging its parent company's ecosystem to streamline operations and foster environmental stewardship. This case highlights Zhuan Zhuan's role in sustainable commerce and its trajectory towards broader societal and environmental impact in the e-commerce landscape.

DOI: 10.4018/979-8-3693-2921-4.ch027

DESCRIPTION OF ZHUAN ZHUAN

Brief History of Zhuan Zhuan

Launched on November 12, 2015, Zhuan Zhuan is a second-hand e-commerce platform in China that the 58 Group incubated. It was developed with the core value of "users first" and the corporate vision of "let resources be reconfigured, let people trust each other more". A year later, 58 Group officially announced that the second-hand channel of 58 & Catch.com had been upgraded to an independent app - "Zhuan Zhuan", realizing the sharing of data and traffic and making every effort to build the most professional second-hand trading platform (Editorial Board of the Journal, 2018). Between 2017 and 2021, after the completion of a total of five rounds of financing totaling more than 1.08 billion U.S. dollars (among the investors include 58 Group, Tencent Investment, Xiaomi Group, Shunwei Capital, etc.) as well as acquiring a 100% equity interest in the operator of second-hand mobile phone trading app Zhaoliangji, Zhuan Zhuan became a unicorn of the second-hand transaction industry in China.

In modern Chinese society, the rise in income levels and decrease in Engel's coefficient have given people more disposable wealth for purchasing commodities other than food, including durable and non-durable goods. With the rapid growth of consumer spending power in China, consumer goods are being iterated at an unprecedented rate, resulting in some goods being considered obsolete before they reach the end of their useful lives. This increase in "out of date" items has made resource efficiency one of the most critical challenges that industries must face. The "idle economy", or second-hand market, is an essential way of rationalizing the utilization of resources and has received increasing consumer affirmation in recent years.

Zhuan Zhuan encompasses over 30 categories of second-hand trade, including mobile phones, books, 3C digital products, clothing, footwear, maternity and baby supplies, furniture, and household appliances. The company is dedicated to establishing standardized services, offering comprehensive second-hand mobile phone inspections, and ensuring quality assurance service. With continuous development and growth, Zhuan Zhuan has won several honors inside and outside the industry. On April 9, 2024, Zhuan Zhuan was listed on the Global Unicorn Index 2024 at 320th with an enterprise valuation of RMB 21 billion. It has been named one of the most trusted brands by consumers for many consecutive years, which is not only a recognition of its quality assurance and user experience but also an affirmation of its good reputation in the industry. Behind these honors are the unremitting efforts of the operational team and the constant pursuit of users' interests.

Customers

The current consumers of the domestic second-hand industry are primarily young people in first- and second-tier cities. Compared with the older generation, they have a higher level of education, a more vital ability to accept new things and think independently, and a greater acceptance of the concept of sharing, environmental protection, and improving resource utilization. According to the Baidu Index (2022), the primary user group of Zhuan Zhuan is predominantly aged between 20 and 39 years old, with the user base gradually declining. Users are primarily young and middle-aged, and they trade idle goods for the experience, sharing, and leasing. This indicates that trading idle items has become a daily consumption habit and lifestyle for most young people.

Furthermore, the number of male users (69.89%) significantly surpasses that of female users (30.11%). This is correlated with the main categories of goods operated by Zhuan Zhuan. Male users in their middle-aged and young age, with strong purchasing power, are generally more interested in trading goods in the popular categories of 3C digital and second-hand cell phones. Users on Zhuan Zhuan can be classified into two main groups: buyers and sellers.

Buyers

According to research conducted by Williams and Paddock (2003), affluent middle-class individuals may engage in second-hand shopping for enjoyment, social engagement, uniqueness, and the desire to be perceived as making discerning purchases. Conversely, individuals facing financial constraints may turn to second-hand shopping out of necessity, as they have limited options. Similarly, buyers of Zhuan Zhuan can be broadly categorized into two types: online shopaholics and rigid needs groups.

The rigid needs group refers to users with a specific purpose for buying a particular item. This type of user is characterized by choosing second-hand goods to save money and obtain the product's essential functions. They only log on to the platform when they need a particular item, so their behavior is based on search. For instance, college students with limited financial means often tend to buy a used refrigerator from a graduating senior rather than purchasing a brand-new one.

The other users are those intensely interested in a specific category of goods. They spend considerable time browsing on the second-hand trading platform and often purchase second-hand goods. We categorize them as the online shopaholic group. For example, some users who love vintage goods want to "treasure hunt" on second-hand e-commerce platforms and might stumble upon a pair of jeans with historical significance being sold at a low price, which motivates them to continue browsing.

These highly active consumers place an emotional value on specific categories of goods due to their in-depth knowledge of the field. The primary motivation behind the significant transactions by these major players in the secondhand market is the need to discover interesting items, not just to save money.

Sellers

Sellers can be broadly categorized into individual and professional sellers based on their activity on Zhuan Zhuan. The core need of individual sellers is to clear out unused items at a reasonable price, which usually stems from impulsive shopping and premature obsolescence. These users are less active and usually only open the app when new, unused items are uploaded for sale or when a buyer contacts them.

On the other hand, professional sellers use Zhuan Zhuan as an extension of their sales channel. They have specialized knowledge in a particular field and create a sales page more likely to be trusted by buyers across a wide range of product categories, providing superb sales guidance. These users are the most active group on Zhuan Zhuan.

As a reliable second-hand trading platform, Zhuan Zhuan naturally takes into account the needs of both types of users. Combined with the needs of user scenarios and the process and nature of second-hand trading, users' expectations of the platform mainly include the following points:

1. Since second-hand goods are non-standardized, the core focus is on their quality and how to ensure that buyers perceive them.
2. Ensuring the reliability of the other party and how to establish trust in the other party to guarantee the quality of the transaction.
3. Organizing the display of goods to promote the efficiency of the transaction, making it easier for buyers to find goods and for sellers to sell commodities more efficiently.
4. Establishing a guarantee mechanism for the transaction process.

Business Model

The practice of second-hand trading on e-commerce platforms in China can be traced back to 58.com and Catch.com around 2010 (Wei, L & Mengyu, X. 2020). During that time, most of the second-hand trading transactions were carried out by college students in the same area. This type of e-commerce model, where consumers directly trade with other consumers, is known as C2C (Consumer to Consumer). It offers a high level of trade flexibility. In this stage, the entire trading process revolves around transactions between individual users, with the platform primarily acting as a matchmaker. However, as the market scale expanded and more users joined the second-hand trading platform, the traditional C2C model gradually revealed two significant issues: firstly, there was an information gap between the seller and the buyer, including assessing the residual value of the second-hand goods, pricing, and the authenticity of the goods. Secondly, it was challenging to provide after-sale protection under this model. For instance, due to the lack of regulations, sellers could deny that some of the damage to the item was caused by the buyer, making it even harder for buyers to defend their consumer rights when the seller recognizes their dissatisfaction with the goods.

In response to the pain points of information asymmetry in the second-hand trading industry, especially in the field of second-hand cell phone trading, Zhuan Zhuan took the lead in the industry by launching an innovative quality inspection and corresponding warranty service based on the C2B2C (Consumer to Business to Consumer) model and quickly formed a quality inspection and service standard that is generally recognized in the industry.

In this model, Zhuan Zhuan will serve two roles: both seller and buyer. On the one hand, the platform acquires goods from sellers as buyers, and the goods' information will be uploaded with the platform's actual evaluation information of the second-hand goods; on the other hand, after recovering, sterilizing, and refurbishing the goods, Zhuan Zhuan will display the goods information and relevant appraisal reports as sellers for buyers to choose from. Compared with the traditional C2C model, the information presented by Zhuan Zhuan has more detailed product descriptions (inspection reports with relevant indicators) and more beautiful pictures.

Unlike the traditional C2C model, where the platform manages the buyer's funds, Zhuan Zhuan's C2B2C model divides funds into two segments - the C2B segment and the B2C segment. In the C2B segment, after the platform identifies the goods, the platform agrees with the seller, and the funds reach the seller from the platform. In the B2C segment, the buyer places an order on the platform, and the funds reach the platform from the buyer. This approach allows the seller and the buyer to deal directly with the platform, improving trust in second-hand transactions and enhancing the overall selling and buying experience.

In the traditional C2C trading model, logistics costs often lead to communication challenges between the parties involved. Zhuan Zhuan addresses this issue by cleverly dividing logistics into two parts: from the seller to the platform and from the platform to the buyer. In the B2C segment, logistics from the second-hand e-commerce platform are directed straight to the buyer through the platform's logistics delivery. In the C2B segment, the logistics method varies based on the goods' attributes and the region's location. The seller can choose direct delivery to the designated area of the goods or opt for the platform to pick up the goods.

It is essential to acknowledge that second-hand trading is non-standardized, and different user groups have varying needs. Therefore, Zhuan Zhuan retains the more convenient C2C model to provide a "free market" for non-standardized commodities with fluctuating prices. Zhuan Zhuan takes an expansive view of idle goods, including a wide range of items such as celebrity concert tickets, peripheral products, housekeeping services, and education-related goods. This concept of "comprehensive idleness" encourages users to value their unused items, leading to the rapid development of the second-hand market.

Furthermore, Zhuan Zhuan offers a "nearby" function, enabling users to find idle items posted by other users within a 10-kilometre radius, facilitating convenient offline transactions. Offline services inspire trust and provide greater security than online transactions. The physical aspect of offline transactions allows for quality assessment, and the trading parties' proximity enhances trust. This location-based "free market" feature aims to create a familiar community environment, fostering trust and security and helping users with similar interests connect and build a network, ultimately contributing to a positive impression of the platform.

Product and Services

Zhuan Zhuan "Official Inspection"

This feature is based on the B2C segment of the C2B2C model described above. "Official Inspection" is a revolutionary service launched by Zhuan Zhuan to solve the problem of non-standardized second-hand goods. Through cooperation with Foxconn, the quality inspectors from the Zhuan Zhuan platform carry out individualized inspections on each non-standardized commodity. They assess the degree of newness and oldness of the commodity based on its functionality, appearance, and other factors and issue a detailed quality inspection report to make the transaction more transparent. For example, Zhuan Zhuan focused on the used cell phone category and upgraded its quality inspection standards to 66 significant items as early as the beginning of 2019. They promptly updated these standards following market changes and user needs and continuously improve the efficiency and accuracy of their inspection by developing intelligent and automated inspection equipment. To meet the needs of more users in second-hand transactions, Zhuan Zhuan has also gradually expanded its quality inspection service from second-hand cell phones to include books, digital products, sneakers, and beauty products. By creating a mature quality inspection system, the core competitiveness of the enterprise has been built up. According to the professional inspection report issued by the platform, buyers can have a more accurate perception of the quality of the goods when browsing the goods. They can find used goods that meet their purchase expectations faster.

After-Sales Services

Huang Wei, CEO of Zhuan Zhuan, admitted that "the quality inspection of non-standardized commodities is challenging, especially in terms of subjective evaluation such as appearance" (Huanqiu Finance, 2024). As China's leading idle second-hand goods trading e-commerce, Zhuan Zhuan is the first platform to provide C-end consumers with second-hand quality inspection, a 7-day no-reason return policy, a one-year warranty for second-hand cell phones, and other services. Compared with the previous focus on "inspection," the current turn in the service process adds "return" and "compensation" in the after-sales links, aiming to better serve the users with processes like "inspection and then shelving," "unsatisfied can be returned," and "if the inspection is wrong, then compensation."

In 2023, Zhuan Zhuan will start the comprehensive "official inspection," extending from the initial cell phone 3C to various categories like clothing, luxury goods, and more. Based on excellent users experience and positive feedback, the company aims to improve its service level to make "greater, faster, better and more economical" official inspection products available to more consumers.

Multiple Sales Channel

On Zhuan Zhuan, sellers can sell their items in various ways: recycling, consignment, and selling on the "free market". Recycling is the fastest and most hassle-free way, as it involves selling directly to Zhuan Zhuan. Sellers can place an order on the app, provide relevant information about the unused item, and wait for the operator to schedule a home pickup. If the platform verifies the item and the provided information, sellers can receive payment within 24 hours as soon as possible. However, while this method saves time, the price offered by the platform may be lower than the seller's expectations.

The second option is consignment, where sellers use the platform's channels to list their items for sale. Sellers need to send photos of the item to the platform and set their desired price, and the platform will list the product for sale after reviewing the uploaded inspection report. The advantage of this method is that sellers can set their prices without incurring logistics costs. However, after a successful transaction, the platform will deduct a service fee based on the price.

It is worth noting that the first two methods require the platform to inspect the goods, but only some items adhere to strict standards, leading to some items not being eligible for recycling or consignment. For such items, sellers can use the third option: selling in the "free market" on Zhuan Zhuan. In this method, sellers only need to upload explicit photos of the unused items they want to sell and set their desired price. The advantage here is its flexibility, as it covers almost all items. However, it also entails higher communication and logistics costs for the sellers.

Market Analysis

Original Situation of the Market

With China becoming the world's second-largest economy, China's per capita income level is increasing, accelerating consumption growth. However, this has also led to blind and impulsive consumption, resulting in the inefficient use of products and the product's value not being fully realized. Additionally, the rapid turnover of products has led to wasting many items in society. Nevertheless, China's traditional second-hand market needs to catch up to the country's economic and social development. This lag is evident in the need for more business outlets, low transaction integrity, operation of small-scale enterprises, and limited convenience in logistics, which collectively restrict the circulation of second-hand goods and hinder the traditional second-hand market industry's development (Qian et al., 2019).

Evolution of the Market Until Today

In 2002, China's first second-hand e-commerce website operated in C2C mode, Kongfz.com, was established. It developed an online to offline transaction business model (O2O), marking the start of China's exploration period in second-hand e-commerce. Second-hand e-commerce and traditional e-commerce share a competitive and cooperative relationship. Second-hand e-commerce relies on traditional e-commerce to increase the number of idle sources and develop a logistics system. Additionally, with the sale of idle commodities, user spending power grows, taking advantage of new product iterations and repeat purchases. There is also direct competition in the product demand field between second-hand e-commerce and traditional e-commerce, with cost-effectiveness being key for developing second-hand e-commerce. Thus, traditional e-commerce will not easily give up the potential of the new second-hand e-commerce market. As a result, comprehensive domestic second-hand e-commerce platforms such as Goofish APP (established in 2014) and Zhuan Zhuan APP (officially promoted in 2015) have come online.

Since 2016, the Chinese government has introduced a series of policies to encourage the development of the sharing economy. China's second-hand goods trade has begun to emerge, and the online second-hand market has proliferated with the entry of large online platforms and e-commerce giants. Data released by the China Internet Economy Research Institute showed that by the end of 2017, the scale of China's idle goods trading had reached 500 billion yuan and was growing at a rate of more than 30% per year. China's online second-hand transaction user scale has reached 0.76 billion people, with a growth rate of 55.1% (Li, 2018).

Domestic e-commerce giants mainly establish the domestic second-hand trading platform under the "sharing economy" mode based on their logistics network, financial capabilities, and extensive data analysis capabilities. They rely on the original mature e-commerce platforms of e-commerce giants, allowing for the second-hand market, to a certain extent, to gradually get rid of the lack of the original standard. In 2022, the transaction scale of the second-hand e-commerce industry will be 480.204 billion yuan, a year-on-year growth of 20%. The user scale of the second-hand e-commerce industry is rising year by year, and the user scale of this industry in 2022 will increase by 33.9% to 620 million compared with the previous year. Consumers are already in the era of material surplus; excessive and impulsive consumption will be compressed in proportion to residents' consumption, consumer psychology tends to be rational, and second-hand products gradually become an essential choice for consumers. In 2022, China's second-hand e-commerce industry penetration rate increased to 33.32%, with room for further increase (Huaon, 2024).

Competition Analysis

China's second-hand e-commerce industry can be categorized into five segments: general, electronics, fashion, luxury, and books. From a market competition perspective, the second-hand e-commerce industry has evolved into a market structure characterized by "three giants + multiple oligarchs". The three giants are Goofish, Atrenew Inc, and Zhuan Zhuan. Additionally, there are several oligarchs in specific verticals, such as Plum, a platform for second-hand luxury goods, and Kongo.com, a platform for second-hand books, both of which are leaders in their respective fields.

Forecast for this Market

Matthew Effect

After years of development in the domestic second-hand e-commerce industry, a mature business model and industrial chain have been established. This has led to a significant advantage for leading platforms, creating a strong Matthew effect. Idle Fish and Atrenew Inc. have formed a closed industrial chain loop. They are leveraging broad pre-category traffic to transition into the second-hand 3C (computers, communications, and consumer electronics) segment. Platform competition may focus on refining user experience and precise operations in the future.

User Trust Enhancement, Standardisation, Normalisation.

Enhancing customer trust can boost user retention and repeat purchase rates while improving the platform's reputation and attracting more traffic through word-of-mouth. According to 2021 data, there is an overabundance of counterfeit products in the domestic market, leading to 37.8% of netizens needing more trust in the platform and refusing to use second-hand e-commerce platforms. This highlights the significant room for improvement in building user trust. The primary advantage of second-hand e-commerce platforms lies in improving transaction efficiency. However, the industry must still grapple with challenges such as inadequate consumer rights protection and substandard goods. Therefore, it is imperative to continue optimizing the platform system, establishing a trust mechanism, and reducing information asymmetry between transaction parties to develop the second-hand market further.

DEVELOPMENT AND STRATEGY

Sustainability

As an essential path and an effective solution to help achieve the goal of carbon neutrality, second-hand goods trading is gradually gaining recognition and support from policymakers and the market. At the same time, it is also the low-carbon environmental protection behavior with the broadest public participation and the lowest participation threshold. As a typical recycling economy business, the trading of second-hand commodity can achieve a carbon emission reduction of 0.3-130 kilograms per single second-hand transaction, with second-hand cell phones leading the way with a reduction of up to 52 kilograms per transaction. With the growing acceptance of idle trading and increased awareness of green consumption, second-hand goods trading is gradually becoming a fashionable green lifestyle.

Zhuan Zhuan, a second-hand e-commerce platform, not only facilitates the discovery of high-quality second-hand products for consumers but is also actively shifting its focus towards a more crucial role in the future development of society and the world through a commitment to the circular economy. Zhuan Zhuan was founded with high hopes from 58 Group CEO Jinbo YAO. He publicly stated at the time of the establishment of Zhuan Zhuan, "Doing second-hand idle trading, in addition to business opportunities, has another level of significance for us. For example, it can connect people and have some 'emotional' impact on users. It also has the opportunity to help China enter a more circular and environmentally friendly society." Starting in 2022, the company's slogan transformed to "save the money-save the world." In 2022, Zhuan Zhuan, together with its users, will complete a cumulative carbon emission reduction of 668,000 tons by facilitating the flow of unused items. From its establishment to the end of 2022, the cumulative carbon emission reduction of the Zhuan Zhuan Group reached 3.258 million tons, equivalent to the carbon emissions of 18.3 billion kilometers of traditional fuel vehicles; the cumulative energy reduction of 4,403 GWh, and the cumulative turnover of 26 million second-hand books, which is equivalent to the preservation of 220,000 forest tree resources (Qin, 2023).

While promoting the flow of unused items, Zhuan Zhuan has continued to practice low-carbon and environmentally friendly business concepts in its development. Zhuan has upgraded its product packaging to be more environmentally friendly, replacing most of the plastics in the original packaging with biodegradable PLA materials and cellulose film and reducing the amount of ink used by 80% (Eastday Finance, 2022). In addition, all cardboard used is renewable. Even though using the new eco-friendly packaging will add ¥2.26 to the cost of each cell phone box. When many industries and enterprises are cutting costs and increasing efficiency, Zhuan Zhuan's insistence on investing in environmentally friendly packaging also reflects the company's determination and confidence in practicing sustainable development and going all out to help the development of the circular economy.

Leveraging on External Partners

Zhuan Zhuan has emerged as one of the leading players in the second-hand general e-commerce sector, mainly due to the support of its partners in areas where its business was weaker. Goofish, Zhuan Zhuan's main competitor in the second-hand e-commerce market, boasts a substantial user base from Taobao and has had a well-established payment system since its inception. Taobao, China's dominant e-commerce platform, has refined its transaction system over decades, ensuring a seamless experience from purchase to delivery, including returns and exchanges. This robust system is a foundation for Goofish's independent platform, augmented further by collaboration with Sesame Credit to standardize valuation processes, enhancing transaction security.

Zhuan Zhuan tackles credit concerns differently by outsourcing the assessment of non-standardized goods for background disassembly and inspection and issuing detailed reports to alleviate user communication and psychological burdens. Collaborating with Foxconn, Zhuan Zhuan's quality inspection team streamlines mailing, disassembly, assembly, virus scanning, and evaluation for mobile phones, assuring consumers of product quality, merchant credibility, and transaction fairness. Moreover, integration with WeChat as the exclusive login and payment portal, alongside prominent visibility within WeChat's third-party services, leverages Tencent's extensive user base to broaden Zhuan Zhuan's reach in the second-hand market. This strategic move mirrors the significance of Taobao for Goofish, poised further to shrink the gap between Zhuan Zhuan and its competitors.

THE PEOPLE BEHIND THE UNICORN

CEO Huang Wei

Graduating from Tsinghua University, Huang Wei's significance to Zhuan Zhuan is that he staunchly advocated and promoted implementing the "Official Inspection" program. Confronted with the issue of non-standardization in the second-hand goods market, Huang Wei realized that it posed efficiency challenges for the market. Despite the potential increase in labor costs and R&D investment, he persisted in launching the "Official Inspection" program, ensuring that every item is verified before it can be sold on the Zhuan Zhuan APP or in offline stores through the establishment of a rigorous quality inspection process. To achieve this, Zhuan Zhuan established a large quality inspection team comprising 2,000 warehouse inspection engineers, 400 stores, and nearly 2,000 door-to-door personnel, totaling almost 5,000 individuals involved in the quality inspection work (Huanqiu Finance, 2024).

This initiative not only enhances consumer confidence in the quality of goods but also bolsters the credibility and competitiveness of the entire platform. Huang also formulated a series of management specifications covering the entire life cycle of commodities and ensured the quality of goods through multi-link inspections. Whenever problematic items are discovered, Zhuan Zhuan promptly removes them from the shelves and penalizes the sellers accordingly. In 2023, Zhuan Zhuan rectified and punished over 600 sellers, retired 35, permanently banned 536,000 non-compliant accounts, and took down 16,349,000 non-compliant goods (Huanqiu Finance, 2024). These rigorous management measures have effectively curbed irregular trading behavior and boosted users' trust and satisfaction with the platform.

Yao Jinbo (Michael)

As the founder of 58 Group, Michael's significance to Zhuan Zhuan cannot be underestimated. He is a cerebral and passionate person who started from 58.com on the Craigslist model (a successful example of a classified advertisement website) but keenly realized the opportunity to shift from information flow to deep transactions. He pursued to make 58.com into a comprehensive platform covering recruitment, buying and selling used cars, renting houses, decoration and repair, unused items, and other types of information so that users can easily find the information they need. However, with the rise of the mobile Internet, the gap between 58.com and Taobao has gradually widened.

Michael states, "We believe that the combined horizontal and vertical model provides unparalleled strengths for classifieds marketplaces. We intend to replicate our proven success with the combination of 58.com, a horizontal classifieds platform, and Anjuke, an online housing vertical acquired in 2015. We believe Zhuan Zhuan, a horizontal used goods platform, and Zhaoliangji, a used cell phone vertical, will create another powerful combination" (China Telecom, 2020). Although 58.com has spawned several vertical platforms like ANJUKE, ChinaHR.com, and others, Yao has only shown great attention to Zhuan Zhuan. He believes that as an idle goods trading platform, Zuanzhuan has a high-frequency demand, which is different from the low-frequency demand of other platforms. Users make frequent transactions on the Zhuan Zhuan platform, not just limited to buying a caravan or looking for a job, which gives it the potential to become an e-commerce giant like JD.com and Taobao. As a result, 58 Tongcheng gave Zhuan Zhuan its valuable WeChat nine-gallon entrance, hoping to draw on 58—com's experience to attract consumers and make it an essential part of the e-commerce space. At a time when the second-hand e-commerce trend is just emerging, Zhuan Zhuan has a huge imaginative space in which Yao has great confidence, and his support and investment are crucial to the development of Zhuan Zhuan.

FUTURE PROJECTS

Deeper Collaboration With Tencent

Zhuan Zhuan's CEO, Wei HUANG, has stated that he accepted investment from Tencent not only for the capital but also for Tencent's resources in terms of users, community, and e-commerce. Zhuan Zhuan plans to form a dedicated team with Tencent to integrate resources for future cooperation in users, community, e-commerce, and the credit system. According to Huang, the number of users is a significant variable in the late Internet era. The cost of acquiring users has become exceedingly high, surpassing the cost of offline channels. Tencent holds an advantage in terms of the number of users and their engagement, primarily through its social platforms, QQ and WeChat.

In China, less than 10% of second-hand transactions are conducted through mobile channels, and a substantial number of transactions occur offline, often within QQ and WeChat neighborhood groups. Zhuan Zhuan aims to leverage the social relationship chain on WeChat to enhance the trustworthiness of user transactions. Their vision involves using WeChat to provide a certain level of social trust for transactions. For instance, buyers could view the seller's connections and see which WeChat friends have joined the app. Users can also share the goods they have posted with their WeChat circle of friends or in group chats with close connections. This social relationship-based approach to disseminating second-hand transactions is expected to address the challenge of limited user volume, thereby mitigating the high operational costs mentioned in the competition analysis.

In addition to leveraging Tencent's resources, Zhuan Zhuan intends to maintain collaborative relationships with various businesses under the 58 Group. Huang Wei emphasized that "the time when people most want to sell things is when they need to move or rent a house. These needs are interconnected." Therefore, Zhuan Zhuan's services, such as rental and moving services, can be integrated with the businesses of the 58 Group.

Enhancing the Category Richness of Idle Items

With the introduction of Plum, the influx of second-hand fashion goods has brought many young people's favorites to Zhuan Zhuan. Relying on the service system of "supply chain + standardization," more than 2,000 fashion brands have easily achieved circulation. Based on this experience, expanding the variety of second-hand recycled goods will be the secret to Zhuan Zhuan's continued success.

Currently, the commodities traded on Zhuan Zhuan's platform are mainly small home appliances and other items that are easy to overhaul and facilitate logistics. However, large household appliances such as refrigerators, washing machines, and large TVs, although having higher residual and recycling values, have yet to become mainstream commodities in second-hand trading due to higher transportation and logistics costs. Usually, these large items are circulated within the community, but there needs to be more supply and demand, resulting in the possibility that these items may be scrapped outright. Considering that these large appliances are essential in daily life, addressing their circulation and recycling is crucial.

In the future, Zhuan Zhuan plans to start building its own supply chain and logistics system to significantly reduce the cost of recycling large items and to promote the trend of recycling large goods. By relying on 58 Group's accumulated users and business base in its same-city business to establish an efficient logistics network and reasonable transportation solutions, Zhuan Zhuan can handle and transport these large appliances more efficiently, thus providing users with more choices and a more convenient shopping experience. This move will not only help extend the service life of these bulky items and reduce the waste of resources but also contribute to reducing carbon emissions and promoting sustainable development. Through its efforts and innovations, Zhuan Zhuan hopes to promote the development of the second-hand bulky goods market and contribute to the cause of environmental protection and sustainable socio-economic development.

REFERENCES

Editorial Board of the Journal. (2018). [Zhuan Zhuan brand development events]. *Sound Screen World-Advertiser*, (03), 83.

Finance, E. (2022). [Double 11 is full of "green" intention. Zhuan Zhuan: Shipments use environmentally friendly packaging and promote resource recycling]. *Chinadaily*. https://caijing.chinadaily.com.cn/a/202211/15/WS637347d3a3109b d995a501b7.html

Finance, H. (2024). CEO [Huang Wei, CEO of Zhuan Zhuan: The road to standardisation in the second-hand non-standard industry is like a fool's errand, but we will insist on it]. Xueqiu. https://xueqiu.com/8545085170/277358929

Huaon. (2024). *2024- [In-depth Research Report on China's Second-hand E-commerce Industry, 2024]*. Huajing Industrial Research Institute. NetEase. https://m.163.com/dy/article/IT2RPA1C0552SV13.html?clickfrom=subscribe

Li, Z. (2018). [China's rapid rise in second-hand trading platforms]. *People's Daily Online*. http://industry.people.com.cn/n1/2018/1022/c413883-30354591.html

Qian, Z., Xinyu, Z., Changshan, B., Min, T., & Zhengzheng, D. (2019). [Analyzing the development of the second-hand market under the sharing economy]. *Market Modernization*, (10), 182–183. DOI:10.14013/j.cnki.scxdh.2019.10.106

Qin, X. (2023, October 30). :"" [Turnaround Group's Xu Jian: Circular Economy Helps Realize 'Dual Carbon' Goal]. *China Business Journal*, B16. DOI:10.38300/n. cnki.nzgjy.2023.002504

Report, H. (2024). · . *[Hurun Global Unicorn Index]*. Hurun. https://www.hurun.net/zh-CN/Rank/HsRankDetails?pagetype=unicorn

Telecom, C. (2020). 58. com's Zhuan Zhuan to Acquire Used Handset Trading App Zhaoliangji. *China Telecom Newsletter*, 12-13. https://web.p.ebscohost.com/ehost/pdfviewer/pdfviewer?vid=3&sid=c4953976-774e-4664-85fe-27211bef7aec%40redis

Wei, L., & Mengyu, X. (2020). C2B2C—"" [Exploring the development of second-hand e-commerce platform under C2B2C model—Taking "Zhuan Zhuan" second-hand e-commerce platform as an example]. *Morden Business*, (28), 34–36. DOI:10.14097/j.cnki.5392/2020.28.013

Williams, C. C., & Paddock, C. (2003). The meaning of alternative consumption practices. *Cities (London, England)*, 20(5), 311–319. DOI:10.1016/S0264-2751(03)00048-9

KEY TERMS AND DEFINITIONS

3C Digital Products: 3C products mainly refer to computer-type, communication-type, and consumer electronics products, such as computers, tablets, cell phones, or digital audio players.

Dual Carbon: "Dual carbon" is short for Carbon Peaking and Neutrality. Carbon Peaking refers to the process whereby carbon emissions reach a peak, stop growing, and gradually decline. Carbon neutrality refers to the process whereby the amount of carbon emitted is equal to the amount of carbon absorbed by each object in the future at a given time.

Matthew Effect: The "Matthew effect" is the tendency of individuals to accrue social or economic success in proportion to their initial level of popularity, friends, and wealth. The adage or platitude sometimes summarizes it, "The rich get richer, and the poor get poorer."

Compilation of References

36Kr. (2022, April 12). *The journey of ten thousand miles begins with the landing of the road to the commercialisation of Uishi technology autonomous driving.* 36KR. https://www.36kr.com/p/1695459324366855

36Kr. (2023, February 6). *[6 Things to Watch on the Education Smart Hardware Track in 2023].* 36 Krypton. https://36kr.com/p/2119647329831299

36. Krypton Research Institute. (2022). *China Service Robot Industry Research Report 2022.* 36Krypton. https://www.36kr.com/p/2030626518920196

36Krypton. (2021, January 5). *2020, The Year of Gains and Losses in the Education Industry.* 36Kr. https://36kr.com/p/1040939156160646

36Krypton. (2024, January 16). 2023 Head Education Company Transformation Review: The business landscape blossoms, and technology becomes an essential driver of transformation. 36Kr. https://36kr.com/p/2606033145526913

A3 Robotics. (n.d.). *Association for Advancing Automation.* Automate. https://www.automate.org/robotics

Academic Headlines. (2018, July 27). *Historical changes in the development of autonomous driving from the 1970s to the present.* Baidu. https://baijiahao.baidu.com/s?id=1607101656119496661&wfr=spider&for=pc

ACOLINK, LTD. (2018, September 25). *Little Red Book (XiaoHongShu) paves the way for China's new social consumer culture.* ACOLINK, LTD. https://acolink.com/news/2018/little-red-book-ecommerce-social-consumer-culture

Adams, H. (2021, October 8). Online-to-Offline (O2O): Commerce definition and trends. *Investopedia.* https://www.investopedia.com/terms/o/onlinetooffline-commerce.asp

Ai, J., & Shi, D. (2022). Wenheyou: Escaping the troubles of Changsha. *Business School*, (05), 48–51.

Amber. (2023, March 7). Dismantling Tuhu car: The last stand of the industry's top students. *The Paper*.https://m.thepaper.cn/baijiahao_16955522

Amit, R., & Zott, C. (2001). Value creation in E-business. *Strategic Management Journal*, 22(6–7), 493–520. DOI:10.1002/smj.187

An, W. (n.d.). *[Annual GDP growth of 5.2% year-on-year in 2023]*. CN Gov. https://www.gov.cn/yaowen/liebiao/202401/content_6926714.html

Bai, J. (2018). Research the business model of Chinese auto aftermarket e-commerce platform enterprises. Take Tuhu as an example. *Economic Forum*.

Bai, M. (2024, March 6). *WeRide's self-developed autonomous driving middleware receives ISO 26262 ASIL-D functional safety product certification*. Sohu. https://sports.sohu.com/a/762272100_120159294

Baidu Index. (n.d.). *[Mafengwo Travel - Crowd Portrait.]* Baidu Index. https://index.baidu.com/v2/main/index.html#/crowd/

Baidu. (2024). *Kenglang Intelligence CEO Tom Lee: Leave the mechanical things to the robots and let people do more meaningful things*. Bajiaho. https://baijiahao.baidu.com/s?id=1622717804465260603&wfr=spider&for=pc

Baidu. (n.d.).*[UISEE Technology (Beijing) Co., LTD]*. UISEE Technology (Beijing) Co., LTD. Baidu Baike. https://baike.baidu.com/item/%E9%A9%AD%E5%8A%BF%E7%A7%91%E6%8A%80%EF%BC%88%E5%8C%97%E4%BA%AC%EF%BC%89%E6%9C%89%E9%99%90%E5%85%AC%E5%8F%B8

Bakhmutov, S., Saykin, A., Endachev, D., Evgrafov, V., Shagurin, A., Kulikov, I., & Fedoseev, K. (2018). Prospects of development of land driverless trucks. *IOP Conference Series. Materials Science and Engineering*, 315, 1. DOI:10.1088/1757-899X/315/1/012001

Bao, Y., Chen, B., Chen, X., Wang, Q. Y., & Kang, J. (n.d.). *"Data analysis of Chinese Doctor group."* McKinsey Greater China. https://www.mckinsey.com.cn/%E6%95%B0%E8%AF%B4%E5%8C%BB%E7%94%9F%EF%BC%8C%E4%B8%AD%E5%9B%BD%E5%8C%BB%E7%94%9F%E7%BE%A4%E4%BD%93%E7%94%BB%E5%83%8F/

Baobao. (2020). *Focusing on Unmanned Delivery Robots, "Optimus Intelligence" Receives 200 Million RMB Series B Financing Led by Source Capital.* 36Krypton. https://www.36kr.com/p/1724969369601

Beisen Holdings Limited. (2023). *Beisen 2023 financial reports [Financial reports].* Beisen Holdings Limited. https://ir-upload.realxen.net/iis/9669/uploads/iis/2023/10827405-0.PDF

Bergen, L. Y. C., & M. (2018, October 1). The unknown 35-year-old behind the world's most valuable startup. *The Sydney Morning Herald.* https://www.smh.com.au/business/companies/104b-goliath-the-unknown-35-year-old-behind-the-world-s-most-valuable-startup-20181001-p5072r.html

Bhaskar, S., Bradley, S., Sakhamuri, S., Moguilner, S., Chattu, V. K., Pandya, S., & Banach, M. (2020). Designing Futuristic Telemedicine Using Artificial Intelligence and Robotics in the COVID-19 Era. *Frontiers in Public Health*, 8, 556789. DOI:10.3389/fpubh.2020.556789 PMID:33224912

Big news. (n.d.). The year of Yuanfudao: rediscovering the rhythm. *Big News.* https://www.bianews.com/news/details?id=179070

Bizinnolab. (n.d.). *Jack's Column | The 2020 Epidemic: Yuanfudao's Business Model: Is Online Education Ready?* Bizinnolab. https://www.bizinnolab.com/h-nd-41.html

Bogumil, V., & Vlasov, V. (2018). Analysis of the main risks in developing and implementing uncrewed vehicles for urban passenger transport. *Transportation Research Procedia*, 36, 63–67. DOI:10.1016/j.trpro.2018.12.044

Brice, M., & Shepardson, D. (2024, February 1). *Tech CEOs said, "You have blood on your hands" at US Senate child safety hearing.* REUTERS. https://www.reuters.com/technology/meta-tiktok-x-ceos-face-tough-questions-child-safety-us-senate-hearing-2024-01-31/

ByteDance. (2021, May 20). *TikTok's co-founder will step down as chief executive.* BBC News. https://www.bbc.com/news/business-57181225

ByteDance. (2023). *Inspire creativity and enrich life.* ByteDance. https://www.bytedance.com/en/

Caijing. (2024, February 16). *From spicy strips to delicious, Weilong Delicious strongly opens a new era of development in 2024.* Sina. https://finance.sina.com.cn/stock/relnews/hk/2024-02-16/doc-inaifksa4442046.shtml

Canyinjie. (2021). *With a valuation of tens of billions and a rumored listing, is Wenheyou's value worthy of being China's No. 1 Catering Media?* Canyinjie. http://int.canyinj.com/index.php?m=home&c=View&a=index&aid=249

Cao, J. Y. (2020, June 23). Wenheyou [The Crowd-Pulling Popularity King]. *New Hunan·Daxiangcai News.* https://m.voc.com.cn/xhn/news/202006/14651666.html

Carriage House Polytechnic. (2021, December 14). *Getting to Know Enterprises | Phase 7, Zongmu Technology.* WeChat Public Platform; Vehicle Engineering College Youth League Branch Media Center. https://www.36kr.com/p/2450960495483008

CBBC. (2022, January 12). *Will manner coffee conquer Starbucks in China?* China-Britain Business Council. https://www.cbbc.org/news-insights/will-manner-coffee-conquer-starbucks-china

CBinsights. (2024). *Manner stock price, funding, valuation, revenue & financial statements.* CB Insights. https://www.cbinsights.com/company/manner/financials

Ceci, L. (2024). *TikTok—Statistics & facts.* Statista. https://www.statista.com/topics/6077/tiktok/

CEOCLUB. (2018). Zongmu Technology CEO Tang Rui: We Aim to Innovate from 0 to 1. *Technology and Finance*, (07), 43–46.

Chang, Y. (2020). Research on the marketing strategy of burgeoning sugar-free beverages: Taking Yuanqi Forest as an example. *E3S Web of Conferences.* e3s. DOI:10.1051/e3sconf/202021802002

Changsha Evening News. (2019, November 4). *["Wenheyou" wins Germany's Red Dot Design Award.]* ICWSB. https://www.icswb.com/h/152/20191104/627699.html

Changsha Municipal Data Resource Management Bureau. (2020, October 28). 2020 analysis report on the night economy data of Changsha City. *WeChat Official Account: Changsha Releases.* https://mp.weixin.qq.com/s/zq7LerZth9_aPIH5DAJ-ZA

Charlie Mao: Founder. (n.d.). Forbes. https://www.forbes.com/profile/charlwin-mao/

Charlwin Mao (Mao Wenchao). (n.d.). CompassList. https://www.compasslist.com/founders/charlwin-mao-mao-wenchao

Che, C. (2021, November 5). The rise of Manner Coffee. *The China Project.* https://thechinaproject.com/2021/11/05/the-rise-of-manner-coffee/

Chen, G. E., & Li, J. X. (2021). Research on "Internet Celebrity" Consumption Space in the Internet Era: A Case Study of Changsha Super Wenheyou. In *Urban Design Towards High-Quality Development: Proceedings of the 2021 China Urban Planning Annual Conference (07 Urban Design)* (pp. 1210-1220). School of Architecture, Southeast University. https://doi.org/DOI:10.26914/c.cnkihy.2021.026600

Chen, L., & Chen, D. (2022, May 25). *WeRide receives strategic investment from doctorate holders and conducts intelligent driving software development jointly.* Baidu. https://baijiahao.baidu.com/s?id=1733763700373840579&wfr=baike

Chen, P. (2023, July 4). *"China's first medical generative AI milestone, Medlinker MedGPT has over 96% diagnostic consistency with tertiary experts".* Vbdata. https://www.vbdata.cn/1518918039

Chen, R. (2021). Annie Chen: Industrialising comics. *China Entrepreneur*, (04), 55-57+54.

Chen, R., & Ma, R. (2022, February 24). How ByteDance became the world's most valuable startup. *Harvard Business Review.* https://hbr.org/2022/02/how-bytedance-became-the-worlds-most-valuable-startup

Chen, S. (2019). *The Product Life Cycle and Product Design.*

Chen, X. (2017). Research status and prospects of Internet healthcare. *People's Forum: Academic Frontier, 24*, 40-47+95. DOI:10.16619/j.cnki.rmltxsqy.2017.24.005

Chen, B. (2020). *Exploration of China's car-sharing development strategy based on SWOT analysis. Journal of Chongqing Jiaotong University.* Social Science Edition.

Chengxiang, Z. (2023, January 19). Zongmu Technology Files for the STAR Market After Losing 785 Million in Three Years. *National Business Daily.*

Chen, X. (2016). Trial and error in Hokusen. Twenty-first Century. *Business Review*, 12, 52–53.

Chen, X. M., & Xu, H. Y. (2017). Strategic cost management in the start-up and growth period of China's e-commerce enterprises: A case study of Jiuxian.com. *Finance & Accounting Monthly*, (31), 82–87. DOI:10.19641/j.cnki.42-1290/f.2017.31.018

Chen, Z. X. (2022). [Jiuxian.com's IPO has not been bid, so who will become the "second share" of liquor circulation?] *Huaxia Wine News*, A06. DOI:10.28390/n.cnki.nhxjb.2022.000367

Chernavina, K. (2022, June 29). *2021-2022 Xiaohongshu/RED user trends*. HI-COM. https://www.hicom-asia.com/2022-xiaohongshu-red-user-trends-and-statistics/

Chi, R. (2021, June 9). Jump on the rise of Xiaohongshu, China's fastest-growing social media marketing platform. *The Drum*. https://www.thedrum.com/opinion/2021/06/09/jump-the-rise-xiaohongshu-china-s-fastest-growing-social-media-marketing-platform

China Business Industry Research Institute. (2023, November 14). *"Research Report on market prospect forecast of China's Internet medical industry in 2024"*. Netease. https://www.163.com/dy/article/IJGACK2805198SOQ.html

China charging station industry market prospect and investment research report. (2021). Electric appliance industry, (12), 13–33.

China Digital Marketing Agency in Hong Kong. (n.d.). *Mafengwo Guide*. Alarice. https://alarice.com.hk/mafengwo-guide/

China Education Network. (n.d.). *The 2023 World Conference on Artificial Intelligence recently opened. KLM focuses on robotics/artificial intelligence education.* China Education Network. http://www.edu-gov.cn/edu/23510.html

China Education Online. (n.d.). *Ministry of Education: China's higher education gross enrollment rate will reach 59.6% by 2022*. China Education Online. https://news.eol.cn/meeting/202303/t20230323_2331956.shtml

China Electromechanical Recruitment Network. (2023, February 28). *Hebei Provincial Public Security Department charging pile and related equipment procurement and installation project transaction announcement*. China Electromechanical Recruitment Network. https://caizhao.jdzj.com/purchases/2023-02-28.31592b669f424971f973adb4162c7343

China Hunan Province Political Consultative Conference. (2022, June 28). *[Boosting the Hunan Cuisine Industry from Billions to Trillions! Provincial Political Consultative Conference Continues to Focus and Contribute Wisdom to "Creating a Great Table of Hunan Dishes."]* Political Consultative Conference Media. https://www.hunanzx.gov.cn/hnzx/wzsyszx/zxdt/202206/t20220628_26527415.html

China Science and Technology Information. (2019). *The State of K12 China.*

Chine Marketing Agency. (2023, November 23). *From WeChat to Douyin: Navigating Chinese Social Media Landscape*. Do Matters. https://www.domatters.com/most-popular-chinese-social-media-platforms/

Chun, D. (2016, October 20). *[Ximalaya FM business model: Creating a multi-dimensional "ear economy" with "UGC+PGC+Social Scene].*http://www.jiamengpinglun.com/34996

Chu, Y. (2023). Manner Coffees marketing strategies: A review. *Advances in Economics. Management and Political Sciences*, 8(1), 275–279. DOI:10.54254/2754-1169/8/20230325

Civil Affairs Bureau of China. (2023). *2022 China National Aging Development Report*. Civil Affairs Bureau of China.

CNNIC. (2023). *The 51st statistical report on China's Internet development.* CNNIC. https://www.cnnic.com.cn/IDR/ReportDownloads/202307/P020230707514088128694.pdf

Cong, L., & Wu, Q. (2014). Talent management enters the era of a cloud computing platform—Interview with Ji Weiguo, Co-founder of Beisen Assessment. *China Human Resource Development*, 90–97. DOI:10.16471/j.cnki.11-2822/c.2014.12.020

Consulting, A. M. (2023). *[China Sound Economy Digital Application Development Trend Report 2022]*. iiMedia. https://www.iimedia.cn/c400/91728.html

Consulting, A. M. (2023). *[Chinese Knowledge Payment Industry Status and Development Outlook Report 2023]*. iiMedia. https://www.iimedia.cn/c400/92443.html

Cooper, B. (2023). *Challengers to Watch 2023: Genki Forest*. BizCommunity. www.bizcommunity.com

Crunchbase. (2024). *Charlie Mao*. CrunchBase. https://www.crunchbase.com/person/charlwin-mao-wenchao

CSDN. (2020, September 7). *[Competitive Product Analysis Report: How Can Keep Make Sports More]*. CSDN. https://wenku.csdn.net/doc/5qt3z9xd4k

CSDN. (n.d.). *Honour, UISEE Technology recently won an awards review*. CSDN. https://blog.csdn.net/UISEE2031/article/details/130460487

Dai, B.B. (2010). Research on the current situation and development trend of the aftermarket in China. *Economic Research Guide, 21*.

Day, G. (1981). The Product Life Cycle: Analysis and Applications Issues. *Journal of Marketing*, 45(4), 60–67. DOI:10.1177/002224298104500408

Ding, Z. (2022). Wei Long: Reshaping quality standards. *China Quality Supervision*, (12), 90.

DJ Research. (n.d.). *Professional real-time research report sharing, industry research report, industry analysis report, brokerage research report, industry think tank.* DJ Research. https://www.djyanbao.com/report/search?channel=360yanjiubaogao&qhclickid=f11092d753085801

Dong, R., & Li, H. (2024). *"A total of more than 18,000 medical alliances of various forms have been established across the country".* Economic Information Daily. http://dz.jjckb.cn/www/pages/webpage2009/html/2024-03/06/content_96735.htm

Dou, E. (2015). Shou Zi Chew joins Xiaomi as CFO. *WSJ.* https://www.wsj.com/articles/shou-zi-chew-joins-xiaomi-as-cfo-1435719748

Du, C. (2023). Analysis of the current situation and operation path of social content e-commerce under the new media background. *National Circulation Economy*, 13, 24–27. DOI:10.16834/j.cnki.issn1009-5292.2023.13.016

Easemob. (n.d.). *AI+Education is not as optimistic as it seems.* EaseMob. https://www.easemob.com/news/4264

ECS. (2024). *1.4 billion reasons to sell coffee* [The European Coffee Symposium]. China's Coffee Revolution: Opportunities and Challenges Ahead. https://www.europeancoffeesymposium.com/blog/1-4-billion-reasons-to-sell-coffee

Editorial Board of the Journal. (2018). [Zhuan Zhuan brand development events]. *Sound Screen World-Advertiser*, (03), 83.

Education.com. (n.d.). *2023 Education Industry Insight\Add, subtract, multiply and divide to answer the "2023" questionnaire.* Education.com. https://www.jiaoyujie365.com/N/1510.html

Enfodesk. (2016). Special research report on e-commerce in China's auto aftermarket in the first half of 2016. *Auto Maintenance & Repair*, 12.

Enterprise Check. (n.d.). *Enterprise business information query system_Check the enterprise _ check the boss _ check the risk on the enterprise check!* QCC. https://www.qcc.com/

Fan, Z. (2020). Prospecting unlimited possibilities for future traveling in the era of smart connected cars. *Smart Connected Vehicles*, 6, 53–55.

Feng, S.S. (2015). *Tuhu: Deep in O2O*. Chief Financial Officer.

Feng, T. (2016, September 13). *"Academicians such as Zhan Qimin and Yang Huanming praised Medlinker as a 'pioneer of doctors' multi-practice"*. Chinadaily. https://caijing.chinadaily.com.cn/finance/2016-09/13/content_26787915.htm

Finance, E. (2022). [Double 11 is full of "green" intention. Zhuan Zhuan: Shipments use environmentally friendly packaging and promote resource recycling]. *Chinadaily*. https://caijing.chinadaily.com.cn/a/202211/15/WS637347d3a3109b d995a501b7.html

Finance, H. (2024). [Huang Wei, CEO of Zhuan Zhuan: The road to standardisation in the second-hand non-standard industry is like a fool's errand, but we will insist on it]. Xueqiu. https://xueqiu.com/8545085170/277358929

Finance, W. H. (2021, September 15). [Behind Ximalaya's return to Hong Kong, the "merits" and "demerits" of 12.46 million UGC creators]. 36KR. https://www .36kr.com/p/1398444289997575

Financial Sharp Eye. (2021). *[Jiuxian.com, which sprinted to the market, burned more than a billion dollars, false publicity, and sold fake wine]*. Zhihu. https:// zhuanlan.zhihu.com/p/371770835

Fleck, A. (2024, March 14). More Americans turn to TikTok for news. *Statista Daily Data*.https://www.statista.com/chart/31905/us-adults-who-regularly-get-news -from-tiktok

Flexi Classes. (2021, January 12). *Xiaohongshu Vs Instagram | What is ? Should You Get It?* Flexi Classes. https://flexiclasses.com/xiaohongshu-vs-instagram/

Forbes. (n.d.). *Qu Miranda*. Forbes. https://www.forbes.com/profile/qu-miranda/

Foresight Industry Research Institute. (n.d.). *China Online Education Industry Market Status, Segmentation, and Development Trend Analysis in 2021 Further Sinking Trend is Obvious*. Foresight Industry Research Institute. https://bg.qianzhan.com/ report/detail/300/211011-e5f2ee29.html

Fried, I. (2015, July 1). *Xiaomi taps DST investment partner Shou Zi Chew to be CFO*. Vox. https://www.vox.com/2015/7/1/11564020/xiaomi-taps-dst-investment -partner-shou-zi-chew-to-be-cfo

Fu, C., & Wang, Y. (2021). [Research on urban night-time cultural and tourism consumption space from the perspective of the scene: A perspective based on the cultural scene of Changsha Super Wenheyou]. *Journal of Wuhan University (Philosophy & Social Sciences)*, *74*(6), 58–70. DOI:10.14086/j.cnki.wujss.2021.06.006

Fu, C., & Zhong, S. (2014). [Research on the construction of regional cultural tourism themes from the perspective of cultural identity experience: A case study of the Hexi Corridor]. *Journal of Wuhan University (Philosophy & Social Sciences)*, *67*(1).

Fu, Z. (2022, August 19). *The rise of Xiaohongshu: the little red's big ambition.* PingWest. https://en.pingwest.com/a/10594

Fuller, T., & Maheshwari, S. (2023, May 12). Ex-ByteDance executive accuses the company of "lawlessness." *The New York Times.*https://www.nytimes.com/2023/05/12/technology/tiktok-bytedance-lawsuit-china.html

Future Think Tank. (n.d.). Autonomous driving industry competition pattern and future outlook analysis. https://www.vzkoo.com/read/20240305ea109edebbab09d2d89f077b.html

Gao, S. Y., Ma, X. H., & Zhang, Y. (2019). Research on the driving factors and driving mechanism of business model innovation of shared medical enterprises: A case study based on WeDoctor. *Lanzhou Journal*, 09, 149–163.

General Office of State Administration of Radio and Television. (2021). *[Notice of the General Office of the State Administration of Radio, Film and Television on releasing the digital copyright management standard system for distributing audio and video content].* General Office of State Administration of Radio and Television. https://www.gov.cn/zhengce/zhengceku/2021-02/24/content_5588584.htm

General Office of the State Council. (2018, April 28). *"Opinions of the General Office of the State Council on Promoting the Development of 'Internet + Healthcare'".* Central People's Government of the People's Republic of China. https://www.gov.cn/zhengce/content/2018-04/28/content_5286645.htm

Goh, I. (2023, January 11). You Probably Didn't Know These 10 Facts About Xiaohongshu. *Goody Feed.* https://goodyfeed.com/xiaohongshu/

Grewal, D., & Levy, M. (2020). *Marketing* (7th ed.). McGraw-Hill Education.

Guan, W. (n.d.). *IPO53-year-old boss sells hotpot ingredients, opens nearly 10,000 stores, worth $5 billion, sprints to IPO*. cyzone. https://m.cyzone.cn/article/739918.html

Guanyantianxia. (2022, October 14). *Analysis of the advantages and disadvantages of the aftermarket industry in our country: The market scale is expanding, and the service level needs to be improved.* 360doc.com. http://www.360doc.com/content/12/0121/07/13672581_1051684870.shtml

Guo, J. (2022). The postfeminist entrepreneurial self and the platformisation of labour: A case study of yesheng female lifestyle bloggers on xiaohongshu. *Global Media and China*, 7(3), 205943642210958. DOI:10.1177/20594364221095896

Guoquan. (2024). *Guoquan Shihui brand advantages—Guoquan Shihui Hot Pot BBQ ingredients supermarket*. ZZHQSH. https://www.zzgqsh.com/website/advantage

Guo, W. (2021). *Driverless taxis are edging closer from manned tests to eliminating safety officers*. Smart Connected Cars.

Han, W. J. (2023, April 8). Moutai invested in hot pot supermarket to IPO, valuation of more than 10 billion]. *Foodaily*. https://www.foodaily.com/articles/32383

Han, X. (2019). Progress and outlook of L4-level autonomous driving. *Intelligent Networked Vehicles*.

Han, X. C. (2021, April 20). *[Online Fitness: A gym at home]*. Zhongtai Securities. https://pdf.dfcfw.com/pdf/H3_AP202204271561920041_1.pdf?1651069207000.pdf

Hang, H. C. (n.d.). *[Industry Research Databases]*. Hang Cha. https://www.hanghangcha.com/pdf.html

Hao, X.C. (2023). Tuhu Car Maintenance - The growth path of an automotive aftermarket leader. *Academic Journal of Management and Social Sciences, 2*(1).

Hastam, J. (2024, February 29). *What is Xiaohongshu? Marketing Guide for Brands*. Nativex. https://www.nativex.com/en/blog/exploring-xiaohongshu-chinas-answer-to-instagram/

He, L. (2024, March 18). *Analysis: Wait, is TikTok Chinese?* CNN. https://www.cnn.com/2024/03/18/tech/tiktok-bytedance-china-ownership-intl-hnk/index.html

He, Q. (2024). Shanghai pushes China's coffee industry to nearly $40b. *China Daily*. https://www.chinadaily.com.cn/a/202405/01/WS6631eea3a31082fc043c5022.html

He, Y. (2021, April 25). *[Quanjude faces a massive loss of nearly three years of profit in one year, with a 2020 deficit of 262 million yuan]*. China Business Network. http://www.zgswcn.com/article/202104/202104251534511141.html

HelloRide. (n.d.). *Helloride shared micromobility: World's leading shared E-mobility operator*. HelloRide. https://www.helloride-global.com/

Heytea. (2024, January 3).*[Heytea Decennial Report]*. Heytea. https://www.heytea.com/

Hongwang. (2019, December 25). *[Changsha Pozi Street and Taiping Street become the first national "Must-Eat Streets" recognized by Dianping]*. SOHU. https://m.sohu.com/a/362638374_100180399

Hou, J. (2022). The evaluation of Hellobike. *Proceedings of the 2022 2nd International Conference on Economic Development and Business Culture (ICEDBC 2022)*, (pp. 1736–1742). Atlantis Press. DOI:10.2991/978-94-6463-036-7_259

Hu, Z. (2024). Sprint IPO Star Charge: Expansion, pressure, transformation. *Zhihu column*. https://zhuanlan.zhihu.com/p/681012997

Hua Jing Intelligence Network. (n.d.). *2022[An immense talent demand gap and voice training emerge in the analysis of the development status and trends of China's sound economy industry in 2022]*. Huaon. https://www.huaon.com/channel/trend/878350.html

Huajing Industrial Research Institute. (n.d.). Huajing Industrial Research Institute - focuses on industrial economic intelligence and research in Greater China. https://www.huaon.com/

Huaon. (2024).*2024[In-depth Research Report on China's Second-hand E-commerce Industry, 2024]*. Huajing Industrial Research Institute. NetEase. https://m.163.com/dy/article/IT2RPA1C0552SV13.html?clickfrom=subscribe

HuffPost. (2020, December 15). The $15.5 Billion Giant Yuanfudao: The Underlying Capabilities Behind Crazy Growth. *Huffington Post*.https://www.huxiu.com/article/400201.html

HuRun Research Institute. (2023, April 18). *2023 Global Unicorn List*. HuRun. https://www.hurun.net/zh-CN/Info/Detail?num=PH71LJQJPANH

Hurun Research Institute. (2023, April 18). *Hurun Report 2023 Global Unicorn List*. Hurun Research Institute. https://www.hurun.net/zh-CN/Info/Detail?num=PH71LJQJPANH

Hurun. (2023). *Hurun global unicorn list*. Hurun. https://www.hurun.net/en-US/Rank/HsRankDetails?pagetype=unicorn

Husni, M. A., Nugroho, A. K., Fakhrudin, N., & Sulaiman, T. N. S. (2021). Micro-encapsulation of ethyl acetate extract from green coffee beans (coffea canephora) by spray drying method. *Indonesian Journal of Pharmacy*, 221–231. DOI:10.22146/ijp.1457

Huxiu technology. (2023, September 4). *WeRide focuses on innovative business models and accelerates the implementation of autonomous driving technology*. Dongchedi. https://www.dongchedi.com/article/7274776701589094973

Ifeng Finance. (n.d.). *UISEE Technology - The future global AI driver covering all models*. Ifeng Finance. https://finance.ifeng.com/c/8PrdFAPWzk9

IFR International Federation of Robotics. (n.d.). *IFR presents World Robotics 2021 reports*. IFR. https://ifr.org/ifr-press-releases/news/robot-sales-rise-again

Iimedia. (2019). *Ai media research report: 2019H1 submarine operation status and industry trends research report*. iiMedia. https://www.iimedia.cn/c1000/65350.html

iimedia. (2019, April 8). *[Analysis of the burden of primary and secondary school workload report: nearly 30% of students learning pressure, more than 50% in the holidays have extracurricular tutoring classes]*. AiMedia.com. https://www.iimedia.cn/c460/64040.html

iiMedia. (2020, August 10). *Top 10 charging pile operators in China in the first half of 2020*. iiMedia. https://www.iimedia.cn/c880/73400.html

iiMedia. (2021, November 5). *2021 "China Internet Hospital Industry Development Research Report 2021"*. https://www.iimedia.cn/c400/81955.html

iiMedia. (2022). *2021[China New Style Tea Drink Industry Research Report 2021]*. iiMedia. https://www.iresearch.com.cn/

Ikanchai. (2019). *Keep won the 2019 Responsible Brand award, delivering a new way of healthy living through internet technology express chopping network*. Ikanchai. http://news.ikanchai.com/2020/0115/332495.shtml

iMedia. (2024). *The poor boy, whom his ex-girlfriend abandoned, became a student of Jack Ma and opened three stores with a valuation of 10 billion*. iMedia. https://min.news/en/entertainment/722bc88fc8d6d4fb5135872cfc33ac71.html

iMedia. (2024). *Yuanqi Forest deepens cooperation with Fenxiang Sales: Using data to connect businesses to drive decision-making.* iMedia. https://min.news/en/economy/d97291f425e4b78e19e83f0fa89d9452.html

iNEWS. (2023). *Tang Binsen: Before the success of Yuanqi Forest, I had a "Ten Billion Dollar Lesson" [Interview].* iNews. https://inf.news/en/economy/b46674018582 5621db468760de59c973.html

Interface news. (2024, January 12). The next ten years of Chinese snacks. *Interface News.* https://finance.sina.com.cn/jjxw/2024-01-12/doc-inachqhs1822188.shtml

Interface News. (n.d.). Yuanfudao Becomes the Official Sponsor of the Beijing 2022 Winter Olympics. *Interface news.* https://www.jiemian.com/article/4664407.html

iResearch Consulting. (2021). *iResearch Awards[2021 iResearch Awards Gold Award-winning Companies Announced].* iResearch Consulting.

iResearch Consulting. (2022). *Research Report on Digitalization of Human Resources in China,* 557–615. iResearch Consulting.

iResearch. (2018). *Research Report on China's Animation Industry.* iResearch. https://report.iresearch.cn/report_pdf.aspx?id=3309

iResearch. (2019). *White Paper on the Marketing Value of the Anime and Manga Culture Crowd.* iResearch. https://report.iresearch.cn/report_pdf.aspx?id=3496

iResearch. (2021). *China's Anime and Manga Industry Research Report.* iResearch. https://report.iresearch.cn/report_pdf.aspx?id=3865

iResearch. (2022). *Iresearch: The Tide of China Tradition.* iResearch. https://report .iresearch.cn/report_pdf.aspx?id=3940

Iresearch. (2022, September). *[China Education Smart Hardware Market and User Insights Report 2022 Report. Research].* Cn. https://report.iresearch.cn/report_pdf .aspx?id=4069

IT information. (2019, December 8). Xueqiu. https://xueqiu.com/8175691790/ 137009115

Janssen, D., & Carradini, S. (2021). Generation Z workplace communication habits and expectations. *IEEE Transactions on Professional Communication,* 64(2), 137–153. DOI:10.1109/TPC.2021.3069288

Jian, Y. (2023). *Charging pile industry data analysis: Star Charge's market share was 19.6%*. IIMedia. https://www.iimedia.cn/c1061/90253.html

Jiang, T. Y. (2021, July 9). The road of China's digital healthcare from the growth of WeDoctor. *Health Newspaper*, 6.

Jiang, Z., Lin, H., Zhong, Y., Huang, Q., Chen, Y., Zhang, Z., & Ye, J. (2024). *MegaScale: Scaling large language model training to more than 10,000 GPUs*. arXiv preprint arXiv:2402.15627.

Jiang, C. (2023). Weilong Food: Turning a 50-cent business into billions. *Zhongguancun*, (01), 32–33.

Jianping, L. (2023, September 28). *Zongmu Technology IPO Terminated: Pre-Investment Valuation of 8 Billion, Xiaomi Junlian Tongchuang is a Shareholder*. 36Krypton. https://www.36kr.com/p/2450960495483008

Jiuxian. (2021). *[IPO prospectus]*. Huatai United Securities Co., Ltd. https://pdf.dfcfw.com/pdf/H2_AN202109291519304688_1.pdf

Jiuxian. (2023). *Company description*. Jiuxian.com. https://help.jiuxian.com/view-0-105.htm

Kelly, M., & Williams, C. (2019). *BUSN11: Introduction to business*. Cengage.

Kesan, J. P., & Shah, R. C. (2013). Setting software defaults: Perspectives from the law, computer science, and behavioural economics. *The Notre Dame Law Review*, 82, 583.

KrASIA. (2023, December 14). *With 1,000 stores established, can Manner Coffee fend off the likes of Starbucks, Luckin, and Cotti to keep growing?* KrASIA. https://kr-asia.com/with-1000-stores-established-can-manner-coffee-fend-off-the-likes-of-starbucks-luckin-and-cotti-to-keep-growing

Lai, L., Wan, B., & Li, Y. (2023). Scene, interaction, and consumption: The power characteristics and realisation mechanism of online shopping platforms—A "Dewu APP" case study. *Media Forum*, (08), 38-40.

Lai, Y. (2023, January 13). *[Two Sessions Connection: Chen Gang, Founder and CEO of Mafengwo Tourism Network: This data city will grow into a world-changing enterprise]*. Contemporary Pioneer Website. http://www.ddcpc.cn/detail/d_guizhou/11515116071350.html

Lantu. (2023). Tuhu car digital practice - Leveraging technology to drive the new transformation of automotive aftermarket service. *Zhang Jiang Technology Review, 4*.

Lei, A. (2020). Comparative study on short video function of animation apps: A case study of "Kuaikan Manhua" and "Tencent Animation". *New Media Research*, (09), 35–37.

Lei, X. (2022). China Inspection Forms Joint Identification Research Team with Depwu. *China Quality Milestone Journey*, 11, 50–52.

Li Jing. (2023, February 20). Zuoyebang's hardware success. Economic Observer, p. 004. DOI:10.28421/n.cnki.njjgc.2023.000279

Li, B. (2016). [1919 & Jiuxian: The Coopetition and Cooperation of Liquor E-commerce]. *China Business News*, C07.

Li, L. (2021, March 3). *Behind the mass production of automatic driving before loading, the breaking work of Wen Yuan knows the line.* Sohu. https://www.sohu .com/a/453812593_99919085

Li, M. (2023, December 8). *Insight Magazine | Xiaohongshu: A Social Commerce Platform You Cannot Miss.* Amcham-Shanghai.org. https://www.amcham-shanghai .org/en/article/insight-magazine-xiaohongshu-social-commerce-platform-you -cannot-miss

Li, X. (2021). China's education companies diversify their businesses after regulatory updates. *Beijing Review*. https://www.bjreview.com/Special_Reports/2022/ NPC_CPPCC_Sessions_2022/Economy/202203/t20220303_800277655.html

Li, X. (2021, September 16). Identify first, then ship: Dewu App's quality online shopping stimulates consumption potential. *China Consumer News, 007*.

Li, Z. (2018).[China's rapid rise in second-hand trading platforms]. *People's Daily Online*. http://industry.people.com.cn/n1/2018/1022/c413883-30354591.html

Lin, H. (2021, July). *"China Internet Medical Content Industry Research Report in 2021".* iyiou. https://www.iyiou.com/research/20210707877

Lina. (2021). *DynaLang Intelligence Closes $200 Million Series D Funding Round Led by Softbank Vision.* 36Krypton. https://www.36kr.com/p/1397821032561417

Lin, H. S., & Wang, Y. B. (2023). Research on the Current Situation and Development Strategy of Keep Fitness Software Sports Marketing. *Sports Boutique*, 42(02), 51–53.

Lin, S. (2022). Analysis of Weilong's marketing strategy. *The China Business Review*, (05), 44–47. DOI:10.19699/j.cnki.issn2096-0298.2022.05.044

Liu, J. (2020). The driverless era accelerates. *Economic Journal*.

Liu, Q. (2023, July 13). *[AI Education Industry Research (I): Bullish on Smart Education, Education Informatisation and AI Talent Training]*. Data.eastmoney.com. https://data.eastmoney.com/report/zw_industry.jshtml?infocode=AP202307131592237453

Liu, Y. (2023). Analysis of the Development Environment of China's Intelligent Driving Industry in 2023 (PEST): Policies remain favourable, and market competition is fierce. https://www.chyxx.com/industry/1153277.html

Liu, Z. W. (2023, December 28). *[China's largest online fitness platform, deep cultivation of online fitness to form a diversified realization]*. Doc88. https://www.doc88.com/p-95929899267358.html

Liu, Y. (2023). Analysis of Xiaohongshu's Internet Marketing Strategy. *BCP Business & Management*, 43, 110–116. DOI:10.54691/bcpbm.v43i.4629

Liu, Y. (2023, March 21). Weilong insists on quality first and guards safety on the tip of the tongue. *China Food Safety News*, B03. DOI:10.28737/n.cnki.nspzl.2023.000556

Li, W. G. (2023).[Keep APP Research on the Development Strategy of Fitness APP Based on PEST Analysis Paradigm——Taking Keep APP as an Example]. *Contemporary Sports Science and Technology*, 13(3). DOI:10.16655/j.cnki.2095-2813.2209-1579-3569

Li, X. Q., & Li, N. (2021). Research on the business model of Internet hospitals. *Software*, 12, 1–3.

Li, Z. X., Li, W., Guo, X., Han, W., & Wang, H. L. (2022). Research the intelligent service model based on "Internet Plus Medical Care". *China New Communications*, 14, 87–89.

Lu, Z. (2021, September 9). *WeRide enters the freight field and launches L4 autonomous light passenger vehicles in cooperation with Jiangling and Zhongtong*. Sina. https://finance.sina.com.cn/tech/2021-09-09/doc-iktzscyx3258444.shtml

Luo, M. (2022). *[Reevaluation of the value of Changsha Wen He You from the perspective of urban renewal practices]* [Master's thesis, Hunan University]. https://link.cnki.net/doi/10.27135/d.cnki.ghudu.2022.003410

Luo, X. Y., & Wang, N. N..(2024). *[Research on the development strategy of audio publishing platform based on user experience -- taking Ximalaya FM as an example. Digital publishing research].* Digital publishing research (01),16-24.

Luohuan. (2021). *[Ximalaya FM platform operation strategy research"(Dissertation, Zhongnan University of Economics and Law).* CNKI. https://link.cnki.net/doi/10.27660/d.cnki.gzczu.2021.000824doi:10.27660/d.cnki.gzczu.2021.000824

Luyun. (2020). [Revenue recognition and measurement analysis of knowledge payment platform: A case study of Ximalaya FM]. *Business accounting*, (21), 52-56.

Lv, R. (2017). Charging the Tigers and Roses in operation. *New energy economic and trade observation,* (Z1), 74–75.

Ma, L. (2015). *Interview: Shao Danwei, Chairman of Wanbang New Energy Investment Group Co.* China Government Net. https://www.gov.cn/wenzheng/2015-09/15/content_2931970.htm

Ma, W. (2021). *It is rumored online that Manner Coffee will be listed in Hong Kong next year.* IYIOU. https://www.iyiou.com/news/202110131023145

Mafengwo. (2018, February 26). *[The Evolution of Mafengwo: From New Wave Travel Agency Area to National Tourism Brand].* Magengwo. https://m.mafengwo.cn/travel-news/1424122.html?ivk_sa=1024320u

Mafengwo. (2024). *[About Mafengwo – Mafengwo].* Mafenwo. https://www.mafengwo.cn/s/about.html

Maigoo Travel Website. (n.d.). [Introduction of Chen Gang – Co-founder of Mafengwo Tourism Network]. *Maigoo.* https://www.maigoo.com/mingren/19768.html

Mai, J. H. (2020). [The rebellion of Wenheyou]. *Splendor,* (10), 56–58.

Maimai. (2019, March 1). *WeRide SVP Hua Zhong: Engineers are the people who solve problems.* Maimai. https://maimai.cn/article/detail?fid=1146584014&efid=cS3KDTyj0vQDhAxdXKbcmw

Maluleke, A. M. (2023, January 10). TikTok CEO Shou Zi Chew meets with EU Commission vice-president. *SABC News.* https://www.sabcnews.com/sabcnews/tiktok-ceo-shou-zi-chew-meets-with-eu-commission-vice-president/

Mao, Q. (2021). Research on the interaction mechanism of trend-related platforms from the perspective of interaction ritual chains: A case study of Depwu App. *Journal of News Research Guidance*, 18, 57–59.

McKinsey Greater China. (2024, March 13). China may become the world's largest autonomous driving market. *[McKinsey Future Mobility Research Center: China May Become the World's Largest Autonomous Driving Market]*. McKinsey Greater China.

McKinsey Greater China. (2024, March 14). Making science Fiction Reality: Progress and trends in autonomous driving in China. *[Making Science Fiction Reality: Progress and Trends in Autonomous Driving in China]*. McKinsey Greater China.

Medlinker. (2022, November 1). *"Medlinker's Precision Marketing Platform Goes Live, Helping Pharmaceutical Enterprises Transform Digital Marketing"*. Medlinker. https://www.medlinker.com/pc/news/detail/191

Medlinker. (2024). *"Medlinker empowers doctors to improve the efficiency and quality of patient management"*. About Medical Alliance Honors. https://www.medlinker.com/pc/about/honor

Meng, Q., Yin, X., & Liang, C. (2017). Overview of the current situation and development of "Internet Plus Healthcare" in China. *Chinese Journal of Health Information Management*, 02, 110–118.

Ministry of Education of the People's Republic of China. (2021, March 9). *Notice on issuing the 2021 Work Points of the Department of Science, Technology and Informatisation of the Ministry of Education*. Government Portal of the Ministry of Education of the People's Republic of China. http://www.moe.gov.cn/s78/A16/tongzhi/202103/t20210319_520941.html

Ministry of Industry and Information Technology Information Center. (2019). *2019 China's Top 100 Internet Enterprises Development Report*. Ministry of Industry and Information Technology Center.

Ministry of Public Security. (2024, January 11). *The number of motor vehicles in China reached 435 million, with 523 million drivers, and the number of new energy vehicles exceeded 20 million*. Ministry of Public Security. https://www.gov.cn/lianbo/bumen/202401/content_6925362.htm

Mordor Intelligence. (2024). *Service Robotics Market - Size, Analysis and Companies*. Modor Intelligence. https://www.mordorintelligence.com/zh/industry-reports/service-robotics-market

Mordor. (2024). *China coffee—Market share analysis, industry trends & statistics, growth forecasts 2024—2029*. Gire Research. https://www.giiresearch.com/report/moi1404108-china-coffee-market-share-analysis-industry-trends.html

National Bureau of Statistics of China. (2021). *National Bureau of Statistics of China Yearbook*. National Bureau of Statistics of China. https://www.stats.gov.cn/english/Statisticaldata/yearbook/

National Bureau of Statistics. (n.d.). *Income and Consumption Expenditure of the Population in 2023*. National Bureau of Statistics. https://www.stats.gov.cn/

National Bureau of Statistics. (n.d.-a). *[The situation of residents' income and consumption expenditure in 2023]*. NBS. https://www.stats.gov.cn/sj/zxfb/202401/t20240116_1946622.html DOI:10.14097/j.cnki.5392/2018.20.043

National Health and Family Planning Commission. (2014, August 29). *"Opinions of National Health and Family Planning Commission on Promoting telemedicine services in medical institutions"*. National Health Commission. http://www.nhc.gov.cn/

New Beijing News. (2020, March 31). Good News, No End. *New Bejing News*. https://www.bjnews.com.cn/edu/2020/03/31/711118.html

Ni, A. (2020, July 10). *[Ximalaya, why is it leading the online audio market?]*. WoshipM. https://www.woshipm.com/evaluating/4077639.html/comment-page-1

Octoplusmedia. (2023, June 20). *What is the Audience Profile of Xiaohongshu (RED) Users? A Demographic Breakdown Across Various Industries*. Octoplus Media. https://www.octoplusmedia.com/what-is-the-audience-profile-of-xiaohongshu-red-users-a-demographic-breakdown-across-various-industries/

Office for National Statistics. (2024, January 17). *[Income and Consumer Expenditure of the Population in 2023]*. Office for National Statistics. Www.stats.gov.cn. https://www.stats.gov.cn/sj/zxfb/202401/t20240116_1946622.html

Operations, L. (2023, May 17). *[Product Analysis | Ximalaya FM - The King Who Deserves the Name]*. iYunYing. https://www.iyunying.org/pm/257572.html

Osterwalder, A., & Pigneur, Y. (2010). *Business model generation: A handbook for visionaries, game changers, and challengers*. Wiley.

Pang, H. W. (2022). *[Factors affecting the precise operation of orderly parking of shared bicycles]*. [Master's thesis, Beijing Jiaotong University].

Pemarathna, R. (2019). *Impact of Xiaohongshu on Its User Based and Society: A Review*. ResearchGate. https://www.researchgate.net/publication/333974009_Impact _of_Xiaohongshu_on_Its_User_Based_and_Society_A_Review

Peng, F. (2023). *[Research on customer relationship management strategy of Hello Travel platform]*. [Master's thesis, Huazhong Agricultural University].

People's Public Transport. (2024). International News. People's. *Public Transport (Berlin)*, 1, 90.

Phoenix News. (2017, December 30). [Interview with Lv Gang from Mafengwo: I believe the world rewards courage more than wisdom.] *Pheonix*. https://news.ifeng .com/c/7fa2Op7pUYj

Platform, X. O. (n.d.). *[Join the Ximalaya open platform and connect the world with voice!]*. Ximalaya. https://open.ximalaya.com/doc/detailQuickStart?categoryId =21&articleId=43# Zhang

Pro, I. (2022, March 30). *[Sound economy is challenging to make money: Ximalaya's three breakthroughs in the Hong Kong Stock Exchange with a loss of 5.1 billion yuan a year]*. 36KR. https://36kr.com/p/1677147148428549

PubLink. (n.d.). *After-sales service, creating "zero distance" between customers*. SHB. https://www.shb.ltd/customerCase_49/255.html

QCC. (n.d.). Hunan Wenheyu Cultural Industry Development Group Co., Ltd. *QCC*. https://www.qcc.com/firm/cfd3bfb144580a8b8112a1a6633d37a2.html

Qianji Investment Bank. (2023, September 18). *"2023 Internet medical industry research report"*. https://www.21jingji.com/article/20230918/herald/57dee0449c71 b1ba2ce449391a9e3bc7.html

Qian, Z., Xinyu, Z., Changshan, B., Min, T., & Zhengzheng, D. (2019). [Analyzing the development of the second-hand market under the sharing economy]. *Market Modernization*, (10), 182–183. DOI:10.14013/j.cnki.scxdh.2019.10.106

Qi, C. (2021). *Research on the current situation and development trend of car sharing*. Automobile Maintenance and Repair.

Qiming Venture Partners. (2020, April 22). *WeRide: Robotaxi brings autonomous driving to the masses*. Sohu. https://www.sohu.com/a/390071500_313637

Qin, X. (2023, October 30). [Turnaround Group's Xu Jian: Circular Economy Helps Realize 'Dual Carbon' Goal]. *China Business Journal*, B16. DOI:10.38300/n.cnki. nzgjy.2023.002504

Qpzone. (2022, January 12). *In 2022, China's auto aftermarket faced three pain points*. Qpzone. http://www.qpzone.com.cn/Wap/hynews/10735.html

Ren, Z., & Xin, X. (2022). Analysing the word-of-mouth marketing strategy of Netflix products based on the 5T theory - Taking "Genki Forest" as an example. *Modern Marketing*, 18, 67–69. DOI:10.19932/j.cnki.22-1256/F.2022.06.067

Report, H. (2024). *[Hurun Global Unicorn Index]*. Hurun. https://www.hurun.net/zh-CN/Rank/HsRankDetails?pagetype=unicorn

Reuters. (2020, September 5). *TikTok troubles narrow gap between Beijing and ByteDance founder Zhang Yiming*. Reuters. https://www.reuters.com/article/us-usa-tiktok-bytedance-insight-idUSKBN25W0EM

Reuters. (2021, March 26). *TikTok owner ByteDance hires CFO in a step towards IPO*. Reuters. https://web.archive.org/web/20210326005416/https://www.reuters.com/article/us-bytedance-moves-xiaomi-idUSKBN2BG1JK

Richardson, J. (2008). The business model: An integrative framework for strategy execution. *Strategic Change*, 17(5-6), 133–144. DOI:10.1002/jsc.821

Rodan. (2020). Delivering Chinese Culture and Chinese Spirit in Comics - Remembering Annie Chen, Founder and CEO of Kuaikan Manhua. *Business Culture,* (35), 5-7+4+130.

Rometty, G. (2018). The era of cognitive business. *Harvard Business Review*, 96(1), 72–81.

Ruiyan World Report Network. (n.d.). https://baogao.ruiyanshijie.com/?tag=360search&actID=home&word=pinpaici5-2&qhclickid=06dd4342f1734eb4

Runwise. (2022, July 6). *Yuanfudao Product Analysis|In-depth analysis of the growth logic of online education platform*. Runwise. https://runwise.co/digital-growth/63943.html

Safdar, M. (2023, April 2). *The Rise of Social Commerce: Opportunities and Chal-lenges for Brands*. Hannan Muhammad. https://hannanit.com/2023/04/02/the-rise-of-social-commerce-opportunities-and-challenges-for-brands/

Schmitt, B. (1999). Experiential marketing. *Journal of Marketing Management*, 15.

Schwartz, P. M. (2013). The EU-US privacy collision: A turn to institutions and procedures. *Harvard Law Review*, 126, 1966.

Securities Times. (2021, April 2). *[Over 50,000 people queue up, and Shenzhen Wen He You goes viral]*. WeChat Official Account: Securities Times. https://mp.weixin.qq.com/s/n3JG-MOYkP55o8JbeSlPVSQ

Security, M. (2023, March 30). *Gluttony Research Report 2023 Twenty-four years of deep plowing into the restaurant industry, diversified operations to create in-dustry leaders*. Xue Qiu. https://www.vzkoo.com/read/20230330cb177433bf45bed668310ae5.html

Shandong University Cultural Industry Key Laboratory. (2021, May 7). *[Marketing Model Research on the "Wenheyou Phenomenon" in the Context of Internet Celebrity Economy]*. CS Lab. http://www.cslab.sdu.edu.cn/info/1078/2416.htm

Shang, Z. Z. Q. (Ed.). (2023). *[Gluttony in-depth report: reorganisation and start again, fresh clothes and angry horse teenagers]*. Maverick Research. https://www.hangyan.co/reports/3040103611704018909

Shanghai Observer. (2020, July 21). The new generation of Internet: The impres-sion of Chen Min, the founder of Tuhu Car. *Shanghai Observer*. https://sghservices.shobserver.com/html/baijiahao/2020/07/21/227493.html

Shanghai Office for Promoting the Construction of Science and Technology Innovation Centre. (n.d.). *Kenglang Intelligence Li Tong: "The 'China Smart Manufacturing' we represent is being seen by the world!"* KCB. https://kcb.sh.gov.cn/html/1/168/151/155/3234.html

Shanghai SAIC Anyue charging Technology Co. (2024, March 25). *Ltd.-Love enter-prise check*. Aiqicha. https://aiqicha.baidu.com/company_detail_83402490651136

Shen, J., & Zhang, Y. (2020). Research on platform innovation in the value chain of internet trend items: A case study of Dewu App. *China Economic & Trade Guide (Middle)*, 08, 111–113.

Shi Mei Kan Changsha. (2020, May 14). *[A decade of innovation: How Changsha's Wen He You moved from street stall to the world stage]*. Xingchen Online. https://news.changsha.cn/cslb/html/111874/20200514/78683.shtml

Sina Education. (2019, January 13). *Yuanfudao joins forces with The Strongest Brain for a full strategic partnership to synchronise and push customised lessons.* Sina Education. https://edu.sina.com.cn/l/2019-01-13/doc-ihqfskcn6781910.shtml

Sina Finance. (2024, April 25). *Xu Han: Change human travel with unmanned driving.* Baidu. https://baijiahao.baidu.com/s?id=1797315237395513217&wfr=spider&for=pc

Sina Mobile. (2020, October 22). *The first place of the global education technology unicorn came Yuanfudao, who announced the completion of 2.2 billion U.S. dollars in financing.* SINA. https://finance.sina.cn/tech/2020-10-22/detail-iiznctkc7014466.d.html?fromtech=1

Sina Mobile. (2021, January 4). *"Super" Yuanfudao, now online.* SINA. SINA. https://finance.sina.cn/tech/2021-01-04/detail-iiznezxt0432396.d.html?fromtech=1&from=wap

Sina Website. (2021). *[Beisen was listed in the Forbes China Enterprise Technology Top 50 , all-in-one HR SaaS was praised].* SINA. https://client.sina.com.cn/2021-12-08/doc-ikyakumx2790566.shtml

Snowball. (n.d.). *K12 Education Industry Development Prospect Research: forecast market size of about 400 billion yuan.* Xueqiu. https://xueqiu.com/9569737096/266323310

Snowball. (n.d.). *Online Education Institution Ads Land on Spring Festival Gala Wen.* Xueqiu. https://xueqiu.com/7423950559/140050028

Sohu. (2023, April 10). *Tuhu updated its prospectus, Tencent, Pleasure Capital, and Sequoia Capital as shareholders, and monthly active users reached 9 million.* Sohu. https://www.sohu.com/a/665128256_100157908

Sohu. (2023, August 31). *When the world auto industry comes to the "Great Age of China", Tuhu car is the result: The business of an independent car service market leader.* Sohu. https://news.sohu.com/a/716612257_585920

Sohu. (2023, June 15). *Behind the "Tuhu Eight steps": Doing a good job in technology and service standardisation is the basis for improving user satisfaction.* Sohu. https://www.sohu.com/a/685616764_118560

Sohu. (n.d.). *Behind the $10 billion Yuanfudao, founder Li Yong's entrepreneurial story is Li Yong.* Sohu. https://m.sohu.com/a/54123652_172472/?pvid=000115_3w_a&spm=smmt.mt-it.fd-d.3.1603943415501QIJMZ9R

Sohu. (n.d.). *Making science Fiction Reality: Progress and trends in autonomous driving in China.* Sohu. https://www.sohu.com/a/524648166_121207965

Sohu.com. (n.d.). *Interview with Guo Changzun of Yuanfudao: "AI+Education" is not as optimistic as imagined.* Sohu. https://www.sohu.com/a/242185243_350699

Song, J.T. (2016). How does Tuhu become a car O2O market survivor? *Innovation*, *86.*

Song, H. (2021). Research on the development of web comics in China. *Art Review*, (09), 183–185.

Song, Z. (2017). Exploring the development of e-commerce from C2C to C2B2C in the context of consumption upgrading. *Commercial Economic Research*, (14), 66–68.

Spence, P. (2019). *ByteDance cannot outrun Beijing's shadow.* Foreign Policy. https://foreignpolicy.com/2019/01/16/bytedance-cant-outrun-beijings-shadow/

State Grid Company Limited 2021 annual report. (n.d.). SH Clearing. https://www.shclearing.com.cn/xxpl/cwbg/nb/202204/t20220429_1048012.html

Statista. (2023, February 17). *China: Most Popular Social Media Platforms 2018.* Statista. https://www.statista.com/statistics/250546/leading-social-network-sites-in-china/

Statista. (n.d.). *China: most active industries in Xiaohongshu recommendation marketing 2023.* Statista. https://www.statista.com/statistics/1412241/china-recommendation-marketing-by-industries-on-xiaohongshu/

Sun, H., & Xu, J. (2022). Research on the business model of platform enterprises under the background of the digital economy: A case study of Dewu APP. *Open Management*, (04), 19–24. DOI:10.16517/j.cnki.cn12-1034/f.20211231.001

Sun, X., Feng, Z., Zhou, X., Kong, Y., & Zhao, Q. (2023). Analysis of AR technology empowerment path under the background of new e-commerce formats. [First Half of the Month]. *Modern Marketing*, 08, 92–94. DOI:10.19921/j.cnki.1009-2994.2023-08-0092-030

Tang, H. Y. (2018, February 6). *[The way to win for retailers in the era of "new retail."]* PwC. https://www.strategyand.pwc.com/cn/zh/reports-and-studies/2018/new-retail-era.html

Te, Y. T. (2022). *[Supply chain of Haidilao]*. Zhihu. https://www.zhihu.com/tardis/zm/art/412681115?source_id=1003

TechNode. (2023, April 23). *Tencent-backed Yuanfudao will launch an AI-powered design tool*. TechNode. https://technode.com/2023/04/23/tencent-backed-yuanfudao-to-launch-ai-powered-design-tool/

Telecom, C. (2020). 58. com's Zhuan Zhuan to Acquire Used Handset Trading App Zhaoliangji. *China Telecom Newsletter*, 12-13. https://web.p.ebscohost.com/ehost/pdfviewer/pdfviewer?vid=3&sid=c4953976-774e-4664-85fe-27211bef7aec%40redis

Tencent News. (2023). Dialogue "Star Charge," glimpse "unique innovation". *Tencent News*. https://new.qq.com/rain/a/20230421A00YNU00

Tencent News. (n.d.). Autonomous driving company "UISEE Technology" introduced the national team strategic capital injection and completed more than 1 billion yuan of financing. *Tencent News*. https://new.qq.com/rain/a/20210125A01C3O00

Tencent News. (n.d.). *Yuanfudao founder Li Yong steps down as Beijing Stranger, its Chalk Technology sprints to IPO*. Tencent News. https://new.qq.com/rain/a/20221201A03OTD00

Tencent News. (n.d.). *Yuanfudao is valued at $15.5 billion and leaps to the top of global education unicorn companies*. Tencent News. https://new.qq.com/rain/a/20201022A0C9N600

The Beijing News. (2023, December 29). From spicy strips to spicy snacks, Weilong multi-layout puffed snack track what? *The Beijing News*. https://finance.sina.com.cn/jjxw/2023-12-29/doc-imzzsqhx5780830.shtml

The Business of Fashion. (n.d.). *Miranda Qu | BoF 500 | The People Shaping the Global Fashion Industry*. The Business of Fashion. https://www.businessoffashion.com/community/people/miranda-qu

The Economic Observer. (2023, December 14).[What does Mafengwo rely on to survive in the "New Golden Decade of Free Travel"?] *The Economic Observer*. https://mp.weixin.qq.com/s?__biz=MjM5OTExMjYwMA==&mid=2670192453&idx=5&sn=df3910ba5a3baf0d3aa4e019d32f028a

The first strand of the spicy strip. (2023, March 2). Weilong Delicious. https://www.shiyetoutiao.cn/article/110193.html

The Paper. (2023, May 2). [Report on the Recovery Trends of China's Tourism Industry in 2023]. *The Paper*. https://www.thepaper.cn/newsDetail_forward_22926623

The Paper. (n.d.). [Wired founder] Wu Gansha of UISEE Technology: I hope to change the world's traffic with uncrewed vehicles. *The Paper.* https://www.thepaper .cn/newsDetail_forward_11233736

The Paper. (n.d.). Autonomous Driving Insights: Changing roles and challenges for suppliers and OEMs. *The Paper.*https://www.thepaper.cn/newsDetail_forward _23806166

The Paper. (n.d.). Yuanfudao completed a new $1 billion round of financing, led by Tall Capital and Tencent's participation. *The Paper.* https://www.thepaper.cn/ newsDetail_forward_6768070

Tian, Z. (2021, June 17). *17 "former" Microsoft people have achieved another Whampoa Military Academy for China's automatic driving.* Lepiphone. https://www .leiphone.com/category/transportation/LeSYLRm3ozHsR0yZ.html

TMI & CADA. (2023). *2023 white paper on consumption in China's liquor industry* [White paper]. TMI. https://file.tencentads.com/web/pdf/index/f90b46878551cdba

TMTPost. (n.d.). *[After the wind, can the three audio giants still fight? Litchi, Dragonfly and Ximalaya status analysis].* TMT Post. https://www.tmtpost.com/ 6256669.html

Tu, J.J. (2022). UFI Group signed a strategic cooperation agreement with Tuhu. *Auto Maintenance & Repair.*

U.I.S.E.E. (n.d.). *IC design industry chain and domestic substitution in-depth research report.* UISEE. https://zhuanlan.zhihu.com/p/421016440

UISEE. (2022). *Won the second prize in the Beijing Science and Technology Award.* UISEE Award. https://www.uisee.com/en/article91.html

UISEE. (n.d.). Core technology. https://www.uisee.com/core.html

Uncle Cars Talk Cars. (2019, December 13). *Why did autonomous taxis choose WeRide?* Zhihu. https://zhuanlan.zhihu.com/p/97253961

Verot, O. (2023, August 10). *How Do Different Generations Use Chinese Social Media Platforms? - Marketing China.* GMA. https://marketingtochina.com/how-do -different-generations-use-chinese-social-media-platforms/

Verot, O. (2023, September 21). *Xiaohongshu Statistics and Trends For The Upcoming Years - Marketing China.* GMA. https://marketingtochina.com/xiaohongshu -statistics-and-trends/

Viewpoint Institutions. (2023, November 20). *WeRide approved the launch of commercial autonomous driving mobility services in Beijing.* Wangyi. https://www.163.com/dy/article/IK015R7U0519D45U.html

Wancaishe. (2023). *Generation Z Consumer Trend Insight Report 2023.*

Wang, C. (2021). Yuanqi Forest will own Netflix's ready-to-drink coffee brand, Never Coffee. *Food Safety Magazine*, 7-15.

Wang, C. M. (2014). *Research the wine b2c website for vertical development strategy – take the example of jiuxian.com.* [Unpublished doctoral dissertation. Tianjin University of Commerce. Tianjin].

Wang, H. (2019, December 6). *What is "New Retail"? What are the key points?* Zhihu. https://www.zhihu.com/question/52950329/answer/179975491

Wang, J., Wang, Y., & Jin, Y. (2021). *Marketing and Future of Mobile Audio Apps - case study of the Ximalaya FM.*

Wang, Q. (2024, February 28). *[Deep ploughing into education and technology The underlying logic of Zuoyebang's hardware outbreak. Finance].* Finance China. https://finance.china.com.cn/roll/20240228/6086294.shtml

Wang, S. (2022). *The Current Situation, Dilemma and Way Out of the Auditory Transmission of Online Novels—The Example of Ximalaya FM.*

Wang, J. (2023). The tripartite pattern of sharing bicycles in China: Future development of Hello Bike. Highlights in Business. *Economics and Management*, 11, 125–130. DOI:10.54097/hbem.v11i.7956

Wang, M. (2021). Analysis of network marketing strategies in China's sneaker market: A case study of Depwu App. *Western Leather*, 03, 38–39.

Wang, Q., & Zhu, J. (2023). Research on the impact of the accurate push of commodity information on consumers' online shopping behaviour on e-commerce platforms. *Office Automation*, 11, 23–26.

Wang, S. (2021). Depwu App: We are committed to meeting the enthusiasm of young people. [Marketing Edition]. *Sales & Marketing*, 02, 23–25.

Wang, X. (2020). *The unmanned taxi race: Ambitions, bottlenecks and counterattacks.* China Entrepreneur.

Wang, X. (2021). *WeRide dances with self-driving giants.* China Entrepreneur.

Wang, X. L., Wang, L., Bi, Z., Li, Y. Y., & Xu, Y. (2016). Cloud computing in human resource management (HRM) system for small and medium enterprises (SMEs). *International Journal of Advanced Manufacturing Technology*, 84(1–4), 485–496. DOI:10.1007/s00170-016-8493-8

Wang, Y., & Zheng, Y. (2021). Intelligent educational products: constructing a new ecology of intelligent education based on AI. *Open Education Research*, 27(6), 9.

Wangyi. (2024, April 28). *[Subscription services prop up half of the revenue, Ximalaya paying users pay lower rates]*. Wangyi. https://www.163.com/dy/article/J0T9D11Q0553YQCC.html

Wang, Z., Huang, W.-J., & Liu-Lastres, B. (2022). Impact of user-generated travel posts on travel decisions: A comparative study on Weibo and Xiaohongshu. *Annals of Tourism Research Empirical Insights*, 3(2), 100064. DOI:10.1016/j.annale.2022.100064

Wan, L., & Liu, J. (2024). Analysis of consumer acceptance of driverless internet taxi - Based on UTAUT2 theoretical model paradigm. *Business and Economic Review*, 5, 80–83.

WCP. (World Coffee Portal). (2024, March 22). *China: 1.4 billion reasons to sell coffee*. World Coffee Portal. https://www.worldcoffeeportal.com/Latest/InsightAnalysis/2024/March/China-1-4-billion-reasons-to-sell-coffee

WeDoctor. (2024). *WeDoctor-Internet Hospital [Mobile application software]*. Huawei AppGallery. https://appgallery.huawei.com/app/C10193357

Wei, J., Su, Z. H., & Liu, Y. (2023). Research on the entrepreneurial process mechanism of emerging field platform-type enterprises. *Management World*, 09, 158–177. DOI:10.19744/j.cnki.11-1235/f.2023.0113

Wei, L. (2022). *The commercialization of uncrewed sanitation vehicles speeds up to increase quality*. Intelligent Networked Vehicles.

Wei, L., & Mengyu, X. (2020). C2B2C[Exploring the development of second-hand e-commerce platform under C2B2C model—Taking "Zhuan Zhuan" second-hand e-commerce platform as an example]. *Morden Business*, (28), 34–36. DOI:10.14097/j.cnki.5392/2020.28.013

Weilong latiao is a unique choice for contemporary young people. (2023, September 7). Zhuan Lan. https://zhuanlan.zhihu.com/p/654842663

Weilong. (2021). *Weilong Delicious's Photovoltaic power station grid-connected power generation ceremony was successfully held*. Weilong. https://www.weilongshipin.com/en/xinwenjujiao/134.html

Weilong. (2024). *Weilong Spicy Tiao sells well in 40 countries around the world, capturing the preferences of young people and demonstrating brand competitiveness—China Net*. Weilong. http://zjnews.china.com.cn/yuanchuan/2024-03-28/418541.html

Weixin Official Accounts Platform. (n.d.). *Wu Gansha: Driverless is your yearning for a better life*. Weixin. https://mp.weixin.qq.com/s?__biz=MzA4OTMyNzIzOA==&mid=2650832005&idx=1&sn=d0ba287b71f0599fea4bea8f4def9bbc

Wen, H. (2022). *[Research on the business model of knowledge payment platform under the background of Internet]*. CNKI. https://link.cnki.net/doi/10.26962/d.cnki.gbjwu.2022.001066doi:10.26962/d.cnki.gbjwu.2022.001066

Wen, N., & Liao, Q. (2016, July 20). [Wen Bin: Even with a street stall, I aim to create a brand]. *Hongwang*. https://hn.rednet.cn/c/2016/07/20/4039241.htm

WeRide. (2022). *WeRide Inc. environmental social and governance report*. WeRide. https://d2s675kp4ttxrq.cloudfront.net/uploads/We_Ride_Inc_2022_Environmental_Social_and_Governance_Report_EN_c474448943.pdf?updated_at=2023-09-08T06:29:25.000Z

What changes has the spicy strip industry experienced, from snacks at the school gate to a hundred billion industry? (2023, May 31). Bajiahao. https://baijiahao.baidu.com/s?id=1767381814629528454&wfr=spider&for=pc

Why does Weilong stand out in the spicy snack industry? (2023, June 13). Sohu. https://business.sohu.com/a/685424521_121123922

Williams, C. C., & Paddock, C. (2003). The meaning of alternative consumption practices. *Cities (London, England)*, 20(5), 311–319. DOI:10.1016/S0264-2751(03)00048-9

Wirtz, B., Pistoia, A., Ullrich, S., & Göttel, V. (2016). Business models: Origin, development and future research perspectives. *Long Range Planning*, 49(1), 36–54. DOI:10.1016/j.lrp.2015.04.001

Wu, A. H. (2022). *Big Data Boosts the Development of China Fitness Industry - Take Keep App as an Example*. Shandong University., DOI:10.2991/978-94-6463-036-7_144

Wu, R. (2021). Research on developing new e-commerce platforms under the C2B2C model: A case study of Dewu App. *Hebei Enterprise*, 11, 54–56. DOI:10.19885/j. cnki.hbqy.2021.11.013

Xiaohongshu. (2001, September 15). Xiaohongshu debuts the WILL Awards to recognise extraordinary up-and-coming Chinese brands. *PR Newswire*. Www.prnewswire .com. https://www.prnewswire.com/news-releases/xiaohongshu-debuts-will-awards -to-recognize-extraordinary-up-and-coming-chinese-brands-301377677.html

Xiaohongshu. (2022, November 11). Xiaohongshu invites top brands to share insights into China's Gen Z consumers during CIIE. *PR Newswire*. Www.prnewswire .com. https://www.prnewswire.com/news-releases/xiaohongshu-invites-top-brands -to-share-insights-into-chinas-gen-z-consumers-during-ciie-301675472.html

Xiao, L., Guo, F., Yu, F., & Liu, S. (2019). The Effects of Online Shopping Context Cues on Consumers' Purchase Intention for Cross-Border E-Commerce Sustainability. *Sustainability (Basel)*, 11(10), 2777. DOI:10.3390/su11102777

Xie, L. Y. (2023, December 3). *[In-depth discussion: Can Keep's unique business model run through?].* Topsperity Securities. https://pdf.dfcfw.com/pdf/H3_ AP202312041613226542_1.pdf

Xie, Y., & Yan, L. (2023). "Enterprise strategic risk management of Hello Trans Tech". *Modern Business*, 02, 16–19. DOI:10.14097/j.cnki.5392/2023.02.02

Ximalaya Marketing Model Problems and Countermeasures Research. (2023a, May 20). *[Ximalaya marketing model problems and countermeasures research].* Ximalaya Marketing Model Problems and Countermeasures Research. https://www .sbvv.cn/chachong/142302.html

Xing, W. Y. (2019). *[Research on the development strategy of sports fitness APP under the background of "Internet +].* Yanshan University. DOI:10.27440/d.cnki. gysdu.2019.001044

Xinhua Finance. (2022, September 7). *Tuhu Car's "burning cash model" encountered a bottleneck: Revenue declined, and the number of cooperative stores decreased by 6,302.* Baidu. https://baijiahao.baidu.com/s?id=1743265642732411071&wfr= spider&for=pc

Xinhua New Media. (2024). *Hello releases annual sustainability & ESG report, cumulative carbon reduction exceeds 13.1 million tons.* SH News. http://sh.news .cn/20240606/3df28c748d034b21944145af60d74207/c.html

Xiong, Y. (2022, November 1). *[2022 China (Changsha) New Consumption City Summit inaugurated, establishing the Changsha New Consumption Research Institute]*. Huasheng Online. https://hunan.voc.com.cn/article/202211/202211010711551222.html

Xplore, I. E. E. E. (n.d.). Robotics: Science and Systems VII https://ieeexplore.ieee.org/book/6276859

Xu, G. H. (2023, March 17). *[Gluttony Research Report: Kicking into gear, restarting the road to growth.]* Xue Qiu. https://xueqiu.com/9508834377/244728717

Xu, J. (2021, September 9). *WeRide officially entered the unmanned freight transportation field and cooperated strategically with Jiangling and Zhongtong.* Tencent. https://new.qq.com/rain/a/20210909A071UZ00

Xu, M. J. (2022, March 31). *[How to View the Model of Online Fitness Platform?]* Sinolink Securities. https://pdf.dfcfw.com/pdf/H3_AP202204011556478581_1.pdf?1648818722000.pdf

Xueqiu. (n.d.). *To help enterprises, scientific research institutions, investment institutions, and other units understand the development trend and future trends of the autonomous driving industry, China Economic Research Institute has launched.* Xueqiu. https://xueqiu.com/1973934190/273329499

Xu, H., Zhou, Q., & Yu, C. (2021). Empowerment mechanism of internet platforms under sudden changes: A longitudinal case study of WeDoctor platform. *Research and Development Management*, 01, 149–161. DOI:10.13581/j.cnki.rdm.20201854

Xu, Y., & Zhang, A. (2023). *Yuanqi Forest: Beverage Market Breaker*. Business Management. DOI:10.3969/j.issn.1003-2320.2023.02.018

Yan, M. H. (2023, October 12). *[Yang Mingchao: A Boss Who Lets Moutai Back Him Up]*. China Financial Online (CFO), a financial newsletter. http://mp.cnfol.com/31441/article/1697101223-141111304.html

Yan, X. Q., & Guo, L. L. (2024). Exploring the Dilemma of Food Safety Supervision and Legal Regulation of Prepared Dishes. *Preservation and Processing, 24*(01), 64–69.

Yang, M. H. (2023). [Instant retail reshapes the trillion-dollar market of the wine industry]. *Huaxia Wine News*. A08.

Yang, G. (2024, January 29). Competitiveness is the foundation for enterprises to go global. *Henan Business Daily*, A06. DOI:10.28373/n.cnki.nhnsb.2024.000082

Yang, M. H. (2022). Behind Jiuxian.com's "off-grid", the first generation of e-commerce has accelerated its transformation. *Huaxia Wine News*, A06. DOI:10.28390/n.cnki.nhxjb.2022.000248

Yang, W. M., & Chen, M. Z. (2020). *[Keep: The entrepreneurial road of fitness "little white"]. Tsinghua Management Review*, 03, 104–111.

Yang, X., Lu, S., Zhou, M., Tian, Z., & Tan, W. (2019). GPS attitude measurement with a baseline-constrained optimization algorithm for the unpiloted car. *Wireless Networks*. DOI:10.1007/s11276-019-02062-y

Yang, Y. (2019). Weilong Latiao's Internet Celebrity Training Manual. *Business Observation*, (Z1), 60–63.

Yao, L., & Tan, R. Q. (2021, April 20). *[KEEP in-depth report: Sports + technology first stock, content + consumption dual drive]*. Sealand Securities. https://pdf.dfcfw .com/pdf/H3_AP202204211560651758_1.pdf?1650558366000.pdf

Yao, Z. (2020). Analysing the marketing strategy of Kuaikan Manhua based on the 4I principles of network integration. *Theatre House*, (09), 210+212.

Yao, F. (2017). Analysis of the rise of Weilong Spicy Tiao from the perspective of strategic management. *Chinese and Foreign Entrepreneurs*, (19), 99.

Ye, T. (2023). Shao Danwei: Strengthen the construction of new energy vehicle charging and replacement infrastructure. *Intelligent connected car*, (02), 44–45.

Yicai. (n.d.). *What are the barriers to large-scale commercialisation in the field of autonomous driving?* Yicai. https://www.yicai.com/news/101004523.html

Yin, G. (2012). Read the report and see the change II National Grid: Integrating the concept of social responsibility into strategic goals. *WTO Economic Guide*, (04), 60.

Yipai, H. (2021). [Beisen Progress Rapid]. *21*, (08), 72-73.

Yipai, H., & Qi, Z. (2022). [A new way to use HR SaaS]. 21(03). *21st Century Business Review*(03), 46-48.

Yisi, X. (2024, January 22). Autonomous Driving Companies Enter the Field as "Mobile Power Banks" for Cars. *Yicai Daily*.

Youjia. (2023, September 25). *Analysis of competitive products in the aftermarket: Ping An Good car owner, DCar, and Tuhu Car maintenance.* Youjia. https://www .yoojia.com/ask/17-11763544949897401698.html

Yuan, S. Y. (2023). *Study the profit model and its effects on "Internet Plus" medical health enterprises* [Master's thesis, Chongqing University of Technology]. https://kns.cnki.net/kcms2/article/abstract?v=HR7ide6_o4T_JzBSpff75560rNIkr 39nFAyjl4qfQWXRvRzPx-yox8TqYaO0C_YEEPErjYhYWSCzgpMEDMyFi-smQzTzrcc4Yc6xz-BN-HKBX0X_4JnQ1VW6RkXMxfQE&uniplatform=NZKPT &language=CHS

Yuanfudao. (n.d.). *Yuanfudao, online education technology leader*. Yuanfudao. https://m.yuanfudao.com/

Yuanqi Forest. (2023). *2023 Global Challenger Brand List*. Yuanqi. https://www .yuanqiForest.com/news/86

Yuanqi Forest. (2024). *About us*. Yuanqi Forest. https://www.yuanqiForest.com/ about/recommend

Yue, P. (2023). "Identify first, then ship" carries quality trust. The "Dewu" service trademark was selected as one of China's top ten trademark protection cases. *China Quality Walk*, (05), 70–71.

Yue, P. (2023). Robust quality, emphasis on quality, excellent experience: Dewu App injects youth vitality into boosting consumption. *China Quality Walk*, (03), 64–67.

Yunfan, Z. (2022, December 13). Zongmu Technology's A-Share Autonomous Driving Debut: Braving the Winter of the Race Track. *21st Century Business Herald*.

Yunjiu. (2018). [In two years, 5 Jiuxian International Wine & Spirit Centre stores have been opened, and what is the store's profit?] *Business Culture,* (16), pp. 78–80.

Zhang, Q. L. (2023). [Analysis of Consumption Trends and Influence Mechanisms of Prepared Vegetables Based on SOR-SEM Modeling.]. *Operations and Management, 1*(12). doi:10.16517/j.cnki.cn12-1034/f.20230712.005

Zhang, S. (2016). "Dream Sports Ground" Charity Plan 6 Years: Multiple playgrounds launched in remote areas. *China News*. https://m.chinanews.com/wap/detail/zw/sh/ 2021/06-01/9490405.shtml

Zhang, S. (2022). *SWOT Analysis and Recommendations for Genki Forest - The Case of Soda Sparkling Water*. CHN. DOI:10.13939/j.cnki.zgsc.2022.02.128

Zhang, L., Zhou, F., & Zhou, C. F. (2024). Bottleneck Constraints and Path Choice of China's Prefabricated Vegetable Industry in the Perspective of High-Quality Development. *Shipin Yu Fajiao Gongye*, 1(11). doi:10.13995/j.cnki.11-1802/ts.037771

Zhang, T., & Liu, L. (2022). *Research on brand innovation of Yuanqi Forest*. Cooperative Economy and Technology. DOI:10.3969/j.issn.1672-190X.2022.06.038

Zhang, Y., & Peng, L. (2022). Competitiveness analysis of the trend e-commerce platform Poizon APP under the C2B2C model. *Open Management*, 10, 46–51. DOI:10.16517/j.cnki.cn12-1034/f.20220426.001

Zhang, Z. (2022). *Analysis of the recent development of the ready-made tea industry in China based on the innovation of Heytea.*, DOI:10.2991/978-94-6463-052-7_168

Zhao, A.L. (2023). How do unicorn enterprises stay innovative? *China's Foreign Trade, 08.*

Zhao, B. H. (2017). [Hao Hongfeng, Chairman of Jiuxian: The liquor industry is transitioning from the marketing era to explosive products]. *North Daily*, B03.

Zhao, L. (2023, October 11). *Analysis: Why Brands Are Flocking To China Instagram Rival Xiaohongshu.* Provoke Media. https://www.provokemedia.com/long-reads/article/analysis-why-brands-are-flocking-to-china-instagram-rival-xiaohongshu

Zhao, Y. N. (2023, October 17). *[Pot Circle Food Prospectus Sorting Eat-at-home meal leader, scale operation first breakout].* DFCFW. https://pdf.dfcfw.com/pdf/H3_AP202310221602714879_1.pdf?1697983474000.pdf

Zheng, R. (2019). Exploration of the development strategy of China's comic app under the trend of pan-entertainment—Take the example of Kuaikan Manhua. *Audiovisual*, (08), 173–174.

Zheng, Y., Bao, H., & Xu, C. (2018). A method for improved pedestrian gesture recognition in self-driving cars. *Australian Journal of Mechanical Engineering*, 16(sup1), 78–85. DOI:10.1080/1448837X.2018.1545476

Zhong, J. (2022). *[Ximalayan business model, implications for the rise of the online audio industry].* China Daily website. https://caijing.chinadaily.com.cn/a/202204/14/WS6257d741a3101c3ee7ad07ab.html

Zhong, J., Sun, L. J., Li, H. Q., Cai, Y. H., Guan, R., & Tian, Q. (2023).[Research Progress, Problems and Suggestions of Prefabricated Vegetable Standard System in China]. *Preservation and Processing, 1*(11). https://link.cnki.net/urlid/12.1330.S.20231025.1323.002

Zhong, Y. (2022, March 10). How the Chinese version of Instagram is outgrowing Instagram. *Medium.* https://uxdesign.cc/how-the-chinese-version-of-instagram-is-becoming-much-more-than-instagram-61eb70e89b54

Zhong, H. (2021). *Robotaxi's scaled-down operational system on the ground.* Intelligent Networked Vehicles.

Zhou, B., Pei, H., & Wenyin, L. (2016). *The function cognition and implementation suggestions of network security legislation.* DEStech Transactions on Computer Science and Engineering.

Zhou, E. (2021). *[The research report on the operation strategy of the Ximalaya FM audiobook channel].* Nanjing University. https://link.cnki.net/doi/10.27235/d .cnki.gnjiu.2021.000550

Zhou, Y., Chen, T., & Yang, L. (2021). [Research on the Development Status and Trend of High School Online Education--Taking Zuoyebang as an Example]. *18,* 127–129. DOI:10.19699/j.cnki.issn2096-0298.2021.18.127

Zhou, C. (2023). "Current situation and countermeasures of internet shared bicycle operation". *Journal of Jinhua Vocational and Technical College*, 02, 23–29.

Zhou, H., & Liu, Q. (2018). Exploration of Multidimensional Communication Strategy in the Internet Comic Industry—Taking Kuaikan Manhua as an example. *Today Media*, (03), 22–24.

Zhou, J. (2022). Development strategy research of the Poizon APP based on SWOT analysis. *Economic Research Guide*, 18, 44–46.

Zhu, Y. Y. Julie. (2020, March 13). *Zhang Yiming, founder of TikTok owner ByteDance, gears up for the global stage.* Reuters. https://www.reuters.com/article/us -china-bytedance-ceo-idUSKBN21014Y

Zongmu. (2021). *About Zongmu Technology.* Zongmu. https://www.zongmutech .com/our.html

About the Contributors

Elhaoussine Youssef is a researcher and professional from France. He has a scientific background in Physic-Chemistry and Analytic Chemistry and Marketing and Entrepreneurship background. He has been working in China for more than 5 years as a production manager for a French printing consumable retailer, developing a manufacturer network and monitoring the production in in China and Europe. In 2013, he decided to turn to a more academic career. His research focused on consumer behavior in China. After that, he became a researcher for the Sun Yat-sen International School Of Business And Finance specializing in B2B Branding strategies for Chinese factories and the Belt Road Initiative. He is regularly invited by trade organization to provide the latest development on brand strategies.

Henni Appelgryn started teaching in China in 2007. He is a Lecturer in the Division of Business and Management (DBM) at United International College (UIC), where he has been since 2014. He received his PhD and DBA in Business Administration from the Swiss Management Center University, Switzerland in 2015. Additionally, he received his MBA from the University of South Africa. Before moving to China, he was an entrepreneur with more than 20 years of business experience in South Africa. Amalgamate his subject knowledge in Marketing Management and Entrepreneurship with his extensive experience in business complement his understanding of the global competitive entrepreneurial environment.

***

Ke Chen is a marketing management major student at Beijing Normal University - Hong Kong Baptist University United International College. Her business interests lie in enhancing marketing strategies through digital and sustainable practices. With internships at WOOK Technology, SONGMICS HOME Technology, and Zhuhai Coca Cola, Ke has honed skills in operation strategies, content management, and brand promotion. Actively involved in academic and extracurricular leadership roles, Ke demonstrates a strong commitment to applying marketing principles in practical settings.

Fang Jingtian is majoring in Applied Economics at Beijing Normal University - Hong Kong Baptist University United International College. After three internships and many business imitation contests, she found that she is more interested in micro-analysis, especially the behavior of the enterprise in the industry and its influencing factors

Shuyi Feng is an accounting student at Beijing Normal University-Hong Kong Baptist University United International College. She is passionate about applying her knowledge to practice, particularly in the areas of data analysis, financial statement production, and financial management. Her main research areas are the application of accounting to the ESG field, cost and management accounting, environmental accounting and sustainability and other hot topics. Her purpose in writing this chapter is to give academics access to more comprehensive academic resources through investigating unicorn companies' development processes and marketing strategies. And to provide successful experience and resources for corporates with development potential.

He Jiantao is a college student studying marketing management in Beijing Normal University - Hong Kong Baptist University United International College. He devotes himself in conducting searches on different kinds of business in China and has high enthusiasm in the field of marketing strategy. As a student in business, he has attended several business competitions including CMAU and has composed articles on IGI website. Aiming to be a business leader, he is planning to go to America for further study.

Zhuoxi Jiang is currently pursuing her Bachelor of Business Administration (Honors) in Accounting at Beijing Normal University - Hong Kong Baptist University United International College. Her interests include but not limited to the relationship between the accounting information and market efficiency, the role of audit in corporate governance, accounting and financial ratios.

Zhuoyuan Li's major is Applied Economics, with primary research areas focusing on economic theory and practice, business analysis, market planning, company management, marketing, and more.She has work experience in the music and arts industry, private equity investment industry, technology innovation industry, construction industry, and telecommunications industry.

Li Ziyi is a senior undergraduate majoring in Accounting in Beijing Normal University-Hong Kong Baptist University United International College. She is interested in how macroeconomics policies affect the financial market and a company's operation.

Danyu Luo is pursuing a major in Applied Economics at Beijing Normal University – Hong Kong Baptist University United International College. Her research interests include strategic management, economic theory application, and business analysis. She has participated in numerous business competitions organized by KPMG, OliverWyman, Schwarzkopf, and others. Through these experiences, along with internships in audit and market consultation, she has deepened her understanding of the business world, further solidifying her passion for exploring business dynamics

Wei Min is a student with a keen interest in ESG practices, particularly in the context of tech companies and enterprises. I enjoy integrating business and consulting concepts to gain insights into economic and social issues. My passion lies in understanding how human capital, finance, and marketing intersect and collaborate. Eager to expand my knowledge, I strive to make a positive impact through thoughtful and strategic actions in my studies and beyond

He Qinghao focuses on market and data analytics, and is interested in artificial intelligence, machine learning, and e-commerce. Currently, she has obtained the certificate of market analysis researcher level1. In the competition, the artificial intelligence robot in the medical field that she leads to develop and design got the silver prize in the China "Tiao Zhan Cup" Guangdong Provincial Competition and the first prize in the school. In terms of research, she successfully published a paper entitled *A Case Study of Implementing Simulation Game in Management Accounting Teaching* in the 24th International Conference on Electronic Business (ICEB 2024). In terms of internships, she has been involved in product development for a subsidiary of Alibaba, and has also had extensive experience in marketing the NFT art collection at IBA Art Hong Kong Ltd.

Hailin Wang is currently a postgraduate student of Intercultural Communication at the University of Manchester. In addition to her background in communication, she has extensive work experience in marketing and branding, and data analysis skills. Her research interests focus on social media and intercultural marketing for brands

Yiru Wang is a sophomore accounting student from China. She has established a start-up enterprise to promote the intangible cultural heritage in Zhuhai China, through the popular online and offline board role-playing games. Also, she served as an intern in the strategic and development department of one listed company to experience the actual commercial operation. She has a strong passion in corporate finance, strategy planning, and enterprise innovation. In 2020, she became a university student at BNU-HKBU United International College to pursue further studies

Zizhen Wang is a hungry student with a first-class honours Bachelor's Degree in Finance at UIC is studying for a Master's Degree in Digital Innovative Build Asset Management at UCL, but enjoys marketing and would like to pursue a career in marketing.

Chenyu Wu, a junior grade student from Beijing Normal University-Hong Kong Baptist University United International College, is now majoring in Applied Economics. Academically, he was on the Dean's Honor list for several times. His business interests mostly lie in studying macro trends and drivers of economic development through international geopolitical relations. In terms of social practice, he has interned in the business Analysis Department of a state-owned bank, the Strategic Energy and Development Research Office of an Energy Research Institute of the Chinese Academy of Sciences, and the Strategic Customer Management Department of a state-owned securities company, and is relatively proficient in financial and economic tools. In the future, he plans to continue his studies in the field of macroeconomics.

Jiarui Yang is an undergraduate student majoring in Applied Economics at Beijing Normal University-Hong Kong Baptist University United International College. Her primary academic interests lie in International Economics, China Economy, and Industry Organization and Market. Jiarui has completed two internships at financial subsidiaries of Huaxi Securities Co., Ltd, where she gained practical experience in the financial sector. She has also participated in multiple business competitions, including the "China National Undergraduate' Innovation, Creativity and Entrepreneurship' Challenge" and the "L'Oréal Brandstorm Innovation Competition (BRANDSTORM)". Jiarui plans to pursue graduate studies in International Business and Marketing.

Yang Zihui is currently a student at the Beijing Normal University-Hong Kong Baptist University United International College, majoring in Accounting. She has a strong interest in research related to finance, marketing, and ESG (Environmental, Social, and Governance) topics.

Wang Yiru, a sophomore accounting major, wrote this chapter due to her interest in Guoquan Shihui, a unicorn company in the new retail market and prepared dishes market, in hopes of providing assistance to scholars who are also interested.

Xintong Yu is a college student majoring in Applied Economics, interested in the field of economics and finance, and has won the Bronze Award in Sephora's Creative Marketing Competition

Zhixuan Yu is a master's student at EDHEC Business School in France, specializing in Data Analytics and Artificial Intelligence. Prior to this, Zhixuan earned a bachelor's degree in Finance from Beijing Normal University - Hong Kong Baptist University United International College, graduating with First Class Honors. With a strong academic foundation in finance and a growing expertise in data analytics, Zhixuan is passionate about leveraging data-driven insights to address complex challenges

Liu Yuan is a student Master of Project Management from the University of Warwick, is dedicated to academic research in the fields of business management, corporate ethics, and project management. His research aims to assist companies in building a socially responsible image through systematic studies and explores the benefits and ethical standards of artificial intelligence in corporate development to promote the collaborative growth of AI technology, enterprises, and society, thereby fostering a more harmonious and just social environment.

Enyi Zhang is a student majoring in human resource management. She loves this major and hopes to contribute academically. She has a profound understanding of the human resources profession, and her main research areas are employee health in the workplace, gender equality, equal pay and other hot topics.

Sijing Zhou is currently pursuing a Bachelor of Management at Beijing Normal University-Hong Kong Baptist University United International College (UIC), majoring in Finance. She participated in exchange programs at Hong Kong Baptist University and The London School of Economics and Political Science, further enhancing her expertise in Financial Statement Analysis.Her research interests include corporate financial management, data-driven financial decision-making, and cost optimization strategies. Sijing has completed internships at Shenzhen Securities Information Co. Ltd. as a Data Analysis Intern, and at SINOAGRI E-Commerce as a Cost Accounting Intern, where she gained hands-on experience in SQL data collection, financial analysis, and cost management. Her work at the Industrial and Commercial Bank of China as an Account Manager Assistant also provided her with valuable skills in client service and financial product promotion

Index

9 798369 329214